DATE			

Making and Marketing Arms

EDWARD A. KOLODZIEJ

Making and Marketing Arms

The French Experience and Its Implications
for the International System

PRINCETON UNIVERSITY PRESS
PRINCETON, NEW JERSEY

Published by Princeton University Press, 41 William Street,
Princeton, New Jersey 08540
In the United Kingdom: Princeton University Press, Guildford, Surrey

Library of Congress Cataloging in Publication Data will be
found on the last printed page of this book

ISBN 0-691-07734-7

Publication of this book has been aided by the
Whitney Darrow Fund of Princeton University Press

This book has been composed in Linotron Baskerville

Clothbound editions of Princeton University Press books
are printed on acid-free paper, and binding materials are
chosen for strength and durability. Paperbacks, although satisfactory
for personal collections, are not usually suitable for library rebinding

Printed in the United States of America by Princeton University Press
Princeton, New Jersey

To Peter, Andrew, Matthew, and Daniel

CONTENTS

Appendixes

THIS STUDY explains why the French Fifth Republic makes and markets arms and military technology. Compelling aims—independence, national security, economic welfare, foreign influence, *grandeur*—propel French arms production and transfer behavior. The military-industrial complex, created by the French state and cultivated by successive French regimes, institutionalizes these aims and ensures the making and marketing of weapons as a top governmental priority. Broad elite and public support, tied inextricably to these governmental aims and bureaucratic and industrial interests, sustains France's unwavering commitment to a nationally determined strategic policy based on nuclear weapons and an indigenous arms production and sales effort of global proportions. The stability of France's governing institutions and the very legitimacy of the French Fifth Republic have been progressively linked since 1958 to the success of French arms and arms sales.

French aims and interests respond to two systemic imperatives of contemporary international politics. The first derives from the nation-state system, now globalized with the demise of colonialism, and the incentives generated by the incipient anarchical character of this war-prone security regime. To survive and prosper, a state attempts to pursue autonomous strategic policies; correspondingly, it seeks to control access to those arms that provide for its independence and security. Indigenous production guarantees needed weapons and equipment, minimizing a state's dependence on other suppliers while maximizing its capacity to use or threaten force in support of its purposes.

The second imperative has until now been less clearly articulated than the security dilemma as a principal determinant of producing and selling arms and military technology. It arises from the demands of national populations everywhere for greater material welfare and a more equitable share of national wealth and the world's resources. An independent, national capacity to design and develop arms and an open-door policy to transfer them—*ventes d'armes tous azimuts*—has been one of the principal policy instruments relied upon by Fifth Republic policy-makers to assure French security and welfare.

Viewed from these systemic imperatives, arms and military technology transfers are simultaneously an instrument and an aim of French foreign policy. As instrument, they fulfill the traditional function of foreign policy. They project the power and purposes of the French

state abroad to influence the behavior of other international actors—
principally states—and to shape the international system in ways congenial to its interests and compatible with its preferred values. As aim,
French diplomacy paves the way for expanded sales of arms and military technology to support France's arms complex and to promote economic growth and technological progress, key concerns of the welfare
state.

The analysis of these determinants of French arms production and
transfer policy is divided into four parts. Part I traces French arms production and transfers from the inception of the French state to the present. Chapter 1 carries the discussion to the close of the Fourth Republic
in 1958. It underlines the sometimes forgotten point that producing
arms in France has been almost coterminous with the rise of the French
state. If history is a guide, there is little likelihood, short of invasion and
occupation, as in World War II, that France will cease to produce arms,
the final guarantor of its independence and security and the symbol of
its status as a great power.

Chapter 2 defines the impact of French military strategic policy under the Fifth Republic on arms production and sales. The de Gaulle
government (1958-1969) and its successors affirmed the traditional
goal of a militarily self-reliant France possessing its own capacity to produce arms. The *force de dissuasion* and the Evian accords granting Algerian independence signified France's abandonment of its centuries-old
strategy of empire and colonial holdings that had been relied upon until the Fifth Republic to foster French security and economic well-being.
A nuclear strategy, implying a radical reduction in requirements for
conventional arms and a large ground army, posed the problem of
maintaining a viable arms industry capable of producing a full panoply
of arms for France's military services. Within a limited defense budget
keyed to nuclear arms, French leaders recognized that internal demand
for arms would inevitably fall well below full employment and efficient
levels of production within the arms industry. The French answer was
to sell arms abroad and even to stimulate demand to preserve the arms
complex intact. Correspondingly, French arms control and disarmament policy was adapted to the protection of the arms complex, particularly on issues of nuclear and conventional proliferation.

Pressures to export arms, arising from strategic necessity, swelled
others unleashed by popular demands for economic growth and technological development. The view gradually arose in postwar France
that arms production and sales could stimulate economic expansion,
renovate industry, enhance competitiveness, and promote scientific
and technological modernization. Part II links these expectations to the

development of the arms industry and to France's climb to the rank of the world's fourth leading exporter and third leading supplier of arms and military technology. Between 1956 and 1980, France transferred, by conservative estimates, more than $30 billion in arms and military technology. Two-thirds of this amount was delivered after the oil crisis in the middle 1970s, mostly to developing states. Not surprisingly, Middle East oil producers have been the principal recipients of advanced military systems. France currently controls about 12 percent of the world's arms market. Its weapons of all kinds are found in the inventories of over 100 states on all continents.

Part III describes the organization and governance of the military-industrial complex. Chapter 4 traces the evolution of industrial concentration in the arms industry, the emergence of state-designated national champions, and the nationalization of key segments of the arms industry. Chapter 5 identifies the major players within the arms complex and the process by which decisions are reached about what arms will be produced, in what quantities, and for whom. It also evaluates how decision-makers are held accountable and submits the analysis of the governing process and the politics of arms production and sales to minimal democratic tests.

Part III also argues that the arms complex is ruled by a loose coalition of high bureaucratic functionaries, located primarily within the General Delegation for Armament (DGA), military engineers, industrialists, and armed services chiefs. This oligarchy is largely insulated from daily governmental direction and control and shielded from close public scrutiny. Like the force de dissuasion, arms sales policy has been gradually depoliticized and bureaucratized under the Fifth Republic. The leadership of the arms complex, primarily military technocrats occupying posts in the DGA, possesses the requisite powers and mechanisms to order its own affairs and to resolve internal conflicts that might prompt external intervention. It controls the recruitment, training, and incentive structure—pay, privileges, and promotion—within which arms operatives work, and it commands impressive resources to advance its own interests within the governmental bureaucracy and to project a favorable public image of its activities. As a state-anointed enterprise, charged with the responsibility to be guardian and guarantor of the nation's security and welfare, the DGA enjoys access to some of the most powerful emotive symbols of national pride and unity—symbols susceptible to manipulation in advancing its own, self-interested claims to governmental and public support.

Part IV examines arms sales as the instrument and aim of French foreign policy. Chapter 6 defines France's role and status within the global arms transfer system. The value of the arms as well as the kinds and amount of major weapon systems delivered by France to other countries and regions are compared to those of other arms producers to assess France's importance as a supplier. Sketched, too, are the responses of other arms suppliers and recipients, especially those in the developing world, to the systemic factors shaping French arms production and transfer behavior.

The French experience foreshadows the strategies apparently adopted by many key developing states in responding to the incentives arising from the very structure of the nation-state system and from demands of their populations for greater material welfare and for the modernization of their societies. Nation-state leaders bias the international community toward military solutions in managing and resolving external conflict and in relying, in varying measure, on indigenously produced arms and exports to address internal socio-economic imperatives and pressures for domestic reform.

Chapter 7 rationalizes, through a regional approach, the crazy-quilt pattern of French arms transfer behavior under the Fifth Republic as an instrument of foreign policy in pursuit of systemic and particular national interests. The security, welfare, and bureaucratic dimensions of French arms sales obscure their use in support of traditional French diplomatic objectives. Chapter 7 attempts to remedy this oversight.

The concluding chapter summarizes the findings of the study. French behavior is explained primarily in terms of the systemic imperatives driving French arms transfer practices. These elicit the specific aims and interests that appear only on the surface to be primary determinants of French behavior. The French experience is then related to the efforts of other states, sketched in Chapter 6, to make and market arms as a solution to their security, welfare, and modernization needs.

The very aims and interests pursued in adopting independent national arms and arms production strategies—security, socio-economic welfare, and political modernization—are threatened by the imitation of the French approach by other states and its propagation throughout the system. The short-term rational strategies of states, like France, in adapting scarce national resources to systemic constraints, create an irrational international system which places national security and well-being at risk. As the French case suggests, the dismal implications of this diagnosis of the adverse effects of uncontrolled arms production and sales will not be readily recognized, much less accepted, by weapons makers, since making and marketing arms is so deeply institutionalized in the security and welfare systems of national states.

Remedies will also not be easy to devise or to apply. Nothing less than the restructuring of the international system must be undertaken in tandem with national reform to ameliorate, if not cure, the symptoms and the sources of our current discontents. Diagnosis is a precondition for effective remedy. This effort to explain French arms transfer behavior is in partial fulfillment of the efforts that remain to be made to identify the impact of specific and systemic determinants on the behavior of other arms producers and to devise ways and strategies to moderate and resolve the multiple causes of international conflict.

ACKNOWLEDGMENTS

I AM INDEBTED to many individuals and organizations for help in completing this study. A Ford Foundation fellowship launched the research. The Centre d'Etudes de Politique Etrangère under Jacques Vernant and its successor, the Institut Français des Relations Internationales (IFRI) under Thierry de Montbrial, furnished on several occasions indispensable research facilities in Paris. The University of Illinois at Urbana-Champaign (UIUC) provided support through several avenues. The Department of Political Science, headed successively by Richard Merritt and Roger Kanet, and the Center for Advanced Studies, directed by Daniel Alpert, afforded me leave and resources at different times to speed progress on the manuscript and deepen the analysis. Robert Crawford, Director of the School of Social Sciences, supported these leaves and, with the Research Board, supplied needed funds at crucial times for research assistance, materials, and travel. The Program in Arms Control, Disarmament, and International Security (ACDIS) supplied valuable secretarial and editorial assistance. A NATO fellowship assisted my research in Brussels where Fernand Welter led me through the NATO labyrinth.

Many people, more than there is space to cite, were generous with their time, expertise, and encouragement. Special thanks go to Jean Klein, David S. Yost, and Andrew Pierre whose thoughtful comments on the entire manuscript saved me from countless errors. Walter Schütze of IFRI was a mine of information and insight. Charles Zorgbibe, Dean of the School of Law at Paris-Sud, provided several occasions to test ideas with French colleagues. Jean-Pierre Thomas, one of France's foremost military sociologists, shared his impressive knowledge of France's defense establishment and was considerate in placing the resources of the Centre de Sociologie de la Défense Nationale at my disposal.

Many others furnished information, guidance, and criticism. Notable are Philippe Moreau Defarges, Michel Dobry, Pierre Gallois, Richard Grimmett, Alfred Grosser, Robert Harkavy, Pierre Hassner, Claude Lachaux, Pierre Lellouche, Michel Martin, Stephanie Neuman, Lucien Poirier, and Hugo Sada. Fred Pearson was particularly helpful in his critique of Chapter 7. Several French journalists, political commentators, and legislators should also be mentioned. Prominent are Paul Marie de la Gorce, Jacques Isnard, Pierre Messmer, Jean-Pierre Mithois, and the late Raymond Aron. Joël le Theule, a major behind-the-scenes force in shaping Gaullist security policy, merits special tribute. I profited from his healthy skepticism about governmental reports in interviews with him during the 1960s and 1970s before his untimely death just months after he had assumed the post of Minister of Defense for which he was uniquely suited. Professors Christian Schmidt and Pierre Dussauge assisted especially in developing the economic dimensions of the study. Stanley Hoffmann, Director of the Center for West European Studies at Harvard University, provided useful venue for the presentation of research findings en route to this study.

Although they must remain anonymous, I am also grateful to busy political leaders and government officials within the French arms complex for granting me over a hundred interviews, for correcting misguided views, and for directing me to other specialists and to primary documentation. This work would have been impossible without their cooperation. I hope the facts are right, although my interpretation of their significance for global security and economic welfare clearly diverges from most practitioners engaged in the French arms complex.

I was also fortunate in gaining access to a wide range of documentary and library sources in Paris and elsewhere. I am pleased to acknowledge permission to use source material at the Stockholm International Peace Research Institute and the International Institute for Strategic Studies. In Paris, several libraries and research centers deserve mention for access to materials and for staff assistance: the Atlantic Institute, the National Assembly, the Ministry of Defense, the Direction Nationale des Statistiques du Commerce Extérieur, the Paris Chamber of Commerce, Documentation Française, Fondation des Sciences Politiques, Institut National de la Statistique et des Etudes Economiques, the Service Historique at Chateau de Vincennes, the Organization for Economic Development and Cooperation, *Le Monde*, and the International Monetary Fund.

Specialized institutes which were helpful include the Fondation pour les Etudes de Défense Nationale under General Henri de Bordas, the Centre d'Etudes Politiques de Défense under Pierre Dabezies (later reorganized as the Institut National Supérieur d'Etudes de Défense et de Désarmement under Jacques Soppelsa), the Institut Diplomatique International under Madame Bodart, the Institut Français de Polémologie under Jean Paucot, and the Centre Lyonnais d'Etudes de Sécurité Internationale et de Défense.

Cheerful and professional secretarial aid was provided by Janie Carroll, Eileen Yoder, Ginger Lottman, and Sandy Setters of UIUC, and Madame Yvonne Cressel of IFRI. Mary Anderson was unfailing in seeing the final manuscript preparation to completion. Mary Hoffman and my wife Antje Heberle Kolodziej contributed their impressive editorial skills and research knowledge to improve the manuscript throughout. Judy Jones helped in countless ways to ease my research and writing. My research assistants, Jeffrey Starr, Eberhard Schubert, and Nancy Gallagher-Wiesler were invaluable in collecting data and in hunting down fugitive materials and footnotes. Peter Kolodziej read galleys with an attentive and discerning eye. Jeffrey Mellander and Precision Graphics assisted in the design of selected figures and tables.

While this study would have been impossible without the aid and encouragement of everyone cited above, only I am responsible for what follows.

Urbana-Champaign
January 4, 1987

ACDA	Arms Control and Disarmament Agency
ACF	Future Combat Fighter (Avion de Combat Futur)
AMD-BA	Avions Marcel Dassault-Bréguet Aviation
ASM	Air to surface missile
ASMP	Air-sol moyenne portée (medium range air-to-ground missile)
ASW	Antisubmarine warfare
AWACS	Airborne Warning and Control System
BEG	Bureau of General Studies (Bureau d'Etudes Générales)
BFCE	Banque Française du Commerce Extérieur
CAP	Common Agricultural Policy
CAR	Central African Republic
CBM	Confidence Building Measures
CDE	Conference on Disarmament in Europe
CDNFA	Commission de la Défense Nationale et des Forces Armées
CEA	Atomic Energy Commission (Commissariat à l'Energie Atomique)
CELAR	Center for Electronic Armaments (Centre d'Electronique de l'Armement)
CEPODE	Centre d'Etudes Politiques de Défense
CF	Commission des Finances
CFDT	Confédération Française Démocratique du Travail
CGE	Compagnie Générale d'Electrique or Central Govermental Expenditures
CGT	Confédération Générale du Travail
CHEAR	Center for Advanced Armament Studies (Centre des Hautes Etudes de l'Armement)
CIEEMG	International Committee for the Study and the Export of War Materials (Commission Interministérielle pour l'Etude et l'Exportation des Matériels de Guerre)
CII	Compagnie Internationale de l'Informatique
CIRPES	Centre Interdisciplinaire de Recherches sur la Paix et d'Etudes Stratégiques
CLICAN	Centre Local d'Information et de Coordination pour l'Action Non-Violente
CMN	Constructions Mécaniques de Normandie

CNES	National Center for Space Studies (Centre National d'Etudes Spatiales)
CNIM	Constructions Navales et Industrielles de la Meditérranée
CNRS	National Center for Scientific Research (Centre Nationale de Recherche Scientifique)
COFACE	Compagnie Française d'Assurance pour le Commerce Extérieur
COFRAS	Compagnie Française d'Assistance Specialisée
DAI	Directorate of International Affairs (Direction des Affaires Internationales)
DAM	Directorate for Military Applications (Direction des Applications Militaires)
DAT	Directorate for Ground Armaments (Direction des Armements Terrestres)
DCAé	Directorate for Aeronautics (Direction des Constructions Aéronautiques)
DCMAT	Central Directorate for Materiel of the Ground Army (Direction Centrale du Matériel de l'Armée de Terre)
DCN	Directorate for Naval Construction (Direction des Constructions Navales)
DEI	Directorate for Electronics and Computers (Direction de l'Electronique et de l'Informatique)
DEN	Directorate for Missiles (Direction des Engins)
DGA	General Delegation for Armament (Délégation Générale pour l'Armement)
DGRST	General Delegation for Scientific and Technical Research (Délégation à la Recherche Scientifique et Technique)
DMA	Ministerial Delegation for Armament (Délégation Ministérielle pour l'Armement)
DMS	Defense Marketing Services
DPA	Delegate for Armament Programs (Délégué aux Programmes d'Armement)
DPAG	Directorate for Personnel and General Armament Affairs (Direction des Personnels et Affaires Générales de l'Armement)
DPAI	Directorate of Armaments Programs and Industrial Affairs (Direction des Programmes et Affaires Industrielles de l'Armement)
DREE	Directorate for Foreign Economic Relations (Direction des Relations Economiques Extérieures)
DRET	Directorate for Research, Development, and Techniques (Direction des Recherches, Etudes et Techniques)

DRI	Delegate for International Relations (Délégué aux Relations Internationales)
DRME	Directorate of Research and Testing (Direction des Recherches et Moyens d'Essais)
EAA	Ecole d'Administration de l'Armement
EC	European Community
ECSC	European Coal and Steel Community
EDC	European Defense Community
EMAT	General Staff of the Ground Army (Etat Major de l'Armée de Terre)
EMD	Electricité Marcel Dassault
ENICA	Ecole Nationale d'Ingénieurs de Construction Aéronautique
ENSAE	Ecole Nationale Supérieure de l'Aéronautique et de l'Espace
ENSIETA	Ecole Nationale Supérieure des Ingénieurs des Etudes et Techniques d'Armement
ENSTA	Ecole Nationale Supérieure des Techniques Avancées
ERP	European Recovery Program
ETA	Ecole Technique Nationale
ETNA	Ecole Technique Normale de l'Armement
FAN	Armed Forces of the North (Forces Armées du Nord)
FAR	Rapid Action Force (Force d'Action Rapide)
FBIS	Foreign Broadcast Information Service
FO	Force Ouvrière
GATT	General Agreement on Tariffs and Trade
GE	General Electric
GIAT	Groupement Industriel des Armements Terrestres
GIFAS	Groupement des Industries Françaises Aéronautiques et Spatiales
GUNT	Transitional Government of National Unity (Gouvernement d'Union Nationale de Transition)
IAEA	International Atomic Energy Agency
IETA	Engineers of Arms Studies and Techniques (Ingénieurs des Etudes et Techniques d'Armement)
IFRI	Institut Français des Relations Internationales
IISS	International Institute for Strategic Studies
IMF	International Monetary Fund
INSEDD	Institut National Supérieur d'Etudes de Défense et de Désarmement
INSEE	National Institute of Statistics and Economic Studies (Institut National de la Statistique et des Etudes Economiques)

IRBM	Intermediate Range Ballistic Missile
ISL	Institut de St. Louis
MBB	Messerschmitt-Bölkow-Blohm
MBFR	Mutual Balanced Force Reductions
MIRV	Multiple Independently Targeted Reentry Vehicle
MLF	Multilateral (Nuclear) Force
MW	Megawatt
NATO	North Atlantic Treaty Organization
OAU	Organization for African Unity
OFEMA	Office Français de Exportation de Matériel Aéronautique
OGA	Office Général de l'Air
ONERA	Office National d'Etudes et de Recherches Aérospatiales
PEF	Politique Etrangère de la France
PLO	Palestine Liberation Organization
R&D	Research and Development
RITA	Réseau Intégré de Transmission Automatique
RSI	Rationalization, Standardization and Interoperability
SAM	Surface-to-Air Missile
SAMRO	Satellite Militaire de Reconnaissance et d'Observation
SCAI	Central Service for Industrial Affairs of Armament (Service Central des Affaires Industrielles de l'Armement)
SDI	Strategic Defense Initiative
SEP	Société Européenne de Propulsion
SEREB	Société d'Etude et de Réalisation d'Engins Balistiques
SGDN	General Secretariat for National Defense (Sécrétariat Général de la Défense Nationale)
SIAR	Service of Industrial Surveillance of Armament (Service de la Surveillance Industrielle de l'Armement)
SIPRI	Stockholm International Peace Research Institute
SIRPA	Service d'Information et de Relations Publiques des Armées
SLBM	Sea-Launched Ballistic Missile
SNCAC	Société Nationale de Constructions Aéronautiques du Centre
SNCAN	Société Nationale de Constructions Aéronautiques du Nord
SNCASE	Société Nationale de Constructions Aéronautiques du Sud-Est
SNCASO	Société Nationale de Constructions Aéronautiques du Sud-Ouest

SNECMA	Société Nationale d'Etude et de Construction de Moteurs d'Aviation
SNIAS	Société Nationale Industrielle Aérospatiale
SNPE	Société Nationale des Poudres et Explosifs
SODETAG	Société d'Etude Technique et de Gestion
SOFMA	Société Française de Matériels d'Armement
SOFRANTEM	Société Française de Vente et Financement de Matériels Terrestres et Maritimes
SOFREMAS	Société d'Exportation d'Equipements et Matériels Spéciaux
SOFREXAN	Société Française d'Exportation d'Armement Naval
S.O.M.V.A.	Rapid Tanks
SSM	Surface-to-Surface Missile
STAT	Technical Section of the Ground Army (Section Technique de l'Armée de Terre)
STOL	Short Takeoff and Landing Aircraft
UNIFIL	United Nations Interim Force in Lebanon
USIAS	Union Syndicales des Industries Aéronautiques et Spatiales
WEU	Western European Union

Part I.
Arms and International Security

CHAPTER 1

From the Beginning through
the Fourth Republic

INTRODUCTION

FRENCH ARMS production and strategic military policy, including the raising, training, and equipping of armed forces, are inextricably entwined. However much French regimes—royal, imperial, or republican—may have differed in composition, claims to legitimacy, or objectives, they could agree that France's independence, security, big-power role—grandeur no less—required an autonomous military strategy and national armed forces free from outside control. These imperatives generated yet another, until now largely overlooked, feature of the evolution of the French nation and state: making and marketing arms. French will to be French—to forge a nation and to fashion a state—explains much of the efforts of French governments to ensure an indigenous capacity to fabricate arms. Under the Fifth Republic, heir to a legacy of over a millennium of national independence, arms production has grown increasingly more complex and sophisticated. Making arms, conventional and nuclear, is now woven deeply into the fabric of France's scientific and technological establishment, industrial plant, business practices, governing process—even its cultural mores. And, for the first time in France's history, the arms complex depends for its survival on a global sales network tied to over 100 states around the world.

However important other factors are in explaining French arms transfer policy—and these are increasingly powerful as we will soon see—the real and perceived imperatives of political independence, physical security, and grandeur form, through the centuries, the tap roots of current French arms production and transfer behavior. Conflicts between the Right and Left over generations have thus turned less on the question of whether there should be an arms industry than on secondary, if still fervently disputed, issues: how the arms industry should be organized, whether under the aegis of the private sector or the state; who should direct it; and who should receive French arms and know-how and under what conditions.

This chapter and the next trace the evolution of French military strategic policy and its implication for arms production since the inception of the modern French state. Chapter 1 carries the discussion through the Fourth Republic; Chapter 2 focuses on the strategic policy of the Fifth Republic in which arms production has played a central role in the security policy of successive governments, in the rapid industrialization and progressive competitiveness of the French economy in world markets, and in the modernization of French society. The most powerful forces in contemporary society drive French arms making and selling: national security, welfare, modernization, and a profound concern for France's status in world affairs.

Strategic policy refers to the overall plan for the use or threat of force to shape the exterior political environment in ways considered to be congenial to the interests and values of the French nation and leadership. While arms production has always been a key component of French national strategy, arms transfers, until the modern period, have played a lesser role. This is not to denigrate the historical importance of arms transfers; the outcome of the American Revolution or World War I might well have been different without them. Rather, it is to recognize that arms transfers have never been as important a part of French national strategy as they are today. Their current significance stems from the broader conception of national security policy that governments today must adopt in comparison to the narrower view of defense held by their counterparts centuries ago.

National security today goes beyond the question of threatening or using force to include, given the destructive uses of modern weapons, strategies for its control and elimination. It also encompasses, certainly in French eyes, the maintenance of a welfare state, corporate profits, and personal gain. Out of these broader incentives arise the economic, technological, social, and political supports of a popularly based arms system. Arms production and transfers not only help to provide physical security and to project the nation's power and influence abroad, they also are used to promote economic growth, high employment, and at least a tolerable, if not always an equitable, division of economic wealth. Elites in control of these critical state functions have inevitably assumed increasing influence and sway over the allocation of inherently scarce national economic resources. These elites, defined by their technical, administrative, and industrial roles in making and selling arms, populate and dominate powerful new and broadly based structures fused indissolubly to the apparatus of the French state. The political support and legitimacy of the Fifth Republic also partially depend on the success of a new leadership class to maintain a competitive arms industry capable of simultaneously servicing France's welfare, security, and foreign policy goals and of motoring the modernization and the reform of French society. Arms transfers, as succeeding chapters describe, serve these varied functions. But the starting point is arms production itself which derives from the self-help, incipiently anarchical character of the modern state system.

Several lines of argument are advanced in the succeeding discussion: that the development of the French state and national armed forces are essentially coterminous; that the gradual emergence of a royal army and navy inevitably prompted a need for gradual state oversight, control, and eventual production of military equipment to arm national forces; that France has been in the war-making, war-implementing, and arms transfer business for centuries; that any departure from this pattern would entail an abandonment of France's pursuit of an independent foreign policy whose supportive and nurturing roots lie deep in French history and culture and in current French political practice and institutions; and that one of the principal determinants of French arms production and sales policy under the Fourth and Fifth Republics has been the drive for national independence, military autonomy, and a big power role in using and threatening force in the service of France's security and foreign policy interests.

RISE OF THE MODERN FRENCH STATE AND ARMS PRODUCTION: ORIGINS TO THE NAPOLEONIC WARS

The rise of France as a nation-state and its initial direction, first under the Capetian, then the Valois, and finally the Bourbon kings, have been almost as one with the history of France's armed forces and their armaments. While feudal armies in the service of the king largely provided their own weapons, produced by local artisans, the monarchy was not indifferent to the quality and effectiveness of the arms that were supplied. Geoffroy Martel, Phillippe-Auguste's chief of armed forces, pressed for up-to-date arms to meet the crown's needs. The English bow and crossbow, war machines, and rolling towers were introduced and became key parts of the crown's arms inventory. These efforts were rewarded in the victory at Bouvine in 1214.[1]

As early as the fourteenth century, the crown assumed monopoly control over the production of powder. The right to make or buy powder was conferred upon masters in artillery who were placed eventually under the supervision of the king's Grand Master of Artillery, a post that continued to 1750. These efforts to ensure the crown's access to ground and naval armaments marked the first notable sallies of the French state into the direct fabrication of arms and munitions. Following the practices of the period, the design and manufacture were left largely to local artisans who produced weapons under royal tutelege.[2]

The control of the crown also extended to the extraction and sale of saltpeter. essential to the early use of gunpowder. Only royal arsenals or authorized dealers could sell saltpeter. Francis I prohibited its export to assure the crown an adequate supply. For over 100 years the privilege of gathering this valued element was assigned to a special class, so-called *fermiers généraux*, who retained a monopoly over its collection almost to the time of the French Revolution. Responsibility for producing gunpowder and saltpeter was brought under state control during the revolutionary upheaval in a law passed in 1797 and kept in force for a century thereafter. It transformed those connected with these materials into state functionaries. The state-controlled system had several advantages: it assured supplies for French forces, controlled transfers to foreign states by crown officials, and provided profits from sales to enlarge the public treasury.

The production of hand weapons and firearms similarly fell under progressive state control. Corporations of master craftsmen were engaged to produce and sell arms. Regulations governing their work can be traced to the beginning of the fifteenth century. These corporations initially furnished weapons to individuals in the service of the crown and, later, with the creation of the embryo of a permanent army under Charles VII, directly to the king's own troops. Until the revolution, French arms production was insufficient to satisfy state demand. Extensive foreign purchases were made in Holland, Italy, and Germany to supplement national production. By the time of Louis XIV, efforts were in train to bring small arms production for export or private use under royal direction. These measures were not wholly successful. A report to the crown in 1637 noted that there were enough weapons in private hands to arm 40,000 men. Exercising control over these weapons and the ateliers where they were fabricated became a test of royal authority and was pursued with varying degrees of success and enthusiasm until the collapse of the ancien regime.

The production of heavy armaments, including artillery and mortars, was of particular interest to the French crown.[3] The Grand Master of Artillery was responsible for supplying the crown's military forces with cannon, mounts, and equipment. These were largely produced by master iron forge craftsmen. A decentralized system of supply was organized in which many of these craftsmen were commissioned to produce heavy armor as part of their other commercial ventures. The feudal practice of obliging noblemen, owing fealty to the king, to supply their own arms was not without its inconveniences. It could guarantee neither an adequate supply of arms nor the safety of the crown against disgruntled nobles who were often better equipped than the French king.

From the time of Charles VIII in the fifteenth century, arsenals serving the crown were already operating in Lyon and Strasbourg. The first attempt at standardizing production was made by specifying bronze as the desired metal. Under Pierre Bessoneau and the brothers John and Gaspard Bureau, the French crown quickly drew abreast of England as the leading developer of artillery in Europe. Caissons were lightened and streamlined and gun calibers simplified.[4] Louis XI carried this work forward. Iron cannonballs were employed and artillery calibers were reduced to increase the range of fire. Jean d'Estrées, Henry II's Grand Master of Artillery, created heavy and light sets of artillery pieces. Specifications were established for artillery. One-third of the crown's artillery was to be heavy cannon capable of firing projectiles between 15 to 33 pounds; the remaining two-thirds of light cannon were supposed to launch cannonballs of 1 to 7 pounds. Francis I had earlier constructed a foundry and munitions magazine in Paris which was placed under the direction of a private entrepreneur. This marks the first real attempt to develop an arsenal system devoted to crown needs. Henry II, the son of Francis I, extended the Paris works by creating a regional network of 14 arsenals to produce cannons, powder, and projectiles. The arquebus, employed extensively in the religious wars, gave way eventually to the lighter and more manipulable musket.[5] Perfections were gradually introduced with the flintlock musket, and the pike was replaced during the reign of Louis XIV with what became the modern bayonet.[6]

The standardization of equipment—caliber, shot, mountings, charge, and moving platforms—developed slowly. Often in battle, cannons issuing from different royal suppliers could not use interchangeable munitions even when the weapons ostensibly had the same caliber. Thanks to the initiative of Jean-Florent Vallière and Jean-Baptiste Gribeauval, private and public arsenals supplying the state became progressively more uniform in their production of heavy armaments. Vallière, the first inspector-general of the royal artillery (1732), regulated the form and bore of firing, standardized some manufacturing processes, and reduced gun calibers to five. Gribeauval introduced into France successful Prussian techniques in producing artillery pieces. Oversight was assured by the General Director of the Forges.[7] A national system of heavy armaments was installed, covering field, siege, defense, and coastal artillery. Gribeauval's system, adopted in 1765, continued through the revolution and the Napoleonic period. The science of ballistics was also advanced by the crown in artillery schools organized in the aftermath of the Seven Years' War. It was first at Brienne, one of the most renowned of these technical schools, and later at the Paris Military School that Napoleon was trained as an artillery officer.[8] The successes of French armies between 1792 and 1814 owe much to the legacy of the military engineers who had been servants of the crown.

The irregular but increasing control of the French state over naval construction and armament paralleled the expansion of its direction of small arms and artillery manufacture.[9] A royal arsenal and shipbuilding system slowly developed, although it never fully replaced private works. Philip IV (Le Bel) erected the *Clos de Galées* on the Seine at Rouen to construct a royal fleet. The latter eventually grew to include 4 galleys, 24 sailing vessels, and 20 transport ships, supplemented by foreign vessels and the Norman commercial fleet. The rank of admiral was created in 1244. Philip VI and Charles V furthered the idea of a royal navy. Jean de Vienne, a minister of Charles V, built for the first time warships weighing over 300 tons mounted with heavy cannon.[10]

Distracted by English occupation during the Hundred Years' War (1337-1453) and by internal revolt, French kings in the fifteenth century were in no position to advance the development of a national navy. With the English at bay (though they held Calais until 1558) and domestic opposition on the defensive, Francis I was able to revive this effort by constructing the port at Le Havre and by building several major fighting vessels. Lack of funds prevented the erection of a fleet capable of challenging English sea power. Like his predecessors, Francis I relied on mercenaries, principally Turks and Italians, to harass English shipping. Henry II had more success in creating a royal fleet. With the assistance of Antoine Escalin, as admiral of France, Henry II commanded by 1548 a respectable fleet of 50 sailing vessels capable of transporting 10,000 men and naval cannon whose size and caliber were prescribed by the crown.[11] Henry IV is credited with having rebuilt France's Mediterranean fleet leading to French naval dominance over the Spanish fleet during the reign of his son, Louis XIII (1610-1643).[12]

Cardinal Richelieu was the first to put the French Navy on a solid financial and administrative footing. Partly to meet the Huguenot challenge centered at La Rochelle, he worked industriously to build a dependable navy. He established a system for retaining master naval craftsmen and ship personnel on a regular basis. Dutch shipbuilders, more technologically advanced than French craftsmen, were engaged as a model for their French counterparts. By Colbert's time, in the second half of the seventeenth century, royal ports or arsenals existed at Dunkirk, Le Havre, Brest, Brouage, Marseilles, Toulon, Bayonne, and

Lorient. Rochefort subsequently replaced Brouage as a royal arsenal. Brest became Louis XIV's principal naval arsenal. Ship construction and naval armaments were placed under the direction of an intendant who was "l'homme de sa Majesté." Naval foundries were established at Chaussade, Guérigny, and St. Gervais. Alongside these royal ports and arsenals there continued to prosper private works which were indispensable in meeting the needs of the crown. By 1685, Louis XIV had 120 large men-of-war, each with 50 cannons, at his disposal.

After the disaster of La Hogue in 1692, French naval ambitions were again checked. Unable to confront the English fleet directly, French strategists devised a *guerre de course*, based on fast, light ships to inflict damage on English commerce. Parallel to the work of Gribeauval, a line of naval ministers laid the foundation for the navy of the revolution and empire. John Maurepas increased crown spending for naval vessels and arms. Rouillé created the naval foundry at Ruelle, which is still in operation, as well as the naval academy. The Seven Years' War (1756-1763) stimulated further constructions that resulted by one accounting in a naval force on the eve of the revolution of almost 300 ships, with 9,000 cannons. Uniform standards for ship size and armor—grouped into vessels of 118, 80, and 74 cannons—were also specified.[13]

The actual number of battle-ready vessels was much lower than 300. Many were in a bad state of repair, unseaworthy, or ill-equipped to engage enemy forces. The British attack on Toulon in 1793 depleted the Republic's ships of the line by almost half.[14] The Committee of Public Safety, into whose hands the protection of the revolution had fallen, launched an ambitious naval rebuilding program at Brest, Lorient, and Rochefort. To meet urgent defense needs, economic controls were instituted to force suppliers to furnish services and materials below market prices, and workers in naval arsenals were forbidden to strike or disrupt construction or repairs.[15] By 1794, the number of vessels of the line and frigates under construction was twice that of Great Britain.[16] At the rate of construction begun in the early years of the revolution, the French fleet might well have been a match for Britain. Losses in battle, continued internal upheaval, and failure of those in control of the revolution to sustain a long-term naval building program conceded the dominance of the seas to England.[17]

ARMS PRODUCTION BETWEEN THE NAPOLEONIC WARS AND WORLD WAR I

The Industrial Revolution, the growth and expansion of the French economy, and the gradual harnessing of scientific discovery and technological innovation to warfare gradually transformed the French armaments industry during the nineteenth century. In earlier times, when progress in arms was slow, finances short, and royal authority disputed, most of the attention of the crown was devoted to the problem of recruiting and financing armies and navies for war and of controlling disbanded units in peacetime. After 1800, the state had to be concerned as never before with the nation's capacity to produce large quantities of a progressively expanding number of technologically advanced weapons for a nation in arms. Before the Industrial Revolution, military strategy on land was tied largely to relatively small forces. The firepower of foot soldiers, bolstered by slow-moving armor and inaccurate artillery, was the principal means of delivering munitions against opponent forces. At sea, military operations depended on the hazards of sail and wind and the number of cannon that could be marshaled for broadside fire. Battlefield success hinged more on an adequate supply of muskets, shot, cannon, and powder—not to mention luck—than on improvements in weapons design. To protect the revolution against its enemies at home and abroad, the Committee of Public Safety, under Lazare Carnot's impulsion, created hundreds of arms manufacturers to supply the newly developing republican army. By 1794 Paris was producing 750 muskets a day, an output greater than the rest of Europe.

The restoration monarchies of the Bourbons and Louis-Philippe (1814-1848) were more concerned about internal stability than foreign foes. The efforts of the crown to restore royal control over weapons manufacture was aimed more at domestic opponents than at rebuilding France's arms production capacity for foreign conflict. Keeping, selling, importing, or exporting arms were prohibited. The Prussian victory at Sedan, which led to the military defeat and fall of the government of Napoleon III, shocked French leaders of the Third Republic into re-examining the nation's military preparedness. The superiority of Prussian military planning and deployment, as well as the technical proficiency of Prussian armaments, could not be ignored. The introduction of new weapons like the breech-firing needle gun and use of railroads to speed troops to the battlefield forced a major reform of French thinking about war and arms manufacture. The Prussian concept of the general staff was adopted by French armed forces. The private sector was encouraged to develop new arms as a stimulus to state arsenals.

That more than numbers were needed became evident after the stunning Prussian victory of 1870. Until the Franco-Prussian War, expenditures for arms and equipment were generally quite low. Table 1-1 summarizes these expenditures over ten-year intervals from 1820 to

Table 1-1. Production of War Materials for French Forces: 1820-1913
(In millions of francs)

Period	Ground Arms	Naval Arms	Total Arms	Ground Arms[a]	Naval Arms[a]	Total Arms[a]
1820-1824	4.8	12.6	17.4	10	9	9
1825-1834	10.3	14.0	24.3	21	10	13
1835-1844	6.0	15.3	21.3	12	11	11
1845-1854	5.3	17.5	22.8	11	12	12
1855-1864	6.5	39.6	46.1	13	28	24
1865-1874	28.4	31.1	59.5	57	22	31
1875-1884	69.9	49.3	119.2	141	35	62
1885-1894	46.3	76.6	122.9	94	54	64
1895-1904	35.8	115.5	151.3	72	81	79
1905-1913	49.5	142.1	191.6	100	100	100

SOURCE: Adapted from François Crouzet, "Recherches sur la production d'armements en France," *Revue Historique*, No. 509 (January-March 1974), 50-51.

[a] Index: 1905-1913 = 100.

the eve of World War I. It is clear that spending on arms was modest for the first half of the century after the conclusion of the Napoleonic Wars. Arms spending for the Navy began to rise in the 1850s and for the Army a decade later. Both trends were given some slight impetus by the Second Empire.

Spending for arms as a proportion of overall governmental expenditures for ground forces was never great. As Crouzet shows in two articles in *Revue Historique*,[18] equipment purchases never rose above 4 percent of defense spending in the successive ten-year periods between 1825 and 1864. Thereafter, the highest percentage spent for weapons was 9.24 percent in the decade after the German victory in the Franco-Prussian War. In the decade before World War I, spending for arms only attained a level of 5.12 percent of expenditures for ground forces during the period. Most funds were devoted simply to the daily maintenance of the Army. What fluctuations occurred during this century appear related to changing economic conditions, to foreign crises, like Fashoda or the Moroccan scare of 1905-1906, as well as to weak, but steady, pressures from the military for modernization. Even such crises as the Crimean War did not stimulate much of an increase in spending on hardware. In the decade between 1855 and 1864, arms procurement represented less than 1.5 percent of the military budget.[19]

After the French defeat in 1870 and the creation of the Third Republic, an additional restraint on large ground-force expenditures was introduced. The hesitant commitment of the Third Republic to a large and powerful army may partly be explained by the struggle between conservative elements within the armed forces, suspicious of popular rule, and the liberal leadership of the Third Republic, a tension dramatized by the Dreyfus affair at the turn of the century. The loyalty of the professional army corps to republican principles was always ambiguous. World War I did not resolve these doubts. Since the principles of nationalism and republicanism were simultaneously at stake, the Army's commitment to popular rule was never fully tested. The nationalistic fervor of the Left also eased the tension between the Army and the nation that might otherwise have irreparably split the republican regime from the armed forces.

Whatever the combination of factors explaining the vacillating support of the Third Republic for ground-force modernization, France was clearly unprepared for the scale and intensity of World War I operations. The modest expenditures for arms in the nineteenth century did not preclude modest technological progress along several fronts in equipping French forces with new weapons. Napoleon III adopted a field howitzer with a single caliber. By 1858, rifled cannons (although still of bronze and front-loaded) were progressively introduced. After the defeat by Prussia, spending for new arms increased rapidly for a decade, attaining 104 million francs in 1877. Average spending reached 70 million francs between 1875 and 1884 or ten times prewar levels. Breech-loading artillery, made of steel, was gradually substituted for less efficient cannons. Between 1877 and 1886, artillery of various calibers was produced; inventories grew from 1,229 to 12,664 units. By the end of the century, the rapid-firing 75 mm. cannon was being produced as a standard field artillery piece. The same record of progress was not achieved in heavy artillery where German producers maintained a clear lead. A program for the construction of these weapons was passed by the French Parliament on July 15, 1914, only a month before the start of World War I.

Along with artillery, ground forces were supplied with successive generations of new hand weapons. The breech-loading, rifled *chassepot* was distributed to troops in 1866; 1,200,000 copies were produced in four years. The chassepot was subsequently modified and a metallic cartridge substituted for the primitive paper binding that had been previously used. Three times as many of this later model were produced over a twelve-year period as the original model. The new Lebel rifle as well as an array of improved munitions and explosives came into service at the close of the nineteenth century.

Arms expenditures for naval forces followed a somewhat smoother course, partly due to the heavy capitalization needs of the service and the longer lead time needed to construct warships. Naval weaponry underwent a more fundamental revolution than ground armaments. After 400 years of subservience to galleys and sails, a steam-driven navy could now dominate wind, waves, and currents. Ironclads rapidly replaced wooden vessels. Successive European naval arms races at the end of the nineteenth century ensued in which states vied for naval supremacy. The Anglo-German competition dominated the continent. The rise of the United States and Japan as global powers was due directly to their development of modern navies, signaled by the victory of Admiral Dewey over the Spanish squadron at Manila in 1898 and of Admiral Togo at Tsushima over the Russian fleet in 1905.

A race also developed between offensive and defensive naval warfare. It was propelled, on the one hand, by advances in firepower, resulting from improved artillery and munitions, and, on the other, by the ability to protect ships with thicker and tempered armor plating. France was somewhat slow in joining these national and technological races. The defeat at Sedan in 1870 signaled Germany's rise as the dominant continental power, replacing France as Britain's principal competitor in Europe. Its larger population and industrial base outstripped French efforts to keep pace. Spending for French naval armaments averaged below 24 percent of overall spending for the Navy in successive ten-year periods between 1824 and 1874. It began to rise under the impact of modernization pressures to 27 percent in the decade between 1875 and 1884 and reached a level of approximately 38 percent in the twenty years preceding World War I.

The revolution in naval armaments began with the launching in 1852 of the *Napoleon*, the first armored frigate to join the French Navy; 18 frigates and 7 corvettes were subsequently launched. Tonnage also increased from the 5,600-ton *Gloire* to the 14,900-ton *Patrie* in 1901, rising to over 25,000 tons for armored vessels produced at the outset of World War I. Between 1910 and 1914, the keels of 12 dreadnoughts were laid. Naval artillery also experienced a revolution. In advance of army modernization, naval artillery pieces were rifled, breech-loaded, and fitted to fire more accurate and powerful shells.

Exports of French arms were small in the century after the Napoleonic Wars. Table 1-2 summarizes the export of ground and naval arms by ten-year periods between 1825 and 1913. The pattern is irreg-

Table 1-2. Export of French Ground and Naval Armaments: 1825-1913[a]
(In millions of francs)

Period	Ground Arms	% of Ground Arms	Naval Arms	% of Naval Arms	Total Arms	% of Total Arms Produced	Total Arms (1905-1913 = 100)
1825-1834	.4	3.7	—	—	.4	1.6	—
1835-1844	.5	7.7	—	—	.5	2.3	—
1845-1854	1.7	24.3	—	—	1.7	6.9	—
1855-1864	5.8	47.2	3.5	7.1	9.3	16.8	57
1865-1874	2.9	9.2	4.1	6.4	7.0	10.5	43
1875-1884	4.9	6.6	5.2	4.2	10.1	7.8	62
1885-1894	7.6	13.6	10.6	7.9	18.2	12.9	111
1895-1904	6.6	15.6	11.3	6.9	17.9	10.6	109
1905-1913	12.8	20.5	3.6	2.0	16.4	7.9	100

SOURCE: Table 1-1, Crouzet, "Recherches sur la production d'armements en France," pp. 50-51.
[a] Averages by decades.

ular. Exports as a percentage of total production rose slowly from the 1820s, reaching a high point of almost 13 percent in the period 1885 to 1894, while dropping to 7.9 percent of total production in the decade before World War I.

To look only at total exports, without differentiating between ground and naval armaments, is deceiving. As Table 1-2 notes, ground arms were exported at a much higher rate of total production than naval armaments. In the decade between 1855 and 1864, almost 50 percent of all ground weapons produced were sent abroad. Just before World War I, France was sending one-fifth of its ground arms to other countries. Table 1-3 lists the value of ground arms and munitions exported by

Table 1-3. Export of French Ground Arms: 1885-1913
(In millions of francs)

Period	Portable Arms	Artillery	Projectiles
1885-1894	2.7	3.7	1.2
1895-1904	1.6	2.5	2.5
1905-1913	0.8	6.5	5.4

SOURCE: Table 1-1, Crouzet, "Recherches sur la production d'armements en France," p. 64.

France in the three decades preceding World War I. In contrast, a much smaller proportion of naval production was exported, although much more was spent on naval arms. The value of exported naval arms and material never exceeded 7.9 percent of overall production during the nineteenth century. Naval exports ceased shortly before World War I, suggesting that there was little excess production capacity. Preparation for war absorbed most of France's shipbuilding effort. Much of what was exported was not ships but armor plating.

Most of the arms produced for domestic or foreign consumption came from national arsenals and naval yards. Private manufacture remained negligible until the middle of the nineteenth century. In 1885, legislation reinstituted the private manufacture of arms.[20] This shift in supply policy accorded well with the bourgeois leadership of the fledgling Third Republic. There were widely held expectations that private manufacturers would produce more and better arms to promote France's commercial position and to ensure access to arms from a wider range of commercial outlets than governmental arsenals. Arms merchants and the marketplace, later to be attacked after World War I as contributing factors to the conflict,[21] were called upon to stimulate arms programs and meet national needs. These expectations were only modestly fulfilled. "Privatization" of the arms industry was slow. Most of what the Army needed was supplied by the arsenals at Puteaux and Tarbes and the foundry at Bourges. Major Army contracts to private firms were not let on a significant scale until just shortly before the outbreak of war in 1914. The private sector experienced losses through most of this period. Several companies were forced to sell or to go out of business for lack of sufficient orders. Naval construction rested largely in governmental hands, although those private firms that were able to establish themselves as suppliers flourished. Production of ground and naval arms fell into the hands of a small number of firms. Schneider was the largest private arms supplier of ground equipment. With Marene-Homecourt and Chatillon-Commentary, it was also among the three major producers of naval armaments.

Exports of arms from private sources fell below expectations. The German Krupp firm proved more resourceful than French arms entrepreneurs, and Germany's share of the world market was twice as large as France's. Only the Schneider group proved to be a formidable competitor for German firms. It sold its arms, artillery, and munitions to 23 countries, including the Balkans, where French arms were purchased by Bulgaria, Serbia, and Greece.

Whatever the shortcomings surrounding the French arms industry before World War I might have been, it was still able to respond heroically during the four years of hostilities. Its success may be measured by the quantity and quality of the arms supplied to French and allied forces. By the end of the war, France was the largest manufacturer of warplanes in the world and supplied much of the equipment used by American expeditionary forces. Its 75 mm. light artillery proved a match for what the German industry was able to field. Table 1-4 presents selected data for French military production during World War I. Production reached unparalleled levels.

Table 1-4. Selected Artillery, Explosives, Machine Guns, and Portable Arms Procured by French and Allied Armed Forces: 1914-1917

	1914	1915	1916	1917
Materiel				
75 mm.	4,050	3,240	4,260	5,890
105 L (1913)	—	78	303	643
155 C Schneider	—	—	66	474
155 C St. Chamond	—	—	16	358
Shells (daily production, Aug. 1)				
75 mm.	8,000	210,000	230,000	175,000 (record of 292,000, May 1917)
105 mm.	200	7,400	17,500	2,500 (record of 18,900, June 1917)
155 mm.	200	29,500	47,000	37,700 (record of 52,000, Sept. 1917)
Powder (in tons)	—	28,865	55,280	111,045
Machine Guns	5,100	10,332	24,991	39,987
Rifles (in millions)	2.88	2.09	2.137	2.494

Source: France, Ministère de la Guerre, *Les Armées françaises dans la grande guerre* (Paris: Imprimerie Nationale, 1937), xi, 567-571.

Each of the services had its own technical directorate charged with overseeing the production of equipment and the introduction of new weapons into the inventory of the armed forces. Overall direction was placed in a Minister of Armaments to whom arsenals and private manufacturers were responsible. The Navy relied heavily on its own yards and workshops. Private firms, like Schneider, provided torpedoes and cannon. Ground forces, which bore the bulk of the fighting, drew from a mix of public and private sources. Many of the newer and most effective weapons came from private firms. The factories of Creusot, within the Schneider group, supplied mortars and fuses; Brandt, machine guns; Hotchkiss and Renault, tanks, motorcars, and trucks. Arsenals at Bourges, Roanne, and Tarbes provided various kinds of artillery, powder, and shells. Rueil and Satory furnished tanks and armor.

Military aircraft was largely the preserve of private industry. Until the 1930s, the War Ministry preferred to rely on financial inducements and close working relations with firms in the private sector rather than press for the development of separate state manufacturing capabilities to compete with them. Part of the explanation for this development lies in the slow recognition by the French High Command of the military value of the airplane. Flying was considered a sport, an interesting distraction but with few, and limited, military applications.

The French military were also slow to learn how to use effectively the weapons that were available to them.[22] One war behind in their thinking, they placed almost total reliance on an offensive strategy. Plan 17, France's counter to the German Schlieffen Plan, envisioned a French defeat of the main elements of Germany's army on France's eastern frontier before German troops could mobilize and sweep through Belgium on their way to Paris.[23] Such a thrust was also calculated to assure French occupation of the lost provinces of Alsace and Lorraine and open the road to Berlin.

French strategists profoundly misunderstood the destructive power of modern armaments. Aircraft was initially confined to a reconnaissance role. Rapid-firing, accurate artillery and deadly machine guns were treated as support for attacking ground forces. Only after heavy battlefield losses were suffered was the lesson learned that they were primarily useful to negate concentrated troop assaults against fixed, entrenched positions. Tanks were employed late in the war. When used, their capacity to pierce enemy lines was neither clearly understood nor were military commanders alert to the opportunity of exploiting breakthroughs occasioned by their use.[24] Slowly, the French military came to understand that the massed artillery, machine guns, and mortars— used by concealed troops protected by fortifications and barbed wire— made offensive war so costly as to bring into question the utility of war itself. Of the 8,410,000 men mobilized for the war, 73 percent are estimated to have either been killed (1,357,000), wounded (4,266,000), or taken prisoner or missing in action (537,000).[25] The attackers suffered greater casualties than the defenders. Gains, measured often in yards, not miles, were paid for with hundreds of thousands of casualties.

France's eventual success lay more in its alliance ties and the imperial resources at its disposal than in its masterful use of arms. The Entente Cordiale furnished France access to Britain's navy and to the manpower, industrial resources, and raw materials of the British Empire. Germany's naval inferiority dictated its reliance on submarine warfare as a counter to allied control of the seas, whose unintended result was American entry into the war as a consequence of attacks on U.S. shipping. Not the genius of French military strategy, but the productive capacity of the French arms industry and the superior resources of France's allies proved to be decisive. As the military balance tipped against Germany and as German domestic support for the war finally eroded, the stage was set for the armistice of November 1918.

THE INTERWAR PERIOD

The French military prepared for World War II by refighting World War I. French planners envisioned a future armed conflict as a long war of attrition similar to World War I. The primary task of French forces was to deny a quick victory to an attacking foe, preparing the way for the greater weight of indigenous, colonial, and allied resources at France's disposal to win the war. Planning rested on a number of assumptions: (a) a strong defensive posture based on the Maginot Line; (b) low defense expenditures in peacetime to minimize the defense burden on the French population and economy; (c) a reserve system capable of rapid mobilization of national and imperial manpower in time of war; (d) a network of bilateral and multilateral alliances to check Germany—and to defeat it if war should erupt; and (e) reliance on international pledges renouncing war, like the Kellogg-Briand Pact, and on arms limitation accords, like the Versailles Treaty and the Washington naval disarmament agreements, to maintain France's military ascendancy over Germany.[26]

This strategy had a deadening effect on French military strategy and practice. The retarded development of French military thinking in the interwar period is reflected by the outdated notions about tank and air warfare widely held throughout the French military establishment. Armor and aircraft were considered appendages to the infantry. Neither was conceived as capable of independent, much less decisive, military action. The instruction manual issued by the French High Command for the use of tanks laid down these confining guidelines for the use of ground armor: "Combat tanks are machines to accompany the infantry. In battle, tank units constitute an integral part of the infantry. . . .

Tanks are only supplementary means, put temporarily at the disposition of the infantry. They strengthen considerably the action of the latter but they do not replace it. Their action, to be effective, must be exploited by the infantry at the moment of their impact; the progress of the infantry and its seizing of objectives are alone decisive."[27]

The airplane fared no better. The High Command's instruction manual devoted only 3 of 177 pages to airpower. There was no discussion of strafing, interdiction, or troop support missions. "Direct action of air forces in the battle is illusory," wrote General Philippe Pétain, hero of Verdun, commander of the French armed forces, and one of the most influential military thinkers in the interwar period. "There is no such thing as the aerial battle. . . . There is only the battle on the ground."[28] Pétain summarized his position in 1939 in a much quoted preface to General Chauvineau's book, *Is an Invasion Still Possible?*[29] He rejected ideas advanced by Colonel Charles de Gaulle and General J.E.B. Estienne, who advocated the combined use of armor and motorized infantry in conjunction with aircraft along a wide, long movable front. He dismissed the view that these forces, acting in unison, could decide the outcome of battle by splitting enemy forces, harassing rear supply lines, and spreading panic in the ranks: "It would be imprudent to conclude that an armored force . . . is an irresistible weapon. The decisive results obtained by this force would have no tomorrow. . . . Before a barrage of antitank guns and mines the armored division would be at the mercy of a counterattack on the flanks. . . . As for tanks, which are supposed by some to bring us a shortening of wars, their incapacity is striking."[30]

The French High Command translated its defensive strategy into a coherent, if increasingly irrelevant, set of plans and policies. Spending for new equipment, especially for ground and air forces, all but stopped until the rearmament program of the middle 1930s that responded belatedly to the German military buildup. France emerged from World War I with the largest army in Europe. Its weapons arsenal and supplies exceeded all other states. Its military predominance seemed assured. The notion that innovation in weapons design might overturn the perceived superiority of the defense was dismissed since the peace treaties forbade Germany from developing or producing new weapons. Meanwhile, French ground and air forces fed on their existing inventories. New prototypes, such as the Hotchkiss antitank and Schneider 75 mm. antiaircraft cannon or the Renault, Somua, and Hotchkiss tanks, were delayed for adoption until after 1934.[31] Between 1920 and 1934 only 10 percent of the military budget was devoted to new military equipment.[32]

Table 1-5. Distribution of Funds for New Military Equipment for
French Armed Forces: 1920-1939
(In percentages)

	1920-1936	1937	1938	1939
Navy	42	28	22	17
Army	31	40	36	32
Air Force	27	32	42	51

SOURCE: Robert Jacomet, *L'Armement de la France: 1936-1939* (Paris: Lajeunesse, 1945), pp. 137-143.

Table 1-5 outlines the proportion of funds assigned to the various military services from 1920 to 1939. Until 1937, the Navy enjoyed the largest share of a progressively falling total. Given the defensive mentality of French military planners, it made sense to favor the Navy. It linked France to its empire and allies. Guided by lessons drawn from World War I, French strategists relied on access to these resources to tip the scales against Germany. Even Charles de Gaulle, who vigorously dissented from official thinking about armor, conceded France's strategic dependence on its imperial possessions and on British and American assistance. In his appeal for support on June 18, 1940, de Gaulle condemned Vichy for failing to resist German power although imperial resources and allied help were still available to carry on the struggle. De Gaulle had argued unsuccessfully for an offensive strategy. Quick-moving armor and fighter aircraft would block a German advance for a long enough period to permit France to invoke the superior resources at its disposal to defeat Germany. Such a posture was also viewed as suited to France's treaty obligations, particularly with the East European states. France could hardly assist its allies, much less itself, from a fixed defensive position if confronted by a foe possessing superior local firepower and strategic maneuverability.

Most interwar French strategists and political leaders rejected proposals to increase spending on new equipment or to maintain a large standing army—or even, as de Gaulle had suggested, to strengthen the professional army corps. Neither economic resources nor political will appeared available to support higher levels of preparedness. After naval needs were met, what remained of the National Assembly's capital authorization for weapons was allocated for an elaborate network of fortifications on France's western frontier. The Maginot Line was supposed to check a German attack launched from the east. The bulk of French forces were then to be deployed along a line running from the

Maginot Line to the Belgian frontier and the English Channel. These elements were to carry the war against Germany onto Belgian soil, shielding France from invasion over the Belgian plain and protecting its mining and industrial plants concentrated north of Paris. Behind this defense line, France's arms production capabilities could then be mobilized for a long war. Troops would assume a defensive posture, relying on concealed positions and high firepower, until allies and empire could join France to wear down Germany before the final knockout blow, an offense against a foe fatally weakened by attrition.

Other factors also encouraged a defensive strategy built on a triad of fixed fortifications, an overseas navy, and a mobilization strategy keyed to the rapid conversion of the civilian population and industry into a war machine once armed hostilities became imminent. The firsthand experience of officers of the French High Command in World War I hampered reevaluation of strategic doctrine in light of increased firepower and mobility in ground armor and attack aircraft. It reinforced wishful thinking about German military plans. German strategists were expected to be as paralyzed by memories of the carnage of World War I as their French counterparts. There was also the widely held assumption within the French general staff that there were sharp limits to the endurance and sacrifice that could be expected from the French nation and armed forces. French military commanders still remembered the harsh measures that had to be used during World War I to suppress repeated mutinies in the ranks.

French strategists argued further that France was a status quo, not a revisionist, power. Having no territorial claims, its defensive military posture presumably complemented its political stance. The French military and political leadership also banked on the Versailles settlement to check Germany. The Versailles Treaty placed limits on German personnel under arms and forbade Germany to produce tanks, heavy artillery, or submarines. It also neutralized the Rhineland. The League of Nations created a collective security framework within which the victorious allied powers were expected to play central roles in deterring and defeating aggression, should it occur. Articles 8, 23, and 24 of the treaty also envisaged disarmament talks, including the control of the arms trade, among the major powers. The limitations defined by the Washington naval disarmament agreements in the early 1920s guided French naval construction for most of the interwar period. They also raised hopes, inflated by pacifist sentiment, that progress in limiting naval tonnage could be extended to ground and air forces. These efforts were also accompanied by well-intentioned but quixotic diplomatic initiatives to outlaw war.

Decreased military spending was consistent with French interwar economic means. Since deficit spending had to be continued after the war, lowered expenditures for military forces freed resources for debt management and rising demands for greater social welfare. Internal financial controls applied by an overbearing bureaucracy also put additional limits on spending for the armed services. The practice of extending funds to the military branches through multiyear authorizations and paying for deliveries through annual appropriations was not introduced into France until the late 1930s. Before this reform, funds had to be committed and spent with no appreciable carryovers during the year that materials were ordered and delivered to the armed forces. Paper savings in spending were recorded at the expense of army preparedness. Only the Navy partially escaped these restrictive accounting procedures since its building program necessarily carried over several years. Through the simple expedient of controlled annual spending, the Minister of Finance held sway over the Minister of War. Had the government wished to spend more on defense, the global depression and the diminution of French economic productivity largely precluded greater expenditures. Expected German reparations failed to materialize, and the French were compelled to default on the foreign loans floated to finance the war.

French diplomacy failed to compensate for the shortcomings of French military power. The alliance structure erected after World War I produced unreliable and burdensome allies. Meanwhile, France's military capabilities decreased in inverse proportion to the expansion of its exterior security obligations. In the west, the French advanced the notion of an Anglo-American security pact to turn the League of Nations into a guarantee pact against Germany. American rejection of the Versailles Treaty and the reluctance of Britain to tie itself to the European continent—even less so to French security needs—reduced France again to its own sparse resources and to its diplomatic wits and resourcefulness. A Sovietized Russia was no longer available to counterbalance a resurgent Nazi Germany. French and allied efforts to use the Versailles Treaty to enforce a vindictive peace on Berlin contributed to the German-Soviet Rapallo Pact (1922) which joined the two outcasts in opposition to the postwar power balance in Europe, even before Hitler's rise to power in 1933.

France's alliances with unstable regimes in eastern Europe were also weak reeds to lean upon. France and Poland signed a treaty of friendship in 1921 and a secret protocol of military assistance. France also aligned itself with the security interests of the states of the Little Entente—Czechoslovakia, Romania, and Yugoslavia—that had been carved from the remains of the Austro-Hungarian and Russian empires as well as Serbia and Montenegro. The hazards of these accords are succinctly described by E. H. Carr: "France was now definitely committed to the maintenance not only of the Versailles Treaty, but of the whole European peace settlement. It was no longer her concern merely to keep Germany at bay on the Rhine and prevent her from strengthening her position in the east. It became a recognized French interest to support Poland against Lithuania, Czechoslovakia against Hungary, and Yugoslavia and Romania against Bulgaria. . . ."[33] As long as France held the military upper hand in Europe with the largest army in Europe, its own security and that of its allies could be guaranteed. In the 1920s, facing a defeated Germany beset by grave economic crisis, these conditions seemed immutable. Forever lasted only a decade.

French arms transfer policy was only partially responsive to France's military needs and international obligations. According to League of Nations tabulations, France, compared to other states, was not in the forefront as an arms supplier. Only part of its exports can be attributed to alliance ties. Most arms and military equipment were sent to nonalliance states. Table 1-6 presents the average annual sale of small arms and ammunition from 1929 to 1938 for the nine leading supplier states which controlled approximately 90 percent of the arms trade covered by League data. France is listed fourth, accounting for 10.7 percent of total trade. In the period 1931 to 1935, for which statistics are available on a country-specific basis, France sold the bulk of its war materials to nine countries. These are listed in Table 1-7. Most sales were to non-European states. Argentina was France's principal customer, with Japan and China, antagonists in the 1930s, slightly exceeding Argentina's total. In Europe the leading recipients of French materials were Poland, Yugoslavia, and Belgium.

These figures would appear to underestimate the volume of French arms shipments. American military intelligence reports[34] present what seems to be a more realistic picture of French transfers, although the number of different forms of military equipment sent to specific countries is not presented. Table 1-8 summarizes these transfers in the period between 1930 and the outbreak of World War II for the six leading suppliers in each category.

In the interwar period, the U.S. led in the sale of combat, transport, and trainer aircraft; the United Kingdom was first in submarines and warships; Austria outstripped all other countries in the delivery of armored cars. France led in only one category—tanks, an area where it had been traditionally thought to be lagging. French export success is surprising since the rearmament program began late. Robert Jacomet,

Table 1-6. Exports of Arms and Ammunition of Principal Exporting Countries: 1929-1938
(In millions of former gold dollars)

	1929	1930	1931	1932	1933	1934	1935	1936	1937	1938	Annual Average of 10 Years	% of Grand Total
Great Britain	21.8	17.0	13.4	10.1	10.1	8.5	9.6	9.7	11.9	17.1	12.9	25.0
Czechoslovakia	3.2	5.3	3.9	1.4	3.2	8.7	10.5	7.7	7.2	14.3	6.5	12.6
Germany	7.5	6.5	5.2	3.8	4.1	3.3	2.5	5.3	9.0	8.4	5.6	10.9
France	9.4	7.0	2.7	9.3	8.5	8.0	6.6	10.6	6.7	6.8	7.6[a]	10.7
United States	10.7	6.5	3.9	2.9	3.2	3.7	3.3	4.3	5.6	6.9	5.1	9.9
Sweden	3.0	4.3	3.7	3.7	3.4	3.7	3.3	2.9	5.7	7.8	4.2	8.1
Belgium	3.0	2.5	1.5	1.5	1.4	2.1	2.5	2.4	3.2	6.1	2.6	5.0
Switzerland	0.5	1.0	1.1	0.7	1.1	0.8	0.4	2.4	5.0	5.8	1.9	3.7
Italy	3.7	3.8	2.2	0.6	1.5	1.6	0.7	0.7	1.6	2.2	1.9	3.7
TOTAL	62.8	53.9	37.6	34.0	36.5	40.4	39.4	46.0	55.9	75.4	46.2	89.6
Other Countries	9.6	8.3	2.8	4.6	5.6	4.6	3.7	3.9	4.5	6.5	5.4	10.4
GRAND TOTAL	72.4	62.2	40.4	38.6	42.1	45.0	43.1	49.9	60.4	81.9	51.6	

Source: N. M. Sloutzki, *The World Armaments Race, 1919-1939* (Geneva: Carnegie Endowment for International Peace, 1941), p. 71.
Note: The exports do not include aircraft.
[a] The original table cites 5.5, an error in calculation.

Table 1-7. French Exports of Arms and Ammunition: 1931-1935
(In thousands of former gold dollars)

Countries of Destination	1931	1932	1933	1934	1935	Five-Year Totals
Principal European Countries						
Belgium-Luxembourg	286.1	277.2	149.6	278.7	129.4	1,121.0
Spain	48.8	45.1	36.6	119.3	213.2	463.0
Lithuania	—	—	2.0	245.7	6.7	254.4
Netherlands	41.2	24.0	3.8	7.8	—	76.8
Poland	417.3	2,018.8	1,185.6	1.275.7	259.7	5,157.1
Romania	78.5	1,507.2	58.6	2.8	390.0	2,037.1
Yugoslavia	—	300.3	1.5	—	—	301.8
TOTAL	871.9	4,172.6	1,437.7	1,930.0	999.0	9,411.2
Principal Non-European Countries						
Argentina	434.8	1,745.0	758.9	973.8	1,856.4	5,768.9
Brazil	130.7	539.6	161.9	29.4	6.5	868.1
China	120.9	606.9	1,841.3	93.6	284.4	2,947.1
Japan	—	1,185.6	1,090.6	361.7	538.9	3,176.8
TOTAL	686.4	4,077.1	3,852.7	1,458.5	2,686.2	12,760.9
Colonies and Protectorates	1,079.1	773.9	640.9	719.8	663.8	3,877.5
Other Countries	415.8	1,447.8	2,700.0	4,036.2	1,862.5	10,462.3
GRAND TOTAL	3,053.2	10,471.4	8,631.3	8,144.5	6,211.5	36,511.9

SOURCE: See Sloutzki, *World Armaments Race*, p. 79. The figures for Table 1-7 and Table 1-6 do not conform because two different sources were used by Sloutzki. The totals in Table 1-7 are more complete.

former Comptroller General of the French Army, lists only 194 new tanks produced as of June 1936.[35] In no other category did France place higher than third. In patrol vessels it was not among the six major suppliers.

There were complaints throughout the 1930s that French military equipment, even in the modest numbers recorded in Table 1-8, was often exported even when it was needed by French units.[36] Fault would seem to lie in the profits sought by private arms manufacturers and in the careless oversight exercised by French military authorities in ap-

Table 1-8. Transfer of French Military Equipment by the Six Leading Suppliers in Selected Categories: 1930-1939

	Aircraft	%	Transport Aircraft	%	Trainer Aircraft	%	Tanks	%	Armored Cars	%
U.S.	3,218	22.8	158	53.6	1,311	25.6	574	14.7	288	18.0
U.K.	2,435	17.3	30	10.2	1,231	24.0	1,071	26.1	—	—
France	2,204	15.6	31	7.1	834	16.3	1,091	27.9	189	11.8
Italy	1,786	12.7	38	12.9	146	2.8	424	10.9	—	—
Germany	1,336	9.5	29	9.8	954	18.6	—	—	183	11.4
U.S.S.R.	784	5.6	—	—	—	—	220	5.6	160	10.0
Sweden	—	—	12	4.1	—	—	—	—	—	—
Czechoslovakia	—	—	—	—	152	3.0	270	6.9	165	10.3
Austria	—	—	—	—	—	—	—	—	400	25.0

	Submarines	%	Warships	%	Patrol Vessels	%
U.S.	4.0	8	3	2.3	11	3.6
U.K.	18.0	36	76	58.9	62	20.5
France	5.0	10	13	10.1	—	—
Italy	12.0	24	23	17.8	143	47.2
Germany	4.0	8	—	—	40	13.2
Spain	—	—	5	3.9	10	3.3
Czechoslovakia	—	—	—	—	—	—
Japan	4.0	8	5	3.9	8	2.6

Source: Robert Harkavy, *The Arms Trade and International Systems* (Cambridge. Ma.: Ballinger, 1975), pp. 49-78.

proving sales. Arms shipments to Latin America, Japan, and China seem to have been guided largely by considerations of commercial gain. Sales to Japan ill-served French security interests in Asia, even when offset by arms export to the Chinese Nationalist regime.

Lapses in French High Command thinking were also apparent in its approval of tank deliveries to European states after the outbreak of hostilities with Germany. Poland, Romania, Yugoslavia, and Turkey received 235 of the latest 400-model Renault-35 tanks produced up to May 1940. Only 90 of these systems were in French units at the time of the German attack. During the *drôle de guerre*, 830 25 mm. antitank guns and over 500 pieces of artillery and ammunition were reportedly sold to foreign powers.[37] Some of these sales could be justified as elements of France's security obligations to Poland and the Little Entente. If France's rearmament program had not started so late, beginning in earnest in 1935, some of these sales might have been justified in support of its exterior security obligations. However, its tardy rearmament program essentially precluded France from meeting its own foreign security needs and, simultaneously, those of its newly acquired allies.

In the 1930s, the Hitler regime rapidly completed the dismantling of what the Weimar Republic had begun of the delicate military, economic, and diplomatic structure on which French hegemony in Europe rested. Efforts to reach accord on disarmament with Germany within the framework of the League of Nations failed.[38] In 1935, Hitler renounced the restrictions on German armed forces and on arms production. The remilitarization of the Rhineland in 1936 removed a critical buffer between France and Germany. American isolationism and British vacillation over German rearmament, implied by London's 1935 agreement with Germany on submarine production, meant that France could not rely on its allies for timely support against German expansionism. The Nazi blitzkrieg against Poland, employing mass armor, mechanized infantry divisions, and combat aircraft over a fluid front, revealed fatal weaknesses in French military planning. One by one, and in rapid succession, the foundation stones of France's national strategy were weakened or undone by a resourceful and ascendant Germany.

The breakdown of disarmament talks in the 1930s, Germany's repudiation of the military clauses of the Versailles Treaty, and the deterioration of the international order, signaled by Japanese aggression in China, Italy's invasion of Ethiopia, and the Spanish Civil War, induced a reluctant France to rearm. Defense spending slowly increased after 1935. New legislation granted the government increased oversight over military production under private auspices. The pace of the rearmament program accelerated in each successive year until the German victory. Production facilities which had fallen into disuse and disrepair since World War I were modernized.[39] Between 1935 and 1939, authorizations for military expenditures rose tenfold from approximately 2.8 to 28.9 billion francs.[40]

Economic and political upheaval in France, occasioned by the worldwide economic depression of the 1930s, complicated French rearmament. The election of the Popular Front in 1936 paved the way for the nationalization of selected, but key, private firms engaged in arms production.[41] Whereas the reforms of 1885 had enlisted profits in the service of arms, with an emphasis on private sector responsibility for armaments, the Leon Blum government, with Socialist, Communist, and Radical support, sought to cut the tie between arms and economic gain without jeopardizing French security or welfare.[42] Contradictory claims were inevitably advanced to justify nationalization. Many argued that "merchants of death" started the arms races that led to World War I. Nationalization would presumably tighten governmental control over the arms trade and by that token contribute to peace. A socialized arms industry was by definition a tribune of peace. Other partisans of public ownership of the means of arms production also argued that a governmentally controlled arms industry would produce arms more cheaply and efficiently. The controls needed to restrain private manufacturers would presumably not be needed by the government to control itself. Ostensibly not driven by a profit motive, arms exports would exclusively serve France's security and diplomatic requirements, and not the need for corporate or private gain. If arms sales proved profitable, the public treasury, not corporate interests, would be the beneficiary; the nation, not private firms, would receive a return on the subsidies accorded the arms industry through taxes and domestic arms purchases.

These conflicting impulses produced a mixed and confusing system of governmental ownership and control of the arms industry. Since the Army and Navy had a long history with arsenals, they preferred to seize private facilities and to operate them with their own engineers and personnel. The Army's creation of a corps of military engineers in the 1930s, patterned after the Navy system, facilitated the takeover process, although the newly formed cadres were too small and inexperienced to assume full and immediate direction of nationalized arms centers.

The Air Force, having relied primarily on the private sector for its equipment, favored the purchase of a majority share of stock in private firms to gain control over corporate decisions and resource allocation. Between October 1936 and March 1937, the Army and Navy transformed twelve groups of factories into state installations under the na-

tionalization law of August 1936. The Air Force's method of nationalization was simpler and easier to apply. In many instances, private
manufacturers, like Marcel Bloch (later to be known as Dassault), and
their managerial teams were incorporated wholesale into the newly created state-run system. Through this device the French state and the Air
Force gained control over much of France's airframe industry. These
purchases and expropriations were grouped into six national air construction corporations. After the war, the state extended its control
over the aircraft engine industry, creating SNECMA (Société Nationale
d'Etude et de Construction de Moteurs d'Aviation) as France's principal
aircraft engine developer.[43]

Much controversy has surrounded the question of whether nationalization helped or hindered France's prewar rearmament. Whatever
the final answer may be, there is evidence to suggest that by the outbreak of hostilities in September 1939, French production was actually
gaining substantially on Germany output. It can be argued that the two
countries were roughly equal with respect to the quantity and quality of
the ground equipment available to their armed forces.[44] The same
could be said for their air forces.[45] With the application of Plan V in late
1937 until the fall of France in June 1940, the French aeronautics industry grew from approximately 38,000 to 250,000 workers and delivered in this time period 4,010 aircraft to the Air Force.[46] According to
one estimate, the French had accomplished in two years what Germany
had done in four.[47] The nationalization of much of the aircraft industry
did not appear to have been the determining factor in France's defeat.[48]
Had the war been deferred for another year, France was also scheduled
to receive substantial numbers of American combat aircraft, thanks to a
contract initialed by the Daladier government five days after the Mu-
nich capitulation.[49] As for France's naval preparations, they appeared
in advance of those of Germany. France's Navy, the second largest in
Europe after Britain's, exceeded Germany's, whose fighting strength
was primarily concentrated in its submarine fleet.

Table 1-9 outlines French output of ground armor and weapons. It
shows a dramatic increase after 1936. For key arms, production expanded severalfold: by a factor of approximately 14 for motors, 9 for
armored personnel carriers, and 23 for heavy tanks. Light and rapid
tanks as well as 47 mm. antitank cannons were not even manufactured
in 1936. Table 1-10 presents a similar picture. It compares Anglo-
French and German air power on the western front in May 1940. It ex-
cludes an additional 1,000 aircraft imported from the United States.

While there is considerable disagreement over France's use of the
military equipment at its disposal in 1940, there is less controversy

Table 1-9. Selected French Arms Production for Ground Troops:
1936-May 1940

	1935 Stocks	1940 Stocks
Brandt 60 mm. Mortars	450	6,200
25 mm. Antitank Cannons	1,280	6,000
Armored Personnel Carriers	700	6,000
Light Tanks (Renault, Hotchkiss)	0	2,665
Rapid Tanks (S.O.M.V.A.)	0	416
Heavy Tanks, Type B	17	387
47 mm. Antitank Cannons	0	1,280
Modernization of 75 mm. Cannon	25	400

SOURCE: Jacomet, *L'Armement de la France: 1936-1939*, pp. 288-291.

Table 1-10. Anglo-French and German Air Forces Engaged on the
Western Front: May 1940

Type of Aircraft	German Air Force	British Air Force	French Air Force	Difference
Fighters	1,000	954	764	+718
Bombers	1,200	612	220	−368
Dive Bombers				
(Stukas)	400	0	0	−400
Reconnaissance	450	180	516	+246
Transport	300	0	0	−300
Liaison	150	0	0	−150
TOTAL	3,500	1,746	1,500	−254

SOURCES: Lieutenant Colonel Rose, "Les Aviations allemandes, françaises, et anglaises," *Revue de Défense Nationale* (February 1951), 170-176. See also the following for different estimates: Colonel Paquier et al., "Combien d'avions allemandes contre combien d'avions français le 10 Mai 1940?" *Revue de Défense Nationale* (June 1948), 741-759, and General Charles Christienne, Chef du Service Historique de l'Armée de l'Air, "L'Armée de l'air française de mars 1936 à septembre 1939," mimeo. (n.d.); and Jacomet, *L'Armement de la France: 1936-1939*, pp. 293-294.

about the balance of military forces and equipment existing on the western front in May 1940. One estimate placed France in the ascendancy vis-à-vis German forces at the time of the German attack on Poland.[50] Some official sources support this view. In an investigation of France's collapse, General Gamelin, French Commander-in-Chief, conceded that French armed forces were as well equipped as their German adversaries: "It is important to recognize, and to be fair one should recognize that if we did not have the superiority wished for by the [French High] Command, we had, all the same, an honorable equality on the northeast front for a war that the Government had estimated inevitable in October 1939."[51]

What was lacking in French preparations was a relevant doctrine for the effective use of France's military forces. Despite a new accent on armor and air forces in the late 1930s, a defensive mentality and the notion of a war of attrition still dominated French military thinking. France possessed enough tanks and armored vehicles to organize more armor and motorized infantry divisions than it had in 1940. As General George, Commander-in-Chief of theater operations in the northeast, declared: "Germany had an indisputable superiority in armored divisions. I do not say tanks, I insist on the words armored divisions."[52] Charles de Gaulle, newly appointed to the rank of brigadier general, having been among the few French military officers to have led a successful armored counterattack against German columns, concurred in George's assessment: "There existed . . . 3,000 modern French tanks and 800 self-propelled machine guns. The Germans did not have more, but ours were, as predicted, divided in sectors of the front. They were not, . . . for the most part, in any way constructed nor armed to take part in a mass maneuver."[53] Losses in German aircraft also suggest that Anglo-French forces, if properly deployed and coordinated, might have conceivably been a match for the Luftwaffe. Between May 10 and June 25, 1940, Germany lost 1,900 aircraft, 850 of which were downed by the RAF, while Britain and France suffered losses of 760 and 960 planes, respectively.[54]

Only after the German blitzkreig had been launched against France in May 1940 did the French High Command grasp the new warfare of mobile fronts and concentrated firepower against weak enemy points with combined ground armor and air assaults. The unanticipated German invasion through the Ardennes divided France's forces, thrusting half against their own defenses in the west while German units destroyed isolated elements and sowed panic in rear areas already clogged with fleeing refugees. Large quantities of French tanks, machine guns, artillery, and aircraft remained unused as German forces overran French defenses. Within a week, Paris was open to invading German armored divisions. The sky belonged to the Luftwaffe since French and British aircraft, like tanks and armor, were dispersed throughout France rather than concentrated against attacking forces. The Battle of

France was lost before it could be joined; in less than a fortnight France fell under Nazi occupation.

FOURTH REPUBLIC: NATIONAL STRATEGY, ARMS PRODUCTION, AND TRANSFERS

France's rise to become the third largest exporter of arms by the 1960s must be traced to the Fourth Republic. The return of France to the front ranks of the world's arms producers must be viewed against the backdrop of its slow recovery after World War II and its determined effort to remain a force in global affairs. France's defeat dropped it from the ranks of the major powers for the first time in three centuries. The war profoundly weakened the nation's morale and social structure, severely damaged its economy and industrial capacity, undermined the internal unity of its armed forces, sparked civil strife, and dealt a mortal blow to its empire. Like the Weimar Republic, the Fourth Republic appeared doomed from the start. In adjusting to a superpower world and to the end of the Eurocentric system based on colonial empires, it was asked to do too much in too short a time with too few resources. It was expected to return France to big-power status as an equal of the United States and the Soviet Union while relying on them for diplomatic support, or economic and military assistance, to maintain France's empire as pledge and symbol of its world status. It was also supposed to hold on to its sprawling empire in creating a French Union, while continuing to fight colonial wars in the midst of efforts to mount an effective economic and social recovery program. With the emergence of the Cold War, it was torn between the demands of allies, especially the United States, to assume its responsibilities within NATO's integrated command structure and domestic pressures arising on the Right and Left to pursue an autonomous security policy and to assert an independent national stance.

These elusive and conflicting goals were to be sanctioned and supported by a volatile democratic consensus expressed through a multiple party system exercising fluctuating and ever-faltering control of the National Assembly. For its pains in engineering France's recovery, in dismantling its costly colonial holdings in Asia, and in reconciling the nation to its loss of big-power status, the Fourth Republic was toppled from power by forces beyond its measure to control or resist. The surface explanation for its downfall was the revolt of the overseas army demanding more vigorous prosecution of the Algerian War. The deeper causes lay elsewhere: in the long decolonization process, marked by the humiliation of Indochina and Suez; in the contending pressures of the Cold War; and in profound divisions within France's social and political fabric, rent by a generation of warfare and incipient civil war and by an even longer period of internal unrest and economic dislocation. At the moment of truth, when the mob and army ruled Algeria, even its friends, largely from the narrowly based center of French politics, recoiled from its defense.

Given the burdens under which the Fourth Republic labored, it is astonishing that it should have survived as long as it did. No less surprising is the success of its alleged failures. The ability of the Fifth Republic to assert, if not assure, an independent foreign policy posture, to pursue an autonomous if yet circumscribed military strategy, to modernize France's lagging economy and to make it competitive in world markets—to do all these things while maintaining an open society and democratic institutions—owed much to the efforts of its much maligned predecessor. The Fourth Republic laid the industrial, scientific, and technological foundation for France's emergence as a nuclear power, an independent arms producer, and a global arms supplier. It also was a founding member of the European Coal and Steel Community (ECSC) and the European Economic Community (EC). Notwithstanding the defeat of the European Defense Community (EDC), discussed below, Franco-German reconciliation after World War II owed much to the vision of French leadership under the Fourth Republic.

French foreign and security policy under the Fourth Republic may be divided into two periods. The first covers the period from the Liberation in the spring of 1944 to the departure of Communist deputies from the French government in May 1947. This is the period of an illusionary return to normalcy—a *drôle de paix*—and the eventual capitulation of the French government to the imperatives of the Cold War and economic recovery. The second period stretches from 1947 to the fall of the Fourth Republic in May 1958. This decade is preoccupied with concerns about French recovery, external security, Europe's economic and political integration, and the continuing but losing struggle to retain France's empire in Southeast Asia and North Africa.

The provisional government of General Charles de Gaulle and the early Fourth Republic attempted to pursue an evenhanded policy between the United States and the Soviet Union. A neutralist posture assumed that France still possessed sufficient power and prestige to stand apart from growing East-West differences. De Gaulle maintained the fiction that France was still a great power. German occupation was a setback, not a defeat. In his famous appeal of June 18, 1940, on the BBC, he argued that France's allies and empire were still powerful weights that could tip the balance against Nazi Germany.[55] De Gaulle was essentially correct about the resources at France's disposal, but he consistently refused to accept, whether through practiced blindness or tactical need, the constraints that dependency implied. Vichy, moreover, divided France against itself. Its armed forces, neutralized or compromised, were fitfully engaged against allied forces in the Levant, Africa, and on the high seas. Meanwhile, de Gaulle's Free French were totally dependent on American and British assistance to equip, transport, and arm their military forces. Over $3 billion in lend-lease aid was officially extended to French fighting forces. Additional assistance, amounting to hundreds of millions of dollars, was furnished in civilian goods and military equipment during the liberation process and, later, through emergency loans.

It was not until 1944 that de Gaulle's claim as the legitimate head of the French government was recognized. He was not invited either to Yalta or Potsdam where the structure of Europe's security and political division was initially decided. France owed its inclusion in the Allied Control Commission for Germany to British sponsorship and reluctant American support, and not to the success of its arms as an equal partner to the Big Three in the victory over Nazi Germany. Despite a security pact signed by de Gaulle with Soviet Russia in 1944, Moscow was prepared to exclude France from big-power decisions over Germany's political fate, including questions of boundaries, internal organization, future security posture, or reparations liabilities.

The principal priorities of the provisional government were the reestablishment of France's international standing and big-power status, permanent security guarantees against Germany, reassertion of its authority over the French Union, and internal economic recovery. Toward the West the de Gaulle regime continued its policy of forcefully asserting France's national sovereignty and independence, even to find honor in a straw, as proved often the case during World War II, if France's standing would thereby be enhanced through opposition. Throughout the war, de Gaulle resisted allied attempts to limit the role of the Free French in wartime planning or of the French government, once reestablished, in postwar reconstruction. Early in the war, de Gaulle opposed British military occupation of Lebanon and Syria, France's former mandates, to preserve the appearance of French influence within those two states. Toward the war's end, de Gaulle refused to follow allied directives in investing Stuttgart, key to French claims to a separate occupation zone in Germany, and opposed the wishes of the allied military government over cantons in northern Italy.

Meanwhile, the Paris government pursued allied support for its efforts to regain control over its colonial possessions in Southeast Asia, Africa, and the Levant. The French-Soviet treaty of December 1944 served these several purposes. It signified, at least in French eyes, France's reemergence as a major power on a par with the Big Three. It also purportedly afforded a balance to western allied pressures. The treaty also provided a basis for Germany's permanent subordination to French political and military interests.[56] These were served by Germany's internal division and partial dismemberment as well as through its disarmament, demilitarization, and occupation. Germany was no longer to be ruled by a central authority. Several German states would be created to rule one German people. In addition, the Rhineland and Saar would be placed under French control and the Ruhr, the productive center for German arms production, would be organized under international direction. As these policies were being implemented, Germany was also expected to underwrite French economic recovery through substantial reparations payments.[57]

Postwar France was alone too weak to achieve these varied aims. The provisional government presided over a nation on the brink of civil war, with armed forces split by conflicting political loyalties, notwithstanding the temporary unity and euphoria created by Germany's defeat. The provisional government was faced with the task of purging the Army of Vichy collaboration, while attempting to integrate diverse elements of the Free French, the regular army, the African army, and cadres from the underground into a loyal and usable military body. Wartime memories of battles where Frenchmen were on opposing sides hindered unity efforts. The performance of many units against German forces was also not uniformly high.

There was widespread concern about the Army's future role abroad and as the guarantor of a reconstituted republican France. In light of the Vichy episode, the Army's political orientation as well as its social composition were very much at issue. Before this flawed instrument could be purified and reforged, however, French armed forces were thrust into occupation duties in Germany and propelled into a long, costly, and futile struggle to maintain France's colonial possessions. Set against itself and burdened by the psychological weight of defeat, the French Army was sent to fight in faraway places to control alien populations with little clear direction and often less real moral or material support from France's political leadership or from the French nation.[58]

The allied victory over Germany hid rather than repaired the weakened ties that had hitherto bound the Army to the nation; the colonial wars gradually severed the tattered fragments that remained and produced the final rupture with civil authority in May 1958. The strains were evident early in the postwar period when de Gaulle resigned from office in January 1946, partly in response to modest decreases imposed by the French Parliament and parties on military expenditures.[59]

From Neutralism to Alliance

The Fourth Republic was unable to maintain a neutralist posture in the face of Cold War polarization between East and West, to stem independence demands abroad, or, alone, to launch France's economic recovery.[60] The expectations on which postwar German policy were initially based proved hopelessly unrealistic. Reparations could not be met, and allied support for French claims never materialized. Neither the Rhineland nor the Ruhr was detached from Germany. Both were viewed as parts of Germany and indispensable for its economic and political rehabilitation. Germany's division, a French objective, was largely determined by the position of the western and Soviet armies after World War II rather than by French arms or argumentation.

Unable unilaterally to pursue independent security and economic policies, the Fourth Republic was compelled increasingly to depend on the United States to block Soviet expansion, to revive its economy, and to underwrite its colonial wars. By 1947, it had become apparent to most French officials that the Red Army, in league with domestic subversive elements, posed a greater threat to France's security and open institutions than a defeated Germany. The Franco-British treaty, signed at Dunkirk in April 1946 and ostensibly aimed at Germany, led to the broader-based Brussels treaty of March 1947. The Brussels pact paved the way for the Atlantic Alliance of April 1949 and the formal commitment of the United States to French security.

The United States became the primary support for France's recovery. There was general recognition of the need for France's economic reconstruction if the French nation was to regain its former international stature, sustain its armed forces, and meet internal demands for economic rehabilitation and equity. The conclusions of the Jean Monnet report, outlining a plan for postwar French recovery, were generally shared: "The preconditions of a modern military plant are the augmentation of industrial potential, the modernization of the economy and scientific research. The true significance of the war potential of a country is measured henceforward by the degree of development of its heavy industry. . . ."[61]

France lacked the resources for its "recovery and independence."[62] In 1946 over five million tons of coal were imported from the United States. Industrial production by the end of 1946 was 87 percent of 1938

levels, while the price index, based on 1938 prices, rose threefold between 1946 and the end of 1948. Over a billion dollars in loans from the
United States were unable to reactivate the French economy.[63] Only the
infusion of large sums of capital and a recovery effort mounted at a European level would suffice to shake France from the grips of economic
depression. As late as July 1947, sentiment lingered in the National Assembly for close association with other European nations and opposition to bloc politics.[64] By late summer, resistance to the polarizing force
of the Cold War struggle collapsed. The French government embraced
the American European Recovery Program (ERP) as the major vehicle
of France's economic recovery. France was now firmly in the western
camp and linked by strong security and economic needs to the United
States. The departure of Communist ministers from the cabinet of Paul
Ramadier in May 1947 signaled the adjustment of domestic politics to
harsh but compelling security and economic realities. Neither alignment with Russia against Germany, a traditional alliance strategy, nor
neutrality between the superpowers was a viable option, although there
were strong domestic forces urging these alternatives when the Fourth
Republic cast its lot with the West.

The Fourth Republic made a virtue of necessity. Tight alliance with
the United States and its European allies was relied upon, paradoxically, to restore France's independence and grandeur. What the Fourth
Republic was unable to achieve through its own resources and will—
French independence, economic recovery, and grandeur—it now
sought through alliance. In security policy the French pressed for
American troops in Europe to contain the Soviet Union under terms of
the Atlantic Treaty. Under American pressure to rearm Germany in
the wake of the Korean War, the French took the lead in proposing the
European Defense Community. The French also lobbied for the extension of the Atlantic Alliance to the developing world to bolster France's
sagging colonial position in Southeast Asia and North Africa. Parallel
with these initiatives, Paris also used the ERP to promote European economic integration. The European Coal and Steel Community and the
European Economic Community were of a piece with French reliance
on allied support to solve national problems. Most French were agreed
that these could be managed or resolved only at regional and global levels of cooperation. Defying Gaullist critics on the Right and Communists on the Left, the leadership of the Fourth Republic was willing to
risk ensnaring France in a web of multilateral ties if national revival
could be fostered. While many, like Jean Monnet, may have been committed Europeanists, most French Fourth Republic leaders were still
basically French nationalists who disagreed with their opponents more

over method and strategy than over objectives and political priorities.[65]

American economic and security assistance on which French recovery depended encouraged French cooperation within Europe and the western alliance. A precondition of American economic aid under the Marshall Plan was the development of a European recovery plan to which all of the benefiting states were expected to contribute. American military assistance was equally predicated on the assumption of European cooperation. The Pleven Plan leading to the European Defense Community treaty was prompted by American insistence on a rearmed Germany. The EDC provided a mechanism to subordinate German rearmament to European control. It was also consistent with the American design for a united Europe. Such an entity was supposed to end centuries of fratricidal wars between the European states, a feature of the international system since the inception of the nation-state. It was also expected to speed European economic recovery and strengthen Europe's military contribution to the Cold War fight. Washington also conceived a united Europe as a simpler and more efficient entity with which to deal than a collection of single-minded states. Once united and strong, Europe would again become a world force. As a partner of the United States, the western system would prevail in the East-West conflict and absorb Europe's former colonies into an American-dominated global order. For American policy-makers, France was an indispensable element of a united Europe and their global design; for most French, at least those whose opinion would eventually count, Europe and the United States were useful tools for French national regeneration. So long as the two perspectives were complementary, no conflict erupted. Only when one was the obstacle to the other was a clash unavoidable, as much under the Fourth as under the Fifth Republic.

In the minds of most influential Frenchmen (the Communists partly excepted), empire, grandeur, and national security were a holy trinity, indissoluable and—for critics—no less a mystery. There was no gainsaying the critical role played by France's colonial possessions in World Wars I and II and in the fight for the liberation of the metropole. Thousands of colonial troops fought in both wars, not only in their homelands but on the western front, and contributed to allied victories in North Africa, the Middle East, and Europe. They came from as far away as Algeria, Morocco, Tunisia, Senegal, and the Ivory Coast. The colonies also furnished important bases from which French air, sea, and ground forces could operate, such as Dakar, Mers-el Kebir, and Bizerte.

Since the experience of two world wars confirmed the empire as indispensable for the defeat of the Kaiser's Germany and of Hitler's Third Reich, it was hardly surprising that there was a broad political consensus within France on the need to keep France's colonies in some form or another after the end of hostilities in Europe. The postwar solution was the French Union. This loose federation, while theoretically permitting more local control, was in reality closer to an imperial model where Paris still decided all important questions affecting French interests and those of the local French population. Leon Blum, leader of the Popular Front in 1936 and Socialist Prime Minister in the early years of the Fourth Republic, was as one voice with General de Gaulle and his conservative supporters who insisted on suppressing local uprisings against French authority, whether in Syria, Lebanon, Madagascar, or Vietnam. While partisans on the Right and Left applied different tests to union with France, neither group envisioned France's relinquishment of its privileged position. On December 23, 1946, Prime Minister Leon Blum told the National Assembly: "Once this [present] crisis [in Vietnam] is surmounted, our goal will remain exactly the same. . . . We must faithfully take up the work now interrupted, that is, the organization of a free Vietnam in an Indochinese Union freely associated with the French Union. But first of all, peaceful order, the necessary base for the execution of contracts, must be restored."[66] On the Left, Guy Mollet, Socialist Premier from 1956 to 1957, and, on the Right, Jacques Soustelle, who would help overthrow the Fourth Republic, agreed on holding Algeria at all costs. After fifteen months in office, Mollet would answer critics of his Algerian policy in these combative terms: "The Government has never ceased to give an absolute priority to the necessities of Algeria. . . . Let us then affirm the essential, and first of all this important affirmation: the demonstration of a unanimous will that France remain present in Algeria."[67]

These widely shared strategic views about the importance of the French Union for France's security and rehabilitation as a world power had profound implications for French cooperation within the Atlantic Alliance. The French did not distinguish between French and European security or between the security of France and the French Union. They were a composite of a single strategic field for action and control. For the French, the Atlantic Alliance was valued principally for what France's allies would contribute to help France solve its security problems. The French pressed, albeit unsuccessfully, for privileged status, on a par with Great Britain and the United States, within the western grouping. These efforts assumed several forms, including proposals for a directorate within the alliance, closer consultations on security is-

sues, and support for the military standing group within NATO to facilitate a Big Three definition of alliance measures within and outside the
European theater.[68] The division of labor implied by NATO was viewed
as militarily sound and acceptable only if the alliance supported French
strategic needs as these were defined by Paris. Otherwise French forces
would be servicing allied interests without reciprocal benefit. The colonial wars, in Southeast Asia and North Africa, as successive French military officers explained, were viewed as major contributions to western
security.[69] The doctrine of revolutionary warfare, advanced by French
strategists, was presented as a set of countermeasures to defeat Soviet
reliance on surrogates to expand its influence in the Third World.[70] For
most French governmental leaders and military officers, western values
and interests were at stake in France's efforts to hold the French
Union.[71]

The benefits of cooperation with the western alliance were compelling from the late 1940s until the fall of Indochina and the defeat of the
European Defense Community. The Marshall Plan substantially aided
the French economy. According to one careful accounting, France received from the United States over $4 billion in grants, loans, and stim-
ulants to production.[72] Needed capital goods were acquired and scarce
dollars were accumulated with which to make additional investments in
plants and machinery. In 1949, one-half of all governmental investments were attributable to ERP funds. These were devoted largely to repair of war damage and the rebuilding of the nation's railway system
and naval fleet. The role of American assistance in maintaining the
French budget and trade in balance was also impressive. From 1948 to
1954, American aid covered approximately 28 percent of the annual
French deficit and almost the entire balance of payments deficit. Between 1951 and 1954, American aid actually contributed to a net surplus in French exterior transactions.[73] As one French analyst concluded
in 1956 about France's economic condition: "Contrary to what one
might think, the improvement of France's situation stems in part from
the dollars received under the title of American military assistance and
not as much from a modification of the structure of the commercial ex-
changes of France with the Sterling Zone or the member states of the
European Payments Union."[74]

No less important for France's recovery was American military assistance from World War II through the end of the Vietnam War. French
forces in World War II were largely equipped with American arms.
French dependence on American aid continued after the war because
of the inability of France to mount a rearmament effort proportionate

to its security needs in Europe and throughout the French Union. American aid must be measured both in equipment and financial transfers. Almost one-fifth of all French military expenditures in 1954, the height of the French phase of the Vietnam War, were derived from the United States. Comparable percentages for 1952 and 1953 were 4.8 and 7.3 percent.[75] If military assistance in the form of equipment, arms, and munitions is added to financial aid, the percentage of American support of the French military establishment increases dramatically.

Table 1-11 presents estimates of largely American and some allied financial and material support for French armed forces. By 1954, 30 percent of the total amount of annual resources at the disposal of the French military were from American sources. From 1951 to 1953,

Table 1-11. American and Allied Military Assistance to France: 1951-1954 (In billions of old francs)

Year	Military Spending A	Aid in Kind B	Military Resources A + B = C	Financial Aid D	Total Aid B + D = E	Percent E/A
1951	806	207	1,013	2	209	20.5
1952	1,257	298	1,555	61	359	28.6
1953	1,290	380	1,670	95	475	28.0
1954	1,272	235[a]	1,507[a]	240[b]	475[a]	30.0[a]

SOURCE: Jean Godard, "La Contribution alliée aux charges militaires de la France," *Revue de Défense Nationale* (April 1956), 436-445.

[a] Estimates.

[b] Less than one-quarter of financial aid can be attributed to non-American sources.

American assistance accounted on the average for one-quarter of the French military budget. The significance of American assistance becomes even more pronounced when it is related specifically to French spending on military equipment. Table 1-12 summarizes American assistance as a ratio of French expenditures for arms and material. On the average, American assistance comprised approximately 50 percent of the French spending for arms and equipment between 1951 and 1954.

When economic and military assistance are combined over the first decade of the postwar period, ending with the close of the French phase of the Vietnam War, France received approximately $10 billion in aid

Table 1-12. American and Allied Contributions to French Spending on
Military Equipment: 1951-1954 (In billions of old francs)

Year	Military Equipment Expenditures A	Aid in Kind B	Allied Financial Aid C	Total Resources D	Total Aid B + C = E	Percent E/D
1951	178	207	2	387	209	54.0
1952	448	298	61	807	359	44.0
1953	521	380	95	996	475	47.7
1954	467	235	240	942	475	50.4

SOURCE: Based on Table 1-11 above, and on Jean Godard, "L'Aide américaine à la
France," *Revue de Science Financière*, XLVII, No. 3 (July-September 1956), 453.

and in additional compensations for the use of its territory for joint
western defense. It thus received more aid than any other NATO ally.
Neither France's rearmament effort nor its pursuit of the Vietnam War
would have been possible without massive American assistance. France
received almost twice as much military assistance as the next highest recipient—Italy—and four times more than the United Kingdom whose
perceived privileged relation was so envied by French leaders. To support the war in Indochina, the Truman and Eisenhower administrations subsidized slightly more than one-quarter of France's defense
budget and over one-half of its reequipment.[76]
   To this level of support for the French economy and military forces
should be added the now largely forgotten offshore procurement program, launched in the first half of the 1950s to speed European rearmament while the United States was preoccupied with the Korean War.
It was especially helpful in reconstituting France's arms industry. Under this program, several billions of dollars in contracts were let over
half a decade. In fiscal years 1952 and 1953, they amounted to $2.26
billion in value. Of this value France received more than half of these
orders. Of $1.25 billion in contracts, $619.7 million was directed to the
Army, $180 million to the Navy, and $226.1 million to the Air Force.[77]
These contracts provided the additional margin of support needed to
develop France's arms industry as a self-sustaining system. It permitted
France to accelerate its long-term program of meeting all of its military
requirements through indigenous capabilities and of positioning the
French arms industry to meet rising world demand for armaments.
The intent of the offshore procurement program was to respond to
what was perceived as an imminent Soviet threat in Europe by supply-

ing NATO forces with weapons and material through local sources. The unwitting result was, as two observers recognized, to put "the United States into the business of building an armaments industry abroad,"[78] and of creating in France a potential competitor for arms markets.

Immediately after World War II, France's armaments industry was in shambles and unable to meet French military needs. Plants lay damaged and destroyed; workers were scattered or idle; governmental direction of privately and publicly owned facilities was ineffective or nonexistent. Fifty to 75 percent of available production space was out of commission. Available surface area for production was 30 percent of what had existed in 1939.[79] Shipyards were particularly hard hit and had to be almost totally rebuilt.

Only one-third of the 1.4 million square meters of space available for naval arms construction remained intact or in repair.[80] Three years after the war, naval tonnage was 42 percent of 1938 levels.[81] Arsenals devoted to production of weapons for ground forces were converted to civilian production to meet pressing needs. By 1947, 62 percent of France's postwar arms production capacity was devoted to the civilian production of tractors, machine tools, trucks, and even canning materials.[82]

From the outset of the postwar period, rebuilding France's arms production plant was a major priority. By 1947, a five-year plan, linked to economic recovery, was sketched for the development of the French armaments industry.[83] A special report was also prepared for the aeronautics industry that outlined its systematic development.[84] Production of military aircraft was viewed not only as a prerequisite for an independent military policy but as the key to France's reemergence as a world leader in civilian aircraft design. These ambitions bore little relation to the meager resources available. Until 1950, almost no funds could be specifically earmarked for military plant renovation. In 1947, less than $4 million was allocated to arms production and only $200,000 for the reconstruction of arms production facilities.[85] As late as 1954, almost a decade after the war, less than 25 percent of French defense expenditures, otherwise not derived from allied contributions, was allocated to military equipment.[86] A series of plans, developed throughout the Fourth Republic for each of the armed forces, had to be repeatedly scrapped and revised downward.[87] These setbacks, occasioned by the demands of economic recovery, defense preparedness in Europe, and colonial wars, seriously impeded but did not arrest the slow, inexorable reconstruction of the French arms industry. If France remained dependent on American assistance through much of the 1950s, the French arms industry was able gradually to reconvert from civilian to military production during this period. At the start of the Korean War, 80 percent of French aircraft production capacity was devoted to military purposes.[88]

French leaders used American support to develop an independent arms production capacity in much the same way that they employed American aid to support its colonial wars. Military assistance, Marshall Plan funds, and offshore procurement contributed to the modernization of the arms industry. In the early 1950s, when the offshore program appeared in doubt, French Prime Minister René Pleven threatened his own agonizing reappraisal of French allied commitments if American equipment and arms orders were not forthcoming.[89] Industrial spokesmen counted on foreign sales to bolster weak internal demand for French military aircraft.[90]

Pierre Montel, French Minister of Air, declared at the opening ceremonies of a NATO meeting in France that the French government sought a more significant role within the alliance than as a furnisher of cannon fodder. "It is my responsibility to tell you," Montel told NATO Commander General Lauris Norstad, "that we expect of you . . . not only discussions of military committees and directives of the general staff but also effective military assistance permitting us to bring to the common combat not only French bodies."[91] French arms, too, were important. Georges Herteil, president of France's most important aeronautics trade association, the Union Syndicale des Industries Aéronautiques Françaises, criticized NATO's early spending program which gave priority to base construction over European arms production capacity: "Instead of participating in the construction of runways where one could not see any French aircraft one should think first of producing material from aviation plants, that might well signify a new orientation of French military and foreign policy."[92] These were not isolated assertions of independence; they represented governmental policy. As one analyst of the offshore program concluded, there was "a natural reluctance by European countries to embrace any plan that makes them rely upon a neighbor country for military equipment needs, and there is a reluctance to chance the loss of orders for their own plants through participation in a multinational program."[93] France's Minister of Defense insisted on France's need "to avoid being dependent on any other powers"[94] in pursuing its security policies.

The offshore program spurred industrial production for French armed forces and helped lay a new and broad-based foundation for a revitalized armaments industry. American military planners, who focused on the short-run need to meet the perceived threat to Europe, were eager to bolster French arms production capabilities. As one Defense Department directive of January 1954 indicated: "A sound logistics future for friendly foreign forces requires that they be able to support themselves in combat from local sources. The establishment of a substantial indigenous production base is therefore an indispensable part of any defense plan. It is the policy of the Department of Defense to foster a self-supporting military production capacity in friendly foreign countries which will become self-sufficient and while [sic] at the same time will not conflict with the security interests of the United States."[95] Thanks partly to such assistance, France would emerge by the end of the de Gaulle regime in 1969 as the world's third largest arms supplier, a position that it firmly held until the middle 1980s without serious challenge from other European suppliers.

The offshore program made possible the expansion of France's military production facilities along a wide front. Almost $100 million was earmarked for the expansion of ammunition production for France and Italy to bring allied capacity to 25 percent of wartime requirements.[96] British Centurion tanks were also licensed for French manufacture.[97] Heavy cannon, artillery, mortars, bazookas, machine guns, and light arms were purchased by American funds for French and European forces.[98] The Navy launched several construction programs, including escort and small combat ships. Aid for French-designed fighter prototypes was also made available. The AMX series of armored vehicles and tanks was also first developed in this period.[99]

The reconstruction of the military aircraft industry proved in many ways the most difficult challenge facing French planners. Little was left of French productive capacity at the end of World War II. The French Air Force was almost totally equipped with American and British bombers and fighters. Except for obsolete Dewoitine 520s, French fighter pilots primarily relied on Republic P47s, Lockheed P38s, Curtiss P36s and P40s as well as aging British Spitfires. Bombers included American B26s and British Wellingtons.[100] The nationalized aircraft firm of Sud-Est launched the Espadon (Swordfish) as early as 1945, but the aircraft was never developed for series production. It also produced under license the British Vampire as the Mistral. It was not until 1949, after two years of design and development, that the private firm of Marcel Dassault flew the Ouragan 450, the first indigenously produced jet fighter aircraft of the postwar period. Series production began in 1952.[101]

The offshore program was a breakthrough in the development of France's military aircraft industry. The United States purchased from Dassault 225 Mystère IVs, a follow-on to the Ouragan 450, for the French Air Force.[102] The experience learned from the Ouragan and Mystère furnished the design capital and trained cadres that launched the highly successful Mirage III series that became the mainstay of the French Air Force in the 1960s and early 1970s and the principal combat fighter of several air forces around the world. The Mirage III first flew in 1956, followed by the twin-engine Mirage IV in 1959. By the end of the 1950s, French aircraft inventories swelled with the introduction of the additional fighter aircraft (Dassault's Super Mystère), Sud-Ouest's fighter-bomber (Vautour), transports (Noratlas 2500), and trainers (Potez's Fouga-Magisters). New aircraft engines like the Nene were also being produced to power the Mistral, SNECMA's celebrated Atar engines for Dassault's series of fighter aircraft, and Turboméca's Marbore for the Fouga-Magister.

Foreign sales followed indigenous production. Table 1-13 lists aircraft, helicopters, and vessels developed under the Fourth Republic for which significant domestic and foreign sales had already been placed by the collapse of the regime in 1958. Much of the success of Fifth Republic sales of these items can be attributed to the solid arms production base laid by the Fourth Republic. By the end of the 1950s, France was largely supplying its Air Force with equipment made in French plants and had already launched a modest but still significant foreign sales program for military aircraft. The Indian and Israeli air forces bought the Ouragan 450 and Mystère IV. The Fouga-Magister, a jet trainer, especially enjoyed broad currency. By the end of the 1950s, close to 600 Fouga-Magisters had been ordered or were under contract for licensed production in West Germany, Belgium, and Israel. European purchases were spurred by the recommendation of NATO's Military Agency for Standardization that the Fouga-Magister be adopted by alliance members for basic and intermediate training.[103] Sud-Ouest's Vautour was also sold under license to Israel.[104]

French engineers also moved to the forefront in the development of a wide range of tactical missiles. The SS-10 and SS-11, surface-to-surface missiles, and wire-guided antitank missiles were sold to West Germany, Sweden, Belgium, Israel and the United States as well as to French armed forces.[105] Israeli forces reportedly acquired 200 SS-10s[106] and used them effectively against Egyptian armor in the Suez War, not the last time that French equipment would prove itself in battle. The value of French military exports, principally aircraft, helicopters, and missiles, steadily grew to approximately $200 million by the end of the 1950s.

Sales of French ground equipment also slowly advanced. French arsenals successfully designed a new AMX series of armor. AMX vehicles, especially the AMX-13 light tank, met French ground force requirements and attracted considerable interest abroad. Table 1-14 lists

Table 1-13. Selected Military Aircraft, Helicopters, and Missiles:
Domestic and Foreign Orders under the Fourth Republic

Designation	First Flight	Domestic Orders	Foreign Orders
Fighter Aircraft			
Ouragan MD 450	1949	350	164[a]
Mystère IV	1952	225	170[b]
Trainers			
Fouga-Magister	1952	195	109[c]
Transport			
Noratlas (2500/2501)	1949	192	41[d]
Helicopters			
Djinn	1953	100	50[e]
Alouette II	1955	180	71[f]
Missiles			
SS-10	Late 1950s	—	200[g]

SOURCES: *Jane's All the World's Aircraft* (London: Jane's Publishing Company Limited, 1952-1953 to 1960-1961, and 1967-1968). Stockholm International Peace Research Institute (SIPRI), *Worksheets* and SIPRI, *The Arms Trade Registers* (Cambridge: The MIT Press, 1975).

[a] For India, 104; for Israel, 60.

[b] For India, 110; for Israel, 60.

[c] Includes an order of 250 for West Germany, of which 40 were delivered by 1958; the rest were assembled and license built in Germany. Another order for 45 was placed by Belgium, 6 for Austria, and 18 for Finland. None of these orders was delivered during the Fourth Republic, i.e., by October 4, 1958. In addition, license agreements were signed with Finland for 62, with Israel for 100, and with Austria for an unspecified number.

[d] *Jane's All the World's Aircraft*, 1960-1961 cites 10 deliveries to "non-military operators" in addition to 25 deliveries to West Germany and 6 to Israel. West Germany also signed a license to build 129 more Noratlas transports.

[e] *Jane's All The World's Aircraft*, 1960-1961, notes that a total of 100 Djinns were delivered by the end of 1958 and a total of 150 had been ordered, 100 for the French Army, 6 by W. Germany, 3 by the U.S. Army, and the rest by "civilian customers in many different countries."

[f] Foreign purchasers include Belgium (27), Austria (16), Sweden (11), Switzerland (8), Portugal (7), Morocco (1), and Peru (1). Total Alouette II sales are found in Chapter 2.

[g] Exact sales figures are not available. By 1960, production reportedly reached 450-500 a month. The SS-10, surface-to-surface, wire-guided antitank missile was purchased by France, West Germany, Sweden, the United States, and Israel. Israel reportedly acquired 200 SS-10s and used them effectively against Egyptian armor in the 1956 Suez engagement.

Table 1-14. Sales of AMX-13 Light Tanks to Foreign States under the Fourth Republic

State	Delivery Date	Number
Switzerland	1951	200
Israel	1954	150
Egypt	1957	20
Venezuela	1954	20
Peru	1954	40
Morocco	1956-57	45
Tunisia	1957	20
India	1957	150
Lebanon	1957	42
Dominican Republic	1958	20
South Vietnam	1958	50
TOTAL		757

SOURCE: SIPRI, *The Arms Trade Registers* (Cambridge: The MIT Press, 1975), *passim.*

eleven countries that purchased the AMX-13 by 1958. Sales span several regions, including Europe, Latin America and the Caribbean, Southeast and South Asia, and the Middle East. Additional sales of AMX-105s were made to Tunisia (10), Egypt (20), and Israel (30). These sales would not have been possible without the active support of the French government and a sales effort to penetrate emerging world military markets.

As early as the 1950s, France was already selling arms to regional rivals, a pattern that was to become more pronounced under the Fifth Republic. Egypt received AMX-105s in 1954, a year before Israel. These sales in no way inhibited the French and Israeli attack on Egypt in 1956. Even after the Suez crisis, Egypt was still receiving French AMX-13s along with Israel. The French also transferred previously supplied allied equipment to other states, especially Israel, as newer, indigenously produced equipment entered the inventories of French armed forces. Exports included tanks and armored vehicles, World War II light Mosquito bombers, and small naval craft, much of which was sent to Southeast Asia.[107]

Nuclear Weapons Program

Any discussion of the slow rebuilding of France's arms production capacity must address its military nuclear program.[108] As early as October 1945, the provisional government under Charles de Gaulle established a public agency with broad administrative and financial authority, largely outside the traditional French bureaucracy, to develop the atom. The program of the Commissariat à l'Energie Atomique (CEA) can be divided into three periods. From 1945 to 1952, the program was devoted primarily to scientific research and development. By 1948 the French had constructed the first atomic pile on the West European continent and a year later, a nuclear test center at Saclay.

The second phase of the French program concentrated on industrial development and laid the groundwork for the military component of the French nuclear effort. The first five-year plan was adopted in 1952. Plans were laid for sufficient plutonium production to meet civilian needs and military requirements and, if a timely decision were made, to explode an atomic device. Two atomic piles were established at Marcoule from which the plutonium needed for France's first atomic explosion was eventually drawn. In 1954, the Bureau d'Etudes Générales (BEG) was established within the CEA. It was later reorganized in 1956 and subsequently under the title of the Direction des Applications Militaires (DAM). In 1955 the CEA and the defense ministry reached accord on the extension of basic and technical nuclear research to military needs. In return for funding support, including a third plutonium reactor, the CEA agreed to provide technical data on nuclear energy and fissionable materials. The Navy transferred funds to the CEA for atomic submarine development.

In the 1950s, a small group of military officers, spearheaded by Colonel Charles Ailleret, began advocating the development and use of atomic weapons. In 1954, articles began appearing in the *Revue de Défense Nationale* in support of the military applications of atomic energy.[109] Matters came to a head in 1956. In the fall, the CEA and the defense ministry signed a five-year protocol which clearly defined a military program within the CEA. Basic research work started on long-range missiles. Colonel Ailleret was placed in charge of preparations for the first atomic tests to be held in Algeria. In the spring of 1957 Defense Minister Maurice Bourgès Maunoury and his advisers agreed that a nuclear force should be organized. As early as 1956, the Mirage IV, a twin-engine fighter-bomber, was provisionally designated as the delivery vehicle for France's emerging atomic force.

The decision to explode an atomic weapon advanced along a more tortuous political path. In December 1954, the government of Pierre Mendès-France fell before the issue of militarizing the nuclear program could be joined. While its successors vacillated over the question, the CEA, under the impulse of Gaston Palewski, doubled the outlays for CEA military activities. The government of Socialist Guy Mollet hesitated before the decision to explode an atomic weapon and confined its support to more research on military applications of atomic energy. The second five-year plan also included funds for an isotope separation plant. In April 1958, a month before the Fourth Republic would be dissolved, the government of Premier Felix Gaillard finally ordered the construction of a test site and the explosion of a plutonium device.

Shifting motives and objectives shaped and directed the military nuclear program. Their importance varied with circumstance but, cumulatively, they led irresistibly to the nuclear strike force. The principal difference between the leadership of the Fourth and Fifth Republics regarding nuclear weapons was the strategic and political framework within which they were to be developed and deployed. Fourth Republic civilian and defense officials conceived nuclear weapons within the structure of NATO; the de Gaulle government and its successors defined nuclear weapons in purely national and unilateral terms. The practical consequence of this difference can be exaggerated since both were agreed that the only legitimate measuring rod of alliance with other states was French national interests. From this perspective, most French leaders believed that nuclear weapons would bolster France's position vis-à-vis its allies and adversaries. General Paul Ely's proposal for a tripartite directorate to guide alliance policy presaged General de Gaulle's proposal to establish such a group composed of France, Britain, and the United States.[110] The bomb was also seen as a check on Germany as well as a response to strategic imperatives posed by France's attempt to maintain its colonial empire and to respond to the Soviet military and political challenge. Narrower military and bureaucratic concerns supplemented these supports for a military program. Ailleret and his associates were intent on modernizing France's military forces and on applying nuclear weapons to France's strategic aims and battlefield needs. Cutting across these considerations was the shared view that a strong nuclear program, including a military component, was a key determinant of France's economic development. The CEA's military program was viewed as much a means for advancing France's technological base as for enhancing its military capabilities: military and civilian modernization were seen as different sides of the same coin.[111]

CONCLUSIONS

Thanks partly to the alliance policy of the Fourth Republic, the regeneration of France's arms industry and its emergence as an important exporter of military arms and technology were clearly in evidence by 1958. France received more economic and military aid in the postwar period than any other NATO country—more even than Great Britain, which was supposed to have a special relation with the United States. Diplomatic support for France's efforts in Vietnam was steady until the closing stages of the war. If American assistance was not always as strong as French leaders might have wished, it was no less forthcoming than the support of the French public for the conflict. French armed forces were equipped in large measure with American arms. In the last year of the struggle, more than half of France's military procurement was derived from surplus American stocks or from purchases underwritten by the American treasury. The Atlantic Alliance pledged American military power to French security; American forces in Europe were hostage to American intentions.

The Marshall Plan aid enabled the Fourth Republic to concentrate on economic recovery and on the regeneration of the arms industry. American funds, machine tools, and equipment significantly contributed to this effort. Funds otherwise diverted to domestic purchases of equipment could gradually be accumulated to finance plant expansion and renovation. Offshore purchases guaranteed work for France's arms industry and relieved unemployment in this vital sector. As the economic and technological foundation of France's arms industry enlarged, its capacity to compete for sales in foreign markets increased, evidenced by expanded sales of high technology items. Largely through its own efforts, the Fourth Republic was also able to develop a nuclear weapons program and lay the groundwork for the *force de frappe*.

The limits of cooperation within the Atlantic Alliance in pursuit of French-defined security interests, including the development of an arms industry and foreign sales, had been reached by the end of the Fourth Republic. In Europe, the EDC controversy pitted French and American conceptions of European security against each other. Washington did not accord the privileged position sought by Paris within the Atlantic Alliance, and remained unconvinced by French entreaties for reliable guarantees to compensate France for the risks run in rearming Germany. Lacking other alternatives, the leadership of the Fourth Republic acceded to the British proposal to revive the Brussels treaty, under the title of the Western European Union, to secure guarantees not available explicitly through the Atlantic Alliance. In adhering to the treaty, West Germany renounced development of nuclear weapons and accepted allied oversight over German rearmament.

American planners viewed skeptically French acquisition of nuclear arms. Although marginal concessions were made, such as in providing 440 kilos of U-235 for atomic submarine engines,[112] Washington gave France little access to American nuclear know-how and material. Under the McMahon Act and its amendments, only Great Britain was granted this privilege. The discrimination, cited repeatedly by the de Gaulle government to justify a French nuclear force, was not lost on French leaders.

Divergencies between American and French perspectives in the developing world became acute by the middle 1950s. The American demurrer to intervene militarily in Vietnam during the Dienbienphu crisis destroyed whatever hope existed that France could cling to the southeast salient of its colonial empire. The Suez crisis deepened the division of interests and global perspectives between the United States and France. Washington joined with Moscow against Paris to force French, British, and Israeli withdrawal from Egyptian territory. For many French, on the Right and Left, the need for an autonomous military posture was never more clearly demonstrated. Conflicts between France and its allies over Algeria reinforced the conviction in ruling French circles that France could not rely on alliance support for its efforts to save the faltering French Union or, as de Gaulle and his advisers later suggested,[113] its orderly dissolution once the untenable character of France's colonial policies was acknowledged. Adding to the tension between Paris and Washington over alliance support for extra-European French security interests was the dismantling of three modernized divisions between 1956 and 1958 and their dispatch to Algeria. Only 50,000 French ground troops and 8,000 air force personnel were left in Germany to meet French alliance commitments.[114]

Even if the varied limiting elements of French-Allied relations had not appeared before de Gaulle's re-entry onto the French scene, the economic rehabilitation of France and the growing strength of its arms production capacity would have required a redefinition of allied relations and of France's role within the alliance once the Algerian War was resolved. The development of an increasingly autonomous arms industry capable of equipping French forces with indigenously produced weapons provided both impetus and a perceived margin of safety in the pursuit of a more independent stance for France in world affairs. For its pains the Fourth Republic was repudiated as an obstacle to France's resurrection as a European power with a global voice. Obscured from vision by self-serving Gaullist arguments was the shared conviction of leaders of both regimes that security policy began at home in the service of national—not alliance—needs and interests. These implied continuation of France's centuries-old policy of raising and equipping its own forces with arms. On this point monarchy, empire, and republic were joined as one.

The Fifth Republic: National Independence, Military Autonomy, and a New World Order

INTRODUCTION

FRENCH SECURITY and arms control policies have had a profound impact on French arms production and transfers under the Fifth Republic. While not the only factors, as succeeding chapters suggest, they play a critical role in determining why the French make and sell arms. In response to the superpower struggle and to the security threats raised by the globalization of the nation-state system, the Fifth Republic expanded the size of the arms industry to unprecedented levels and scaled it to global demand for arms and a worldwide market. Building on the work of its predecessor, it constructed an arms industry as sophisticated and complex as any in the world outside the superpowers. This impressive effort was driven by an unwavering determination to underwrite an independent national defense policy freed from reliance on other states for arms and equipment. The shift to a strategy based on nuclear weapons was also calculated to broaden and deepen France's technological development and to ensure that France, as a major industrial power and product innovator, would remain competitive in world commerce. Arms production and sales aimed at several overlapping targets: national independence, strategic military autonomy, and, as succeeding chapters argue, economic growth, increased domestic welfare, and accordingly, internal political stability as a function of internal consensus on security and foreign policy and satisfaction with France's socio-economic development and modernization.

Fifth Republic foreign policy has been unique in its sustained pursuit not only of certain preferred foreign policy outcomes—e.g., maintenance of French influence in Europe or Francophone Africa—but also of a new international order to replace the bipolar division arising from World War II. The Fourth Republic initially tried to withstand the polarizing force of the superpower struggle. It eventually succumbed to the pull of American power, notwithstanding periodic but failed assertions of independence, evidenced in the fiasco over the fight for the European Defense Community treaty and the Suez debacle. The Fifth Republic was more single-minded and relentless—and successful—in its quest for independence and freedom of maneuver. If, like its predecessor, it has had to recognize the limits of its independence and its reliance on allied and, specifically, on American support to attain its specific strategic and political objectives, it has also striven, albeit with varying degrees of enthusiasm and consistency, to dismantle or to modify the bipolar structure—or failing in these endeavors, to inflect the system to suit its interests. Championed has been a multipolar system within which French grandeur could flourish as a consequence of heightened French power, status, and prestige vis-à-vis the relative decline of influence of the superpowers, neutralized by their own struggle and preoccupied by the threats and opportunities arising from the emergence of new centers of military and economic power in Europe and in the southern hemisphere.

The first two parts of this chapter outline French international and security policies. They identify the principal implications of French global diplomacy and military strategy for the development and expansion of France's arms system. Never before has the French state been involved in selling arms and military technology on so large a scale, defined by the quantity, sophistication, variety, or value of French arms, or on so wide a geographic front, represented by the number of states receiving French arms and military know-how. The ceaseless and focused quest for independence and military autonomy, under conditions of stringent domestic socio-political constraints and of inherently limited economic and technological resources, generated irresistible incentives prompting French leaders, including weapons planners and producers, to search for arms markets abroad to support an indigenous arms production complex. The decision of the de Gaulle government and successive Fifth Republic administrations to assign the highest priority in defense spending to nuclear forces, which were not for sale, further bolstered the incentives to seek foreign buyers to compensate for lagging internal demand for conventional arms.

A final section traces the impact of France's open-door approach to arms sales on key elements of its arms control policy. If official French pronouncements are taken at face value, French arms control policy hardly exists. The French insist on disarmament and resist the notion of arms control, viewed as a superpower bargaining device to check the military capabilities of challenger states. The French protest too much. Like Molière's Monsieur Jourdain, they speak the prose of arms control, especially during the presidencies of Giscard d'Estaing and François Mitterand, but in a different idiom than the superpowers. French arms control policies are tributary to France's international and security objectives. They protect these pursuits from challenges, mounted prin cipally by the superpowers, to restrain France's development of an independent nuclear deterrent and to inhibit France's sale of conventional arms and civilian nuclear technology and materials.

France has shown little interest in an international regime for the control of conventional arms sales. Until President Giscard d'Estaing assumed office, it also evidenced little enthusiasm for international efforts to stem the spread of nuclear arms. Even on the latter score, its support for international constraints has been conditional on the compatibility of an international regime with France's systemic interest in pursuing an independent course, its military and energy needs, and its determination to be a world leader in the supply of nuclear reactors, equipment, fissionable materials, services, and technical know-how. France's nuclear export policy was essentially an extension of its arms production system and the compelling incentives that it generated to sell arms and military technology abroad. Changes in French civilian nuclear policy, registered in the middle 1970s, responded to a reassessment of the effectiveness of France's essentially go-it-alone strategy, rather than an abandonment of Gaullist-defined aims of political independence, military autonomy, and increased competitiveness in world markets through the penetration of French technology in fields like civilian nuclear power.

French International Policy and the Fifth Republic

Breaking with the bloc mentality of the Fourth Republic, President Charles de Gaulle condemned the superpower-dominated structure of global politics as inherently unstable and illegitimate.[1] According to de Gaulle, it was prone to war because of the implacable, ideological split between Moscow and Washington and their proclivity to expand their imperial spheres. Nuclear war could erupt directly between them at any time and from any point in the world. The crises over Lebanon and Formosa in the late 1950s or the Congo and the Cuban missile confrontation in the 1960s illustrated the problem. Crises over Lebanon and Central America in the 1980s later confirmed the Gaullist analysis. The superpower competition threatened to overwhelm other states against their wishes or interests. States were under pressure, as France had been after World War II, to align with a bloc. Probes, occurring anywhere along the long frontier between the spheres of interest of the superpowers, from Berlin to Saigon, could conceivably spark a global conflagration. As smaller states were absorbed into the superpower struggle, their localized quarrels—rooted in longstanding historic, racial, ethnic, and national conflicts—created new and multiple opportunities to spark a superpower confrontation. The probability of a nuclear "Fashoda" was inherent in the global bipolar struggle.

Since a superpower nuclear war could develop at almost any flash-point around the world, even over issues of secondary importance, the bipolar system was pronounced by President de Gaulle as fundamentally unstable. There was little space for maneuver, negotiation, or compromise between blocs. The claims of other states, according to the Gaullist analysis, had to be mediated through the rigid military systems erected to promote superpower, not third-state, interests. Local disturbances, moreover, could not be contained easily since neither superpower felt that it could be indifferent to the outcome of these disputes. They also risked rapid expansion and escalation along the multiple networks of conflict created and reinforced by the Cold War split.

According to de Gaulle, relevant actors, like Communist China and West and East Germany, were disenfranchised from regional and global affairs since one or the other of the superpowers was able to limit their participation in resolving security issues of vital concern to them. Neither belonged to the United Nations during de Gaulle's tenure in office, yet peace in their regions depended entirely on their cooperation. France, too, was pictured as excluded from big-power dealings on matters vital to French national interests. Gaullist spokesmen repeatedly cited the absence of French representatives at Yalta in 1944 as the starting point of the superpower-dominated system.[2] The handiwork of Yalta had to be undone by a new system affording other states more influence and an opportunity for greater participation in deciding issues of importance to them. "Since the division of the world between two great powers, and therefore into two camps, does not benefit the liberty, equality, and fraternity of peoples," announced a defiant de Gaulle, "a different order, a different equilibrium are necessary for peace."[3]

The alleged instabilities of the bipolar system also led de Gaulle to reject the system as illegitimate. The chain of logic was deceptively simple. Gaullist thinking, shared even by those opposed to de Gaulle, contended that the nation-state was the primary source of authority in international relations. Only states could make valid laws and reach binding accords in international relations. The state ultimately derived this right to bind and loose from the protection that it provided those over whom it asserted authority and from whom it expected loyalty. The capacity of a state to assure national and personal security hinged on its control of the issue of war and peace. In eroding the ability of a state to decide on war and peace—or, more broadly, the circumstances under which it would use or threaten force—its claim to sovereignty was weakened; its right to demand the loyalty of citizens, diluted; and its legitimacy, correspondingly, questioned.

A multipolar system was judged by Gaullist partisans as more stable and legitimate because of the internal accord of the participating states on the terms of its maintenance and the outcomes of its processes of bargaining and negotiation. The superpowers hindered other states from developing relations beyond those defined by the Cold War conflict. Impeded, too, was interstate accommodation. Local conflicts assumed global proportions, and were transmitted vertically along the superpower global structure rather than confined to conflicting states. Alternatively, legitimate small-state demands had to be ignored or compromised to preserve a brittle global stability resulting from the rigidity of the two blocs.

The key to the Gaullist solution to the threat to national survival and independence posed by the superpower struggle was the creation of nuclear forces. A nuclear deterrent—a force de dissuasion—was central to Gaullist thinking about the military arms needed by France to stimulate technological innovation and economic development, and to enhance France's status in world affairs.[4] For de Gaulle, the nuclear force reinforced France's big-power credentials. These were rooted in history and confirmed by the special circumstances of its postwar position as a victor state in World War II, as one of Germany's four occupying authorities, as a permanent member of the United Nations Security Council, and as the primary actor on the West European continent, with a sphere of influence in the Mediterranean basin and Francophone Africa. In reshaping the international environment, an autonomous military strategy, resting on nuclear weapons, was expected to enable France to regain control over the decision of war and peace; to diminish dependence on the United States; to underwrite new initiatives to weaken bloc politics and end the Cold War—at least in Europe; to expand global support, swelled already by demands for self-determination; and to promote a multipolar system, a check on superpower pretensions and a bar to the spread of their struggle. The attack on superpower hegemonial tendencies and the dangers of the Cold War were enshrined in French policy pronouncements. So, too, was the call for an end to bloc politics and a more open, fluid system of nation-state alignments.

The nuclear force, however much opposed by the Left when out of power or viewed with skepticism by the Center, was eventually accepted by all political parties as the core element of France's independent military and foreign policy.[5] Except for the extreme Right, all factions eventually endorsed the abandonment of colonialism as a strategy to promote French security and economic interests and to recapture some of its lost grandeur. Successive presidents under the Fifth Republic, starting with de Gaulle, projected the image of France as conciliator and mediator, if not arbiter, of the East-West conflict and as moderator of the North-South dialogue. It was an attractive self-image to most segments of the French political elite and public and an *image de marque* that, wittingly, promoted France's reputation as a willing and reliable major arms supplier. On these matters, as de Gaulle's prescience dictated, everyone would eventually be Gaullist.

The Gaullist rationale for the transformation of the bipolar system lent impetus and legitimacy to postwar efforts to recreate a modern, autonomous arms industry and a worldwide sales network. The success or failure of de Gaulle's design or the ability of his successors to achieve— or even expect—total independence in making strategic and foreign policy decisions is less significant as an explanation of French arms transfer policy than is the goal of an independent stance itself. The pursuit of independence provided moral and political justification, as it had in the past, for the development of indigenous arms production. Like the force de dissuasion, this capacity was accepted as central to France's claim as a major power. Through a sophisticated arms complex and a liberal arms transfer policy, the Fifth Republic reinforced the postwar trend, in spite of countervailing superpower efforts, to globalize the self-help international system based on nation-states supported by national military forces. Fifth Republic governments not only perfected the sale of arms as an instrument of national policy but also transformed it into a systemic obligation to equip foreign armies. In a defense ministry *White Paper* published in 1972, three years after de Gaulle's departure from office, his trusted lieutenant, Michel Debré, serving as defense minister under President Georges Pompidou, affirmed France's determination to sell arms as a contribution to the dissolution of bloc politics: "It is difficult to avoid the duty of responding to the requests for arms of certain countries, [who are] concerned for their defense and who desire to assure it freely without having to have recourse to the dominant powers of the two blocs. Not to respond to these requests would accentuate the hegemony of the big powers and would also preclude all moderating actions attached to our exporting position."[6]

President Valéry Giscard d'Estaing entered office in 1974 deploring France's record of arms sales. To a journalist's question about his administration's interest in developing new arms markets, he replied: "I do not think so. Certainly there are arms sales and we have a capacity to sell, but I do not think it is a sector in which we ought to accent our effort."[7] Giscard failed to turn back the clock. His administration was swept forward by the onrush of the search by the arms complex for markets abroad. When he was voted out of office in 1981, he had pre-

sided over the largest expansion of arms and military technology transfers, including nuclear know-how, equipment, and fissionable materials, in French history. France's arms control policy under Giscard
d'Estaing essentially sidestepped any consideration of international
controls over arms sales and technology.[8]

Upon taking office, François Mitterrand, Giscard d'Estaing's Socialist
successor and a longtime critic of French arms sales, particularly to authoritarian regimes abroad, followed his predecessor's lead. One of his
first acts as president, was to notify foreign arms buyers that contracts
signed by the previous French governments would be honored.[9] In
keeping with the practice of defying American leadership, Paris also
sent helicopters, tactical missiles, and missile-firing patrol boats to the
Sandinista regime in Nicaragua, overriding Washington's objections.[10]
It was important for the new Socialist government to maintain its Leftist
credentials in good order and, certainly, to do at least as much for revolutionary governments as the de Gaulle regime. There was little significant difference between the systemic justification offered by Socialist Prime Minister Pierre Mauroy for France's open-door arms policy
and that of Michel Debré more than a decade earlier: "France has no
vocation to be an arms merchant. But France cannot prohibit itself
from exporting military materiel. With respect to itself, of course. With
respect to its partners also, since it permits them to increase their margin of independence by avoiding the need to turn to one of the two superpowers with all of the consequences created by that type of relation.
The spread of our arms industry flows first, let's not forget, from its independence."[11]

Along with the force de dissuasion, arms and military technology
transfers have been the most important instrument of France's global
policy. They have survived the collapse of the Gaullist design as well as
the frustrations experienced by de Gaulle's successors in their attempts
to change the structure of international power. If Fifth Republic France
has been unable to increase appreciably its influence within the Atlantic
Alliance, Europe, or in world councils, it has contributed, through its
transfer of arms and technology, to the emergence of multiple centers
of state power. If the nuclear arms structure essentially remains bipolar
at the global level, one can discern at regional levels the rise of important nuclear powers including China, Britain, and France, and states
with civilian nuclear technology which may be on the way to developing
nuclear arms. At nonnuclear levels, the global security system has
grown more decentralized and has diffused into distinct regional
groupings. While the superpowers have been principally responsible
for the dissemination of increasingly greater quantities of advanced
military equipment around the world (e.g., Soviet MiG fighters to India

and American F-16s to Pakistan) and have aided the nuclear arms programs of other states, France, measured by its size and resources, has proportionately done as much as the superpowers to create a self-help system progressively beyond the control of any one power or even the superpowers in collusion.

The de Gaulle government moved along several fronts, often as not simultaneously, to change the global balance in France's favor. These initiatives can be grouped into four overlapping circles of activity, aimed at enhancing France's influence with the states within each circle: the Atlantic Alliance, the European Community, the Soviet Union and the eastern bloc, and the developing world.

Although beset by the Algerian War, de Gaulle moved quickly to establish France's claim to a privileged position in NATO. In a memorandum of September 17, 1958, sent to British Prime Minister Harold Macmillan and President Eisenhower, de Gaulle proposed creation of a tripartite body, composed of France, Great Britain, and the United States, to oversee and direct western security interests. It was designed to deal with two critical problems: the formulation and direction of allied nuclear policy and global security. Adoption of the de Gaulle proposal would have made France the equal of its Anglo-Saxon rivals. What French power could not attain directly, its association with American power would achieve through diplomacy. France would have been granted a veto over American nuclear strategy while presumably gaining access to American military might and influence to support French objectives and security needs.

The timing and scope of the de Gaulle proposal were bold since French bargaining leverage within the western alliance had never been weaker. When it was advanced, French military forces, earmarked for Europe, were bogged down in Algeria; France had still to explode a nuclear device; and plans for a nuclear strike force were only at an early stage of formulation. De Gaulle was seeking a greater say over American military power in return for the dubious and fleeting benefits of possible French cooperation. The expectation that France would eventually have a nuclear force was being traded upon to enhance France's international position at a time when the Fifth Republic's own future was in question over Algeria and its claim to legitimacy was under a cloud as a consequence of the coup d'état that overturned the Fourth Republic. These were shaky grounds on which to resurrect western Big Three collaboration. Remembrance of the bitter experience with de Gaulle during World War II also reinforced allied suspicions that close French/Anglo-Saxon cooperation would be feasible on any terms other than those defined by de Gaulle.

The weaknesses of de Gaulle's proposal did not preclude his government from joining the issue over NATO integration and American domination of alliance nuclear strategy. NATO's integrated arrangements were criticized for having placed "everything . . . under the command of the Americans"; only they could "decide on the use of . . . atomic weapons."[12] "Given the nature of these weapons, and the possible consequences of their use," de Gaulle concluded, "France obviously cannot leave her own destiny and even her own life to others."[13]

The proposal to extend the western alliance beyond Europe was of more immediate significance for the de Gaulle regime. The survival of republican institutions and the Fifth Republic depended on the successful resolution of the Algerian War. Fourth Republic attempts to extend the Atlantic Alliance to cover Algeria, treated in French law as an extension of the Metropole and not as a colonial possession or protectorate, were unavailing. For de Gaulle, moved by classical notions of alliance, the worth of allies was a function of French national needs (and those of his beleaguered regime). Since Gaullist France purported to be a global, not a regional, power, it followed that Allied discord, confusion, or lapses in coordination outside Europe would adversely affect harmony over policy in Europe. President de Gaulle posed the issue in his news conference of September 5, 1960: "We felt that, at least among the world powers of the West there must be something organized— where the Alliance is concerned—as to their political conduct and, should the occasion arise, their strategic conduct outside Europe, especially in the Middle East and in Africa, where these three [the United States, Britain, and France] are constantly involved. . . . If there is no agreement among the principal members of the Atlantic Alliance on matters other than Europe, how can the Alliance be indefinitely maintained in Europe?"[14] De Gaulle's prime minister, Michel Debré, was more explicit about the implications of the de Gaulle proposal for France's plight in Algeria. In terms reminiscent of Fourth Republic complaints, Debré asserted that "it belongs to a renewed France to make its allies understand that it is right to demand from all of them the support for a cause [Algeria] which is much greater than one people or one generation."[15]

Implementation of the de Gaulle proposal would have allegedly precluded future Suez crises since American support would have presumably been assured before mounting such an operation. Traditional French interests in North Africa and the Middle East, noted in the September memorandum, would be protected since France would be engaged in the decision-making over American foreign intervention. There would be no repeat of the Lebanese case of 1958 where traditional French interests were at stake. Before American troops would be dispatched, France's approval would first have to be sought. If de Gaulle had had his way, American support for France's colonial empire—or at least for a negotiated solution over Algeria favorable to France and the de Gaulle government—would be reinstituted after the break that had occurred in Franco-American cooperation with the fall of Dienbienphu, the French withdrawal from Vietnam, and the Suez incident.

Anglo-American reticence to discuss, much less adopt, de Gaulle's scheme paved the way for France's gradual withdrawal from the Alliance's military organization and the departure of NATO forces from France. As negotiations over the tripartite proposal lagged, the de Gaulle government in early 1959 withdrew the French Mediterranean fleet from NATO's jurisdiction. In June, American fighter-bombers were shifted to other NATO countries after Paris refused to accept American-controlled tactical nuclear weapons on French soil. These moves were only the start of a series of moves, culminating in de Gaulle's news conference of February 21, 1966, that announced France's formal withdrawal from NATO's integrated military structure and the dismantling of all foreign bases on French soil. France would remain within the Atlantic Alliance, but its forces would not be placed under American or allied command, nor would its territory be used for purposes, within or outside Europe, other than those explicitly approved by Paris. France's independence and sovereignty would be re-established: "that which is France as regards soil, sky, and [military] forces, and any foreign element that would be in France," de Gaulle affirmed, "will in the future be under French command alone."[16]

Parallel with the efforts to exert more influence and gain more status for France within the Atlantic Alliance were initiatives taken with France's European partners to bolster its European position. First was de Gaulle's acceptance of the European Economic Community, confirmed in meetings with German Chancellor Conrad Adenauer. France would open its borders to the industrial products of its partners, provided that a common agricultural policy (CAP) was adopted to protect French farmers and that special trade considerations and financial support, largely underwritten by West Germany, were accepted by other Community members to ease the adaptation of France's traditionally protected industries to the competitive demands of Community and world markets.

Second, accord was reached on opening negotiations on political union among the European Six. What the Gaullist government had in mind in launching the Fouchet Plan talks in October 1961 was more a confederation of states than a united Europe along American federal lines.[17] The French plan was received with skepticism by France's European partners. The inclusion of defense responsibilities for the proposed union threatened to drive a wedge between the United States within the Atlantic Alliance and the European Community. France's nuclear status might improve its stance within the Six, but French security guarantees were no substitute for the American nuclear umbrella, however leaky it might be in light of growing Soviet capabilities. Britain's exclusion was no less disturbing to France's EC allies, especially to the Netherlands and Belgium, which viewed London as a balance to Paris and Bonn and as a more reliable alliance partner with a historic commitment to democratic institutions. The French plan was also a source of concern because it was vague about the role and authority of EC institutions and the responsibility of the contracting states to make progress toward political union, including the development of common institutions and democratic controls within the meaning of the Rome treaty.

The Fouchet talks collapsed in 1962 under the weight of these objections. From them, France salvaged a bilateral treaty of cooperation with West Germany, signed in January 1963. The treaty, however, lost much of its force and attraction when the Bundestag insisted on a preamble that essentially subordinated its provisions to commitments assumed under the Atlantic, EC, and GATT treaties. West Germany was not prepared to forego the protection and economic benefits of these international arrangements for the promise of closer ties with France—largely at France's behest to define or to exploit.

Meanwhile, de Gaulle was able to block British entry into the Common Market. Justification for rejection revolved around Gaullist assumptions about Britain's inability to accept EC rules and policies and the diluting effect that British participation would have on European cohesion. De Gaulle heaped doubt on Britain's ability and willingness to accept the CAP and Community preference, to relinquish its Commonwealth privileges, or to abandon its partners in the European Free Trade Association, organized as much to compensate for the advantages enjoyed by the Six through customs cooperation as to provide an alternative form of loose economic organization to the EC which was less threatening to traditional British concerns about continental union. According to de Gaulle, Britain's presence would also entail American influence since London and Washington were wary of a protectionist Europe within the American orbit. It would also draw the EC closer to the Atlantic Alliance and into the American sphere. France's hold on Germany, whether as a claimant on its economic resources or as an instrument of its security needs, would be correspondingly weakened.

The British-American decision to create a NATO multilateral force (MLF) and to link the British nuclear deterrent to the MLF in exchange for American nuclear assistance confirmed in de Gaulle's mind Britain's dependency on the United States. In the same news conference of January 14, 1963, announcing France's veto of Britain's application, de Gaulle rejected the Anglo-American offer to join the MLF. It was viewed as a challenge to France's nuclear deterrent and French independence. American influence over French nuclear forces would be increased in much the same way that Washington had succeeded, according to Paris, in limiting British nuclear autonomy. French opposition to MLF highlighted less vocal resistance registered in other NATO capitals, including London, to the American proposal. It eventually fell under the weight of allied pressures, not to mention its dubious strategic value (redundant to the American nuclear guarantee), cost, and political sensitivity associated with West German participation in planning and using nuclear weapons.[18]

Adding to the difficulties over security policy between Gaullist France and its EC partners was the issue of the Community's political development. The line between Community and French national authority was drawn by de Gaulle in a dispute over Commission and European parliamentary control of a small segment of the EC budget.[19] The controversy dragged through the end of 1965 into early 1966 before a compromise settlement was reached. Community institutions were not dismantled, but the right of a state to veto Community decisions if it concluded that issues of national interest were at stake was successfully asserted. The EC Commission's ability to act independently of member state consent was more sharply constrained than before. If the Five rejected de Gaulle's notion of a confederacy of states as a working model for the development of a united Europe, they had to concede that Europe could not be built without France on Gaullist terms.

The battles over the authority of NATO and the EC, however significant, were preliminary bouts to the main contest for a transformation of the European security system and France's role and influence within it. Germany was the immediate object of the battle; the end—or at least the relaxation—of the Cold War in Europe was the longer-run aim. Success in resolving Germany's future and in diminishing the superpower conflict in Europe depended on Soviet cooperation. The Soviet Union insisted on acceptance of Germany's postwar borders, international recognition of the East German regime, and Berlin's closure as a passageway to the West. A loosening of West German-American security ties also held interest for Moscow. The problem confronting de Gaulle was to gain German adherence to these shifts in political posi-

tions and alignment strategies without necessarily jeopardizing European and French security, still based on the United States guarantee.
Partial answers were found in France's withdrawal from NATO (but not
the Atlantic Alliance), closer ties with Germany (symbolized by the
Franco-German treaty), an independent military policy (resting on a
force de dissuasion), and an indigenous arms production capacity.
These conditions appeared sufficient to risk approval of the Soviet
Union's sphere of influence in eastern Europe in exchange for a Germany reconciled to its division and postwar frontiers and for a western
Europe distancing itself from the United States and disposed more to
the politics of détente than of defense.

Possessed of its own means of national survival, France would enhance its position in Europe as an *interlocuteur valable*, transcending the
subordinate role that it played in alliance politics under the Fourth Republic. The Cold War would be on its way to solution in Europe. Its evolution in the developing world would be guided partially by French
needs and interests. France's privileged European position would bolster its authority and influence in the developing world, especially in the
Mediterranean basin and Black Africa where its interest has been asserted for centuries.

Liquidation of France's colonial empire and manipulation of the developing world for French systemic and national purposes were the remaining key parts of the Gaullist strategy to create a new international
order. French colonies had for several centuries been considered critical supports of France's national security and welfare. The experience
of World Wars I and II appeared to confirm the importance of overseas
bases and a Francophone community, at the ready, to defend the Metropole. So, too, arose the need for a large colonial army to protect the
empire. Postwar efforts to retain French holdings in Southeast Asia and
in sub-Saharan and North Africa were of a piece with policies whose
roots extended to monarchical France four centuries earlier in its attempt to develop settlements in the New World. In the war of American
independence, the New World was used to balance rising English
power in the wake of its victory in the Seven Years' War; the Third
World would now be weighed on the scales to balance—or at least complicate—the spread of superpower influence and, specifically, the as-
cendance of the United States as the premier power within the international system and the principal threat to the Gaullist design.

France's defeat in Indochina and its embattled position in Algeria,
self-destructive at home and draining abroad, prompted de Gaulle to
abandon France's centuries-old colonial strategy. The costs of maintaining the empire exceeded French resources and will. It divided the

nation against itself to the point of incipient civil war. It also pitted the Army against the nation. Its colonial empire, rationalized as a defense of national interest and western values, was invoked to justify the overthrow of established political authority. The survival of the Fifth Republic, the loyalty of the officer corps, and the transformation of France's global position hinged on terminating the Algerian War and on renouncing (if not shedding) all imperial claims.

The principle of self-determination animating the decolonization process suited Gaullist ideology and French interests, especially those linked to arms sales abroad to open new markets and to bolster the independence of third states, most notably those in the developing world. The French government could not very well demand greater independence from superpower imperial pretensions and deny other peoples the same right or fail to respond with arms to promote autonomous centers of military power free from superpower control or manipulation. De Gaulle's condemnation of the superpower conflict and his pointed attack on American expansion in Southeast Asia,[20] the Middle East, and Africa[21] also accorded well with his charges of American domination in Europe. Attacking the United States had the added virtue of aligning Paris and Moscow vis-à-vis a shared perspective of growing American power and inclination to expand. In de Gaulle's eyes, superpower bipolarity threatened to become a unipolar, American-dominated system. Not only did American military power and foreign intervention have to be attacked but also the dollar (the so-called Gold War),[22] American multinational corporations, and American technological superiority had to be challenged to ensure the independence not only of the European states but of the developing world.[23]

The Fifth Republic moved with deliberate speed to grant independence to its colonies in Black Africa and Algeria. France's Black African possessions became independent in the early 1960s, followed by Algeria in 1962 with the signing of the Evian accord. De Gaulle portrayed these acts of necessity as disinterested gestures in the service of national self-determination. The accent on cooperation with even former adversaries was contrasted with American policy toward the developing world. Unlike Cuba's place in American foreign policy, Algeria was presented as France's gateway to the developing world, not as a cul de sac. The global application of the principle of self-determination delegitimated the superpower hold on world politics, fostered opportunities for French diplomatic maneuvers and influence, and opened markets for French arms. Greater participation by the developing world in global affairs also relaxed the rigidities of Cold War bipolarity. (France's example and policy would thus lead the Third World to revise the Old

World balance, upset by World War II, in France's favor.) De Gaulle's revisionist world meanwhile checked the perceived expansion of New World power in the form of an expanding America.

The limits of French international policy were largely tested before de Gaulle's departure from office. The May 1968 upheavals within France eroded popular support for defense spending and forced the government to give greater priority to social and economic welfare programs. The de Gaulle government needed its European Community allies and the United States to bolster the franc and to prevent further deterioration of France's international trading position, financial solvency, and attractiveness to foreign investors. It had already been forced to back away from the brink in the 1965-1966 Community crisis. France's welfare, tied closely to increased trade, investment, and full employment, depended on its membership in the EC. The prosperity of French agriculture no less owed much to the CAP and to Germany's heavy financial burden within the Community system.

The Soviet invasion of Czechoslovakia in 1968 also exposed the limits of an independent French security policy. The Soviet Union was prepared to use force to retain its East European empire. French or even West European military power was no match for Soviet strength. Only the United States and the Atlantic Alliance could counter Moscow's armed might. Gaullist France also lost control over the politics of détente. When the détente process in Europe again regained momentum in the late 1960s, after the Czech crisis had passed, French leadership passed increasingly to Bonn and Washington which had more to offer Moscow than Paris.

De Gaulle's successors had largely been forced to live within the constraints set by American-Soviet power and by France's European allies. Expansion of the European Community, including British entry, during the Pompidou administration has not appreciated France's power or influence, nor reduced its economic dependence on Europe and the United States. France relies on an American-dominated regime for access to Middle East oil. France's efforts to establish privileged ties with oil producers have been unavailing.[24] The special oil arrangements wrung by the de Gaulle government from the Evian accord and subsequent understandings have since been revised in Algiers' favor. American economic policies continue to define the range of France's economic possibilities. The Socialist government's criticism of high American interest rates during the first half of the Reagan administration as a brake on French economic growth was little different in substance from earlier Gaullist complaints over lax American monetary practices. At the same time, no counterweight to growing Soviet military power in Europe and elsewhere, other than the United States and the NATO structure, is readily available.

Constraints notwithstanding, Fifth Republic governments have persisted in their pursuit of an independent international policy and an autonomous military strategy. France has contributed through its example to the decentralization of decision-making and the diffusion of power within the international system. It has lent substantial material support to these trends through its transfer of arms and military technology. Neither superpower has been able to slow the dissemination of arms from third sources that now reach around the globe. The value of French arms transfers has grown steadily under the Fifth Republic. As Chapter 6 suggests, other states in Europe and in the developing world are following France's example.

While France's response to the growing international demand for arms must be explained by reference to several sets of factors, the Gaullist rationale of a multipolar system, as a prerequisite of national independence and freedom for diplomatic and strategic maneuvering, remains fundamental for an explanation of French behavior. Gradual movement toward such a system, whatever its hazards, is still viewed as beneficial for France by de Gaulle's successors. Largely lacking other means to reinforce the decentralizing trends now current in international relations, the transfer of arms and military technology is still the preferred instrument of French international policy. It accords well with an autonomous military strategy and, as subsequent chapters delineate, it is consistent with welfare goals and efforts to bolster France's economic position. These real outcomes—and perceived benefits—reinforce the influence of the elites controlling the military-industrial complex within the French government and sustain public support, on the Right and Left, for a large, well-financed arms industry and foreign sales effort.

FRENCH MILITARY DOCTRINE AND ARMS SALES

President de Gaulle's rationale for France's international policy, reaffirmed and reinforced by his successors, confirmed the legitimacy of the nation-state and its unconditional right to produce arms in its own defense. From these age-worn premises, it was but a small step to the proposition that France had both a right and a duty to supply arms to other states lacking means to equip their military forces. Since these politico-moral imperatives took no specific shape, it was left partly to

French military doctrine to define the force levels and weapon systems that would be needed to support France's quest for independence and for big-power status.

Bound by serious economic and technological resource constraints and domestic political limitations, French strategists put primary reliance on a force de dissuasion. Abandoned was the strategy of a large standing army to defend France's European and imperial interests. Downgraded, too, was the comprehensive mobilization program of the prewar era based on the notion of a long conventional war. A large surface fleet and extensive airlift capacity also lost their centrality in the new push for nuclear arms, although France committed itself to extensive security obligations with most of its former colonies. The specter of nuclear war—evoking the prospect of swift, wholesale destruction—challenged the traditional assumption of a war of attrition, the need for long-term allied support, or imperial holdings in the direct support of Metropole security.

France's nuclear forces were supposed to prevent such a costly conflict from erupting. The American deterrent, however necessary, along with its links to the security interests of France's European partners, was no longer considered sufficient to deter aggression in Europe. The growing balance of terror, signaled by Sputnik, convinced the leaders of the Fifth Republic (and many under the Fourth Republic) that France needed its own nuclear force to supplement the American and NATO deterrents and to influence Washington's use of its nuclear forces. Political leaders of different persuasions came progressively to the conclusion that the United States could not be counted upon automatically to risk its existence by attacking the Soviet Union in order to defend France and Europe. The long-range striking power of nuclear weapons also made European bases less attractive to American planners,[25] a concern that grew in French thinking with the withdrawal of American Thor and Jupiter intermediate range missiles in the 1960s. An active deterrent strategy thus replaced the passive defense posture that had served French foreign policy and security after World War II.

As suggested earlier, a nuclear strategy was aimed at several targets simultaneously: France's return to the ranks of the great powers; a nationally based military strategy independent of allied control, yet possessing increased leverage over American and allied strategy and decisions; security against real and perceived adversaries (immediately the Soviet Union and, residually, the possibility of a resurgent Germany); adherence of the officer corps to a military doctrine commanding loyalty to established political authority; and stimulation of technological development and economic renewal. A European nuclear force failed to respond to these needs. Europe was unable to create a viable and credible nuclear force. Divided into nation-states, its interests diverged. Britain stood apart with its own nuclear force, closely aligned with American policy. Germany was precluded from producing nuclear arms; the other states of Europe could not, like their more powerful allies, agree on a single political authority to control or use nuclear weapons.[26]

The setting of arms requirements and priorities for the arms industry can be understood fully only by reference to the centrality of nuclear weapons to French strategic thinking and to the formation of broad and sustained public support for the force de frappe. An independent strategic policy, based on nuclear weapons, within a tight defense budget, generated powerful incentives to sell arms and military technology abroad—policies now supported by all significant French elites and the overwhelming majority of the French public. Nuclear arms production and conventional arms sales do not stand apart from each other. They are the structural, load-bearing walls of a single coherent strategic design. This strategic edifice was not constructed in a day or a week. Like an ancient cathedral, it took more than a generation to erect, sometimes over the fierce opposition of opponents, principally among Socialists and Communists, who are now among its most ardent supporters. Nuclear weapons and arms sales are now enshrined in French strategic thinking and consecrated in the daily routines of French officials. Both policies are perceived to meet critical national needs in much the same way that colonies, overseas bases, and empire did before.

The priority assigned by French military strategy to nuclear weapons had significant implications for French arms sales. As Chapter 3 indicates, the French economy could not simultaneously support major increases in defense spending and the maintenance of large nuclear and nonnuclear forces. Hard choices had to be made about what and how many arms would be produced. These choices increased incentives to sell arms abroad. Domestic demand for conventional arms was inevitably reduced, compared to the colonial period, and subordinated to spending for nuclear forces. Decreased internal spending on conventional armaments threatened to increase the costs of their research, development, and maintenance. Sustaining employment within the industry and keeping design teams together also became serious problems under conditions of weak governmental demand for nonnuclear arms. The obvious need to restrict foreign access to French military nuclear technology, weapons, and delivery systems for security reasons reinforced pressures to find foreign markets for France's excess capacity to produce conventional arms and equipment. Once embarked on selling abroad, it was quite logical and almost inevitable that military requirements set for the arms industry, while initially French in content and aim, would gradually be influenced progressively by foreign demand and needs. New sets of choices arose requiring priorities to be established between design and production for the domestic and foreign markets—orders from both quarters being indispensable for the viability and competitiveness of France's arms industry.

France's military forces must now compete with foreign purchasers for access to France's arms industry. If the strain has not been great for the units associated with the force de frappe, the same cannot be said of the traditional services. They have had to fight hard to get the conventional arms they want. They have been hobbled from the start in the annual budgetary battle because their claims first had to be justified in terms of how well they served French nuclear doctrine and needs. A brief review of evolving French nuclear thinking reveals the tenuous bargaining position of conventional forces and the pressures that a weak demand for nonnuclear arms has had on incentives to sell abroad.

Evolution of French Military Doctrine

While the French commitment to a nuclear posture is clear, many of the principal elements of Fifth Republic strategic doctrine can be traced to the strategic debates of the Fourth Republic.[27] General Paul Gerardot was among the first to suggest, when confidence in the American nuclear guarantee was at its height, that France needed an independent nuclear posture to deter or to launch reprisals against enemy attacks.[28] Following classical lines of thinking, Gerardot envisioned nuclear arms as an economy measure: nuclear weapons could project greater firepower over longer distances than ever before; fewer troops would be needed to defend Europe; and reserves could be used for the conventional defense of the empire.

Generals Pierre Gallois and Charles Ailleret extended these lines of analysis. Nuclear weapons were viewed as equalizers between states of unequal conventional power. A smaller state, like France, could deter a more powerful adversary because it could inflict greater proportional damage on the adversary's cities and industrial centers than the latter would gain by attacking French vital interests. Crystallized from the debate in the late 1950s were many key concepts to be used by French strategists for a generation. Along with proportional deterrence, there emerged the notion of a national sanctuary, defense of the hexagon, the creation of a nuclear *armée de métier*, and insistence on national, not allied, determination of what risks should be run by France in planning for nuclear war.[29] A strategy of nuclear deterrence no longer appeared to require a large conventional defense for Europe, or an empire to balance threatening European powers. Allies could be as much a liability as an asset. Faced with nuclear extinction, they could not be counted on when they were most needed since they risked their existence in defending French national interests; alternatively, they might react to aggression too precipitately or draw France into a regional conflict against its will or interest, with implications for escalation to nuclear war. These arguments were also compatible with Gaullist assumptions about the egocentric tendencies of nation-state behavior, the unreliability of allies, the destabilizing features of the superpower conflict, and the intolerable political and economic burdens of colonial rule.

French armed services were organized on functional lines to respond to four missions: deterrence, European defense, territorial security, and exterior intervention. The first was uppermost. Nonnuclear forces, especially those earmarked for Europe, were largely defined in terms of their contribution to strategic nuclear deterrence. This raised serious questions—still fundamentally unresolved—about the independent role of conventional and tactical nuclear forces as well as their availability and reliability in alliance military planning and crisis management. French strategists have given conflicting answers to these questions over the past twenty years. The first and most extreme response was given by General Ailleret, the military architect of the force de dissuasion, and, later, chief of staff of the French armed forces. Ailleret argued for an all-horizon defense posture (*tous azimuts*) capable of meeting threats from any point in the globe independent of allied commitments. Within the European theater, conventional infantry, armor, artillery, and air forces were narrowly restricted to the role of "covering, exploiting, and completing nuclear moves."[30]

The defense ministry's *White Paper* published in 1972 reflected a somewhat broader view of the role of conventional forces to meet limited incursions or to punish minor transgressions. Using nuclear weapons under these circumstances did not appear credible to Defense Minister Michel Debré and his advisers. "To cross the threshold of the atomic threat can be justified," argued the Minister of Defense, "only in really critical situations."[31] Earlier, Defense Minister Pierre Messmer also had voiced skepticism about the claim that an adversary would immediately use nuclear weapons at the outbreak of hostilities, especially against territory that he proposed to occupy. This view assumed that conventional and selected nuclear weapons would be used before a full-scale strategic nuclear strike would be contemplated. French conventional and tactical nuclear weapons had a small, supportive role in meeting the initial threats of an adversary.

These possibilities of limited use of conventional and tactical arms preceding a French nuclear strike to stop incoming enemy forces led to the notion of "two battles." The main body of French conventional and tactical nuclear forces, along with territorial defense units, were to be reserved for the protection of the national sanctuary and the approaches to its frontiers. They would not be available to support NATO forward defense posture designed to meet attacking enemy forces as close to West Germany's eastern borders as possible. This implied that the French divided European defense into two spheres, with the bulk of French forces committed to the Metropole and deployed independently of NATO plans. French nonstrategic forces, organized into a *force de manoeuvre*, were to be used to test enemy intentions before nuclear weapons were unleashed. These forces were conceived as integral but subordinate parts of the government's management of deterrence.[32] They would have to be strong enough to provide a test of adversary intentions but not so weak that they would convey a reluctance on France's part to use atomic weapons or to delay timely use of nuclear forces. The NATO strategy of flexible response was specifically rejected for this reason. Under American control, according to French analysts, it risked turning Europe into a battleground between the two rival blocs while preserving superpower homelands as sanctuaries against nuclear attack.

Complicating the French debate was uncertainty about the composition and role of tactical nuclear weapons. In the mid-1960s, controversy between army and air force flared over the assignment of these weapons. Army officers saw the possible usefulness of tactical nuclear weapons as battlefield weapons.[33] Although this argument, blocked by doctrinal and budgetary considerations, made little headway in governmental circles, the Army was still anxious to acquire a nuclear mission that would upgrade its position and prestige among the armed services. General of the Army Le Puloch argued for nuclear weapons to break the initial attack of an invading force. Selective use of tactical nuclear weapons was proposed to test enemy intentions and to signal French determination to use its strategic nuclear arsenal.[34] The Army, too, would have a central role in the deterrent game played by the government.

Air Force chief General André Martin rejoined that Army units would not be able to separate themselves sufficiently from an advancing enemy to use nuclear weapons. Nor would they be as efficient as aircraft for interdiction of an aggressor's transportation and supply system. Their destruction would leave advance units disoriented and isolated. According to Martin, the Army should be confined to an alarm-bell role—a *sonnette*—to alert French forces and to protect air and seaborne strategic and tactical nuclear forces.[35]

Defense Ministers Messmer and Debré were more reluctant than the Air Force hierarchy to choose sharply between these rival positions. Messmer saw more utility for air and ground tactical nuclear forces than did Ailleret. While Ailleret focused primarily on the deterrent value of nuclear forces, Messmer saw advantages in lesser responses than an all-out reprisal in case of hostilities.[36] He viewed tactical and strategic nuclear weapons as complementary parts of a credible French deterrent posture. This view was later echoed by Prime Minister Jacques Chirac. Tactical nuclear weapons were portrayed as extensions of the deterrent system. They were needed to meet forms of aggression for which a strategic nuclear response would not be credible. In their absence, France would be reduced to a choice between capitulation or a full-scale nuclear attack.[37] The *White Paper* also observed that the threat of using tactical nuclear weapons would induce the enemy to disperse his troops, a maneuver that would "reduce the numerical importance of [French] forces and guarantee the delay needed by the government."[38] The manifold uses for tactical nuclear weapons deterred political leaders from delegating to any one service exclusive control. All claims were honored as each of the services was armed with tactical nuclear weapons. In the scramble to play a part in the nuclear game, conventional forces and their equipment needs were downgraded further. Even Army insistence on more conventional forces slackened. Pressures to sell these weapons abroad rose accordingly as domestic orders were either cut or stretched out over time while productive capacity remained at existing levels.

French strategic doctrine was significantly modified shortly after the events in May 1968, which almost toppled the de Gaulle regime. In an article published in the semiofficial *Revue de Défense Nationale*, General Michel Fourquet, armed forces chief of staff, departed at several key points from the views of General Charles Ailleret, his predecessor.[39] First, the threat facing France was identified as arising from the east, a return to France's previous stance. Second, to meet this threat, France's frontiers on the north and east were to be defended. Conventional and especially tactical nuclear weapons were upgraded to stop an enemy advance and to test his intentions preceding a strategic attack, a point on which Ailleret had remained ambiguous. Third, the still dim prospect of French cooperation with allied forces improved, although NATO's flexible response strategy was again condemned as incompatible with French strategic needs. French forces would remain under national control, and they would be used independently of NATO.

Fourquet envisioned a more active role for conventional forces within the framework of France's deterrent strategy than the essentially static posture proposed by Ailleret. Like Messmer and Debré, Fourquet closely tied the use of conventional and tactical nuclear weapons to the strategic deterrent. He implied that these forces would be engaged as far as possible from France's frontiers as part of the preparations for a nuclear strike if they were unable to stop an enemy advance. This suggested French participation in Germany's defense. Blurred was the distinction between "two battles" emphasized in previous doctrinal pronouncements. The way was open for French cooperation with NATO, albeit on French terms—or perhaps not at all. Circumstances would decide the degree to which this implied option might be exercised. Fourquet's reformulation of French strategic doctrine edged toward NATO's strategy of flexible response but only as a function of France's limited nonstrategic capabilities rather than in terms of the greater range of resources at the disposal of the alliance. While the French were now willing to contemplate the use of nonnuclear forces in the opening moves of deterrent maneuvering, there were fewer rungs to ascend on the French escalatory ladder than the ones proposed by NATO before strategic nuclear weapons were unleashed. Fourquet's formulation essentially defined the parameters of French nuclear policy ever since with respect to NATO and European security: deliberate ambiguity.

The next major attempt to revise announced policy occurred seven years later. Early into the administration of President Giscard d'Estaing, General Méry, armed services chief of staff, signaled several shifts in French strategic thinking.[40] He criticized two extreme views of French military strategy. The first, a strategy tous azimuts, was judged beyond France's means. The other was a posture of national sanctuarization in which French defense, based almost exclusively on strategic nuclear weapons, would be essentially identified with the protection of French territory. Taking issue with these conflicting legacies of the de Gaulle and Pompidou eras, Méry identified French security with the notion of an enlarged sanctuary (sanctuarisation élargie). It encompassed not only French national territory but "Europe and its immediate approaches, including in particular the Mediterranean basin."[41] According to Méry, French military forces should be prepared to operate throughout this geographic sphere, whether alone or in concert with France's allies. Pointedly rejected was the distinction between the defense of France and of Europe which had figured prominently in previous formulations of official doctrine.

Méry's views fundamentally challenged the Ailleret-Gallois insistence on strategic nuclear arms and their almost total exclusion of conventional and tactical nuclear forces, operating either independently or co-operatively with allied forces. Méry also went beyond Fourquet's tentative expansion of the Army's role in deterrence maneuvers. Méry's proposal for a forward strategy upgraded the role assigned to conventional and tactical nuclear forces in communicating France's deterrent moves to a possible adversary. His notion of active deterrence and NATO's reactive flexible response implicitly overlapped along a broad front. Like Fourquet, Méry still affirmed the autonomy of French forces, and their national political direction. His implicit acknowledgment of French interest in maintaining a strong NATO posture, as well as the presence of American troops and European access to the American nuclear deterrent, inevitably shifted, as critics charged, the emphasis in French doctrine from national means and independence to possible cooperation with allied military forces and deterrent capacity in executing France's deterrent moves to forestall or blunt a Soviet attack. Méry suggested that the contingencies under which French forces might be engaged in a forward battle in Europe might be enlarged. This line of analysis was given additional weight by the remarks of President Giscard d'Estaing, published a month after the Méry statement in *Défense Nationale*: "Some people reason that any conflict taking place outside France would completely spare the national territory from battle. . . . This concept is unrealistic. In fact, in the event of conflict there would be only one zone, because of the speed of transportation and communications, especially by air, and from the outset French national territory would be included in this generalized battle area. . . . For this reason there must be only one military system in this zone, since there will only be one zone."[42] Spending priorities reflected these signaled shifts. Nonstrategic arms were to be modestly upgraded within a defense budget, projected for the late 1970s and early 1980s, to be held to approximately 4 percent of GNP. Méry's proposed reorientation, however, quickly ran into strong opposition from the Gaullist Right, Giscard's coalition partner, and from the Left, particularly from the Communist party. Faced with a possible serious split over defense policy, the Giscard d'Estaing government repaired to the major tendencies of a growing and soon-to-be-solidified consensus on the force de dissuasion, with the adoption by the Left of the independent French nuclear deterrent force and qualified support for greater cooperation with France's European allies in responding to mutual security imperatives.

Renewed interest in conventional forces since the middle 1970s did not signify by any means the abandonment of nuclear weapons as the center of French strategic thinking. Socialist President François Mitterrand embraced the principal elements of Gaullist strategic doctrine. In a news interview he affirmed: "I will ensure that our deterrent force remains level with the competition and all risks. . . . To think that France could even slightly reduce its actual arms is something about which one can dream."[43] Defense Minister Charles Hernu was equally firm about the commitment of the Socialist government to nuclear deterrence: "Nuclear deterrence has been the best means of preventing conflicts for more than 30 years and it still is. . . . Our aim is to prevent war and only nuclear deterrence is capable of doing that."[44] Abandoned was the position adopted less than a decade earlier in the Common Program signed by the Communist and Socialist parties to dismantle the French nuclear strike force.[45] Affirmations issuing from the Mitterrand government about the priority attached to nuclear strategy did not differ essentially from those of its predecessors. This provided some credence for the view of news media commentators that France's "deterrence strategy has not changed since de Gaulle's days."[46]

On the surface, the Mitterrand government hewed closer to Gaullist orthodoxy than its immediate predecessor who attempted, with little success, to upgrade and expand French cooperation with allies in a forward battle. French officials under Mitterrand—and the President himself—repeatedly stressed France's retention of the options of nonbelligerency and nonautomaticity in aiding allies, as well as the preservation of France as a sanctuary and the principles of presidential prerogative in using or threatening nuclear weapons.[47] At a ceremonial dinner in the Kremlin in 1984, President Mitterrand underlined France's nuclear "autonomy of decision" and his singular command and control of nuclear weapons: "The President of the French Republic alone can use them [nuclear weapons]. These are not words devoid of reality. We know in all certitude that our fate, our independence, our very survival, depends on our autonomy."[48] A year earlier, Defense Minister Hernu, in presenting the government's military five-year plan to the National Assembly, stressed the sanctity of French national territory: "Our forces . . . can be called upon to intervene in three circles where our defense policy is being applied. The first . . . is quite evidently to defend national territory . . . and to preserve . . . the liberty of the nation. In this regard, nuclear deterrence, the expression of the will of a unified nation, remains the . . . foundation of our society. This first circle is the sanctuary, the permanent, the untouchable or, again, what makes France what it is."[49] Nonbelligerency, nonautomaticity, sanctuary, and presidential control had one implicit and three explicit purposes. They were alleged to foster France's political independence, maximize its maneuverability in executing deterrence, and insulate it from the conflicts of others foreign to its interests.[50] These principles also preserved the uneasy domestic consensus between the Right and Left on the force de dissuasion.[51]

The reassertion of Gaullist principles should not obscure important shifts in French thinking after 1981. The Socialist government went beyond Gaullist and Giscardian notions of deterrence in at least two fundamental ways, both with critical implications for French cooperation with its allies on European defense. First, new emphasis in announced and operational policy was attached to tactical nuclear weapons. As described more fully in the next section, spending for all of the armed services on these weapons was increased. The Army is scheduled to replace its Pluton artillery divisions with the Hadès missile in 1992. Hadès is more mobile, lethal (20-60 kt. vs. 12-25 kt.), purportedly more accurate, and has greater range (350 km. vs. 120 km.) than the Pluton. Tactical nuclear aircraft—Jaguars and Mirage IIIs—are also to be replaced by a fleet of ground- and sea-based aircraft, including Mirage 2000s and Super Etendards. Renovated Mirage IVs carrying medium-range air-to-ground nuclear missiles (ASMPs) retain a strategic role.

The increased number, range, accuracy, and lethality of these weapons generated extensive official and semiofficial commentary about the roles that these more capable weapons might play. From a battlefield perspective they will be able to strike targets in East Europe from French bases. Unlike the Pluton or even Hadès, aircraft armed with ASMPs would not have to be moved close to the eastern border of West Germany to be used against Warsaw Pact forces or be compelled to attack enemy targets in an occupied West Germany. These forces can conceivably attack opportunity targets, like massed formations, logistical bases, and choke points. These enlarged operational possibilities are presumably added to the armed forces' capabilities to strengthen the deterrent role that tactical nuclear weapons are primarily expected to play as supporting elements of France's strategic strike force. Once employed, they are a warning of worse to come—a shot across the bow—unless the aggressor desists. This warning, explained French armed forces chief of staff, General Jeannou Lacaze, "must have *military effect*, which is to say that it must be effective and brutal, which means a relatively massive employment and therefore limited in *time and space*. But above all this warning must be well integrated in the general deterrent maneuver."[52]

The nuclear role of these forces was underscored by two additional operational changes. First, they were redesignated prestrategic forces in contrast to tactical nuclear forces, a term criticized by officials in the defense ministry as implying traditional military battlefield usage. Second, and more significantly, Pluton regiments were detached from the command of the First Army assigned to Germany and placed under a new army unit. This reorganization was aimed at more clearly differentiating the nuclear and nonnuclear roles of the First Army and France's potential contribution to West European and NATO defense forces. The tactical nuclear forces coming on line in the 1990s will reportedly be placed into a separate command structure directly under the chief of the armed forces.[53]

The second major drift in French strategic thinking under President Mitterrand concerns the reorganization of the Army and the formation of the Force d'Action Rapide (Rapid Action Force, FAR). This change has been widely interpreted as a way to emphasize a renewed French interest in taking concrete steps to shore up western conventional defenses by creating a force that could be rapidly deployed to assist allies in repelling or deterring an attack from the east.[54] It also had the effect of reinforcing French-German bilateral cooperation, a device to anchor Germany to the western defense system in tandem with French efforts to induce Bonn to accept U.S. Pershing missiles to bind it closer to the West as a counter to neutralist sentiment within West Germany. The Army was organized into fifteen divisions. Five of these, comprising 47,000 men, were grouped into the FAR. This new strike force was principally designed for quick deployment to assist France's allies in meeting an attack if the French president believed that it was in France's interest to be joined in the forward battle for Europe against an attack from the east. The FAR was expected to have about 200 helicopters for antitank, troop protection, and attack purposes. This would permit it to have greater mobility and firepower than would have been possible under the previous organization of the First Army. The FAR is also expected to provide a faster reacting force in intervening in trouble spots in the developing world and in meeting France's treaty obligations, principally in Francophone Africa. This role is discussed at greater length in Chapter 7.

Mitterrand government changes in strategic doctrine both relaxed and reinforced the dilemmas underlying French defense policy since its transformation under President Charles de Gaulle. While all of the dimensions of these shifts are not relevant to the focus of this discussion—explaining French arms production and sales and defense priorities—this treatment of the key implication of the Socialist contribution to defense policy is warranted because it sets the stage for the following section which analyzes French attempts to square external treaty obligations and security needs dependent on allied support with national independence within a defense budget of inherently limited resources. The result has been a chronic gap, since the inception of the Fifth Republic, between treaty commitments and national military requirements, on the one hand, and armed force capabilities, on the other, to meet external imperatives.

On the positive side, the Mitterrand regime's differentiation of tactical nuclear and nonnuclear roles and the regrouping of these forces in a separate command potentially clarified, in an adversary's mind, moves up the escalatory ladder in moving from conventional to tactical nuclear forces. It also permitted the French President discretion in using conventional forces in cooperation with allies or as part of the deterrent posturing of French forces without having to join necessarily the issue of using or losing nuclear weapons in defending French and European security. The FAR also had the potential effect of strengthening allied cooperation, specifically French-German coordination, while leaving aside whether French forces were actually being reintegrated within the NATO military structure. The latter raised serious problems in domestic politics where the consensus on nuclear weapons was broad but brittle.[55] The Mitterrand government could at once portray itself in favor of more cooperation in security policy with West European states—consistent with Gaullist precedent in the Fouchet talks—while remaining resistant to American leadership or straightforward integration as a role player in executing NATO's flexible response strategy.

The negative elements of Socialist changes are no less important to recognize. Increasing tactical nuclear weapons capabilities raised more issues than it settled. Modernization of nonstrategic nuclear capabilities for all of the services, as sketched below, produced too many to be made easily consistent with the minimal nuclear posture which was fundamental to traditional Gaullist notions of deterrence, yet these forces were likely to be too small to be taken seriously for independent warfighting purposes. While the latter role can conceivably be played within an alliance framework, it is doubtful whether it can be executed solely and exclusively from French soil. French refusal to discuss the contingencies under which current and future nonstrategic nuclear forces will be used can perhaps be generally rationalized as a contribution to deterrence because of its very ambiguity, but that lack of definition carries several serious disadvantages. Allied cohesion is hardly fostered since allies either will not be able to count on French forces when they are most needed or, worse, they may be compelled to count on them all too well as French nuclear arms may be unleashed prematurely, triggering a rapid escalation of an armed East-West confrontation in Europe. Developing a coherent western strategy, based on an articulated and militarily effective escalatory response ladder to Warsaw Pact aggression, is rendered all but impossible. French air, ground, and sea-based nuclear prestrategic forces become, like the IRBM force, attractive targets for the Soviet Union rather than deterrents.[56] West German concern should not be ignored either about the first-use issue or about the question against whom or what targets would be hit by French missiles. Bonn has openly allowed that the French nuclear forces might not only attack East German military installations but also civilians, who "are Germans, too."[57]

Socialist conventional planning also confuses. The creation of the FAR is at the expense of a 22,000-man cut in ground forces. The FAR may be able to intervene more promptly and effectively at the start of nonnuclear hostilities, but the staying power of French conventional forces is scheduled to be reduced. Little new equipment is being purchased to arm the FAR. The First Army was expected to supply the FAR from its stores. Peter was robbed to pay Paul. The FAR became as much a diplomatic and psychological gesture, keyed to the interest of allies in drawing France into their security planning and commitment strategies rather than a military instrument calculated to respond effectively to battlefield needs. The dismissal by Defense Minister Charles Hernu of opponents to his plan to create the FAR and to decrease troop strength was revealing: "Anyone who tells me that he prefers an additional division of soldiers to a nuclear missile-launching submarine is living in the wrong age."[58] The designation of the FAR for extra-European duties, principally in Francophone Africa which has different and often conflicting weapons and equipment requirements from the European theater, deepens doubts about how useful and responsive Socialist innovations have actually been in meeting allied needs and expectations.[59]

Decreasing numbers in the ground army and increasing expenditures for strategic and tactical nuclear forces inevitably reduced national demand for conventional arms. This circumstance bolstered the long-run trend in French arms production policy which was to become increasingly export dependent. The following discussion sketches how this trend has evolved under the Fifth Republic and how this pattern of dependency is likely to persist as future French governments throughout this century and beyond struggle to keep pace with the superpower arms competition, continued high spending for nuclear arms and weapon systems, and a limited economic and domestic-support base on which to pursue an autonomous strategic policy.

Military Capabilities: Implications for Political Independence,
Military Autonomy, and Arms Export Dependency

Fifth Republic determination by governments of the Right and Left
to pursue independent security policies dictated the need for an expanded arms industry, larger and more complex than the one conceived under the Fourth Republic, to produce both nuclear and conventional arms. Both were needed to equip France's force de
dissuasion, its conventional forces of maneuver and intervention in
support of its nuclear posture, and its territorial forces for the protection of the homeland. Needed also was an expanded and increasingly
more technologically sophisticated military-industrial-techno-scientific
structure which could underpin French political and strategic aspirations. Left to its own economic and technological resources, such a complex was beyond France's capacity or the political will of its people to
erect and sustain. Fifth Republic planners understood from the start
that the creation and maintenance of an autonomous, militarily effective, and economically competitive arms production capacity implied a
policy of greatly expanded sales of arms and military technology
abroad.[60]

Several fundamental considerations coalesced to fashion a chain of
logic to bind France tightly to an arms export policy tout azimuts if it
was to develop its own weapons rather than acquire them through
grants or purchases from other states, principally the United States, as
the Fourth Republic had done. First, if public support for France's defense policy were to be sustainable, after a generation of almost continual warfare, a ceiling would have to be placed on military spending. Second, these socio-political constraints set economic limits, explored in
more detail in Chapter 3, on the quantity and quality of French arms
that could be furnished to French forces if the arms industry were to
rely solely for its support on domestic demand through the defense
budget. The unit cost of weapons would be prohibitively high. In the
case of high-priced systems, carried to the extreme with weapons like
missiles and aircraft, French armed forces would have funds to purchase only a few copies of each weapon, hardly enough to meet its strategic missions. Funds would also be lacking to cover mounting research
and development costs for new weapons to underwrite the expense of
phasing out production of obsolete arms and the investments needed to
tool up for series runs of new weapons. The May demonstrations of
1968 further weakened the budgetary claims of the defense establishment in two ways. They forced a reduction in the percentage of GNP
available for arms in favor of welfare expenditures and the share of the

government's budget devoted to defense; within the military budget, they shifted spending away from equipment to personnel to upgrade the quality of military life measured in increased pay, housing, services, and pensions.[61] Efforts by the Giscard d'Estaing and Mitterrand governments to compensate for these increases in military personnel expenditures by decreasing the size of the armed forces translated inevitably into reduced equipment demand. Reduction in troop strength heightened the need for external markets to offset overall decreases in arms purchases at home.

These varied constraints narrowed the range of options available to French strategists in translating Fifth Republic international and security policy into weapons systems and force levels. First priority was given to nuclear weapons even before the close of the Algerian War. A series of program-laws (*loi-programme*) was devised to rationalize and coordinate defense development and production to meet French strategic needs within a squeezed military budget. Second priority was assigned to French conventional forces in support of European or postcolonial responsibilities in the Mediterranean and Black Africa or in defense of the national territory. The decision to base France's defense on strategic and tactical nuclear weapons also lent greater urgency to the need for foreign exports since demand for conventional arms was lower than it might otherwise have been since a large share (and in some years more than half) of France's research and development and weapon funds were keyed to nuclear systems. Because political and strategic considerations precluded the sale of these weapons, the government counted upon the export of nonnuclear arms to underwrite a significant part of overall procurement and development costs for all weaponry. The stimulus given to the nuclear industry, through major outlays for nuclear arms, also strengthened France's position in the global competition to export civilian nuclear energy. However opposed French regimes may have been to the proliferation of arms, powerful economic and domestic political incentives, tied to ambitious foreign and strategic aims, encouraged a liberal conventional arms and civilian nuclear export policy, with potentially damaging security implications for France and for other states.

Table 2-1 summarizes annual spending for research and development, infrastructure, and procurement for nuclear and conventional arms from 1963 to 1980. From a low point of 21 percent in 1963 of the ratio of nuclear spending to overall expenditures, spending on nuclear forces climbed rapidly to slightly more than 50 percent in 1967. It has steadily dropped since then in each successive year and rested at approximately one-third of all French capital spending on arms in 1980,

Table 2-1. Capital Expenditures for French Conventional and Nuclear
Arms (In billions of dollars)

	Total Arms Expenditures	Nuclear Arms		Nonnuclear Arms	
		Total	Percentage[a]	Total	Percentage[a]
1963	1.57	.33	21.0	1.24	79.0
1964	1.84	.75	40.8	1.09	59.2
1965	2.11	1.02	48.3	1.09	51.7
1966	2.28	1.13	49.6	1.15	50.4
1967	2.49	1.26	50.6	1.23	49.4
1968	2.53	1.25	49.4	1.28	50.6
1969	2.49	1.03	41.4	1.46	58.6
1970	2.31	.92	39.8	1.39	60.2
1971	2.37	.92	38.8	1.45	61.2
1972	2.83	1.01	35.7	1.82	64.3
1973	3.58	1.24	34.6	2.34	65.4
1974	3.55	1.26	35.5	2.29	64.5
1975	4.45	1.49	33.5	2.96	66.5
1976	4.38	1.47	33.6	2.91	66.4
1977	4.87	1.62	33.3	3.25	66.7
1978	6.31	2.05	32.5	4.26	67.5
1979	7.83	2.55	32.6	5.28	67.4
1980	9.44	2.94	31.1	6.50	68.9

SOURCES: France, Assemblée Nationale, Commission de la Défense Nationale et des
Forces Armées (1977), *Avis sur le projet de loi de finances pour 1978, Défense: Dépenses en Ca-
pital*, No. 3150, pp. 22-23; *idem*, Commission des Finances (1978), *Rapport sur le projet de loi
de finances pour 1979, Considérations Générales et Dépenses en Capital*, No. 570, p. 84; and *idem*,
Commission des Finances (1979), *Rapport sur le projet de loi de finances pour 1980, Défense:
Dépenses en Capital*, No. 1292, p. 22. Exchange rates are drawn from International Monetary Fund, *International Financial Statistics, 1977*, XXI, No. 5 (May 1977), 166-167, and *idem*
(May 1981), 151-152.
    NOTE: The figures include procurement, research and development, and infrastructure
expenditure.
    [a] Errors due to rounding.

reaching its lowest point of 30 percent of equipment expenditures in
1981, the final year of the Giscard government.
    The Socialist government gradually increased spending for nuclear
arms. France's defense budget for 1983 projected an increase in spending for tactical and strategic systems of 14.3 percent in annual appropriations while the military budget as a whole increased by only 8.5 percent. Authorizations for nuclear arms jumped 31.8 percent,
underlining the priority status accorded nuclear forces and their mod-

ernization.[62] Spending for 1984 and 1985 was almost at 33 percent of the capital budget. The rise in expenditures for tactical or prestrategic forces was especially dramatic, increasing approximately 30 percent between 1984 and 1985. With 1979 as a base, spending for nuclear arms in constant francs grew by almost 25 percent from 100 to 124.[63]

The strategic and prestrategic nuclear forces marshaled by France in the early 1980s are sketched in Table 2-2. They are divided into three groupings depending on the basing mode and means of delivery. In 1986, 21 Mirage IV aircraft, capable of being refueled in air, carry a payload of one and possibly two 60- to 70-kiloton (kt.) AN-22 bombs. These aircraft are to remain operational until the end of 1986, when they will be replaced by 18 advanced model Mirage IVs, equipped with ASMP medium-range air-to-ground missiles.[64] The ASMP, with an attainable speed of MACH 3, has a range of 100 kilometers at low altitude and 300 kilometers at high altitude. Eighteen ground-based S-3 IRBMs, each armed with a single fusion 1-megaton (meg.) warhead, form the second leg of the French triad. The principal leg is the sea-launched ballistic missile (SLBM) system, carried by nuclear-powered submarines. Six nuclear submarines have now been launched, the last being the *Inflexible*, begun with the Giscard government and completed by the Mitterrand administration in May 1985. The first five SLBMs carry 16 missiles, each topped by a 1-megaton M-20 warhead. The *Inflexible* is equipped with an M-4 missile with 6 warheads. Four of the other 5 SLBMs will subsequently be retrofitted with M-4s.[65]

A seventh nuclear submarine is planned although it is likely to come into operation at the time that the first nuclear submarine will be deactivated. When completed, France will deploy up to 576 warheads, half of which are expected to be on station at all times. Studies were launched to develop an M-5 missile with greater range and throwweight than the M-4 and to design a new mobile IRBM to replace those on the Albion Plateau and the aging Mirage IV force as part of a new five-year plan introduced by the government of Prime Minister Jacques Chirac in the fall of 1986. These efforts to upgrade France's strategic forces were supplemented by a program to enhance the effectiveness of France's strategic nuclear command, control, and communications systems and to harden them against attack.

The projected increase in prestrategic nuclear weapons was particularly striking. By the mid-1990s, the ground army was expected to possess 90 Hadès missiles with two nuclear warheads. The Air Force will replace its tactical nuclear forces consisting of 45 Jaguars and 30 Mirage IIIs with 75 Mirage 2000s, armed with ASMPs to complement the Mirage IVs. The Navy will also have 24 Super Etendards, based on carriers, fitted to deliver nuclear warheads with ASMPs.[66]

France's impressive effort in building a powerful nuclear force has not been easy.[67] It has taken France over twenty years of arduous work, with little outside assistance, to construct a force de dissuasion. Its centerpiece today is its submarine fleet, to be progressively armed with multiple, flexibly targetable, long-range warheads. These accomplishments have been costly. They required the construction of nuclear testing sites in Algeria and the South Pacific; missile development centers in France, in Latin America, and in the Azores; the creation of a complex nuclear energy industry to produce plutonium (Marcoule) and enriched uranium (Pierrelatte). Reprocessing facilities were erected at La Hague and Marcoule. The aircraft industry also had to be modernized to meet France's needs for long- and short-range missiles and satellite launchers. The electronics industry was given a major boost by the nuclear program. During its initial expansion phase in the 1960s, more than 50 percent of its resources derived from the military and a large proportion of this subsidy was tied directly to the nuclear strategic program.[68] Even so, more than a decade passed before the first IRBMs were installed on the Albion Plateau and the first nuclear submarine was placed on patrol. The Mirage IV force was operational earlier, but perfection of the system continued into the 1970s.

The development of France's nuclear forces and the creation of a scientific, technological, and industrial infrastructure to sustain it were made possible partly by retarding the modernization of conventional forces. Spending levels on nonnuclear arms, shown in Table 2-1, were depressed through the 1960s, rising only slightly in the early 1970s once the first elements of the French nuclear triad had been deployed. The severe impact on French nonnuclear forces of the government's decision to accent nuclear weapons is difficult to summarize because of the complex range of ground, air, and sea systems that were adversely affected. The parliamentary reports outlining the first three program-laws all agreed on the negative impact that nuclear expenditures would have on conventional arms purchases.[69] Renewed attention to French nonnuclear forces, signaled by General Méry's revision of French nuclear strategy in 1976, began only with the fourth program-law for military equipment initiated in 1977. Spending gradually climbed from $4.4 billion in 1977, the first year of the fourth plan, to $9.4 billion in 1980, more than double the 1977 figure.

The first 25 years of the Fifth Republic have been lean years for conventional forces. The Algerian War reduced the French Army to a pacification force and stripped the few modernized units that had been assembled. The first program-law, initiated in 1960, held out little hope for speedy modernization. Nuclear forces were given a higher priority even before the war was over with the signing of the Evian accord in

Table 2-2. French Nuclear Forces: 1986

Platform Mode	Delivery Mode	First Year Deployed	Launch Total	Range (km)	Throw Weight (1000lb.)	Warhead Yield	CEP (m)	Warhead/County Total
Strategic								
18 Land-based intermediate range missiles (IRBM)	S3	1980	18	3500	N.A.	1x1 megaton (mg.)	N.A.	18
5 Submarines	M-20	1977-80	80	3000	N.A.	1x1 mg.	N.A.	80
1 Submarine	M-4	1985	16	4400+	N.A.	6x150 kilotons (kt.)	N.A.	96
Aircraft	Mirage IV[a]	1964	21	1500[a]	2.2	1xAN-22, 60 kt. bomb[b]	16	75
	(with ASMP)	1985	6	100-300	3.0	100-150 kt.[c]	19	1
Tactical								
Ground-based missiles	Pluton[d]	1974	44	120	N.A.	1x15 kt. or AN-51, 25 kt.	150-300	100+
Ground-based aircraft	Jaguar A	1974	45	720-750[e]	1.4	1AN-52, 15 kt. bomb (1 or 2) x	10	45-50
	Mirage IIIE	1964	30	600-800[g]	1.8	AN-52, 15 kt. bomb[f]	19	30[b]
Sea-based aircraft	Super-Etendard	1980	36	650	1.0	1xAN-52 15kt. bomb	N.A.	40

SOURCES: The principal source is the International Institute for Strategic Studies, *The Military Balance, 1985-1986* (London: IISS, 1985), pp. 160-161. This source is supplemented by several other sources which differ in some details, partly due to date of publication: David S. Yost, *France's Deterrent Posture and Security in Europe*, Part I: *Capabilities and Doctrine*, Adelphi Paper 194 (London: IISS, 1985), pp.13-29; Robbin F. Laird, *France, The Soviet Union and the Nuclear Weapons Issue* (Boulder, Co.: Westview, 1985), pp. 45-85; William M. Arkin and Richard W. Fieldhouse, *Nuclear Battlefields* (Cambridge, Ma.: Ballinger, 1985), pp. 37-64; Eric J. Grove, "Allied Nuclear Forces Complicate Negotiations," *Bulletin of the Atomic Scientists*, XLII, No. 6 (June-July 1986), 11-23; and *Military Technology* (July 1986), 62-71.

ᵃ The IISS, p. 161, lists a range of 3200 km. See note e and Laird, p. 46.

ᵇ The IISS, p. 161, and Yost, p. 18, cite a payload of one bomb; Laird, p. 46, and Arkin and Fieldhouse, p. 42, indicate two 70 kt. bombs. Stockpile total taken from *ibid.*

ᶜ The 21 Mirage IVs are to be reduced to 18 carrying air-to-surface missiles (ASMP) by 1987. Sources differ on payload. *The Military Balance* and Grove (p. 19) cite 150 kt.; Yost estimates the ASMP at 150-300 kt. (p. 19); *Military Technology* cites 300 kt.

ᵈ The number of Pluton systems cited by sources vary from 30 to 44. These are reloadable with perhaps up to 100 warheads available for firing. See Yost, p. 50; Arkin and Fieldhouse, p. 42, list 120 ANT-51 warheads.

ᵉ The IISS, p. 161, lists a range of 1600 km. based on a notion of "theoretical maximum range at optimum altitude and speed." Laird, Yost, and Grove base their estimates apparently on combat payload.

ᶠ The IISS, p. 161, lists one or two bombs. *Military Technology* rates the AN-52 at 20-25 kt.

ᵍ The IISS, p. 161, lists a range of 2400 km. based on considerations noted in note e. Laird, Yost, and Grove are cited here.

1962. The loss in personnel earmarked for France's forces of maneuver and intervention was particularly marked. By the start of the second military plan in 1965, French armed forces fell from slightly over a million to 545,000. As Table 2-3 outlines, these forces have gradually diminished to a level below a half-million. The long-term trend continues

Table 2-3. French Armed Forces Personnel for Selected Years: 1960-1985

	1960	1965	1970	1975	1980	1985
Army	812,000	350,000	328,000	331,500	321,320	304,500
Navy	68,000	72,500	72,000	69,000	69,950	67,700
Air Force	146,000	122,500	106,000	102,000	103,460	99,150
TOTAL	1,026,000	545,000	506,000	502,500	494,730	471,350

SOURCES: IISS, *The Military Balance, 1960, 1965-1966, 1970-1971, 1975-1976, 1980-1981*, and *1984-1985* (London: IISS, selected years), *passim*.

downward as the cost of maintaining these forces mounts and as French armed forces shift gradually from a conscript to a professional standing army after the American and English models.[70] The Army has been hit the hardest. It fell from a high of 812,000 in 1960 to 350,000 in 1965, a drop of almost 60 percent. It contracted to approximately 320,000 in 1980 and fell even further in 1985 to 304,500, with additional cuts forecast to compensate for the creation of FAR.[71] In contrast, French nuclear forces, for all legs of the French strategic triad, totaled less than 20,000 military personnel, yet this force received approximately one-third of France's expenditures on military equipment and research and development and up to one-half during its early developmental period.

Planners for the first military program-law offered the optimistic assessment that a decade would be needed to bring French ground forces to a level of modernization already enjoyed by other NATO forces in Europe.[72] Its armored units were equipped with obsolete American armor and with light, French-made AMX-13 tanks. A new AMX-30 series of heavy armor, tanks, and engineering equipment was not scheduled to be introduced into the Army until the late 1960s. Its full integration into the French arsenal was projected for the second half of the 1970s. By 1965, only six brigades stationed in Europe were fully equipped, and then only partially with new material. The latter was to consist primarily of transport for ground forces and self-propelled machine guns. While three divisions stationed in Algeria could be transported to Europe on short notice, none possessed modern trucks or armored carriers.[73] Forces stationed in France for use abroad were poorly equipped. Efforts to upgrade their status, as one parliamentary report noted, were not "organized in a way to form a permanent system of coherent forces."[74]

Mirage III fighters to support ground forces fell below stated requirements. A parliamentary evaluation concluded that "after several days of battle [French] air forces would be short of material."[75] Significant numbers of helicopters were not due to enter armed forces inventories until the end of the decade. The imbalance between ground and air modernization was striking. According to a parliamentary assessment that reflected armed forces' thinking, French fighter aircraft would have few French ground forces to support them by the end of the first five-year planning period. Until the end of the decade, they would have been obliged under wartime conditions to confine themselves to a role of reinforcing allied units and to be dependent "on their orders." "It seems doubtful," concluded the report, "that . . . because of this disparity in our forces, that there can be a national use of our means."[76]

In the face of the heavy costs anticipated in developing a nuclear submarine missile fleet, including a sixth and seventh nuclear missile submarine and plans for eight attack submarines, the Navy was compelled to revise its traditional commitment to a large surface fleet in favor of smaller, lighter ships, composed of corvettes, avisos, and fast patrol boats. Naval tonnage gradually decreased through the 1960s and 1970s. In 1960, total tonnage was slightly more than 300,000 tons of which approximately two-thirds was composed of ships ranging from 10 to 30 years of age.[77] Naval tonnage dropped to around 250,000 tons for most of the 1970s.[78] The Navy had to long delay plans for a nuclear-powered carrier to complement the *Foch* and to replace the aging *Clemenceau*. Although included in Chirac's five-year plan, it was not clear how the reported price tag of 10 billion francs could be met, a concern expressed by the Chief of the Navy.[79]

The evolution of conventional ground forces followed a similar, low budgetary trajectory. Spending on conventional forces was lowest for the Navy in the 1964-1970 period. It received only 18 percent of all funds earmarked for conventional arms in the second military plan—less than $200 million over a six-year period. Planning focused on extending the life of the existing fleet rather than on constructing new major vessels.[80] Dropped was a program to build six missile-launching frigates designed to protect France's aircraft carriers. New military construction was limited to two diesel-powered submarines of the 700-ton

"Daphne" class, a nuclear-powered attack submarine to protect the sea-launched missile systems that were being developed, five 2500-ton corvettes, and eight mine sweepers.[81] Expenditures on naval aircraft were proportionally higher than those for surface vessels. The Navy's aircraft fleet included Crusader and Etendard fighters, Neptune and Atlantique patrol planes, and Super Frelon helicopters for antisubmarine warfare.

The second military program-law downgraded conventional forces. Only three of five divisions were scheduled to receive a full complement of new (but not necessarily up-to-date) equipment. Initial equipment orders for the fourth division were to be placed only at the end of the planning cycle. The remaining divisions (one mechanized, the other for intervention overseas) were to be equipped with lighter AMX-13 tanks but with no helicopters. A start was anticipated on a decade-long program to provide 40 Transall cargo planes to airlift personnel and military abroad. Air support for French ground forces was sparse compared to NATO and Soviet capabilities. Concluded a parliament report: "The total number of aircraft to be constructed in six years is extraordinarily weak, even when added to existing equipment. In 1970, the number of operational aircraft in combat formations will be inferior to those of the Luftwaffe. It is certain that they will not be sufficient for [our] needs and possible missions. . . . The conventional means of the two armed forces [ground and air] are not balanced, to the detriment of the air force and finally to the detriment of the entire aeroground maneuver force."[82]

Conventional buildup improved slightly during the 1970s. Much of the research and developmental costs of the French nuclear triad had borne fruit by the early 1970s, releasing some funds for conventional forces. The fourth military program-law authorized expenditures for ground forces equipment. These had fallen to a low of 9.9 percent of capital expenditures in 1965 and had leveled off at approximately 23 percent in the 1970s, reaching a high of almost 26 percent in 1980. Spending on common defense programs, heavily weighted toward nuclear systems, declined slightly. Naval spending slipped to below 18 percent of capital authorizations, indicating that fleet tonnage would continue its downward trend. Aircraft spending, particularly for the F1 and Mirage 2000, was assigned high-priority status.

This marginal improvement in the financial supports created for nonnuclear arms did not substantially upgrade France's conventional forces relative to those of its major allies or, and much less so, to those of the Soviet Union. In the early 1970s, only one-third of the 15 projected motorized brigades were fully organized and equipped. The

Army was estimated to have 500 new combat vehicles, although planning was based on a number eight times that high. By the start of the fourth military program-law, French ground forces were evaluated in some quarters to be among the poorest equipped of major industrial states, despite the ability of France's arms industry to produce conventional weaponry of a high and competitive order. Its ground forces possessed approximately 190 Puma and Alouette II and III helicopters, 190 self-propelled 105 mm. cannons, 2,150 Milan antitank missiles, 1,000 light (and aging) AMX-13s, and only 850 heavy AMX-30 tanks.[83] Germany and Israel had twice as many heavy tanks and more than three times as many light tanks of newer stock.[84] Italy's armored forces compared favorably with those of France.[85] Each of the tank fleets of East Germany, Czechoslovakia, and Poland exceeded France's.[86] In 1980, a parliamentary report still found "a situation which, on many points, [was] not always positive" with respect to French ground force preparedness. Compared to NATO and Warsaw Pact divisions, ground artillery was less powerful and antiaircraft artillery, "nonexistent." "Compared to Soviet divisions," observed the report, "our inferiority in tanks is certain. It is considerable for artillery (relation of 1 to 3). It is clear equally for antitank missiles (relation of 1 to 2), although we are basing our hopes on this type of material. This inferiority is still more manifest for our infantry divisions, feebly equipped in artillery, without armor, and whose sole superiority rests in antitank missiles."[87] Only one-half of France's ground forces were estimated to have up-to-date equipment by 1982.[88]

Several factors besides those associated directly with strategic doctrine accounted for the slow and irregular modernization of French conventional forces. In the 1960s the government consistently underestimated the cost of nuclear development. Skyrocketing costs for nuclear systems, power plants, and facilities for the production of fissionable materials forced the Ministry of Defense to cut back on conventional spending in order to meet its program goals for nuclear weapons and still remain within the prescribed financial limits set by each military program-law. Table 2-4 summarizes some of the important reductions made in conventional purchases in favor of nuclear systems under the first and second program-laws.

The insistence of the three armed forces that they be granted tactical nuclear roles reinforced pressures to cut spending for conventional arms. Spending on tactical nuclear weapons and capability for ground, sea, and air forces cut into the slim amounts available for nonnuclear forces. The May upheaval of 1968 and increased service demands from rank-and-file personnel to spend more on military social welfare, as

Table 2-4. Reductions in Equipment Orders: First and Second
Program-Laws for Conventional Arms

Weapon	First Program-Law: 1960-1964		Second Program-Law: 1965-1970	
	Planned	Ordered	Planned	Ordered
Air Force Combat Aircraft	270	196	270	205
Naval Combat Aircraft	50	40	—	—
Vertical Takeoff Aircraft	—	—	—	Abandoned
Light Patrol Aircraft	80	Abandoned	—	—
Naval Patrol Aircraft	27	20	—	—
Helicopters	220	182	213	210
Light Machine Guns	800	415	—	—
AMX-30 Tanks	—	—	812	195
AMX-10 Armored Vehicles	—	—	1,400	75
AMX-13	—	—	705	598
AML 455	—	—	455	Abandoned
Missile-Firing Frigates	3	2	—	—

SOURCE: France, Assemblée Nationale, CDNFA (1970), *Rapport sur le loi de programme relative aux équipements militaires de la période 1971-1975*, No. 1872, October 2, 1970, pp. 8-30.

noted above, further weakened the thrust of conventional arms modernization. These civil and military social demands swelled inflationary pressures that reached destabilizing levels in the wake of the 1973 oil crisis. With 1970 as the base year, the French industrial price index rose 16 points from 1968 to 1970 and an additional 70 points between 1976 and 1977.[89] As a result, inflation lowered the equipment projections of planned spending programs. Only 85 percent of the third program-law, for example, was achieved as a consequence of unanticipated inflation.[90] Technological bottlenecks like those experienced in developing the AMX-10 armored series also contributed to the modernization slowdown. Series production had to be held up pending testing and improvement of the system. Reallocations within governmental spending to accelerate nuclear arms and programs and to satisfy rising welfare demands set conventional purchases back still further.

The nuclear thrust and slow pace, respectively, of France's modernization programs and the internal economic and political constraints that shaped and influenced their evolution had a telling impact on French arms production and sales. They conspired to make the French arms industry progressively export dependent. French armed forces lacked the resources needed to purchase arms at a rate or level sufficient to absorb the productive capacity of a French industry carefully nurtured and enlarged to produce the full panoply of weapons needed for French defense. Chapter 3 analyzes the economic factors, deriving from strategic necessity, which forced increasing reliance on arms sales to maintain France's arms industry. The implications of this dependency on French security policy are what concern us now.

Table 2-5 summarizes domestic and foreign deliveries of the French arms industry from the 1950s to 1980 for selected weapon systems. Except for the Alouette II, Jaguar, and Alpha-Jet, more than 60 percent of all helicopters and military aircraft have been sold abroad. In the case of six systems (Alouette III, Lama, Gazelle, Super Frelon, Puma, and Transall), foreign deliveries have totaled more than 70 percent. More than a half of all produced vehicles and tanks in each of the three series or families of weapons developed by France since World War II— AMX-10, -13, and -30—have also been sold to foreign countries.

The future growth and competitiveness of the arms industry—and presumably the preparedness of French armed forces, especially nonnuclear elements—critically depend on continued, worldwide sale of French military material. Table 2-6 provides data as of 1980 on foreign and domestic orders of major military systems, including aircraft, helicopters, aircraft and helicopter engines, tactical missiles, and munitions. In only one instance (the Crotale ground-to-air missile) has projected domestic consumption exceeded 40 percent. Foreign deliveries of the Alpha-Jet and Jaguar reached 60 percent of production. In two cases (the Otomat and Durandal penetration bomb), all production is scheduled for export. No helicopter developed in the 1970s falls below 72 percent in foreign orders. The recently developed Ecureuil depends for its success on foreign orders of slightly more than 95 percent of projected manufacture.

Also of interest are the number and geographic spread of countries receiving French arms and equipment. As Table 2-6 notes, helicopter engines lead the list with 103 countries having acquired or being scheduled to receive them. The Alouette III has been sent to 72 countries on

Table 2-5. Deliveries of Selected French Arms to 1980

	— to 1970						1971 to	
Weapon System	Deliveries to French Forces[1]	Deliveries to Foreign Countries[2]	No. of Countries (Foreign)	Total Arms Delivered	% France	% Export	Deliveries to French Forces[1]	Deliveries to Foreign Countries[2]
Aircraft- High Performance								
Mirage III, 5, 50	250-300[a,b,c,g,j]	428	8	678-728	37-41	59-63	190-240	461
Mirage F-1	—	—	—	—	—	—	137[h,i]	222
Jaguar	—	—	—	—	—	—	193[h,i]	154
Alpha-Jet	—	—	—	—	—	—	64[i]	46
Aircraft-Transport								
Transall	33[b]	21	2	54	61.1	38.9	10[g]	98
Helicopters								
Alouette II (SA-313/318)	438[c]	312	31	750	58.4	41.6	—	4
Alouette III (SA-316)	151	620	32	771	19.6	80.4	97[h,i]	370
Lama (SA-315)	—	—	—	—	—	—	—	123[l]
Gazelle (SA-341/342)	—	—	—	—	—	—	189[h,i]	465
Super Frelon (SA-321)	4[f]	29	2	33	12.1	87.9	20[f]	83
Puma/Super Puma (SA-330/332)	—	76	5	76	—	100.0	130[b,g]	400
Dauphin (SA-360/361/365)	—	—	—	—	—	—	—	6
Ground Equipment- AMX Family Series								
AMX-10 (P, PC)	—	—	—	—	—	—	578[g,h,i]	979
AMX-13 (VTT,[b,m] Missile-Firing, Bridge)	1,570[b,n]	1,988	19	3,558	44.1	55.9	402[g]	392
AMX-30 (Tanks, Missile-Firing, Engineering)	446[b]	—	—	446	100.0	—	615[h,i]	1,126

[1] Open sources, including French governmental documents are not clear about the number of aircraft, helicopters, and missiles that were delivered to French armed forces between 1960 and 1980. These are derived from weighing a number of conflicting sources. Those relevant are as follows:

[a] France, Assemblée Nationale, CDNFA (1960), *Avis sur le projet de loi de programme relative à certains équipements militaires*, No. 882, pp. 18-23.

[b] France, Ministère de la Défense, *Compte rendu sur le programme d'équipement militaire présenté par le gouvernement, Année 1971*, p. 10.

[c] France, Assemblée Nationale, CF (1964), *Rapport sur le project de loi de programme relative à certains équipements militaires*, No. 1195, p. 12.

[d] Groupement des Industries Françaises Aéronautiques et Spatiales (GIFAS), *L'industrie aéronautique et spatiale française 1981* (Paris, 1981), p. 36. Figures for total production of listed aircraft and helicopters are drawn from this authoritative industry source.

[e] Defense Marketing Services (DMS), *World Aircraft Forecast to 1985* (Greenwich, Conn., 1976), Volume 1 (see "France"). Helicopters are listed as of March 1, 1969. Note that all helicopters are not necessarily ordered for military purposes, although the vast majority are earmarked for defense functions.

[f] IISS, *The Military Balance, 1971-1972* (London: IISS, 1971), pp. 18-19.

[g] France, Ministère de la Défense, *Compte rendu sur le programme d'équipement militaire, présenté par le gouvernement, Année 1975*, pp. 22-23.

[h] France, Assemblée Nationale, CDNFA (1976), *Avis sur le projet de loi de finances: Dépenses en Capital*, No. 2532, p. 27.

[i] France, Assemblée Nationale, CDNFA (1979), *Rapport d'information sur l'exécution et l'actualisation de la loi de programme militaire pour les années 1977-1982*, No. 1298, October 2, 1979, pp. 111-120.

[j] France, Ministère de la Défense, *Rapport sur l'exécution de la loi de programme*, No. 60-1305, p. 14.

[k] *Jane's All The World's Aircraft* (London: Jane's Publishing Company Limited, 1972-1973).

[l] *Ibid.*, 1969-1970.

1980				Total to 1980					
No. of Countries (Foreign)	Total Arms Delivered	% France	% Export	Deliveries to French Forces[1]	Deliveries to Foreign Countries[2,5]	No. of Countries (Foreign)	Total Arms Delivered	% France	% Export
15	651-701	29-34	66-71	490[d]	889	20	1,379	35.5	64.5
7	359	38.2	61.8	137[h,i]	222	7	359	38.2	61.8
4	347	55.6	44.4	193[h,i]	154	4	347	55.6	44.4
5	110	58.2	41.8	64[i]	46	5	110	58.2	41.8
2	108	9.3	90.7	43	119	4[3]	162	26.5	73.5
3	4	—	100.0	438	316	32	754	58.1	41.9
33	467	20.8	79.2	248[d]	990	51	1,238	20.0	80.0
8	123	—	100.0	—	123	8	123	—	100.0
12	654	28.9	71.1	189[h,i]	465	12	654	28.9	71.1
7	103	19.4	80.6	24[f]	112	9	136[5]	17.6	82.4
34	530	24.5	75.5	130[b,g]	476	35	606	21.4	78.6
3	6	—	100.0	—	6	3	6	—	100.0
5	1,557	37.1	62.9	578	979	5	1,557	37.1	62.9
6	794	50.6	49.4	1,972	2,380	23	4,352	45.3	54.7
7	1,741	35.3	64.7	1,061[p]	1,126	7	2,187	48.5	51.5

[m] France, Assemblée Nationale, CDNFA (1970), *Rapport sur le projet de loi de programme relative aux équipements militaires de la période 1971-1975*, No. 1372, pp. 8ff.

[n] France, Ministère de la Défense, *Compte rendu sur le programme d'équipement militaire, présenté par le gouvernement, Année 1975*, p. 13.

[o] The figures cited only cover items ordered within the terms of successive program-laws. Purchases outside this framework were not available in the open literature. Figures for 1970-1980 include upgrading of selected AMX-13 stock.

[p] France, Assemblée Nationale, CF (1980), *Rapport sur le project de loi de finances pour 1981, Défense: Considérations Générales, Dépenses en Capital*, No. 1976, p. 122. The chart on this page cites materials in use in the armed forces. These numbers only approximate materials actually received by the military and do not include domestic civilian deliveries, which are particularly relevant for helicopters.

[2] See Note on Sources in the Appendix for sources on arms deliveries and for counting rules.

[3] Note the discrepancy with Appendix A for foreign countries receiving the Transall. French sources cite three countries, but do not list them; the SIPRI *Yearbooks* cite Germany, South Africa, Togo, and Turkey, while *The Military Balance* never confirms a delivery to Togo. Transall deliveries to Turkey or Togo may be excluded in the French sources. Turkey received 20 Transalls from Germany in 1971; they were counted here because the Transall was coproduced with Germany (see counting procedure 6 in the Note on Sources). Togo received one Transall from France as part of a military aid package to create an air force, according to the 1976 SIPRI *Yearbook*. Since this was not a sale but most likely a transfer from French stocks, French industry sources may not cite this transfer.

[1] The 1981-1982 *Jane's All the World's Aircraft* cites 285 Lama deliveries by January 1, 1981. *The Military Balance* and *SIPRI* sources only cite 123 deliveries to foreign countries through 1980, while French sources indicate 344 deliveries.

[5] Note the discrepancies between deliveries indicated here and orders in Table 2-6. Some states here are counted twice (e.g. Mirage III to 1970 and 1971-1980.)

Table 2-6. Orders for Selected French Aeronautic Equipment as of 1980

Weapon System	Total	Domestic	Foreign	% Foreign	Total No. of Countries (Foreign)
Aircraft-High Performance					
Mirage III, 5, 50	1,400	490	910	65.0	20
Mirage F1	649	259	390	60.0	10
Jaguar	580	200	380	65.5	4
Alpha-Jet	500	200	300	60.0	7
Aircraft-Transport					
Transall[a]	169	50	119	70.0	3
Helicopters					
Alouette II (SA-313/318)	1,143	438	705	62.0	37
Alouette III (SA-316)	1,424	248	1,176	82.6	72
Lama (SA-315)	344	35	309	89.8	28
Gazelle (SA-341/342)	937	252	685	73.1	34
Super Frelon (SA-321)[b]	99	27	72	72.7	7
Puma/Super Puma (SA-330/332)	729	190	539	73.9	45
Dauphin (SA-360/361/365)	265	31	234	88.3	23
Ecureuil/Astar/Twinstar AS-350B	911	44	867	95.2	24
Aircraft Engines					
Atar 9C (Mirage III, 5)	1,362	409	953	70.0	19
Atar 9K 50 (F1 and Mirage 50)	913	320	593	65.0	4
Helicopter Engines (most of which are for military purposes)	17,938	6,100	11,838	66.0	103
Missiles					
Missiles (17 types)[c]	529,034	148,130	380,904	72.0	49+
R-550 Magic	5,500	2,200	3,300	60.0	11
Crotale	3,200	2,560	640	20.0	9
Otomat	600	—	600	100.0	5
Bombs					
Durandal (penetration bomb)	5,500	—	5,500	100.0	7

Table 2-6 (*cont.*)

Source: Groupement des Industries Françaises Aéronautiques et Spatiales (gifas), *L'Industrie aéronautique et spatiale française 1981* (Paris, 1981), p. 36.

ᵃ See the note on sources in the Appendix.

ᵇ Note discrepancy with Table 2-5 where more Super Frelons are listed as having been delivered than ordered.

ᶜ Includes AS/SS-10, -11, -12, -15, Entac, Harpon, Hot, Milan, AS-20, and AS-30. Pinatel reports deliveries of 334,000 tactical missiles up to 1975, including 30,000 SS-10, 140,000 Entac, 160,000 SS-11, and 4,100 SS-12, sold to more than 20 countries including the United States. Jean-Bernard Pinatel et al., *L'Economie des forces* (Paris: Les Cahiers de la Fondation pour les Etudes de Défense Nationale, 1976), p. 118. Lars Benecke later notes that "by 1985, 183,000 Milan weapons were ordered and 172,000 had been delivered to 32 customers; 58,500 Hot weapons (of which 46,750 had been delivered to 14 customers); and of the 20,181 Roland weapons ordered, 14,750 had been delivered to eight customers." Lars Benecke et al., "Franco-West German Technological Co-Operation," *Survival*, xxviii, No. 3 (May-June, 1986), 235.

all continents, followed by the Puma (45) and Gazelle (34). Over a half-million tactical missiles have been sent to some 50 countries. Most popular among supersonic aircraft have been the Mirage series all-purpose fighters and specialized mission aircraft, which are found in the inventories of 20 countries in Europe, Latin America, Africa, the Middle East, and Oceana.

The arms export dependency of French security policy evidences little abatement in the foreseeable future. Spending for nuclear weapons will have to increase, and a decrease in expenditures for conventional forces—meaning lowered domestic demand—is the likely consequence. Maintaining a competitive edge with the superpowers, themselves engaged in a relentless arms race, remains a fundamental problem for the 1990s. Whether credible nuclear strike forces, strategic and prestrategic, can be maintained is by no means certain. The growth of the Soviet strategic warhead arsenal, estimated at approximately 10,000 in 1985 and counting, avails Soviet planners with first-strike capabilities vis-à-vis small nuclear states. Ground forces are especially vulnerable. The three nuclear submarines on station are also susceptible to detection or tracking as asw improvements advance. The Strategic Defense Initiative pressed by Washington may undermine the survivability and penetrability of French nuclear arms. Cruise missile development may prove necessary if a Soviet sdi goes forward and the abm treaty is formally abrogated or gradually abandoned. Meanwhile, French strike forces need their own early warning network and a space-based reconnaissance and observation capability. The Socialist 1984-1988 program-law provided only for research on such a system known as samro (satellite militaire de reconnaissance et d'observation). C³I systems will have to be modernized, hardened, and made redundant, especially those connected to the sea-based deterrent which operates in low frequencies and with slow reaction times. Additional funding has also been allocated by the Chirac government for the development of the M-5 warhead and for a new mobile ground missile as a hedge against a breakthrough in ASW technology and to replace the IRBMs on the Albion Plateau and aging Mirage IVs.

As expenditures for these strategic arms press on scarce defense resources, the prospects for conventional weapons expenditures are dim. If current trends persist, further cuts in spending for conventional ground forces can be expected. In 1979 constant francs, expenditures for ground forces rose 11 percent by 1982, but then fell to 8 percent over 1979 in 1985. Authorizations for new spending on operations and maintenance and on equipment for 1985 were, respectively, down 10 percent from the previous year.[91] Phillippe Arnold, the commanding officer of the First Tank Division in Germany, was dismissed for complaining to visiting journalists that the AMX-30 lagged behind the technical proficiency of western allied and Israeli tanks. France will not build a new tank using modern laminated-composite armor and a heavy gun. The Army will instead replace part of the MX-30 force with a new B2 model of the old system. Arnold suffered the same fate as the chief of staff of the Army, who, two years earlier was released from service for having objected to cuts in ground force strength. Retiring chief of staff General Lacaze warned, too, that unless spending was increased, the fighting efficiency of the armed forces would be compromised.[92]

Part of the reason for the Socialist government's slow start in developing a five-year plan for defense was the two-year delay in meeting the conventional arms targets set, but not reached, by the Giscard d'Estaing administration.[93] The Air Force chief of staff echoed the concerns of his Army and Navy colleagues over the adequacy of conventional defenses.[94] Delays continued in launching the study of a new all-purpose fighter for the end of the century. Decisions were deferred on buying AWACS or long-range transports. Flying time was cut to hold spending down. Controversy also arose over the proper number of aircraft in service which, critics charged, fell below the targeted ceiling of 500.[95] It is difficult to resist the conclusion that spending for French conventional forces continued to fall behind the expectations of the services and short of fulfilling the ambitious roles assigned to them by the Socialist government or its successor.

THE ARMS TRANSFER DILEMMA:
CHOOSING BETWEEN DEPENDENCIES

The export dependency of the French arms industry raises questions about how successful France has been in developing military capabilities sufficient to underwrite an autonomous military posture and independent foreign and international policy. While these questions fall outside the scope of this study, they are still of considerable interest since the answers they elicit bear critically on the ability of nation-states at France's level of development or lower to attain a position of strategic and foreign policy independence.

The military strategic and foreign policy implications of arms exports are not easy to identify or evaluate. In the French case, the data and expert opinion needed to make an evaluation are not readily available. They are often shrouded by a cloak of secrecy that successive Fifth Republic regimes, the defense ministry, and the military-industrial-techno-scientific complex have spread over France's arms and military technology transfers. A major report in the 1970s on the arms industry, although commissioned by the ministries of defense and of the economy, with the encouragement of the prime minister, was never published because it was critical of inefficient and wasteful practices, ineffectual management, and weak political oversight of the industry.[96] It criticized industrial and governmental leaders for having failed to make sufficient funds available for research and development to keep the industry abreast of foreign competition—corporate and military. The report accepted the need for a vigorous arms industry and a global arms export policy. Its criticisms centered on governmental, administrative, and industrial shortcomings, both in serving the French economy and the needs of the armed forces.

If the friends of the arms industry have had difficulty penetrating the arms production complex, outside critics have had even less success. The armed services are a logical source for critical evaluations of the weapons industry, but they have provided little in the way of substantiated public criticism of the responsiveness of the arms industry to their military needs. With few exceptions, criticism in the open literature has been impressionistic, journalistic, and, partly due to a lack of information, exaggerated.[97] Worse, the arms complex has, at different times, attempted to present its side through planted stories and advertisements which are as self-serving as they are self-congratulatory.[98]

Several lines of critique warrant further investigation. These include the allegations of sacrificed national military requirements on behalf of foreign sales. Allegations assume several forms. First, there are charges that military requirements have been altered to enhance France's prospects of selling arms abroad. Military equipment is designed initially with foreign purchasers in mind, particularly those from the developing world whose needs are not congruent with those of French forces facing a war in central Europe against powerful conventional and nuclear forces. Or, French forces are obliged to adopt systems and arms that they do not want in order to strengthen selling efforts to induce foreign governments to purchase French arms. The remonstrance of the Pompidou administration that the arms industry develop arms that were "simple, exportable, and less costly"[99] lends support to the view that arms have been designed with a double purpose in mind.

It remains an open question whether national requirements and arms trade imperatives can be reconciled. Important figures within the defense policy community have voiced fears on more than one occasion about France's dependency on exports and the potential implications for security: "For the next three years," observed parliamentarian Joël Le Theule in 1976, "our arms industry will be largely tributary to exports for its production program. This situation is not without its risks. One should hope that it can pass through this difficult period without too much damage and that it can preserve a *potential* and a technological level capable of confronting later the new needs engendered by technological change."[100]

In at least two reported instances, elaborated further in Chapter 5, it would appear that a serious conflict developed between the needs of the armed forces and the interest of the arms industry in increased export sales. In the mid-1970s, the Dassault Corporation launched an aggressive campaign to sell the F1 fighter, powered by SNECMA's M53 engine, to four NATO countries in the so-called sale of the century, a contract to replace aging air defense fighters of the Belgian, Dutch, Danish, and Norwegian air forces. To support the Dassault sales package, the French Air Force was obliged to commit itself to the purchase of the aircraft. The Dassault proposal forced the Air Force to accept the modified F1 as its basic fighter for the next decade and to relinquish efforts to develop a future combat fighter—an *avion de combat futur* (ACF). The F1 M53 program promised not only a lower performance aircraft than the projected ACF but higher logistics, operations, and maintenance costs. The award of the contract to General Dynamics for the F-16 relaxed some of the pressures placed on the French Air Force and elements within the General Delegation for Armament (DGA) who opposed the choice being imposed on them. The F1 M53 proposal was dropped, and the F1 with an Atar engine was ordered as a transition aircraft between the dated Mirage III/5 force and the development of the Mirage 2000 as a replacement for the ACF program. The latter was canceled for economic reasons. Cost estimates for the ACF approached those of the financially disastrous Concorde project. One high DGA official characterized the loss of the NATO contract as a victory for the French Air Force.[101]

French ground forces have also apparently objected to equipment that they were obliged to accept to support sales abroad. The AMX-30 chassis, mounted with a 155 mm. cannon, was sold to the Saudi Arabian government during the 1970s. As part of the contract, the French Army was reportedly issued the same self-propelled weapon, although ten towed 155 mm. field guns could have been bought for the $2.9 million price of each AMX-30 copy. The Saudi Arabian contract, like the F1 M53 sale, committed French armed forces to a strategy of modifying equipment based on outdated technology rather than launching a research and development program for a new series of battle tanks that would go beyond the AMX-30 design.[102] Similarly, the Navy absorbed an excess of Nord 262 aircraft when foreign buyers were unavailable.[103]

Second, there are allegations that arms exports have slowed deliveries to French armed forces and have sometimes led to temporary inventory losses as armed forces equipment was sent to a foreign customer to meet contractual obligations or to clinch a sale. Ground forces have apparently been adversely affected, on occasion, by production decisions keyed more to arms sales than to national military needs. The AMX-13 family of weapons was delivered to French forces over the period 1952 to 1971. These deliveries were divided into three overlapping time periods to conform to separate but related elements of the AMX-13 series. From 1952 to 1960, AMX-13 cannons were delivered. In the second time segment, from 1957 to 1967, armored personnel carriers and support equipment became available to French forces. Most deliveries of cannons and personnel carriers were completed in nine to eleven years. The remainder of artillery and engineering vehicles within the series was delivered throughout the period as needed.

In contrast, deliveries of AMX-10 equipment and AMX-30 materials are expected, respectively, to cover fifteen and twenty years. This policy shift to keep in production a full range of weapons within the arms family, as one study observed, "entailed a slowdown in deliveries of each type of material. That poses for the Army problems of stock and operational management. . . . One can wonder whether this phenomenon does not have its origin in the desire of the Ministerial Delegation for Armament to possess a complete catalogue of exportable products; which prompts one to ask about the interest for the armed forces of an arms policy too tuned toward exports."[104]

However necessary they might be, arms exports have contributed, through slowed deliveries to national forces, to the growth of hetero-geneous arms inventories, irregular and unbalanced modernization of the armed forces, and haphazard scheduling of weapon system replace-ments. At times, foreign states were sent new arms before French forces were equipped with copies. Libya reportedly received Crotale ground-to-air missiles in 1973 before the needs of French forces were fully met. Similarly, Saudi Arabia began receiving AMX-30 tanks and armor be-fore the supply objectives of French ground forces were reached.[105] On the other hand, French inventories have on several occasions been drawn down to please foreign customers. Mirage fighters and Atlantic patrol vessels were withdrawn from French inventories and sent, re-spectively, to Spain and the Netherlands, to meet contractual deadlines. In 1983, the French Navy was induced to "lend" five new Super Eten-dards to Iraq to assist that country in its war against Iran by attacking foreign shipping and Iranian oil facilities.

Partisans of the arms industry have defended these practices as a con-tribution to strategic preparedness. Unlike the arms industries of the superpowers, the French system does not have the luxury of producing distinct products to meet differential domestic and foreign needs. As one defender of the arms industry has argued, "France has only the Mi-rage and Jaguar families, and the same production lines serve both do-mestic and export markets. This also results in delivery delays, and it is true that sometimes we delay equipping our own forces to meet a for-eign request. . . . It is common practice to deplete one's own arsenal to arm allies—and it is perhaps wiser to do that early, in order to deter war. . . ."[106] Whatever the merit of this line of logic may be, it does not appear to have been rigorously followed since among the "allies" re-ceiving Mirage or Jaguars one finds neutral states (Switzerland, Paki-stan, Venezuela, and India), outcasts (South Africa), and hostile powers (Libya).

Sales to countries like South Africa raise another problem for French security and foreign policy. What political costs are incurred in sending arms to states which are engaged in bitter conflicts with their neighbors whether over race (South Africa), over charges of aggression (Israel), or over predatory or authoritarian rule (Zaire and Argentina)? As Chapter 7 details, the economic importance of arms sales and their real and perceived internal socio-political benefits have tended to outweigh these negative considerations. They have also overruled concern about transfers of arms and military technology, including civilian nuclear materials and know-how, that risk undermining French defense interests. Libyan possession of the Crotale system poses problems for French aircraft operating in the western Sahara. French arms might well find their way through Libya to military units in North and Black Africa opposed to France's allies.[107] The French were temporarily embarrassed by the sinking of a British destroyer by Argentina with aircraft armed with French-made Exocet missiles during the Falklands War of 1982 and could find themselves in a similar strait in the future. This risk did not dissuade the Mitterrand government from lifting an embargo on arms to Argentina and resuming Exocet deliveries once hostilities ceased, nor from delivering the same, deadly missiles to Iraq which has repeatedly used them against neutral ships carrying oil and goods in the Persian Gulf.[108]

There is also the possibility that French technical advances in arms will fall into the hands of hostile powers, like the Soviet Union, through third-state transfers. These concerns were publicly raised in press reports surrounding the sale to Iraq of Mirage F1s and naval vessels equipped with advanced radar and electronic devices for evasion and countermeasures.[109] At least one French military commander has voiced criticism of France's liberal policy toward the transfer of military technology: "In France one thinks first of exporting arms and of orders for arsenals. The needs of the army come afterward. We sell the Arabs weapons that we know fall into the hands of Soviet experts."[110] Building up the arms production capacity of other states, like Argentina, Israel, and South Africa, also poses problems for French security interests and those of its closest allies in the Atlantic Alliance, the Middle East, and Black Africa. Israel builds the Kfir fighter that draws heavily on the French Mirage III design. South Africa builds Mirages under license from France. India has been granted licenses also to build Jaguars, Puma helicopters (Cheetah), and Mirage 2000s.

Another set of problems concerns the servicing of equipment and the training of foreign military to use it. Not only is France drawn into implicit political ties that it may wish to avoid (e.g., in Iraq), but its own forces are deflected from their operational missions. Sales of submarines, such as those to Argentina and South Africa, entail as much as one year of the time of a regular French submarine crew to train foreign forces. Meanwhile, other mission responsibilities go unfulfilled.[111]

The ability of the military to shift these burdens or to acquire the needed resources to discharge them appears increasingly problematic. Given the pressures to export, the tendency in political circles, reflected in reports of the National Assembly, is to recommend more, not less, military involvement in the after-sale (*après vente*) phase of arms sales to compete with other major arms suppliers, particularly the superpowers which have elaborate support structures as part of their sales arrangements.

Before we turn to the impact of French arms control and disarmament policy on the transfer by France of arms and military technology, it is appropriate to note that the picture just described of an overall distorting and retarding effect of arms sales on the modernization of French conventional forces has implications for French strategic doctrine. This consideration is quite apart from the merits of the French insistence on military autonomy and political independence. French decision-makers are making choices that trade off different kinds of autonomy and independence. The dependency of the Fourth Republic on its allies for arms and economic aid (not to mention political support for successive French governments) risks being transformed into a dependency on arms purchases under the Fifth Republic. Much has been made of the strategic weakness of states which rely on foreign suppliers. Less visible are the damaging effects on the military preparedness of suppliers which need export markets to maintain their arms production systems. These consequences, explored in Chapter 7, are distinct from the unintended and unwitting political commitments that often accompany arms sales.

Aside from the strategic costs and risks of arms sales, French military operations are also threatened in unintended ways. As French armed forces, particularly those assigned conventional missions, fall short of expected levels of equipment, fighting effectiveness, and efficiency, there is a danger that an already heavily favored nuclear strategy and force posture will close off or limit significant military options to French political leaders. Lost may be the opportunity to reinforce effectively and in timely fashion allied conventional moves to deter or defeat Warsaw Pact moves short of using nuclear weapons. By default, if not by design, France also threatens to impose its limited options on its allies in having to resort earlier to nuclear weapons than prudence might advise. The possibility of French assistance for extra-European peacekeeping activities, whether under United Nations or allied auspices, is also not improved except for relatively short, punctual, and surgical interventions.

Arms Control, Disarmament, Arms Production, and Transfers

French arms control and disarmament policies complement France's international and security policies and support its global arms and military technology sales efforts. They have been in tandem with French economic and welfare needs, linked to the development of civilian nuclear power at home and the export of nuclear know-how, fissionable materials, and services as well as conventional arms and technology abroad. French arms control and disarmament policies have been largely defined by these external and internal needs and constraints. Their principal function, if not their announced role, has been to act as a shield, deflecting the efforts of other states, especially the superpowers, to limit France's access to nuclear weapons or its ability to sell arms and military technology to third states.

France's permissive attitude and approach to arms limitation issues have been increasingly challenged by the superpowers, although their arms control accords, formal treaties, executive agreements, or implicit understandings have not resulted in significant arms reductions or, arguably, even in a slower rate of arms modernization. The guiding aim of superpower arms control accords has been placed on maintaining a balance of terror while permitting progressive improvement of nuclear forces. The aim of deep reductions, while repeatedly proclaimed, has been assigned a secondary priority.[112] Viewed against the history of the Cold War struggle, the principal functions of arms control agreements have been to regulate the arms competition, to develop agreed upon rules for the arms race, and to establish a procedure, however fragile or selectively observed, to legitimate the relentless perfection of nuclear arms.

As France's status as a major exporter of weapons and arms technology has grown, its interest in controlling the potential harmful effects of arms transfers has gradually become more pronounced, partly in response to external pressures, notably from the United States, and partly as a result of an internal reassessment of the potential damaging effects on French security and foreign policy objectives. French government leaders, even partisans of an open export policy for military and civilian technology,[113] reluctantly came to the conclusion that limits had to be set to offset or diminish the negative impact of nuclear proliferation. These limits assumed the form of restrictions, particularly on the transfer of civilian nuclear technology, and of tighter review procedures for export licenses. Movement toward controls on conventional arms production and sales as well as the transfer of military technology has been slower. Restrictions on sales or transfers of nonnuclear weapons and know-how derive primarily from national self-limitations and not from foreign pressures. For a set of intertwined reasons, to be discussed below and in succeeding chapters, domestic barriers are few and easily vaulted by the state-led arms complex in France.

Nuclear Arms Limitations: Accent on Disarmament

In light of the Soviet-American experience, arms control implies cooperation between adversaries to preclude war, to lower the costs and risks of the arms race, and to minimize damage and bring hostilities to a quick close if war should erupt. Arms limitation agreements are directed at reducing the probability of nuclear war, prompted by incentives for preemption, misperception, accident, miscalculation or inadvertent use of nuclear weapons. French leaders have looked with suspicion on such superpower arms control proposals. French governmental spokesmen have tended to view them as a means of solidifying their hegemonial status and of inhibiting or denying a role to other states in defining regional and global security arrangements. Superpower accord with respect to European security has also been viewed skeptically as a device to spare the United States and the Soviet Union while making Europe the battleground in a future war. The force de dissuasion was designed partly to forestall these possible consequences of Soviet-American arms control accords and partly to enhance France's security and say about security arrangements in Europe, the Mediterranean basin, and Africa. In tandem with this response, French leaders have generally preferred disarmament measures, calling for reductions in superpower arsenals as a precondition for French participation in arms limitations talks.[114]

The de Gaulle government resisted pressures from domestic opponents and foreign critics, especially from Washington, to scrap the French nuclear force or to limit its size and capability. It was sensitive to France's late start in the nuclear race and to the growing destructive power, accuracy, and flexibility of superpower nuclear forces. Its principal tactic was to withdraw from arms control and disarmament talks rather than to engage in an active diplomatic assault on superpower disarmament positions. An empty-chair policy served Gaullist France quite well. Participation in arms talks, largely beyond its control, risked ensnaring France in a game whose rules were set by the superpowers, even before serious bargaining got underway. The de Gaulle regime might have had to accept restraints on a force that was still to be developed. Most French leaders, not only de Gaulle, blamed the superpowers for proliferation. Superpower vertical disarmament had to precede the horizontal nuclear disarmament of smaller nuclear states and the adoption of an international regime to control proliferation. It was politically, if not logically, consistent for the de Gaulle regime to justify France's nuclear armament as a response to superpower refusal to disarm and to insist that France had first to arm itself before it would negotiate its disarmament.

French resistance to superpower arms control pressures was supposed to bolster global stability and lay the foundation for a new, legitimate world order. The superpowers would have little incentive to take others into account unless they also possessed nuclear weapons. France's possession of nuclear weapons supported its expectation that it had a right to bargain and negotiate with the superpowers as a peer. Its participation in defining international accords allegedly assured other states that their fundamental interests would be promoted. Paris claimed that France's defense of national independence served the security interests of all states. Unlike the superpowers with their imperialist proclivities, France supposedly harbored no expansionist or colonialist ambitions. The de Gaulle regime's self-proclaimed generous settlement of the Algerian war purportedly testified to its disinterest.[115]

The Gaullist position on nuclear arms control and disarmament was essentially discriminatory. According to Gaullist reasoning, the scope and importance of a state's security role depended on its possession of military force. In the postwar period, that meant nuclear weapons. On this score, Gaullist France claimed equality with the superpowers in defining European and extra-European security arrangements. The NATO directorate proposal was designed to institutionalize a two-tier system of authority within the alliance in which the western nuclear states would frame the security policies of the other members. The security and political needs of the nonnuclear states would be determined by the three NATO nuclear powers. Implicit in the French directorate scheme was a client-sponsor relationship in which the representation of nonnuclear state interests would become the charge of one or all of the nuclear powers. Germany's subordinate position within the alliance would be consolidated. Its renunciation of nuclear arms in signing the Western European Union treaty in 1954 assured France's continental superiority among the European liberal democracies once Paris had acquired nuclear weapons. The Fourth Republic set about that task assiduously; the Fifth Republic completed the job while affirming its commitment to global disarmament.

Gaullist disarmament policy, rooted implicitly in the supremacy of the nuclear powers, extended the NATO scheme to a global level. For

French leaders, negotiating over disarmament was of a piece with bargaining over the outstanding political issues separating the major powers. France's possession of nuclear weapons was to ensure it a place around the bargaining table. Accord among the nuclear powers was tantamount to the creation of a global security system guaranteed by their collective nuclear resources. The security interests of nonnuclear states and their political needs were portrayed as a function of big-state diplomacy. Regional security derived then from global entente. From this perspective the de Gaulle government proposed four-power talks between the Soviet Union and the western nuclear powers to resolve the Middle East conflict and between these powers and a nuclear China to settle the Vietnam War. The entry fee to the bargaining table was nuclear arms.

While the French preferred to speak more about superpower disarmament than multilateral arms control, French diplomacy set political accord ahead of either arms control or disarmament measures. During the de Gaulle and Pompidou periods, the French refused to view arms regulation agreements apart from the political conflicts fueling the arms race, the military balance between contending opponents (and allies), and the various objectives to be served by France's possession of nuclear weapons. The road to disarmament passed, first, through détente and political agreement, resting on a military balance among nuclear powers. Early during the de Gaulle administration, French Foreign Minister Couve de Murville explained the French position: "Disarmament can be a factor in bringing about a détente, but without the détente itself, it is inconceivable. . . . There must be a first step which can only be made in the political field. . . . We would all try together to settle the political conflicts that arise, whether in Europe, Asia, or elsewhere. . . . Then everything would become possible, starting with effective disarmament."[116]

Since the de Gaulle and Pompidou regimes viewed nuclear weapons as the admission price to the inner circle of great powers and to equal participation with them in the politics of détente, disarmament proposals were subordinate to larger security and foreign policy needs: an autonomous French military posture resting on nuclear weapons in pursuit of political independence and of the denunciation of superpower influence; recognition of paramount political and security interests, like Germany's political reconciliation with its division and postwar frontiers and its military containment; France's special role in the Mediterranean and Africa; and the legitimacy of its quest for grandeur. One might also note, incidentally, that the tactic of opposing other states on vital issues, particularly the United States, to enhance attention to French demands became part of the baggage of the Gaullist approach to arms control questions.[117] French arms limitation policies thus served several masters at home and abroad. They can be fully understood only within this wider perspective rather than solely as a response to the immediate issues surrounding a specific proposal.

Fourth and the early Fifth Republic leaders shared much the same reservations about the superpower nuclear monopoly. De Gaulle's purist position on nuclear disarmament also made good domestic politics. As long as the force de dissuasion was more a design than a reality and French strategic doctrine more a sentiment than an operational code and arm of diplomacy, President de Gaulle and Jules Moch, his Socialist representative at the United Nations, could agree on the need for nuclear disarmament—starting with the United States and the Soviet Union, not France. The requirements for disarmament were so rigorous that their adoption by other capitals, especially by Washington and Moscow, was not likely; but at the same time the French government could assume the moral high ground while moving swiftly to build its own nuclear force, justified by the failure of the superpowers to heed France's call for restraint.

Insistence on applying strict tests to the superpowers abroad neutralized Gaullist nuclear opponents at home. Moch and de Gaulle, while political opponents at home, could see eye-to-eye abroad on a principle repeatedly pronounced by the French representative at the U.N.: "No disarmament without control, no control without disarmament, but all disarmament presently controllable."[118] Socialist pacifism and Gaullist power politics could march together under so high flying a standard. The control problem was viewed largely as a matter of effective international verification, a principle that has remained solidly anchored to French arms limitation accords until today. If the Soviet Union's reluctance to accept such measures prevented much progress either on its call for general and complete disarmament or on American proposals for more limited approaches, the absence of superpower movement lent legitimacy to France's nuclear effort.

The French proposal first to limit and then to eliminate nuclear delivery vehicles met with little enthusiasm from the superpowers, although this approach was later adopted by them in their bilateral discussions throughout most of the 1970s. Moch initially advanced this proposal before the Committee of Ten and, later, in October 1959, in more elaborate form, before the U.N. Political Committee. In remarks made at a news conference a month later, de Gaulle summarized the French position. Disarmament had to be effective, commencing with the prohibition of delivery vehicles, before France would submit its own nuclear program to external controls. In response to the superpower rivalry, de Gaulle presented the French nuclear program as a source of stability: "In truth, France, in developing a nuclear force, renders a service to the world balance. If the United Nations Organization shows itself capable of putting an effective end to the threat [of the super-power nuclear rivalry] and if, as a beginning, it succeeds in placing delivery vehicles under international control . . . as France proposes through the voice of its delegate on disarmament, M. Moch, then France will apply immediately, without hesitation, and very willingly, international law."[119] De Gaulle reiterated the French either-or position during his visit to the United States in April 1960. The breakup of the Paris summit in May 1960 and the acceleration of the strategic arms race made the French proposal moot.

French resistance to superpower efforts to restrain France's strategic nuclear program continued through the presidencies of Georges Pompidou and Giscard d'Estaing. President Pompidou echoed President de Gaulle's call for superpower disarmament while preserving France's freedom of maneuver to develop its nuclear forces free of exterior constraint. Like de Gaulle, Pompidou stressed the hazards of the superpower nuclear monopoly and the contribution of French nuclear forces to a more stable international system: "Let the great powers that possess the nuclear weapons be ready for simultaneous disarmament, and France will . . . place her nuclear deterrent force on the disarmament table. On the other hand, let us not be asked to approve the system in which the two great powers that are overarmed in nuclear weapons . . . would organize the disarmament of the others, for that is firstly a mockery of disarmament, secondly, a fundamental danger to peace."[120]

President Giscard d'Estaing adopted a similar stance. Giscard's call for a special U.N. disarmament conference did not prevent him from presiding over the most rapid expansion of French nuclear capabilities since the formation of the force de dissuasion. Between the opening of SALT I talks in 1969 and the signature of SALT II a decade later, France increased its nuclear forces from 36 Mirage IV aircraft to 18 intermediate-range missiles and 4 nuclear submarines armed with 64 missiles. All three armed forces also had units equipped with tactical nuclear weapons.[121]

However much the Socialist party may have been committed to disarmament, Socialist President François Mitterrand was no less adamantly opposed than his predecessors to any limitations on the development of France's nuclear forces.[122] Prime Minister Pierre Mauroy reaffirmed his Socialist government's commitment to the nuclear deterrent and the modernization of nuclear forces: "France intends to maintain its independence of choice and of decision in military matters, that ultimate recourse in foreign relations. The means of this independence . . . is the nuclear deterrent. . . . The government completely accepts this option. The military equipment of the country does not . . . give it any other device. . . . Such a strategy . . . must be adapted to changes in threats and technology. . . . This permanent development of nuclear arms obliges France to keep its own potential constantly up to date."[123]

The nuclear disequilibrium perceived by the Socialist regime to exist in Europe and, progressively, at a global level between the superpowers to the disfavor of the western states reinforced the Mitterrand government's reticence to engage in any arms control talks that might hamper the development of France's nuclear forces or, going further than his predecessors, that might weaken the balance of theater nuclear and conventional forces in Europe to the West's disadvantage. Affirmed were previous stances on a partial test ban treaty, reservations about the creation of a nuclear-free zone in Latin America, and French refusal to engage in SALT or START talks. The Mitterrand government also favored the deployment in Europe of 108 Pershing II and 464 Cruise missiles to balance the Soviet modernization program, if an arms accord to limit the deployment of Soviet theater nuclear forces could not be reached.

De Gaulle set French policy on nuclear testing for his successors. Early on he rejected suggestions that France sign the partial test ban treaty: "So long as . . . disarmament is not being carried out . . . we shall continue our tests in any case until the goal is reached, unless . . . the others rid themselves of their means of destruction."[124] The Pompidou administration conducted atmospheric nuclear tests throughout its period in office despite objections from several states affected by fallout. Between 1966 and 1974, 41 above-ground tests were executed, 7 more than all nuclear devices exploded by the United Kingdom.[125] Another 59 underground tests were conducted in the South Pacific between 1974 and 1981. The Socialist government on taking office initially canceled scheduled tests, but this order was rescinded only days after its issuance.[126] In the absence of testing, the French military would be hindered in developing nuclear warheads for new strategic and tactical missiles that were central to the Socialist nuclear program. Following past practice, the Socialist French government also ignored protests of Australia and New Zealand over the leakage of radioactive material from underground tests in the South Pacific.[127] Going further, the Socialist government was responsible for mounting a failed undercover operation leading to the loss of life and the sinking of the *Rainbow Warrior*, a ship used by the peace group Greenpeace to protest French testing. Defense Minister Charles Hernu and the head of France's secret service resigned over the fiasco. The affair revealed the extraordinary lengths to which even past opponents of the French nuclear program were willing to go, once in power, to silence even innocuous, if embarrassingly vocal, peace groups.[128] There was also concern that the declaration of a South Pacific nuclear-free zone by the governments of that region might hamper French testing and movement of nuclear devices through the area and set an unfortunate precedent for Central Europe.

French tergiversations over signing the treaty of Tlatelolco, creating a nuclear-free zone in Latin America, also underlined the unwavering commitment of French policy-makers to a nuclear weapons program, resistant to pressures from third states to impose arms limitations on France. The difficulty of resolving these competing claims has been heightened by French determination to lead the nonaligned states in imposing limitations on the superpower arms race. The treaty of Tlatelolco "prohibits the testing, use, manufacture, production or acquisition . . . , as well as the receipt . . . deployment and possession of any nuclear weapons by Latin American countries."[129] France attached reservations to its signature of the two protocols to the treaty. While Protocol II was signed in 1974, Protocol I, which held non-Latin states, like France, responsible for the application of the treaty, was not initialed until President Giscard d'Estaing's visit to Mexico in March 1978. The French government defined those areas where the treaty would not apply: (1) "transit across the territories of the French Republic situated in the zone of the treaty" and (2) limitations on "the participation of the populations of the French territories . . . in efforts connected with national defense of France. . . ."[130]

If the Tlatelolco treaty were applied strictly to Guyana and the Antilles, French transport of nuclear devices and materials in or through Latin America might be prohibited. In addition, to accept the principle of nonnuclear zones in Latin America is to grant its application elsewhere. What then becomes of the French test sites in the Pacific? On the other hand, French willingness to sign the treaty, subject to reservations covering French nuclear forces and weapons development, opens still another forum for arms limitation discussions in which the French can participate in the continuing effort to harness Third World sentiment to French nuclear diplomacy. Signing the treaty also underscores France's regional interest in Latin America. This assertion of regional status in Latin America is joined to France's more established claims to a significant regional presence in the Mediterranean and in Black Africa, claims that are bolstered by the presence of French troops at different times in Chad, the western Sahara, Zaire, and Lebanon, whether under U.N. command or, as in 1982, as part of an international force to police Israeli-Arab clashes.

The reservations attached to the Latin American nuclear-free zone treaty served more to protect French maneuverability and to mollify the government's domestic opponents, particularly Gaullists on the

Right, than to advance the objectives of the treaty originators. Much like a carousel, circular motion was imparted without forward movement. The Right was granted its reservations; the Left was assuaged in making France a party to an arms control measure sought by the developing world; and French global and regional interests were promoted. What Latin America received is less clear.[131]

Superpower strategic arms talks posed a more serious threat to an autonomous French nuclear effort than did the Latin American nuclear proposal. The de Gaulle and Pompidou governments pictured superpower accord as potentially detrimental to the political and strategic interests of third states, particularly the European members of the western alliance. Either superpower differences would be compromised at European expense or Europe would be implicitly designated, as suggested above, as a battlefield between Moscow and Washington in the event of hostilities while their own countries remained sanctuaries.[132] Or, the United States might concede too much either in global or theater arms control negotiations, and the credibility of its nuclear guarantee would fall below an acceptable level of deterrence—a fear expressed by Europeans in the wake of the superpower summit at Reykjavik in 1986.[133]

These concerns were fueled by American willingness under the Carter administration to place the Backfire bombers and Soviet emplacement of SS-20 missiles on its western borders outside strategic arms limitation talks, as well as its disposition to accept limits on Cruise-missile deployments in Europe and the transfer of Cruise technology to its European allies. According to French analysts, instability in Europe would result either from Germany's acquisition or access to nuclear weapons (a provocation to France and the Soviet Union) or from its accommodations of eastern bloc demands leading to its neutrality (a threat to the West and a blow to the Atlantic Alliance cohesion).[134] Finally, fears were voiced that France would be drawn into the SALT process and international controls on its own nuclear forces would result. Little was said in official circles about the potential benefits of superpower limits on the French nuclear force.[135] The ABM treaty enhanced the penetration capability of French missiles; limits on superpower offensive weapons held the prospect that French nuclear forces might be less vulnerable to a disarming attack.

French regimes under the Fifth Republic have taken a consistent stance toward these conflicting considerations. First, superpower limits on nuclear arms have been encouraged and successive French governments have refrained from taking any step to slow bilateral talks despite discreetly conveyed apprehensions about their potentially destabilizing direction. Concern centered on the possible weakening of U.S. capabilities and the impact of a nuclear arms withdrawal or diminution of American nuclear presence in Europe and the potentially adverse implications of these trends for European security. While Socialist President François Mitterrand proposed Paris as a meeting place for superpower nuclear talks to underscore French interest in reducing superpower nuclear arms, he was careful to distance France from any bilateral superpower agreement that might adversely affect the French nuclear program.[136] Resisted has been any attempt to count French strategic forces in defining the United States–Soviet nuclear balance in Europe.

Second, superpower arms limitation accords, while portrayed as potential contributions to peace, have been disparaged as true disarmament measures. The superpowers are accused of having increased the qualitative buildup of their forces and of having sought to widen the gap between themselves and other nuclear powers through their arms agreements. Third, and most importantly, every French government has rejected overtures either to join strategic arms limitation talks or those aimed at limiting superpower deployment of long-range theater nuclear forces. President Giscard d'Estaing, in the wake of a major campaign in 1978 to organize global disarmament talks, reiterated the French position: "France desires the next conclusion of a balanced strategic nuclear arms reduction accord between the United States and the USSR. She does not foresee participation in an eventual negotiation on the limitation of armaments in the so-called 'gray zone' in Europe for reasons that are related to the independence of her deterrent."[137] The Mitterrand government, affirming France's nuclear weapons as strategic, not theater weapons, insisted on keeping clear of superpower nuclear arms talks. In a news-conference on September 24, 1982, President Mitterrand asserted that France "cannot accept that a part of our nuclear armament is negotiable, because if that were so we would fall to a level at which our deterrent capacity would be destroyed. . . . France's international policy refuses prohibitions. We refuse to accept the prohibition of others."[138] For good measure, President Mitterrand added, "No one will dictate our policy to us; particularly so far as the neutron bomb is concerned."[139]

The determination of the Socialist government to pursue the development of a neutron bomb, although United States deployment of the weapon had been vetoed by the Carter administration, and its encouragement of NATO proposals to deploy long-range theater nuclear forces in Europe in the absence of an arms control accord with the Soviet Union, underscored its rejection of a neutralist stance for France or Europe. "French policy," observed Prime Minister Mauroy, "is in no way neutralist. Even if we worked it to be so it would not, given the geographical situation of the country, be possible."[140]

Whereas President Giscard d'Estaing had limited his regime's attention to the global nuclear balance and, as will be discussed below, to the conventional balance in Europe, President Mitterrand added to French concerns by also focusing on the nuclear balance in Europe. Criticism was specifically aimed at Soviet SS-20 missiles, which were directed at NATO and French forces.[141] In an interview given to the German weekly, *Stern*, several days before his visit to West Germany in July 1981, President Mitterrand charged that the Soviet Union's deployment of SS-20 intermediate-range missiles and Backfire bombers was upsetting the balance of power in Europe: "I do not accept it, and I accept that one must rearm to restore the balance. From that point one must negotiate." Noting the threat of Soviet supremacy in Europe as a "real danger," Mitterrand also affirmed that "the United States has the means to restore the balance of power [and that] France will not hesitate to complete its deterrent weaponry."[142] The perceived conventional and nuclear imbalance in Europe was still very much on President Mitterrand's mind in November 1982. At a news conference he characterized the START and the long-range theater nuclear force talks in Geneva in traditional balance of power terms: "If I notice an imbalance in the world balance of forces, I say so and act accordingly. For example, the Russian nuclear force, tactical or otherwise, combined with its conventional forces, creates an imbalance in Europe which must be remedied, . . . hence the importance of negotiations on disarmament and the need to achieve success."[143]

Nuclear Arms Limitations: Shift to Arms Control

The theater nuclear force issue dramatized the increasing difficulty facing the French government in maintaining the pretense that it could remain indifferent to arms control arrangements reached by other states, especially the superpowers, or that it could forego their pursuit in support of its security interests in light of the expanding nuclear arsenals of the superpowers. President Giscard d'Estaing's "disarmament" initiative at a special session of the United Nations on disarmament in May 1978 had highlighted earlier the growing tension in French policy between an unswerving commitment to disarmament as the only proper approach to arms limitation and the growing realization that global, regional, and, specifically European military balances appeared in the process of being transformed in ways possibly detrimental to French security interests by the superpowers' arms spiral.[144]

France's empty-chair policy—at the eighteen-nation Geneva disarmament talks, at mutual and balanced force reduction discussions in Vienna, in NATO strategic bargaining sessions, and in test ban and non-proliferation negotiations—limited what influence it might have had on whatever might emerge from these arenas. Also conceivably foregone were opportunities to enhance France's modest nuclear forces by restricting superpower capabilities and other potential nuclear competitors in and outside Europe. On the other hand, to engage openly in arms limitation accords risked ensnaring the French nuclear force in entangling commitments. The Giscard d'Estaing government also faced the opposition of its coalition partner, the Gaullists, who were attached to the de Gaulle disarmament legacy and its stiff requirements of national autonomy.

In the 1970s and 1980s, the imbalance in strike forces between the superpowers and Third World nuclear states threatened to grow in the absence of international restraints. Lacking the economic and technological resources of the superpowers, France was increasingly unable to keep pace in the arms race, even though no legal barrier or international accords stood in its way. Conventional and theater nuclear balances in Europe were shifting against France in spite of the rigidity of the French arms control position. Blind adherence to the principle of disarmament risked undoing French security. While the symbolic utility of disarmament was retained—partly to still domestic critics and partly to insulate French nuclear arms development from superpower and third-state interference—French policy under President Giscard d'Estaing's direction moved glacially toward the identification of arms control proposals advantageous to France's needs and of procedural reforms to augment the weight of its bargaining position.

Abandoned gradually, at a pace consistent with the relaxation of domestic constraints, was the traditional attachment to a prewar conception of arms limitation, based on narrow and legalistic conceptions of the strict requirement of disarmament. A consensus slowly emerged which detached itself progressively from opposition to the notion of French noncooperation. The rhetoric of disarmament was retained, but French policy became engaged in arms control bargaining, however tentative the initial moves in this direction. Many questioned whether intransigence had served French interests. France's nuclear forces faced the threatening prospect of being overtaken by the swiftly moving quantitative and qualitative arms race, nuclear and conventional, between the superpowers and, gradually, by the diffusion of military capabilities around the world, signaled by the nuclear explosion of the Indian bomb in 1974.[145]

During the Giscard d'Estaing years, French thinking crystallized around several proposals advanced by the French president in his May

1978 address to the United Nations. Associated with these moves were others taken earlier to reorganize the internal decision-making process within France to ensure tighter political oversight of civilian nuclear exports and to align France's nonproliferation stance closer to that of other nuclear suppliers. These initiatives can be divided into proposals for nuclear and conventional arms limitation accords. They also encompassed recommendations to reform the international process by which accords were to be reached and for a Conference on Disarmament in Europe (CDE). All of these moves were designed to enhance France's and Europe's security through international bargaining. With respect to nuclear proliferation, post-Gaullist France was gradually moving to align itself with the efforts of nuclear suppliers, including the superpowers, who sought to develop international restrictions on the sale or transfer of nuclear technology, fuels, and services. The aims of French strategic policy remained constant—an autonomous and credible force de dissuasion—but tactics changed to impose greater restraints on third state nuclear proliferation whose unregulated development threatened France's special status as a nuclear power within a riskier and less predictable international environment.

President Giscard d'Estaing's proposal before the United Nations to reorganize the Geneva conference on disarmament met with modest success. Following French suggestions, conference membership was expanded and the chairmanship of the group was allowed to rotate, a rupture with the policy of superpower monopoly of the past. With this victory in hand, the French government could return to at least one disarmament table without being accused of abandoning Gaullist principles. Increasing the membership of the Geneva group and rotating its chair did not, however, increase its coherence, nor did these changes make that body more attractive to the superpowers as a forum for discussion. That the French were finally prepared to play a more active role in the Geneva proceedings on their procedural terms was no guarantee that the superpowers would be obliged or interested in upgrading these negotiations. The associated French proposal to create a satellite agency within the U.N. also fell on deaf superpower ears. Neither was prepared to share its monopoly of surveillance technology with the world body, and, indirectly, with France, or to pay the cost of developing such a capacity.

Stemming Nuclear Proliferation

The issue of nuclear proliferation raised more immediate concerns for French policy. In this area, France had a potentially important contribution to make in controlling nuclear armaments since, largely through its own efforts, it gained control over all principal phases of the nuclear fuel cycle. In several areas, principally reprocessing and breeder reactors, it became a world leader. By the 1980s France could furnish experimental and light-water reactors to produce electricity, provide enriched uranium to fuel foreign reactors, and reprocess spent fuel (extracting usable plutonium and disposing of wastes). In the near future, it proposed to furnish know-how to build fast breeder reactors that produced more fissionable material in the form of plutonium than they consumed.[146] To protect these commercial advantages, the French government generally lagged behind other civilian nuclear energy states in adopting steps to prevent the transfer of civilian nuclear technology that might be used for hostile purposes. It refused to sign the 1968 nonproliferation treaty. The de Gaulle government contented itself with behaving, as French U.N. representative Armand Berard observed, "exactly like the states which would decide to adhere to it."[147] Under the treaty, nuclear powers agree not to assist other states in developing nuclear weapons. Nonnuclear states must submit their civilian nuclear programs to international inspection by the International Atomic Energy Agency (IAEA) to prevent "diversion of nuclear energy from peaceful uses to nuclear weapons or other nuclear explosive devices."[148]

This detached stance could be assumed as long as the superpowers were the leading proliferators, whether viewed vertically, as a consequence of their nuclear arms race, or, horizontally, from the perspective of the transfer of nuclear fuel and technology flowing from the near-monopoly position of the United States over the sale of light-water nuclear reactors abroad. By the middle 1970s, France had also assumed a leadership role in civilian nuclear energy development. It could no longer ignore the problem of international controls on proliferation and the potentially adverse impact of its export behavior on its own strategic and foreign policy interests.

The oil crisis of the early 1970s lent urgency to the need for a reexamination of the French position. Expectations grew that nuclear energy might be a viable alternative to oil as an energy source. France's nuclear program, especially its growing reprocessing capability and its Super Phoenix breeder reactor program, promised to furnish large quantities of plutonium for the world market. This new situation increased the possibility of illicit access to bomb-grade materials by foreign governments and terrorist groups. India's explosion of a nuclear device in 1974, using available nuclear technology and fissionable materials unwittingly provided by Canada and the United States, demonstrated that existing international controls were insufficient to stem proliferation. The Giscard d'Estaing administration was forced to face a proliferating world in which France's own security and status might be eroded unless it gained control over its own export policies.

Changing French policy was no easy matter. After much expense and many failures, the French nuclear energy industry had developed a powerful economic position globally that was potentially threatened by the imposition of increased controls on nuclear exports. Pressures, primarily emanating from Washington, to induce French cooperation fueled French suspicions that second thoughts in the United States about its previously liberal stance on nuclear exports, dating back as early as the 1950s with the "Atoms for Peace" proposal of the Eisenhower administration, were aimed at blunting rising European and French competition in world markets. Distinguishing between legitimate American and allied concerns about nuclear proliferation and those seemingly directed at weakening France's hard-won economic position was difficult. Moreover, France's assertion that all states had a right to self-defense and its creation of a nuclear striking force as the sine qua non of an independent defense posture hampered any French government from opposing in principle the acquisition of nuclear arms by other states.

Domestic opinion in France also favored both a military and a broadly based civilian nuclear program. Planning for the latter was based on the assumption of increased reliance on nuclear energy, rising from 10 percent of France's energy needs in 1981 to between one-quarter and one-third in the 1990s. The priority assigned to the expansion of civilian nuclear power at home and to exports by the Giscard d'Estaing government was affirmed by the Mitterrand regime as an essential part of a comprehensive energy program for France and of its plans for sustained economic growth.[149]

Given these perceived needs and opportunities, it is understandable that French nuclear export policy would inevitably be redefined and, in the transition, be subject to charges of inconsistency and contradiction. A major shift in French nuclear policy was signaled on September 1, 1976, when President Giscard d'Estaing established a Foreign Nuclear Policy Council, presided over by the President of the Republic and composed of six ministers and the administrator-general of the Commissariat à l'Energie Atomique (CEA).[150] The council was responsible for determining foreign nuclear policy, notably concerning "the exportation of sensitive nuclear techniques, equipment, and products."[151]

The formation of the council came in the wake of the French decision to adhere to the code of good conduct adopted by the London Suppliers Group.[152] The Group was to establish common standards for the sale of nuclear technology, materials and, especially, facilities for processing and enrichment. These standards struck a balance between several competing objectives: the tightening of international controls on the export of potentially dangerous nuclear technologies, associated especially with plutonium, that are susceptible to conversion for military purposes; the ordered development of the international nuclear industry; and the commercialization of nuclear fuels, equipment, and know-how, which would simultaneously provide outlets for suppliers and respond to the needs of developing states. France agreed to adopt the export rules specified by the nuclear nonproliferation treaty and to apply IAEA controls to the export of any sensitive materials included on the so-called Zangger list. Suppliers are obliged to assure that exported materials are physically protected; exceptional guarantees are required in the particularly sensitive areas of uranium enrichment, the reprocessing of fissionable materials, and the production of heavy water. As one of the founders of the French nuclear program and a longtime director of international relations at the CEA observed, France's acceptance of these controls marked "a turn in the history of non-proliferation because it is the first time that France agreed to join other countries in the search for a solution to this problem of capital importance."[153]

France's participation in the London Suppliers Group did not prevent it from signing contracts with South Korea and Pakistan for the sale of nuclear reprocessing plants. American pressure on the Seoul government forced cancellation of its agreement. The accord with Pakistan proved less amenable to revision. France insisted initially that the contract was consistent with the code of good conduct. According to the terms of the bilateral agreement, signed between France and Pakistan in March 1976, under the auspices of the IAEA, Pakistan agreed to accept the control of the Vienna agency and to desist, for a period of twenty years, from using the knowledge acquired in order to construct a similar installation for military purposes.[154] These lax restrictions opened the French government to criticism. In reaction to these pressures, the Foreign Nuclear Policy Council published in October 1976 a set of six principles guiding French nuclear exports. They affirmed France's commitment to prevent the spread of nuclear arms, underlined its responsiveness to the nuclear needs of other states, and proclaimed its willingness to join other suppliers and buyers in resolving the dilemma arising from the desire both to supply nuclear fuels and technical information and to halt the expansion of the military uses of atomic energy.[155] Two months later a directive of the Foreign Nuclear Policy Council precluded repetition of the Pakistani case. The council decided not to authorize additional bilateral contracts that would assist other states in developing industrial reprocessing plants capable of producing fissionable materials.[156] Paris also participated in President Carter's international fuel cycle evaluation conference in 1977 and expressed interest in defining feasible international controls on nuclear exports.

These various moves had no effect on Pakistan. Informal representations by Paris to renegotiate the contract with Islamabad were adroitly rebuffed. A proposal, announced to the press in January 1978, to modify the retreatment installation to produce a mixture of plutonium and uranium, instead of pure plutonium, was similarly turned down by the Pakistani military government. Although Pakistan had only one major nuclear facility, it insisted on the sale of a process capable of producing plutonium that was potentially useful for military purposes, unlike the plutonium-uranium mixture. On August 9, 1978, the French president requested a renegotiation of the contract and communicated the intent of the French government to suspend supply to Pakistan of the final components of the spent fuel reprocessing plant contracted by Pakistan unless Islamabad agreed—which it refused—to a modification of the contract rendering the plant incapable of producing weapons-grade material.[157]

The Pakistan contract revealed the dilemmas involved in the French position. France hesitated to break its contract with Pakistan partly because it was committed to the development of a free, open market for the sale of nuclear fuels and technology, in response to the energy needs of nonnuclear powers. The French preferred to dampen incentives for the autonomous development of nuclear installations, especially those involving reprocessing or enrichment, by fostering the liberal availability of these facilities and services. As for economic interests, France was unwilling to forego the sale of fissionable materials, fuel cycle services, and technology at a time when it was winning a share of the world nuclear market. Its free-market approach reinforced its image as a champion of the developed states which were opposed to the cartelization and control of the civilian nuclear market by a few producers. In this connection, France, with the Soviet Union, insisted on secret meetings of the London Group. Supplier guidelines were to be announced by the individual states rather than by the London Group as a collective body.

The French argued that the American approach pursued by the Carter administration of tighter international controls, unilaterally imposed if necessary, was likely to have an effect opposite to what was intended. States would be pushed to develop their own reprocessing and enrichment facilities more rapidly, without any international restraints being placed upon them, paralleling the French experience. The Europeans threatened this course if Congress forced them to renegotiate their enriched-uranium contracts with the United States which, under Congressional pressure, sought to impose more stringent controls on use and reexport than those which had been initially negotiated with Euratom. Tacitly supported by Great Britain and Germany, France assumed the European lead in rejecting the American demand. News of what amounted to a cancellation of the reprocessing plant was offset by reports that Pakistani agents had acquired critical materials to develop their own nuclear reactors and reprocessing facilities and had been permitted to operate freely on French territory to acquire needed know-how and materials elsewhere.[158] These lapses were offset by French cooperation, with other suppliers, in discouraging the Pakistanis from going ahead with a military nuclear program or in failing to tender an offer to build a 900-megawatt nuclear power plant at Chashma whose facilities might not be covered by international safeguards despite French Foreign Minister Claude Cheysson's rejection of the American principle that such safeguards were prerequisites for a contract.[159]

French support for the Israeli nuclear program in the 1950s and early 1960s and the Iraqi program in the late 1970s further suggests that immediate political, strategic, and economic considerations have often taken precedence over concern for the development of an effective international regime to arrest proliferation. The French made an important contribution to the Israeli weapons program in supplying Tel Aviv with technical assistance, fuel, and the Dimona reactor.[160] In service by 1964, Dimona, rated at 26 megawatts (mw), is reported to have the capacity to produce annually the fissionable materials roughly equal to one or two Hiroshima-size bombs.[161] Over American protests, French-Israeli nuclear cooperation continued through the 1960s until the Gaullist shift in support of the Arab states in the wake of the 1967 Middle East War. Nuclear cooperation until then had extended, reportedly, to the supply by France of blueprints for a reprocessing facility, reprocessing of spent fuel from Dimona, joint development of the Jericho surface-to-surface guided missile with a range of 260 miles and capable of being fitted with a nuclear warhead, and, possibly, Israeli access to French nuclear testing data.[162]

The French-Israeli connection was one of convenience. Each profited from the exchange of technical information (e.g., Israeli progress in heavy water for French reactor know-how). Until the end of the Algerian War, both also stood together if for no other reason than being equally opposed by the Arab states. Both were outcasts in the world community—the French over colonialism, the Israelis over Palestine and its disputed claims to Arab territory. Cooperation in nuclear development ceased when these conditions no longer prevailed and Gaullist France saw advantage in assuming a pro-Arab stance.[163]

The French sale of the 70 megawatt Osiris reactor to Iraq in the 1970s appeared largely motivated by similar conjunctural needs.[164] France's dependence on Arab and, specifically, Iraqi oil provided ample incentive for the government of Prime Minister Jacques Chirac to sell Iraq the Osiris (named Osiraq) reactor and a less powerful Isis reactor.[165] Both were to be fueled with uranium enriched to over 92 percent, that is, to weapons-grade levels. Although these reactors were small, blankets of natural and depleted uranium can be placed around the reactor core to enhance plutonium production for bomb purposes. Efforts to renegotiate the contract with Baghdad to supply "caramel" uranium fuel enriched to only 7-10 percent—below weapons standards—were initially rebuffed. While France eventually acceded to Iraqi demands, three significant reservations were written into the contract: only 24 kilograms of enriched uranium, not 72, would be supplied at a time to strengthen French monitoring of spent fuel; Iraq agreed to preirradiate the highly enriched uranium fuel for its Isis reactor, rendering it less susceptible for weapons use; and French technicians were to be assigned to Osiraq until 1989.[166] The Israeli raid on the Osiraq reactor of June 7, 1981, afforded the French government an opportunity to deflect Iraq from possible nuclear weapons development and to institute tighter international controls than had been previously applied through the IAEA. After several years of tense and strained negotiations, the Iraqi government finally accepted in September 1983 low-enriched caramel fuel, the presence of French technicians to oversee operations, and the expansion of the reactor's use to service regional research needs.[167] The details surrounding the rebuilding of the reactor have not been fully divulged as of early 1987.

Although France has been able to revise or withdraw from indiscreet contracts for nuclear materials and know-how with South Korea, Pakistan, and Iraq, it has not relaxed its determination to provide reprocessing services or light-water reactors that also produce plutonium as a byproduct of burning enriched uranium. It has contracts with South Korea and South Africa for light-water reactors. South Korea may be restrained in developing a weapons program by its ties with the United States, but the same cannot be said of South Africa. It is widely suspected of having an advanced nuclear weapons program in train.[168] Over protests from Black African states, the Mitterrand government honored the contract signed in 1976 to help build a nuclear plant at Koeberg near Capetown. It approved shipment of a reactor vessel and fuel. Discussions were also undertaken with the South African government to build a second reactor which reportedly would provide 4,000 jobs.[169] South Africa reportedly received low-enriched uranium for the two Koeberg reactors which were scheduled for operation in the 1980s. The French record in discouraging the South African nuclear program from taking a military turn is mixed. Along with western capitals and the Soviet Union, it pressured Pretoria not to conduct possible nuclear tests in the Kalahari desert. Its delivery of fuel to the Koeberg reactors, which are under international safeguards, had the effect, according to one close student of proliferation, of undercutting "the U.S. embargo on nuclear fuel sales to South Africa, an embargo intended to pressure Pretoria to accept full-scope safeguards—or at least penalize it for refusal to do so."[170]

The Super Phoenix or breeder reactor program also opens the way for the production of large quantities of plutonium and facilitates the possible diversion of this material to hostile purposes. The French government is committed to the fast breeder reactor for its own needs and is positioning itself to respond to international demand for these reactors in the later 1980s and 1990s.[171] A liberal trading policy on breeder technology could well offset the steps taken to tighten French controls over nuclear transfers.

Conventional Arms Control and Arms Transfers

Contradictions between the search for national advantage, on the one hand, and the requirements of international security, on the other— evidenced in France's nuclear arms control and disarmament policy— are similarly present in its approach to the transfer of conventional arms and military technology. French concern over the conventional arms imbalance in Europe has not been transferred to its thinking about regional balances outside the European theater. The de Gaulle and Pompidou governments largely ignored the issue as immediately relevant to France's interests. De Gaulle was primarily focused on dismantling France's colonial empire, on withdrawing French troops from abroad, and, most importantly, on creating a nuclear strike force. The Pompidou regime carried forward these policy priorities.

In his U.N. address on disarmament, President Giscard d'Estaing was the first to signal a slight shift in French thinking regarding the implications of conventional transfers. He emphasized the need to create stable regional arms balances. Redefined was the overriding Gaullist emphasis of a global nuclear balance in which France would play a role as the precondition for regionally organized conventional arms balances. Giscard voiced particular concern about the instability of the conventional equilibrium in Europe. A growing imbalance was diagnosed at two levels: between the two military blocs and between the European states of the western alliance because of German conventional preponderance among allied states. To offset the Soviet and Warsaw bloc threat and to strike a better balance among western forces, the French government proposed in May 1978 (on the occasion of President Giscard d'Estaing's address to the United Nations), a European disarmament conference to include all of the signatories of the Helsinki accord. It would be tied directly to the Conference on Security and Cooperation in Europe and, in Gaullist terms, would comprise all of the key states from the Atlantic to the Urals and all armed forces deployed within this geographical zone.[172]

Consistently rejected was the NATO-Warsaw Pact initiative to negotiate conventional arms reductions under terms of the Vienna discussions on Mutual Balanced Force Reductions (MBFR).[173] The ostensible reasons for the French demurrer were the traditional ones of opposition to superpower dominance of the discussions and bloc-to-bloc negotiations. Equally compelling was unvoiced French disquiet about the possible adverse outcome of the Vienna negotiations. Soviet forces might well be excluded from limitations on bloc conventional forces. With France absent from the negotiations, it was also not clear how the conventional balance between the two blocs and within the western camp might be arranged. Little weight was given in the MBFR talks to the mobility of large eastern bloc forces. Their withdrawal and limited geographic reduction in central Europe would not essentially weaken Warsaw Pact forces vis-à-vis the West since they could quickly return in a crisis. Under these circumstances, Paris feared that almost any accord would necessarily be to the disadvantage of the western alliance. There was also concern that the Soviet Union would exercise what one analyst has called a *droit de regard* over central Europe.[174] In practice this would mean a restraint on German force levels. The Soviet Union had proposed formulas for mutual reductions that would have had precisely this effect.

In voicing concerns about the modes and levels of conventional arms reductions in Europe, France was essentially affirming maintenance of the western military system as both a precondition and a guarantee of a lasting détente. Gaullist doctrinal rejection of bloc-to-bloc talks was implicitly amended to signify French opposition to Soviet conventional preponderance in central Europe and reliance on the western alliance and NATO and, specifically, German forces to counter the Warsaw Pact's conventional superiority, to anchor West Germany to the alliance, and to bargain with the East from a position of strength. An accord might be equally damaging in maintaining public morale and support for an adequate western defense since a superficial troop reduction would give the impression of lessened tensions and military stability with little of the substantive assurance derived from a genuine decrease of eastern bloc forces.

In French eyes, several considerations favored a Conference on Disarmament in Europe (CDE) over MBFR. A larger number of participants, representing security interests over a wider geographic area, was more likely to frame European security issues more accurately and comprehensively than the narrowly conceived terms of reference of MBFR. Neutral and nonaligned states, excluded from the Vienna talks, would join the CDE. The CDE also demonstrated a western interest in broad confidence-building measures (CBMs), in disarmament, and in matching Soviet propaganda in this area. The Giscard proposal struck a responsive chord in Socialist domestic circles. Once in office, the Socialists were quick to embrace the CDE initiative as their own. The French Socialists, not unlike de Gaulle, were longtime partisans of the notion that the buildup of mutual trust was a precondition for progress on arms limitation negotiations. The French hoped, too, that CDE might eventually absorb MBFR or at least arrest or preclude some of its potentially damaging tendencies.[175]

The French were firm about the conditions under which conventional disarmament or arms control could be achieved. The French proposal divided progress on reductions into two phases. The first would entail mandatory confidence building measures, such as the exchange of information about troop movements; the second would lead to real cutbacks in forces. Four conditions were set by Paris for the successful completion of the first phase of a European disarmament conference: "The new CBMs should be significant in military terms; they should be binding, not voluntary; there should be appropriate verification; and they should be applicable throughout Europe, from the Atlantic to the Urals."[176] Backed by allied support for linking CDE to CSCE, the French proposal was adopted in September 1983 at the Madrid meeting of CSCE. Deliberations began in Stockholm in January 1984 under the title of the Conference on Confidence- and Security-Building Measures and Disarmament in Europe.

Whereas the French government was prepared under some conditions to discuss arms control and disarmament in Europe where the prospects of nuclear escalation were always present, it was reticent to face the issue of the potentially adverse impact of arms transfers on regional balances and international security. Again, strategic considerations, economic and political advantage, and domestic restraints limited the French government's range of maneuver or interest in international arms transfer restraints.

The issue of limiting French arms sales became increasingly important by the 1970s. France's ascendant position as the third largest supplier of arms was not clearly established until the end of de Gaulle's term. The Pompidou administration built upon this legacy and expanded France's global sales program with little thought given to self-restraint. President Giscard d'Estaing's cautiously expressed willingness to enter into negotiations on limiting arms transfers appeared to depart from previous French hostility or indifference to such suggestions, but not as far as the casual observer might have assumed. The French president set down several stiff conditions for French participation in conventional arms control talks: "that the states under consideration are unanimous in wishing [to halt the conventional arms race] and that no discrimination is admitted among suppliers."[177] In his news conference of February 10, 1978, the president added still other conditions. He asserted that there could be no effective controls on arms sales without the participation of the Soviet Union; nor did he see much utility in convening western suppliers before the Soviet Union had agreed to enter into such multilateral discussions. Limitations also had to be set among buyers and recipients if controls were to work: "It is necessary to combine at once limits on armament purchases with disarmament policy and an accord among the producing countries."[178] The stringency of these conditions largely precluded serious international conventional arms limitation talks while staking out the high ground for France's moral stance on the issue.

The Socialist government also admitted to little more than rhetorical interest in restraining the transfer of conventional weapons and technology. Out of power, the Socialist and Communist parties consistently criticized France's position as the world's third largest arms seller. That role conflicted with long-term Leftist support for reducing conventional and nuclear arms proliferation and for controlling arms merchants. The "banalization" of arms sales under preceding administrations was to be replaced, according to governmental spokesmen, by the "moralization" of arms exports. Prime Minister Pierre Mauroy explained the difference in his interview in Der Spiegel: "French policy aims for peace and détente. Our country will therefore try worldwide to curtail and moralize arms exports."[179]

Deeds did not match words. One of the first actions taken by President François Mitterrand was to send his brother Jacques, a former Air Force general and head of Aérospatiale, the major state-owned arms producer of missiles and helicopters, to assure the Saudi government that French arms contracts already signed by the Giscard d'Estaing government would be honored, a point explicitly made by Prime Minister Mauroy in Der Spiegel.[180] Even before the new French president was sworn into office, his administrative aides were combing through arms contracts to evaluate how they would be implemented.[181] Except for selected contracts with Chile and South Africa, Socialist France filled all of the outstanding contracts held over from the Giscard d'Estaing years. These included shipments of missile-firing fast patrol boats to Iran; missile-launching patrol craft to Libya; a 1,200-ton displacement A-69 frigate, armed with Exocet surface-to-surface missiles, and 14 Super Etendard naval fighter-bombers to Argentina; 16 Mirage 50 aircraft to Chile; and missiles, helicopters, and 56 F1 Mirage fighters to Iraq.[182] Socialist Defense Minister Charles Hernu justified the French government's actions on the same economic, military, and political grounds advanced by his predecessors: "I am always surprised when people talk about arms sales in [a] reproachful tone. . . . Without those arms sales, how would I equip the French Army? . . . they also represent an important aspect of our foreign policy. . . . I have a clear conscience when I sell arms to a country if that prevents it from buying from one of the two superpowers."[183]

Hernu accented the dimensions of French security policy beyond those directly associated with the creation of an independent nuclear deterrent. Building a competitive arms industry in world markets was also a prerequisite of French security, increasingly tied to the continuing export of conventional arms and technology as well as nuclear know-how, fissionable materials, and services. But as French arms exports and those of other suppliers increase (as Chapter 7 suggests), the exterior security environment risks deterioration. As arsenals around the world enlarge and independent centers of military power grow in lethality, the global security systems appear less reliable and tractable. The security interests of the states of the system also tend to be perceived as greater as states are drawn into the logic of the security dilemma endemic to an international community composed of rival nation-states.[184] States are under pressure to set national military requirements higher to respond to what appears as a more threatening international environment partly of their own construction. The result is a vicious circle, where states compete to an appreciable degree with themselves and where incentives are fewer and of decreasing force to break out of the infernal competition for more and better arms.

Conclusions

Several conclusions emerge from the preceding analysis. First and foremost, the Fifth Republic, like its predecessors, identifies national independence and autonomy in military strategy with an indigenous capacity to make arms. National security and the search for freedom of strategic maneuver vis-à-vis rival states give impulse to French arms production quite independently of the economic and technological factors delineated in Chapter 3.[185] Since the formation of the modern French state, French governments, whatever their regime orientation, have been in the business of war-making and of making war implements. That these activities should now extend to nuclear weapons, as a complement to continued development of conventional arms, should come as no surprise.

Second, under conditions of scarce resources and competing societal and military welfare demands, the need to make arms has been extended to selling them. The cost of research, development, and production of arms compels a middle state, like France and other similarly sized or smaller nations, as Chapter 6 relates, to market their arms. The impetus to sell in France's case was heightened by the commitment of successive Fifth Republic regimes to adopt a nuclear strategy. The force de dissuasion promised an easy, if still illusive, answer to the dilemmas posed by Soviet and eastern bloc military powers, to the economic burdens and strategic and diplomatic constraints of membership in NATO's integrated military organization, and to the opposition of Gaullists on the Right and Communists on the Left to participation in Cold War bloc political and military operations. Opting for a nuclear strategy posed hard procurement and force-level choices that have chronically disfavored conventional forces. A depressed internal market for nonnuclear arms and equipment put pressures on political leaders and the weapons complex to seek buyers abroad to sustain an autonomous military weapons production capacity, all the more necessary since nuclear systems were not for sale.

Third, as marketing and making arms became welded to an independent strategic and foreign policy, France's security interests became increasingly dependent on world markets for its arms and tied increasingly and not always comfortably to the defense needs and military requirements of foreign governments, particularly those in the developing world. As France became ensnared in this web of security interdependencies, its continued reliance on allied support to serve its security needs was not appreciably relaxed. The gradual, almost imperceptible shift in French defense policy since the middle 1970s toward cooperation with, and a strengthening of, western allied forces suggests French recognition of this dependency. France's nuclear and conventional strategies remain ambiguously poised between independence and possible cooperation. It still practices the art of "get away closer" toward European allies, with a discernible tilt in the late 1980s toward

closer alignment of France on NATO and West European security policies.

Fourth, French disarmament and arms control policies should be
understood as derivatives of the changing needs perceived by French
leaders of France's security requirements and domestic imperatives
rather than a set of initiatives calculated to achieve arms limitation accords for their own sake. In the early stages of France's nuclear development, a strict disarmament approach and the tactic of the empty chair
suited France well. Once the French nuclear program was both domes-
tically legitimated and recognized abroad by allies and adversaries (a
distinction not always clear in Gaullist thinking), Giscard's France could
address the global nuclear proliferation issue posed by the Indian nuclear explosion. Fashioned was an internal control mechanism at the
presidential level and a more flexible posture toward cooperating with
other suppliers to inhibit the hostile spread of the atom, but with minimal damage to the civilian nuclear export program. Similarly, France's
conventional arms policies strike a balance between controls over the
growth of nonnuclear capabilities and their limitation in the European
arena, where its geo-strategic security interests are directly engaged,
and a less restrictive posture toward extra-European regional arms balances where French arms are marketed.

What is striking about France's arms production and sales complex in
the postwar period is its size, sophistication, and global reach compared
with previous epochs. This expansion of France's arms production capacity and its response to world demand for more and better arms and
know-how can be partly explained as a function of the requirements of
a new strategic posture. The latter induced France to become the
world's third largest arms exporter and to wed French security interests
to the sale of arms and military technology. These strategic considerations were reinforced by other more general and pervasive factors beyond those associated specifically with the rising costs of developing and
producing weapons: socio-economic limits placed on defense spending,
increased expenditures on civilian and military welfare, the techno-scientific and industrial requirements of keeping pace with the arms races
mounted by France's competitors—at first the superpowers but increasingly its European allies and many of its clients in the developing
world—and the demands of the civilian economy to remain competitive
in world markets. We now turn to these considerations to explore their
contribution to the support structure of the French arms complex and
the sale of arms to other states.

Part II.
Arms and the Welfare State

CHAPTER 3

Economic and Technological Incentives to Make and Sell Arms

INTRODUCTION

STRATEGIC FACTORS account only partially for France's export of arms and military technology. They explain more readily why France's arms industry was reconstructed and expanded after World War II than why France sells weapons and arms know-how in such abundance. One must look elsewhere, to technological and economic factors, for a fuller explanation for France's transfer of increasing numbers of arms and military know-how to other states. These factors have become progressively important, and today they are the principal determinants of French arms transfer behavior. This chapter traces the progressive ascendancy and evaluates the relative importance of techno-economic factors in shaping French arms transfer policy under the Fifth Republic.

Postwar French arms production and transfer behavior may be roughly divided into two phases. In the first, from approximately the end of World War II to the 1960s, French arms production and transfer policy was primarily influenced by strategic and foreign policy considerations. Economic and technological incentives, while present, were of lesser weight. The arms industry, viewed as a cluster of several basic industries in support of the armed forces, was not generally conceived as an economic asset or as an independent source of national wealth. Defense spending was still largely understood as a burden on the national treasury. The economic activity of the arms industry was not included in national accounts. Producing arms was viewed as a necessary public expense to provide for France's security, to underwrite its foreign policy objectives, and to restore the nation's lost grandeur.[1]

This was not to say that the reconstitution of an arms industry was pursued in an economic vacuum. French officials were early mindful of the possibilities afforded by defense spending to create advanced, high technology industries. Development of these basic industries was widely accepted as a precondition for France's reemergence as an economic force and as a great power. The arms industry was a part, too, of a larger vision to open gradually France's economy to world trade and to use the incentives of international competition to modernize the French economy.[2] The arms industry was incorporated only slowly into this long-term modernization process.

The task of preserving France's colonial empire limited the degree to which planners and political leaders could make the arms industry a full partner in France's efforts to become a modern industrial power. In the hands of old guard military officers, defense spending was supposed to guarantee the nation's security, not to provide for its welfare—much less to serve as an instrument for the reform of French society. The world was to be fashioned in France's image; France was not supposed to be a reflection of the world. The leadership of the military establishment, associated with the coup d'état that toppled the Fourth Republic in 1958, was concerned with maintaining France's foreign possessions. The military establishment did not view itself as responsible for the transformation of the French economy. The latter was in the service of national security and of France's civilizing mission. Military intervention in the economy, in the form of expenditures for arms and assistance to basic industries, was aimed more at acquiring old arms to support traditional imperial policies rather than using the development of new weapons for the armed forces, symbolized by the force de frappe, as a prod to spur France's technological development and economic growth.

During this first phase, concern for the development of a progressively more sophisticated national arms production capacity and the search for foreign markets for its products were subordinated by the military establishment to immediate security and foreign policy imperatives. One tended to ask what the development of certain key industries could do for national security and arms production, not what defense expenditures and military research and development contracts, subsidies, and credits could do to make French industry more competitive in world markets. While it would be misleading to argue that French officials were unaware of the positive benefits of defense spending on the civilian economy, such concerns were simply secondary. Whatever the possible economic gains to be made from producing arms, the first task was to meet the nation's needs in fighting wars which extended without interruption from 1940 to 1962. There was little time and less incentive under chronic emergency conditions to think about exploiting the nation's arms production capacity for economic and technological gain. The shift in priorities would come later once France's colonial empire had been liquidated. Meanwhile, arms manufacture would be considered in familiar terms as a burden on the treasury and as a tax on the French public.

In this early phase, pressures inevitably grew to sell arms in order to cut the cost of production through longer series runs; to schedule arms production more efficiently through optimal utilization of the factors of production, especially of highly skilled personnel; to seek foreign assistance in covering the mounting cost of research and development and in expanding the nation's weapons development and production capabilities; and to husband scarce foreign reserves depleted by foreign wars and arms purchases. These subsidiary techno-economic considerations progressively assumed an independent character and claim on governmental attention and priorities. Even when guided purely by strategic and foreign policy aims, military planners had to address these economic constraints in deciding on procurement and production targets. Resource limitations hampered France's quest for an indigenous arms industry dedicated solely to national military needs. Arms sales and selective cooperation with other states in weapons development and production, particularly with France's European allies, were the chosen instruments to overcome or lower these limits on the growth and development of the arms industry and on the access of French military forces to adequate supplies of up-to-date arms at affordable prices.

The 1960s ushered in a new phase in the evolution of French arms production. New and powerful economic and technological incentives arose to swell those already at play to modernize French armed forces and to stimulate increased arms production and foreign sales. Under the Fifth Republic, France's arms production complex was drawn into the mainstream of the modernization process of the French economy and society begun after World War II. It was no accident that the old officer corps, wedded more to manpower than machines, was replaced by a younger, technologically attuned elite who, as often as not, had more in common with their counterparts in business and the civilian bureaucracies than with their fellow officers. Warriors gave way to managers of violence.[3]

It was in this second phase, clearly paralleling the life of the Fifth Republic, that the economic thinking shared by early civilian planners was extended to the arms industry. Since World War II there had been widening accord on the preconditions for France's resurgence as a global economic power. Critical among them were the creation of technologically advanced industries and the gradual but inexorable opening of the French economy to world competition. *Ouverture*, as Common Market negotiations demonstrated, would not be all at once, but would proceed in lock step with the progress made by French industries, including the agricultural sector, in organizing themselves to meet the rigors of foreign competition, particularly from German and American firms.

Well before the inception of the Fifth Republic, technological innovation was understood in key sectors of the civilian economy as a factor of production in its own right and a critical component of sustained economic growth. The Fifth Republic systematically applied this notion to military production. Arms development was joined to the widely held view that growth was to be achieved through increased production of goods and services, product development, and the expansion of exports. Increased domestic consumption and the expected growth of foreign demand for French products were counted upon to ensure full employment. The resulting increase in national wealth would respond to heightened pressures for state-assured social welfare.

Under the Fifth Republic, the arms industry was supposed to contribute, like any other industry, to France's technological renovation and modernization. It, too, was to be a product innovator and was expected to mount a global effort to expand French exports. Progress along these fronts was linked directly to the shared objectives of slowly lowering protectionist barriers and of using global market forces as a stimulant to economic expansion and technological development.[4] Government aid to key defense industries, whether in the form of arms orders, research and development contracts, subsidies, credits, or export supports, was gradually merged with ongoing efforts to assist French industries generally in order to place them in the forefront of an expanding and increasingly competitive world economy. Arms exports became central to the realization of this economic vision. By the 1970s, any suggestion to cut arms sales abroad was perceived as tantamount to abandoning economic growth and modernization.

In this second or mature phase of the arms production-sale cycle, arms were treated like any other good or service that could be made and exchanged to enhance public welfare or private gain.[5] While phase one was concerned with the *demand* side of weapons and the ways that the costs and burdens of producing arms could be lowered and the reliability of supply assured, the market or developmental phase dwells on the *supply* side of arms development, production, transfers, and technology. The factors shaping this phase are economic and technological, although the materials and services that are provided are lethal and destructive. What is important is the process of making and marketing arms, not what a client does with these products. Key considerations include maintenance of high domestic employment, economic growth, and investment opportunities.

In pursuit of these objectives, arms sales became increasingly critical to French economic planners. French arms officials faced a host of new marketing problems: development of attractive pricing and concessionary policies to compete with other arms producers; contracts to French firms to stimulate the search for new products through research and development; subsidies to industry to promote exports; easy credit and financial terms for foreign arms purchasers; construction of a global sales and after-sales (après vente) network; identification of specific arms as product leaders to penetrate civilian markets controlled by competitors; and internal regional development through selected arms contracting. Barter arrangements to exchange arms for needed raw materials, especially oil, also became a preoccupation. As one analyst has observed, "The market is characterized by discrete, giant contracts rather than by marginally adjusting commodity flows, and those contracts are negotiated government to government with complex political considerations replacing simple price/quality calculations."[6]

As the French arms industry coped with the challenges arising from selling arms and military technology to a global market, its success inevitably transformed expectations about the role of government in arms sales and about its level of performance. Political leaders both spurred sales abroad and counted on them to strengthen France's competitive position in world trade, to maintain a favorable balance of international payments, to keep the franc strong, and, by these tokens, to create the conditions for a stable yet expanding domestic economy attractive to foreign and domestic investment as a precondition for full employment. A record of success in arms sales thus provided party advantage, bolstered the administration in power, and anchored the Fifth Republic as a viable political regime. Arms and the welfare state were joined.

It is important to recognize that the shift from phase one to phase two occurred gradually and largely imperceptibly. The shift refers to a set of priorities attached by French officials to arms production and transfers. Phase one worries were not ignored in phase two, nor were they necessarily slighted. The pressures they exerted on arms transfers remained. What changed was the larger frame of reference within which these pressures were expressed and managed. Phase two considerations formed a layer of positive incentives reinforcing the cost-cutting concerns of phase one. Together they gave added impulse to arms sales.

To highlight the morphology of French arms sales and the incentives impelling them forward, the discussion below will treat these two phases as distinct, chronologically discrete periods. It emphasizes the principal structural shifts in priorities and perspectives which conditioned French arms sales behavior since World War II. If the need to sell arms had always been strong in the postwar period, especially since the 1950s when the arms industry was well underway toward successful reconstruction, the explanatory incentives driving the transfer of French arms and military technology also multiplied and grew more urgent and powerful over time. These have been particularly pronounced at a systemic level. Traditional national security demands for an autonomous weapons production capability—incentives arising from outside the state as recounted in Chapters 1 and 2—were bolstered by welfare and modernization needs pressing on governments everywhere from within. These systemic imperatives also drive military arms and technology sales. What was new in phase two of the evolution of economic and technological determinants of French arms sales was the marriage of the arms complex, organized initially to respond to France's security needs, to the French welfare state and the maturing identity of interest of these two now indissolubly joined partners. This chapter explains the rationale for this marriage and why it has thrived so far. Chapters 4 and 5 detail the reform of France's socio-economic and political structure occasioned by these systemic security and welfare forces and the impact of these new decisional processes on defining public priorities and resources and on distributing benefits and influence within the French political system.

PHASE I: RESPONDING TO THE ECONOMIC CONSTRAINTS OF WEAPONS DEVELOPMENT AND PROCUREMENT

Three factors conspired in this early period to prompt French political leaders and managers of the weapons industry to adopt an open-door policy toward arms exports: (1) the rising costs of producing modern weapons; (2) insistent demands for greater civilian *and* military welfare; and (3) lowered conventional arms requirements based on France's military strategy regarding nuclear weapons. These same pressures also forced French decision-makers to assume a more flexible, pragmatic posture in developing cooperative research, development, and production accords with other weapons makers than one might have surmised from incessant Gaullist assertions of national independence in fashioning France's defense policy and armed forces.

Rising Costs

The French arms industry has had to confront the problem of steeply rising costs in developing and producing arms. These costs arise from several sources. Most prominent are those associated with research and development and the increasing length of time needed to develop weapons. Holding design teams together and keeping production lines open, even for spare parts, have become increasingly costly and risky. These concerns were very much on the mind of a former head of France's arms complex within the Ministry of Defense: "The cost of developing armaments becomes more and more heavy; the time separating the development of two successive generations of the same material has a tendency to become extended. The length of series runs for French needs is, in counterpoint, more and more limited. If one wishes therefore to adhere to unit cost imperatives, to keep the cadence of production at acceptable levels, one runs the risk of rupturing these production lines with the accompanying dispersion at great cost of established industrial teams."[7]

Figure 3-1 depicts the almost linear growth of the unit cost for French aircraft from 1950 to 1975. The upward sloping curve charts the price of successive generations of French fighter aircraft; the downward sloping curve identifies the decreasing number of these aircraft that can be purchased annually by the French Air Force. In constant 1975 dollars, the Mirage F1, which entered service in the 1970s, cost five times as much as the Ouragan, the first indigenously produced jet fighter after World War II. The Mirage 2000 was estimated to be twice as expensive as the F1. Accelerating costs for high performance equipment dictate the unpalatable tradeoff of smaller numbers of units in armed force inventories. The proposed two-engine Mirage 4000, designed by Dassault-Bréguet for export, was estimated to cost twice as much as the 2000. In the absence of foreign sales, as a cost-cutting measure, the French military runs the absurd risk of pricing itself out of existence.

These mounting costs also confront other arms manufacturers. The trend line for the cost of American tactical fighter aircraft between 1940 and 1980 followed a similar steep upward slope. The unit price of an airplane is conservatively estimated to have climbed from approximately $100,000 at the start of World War II to well over $10 million 40 years later. In constant U.S. dollars that is an increase of 10,000 percent.[8] Price rises for fighter aircraft continue to be dramatic. The price of the F-4 fighter was $3.5 million in 1960 while the F-14 requires an outlay of approximately $20 million a copy.

These same upward cost curves can also be discerned by comparing the cost figures for tanks, carriers, and fighter aircraft between earlier and later models. The Sherman tank which cost $140,000 in 1940 is dwarfed by the estimated price of the newly planned MX-1 tank which will cost over six times as much. The Essex aircraft carrier cost $225 million in World War II; the Nimitz class carrier costs more than five times that amount.[9]

By the middle 1960s, expanding arms exports and cooperative weap-

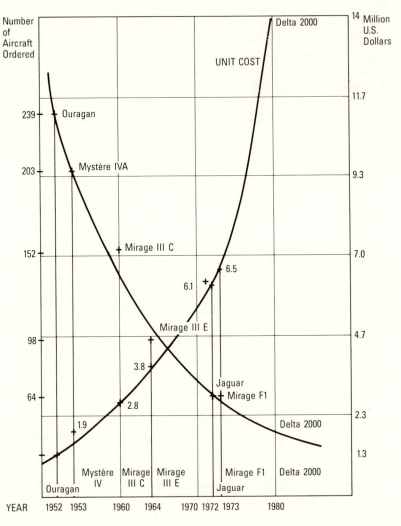

FIGURE 3-1

Evolution of Unit Costs of French Combat Aircraft (Constant 1975 U.S. dollars, in millions)

SOURCE: Adapted from Jean-Bernard Pinatel et al., *L'Economie des forces* (Paris: Les Cahiers de la Fondation pour les Etudes de Défense Nationale, 1976), p. 78.

ons development appeared to be the most feasible strategies to hold down costs and maintain a domestic weapons capability to meet French armed force requirements, despite the risks to independence that these strategies implied. The benefits of cutting military personnel were largely exhausted by the end of the 1960s. Defense Minister Michel Debré, in the only *White Paper* written on defense policy during the Fifth Republic, justified increased arms exports in the name of economic efficiency: "One has already noted the advantages of increased exports: a better balance of production scheduling, an increase of quantities produced, and therefore a spreading of fixed costs over longer series runs. . . ."[10]

Civilian and Military Welfare

In the late 1960s, urgent and widespread demands for greater governmental spending on civilian *and* military welfare multiplied cost-push incentives to sell arms. These pressures culminated in the events of May 1968 which almost toppled the Fifth Republic. The government's failure to diffuse these demands in the elections of 1968 undoubtedly contributed to the resignation a year later of President Charles de Gaulle. Gaullist dreams of a militarily strong and independent France were profoundly disrupted by the insistence of the public on increasing welfare expenditures and on instituting reforms in education, labor relations, and other social areas. Table 3-1 lists French defense expenditures between 1960 and 1980 and relates them to spending for arms and personnel, overall governmental expenditures, and GNP. Several trends are noteworthy. First, the percentage of governmental expenditures devoted to defense has steadily declined since 1960, from almost 30 percent of the French budget in 1960 to just under 17 percent of the budget twenty years later. The same downward curve is evident in the ratio of defense expenditures to GNP. In 1960, at the height of the Algerian War, a little more than 6 percent of French GNP was spent on defense, declining thereafter to a little under 4 percent of GNP in 1980.

Of interest, too, is the sharp break that occurs in these trends immediately after 1968. Public protests accelerated the shift in governmental priorities, already in train, from defense to civilian spending. In one year, between 1968 and 1969, defense spending dropped over two percentage points and the amount of public expenditures devoted to defense fell from 4.6 to 4.2 percent of GNP, although GNP had actually risen despite the internal upheaval. These decreases in military spending are further confirmed by Figure 3-2, which plots the indexed growth of GNP, central governmental expenditures (CGE), and military spend-

Table 3-1. French Defense Budget with Selected Components for Procurement and Personnel as a Percentage of Total Governmental Spending and GNP: 1960-1980 (In billions of dollars)

| Year | Defense Budget | | | | | Govern-mental Total Budget | % of Total Budget | GNP | % of GNP |
	Total (initial)	Procure-ment	%	Per-sonnel	%				
1960	3.35	1.21	36.2	2.14	63.8	11.75	28.5	54.03	6.2
1961	3.41	1.15	33.8	2.26	66.2	12.72	26.8	58.79	5.8
1962	3.50	1.17	33.5	2.33	66.5	14.17	24.7	64.81	5.4
1963	3.76	1.57	41.8	2.19	58.2	15.73	23.9	73.73	5.1
1964	4.02	1.84	45.7	2.18	54.3	17.48	23.0	82.04	4.9
1965	4.21	2.11	50.1	2.10	49.9	18.71	22.5	87.71	4.8
1966	4.46	2.28	51.2	2.18	48.8	20.46	21.8	94.89	4.7
1967	4.77	2.49	52.2	2.28	47.8	23.04	20.7	103.70	4.6
1968	5.06	2.53	50.0	2.53	50.0	25.17	20.1	110.00	4.6
1969	5.08	2.49	49.0	2.59	51.0	28.54	17.8	120.95	4.2
1970	4.90	2.31	47.1	2.59	52.9	27.84	17.6	125.64	3.9
1971	5.21	2.37	45.5	2.84	54.5	29.11	17.9	140.81	3.7
1972	6.17	2.83	45.8	3.34	54.2	34.86	17.7	171.39	3.6
1973	7.81	3.58	45.8	4.23	54.2	44.12	17.7	223.14	3.5
1974	7.95	3.55	44.7	4.40	55.3	45.69	17.4	233.82	3.4
1975	10.22	4.45	43.5	5.77	56.5	60.47	16.9	300.59	3.4
1976	10.46	4.38	41.9	6.08	58.1	61.17	17.1	307.65	3.4
1977	11.89	4.87	41.0	7.02	59.0	68.33	17.4	330.28	3.6
1978	14.99	6.31	42.1	8.68	57.9	88.70	16.9	416.39	3.6
1979	18.12	7.83	43.2	10.29	56.8	107.86	16.8	489.73	3.7
1980	20.97	9.44	45.0	11.53	55.0	124.08	16.9	551.84	3.8

SOURCES: There is considerable variation among French official sources and those of other national and international agencies with respect to French spending on defense, the division of expenditures between personnel and capital purchases, the total of central governmental spending, and GNP. Compare, for example, these differences in French official sources over a period of five years: France, Assemblée Nationale, Commission de la Défense Nationale et des Forces Armées (1977), *Avis sur le projet de loi de finances pour 1978, Défense: Dépenses en Capital*, No. 3150, pp. 13-17; *idem*, Commission des Finances (1979), *Rapport sur le projet de loi de finances pour 1980, Défense: Considérations Générales*, No. 1292, pp. 27, 81, 108-110; France, Sénat, Commission des Finances (1980), *Rapport Général: Défense*, No. 98, p. 7; and France, Ministère de la Défense, SIRPA, *Le Budgèt de la défense nationale pour 1981* (Paris, 1981), pp. 5-7. Defense expenditures are taken from *Rapport*, No. 1292 (1979), p. 81; the percentage division between personnel and capital expenditures for 1960-1974 is drawn from *Avis*, No. 3150 (1977), p. 17 (initial budget figures), and from SIRPA, *Le Budgèt de la défense nationale pour 1981*, for 1975-1980. Central governmental expenditure percentages are taken from *Avis*, No. 3150 (1977), p. 16 (initial budget figures) for 1960-1974 and from Sénat, *Rapport*, No. 98 (1980), p. 7, for 1975-1980. Percentage of GNP spent on defense, calculated in terms of the defense budget, is based on Sénat, *Rapport*, No. 98 (1980), p. 7, for 1960-1980. Percentages are rounded to nearest one-tenth of one percent.

Exchange rates are taken from International Monetary Fund, *International Financial Statistics, 1977*, XXI,

ing between 1959 and 1980. With 1959 as 100, GNP increased tenfold by 1980. The CGE index kept pace with this growth, but defense spending did not. It grew at half the rate, climbing to 562 in 1980.

The significance of these expenditure trends for domestic arms orders is obvious. French manufacturers had to count on a decreasing share of national wealth and governmental spending to sustain output and full employment and to support research and development programs in the arms industry. This downward trend in defense spending and its acceleration after 1968 came at the very time that defense costs began to mount.

Less widely reported but no less important for French arms producers was the changed composition of spending within the defense budget. The May events precipitated pressures to increase spending on military welfare. Until 1967, the percentage of defense spending for equipment and arms climbed from 36.2 percent in 1960 to 52.2 percent. Even in 1968, the procurement percentage held at 50 percent, although there were announced cutbacks in governmental defense spending to meet the demands of May demonstrators and to offset the welfare and labor concessions made by the government to appease an aroused public. Spending for hardware and research and development continued to decline through most of the 1970s, falling to a low of 42.1 percent in 1978 before the modest increases in procurement initiated by the fourth program-law, especially for conventional arms, could be felt.

The Mitterrand government's military five-year plan for 1984-1988

Table 3-1 sources (*cont.*)

No. 5 (May 1977), 166-167, and *idem* (May 1981), 151-152. Note discrepancies between IMF figures for GNP and those deriving from French parliamentary sources, which are lower. The differences are partly due to the different base on which GNP is calculated. The parliamentary reports depend on calculations for *produit intérieur brut*, a formula that generally leads to lower estimates of internal gross national product.

Note also that oscillations in the percentage increase in the budget are partly due to the rate of inflation in France and the shifting exchange rate, expressed in dollars. For example, between 1969 and 1970, defense spending (*crédit de paiements*) increased from 26.4 to 27.19 billion francs. However, the rate of the franc declined relative to the dollar and, therefore, the dollar value of defense spending is shown to have fallen. This distorted effect becomes especially acute after 1981 because of the devaluation of the French franc.

These French sources conflict with other open-literature sources for French defense spending, GNP, and central governmental expenditures. Compare with U.S., Arms Control and Disarmament Agency, *World Military Expenditures and Arms Transfers, 1970-1979* (Washington, D.C.: U.S. Government Printing Office, 1982), p. 124; and SIPRI, *World Armaments and Disarmament, SIPRI Yearbook 1982* (London: Taylor and Francis, 1982), p. 150. These latter sources generally cite higher ratios for defense spending relative to GNP and central governmental expenditures than do the French Ministry of Defense or parliamentary reports.

For an alternative calculation of defense spending estimates from 1945 to 1976, see Michel Martin, *Warriors to Managers: The French Military Establishment Since 1945* (Chapel Hill, N.C.: University of North Carolina Press, 1981), p. 54.

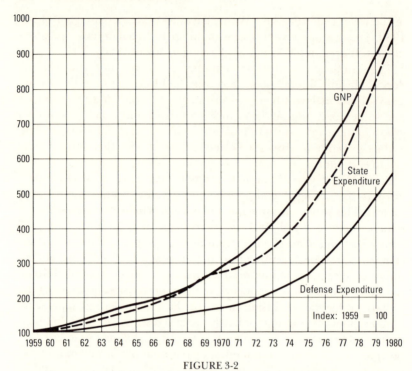

FIGURE 3-2

Indexed Growth of GNP, State Expenditures, and Defense Expenditures: 1959-1980
Source: France, Assemblée Nationale, CF (1979), *Rapport sur le projet de loi de finances pour 1980, Défense: Considérations Générales*, No. 1292, p. 83.

projected a gradual increase in equipment expenditures over operations. Spending for arms, including research and development, was expected to exceed 50 percent of the defense budget somewhere in 1986-1987 and reach 51.5 percent by 1988. As noted earlier, conventional arms were not favored, as spending for tactical and strategic nuclear weapons and delivery vehicles enjoyed priority status.[11]

As long as there is a cap on defense spending, defined as a fixed percentage of GNP, increases in the share accorded to conventional arms procurement and R&D in the defense budget can only be marginal. The personal needs of volunteer enlisted personnel and the officer corps must be addressed. The demands of conscripts after 1968 similarly required attention: "No more cold showers," remarked one military observer.[12] The transformation of large portions of the military establishment from a warrior class to technically proficient managers of violence also placed new liens on hardware spending. Since these officers have readily available job offers in the civilian sector of the economy, the Ministry of Defense must compete for their services with public and private industries whose higher salary levels tend to be a function of world demand for high technology personnel.

Nuclear Strategy and Domestic Procurement

The adoption of a nuclear strategy has also had an unintended and negative impact on domestic procurement of conventional arms. Figure 3-3 charts the percent of the procurement and R&D portions of the defense budget spent on modern nuclear systems since 1963. Spending for the development of nuclear strategic forces hovered around 50 percent of the defense procurement budget between 1965 and 1969. Spending for the force de dissuasion has continued to be substantial even after most of the initial fixed costs had been met in developing the technology, delivery systems, test sites, bases, and communication networks associated with nuclear force. The nuclear program, on the average, has absorbed approximately one-third of the defense procurement budget. Increased spending for tactical nuclear weapons and the requirements of modernization to keep pace with the superpowers have kept nuclear spending high.

The military and civilian leadership of the French arms complex, in the private and public sectors, have been acutely aware for some time of the enlarging internal constraints on domestic demand for arms and the limited availability of adequate capital and technological know-how to mount increasingly burdensome research and development programs. Figure 3-4 plots the growth of French arms exports in constant and current dollars from 1960 to 1980. Except for the 1969-1970 period, in the aftermath of the May 1968 upheaval when French industrial production temporarily declined, the value of French arms deliveries has grown each year in current and constant dollars. These trend lines suggest an inverse relation between the decreasing rate of domestic demand for arms relative to GNP and CGE and the response of the French arms industry to world demand, partly stimulated as we shall soon see by France's efforts to increase foreign sales. The highest levels of the government lent leadership and legitimacy to the search for foreign arms markets. The defense ministry's *White Paper* of 1972 praised foreign sales.[13] Parliamentary spokesmen urged more aggressive efforts to promote arms exports. Minister of Defense Debré, who followed as much as led the surging foreign arms sales program, encouraged the military services to choose weapons and equipment of interest to foreign purchasers.[14] It came as no surprise to discover, therefore, that military requirements for the armed forces, as the sale of the cen-

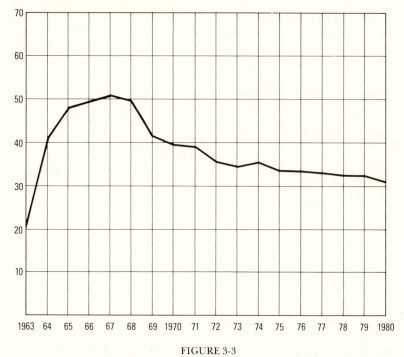

FIGURE 3-3

Percent of Procurement Spent on Strategic and Tactical Nuclear Forces: 1963-1980
Source: France, Assemblée Nationale, CDNFA (1977), *Avis sur le projet de loi de finances pour 1978, Défense: Dépenses en Capital*, No. 3150, pp. 22-23. *Idem*, CF (1978), *Rapport sur le projet de loi de finances pour 1979, Considérations Générales et Dépenses en Capital*, No. 570, p. 84; and *idem*, CF (1979), *Rapport sur le projet de loi de finances pour 1980, Défense: Considérations Général*, No. 1292, p. 22.

tury had demonstrated, were sensitized to these remonstrances to sell arms.

Cooperation with Other Arms Producers

Selling arms and military technology is only one solution to the problem of coping with the increased costs of weapons and rising demands for greater civilian and military welfare. The resource constraints under which the French arms industry must work force the issue of cooperating with other states, particularly France's European allies, to develop new weapons. French officials recognize that the defense budget is too small to maintain a diversified and broadly based industrial complex. Cooperation is accepted as a necessity since an isolated French in-

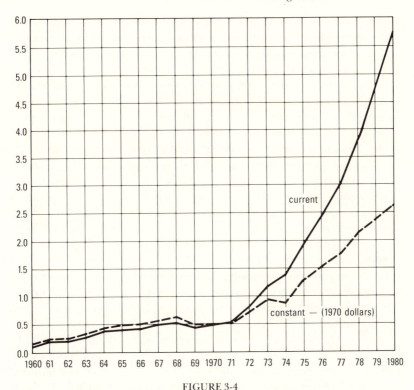

FIGURE 3-4

French Arms Transfers in Constant and Current Dollars: 1960-1980 (In billions of dollars)
SOURCE: See Table 3-3.

dustry would soon atrophy, lacking market outlets and access to new technologies.

Even the Gaullists made cooperation a virtue. The de Gaulle regime ushered in a period of arms cooperation with France's allies that has not been matched since, despite the threat that cooperation potentially poses for French political and strategic independence and autarchy in arms production. These benefits of cooperation were most often cited: (1) access to foreign technology, know-how, and capital to sustain or expand France's arms development and production capabilities; (2) shared development risks and lower national expenditures for new weapons; (3) larger production runs to decrease unit costs; (4) potentially greater third country sales; (5) stronger political and economic ties with cooperating states to advance foreign policy goals; (6) enhanced allied military preparedness; (7) lower costs in maintaining duplicate research and development programs, arms production lines, and logistics support systems; (8) continued employment within the arms industry and the maintenance of design teams and arms production systems; and (9) the stimulation of the civilian economy through spinoffs arising from technological diffusion and advancement.[15]

Simultaneous pursuit of these objectives was not always possible. Cooperative development of weapons among states which seek maximum independence and autonomy inevitably requires mutual compromises in setting military requirements to meet the different needs of national armed forces. Neither the French nor the Germans were satisfied with the Transall, a two-engine cargo aircraft developed by Paris and Bonn. The French preferred a long-range, the Germans a shorter-range, aircraft. Neither received what it wanted.[16] The total cost of cooperative programs was also greater than that of a nationally developed program. Economic efficiency was sacrificed for the sake of lower national expenditures and the perceived political benefits of joint weapons collaboration between Paris and Bonn.[17]

Based on French experience, a former senior French defense official suggested a formula for estimating the costs of a cooperative program. These are equal to the cost of a national program times the square root of the number of participants: $C_c = C_n \sqrt{n}$, where C_c is the cost of cooperation; C_n the cost of a national program; and n the number of participants. Delays can be measured by multiplying the length of time of a national program by the cube root of the number of cooperating members. Difficulties and costs of gaining consent to sell arms to third states are estimated to proceed at a geometric rate—as the cost of a national program times the number of participants raised to the third power (n^3).[18] In other words, and the French have been wary of the problem, as the number of cooperants rises so also do costs and delays, considerations that weighed heavily in France's decision to demur in joining the British-German-Italian Tornado project. Large consortia also imply increased administrative complications and, according to French defense spokesmen, they tend to be less responsive to French control or direction.

It is also not clear that cooperation invariably lowers costs for each cooperating state, even when it must be conceded that overall program costs will almost always be greater than those of a nationally run program. Such programs may equal or even exceed what a purely national program might have cost each participant. The French Cour de Comptes, a body charged to scrutinize governmental program costs, sharply criticized the Transall program for large overruns.[19] The individual costs to Britain and France of the Jaguar, a jointly developed ground support attack plane, are estimated to have been only slightly below those of a nationally sponsored program, suggesting substantial cost overruns. Higher developmental costs also raise unit costs even with long production runs,[20] resulting in arms that are less attractive in world markets than nationally produced weapons. The Tornado is estimated to cost in excess of $20 million a copy, making it an expensive buy for the developers and prohibitive for most foreign purchasers except oil-rich states like Saudi Arabia.

The political purposes driving a cooperative accord may have the unwitting effect of weakening alliance cohesion. The joint desire of the de Gaulle and Adenauer governments to foster closer Franco-German ties encouraged increased Paris-Bonn cooperation in the development of a military cargo plane and tactical missiles. But cooperation also served Gaullist aims to drive a wedge between the U.S. and its European allies, specifically between the U.S. and Germany. One of the main purposes of the Independent European Program Group, formed within NATO and supported by France, is "to ensure the maintenance of a healthy defense industrial and technological base and to strengthen at the same time the European factor in the relationship with the United States and Canada."[21] However, strengthening European arms production bolsters the principal competitor to the American arms industry and challenges its share of NATO and non-NATO markets.

Europe's rise as an arms producer has retarded and even nullified NATO standardization in most arms areas. The European states are also locked in a competitive struggle of their own to assert their political independence and the interests of their arms industries. Within this inner-alliance struggle, the United States government and American private industrial interests act both as arbiters of the European rivalry and as obstacles to European cooperation. The Europeans are hampered in their efforts to achieve equality with the American arms industry. French leaders, joined by their European colleagues, insist that equality is a precondition for long-term and mutually beneficial transatlantic cooperation. General Engineer Marc Cauchie summarized the dilemma facing NATO National Armaments Directors in encouraging greater European and transatlantic arms cooperation: "Our criterion for success will be . . . that both United States and European defense industry [sic] are not disadvantaged relative to what the situation would be if we do not form these [cooperative] programmes."[22] Cast in this light, cooperation becomes a residual of national needs and interest. It is not conceived primarily as a vehicle for increased alliance cohesion, much less integration.

French needs and interest in arms cooperation may be discerned from examining the international accords in which France has participated under the Fifth Republic. Table 3-2 lists the principal military codevelopment and coproduction agreements signed by France with its European allies. Excluded are licensed production items, like Exocet, a surface-to-surface missile, and Roland, a ground-to-air missile licensed and later modified by American firms to meet the all-weather requirements of the U.S. Army. Inclusion of a weapon depends on whether the signatories contracted jointly to design or produce it. In most cases, cooperating states collaborated on development and production within a variety of management frameworks.[23] Each accord reflects a different mix of concerns from the set of objectives, sketched above, that drives arms cooperation.

First, contrary to popular opinion, France has seen more cooperative arms ventures to completion than any other NATO country. It has worked with all major European arms manufacturers and with the United States in the production of the Hawk missile. Second, in all of these arrangements, priority appears to have been given to the contribution of the weapons program to the maintenance of a technologically advanced, financially solvent, and internationally competitive arms industry. The task of filling immediate military requirements has been in every case accompanied by the dominant objective of promoting an independent arms production capacity. Access of French industry to new technology is a continuing concern of the governmentally directed arms complex. Commercial advantage is certainly not unimportant. As the controversy over the proposed sale of Mirage F1 M53 aircraft in the 1970s suggested, this consideration was of great interest to private industrial firms like Dassault. It was, however, of considerably less urgency for the French military or the engineers dominating the General Delegation for Armament (DGA), responsible for maintaining both the long-run competitiveness of the arms industry and its responsiveness to armed service needs. The arms industry is the goose that lays the golden eggs. Except for periodic lapses, attributable to the political clout exercised by French firms, including nationalized corporations, the DGA has focused on the goose and not its eggs.[24]

Third, French officials share a marked preference for cooperative arrangements in which France is the leading member or at least an equal partner. French officials are determined to decide what projects will be pursued, on what terms, and with what nations. Dominance or equality affords France the opportunity to negotiate from a position of strength about organizational responsibilities, cost-sharing obligations, and the allocation of benefits. The strategy followed by the French is to join

Table 3-2. Selected Military Development and Production Programs
between France and Other European States: 1959-1984

Program	Cooperating Nations	Contracted or Start of Study[a]	Cost Sharing	Service
Aircraft				
Atlantic	WG,GB,I,N	1959	Equal	Navy/ Air Force
Transall, Tactical Transport	WG	1959	Equal	Air Force
Jaguar, Dual-Purpose Training and Attack Air-craft (Various Models)	GB	1965	Equal	Air Force
Alpha-Jet Trainer	WG	1970	Equal	Air Force
Helicopters				
Puma,[b] Transport	GB	1967	(F) 100% (GB) 0%	Air Force/ Army
Gazelle,[b] Light Liaison and Antitank	GB	1967	(F) 75% (GB) 25%	Air Force/ Army
Lynx,[c] Transport and Anti-submarine	GB	1967	(F) 25% (GB) 75%	Air Force/ Army
Combat Heli-copter	WG	1984	—	Air Force/ Army
Missiles[d]				
Hawk SAM Missile[e]	I,WG,N,B	1960	—	Army

Table 3-2 (*cont.*)

Program	Cooperating Nations	Contracted or Start of Study[a]	Cost Sharing	Service
Martel ASM Antiradar (AS-37) TV-Guided Version (AJ.168)	GB	1964	Equal	Air Force/ Navy
Milan antitank Missile (Midrange)	WG	1964	Equal	Army
Hot Antitank (Long Range)	WG	1964	Equal	Army
Roland I (Clear Weather) and II (All Weather) SAM	WG	1964	Equal	Army
Otomat (SSM, ASM, Several Successive Versions)	I	1969	Equal	Navy
Supersonic Antisurface	WG	1983	—	Navy
Third-Generation Anti-tank	WG, GB	1983	—	Army
Terminal Guidance[f] Warhead	WG, GB, US	1984	(US) 40% (WG) 20% (GB) 20% (F) 20%	Army
Ground Equipment				
Ratac, Radar-Controlled Artillery	WG	—	Equal	Army
RITA, Communications System	B	1973	(F) 87.5% (B) 12.5%	Army

Table 3-2 (*cont.*)

Program	Cooperating Nations	Contracted or Start of Study[a]	Cost Sharing	Service
Argus, Observation Platform	WG	1974	—	Army
Naval Equipment				
Mine Sweeper	B, N	1975	—	Navy
Motors				
Adour Turbo Jet Engine (Jaguar)	B	1964	Equal	Air Force
Larzac Military Jet Engine	WG	1969	Equal	Air Force

SOURCES: Various sources have been consulted. Most important is the annual review of world armaments, issued by the Stockholm International Peace Research Institute (SIPRI), *World Armaments and Disarmament, SIPRI Yearbooks 1962-1980*, and *Worksheets; Jane's All the World's Aircraft* (London: MacDonald, 1959-1975); Defense Marketing Systems, *Foreign Military Markets, France* (Greenwich, Conn.); and France, Assemblée Nationale, CDNFA (1974), *Avis sur le projet de loi de finances pour 1975, Défense: Dépenses en Capital*, No. 1233, pp. 93-96, and *idem* (1981), *Avis, Défense: Politique de défense de la France*, No. 473, pp. 122-123. Excluded are eight other programs which in 1981 were still in an exploratory stage. See *ibid.*, p. 123, for a listing. The latest and most complete listing is found in France, Assemblée Nationale, CDNFA (1980), *Avis sur le projet de loi de finances pour 1981, Défense: Dépenses en Capital*, No. 1979, p. 45. For motors, see Union Syndicale des Industries Aéronautiques et Spatiales (USIAS), *Informations Aéronautiques, La France dans la coopération européenne*, January 24, 1974. Also Ministère de la Défense, SIRPA, *Armament in France*, Dossier d'Information No. 77, May 1985, p. 29.

NOTE: Belgium = B, France = F, Great Britain = GB, Italy = I, Netherlands = N, United States = US, West Germany = WG.

[a] The sources are not always clear on these two points, i.e., whether a signed accord signifies an immediate start of a program.

[b] Coproduction on French design.

[c] Coproduction on British design.

[d] Note also that the French surface-to-air missile Crotale was subsequently adapted to the needs of South Africa and Saudi Arabia by means of R&D funds received from those states. In South Africa the Crotale is called Cactus and in Saudi Arabia, the Shahine.

France also reportedly assisted Israel in the early 1960s in the development of the Jericho missile, a surface-to-surface missile that could conceivably carry a nuclear charge. Rob-

strength with two or more nations in the same area of technology rather than to encourage cooperative programs in which national units of vastly differing capabilities in two or more technological fields are brought together. The French are skeptical that such asymmetrical arrangements will work. These tend to hinder technology transfers as advanced states resist sharing their specialized knowledge. They also encourage a division of labor that the French fear. Specialization would weaken the French drive to keep abreast of progress in military technology along a broad front. In rejecting an approach to cooperation that would juxtapose vastly differing national specializations into a consortium of unequals, one French official closely involved in international cooperation wryly observed that the best solution for bilateral cooperation does not necessarily consist in perching a paralytic with supereyesight on the superpowerful legs of a blind man.[25]

Collaboration with Germany in aircraft and tactical missile development has yielded the highest dividends for the French arms industry while advancing French foreign and security policy objectives. As early as 1955, in the wake of the French defeat of the European Defense Community and successful American pressure to rearm Germany within NATO, French officials sought ways to control Germany's rearmament. The Coal and Steel Community, established in 1950, provided an implicit French droit de regard over the use of these resources for Germany's rearmament. In joining the Western European Union (WEU), Germany renounced any intent to produce nuclear weapons.

Another, more economically attractive way to control German arms production was through cooperation. In 1955, shortly after the Paris

---

Table 3-2 notes (*cont.*)

ert E. Harkavy, *Spectre of a Middle Eastern Holocaust: The Strategic and Diplomatic Implications of the Israeli Nuclear Weapons Program* (Denver: University of Denver Monograph Series in World Affairs, 1977), pp. 8-9.

France also began development of an air-to-ship missile, Kormoran, with West Germany but then withdrew. Kormoran was produced for West German forces, with Aérospatiale acting as a subcontractor.

As a footnote to history, it is reported by USIAS that Britain underwrote one-sixth of the cost of the Exocet antiship missile which eventually led to the air-to-surface missile which was so damaging to British ships during the Falklands War of 1982. *Economist*, September 8, 1984, p. 37.

[e] Consortium production on U.S. design.

[f] The terminal guidance warhead is to be used with the NATO multiple launch rocket system. It is to be a vital component of NATO's antitank weaponry in the 1990s. The first phase of the development is expected to cost $95 million. Second- and third-phase options could bring the costs to $550 million. *Jane's Defence Weekly*, December 8, 1984, p. 1003; see also *Wall Street Journal*, November 30, 1984.

agreements were signed, the Adenauer government, eager to nurture Franco-German reconciliation, agreed to support a French proposal to promote cooperation in aircraft development.[26] On January 21, 1958, the two countries and Italy agreed to collaborate on weapons development under the auspices of the WEU. Italy soon lost interest, leaving Germany and France to carry on alone. Germany secured French licenses to produce the Noratlas military transport plane and the Potez Fouga-Magister trainer. Codevelopment of the Atlantic, a propeller-driven sea patrol aircraft, and Transall extended the range of cooperation. For Germany, cooperation with the French within NATO (Atlantic) and bilaterally (Transall) legitimated its rearmament effort and the creation of a limited arms production capacity. France gained needed financial assistance to launch two new aircraft programs at the height of the Algerian War when funds for new conventional arms projects other than the force de frappe were in short supply.[27] French interest in expanding its influence over German and European arms production paralleled its long-term efforts on several fronts to weld together a continental grouping which could magnify French power, counter pervasive American influence, and harness German arms production capacity to French purposes.

These foreign and security objectives and industrial concerns overrode the views of military and civilian critics of the two aircraft programs, particularly those associated with the Transall program. Both countries needed a new military cargo aircraft in the late 1950s. The Noratlas did not effectively support France's overseas operations. For these missions, French armed forces needed a long-range aircraft with a large transport capacity capable of operating in desert and southern climatic conditions. German forces, positioned on the central European front, wanted a short-range aircraft with maximum short takeoff and landing (STOL) capability and a smaller payload capacity. Neither wanted the American Lockheed 130-C.

The airplane that finally rolled off the assembly line suited France more than Germany, but neither country was fully satisfied. Despite its STOL capability and fuel efficiency, the Transall resembled Lockheed's Hercules more than the kind of plane sought by the Luftwaffe. Cost overruns on Transall were calculated to be 120 percent over the original estimates; the program took twice as long to complete as planned. Joël Le Theule, rapporteur for the defense committee of the National Assembly, concluded in a 1963 report that "this medium transport aircraft will be expensive. . . . The primary quality of the program would appear to be more political than aeronautical."[28]

The Transall and Atlantic programs subsequently led to cooperation in the development of tactical missiles (Milan, Hot, and Roland) and the Alpha-Jet trainer, a reconnaissance and light, troop-support aircraft. The creation of Euromissile, a jointly owned company between France's Aérospatiale and Germany's Messerschmitt-Bölkow-Blohm (MBB), facilitated work on missiles that enjoy a brisk export trade. The hand-carried Milan and helicopter-transported Hot antitank missiles are in the arsenals of several armies. Production is in the tens of thousands, establishing France and Germany as leaders in this area of weaponry. Between 1949 and 1978, the United States produced an estimated 410,000 antitank weapons while France and Germany manufactured close to 550,000 such arms, including the SS-10, SS-11, and Entac, the latter a highly successful export item incorporated into the inventories of several NATO states and purchased by the United States Army.[29] By 1980, 500 Alpha-Jets had been ordered by France, Germany, and six other countries. This assured the Dassault-Dornier group a successful foreign market with the prospect of additional sales throughout the 1980s.[30]

Franco-British cooperation has been less successful when viewed from Paris. While Gaullist France was optimistic about strengthening the Franco-German alliance and about using it to spearhead a French-led Europe, President de Gaulle was skeptical that Britain could ever be weaned from American dependence or from its Commonwealth ties. It was the British who had to persuade France of the political virtues of British membership in the European Community. Cooperation in arms production and civilian aeronautical projects became one of the chosen mechanisms of the British government to establish Britain's continental credentials. The Labor government under Harold Wilson was particularly insistent in pressing for Anglo-French cooperation. Spurred was work on the Jaguar, the Martel, an air-to-surface missile, and three military helicopters, Puma, Gazelle, and Lynx. Also initiated were the Airbus A-300 and the supersonic Concorde.

French interest in these projects was focused more on their implications for French industrial concerns and military requirements than on facilitating British entry into the European Community. De Gaulle vetoed British entry in 1963 and reaffirmed his veto in 1967 in the midst of cooperative efforts on Jaguar, Martel, Concorde, Airbus, and helicopter projects. The Jaguar project was useful because the Bréguet corporation was in need of a major aircraft program to maintain employment. Matra, a specialist in tactical missiles, and Aviation-Sud were interested in developing ties with their British counterparts and in raising needed capital and market outlets for their arms.[31] While de Gaulle strove to enlarge Franco-German political cooperation through arms accords, he never permitted joint Franco-British weapons programs to interfere with his determination to block British entry into the continental grouping.

The Jaguar and Martel projects, while eventually carried through to completion, never fully met the expectations of either participant. British and French requirements for the Jaguar differed. The British reportedly wanted a heavy supersonic aircraft while the French were more interested in a lighter subsonic plane.[32] Paul Stehlin, a former head of the French Air Force, criticized the Jaguar as "our most costly and ill-conceived aircraft."[33] Many of his Air Force colleagues still in service would have agreed. The French withdrawal from the joint Anglo-French variable-geometry fighter program did nothing to smooth the path of collaboration. The Martel received mixed reviews. In the view of some French experts, it was a successful missile and met the needs of both military services, but like the Jaguar its export possibilities were never fully exploited. The Dassault corporation was lukewarm about promoting Bréguet's Jaguar over its Mirage series when the two firms were merged as a consequence of governmental pressure.[34] Production of the Martel was halted after the British and French met their respective needs.

Helicopter cooperation proved more mutually satisfactory. The French-designed Gazelle and Puma were coproduced in Britain. Both were purchased worldwide. Excluding France and Britain, 33 countries had ordered the Gazelle by the early 1980s while 43 had placed orders for the Puma.

The Airbus A-300 and Concorde projects strained more than solidified Franco-British aircraft cooperation. As for the A-300, the two could not agree on requirements, on the division of financial responsibility, or on project direction and equipment for the mid-range civilian carrier. Only the rescue operation of the A-300 B under Franco-German leadership saved the project while reserving a one-fifth share for the British Aircraft Corporation. The Concorde was a technological wonder but a financial catastrophe. Billions of dollars were lost in the venture. Cost overruns were almost four times projected estimates.[35]

French arms cooperation with other European states has been modest. The Otomat is the major joint achievement with Italy. Work on this naval missile has been limited, and little progress has been made in interesting Italy in other French-related projects. Italy has preferred to work with other European producers, notably Germany and Britain, on other arms projects and on the Tornado, a multirole combat aircraft.

Belgium and Spain have built Mirage aircraft under license. Spain also produces French-designed AMX-30 tanks. France has also developed the RITA communication system with Belgium. Both have joined the Netherlands in developing a new mine sweeper.

French objectives and priorities may also be discerned by tracing France's reaction to American and NATO policies toward cooperation. On the whole the experience has been less than satisfying or reassuring. The fundamental differences between the two states over foreign and security policy, discussed in Chapters 1 and 2, are repeated in the running clashes and misunderstandings that have plagued the two states over weapons cooperation, especially with the onset of the Fifth Republic.

Except for the Hawk missile program, French governments have been largely disenchanted with NATO projects. The French were bitterly disappointed by the NATO decision to choose the Italian G 91 as its basic lightweight strike fighter for the 1960s. Two other competitors, Bréguet's 1001 Taon and Dassault's Etendard IV, were passed over. The consolation prize of the Atlantic did little to quiet French ire. What started as a fourteen-nation NATO project dwindled to five nations—the United States, France, Germany, Belgium, and the Netherlands—which initially agreed on responsibility for financing and directing the project. This group was subsequently narrowed to France and Germany. Expected sales to NATO countries had to be lowered as several of France's NATO partners preferred the U.S. Orion to the French Atlantic.[36] Eventually, 87 aircraft were produced for NATO use. France purchased 40 or almost half; Germany, the Netherlands, and Italy bought the remainder. The poor sales record grated on the French. The Atlantic, noted Defense Minister Pierre Messmer, "has not fulfilled our hopes. We shall in the future remember the results of this experience."[37]

French distress was far greater over repeated attempts to penetrate the NATO market for supersonic fighter aircraft. In the 1960s and again in the 1970s, efforts by Dassault to sell first its Mirages and, later, its F1 M53 to NATO countries were frustrated by successful American promotion of U.S. aircraft. In the 1960s, several NATO governments bought Lockheed Starfighter F-104s. Germany's decision to buy the American aircraft led Bonn to opt for Transall and Atlantic, partly in an effort to assuage French feelings. A decade later Dassault was again unsuccessful in convincing Belgium, the Netherlands, Denmark, and Norway to choose the Mirage F1 M53 over General Dynamics' F-16.[38]

As the discussion in Chapter 5 relates in more detail, French economic concessions and political blandishments fell short in the competition for the sale of the century. Repeated reductions in the unit price of the F1 M53, codevelopment and production guarantees, access to design technology, and the promise of French support for the creation of a broadly based, transnational aeronautics industry in Europe were inviting, but unavailing. Belgium and Holland were offered a consortium in which member states would share responsibilities as single-source suppliers. Payments for aircraft could also be in local currencies. To assure foreign buyers about the technical capabilities of the F1 M53, the French government overruled military objections and imposed the fighter on the French Air Force. The Giscard d'Estaing government also hinted that the French were prepared to "coordinate their air force with the nations that bought the Mirage."[39] The Dutch remained unconvinced that the French had been genuinely converted to Dutch notions of European integration; the Belgians, while drawn to French overtures, reluctantly followed the Dutch; the Danes and Norwegians never seriously considered the French offer. French Air Force officers were also opposed to the F1 M53 because it would delay entry of the F1 coming on line and, worse, halt the development of a new, advanced fighter. The latter was of pressing concern when the *avion de combat futur* (Future Combat Aircraft) project was canceled as a consequence of skyrocketing cost estimates that approached those of the defunct Concorde program.

French-American differences over NATO policy toward the rationalization, standardization, and interoperability (RSI) of alliance armaments illustrate the commitment of French and European NATO arms producers to the maintenance of separate national arms production systems.[40] During the 1970s, the United States launched a major offensive to gain alliance support for increased standardization of NATO arms. This campaign, prompted by a 1974 NATO report written by Thomas A. Callaghan, Jr., identified major weaknesses in NATO's logistics support system, cited wasteful expenditures of billions of dollars for redundant research and development projects, and pinpointed serious gaps in NATO operational capabilities because of the proliferation of national arms.[41] As the French themselves conceded, there was in the mid-1970s a bewildering jumble of different weapons families in NATO: 23 combat aircraft, 7 tanks, 8 armored personnel carriers, 22 antitank missiles, 36 radar-guided firing systems, 8 ground-to-air missiles, 6 antiship missiles, and more than 20 different calibers for small arms. Many NATO units could not communicate with each other, use each other's fuel or spare parts, or interchange missiles, shells, or ammunition among their small arms.[42] The Callaghan report estimated annual redundant expenditures for all weapons at $10 billion. Another study calculated that, for tactical missiles alone since 1949, 43 percent of the $64.2 billion spent by NATO countries on these arms was unnecessary; the $27.8 billion in additional spending produced an estimated 34 more systems than might have been expected if NATO missions and the capabilities of national missiles had been better matched.[43]

These findings, combined with renewed interest in strengthening NATO cooperation and in reducing defense expenditures, galvanized the Pentagon and Congress to press for increased standardization and shared NATO research, development, and production programs. There was much talk of an Atlantic "two-way" street in arms selling, a relaxation of buy-American directives governing offshore purchases, and joint development of weapons families. Only the latter aroused much enthusiasm in Europe. The family approach permitted a national arms producer to concentrate on a particular weapon—say short-range SAM missiles—while maintaining design teams across the entire range of a family of weapons.[44]

The French, quietly supported by British and German arms producers,[45] resisted American standardization proposals. France defined NATO's problem as one of interfacing different national military equipment to facilitate its joint use in battle rather than one of producing common military items for all member states. French military planners focused on interoperable communication systems and the use of common fuel, ammunition, and support systems. On military grounds, standardization was also criticized as encouraging mediocrity in weapons design and simplifying the problems of opponents in developing countermeasures against standardized weapons.[46]

These stock objections, given the evident confusion and cost of arming NATO forces and French recognition of the problem,[47] obscured the driving forces behind the French position. Neither military nor economic efficiency was a primary concern. Access to new technology and calibrated expansion of a globally competitive arms industry were of uppermost importance. Commercial advantage, as the F1 M53 controversy suggested, was not irrelevant. Nor were immediate military requirements and operational readiness ignored. But when choices had to be made, dominant consideration was given to the preservation of a broad-based weapons production capacity. The French behaved like Lee during the Wilderness campaign: the army had to be kept intact at all costs to fight another day; the arms industry had to be continually renovated and improved to meet its international competitors. The stakes for the French were political and strategic independence. Technology was supposed to motor military and civilian modernization, enhance competitiveness, and spur economic growth.

For the French, American-sponsored standardization was a threat to France's arms industries. Whatever the term signified in Washington, standardization meant narrow specialization to Paris. France would have to abandon its efforts to meet its national military needs. It would be forced to concentrate on a limited number of weapon systems in producing for the NATO market. Such a "two-way" street was seen as a snare. First, there was only a "one-way" street since American exports to European allies and non-NATO western powers were sharply tilted in America's favor by a ratio of twelve to one. Between 1967 and 1976, the United States sold $9 billion in military arms and equipment to Europe and bought only $742 million in return. During this period France purchased $200 million in military material but delivered only $32 million in arms to the United States.[48]

Second, NATO cooperation along the American model might conceivably increase American and European purchases of French equipment, but these increases would not compensate France for future losses in extra-NATO markets where the bulk of French exports was concentrated after 1970. The U.S. was also not likely to sanction French third-state arms sales of NATO-produced equipment. Third, there was the fear that NATO market concessions would prove illusory. According to the French, competition for NATO contracts—the favored American approach insisted upon by Congress—would inevitably give an advantage to larger American firms which enjoyed Pentagon support and a large domestic market.[49]

American arms development behavior gave point to French concerns. Buy-American strictures were relaxed but not eliminated. American arms manufacturers, along with their allies in Congress and the defense bureaucracy, were not disposed to relinquish their competitive advantage in the European market or their access to extra-European outlets by agreeing to broader market sharing arrangements with European arms producers. The preponderant position of the U.S. in European arms markets would inevitably mean a loss of revenue for American producers if the "two-way" street principle led to a balance of U.S. and European purchases. The control of the small nation market in Europe to which the bulk of American arms for NATO states flowed would be progressively lost to European suppliers. Over half of the $5 billion of American arms supplied to NATO states between 1967 and 1976 went to smaller NATO powers; the remainder was delivered to France, Great Britain, and West Germany.[50] American armed service insistence on the availability of an American source for arms directly contradicted the announced objectives of the standardization drive. French officials were apprehensive, too, that foreign supplies of arms to France might prove unreliable. The American record was not reassuring. General Cauchie stressed the point before a meeting of American arms manufacturers: "A country which depends upon foreign countries for its military supplies is no longer assured that it will be able to keep [its defense equipment] in [a] proper state. We discovered this with the embargo in Turkey or at the occasion of changes in U.S. foreign policy. After these examples Europe . . . cannot afford, even in hope of a better utilization of resources, to jeopardize its armaments industry. . . . With this lesson of history in memory Europe must therefore maintain, I would say at all costs, its technology and production capabilities necessary to its own defense."[51]

American purchase of a French-German license to produce the Roland surface-to-air missile reinforced French reservations. The Hughes and Boeing corporations purchased the French license and promptly redesigned the system to meet the all-weather requirements of the United States Army. More was spent on developing the American model than had been originally spent by France and Germany in creating the system; cost estimates for deploying the system more than doubled from $942 million to $2.3 billion in three years. Worse, the American corporations, which had purchased the license for Roland, threatened to resell the American version on European markets from which they were supposedly precluded by contract. The Americans felt that their Roland was a new system, nullifying the terms of the marketing agreement with Euromissile. The Franco-German developers were chagrined to discover that the European transfer of technology led to an American Roland whose superior technology put the European Roland potentially in competition with itself. Commercial benefits proved equally fleeting. "The case of Roland is illuminating," General Cauchie observed before a WEU arms symposium. "The United States, with a potential market of $1,500 million, had a splendid opportunity of making a gesture in favor of just such a two-way street, instead of purchasing strictly nothing but a license."[52] Conversely, the French were under no obligation to settle for less. Nor did the Roland episode dampen French efforts to sell military equipment to the United States as evidenced by the sale of the RITA system to the American Army in 1985.

The Roland case illustrated the American preference for competitive research and development contracts and licensed production arrangements over the French interest in negotiated R&D contracts and direct purchase of equipment to assure domestic employment and orderly production schedules. It also revealed how entrenched were the forces in Congress favoring American-made systems and those within the armed forces insisting on U.S.-supplied technology and weapons.

These lessons were not lost on the French whose skepticism about the sincerity of American commitment to two-way street purchases in NATO was certainly not abated by the Roland episode. As for the promotion of standardization in NATO, the Army purchased three, not one, ground-to-air systems—the French-German Roland, the English Rapier, and the American Chapparal.[53]

The French objected further that American firms, in league with their supporters in Washington, actively blocked the development of a European arms industry. There is some truth in this charge, viewed not only as a consequence of the competitive advantages of the American arms industry but also as a result of the pressures that can be exerted on NATO governments by Washington to buy American arms. The French, in complaining about the unwillingness of their European allies to choose European over American arms, were, however, less than candid about their own choices in acquiring American weapons and know-how. When it has been convenient for economic or technological advantage to choose American rather than European cooperation, the French have ignored their own advice. Currently, SNECMA is developing the CFM-56 motor with General Electric for civilian aircraft, and the French are working with their American counterparts on ATLIS laser designators. Earlier, the French bought American nuclear light-water reactor technology to speed their development of a full-cycle nuclear industry, and they participated in the European consortium to build the American Hawk missile when access to new technology on attractive financial terms was available from the American government.

The problem of runaway R&D costs, growing American technological advancement, and faltering West European and British competitiveness, especially in developing high performance combat aircraft, and the prospects of reduced military preparedness if France followed a go-it-alone policy led the Mitterrand government to search for ways to widen arms cooperation in Europe. As Table 3-2 notes, France signed cooperative accords with West Germany to develop a multirole combat helicopter and a supersonic antisurface-vessel missile; with Great Britain and West Germany, to design a third-generation antitank missile; and with these two states and the United States and Italy, to produce a multiple rocket launcher system. The battlefield helicopter was the centerpiece of a renewed effort to regenerate lagging French-German co-operation. Three versions of the helicopter were initially planned to be variously equipped to support troops in the field and to counter tanks either with Hot missiles or third-generation antitank missiles yet to be developed in conjunction with Great Britain. An order of 427 (212 for Germany and 215 for France) was placed on the expectation, moreover, that the helicopter might be mass produced for sale abroad. The Chinese government also announced plans to create a Franco-German group to work on a new tank for the Army.[54]

France also entered serious talks with Germany, Great Britain, Italy, and Spain for the purpose of building a new combat fighter for the 1990s. Envisioned was a market of 1,000 aircraft. The French have rarely been as explicit in citing cost and technological constraints as the basis for their cooperative moves. While national independence was still the aim, allied cooperation and greater interdependence were the preferred strategies if French terms could be met. Defense Minister Charles Hernu joined the issue in an article written for *Le Figaro*:

> Although it seems paradoxical, our main objective in cooperation is to have control over our arms policy and thus an autonomous defense policy. Indeed, without this cooperation, our arms industry would have to abandon the presence it has today in all key spheres; it would have to specialize, which would inevitably lead to a loss of independence in the abandoned sectors.
>
> Through cooperation, however, we remain present in all vital sectors of arms production, by sharing the very high development costs, and reducing production costs by producing greater numbers of models.
>
> In addition, if we refuse to explore the avenues of cooperation for the future fighter plane, we would be likely to isolate our enterprises from the rest of Europe: cooperation programs would then be developed without us. Excluded from this possible European entity, France would have to face—not only in Europe but in the same way in the rest of the world—twofold European and American competition, from which we would obviously not emerge victorious.[55]

Under Hernu's leadership, France signed bilateral accords with Great Britain, Italy, Spain, Greece, Belgium, Norway, the Netherlands, Sweden, and Switzerland to explore ways of cooperating in developing new military equipment.[56] Whether these initiatives will overcome deep-seated resistance to allied cooperation, which might reduce national independence in producing or selling arms, remains to be seen. Despite the French demurrer with respect to the new European fighter, what is noteworthy about the Hernu statement is the willingness of the French government to recognize that limits to national independence do exist in arms making and marketing for middle-range and small powers and only through cooperation can superpower competition be addressed. National sentiment and ethnocentric regard are still formidable obstacles, not to mention the bureaucratic pressures arising from the arms complex to preserve its autonomy and market position. These forces are likely to have less sway as France approaches the limits of a selective policy of cooperation à la carte.[57]

PHASE II: ARMS TRANSFERS AND ECONOMIC GROWTH, TECHNOLOGICAL PROGRESS, AND PUBLIC WELFARE

Overall Dimensions

With several notable exceptions, the notion that the arms industry could be a positive force in advancing France's economic growth, technological development, and public welfare emerged only gradually after World War II. Early on, supporters of the aeronautics industry viewed technological progress in civilian and military sectors as mutually reinforcing. The Pierrelatte enrichment plant contributed to France's development as a world leader in reactor technology and a major supplier of fissionable materials, reprocessing services, and technical know-how. Subsidies given to French industry for military research and development were granted with an eye toward developing new technological sectors of the economy, like electronics, chemicals, and transportation, to enhance economic output and broaden France's industrial base.

The idea that these various parts of the arms industry might form a potentially powerful economic whole grew as French arms sales rose in the middle-to-late 1960s. Armaments, military avionics, and shipbuilding entered national accounts as notable economic activities. Statistics on arms sales and their impact on the French economy were carefully collected and reported in the annual reports of the Minister of Defense.[58] National Assembly reports on military capital expenditures devoted separate sections of each annual report to the arms industry as a whole.[59] Within the arms bureaucracy, efforts to bring costs down through the promotion of arms exports led to the view that arms contributed directly to economic and technological development and high employment, particularly for those in high technology fields.[60] The leadership within the General Delegation for Armaments (DGA), supported by their partisans in business and labor, pressed the argument that arms sales contributed to national welfare. The traditional choice between guns and butter was transformed into an opportunity to acquire both in larger quantities at reduced prices. A choice was not necessary since more guns sent abroad meant more butter at home. France's prosperity was alleged to depend on an internationally competitive and technologically advancing arms industry.[61] Earlier, the French government assisted civilian industries, like aeronautics and electronics, to strengthen France's indigenous arms production capabilities. By the end of the 1960s, with the advent of the Pompidou administration, the relationship tended to be reversed. The arms industry was now cast as a drive wheel of the civilian economy. French ministers of defense progressively widened their conception of their roles beyond military preparedness to encompass the solvency and profitability of the arms industry and the French economy.

Jean-Laurens Delpech, former ministerial delegate for armaments during the Giscard d'Estaing government, highlighted the change: "The public image of our minister of defense is undergoing a radical change. From a minister of expenditures . . . the minister of defense is becoming a minister of receipts who produces . . . foreign exchange indispensable for foreign trade. . . ."[62] Delpech followed a path already marked by Defense Minister Michel Debré, one of the architects of the Fifth Republic, who, like President de Gaulle, was intrigued by the notion that the modernization of France's armed forces was essential to France's quest for military and industrial supremacy in Western Europe: "It is necessary, on the one hand, to maintain and modernize an industrial potential which assures us in the area of armament a sufficient independence in order that the effectiveness of our defense is not tributary to foreign industrial constraints which would compromise our liberty of decision; it is necessary, on the other hand, to contribute to economic development without weighing on the balance of payments, to enrich the general economy by applying useful scientific and technical progress to other purposes than defense, and to relate our [arms production] policy to internal development."[63]

A decade later, Charles Hernu affirmed Debré's commitment to technological development and extended the responsibility of the arms industry to the promotion of full employment within the economy:

People forget that the defense minister is not only responsible for military personnel. Out of 720,000 people who work for the Defense Ministry, there are 143,000 civilians and 90,000 arsenal workers. In addition, there are the armaments enterprises [Aérospatiale], Thomson-CSF, Dassault, Renault. . . . Panhard and the Saint-Etienne Arms Company employ 300,000 workers and engineers. As for subcontracting, do you know how many it employs? One million! . . .

I would like to remind you of the arms industries' contribution to research. Do you know that we are the envy of the Americans in the sphere of lasers, carbon fibers, and the detection of submarines and nuclear weapons? Do you know that Thomson-CSF is one of the world's leading exporters of advanced military technology?

. . . As mayor of Villeurbanne I was unaware that there was a factory in my own city manufacturing carbon fiber elements.[64]

The economic and technological benefits of the sale of arms and military technology have become independent sources of economic activity, clearly distinguishable and progressively detached from the foreign and strategic objectives that initially justified the decision to produce weapons indigenously. Arms are not simply tools of national defense. They are commodities in international trade, instruments of economic growth, and vehicles of technological progress. Such traffic is perceived as contributing to domestic well-being, social harmony, and political stability. These are new and powerful propellants of global arms trade since they fuse two key functions of contemporary government: security and welfare. The Ministry of Defense must respond simultaneously to these imperatives. Its responsibilities are not only limited to cost-cutting measures and administrative efficiency but extend to the generation of national wealth through arms sales as a significant component of GNP and international trade.

Table 3-3 summarizes French arms transfer deliveries between 1956 and 1980. In this period, France sent an estimated $30 billion in arms and military technology to over 100 states. Almost 20 percent of this total was exported in 1980, the final year of the Giscard d'Estaing regime. Estimates of the value of French deliveries during the Mitterrand years suggest a downturn from this high. Distortions are partly due to conversion to dollars. The three devaluations initiated by the Socialist government and the weakness of the franc in these years tended to depreciate the real value of arms and military know-how sent abroad.[65] Current francs figures for each year rise from 1981 through 1984 from 28.5 billion francs at the start to approximately 36 billion francs at the close.[66]

While France is the third largest arms seller in volume, it is the first among the major arms suppliers in the West and in the Communist camp in per capita arms exports. In 1980 about $107 in arms was sold for each French citizen. The Soviet Union, Great Britain, and the United States delivered weapons and military equipment at per capita rates that were approximately one-third the French level.[67]

As Figure 3-4 above suggests, whether measured in constant or current dollars, the growth of French arms exports was spectacular in the 1970s. As Table 3-3 also reveals, the largest gains were in aeronautics and ground equipment. Deliveries of aerospace materials were concentrated in combat aircraft—Mirage IIIs, and 5s, and F1s, helicopters, and a wide assortment of tactical missiles. Appendix B lists the number of countries which have received these weapons. Excluding France, 20 states fly Mirage IIIs and 5s, 72 employ Alouette III helicopters, and over 50 have French tactical missiles in their inventories. Since 1965, aeronautic equipment has accounted for 58 percent or more of the value of French arms exports. High points were 1972 and 1973 when aerospace deliveries reached levels, respectively, of 76 and 74 percent. Ground equipment—particularly AMX-10, -13, and -30 armor, armored personnel carriers, and artillery—has averaged approximately 18 percent of French sales since 1970. With the exception of 1968, naval construction has lagged throughout the 25-year period covered in Table 3-3. Exports have been confined principally to diesel-engine submarines, missile-firing craft (vedettes), coastal patrol vessels, and corvettes. Electronic equipment hovers around 10 percent. This figure is very likely low since aeronautical, ground, and naval materials increasingly contain advanced electronic equipment whose value is not accurately reflected in French statistics. The sale of air defense equipment to Saudi Arabia, the largest arms contract in French history (estimated at 35 billion francs), is listed as ground equipment by the Ministry of Defense, although much of the sale involves sophisticated electronics.[68]

Arms deliveries bulk large in overall French exports. Their importance has grown progressively since the middle 1960s. This trend is depicted in Table 3-4. Arms exports as a percentage of overall exports reached a high of 4.4 in 1964 only to fall to below 3 percent. They slowly inched upward in the 1970s and attained highs in 1978 and 1980 of approximately 5 percent of total exports; they have remained essentially stable at this level throughout the Mitterrand years.[69]

If the trends sketched in Figure 3-5 continue through the 1980s and early 1990s, the French arms industry will continue to preserve its 5 percent position in overall French exports. Except for 1983, new orders have exceeded the value of deliveries in every year between 1974 and 1984. Orders rebounded in 1984 thanks to contracts with Saudi Arabia for an air defense system and Abu Dhabi's purchase of nineteen Mirage 2000s in exchange for oil.[70] The concentration of these contracts on a particular weapon system and the narrow range of countries involved (two Middle East states accounting for more than half of the 75 percent in overall contracts coming from this region in 1984) may lead to imbalances in workload and to unemployment within key sectors of the arms industry. The aeronautics industry is lagging. The Mirage 2000 has not sold as well as expected, partially prompting the Mitterrand government, as noted earlier, to explore possibilities to expand weapons development cooperation with its West European allies.

The significance of these arms export figures may be viewed from several angles. First, French arms exports compose a large proportion of French export of capital goods (biens d'équipement). These are especially important for French trade balances since the value added to the exported product is high in contrast to raw materials or semiprocessed

Table 3-3. French Arms Deliveries by Type: 1956-1980
(In billion current dollars)

Materials Delivered	1956	1957	1958	1959	1960	1961	1962	1963	1964	1965	1966	1967	1968
Air	.028[a]	.075[a]	.054[a]	.054[a]	.043[a]	.071[a]	.087[b]	.128[b]	.190[b]	.246[c]	.285[c]	.287[c]	.355[c]
% of Total	34	60	43	34	40	40	44	48	52	60	66	58	68
% of Annual Change	—	167	-28	—	-20	65	23	47	48	29	16	1	24
Ground	.049	.041	.059	.064	.040	.053	.046	.067	.098	.105	.108	.092	.065
% of Total	60	33	46	40	37	30	23	25	27	25	25	19	12
% of Annual Change	—	-16	44	8	-38	33	-13	46	46	7	3	-15	-29
Naval	—	.002	.0002	.034	.011	.009	.020	.019	.015	.005	.008	.057	.082
% of Total	—	2	—	21	10	5	10	7	4	1	2	12	16
% of Annual Change	—	—	-90	16,900	68	-18	122	-5	-21	-67	60	613	44
Electronics	.006	.007	.014	.006	.013	.045	.046	.054	.062	.056	.029	.059	.026
% of Total	7	6	11	4	12	25	23	20	17	14	7	12	5
% of Annual Change	—	17	100	-57	117	246	2	17	15	-10	-48	103	56
TOTAL[j]	.082	.125	.127	.159	.107	.177	.199	.267	.365	.411	.430	.495	.525
% Annual Change	—	52	2	25	-33	65	12	34	37	13	5	15	6

Table 3-3 (cont.)

Materials Delivered	1969	1970	1971	1972	1973	1974	1975	1976	1977	1978	1979	1980
Air	.319[c]	.319[d]	.375[d]	.607[e]	.867[e]	.871[f]	1.166[g]	1.695[h]	1.832[i]	2.393[i]	2.849[i]	—
% of Total	71	66	70	76	74	63	60	70	61	63	59	—
% of Annual Change	−10	—	18	62	43	—	34	45	8	31	19	—
Ground	.082	.079	.103	.103	.174	.269	.316	.514	.688	.866	1.33	—
% of Total	18	16	19	13	15	19	16	21	23	23	28	—
% of Annual Change	26	−4	30	—	69	55	17	63	34	26	54	—
Naval	.019	.050	.017	.023	.064	.117	.196	.037	.175	.272	.127	—
% of Total	4	10	3	3	5	8	10	2	6	7	3	—
% of Annual Change	−77	163	−66	35	178	84	67	−81	373	55	−53	—
Electronics	.031	.034	.042	.068	.070	.130	.266	.190	.299	.288	.498	—
% of Total	7	7	8	9	6	9	14	8	10	8	10	—
% of Annual Change	19	10	23	62	3	86	105	−29	57	4	73	—
TOTAL[j]	.451	.481	.538	.800	1.175	1.386	1.944	2.435	2.994	3.819	4.807	5.774
% Annual Change	−14	7	12	49	47	18	40	25	23	28	26	20

NOTES: All values were rounded to three decimal points. Totals may not add up due to rounding. All percentages were rounded to the nearest 1 percent; differences are due to rounding. The *Revue de Défense Nationale* cites incomplete information for 1956-1958; thus percentage figures may be distorted.

These estimates of the value of French arms exports are higher and contrast sharply with those issued by the annual publication of the U.S. Arms Control and Disarmament Agency, *World Military Expenditures and Arms Transfers*. See the author's "Measuring French Arms Transfers: A Problem of Sources and Some Sources of Problems with ACDA Data," *Journal of Conflict Resolution*, XXIII, No. 2 (June 1979), 195-227. Breakdowns for air, ground, naval, and electronics exports were not available after the Socialist government took office.

[a] *Revue de Défense Nationale* (June 1962), 1086-1087, and *Revue Militaire d'Information*, No. 350 (June 1963), 67-69, for 1956-1961. Slight discrepancies in table and source figures are due to miscalculations in source totals. The figures cited in these sources are for *authorized* exports of military material, not for the value of actual deliveries. Authorized exports refer to all materials requiring authorization for export whether civilian or military items. Authorized civilian materials are excluded in the table above. Between 1956 and 1970, they are as follows (in millions of dollars):

1956	6.29	1961	160.01	1966	131.86
1957	9.51	1962	105.3	1967	108.16
1958	15.49	1963	85.88	1968	64.82
1959	27.55	1964	75.55	1969	64.82
1960	103.10	1965	129.83	1970	108.03

See citations above and Jean Klein, "France," in *The Gun Merchants*, ed. Cindy Cannizo (New York: Pergamon, 1980), pp. 130-131; and France, Sénat, CF (1974), *Rapport sur le projet de loi de finances pour 1975, Défense: Dépenses en Capital*, No. 99, p. 17.

Authorized exports and arms deliveries should also be distinguished from orders for military equipment. Only deliveries are given here from 1956 to 1980 to emphasize the direct impact of arms deliveries on the French economy and to avoid inflating this impact.

[b] Jean-Bernard Pinatel et al., *L'Economie des forces* (Paris: Les Cahiers de la Fondation pour les Etudes de Défense Nationale, 1976), p. 162, for 1962-1964.

[c] France, Assemblée Nationale, CF (1970), *Rapport sur le projet de loi de finances pour 1971, Défense: Dépenses en Capital*, No. 1395, p. 12, for 1965-1969.

[d] France, Sénat, CF (1972), *Rapport sur le projet de loi de finances pour 1973, Défense: Dépenses en Capital*, No. 66, p. 17. See also J. F. Dubos, *Ventes d'armes: Une politique* (Paris: Gallimard, 1974), p. 134, for 1970 and 1971.

[e] France, Sénat, CF (1974), *Rapport sur le projet de loi de finances pour 1975, Défense: Dépenses en Capital*, No. 99, p. 17, for 1972 and 1973.

[f] France, Sénat, CF (1975), *Rapport sur le projet de loi de finances pour 1976, Défense: Dépenses en Capital*, No. 62, pp. 27-28, for 1974.

[g] France, Assemblée Nationale, CDNFA (1976), *Avis sur le projet de loi de finances pour 1977, Défense: Dépenses en Capital*, No. 2532, p. 57, for 1975.

[h] France, Assemblée Nationale, CDNFA (1977), *Avis sur le projet de loi de finances pour 1978, Défense: Dépenses en Capital*, No. 3150, pp. 102-103, for 1976.

[i] France, Assemblée Nationale, CF (1980), *Rapport sur le projet de loi de finances pour 1981, Défense: Considérations Générales, Dépenses en Capital*, No. 1976, p. 196, for 1977 to 1979. For 1980, consult France, Assemblée Nationale, CDNFA (1981), *Avis sur le projet de loi de finances pour 1982*, No. 473, p. 119.

[j] International Monetary Fund, *International Financial Statistics, 1977*, XXI, No. 5 (May 1977), 166-169, for exchange rates for the period 1956 to 1969. See also the same source, July 1982, pp. 166-169 for the period from 1970 to 1980.

Table 3-4. Arms Transfers Related to Exports, Oil Imports, and
Commercial Balances: 1956-1980 (In billions of current dollars)

	Exports	Arms Exports	(%) Arms Exports	Imports	Oil Imports	(%) Arms Exports/ Oil Imports	Balance: Exports and Imports	Balance Without Arms Exports
1956	4.6	0.1	2.2	5.6	0.6	16.7	− 1.0	− 1.1
1957	5.1	0.1	2.0	6.2	0.7	14.3	− 1.1	− 1.2
1958	5.1	0.1	2.0	5.6	0.6	16.7	− 0.5	− 0.6
1959	5.6	0.2	3.6	5.1	0.6	33.3	+ 0.5	+ 0.3
1960	6.9	0.1	1.4	6.3	0.6	16.7	+ 0.6	+ 0.5
1961	7.2	0.2	2.8	6.7	0.7	28.6	+ 0.5	+ 0.3
1962	7.4	0.2	2.7	7.4	0.7	28.6	—	− 0.2
1963	8.2	0.3	3.7	8.7	0.8	37.5	− 0.5	− 0.8
1964	9.1	0.4	4.4	10.1	0.9	44.4	− 1.0	− 1.4
1965	10.2	0.4	3.9	10.4	1.1	36.4	− 0.2	− 0.6
1966	11.0	0.4	3.6	11.9	1.1	36.4	− 0.9	− 1.3
1967	11.5	0.5	4.3	12.4	1.3	38.5	− 0.9	− 1.4
1968	12.9	0.5	3.9	14.0	1.4	35.7	− 1.1	− 1.6
1969	15.0	0.4	2.7	17.3	1.4	28.6	− 2.3	− 2.7
1970	17.9	0.5	2.8	19.1	1.7	29.4	− 1.2	− 1.7
1971	20.6	0.5	2.4	21.3	2.2	22.7	− 0.7	− 1.2
1972	26.1	0.8	3.1	26.9	2.7	29.6	− 0.8	− 1.6
1973	35.9	1.2	3.3	37.3	3.5	34.3	− 1.4	− 2.6
1974	45.9	1.4	3.0	52.8	9.9	14.1	− 6.9	− 8.3
1975	52.2	1.9	3.6	54.2	9.7	19.6	− 2.0	− 3.9
1976	55.8	2.4	4.3	64.5	11.5	20.9	− 8.7	− 11.1
1977	63.5	3.0	4.7	70.4	11.9	25.2	− 6.9	− 9.9
1978	76.4	3.8	5.0	81.5	12.0	31.7	− 5.1	− 8.9
1979	97.5	4.8	4.9	107.6	17.2	27.9	− 10.1	− 14.9
1980	116.1	5.8	5.0	130.4	26.2	22.1	− 14.3	− 20.1

Sources: See Table 3-3. Trade data are taken from the International Monetary Fund, *International Financial Statistics, 1977*, xxi, No. 5 (May 1977), pp. 166-169 and *ibid.* (July 1982), pp. 166-169.

goods. Between 1971 and 1978, French arms sales rose from slightly under 10 percent of French capital exports to almost 21 percent by 1978. Arms exports rose by over 500 percent during this period while overall capital exports grew less than half as fast.[71] Arms were pushing capital exports upward rather than being pulled along by civilian exports.

Second, the final destination of most French arms sales under the

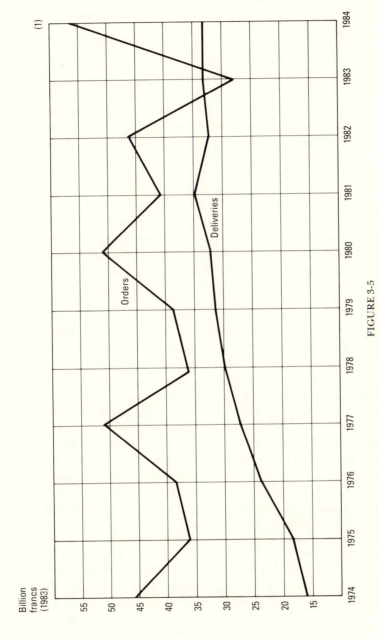

FIGURE 3-5

Total Foreign Orders and Deliveries of French Arms: 1974-1984 (Constant 1983 francs)
SOURCE: Ministère de la Défense, SIRPA, *Armament in France* (Paris, 1985), p. 29. (1) In 1984, total foreign orders came to 61.8 billion francs, or 57.3 billion francs 1983 value.

Fifth Republic has substantially shifted from the developed to the developing world. Until the early 1970s, most of France's arms shipments were to developed states. Twelve countries appeared on France's annual listing of its leading three clients between 1956 and 1967. Of these, seven were western democracies. Germany led all states as France's principal client, being included in ten of the twelve years for which Ministry of Defense data are available.[72] The next leading states were Australia, the United States, and South Africa, which were cited in four out of twelve years. Only three states fit the label as developing states: India, Pakistan, and Brazil. They were listed no more than twice during this twelve-year stretch. Other major purchasers were the Netherlands, Italy, Sweden, Israel, and Belgium. With the exception of the Netherlands (appearing three times), the others appeared twice or less. For 1962, the only year for which data were published on France's top ten arms clients, Brazil was the only developing state listed.[73]

Since the early 1970s, there has been a dramatic shift in French arms exports to the developing world.[74] In 1970, with a major order for French Mirages from Libya and additional large orders from Latin America (Brazil, Argentina, Colombia) and Asia (Pakistan, Malaysia), the French arms trade balance shifted largely to the developing world. Between 1974 and 1982, orders for weapons from other European states averaged only 11 percent each year.[75] For most years after 1970, Europe's share was less than 10 percent of all arms orders. The only year that departed significantly from this pattern was 1978 in which EC countries accounted for 23.3 percent of the total of arms orders recorded by the French weapons industry. Orders to the rest of the world, primarily to developing states, annually averaged about 90 percent of arms orders. Deliveries reflected this pattern of orders. In 1970 and 1971, 49 and 58 percent of French arms deliveries, respectively, were sent to European states. In 1974, one year after the oil crisis, 64.2 percent of French arms transfers were delivered to non-European and non-NATO countries. This ratio steadily increased through the 1970s and stood at approximately 85 percent of annual French deliveries by the close of the decade.[76]

Figure 3-6 lists regional shares of orders for French arms. The overwhelming majority of French arms have gone to Middle East states. Scattered governmental reports provide a glimpse of the size of the Middle East market. The Industrial Group for Ground Arms (GIAT), which was organized to promote exports by governmental arsenals and private firms, reported in 1976 that 78.7 percent of its orders or approximately $200 million came from Saudi Arabia, Qatar, Yemen, and Morocco. In 1982, 83.5 percent of all arms orders came from Arab

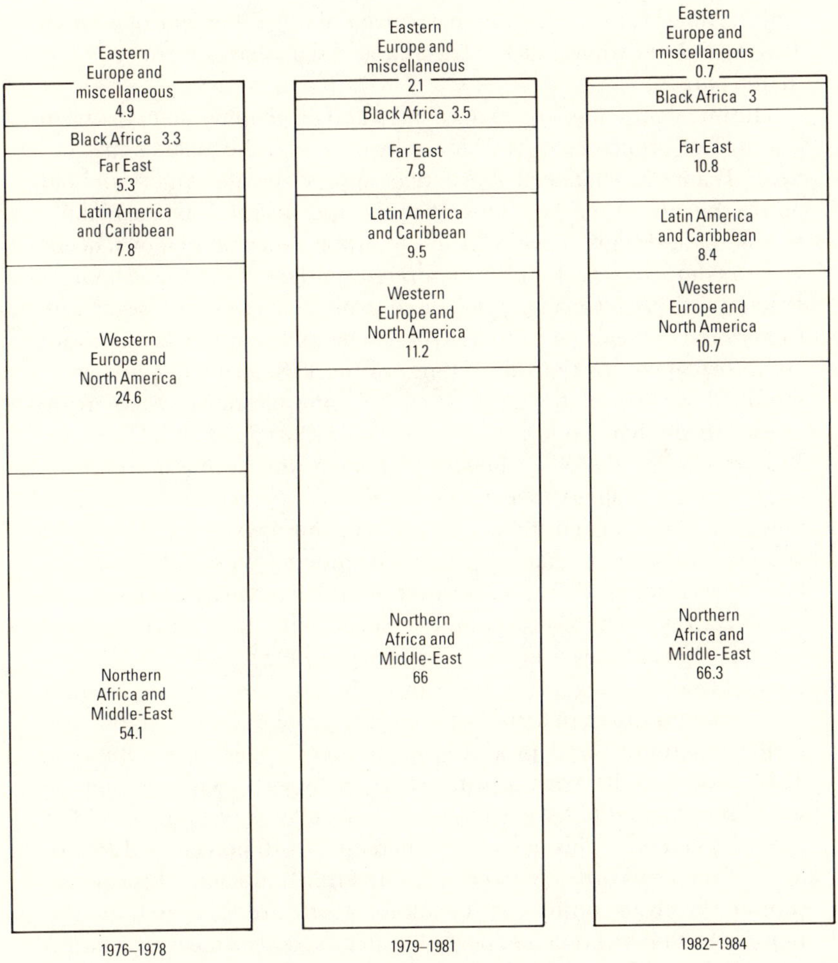

1976–1978

Region	Value
Eastern Europe and miscellaneous	4.9
Black Africa	3.3
Far East	5.3
Latin America and Caribbean	7.8
Western Europe and North America	24.6
Northern Africa and Middle-East	54.1

1979–1981

Region	Value
Eastern Europe and miscellaneous	2.1
Black Africa	3.5
Far East	7.8
Latin America and Caribbean	9.5
Western Europe and North America	11.2
Northern Africa and Middle-East	66

1982–1984

Region	Value
Eastern Europe and miscellaneous	0.7
Black Africa	3
Far East	10.8
Latin America and Caribbean	8.4
Western Europe and North America	10.7
Northern Africa and Middle-East	66.3

FIGURE 3-6

Regional Shares of Orders for French Arms: 1976-1984

Source: Ministère de la Défense, sirpa, *Armament in France* (Paris, 1985), p. 29.

states. In 1980, 78.8 percent of French arms deliveries or approximately $4.55 billion went to Middle East and North African states. Principal recipients were Saudi Arabia, Iraq, and Egypt. European and North American countries each received about 7 percent of French arms deliveries while Black African and Asian shares were each less than 3 percent.[77]

The imbalance in selling to developed and developing states has been a source of French concern.[78] Since its failure in the "sale of the century," France has not been able to dent appreciably the American hold on the European market. The other European states—Great Britain, Germany, and Italy—have been able to supply much of their own needs and to compete with France for foreign markets. Like France, Great Britain and West Germany increased arms deliveries at a faster rate than defense spending in the 1970s.[79] The announced intention (not yet a formal contract at this writing) of the U.S. Army to purchase a modified version of the RITA ground communications system from France through an American corporation with rights from Thomson-Brandt to use and modify the system to meet American requirements, suggests French ability to lead in selected military sectors of high technology.[80] These penetrations into the arms markets of the developed western states are not likely to offset dependency on sales to southern hemispheric states. They are, however, useful. Even marginal success in sales to advanced industrial countries purportedly enhances the attractiveness of French arms in states in the developing world.[81]

Equally disturbing for French officials has been the increasingly heavy concentration of arms in the total value of French exports, particularly manufactured products, to the developing world. Between 1974 and 1978 the arms transfer share of exports to the developing world is estimated to have grown each year, from 9 percent in 1974 to over 15 percent.[82] This percentage increased to 16 percent in 1980. In light of the arms orders currently in the French pipeline, this concentration is likely to continue in the immediate future. Although the volume and value of French export of civilian products have grown dramatically (doubling to the industrialized countries between 1975 and 1981),[83] French penetration of civilian markets in the developing states is still limited by the ability of its competitors to retain and even increase their shares and by increasing competition from developing states, like Taiwan, South Korea, Brazil and India, and developed states, like Israel in the southern tier, which are expanding their arms exports.

Fourth, arms transfers assure France needed energy supplies, especially oil, and the resources to pay for them. Even before the first oil crisis of 1973, French leaders were using arms exports to ensure oil supplies and cover the cost of rising energy bills. Like the other western states in the 1950s and 1960s, French energy policy was founded on the assumption of cheap, plentiful, and reliable sources of oil and gas, principally from the Middle East and North Africa.[84] In only a decade, from 1960 to 1970, France's reliance on oil rose from 34 to 62 percent of all energy consumption. Of this amount, 90 percent had to be imported.

Algeria was initially France's principal oil supplier. The Evian accords settling the Algerian War afforded France generous oil concessions in Algeria. A 1965 Paris-Algiers agreement temporarily facilitated French access. Algeria abrogated unilaterally almost all of these concessions in the late 1960s. Algeria's share of the French oil market fell sharply between 1965 and 1971 from approximately 30 percent to 8.3 percent. American oil companies took up most of the slack as the United States became a major oil and gas importer of Algeria's output.

The loss of the Algerian connection precipitated a major revision in the composition of France's oil suppliers. Since 1970, France has simultaneously narrowed its principal supplier outlets, with Saudi Arabia gradually replacing Algeria as its primary source for oil, and has broadened the number of states which supply its remaining needs. With the latter, Paris has pursued a mixed strategy, moving from one set of suppliers to another, depending on the opportunities of the moment with respect to price, reliability of supply, and prospects for exports, primarily arms and military technology, to pay for imported oil. Table 3-5 traces the shifts in France's oil dependency from 1965 to 1980.

Table 3-5. French Dependency on Oil Imports from Major Suppliers: 1965-1980 (In percentages)

	1965	1970	1975	1980
Algeria	31.1	27.7	6.1	4.8
Saudi Arabia	4.4	10.1	31.3	32.6
Iraq	16.7	12.1	11.5	21.2
Nigeria	0.8	5.3	8.7	11.0
Libya	10.0	16.3	2.0	2.0
Kuwait	14.0	10.5	6.6	2.8
U.A.E.	N.A.	N.A.	11.7	7.1
Iran	10.3	3.9	12.8	1.3
Venezuela	4.2	2.6	0.6	0.7

SOURCE: United Nations, *World Trade Annual 1965-1980* (New York: Walker and Co., 1981), *passim*.

There is a close relation between the pattern of oil imports and arms exports to the Middle East and to oil suppliers elsewhere, like Nigeria. Increased reliance on Libyan oil coincided with a $400 million contract for Mirage fighters and other military equipment.[85] In 1970, 37 percent of France's arms orders were attributable to the Libyan sale. The Libyan relation soured in the 1970s as the Khaddafi regime meddled in Middle East politics and intervened in France's traditional sphere of interest in North and West Africa.

Since the raising of the Middle East arms embargo in 1974, France has signed a series of multibillion-dollar contracts with Arab states. In 1974 it agreed to supply Saudi Arabia with ground equipment. It subsequently sold large stocks of air, sea, and ground material to Iraq. By 1978, France was reported to have had control of 38 percent of the Iraqi arms market, 40 percent of Egypt's (in the pre-Camp David period), and 33 percent of Saudi Arabia's arms purchases.[86] In 1982, France signed large arms contracts with Iraq, Saudi Arabia, and Nigeria—all major oil suppliers. The Iraqi contract, valued at approximately $1 billion, was for ground equipment, including 155 mm. cannons. This equipment supplemented previous purchases of large stocks of French arms, including F1 fighters.

French naval construction was also given a major boost with the signing of a Saudi Arabian contract estimated at $3 billion to equip its navy. The Saudis ordered 4 2000-ton frigates armed with surface-to-surface missiles, 2 oil tenders, and 24 Dauphin helicopters. Created was an estimated 16 million hours of work for France's naval arsenals and for the firms of Thomson-CSF, Aérospatiale, and Matra.[87] This order followed on previous agreements to furnish Riyadh with Shahine and Exocet missiles. The trade of oil for arms continued through the Mitterrand years, culminating in the arms accords with Saudi Arabia and Abu Dhabi noted earlier. To these agreements, France added a $200-million order for Roland missiles from Nigeria and a contract with Egypt for 20 Mirage 2000s and Alpha-Jets.[88]

Arms sales have paid for a substantial percentage of France's oil bill since 1956. As Table 3-4 above indicates, arms transfers covered more than one-third of France's oil imports between 1963 and 1973. The quadrupling of oil prices after 1973, which amounted to a special tax on French consumers, reduced coverage to a low of 14.1 percent in 1974, subsequently leveling off to an average of about 25 percent between 1975 and 1980. Of more interest was the increased value of arms sales needed to balance oil purchases. While successful conservation practices after the 1973 price rise actually led to lower net oil imports, more arms had to be sold than before to pay for imports from Arab oil producers. Up to the middle 1980s, when oil prices fell, France has had to run its arms industry at a faster rate just to stand still.

Finally, arms and military technology transfers are relied upon to off-set chronic trade imbalances. In principle, France's deficits would have been greater by $20 billion in the second half of the 1970s without in-creased arms deliveries abroad. The economic policies of the Socialist government after 1981, aimed at inflating the economy and at increas-ing social benefits, served to accent dependence on the sale of weapons and associated technology to balance foreign accounts. Investors looked elsewhere than France to place their funds. Higher wage and worker benefits and the nationalization of several key industries, in-cluding banking firms, deepened investor distrust.

A series of adverse conjunctural developments undermined further the Mitterrand government's expansionist policies. Among the more negative of these developments were continued high interest rates in the United States and the perception in international financial circles that the economic recovery experienced in the United States in the early 1980s might not extend to Europe. The prospects for investments in France in the early 1980s did not appear bright to foreign and do-mestic lenders. As one analyst concluded: "With profit margins down, credit expensive and growth less certain, business had little to be happy about: the volume of investment was down 10 percent in 1981 and was expected to fall another 7 percent in 1982."[89] The high foreign borrow-ing, the largest in the history of the Fifth Republic, and dwindling re-serves further discouraged private investment. The Mitterrand gov-ernment's introduction of austerity and deflationary measures as well as exchange controls had little immediate impact on domestic and foreign investment. These concessionary signals to the financial community were greeted by an additional fall in the value of the franc, already de-valued three times. With the franc at its lowest value since the inception of the Fifth Republic, with the flight of capital still apace, and with no appreciable reduction of France's high unemployment, the Mitterrand government had little choice but to lean on arms sales even more heav-ily than its predecessors to juggle France's delicate balance of payments position.

Arms Transfers and Comparative Advantage

The preceding discussion has largely been confined to describing *how* arms sales have contributed to France's international trading position. It has not said much about *why* the French have, relative to other arms suppliers, been so successful. What factors explain France's compara-tive advantage? As much by conscious planning as by fortuitous circumstance, the global economic division of labor over the past twenty years has favored French efforts to become a leading arms exporter. Several factors explain France's favored position.[90] First, France's real or potential competitors among the western industrialized countries were occupied elsewhere or followed different industrial strategies during the takeoff period of France's arms sales in the 1960s. The United States arms industry was preoccupied with supplying American forces in Vietnam or meeting the needs of special clients, like Israel and Iran. American forces and inventories in Europe were drawn down to fill immediate shortfalls. France filled some of this void with French-built helicopters, tactical missiles, and supersonic aircraft.

Second, France's European allies did not immediately fill the gap left by the United States. The British Labor government, under strong internal pressure principally from elements within the Labor party, cut back on foreign arms sales.[91] The value of deliveries dropped for almost a decade from 1963 to 1970, falling from $328.6 million in 1963 in constant 1972 dollars to a low of $89.7 million in 1970.[92] Italy lacked the industrial base and marketing network to contest France across the board in weapons sales. It followed the German pattern of relying on foreign sources, particularly the United States and to a lesser extent France, to meet its military requirements.[93] Germany and Japan as defeated powers were initially prohibited from reconstituting their arms industries and, later, when they were rehabilitated, both preferred to cultivate their civilian export markets and purchase the bulk of their arms abroad. Germany was France's principal client in the 1960s.

Third, as excess French arms capacity became available as a consequence of decreased domestic demand in the late 1960s, world demand for weapons, particularly from the developing world, rose. Expanded military conflicts in the Middle East and South and Southeast Asia stimulated arms orders. Nation-building efforts and the modernization of national military establishments, as Chapter 6 recounts, gave additional impulse to the demand for new, sophisticated systems. Much of the 14.8 percent increase in world military expenditures between 1968 and 1977 was attributable to the developing world. During this period, global spending increased from $305 billion to $319 billion in constant 1976 dollars. While the growth in spending in the developed world was estimated to be under 5 percent, military expenditures in the developing world climbed from $54 billion to $92 billion or 70.4 percent. The Middle East led with an increase of 270 percent, followed by Africa (including North Africa). If military spending as a ratio of GNP remained steady in the developing world between 1968 and 1977, it should be noted that GNP increased by 80 percent. More resources were therefore available for arms. Arms spending exceeded the rate of growth in GNP in the Middle East, Africa, and South Asia.[94]

Increases in the amount and rate of arms imports during this ten-year period parallel the rise in military spending by these developing states. Using five-year averages, developing states increased their arms imports by 63 percent in the periods 1968 to 1972 and 1973 to 1977.[95] The growth is all the more impressive since the base for arms imports for developing states was already greater than for developed states. The impact of these imports is evident in Table 3-6, which sketches the growth of advanced military systems among developing states from 1950 to 1977. Dramatic increases can be seen in all major weapons categories: supersonic aircraft, missiles, armored fighting vehicles, and warships.

Fourth, the French were able to offer serviceable, battle-tested products with few political strings attached. French arms worked. Israeli-flown French Mirages destroyed Arab air forces on three fronts in lightning raids during the 1967 war. They also held up well in the war of attrition and the 1973 Yom Kippur war. French arms were used by both sides in the 1971 Indian-Pakistan war. French Exocet missiles were also in the inventories of Argentina and Great Britain in the Falklands War in 1982. Israeli and Pakistani pilots have been employed to demonstrate French equipment to impress prospective customers.[96] France's reliability as an arms supplier compares favorably with the superpowers.

Fifth, the French have a reputation, with some notable lapses, for

Table 3-6. Number of Developing Countries with Advanced Military Systems: 1950-1985

	1950	1960	1970	1980	1985
Supersonic Aircraft	—	1	28	55	55
Missiles	—	6	25	68	71
Armored Fighting Vehicles	1	38	72	99	107
Modern Warships	4	26	56	79	81

SOURCES: Stockholm International Peace Research Institute (SIPRI), *World Armaments and Disarmament: 1978* (New York: Crane, Russak, 1978), pp. 238-253, for 1950, 1960, 1970. The International Institute for Strategic Studies (IISS), *The Military Balance: 1981-1982* (London: IISS, 1981) for 1980, and *The Military Balance: 1985-1986* for 1985. The IISS sources were supplemented by *Jane's Fighting Ships* (1984-1985) (London: Jane's Publishing Company Limited, 1985).

keeping their promises. Keeping contracts, even when politically inconvenient, has been a trademark of the French business approach to weapons. Over much criticism at home and abroad, French arms have flowed to Arab states and to authoritarian regimes and pariah states, like South Africa, once a contract was struck to supply arms. Strong pressures, approaching crisis proportions in some cases, are needed to move the French to violate a contractual obligation to deliver arms which have been duly ordered and paid for. Illustrative are the embargo against Middle East belligerents in the wake of the Six Day War and the decision to end arms shipments to South Africa in order to assuage Black African demands.

Sixth, French officials also take pride in providing arms to developing states to afford them an alternative to the superpowers and to encourage a proliferation of power centers resistant to control by Washington and Moscow. Defense Minister Charles Hernu declared in 1982: "Yes, I have a good conscience when I sell arms to a country if that prevents it from buying them from one of the superpowers."[97] Arrangements are permissive. While restrictions on third-party use are a stock feature of France's contracts with its arms clients, what penalties arms purchasers incur in violating third-party access is not clear. Official embargoes, as Chapter 7 reveals, have also been bypassed, at times with the collusion of French authorities.

Seventh, French firms and engineering have demonstrated a marked capacity to produce a wide range of effective weapons at competitive prices, although like their American counterparts they have been guilty of gold plating and too great a fascination with technical efficiency to the detriment of cost effectiveness.[98] The Dassault Corporation has been particularly successful in selling its Mirage aircraft. Not only have the aircraft performed well, but they have afforded buyers a wide variety of options, including attack, ground support, air cover, and reconnaissance capabilities, at a cost equal or better than that offered by American firms.

Dassault's success as a world supplier of military aircraft can be attributed to several factors: small, highly skilled, integrated design teams which have worked for many years together; a small-step approach to improvements in aircraft design based on proven materials and technology; focused attention on fighter aircraft; tight administrative and financial control of programs; easy access to governmental funds for development and commercialization of projects; and skillful use of subcontractors, like Aérospatiale, to decrease overhead costs in producing component parts.[99] In the early 1970s orders for Dassault aircraft were more than 20 percent greater than the total for the next five leading avionics firms and three times greater than Aérospatiale.[100] A decade later, Dassault remained the leading avionics firm in military exports, although the gap between the major avionics firms narrowed as their military sales expanded.[101]

It is difficult to estimate whether France would have been more successful in world markets if it had followed the Japanese and German examples of emphasizing civilian product development over military arms.[102] Such an option was *never* really seriously considered by any French government during or after the decolonization period in the postwar era. The commitment to a liberal trading philosophy that would have accepted a rationalization of global economic production, increasingly refined specialization, and an international division of labor directed by market mechanisms ran counter not only to traditional French reservations about allowing French industry to compete without support in world markets but also to strictures arising from French foreign and security objectives which had special relevance to the arms industry.

State security and welfare obligations were so intimately linked that Fifth Republic governments have been precluded from adopting a thoroughgoing global liberal trading posture. State planners and bureaucrats have little interest and less desire to relinquish their direction of the French economy and the arms industry. Few state officials, even including the most open-minded within the market-oriented Raymond Barre government, ever considered turning France's arms industry over completely to the private sector after the American model. Internal political limits, resting on broadly shared strategic and foreign policy assumptions about the need for an arms industry, posed the issue of its management and direction differently than would have been the case if an unrelenting internationalist economic policy, keyed to market-determined production levels and pricing, had been adopted. French planners approached the question of market mechanisms and private firms versus state instrumentalities and administrative pricing with a biased answer in favor of the latter option in producing arms.

Using market forces and private firms, like Dassault, in no way implied delegation of the state's responsibility for security and welfare to the hidden hand of the marketplace. It merely tipped the balance of influence in favor of corporate managers of firms, like Marcel Dassault, at the expense of civilian and military bureaucrats and technicians and, then, only temporarily. The Socialist government's nationalization of most key parts of the arms industry still in private hands in 1981 had the effect, as Chapter 5 argues, of formally investing the corporate managers of these firms with state authority and of incorporating them more closely than ever into the insular politics of elite bargaining within the French administrative state.

It would be misleading, however, to conclude that the civilian economy was not competitive or that the French market has been closed relative to other industrial states because of its accent on arms production. France stands fourth on the list of leading trading nations, outstripped only by the United States, Germany, and Japan.[103] Figure 3-7 compares the upward trend of overall French exports and of arms exports. Total exports moved more sharply upward than arms exports through most of the 1970s. The ratios of French imports plus exports over GNP have steadily grown since 1962 (the end of the Algerian War) to 1980. In 1962, the ratio was 22.8 percent; in 1980 it doubled to 44.7, its highest point over this span. Trade is an increasing component of French economic activity, and the French have demonstrated that their success does not depend solely on arms exports, however important they are. Arms exports are a necessary but not sufficient condition for the vitality of France as a trade leader.

Several economic trade indicators underline the competitiveness of French manufacturers and the gradual openness of the French economy to foreign competition. Between 1958 and 1979, exports and imports accounted for an increasingly higher percent of value added in traded commodities. In 1953 these ratios were, respectively, 12 and 15.2 percent. Twenty years later they stood at 44.3 and 51.9 percent.[104] This progress surpassed Japan's and approximated West Germany's record. In six major trading sectors, France's exports and imports outside the franc zone constituted an increasing share in manufacturing production and use.

Table 3-7 sketches the share of foreign trade in selected manufacturing industries between 1953 and 1976. Except for clothing, textiles, and leather, export and import ratios rose in each instance. The dramatic changes in the ratios for manufacturing, machinery, and transport equipment reflect the shift in importance from intermediate products to durables. Export-import ratios for manufactured products were also favorable for France throughout the 1970s. Especially noteworthy, aside from armaments where imports are low, as might be expected, the export-import ratios are high for automobiles, chemicals, and pharmaceuticals. Meanwhile, similar ratios for high-labor, low-capital intensity industries declined.[105] As one close student of the French economy concluded: "These developments, together with the more-than-doubling of industrial production in a period of fifteen years and the shift in exports from intermediate products and consumer nondurables toward producer and consumer durables, show that France established it-

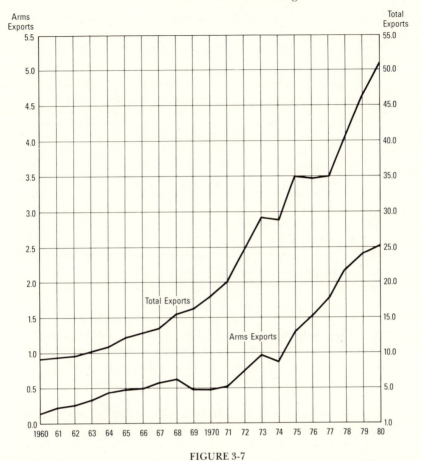

FIGURE 3-7
French Arms Exports and Total Exports: 1960-1980 (In billions of constant dollars, base 1970)
SOURCE: See Table 3-3.

Table 3-7. Share of Foreign Trade in Manufacturing Industries in France:
1953-1976 (Nonfranc zone)

	Manu-facturing Industries	Building Materials & Glass	Machinery & Transportation Equipment	Chemical Industry	Textiles, Clothing, Leather	Wood, Paper, etc.
	1953 1976	1953 1976	1953 1976	1953 1976	1953 1976	1953 1976
Exports as Percentage of Production	11.0 26.2	6.2 12.6	10.2 34.8	12.0 27.2	14.8 20.3	8.2 10.8
Imports as Percentage of Use	12.6 24.3	4.1 14.7	9.1 28.7	14.3 25.6	23.0 21.3	8.0 17.8

Source: Adapted from Bela Belassa, "The French Economy 1958-1978," in *The Fifth Republic at Twenty*, ed. William G. Andrews and Stanley Hoffmann (Albany: SUNY Press, 1981), p. 224.

self as a major industrial power."[106] The GNP rose, too, as civilian and military exports expanded. France's rate of growth was one of the highest in Europe and rivaled Japan's spectacular development.[107]

Arms Sales and Employment

Exact figures on the numbers of workers, technicians, and administrative personnel engaged in armaments production are difficult to acquire. Official estimates vary. Figure 3-8 presents the arms industry personnel figures cited in a 1983 parliamentary report according to regional distribution, domestic-foreign workloads, and industrial groupings. Approximately 310,000 manufacturing personnel work on arms. There may be as many as 1,300 factory sites carrying out defense work. A governmental report in the late 1960s noted approximately 120 factories devoting 80 percent of their work to arms, of which 30 had personnel over 1,000. Another 250 factories employed between 25 and 100.[108]

Approximately two-fifths of France's arms producers are located in Paris with the remainder decentralized throughout France. The major exception is northwest France. Some 118,000 workers are concentrated in the Paris region. The other 192,000 are roughly distributed along three axes. The first two run along the western and southern coasts of France. Here are found naval works at Cherbourg, Brest, Lorient, and

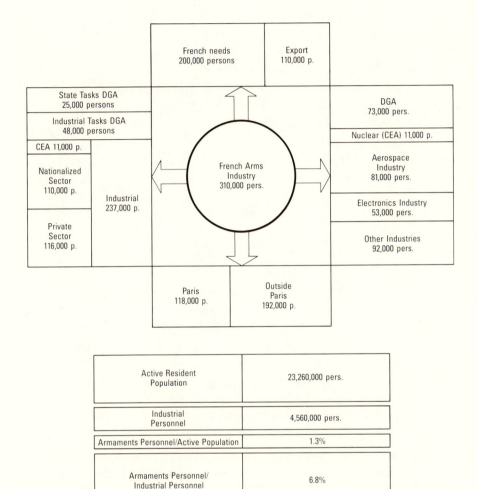

French needs 200,000 persons	Export 110,000 p.			

State Tasks DGA 25,000 persons		DGA 73,000 pers.
Industrial Tasks DGA 48,000 persons		Nuclear (CEA) 11,000 p.
CEA 11,000 p.		Aerospace Industry 81,000 pers.
Nationalized Sector 110,000 p.	Industrial 237,000 p.	
		Electronics Industry 53,000 pers.
Private Sector 116,000 p.		Other Industries 92,000 pers.

French Arms Industry 310,000 pers.

Paris 118,000 p.	Outside Paris 192,000 p.

Active Resident Population	23,260,000 pers.
Industrial Personnel	4,560,000 pers.
Armaments Personnel/Active Population	1.3%
Armaments Personnel/ Industrial Personnel	6.8%

FIGURE 3-8

Distribution of Personnel in the French Arms Industry by Region, Domestic-Foreign Work Forces, and Ratio of Armament Personnel to the Industrial Work Force, 1983
Source: France, Ministère de la Défense, sirpa, *Budget, 1983* (Paris, 1983), p. 26.

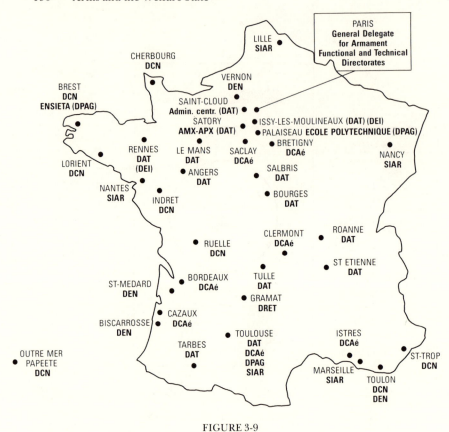

FIGURE 3-9

Installations of the General Delegation for Armament

Source: France, Ministère de la Défense, *Délégation Générale pour l'Armement* (Paris, 1985).

Toulon. The third axis cuts the country in two, starting slightly north of Paris and continuing southward toward Toulouse and Tarbes. Important aeronautic programs are found in the southeast (Marignane) and in the southwest (Bordeaux, Pau, and Toulouse). The arsenal system, implanted throughout France over centuries, is highly decentralized. Figure 3-9 identifies the major installations of the General Delegation for Armament. Local dependency on arms production provides a broad base of support for defense spending and for arms exports. In some departments the percentage of the working population employed in arms production exceeds 20 percent of total employment in industry (Cher, Finistère, Hautes-Pyrénées, and Var).[109]

Based on French estimates for the 1970s,[110] the number of French arms industry personnel has grown at a faster rate than the national av-

erage for manufacturing. The number of workers engaged in manufacturing fell from 5.96 million in 1974 to 5.59 million in 1978, a trend
reflected in other West European states.[111] Service sectors recorded the
largest growth in French employment.[112] According to another calculation, the proportion of employment in manufacturing to total civilian
employment remained essentially static in France between 1955 and
1975.[113] Whichever of these various measures are used, employment
growth in the arms industry ran counter to powerful structural changes
occurring in France and throughout the western world away from manufacturing in favor of service industries.

These downward trends in manufacturing have unleashed strong
protectionist pressures within the developed states.[114] An ironic effect
of the export growth of an essentially protectionist arms industry is to
have it become an unwitting ally of liberalized trade. With so many
workers engaged in arms exports, incentives to restrict international
trade are dampened. Over the decade of the 1970s, the number of personnel working full time on weapons exports, according to government
estimates, increased by approximately 250 percent. In 1972, 45,000
French workers were reportedly occupied in filling foreign arms orders.[115] Less than a decade later, this number grew to 110,000.[116]

Since the middle 1960s, most growth in personnel has occurred in
aeronautics and electronics—major export-oriented industries. Available figures suggest a personnel expansion of approximately 20 percent
in aeronautics and 40 percent in electronics, primarily in response to increased military demand.[117] Naval construction personnel also doubled
from 14,000 to 31,000. The bulk of this expansion would appear to be
related to the atomic submarine program of the force de frappe which
is not available for export.

RESEARCH AND DEVELOPMENT, TECHNOLOGICAL AND INDUSTRIAL GROWTH, AND ARMS SALES

The Gaullist Fifth Republic banked on the modernization of France's
armed forces as one of the principal mechanisms to modernize French
industry. In developing the scientific, technological, and industrial base
to produce the force de frappe, a modern arms industry was also created.[118] Gaullist planners expected that new military-industrial capacity
would spur the civilian economy. France would establish itself as a
leader in nuclear energy, civilian and military supersonic aircraft, electronics, computers, and space launchers and satellites. Under the
Fourth Republic, the arms industry was hampered in spending more
for new technologies, like nuclear power, aeronautics, and electronics,
where only modest gains were scored, because the primary task of the

arms industry was ministering to France's colonial army. The needs of the empire hindered France's modernization of its economy and retarded efforts to increase its competitiveness in world markets.

Gaullist leaders sought to transform the research and development structure underlying the arms industry. Before 1958, military R&D was largely conducted within the state's arsenal system. Little technological progress was recorded beyond the AMX series of ground equipment. The arsenals were ill-equipped to contribute to the development of a modern arms complex. New forms of leadership were also lacking. The engineers in charge were not trained to conduct scientific research. Having little commercial experience, they were unable to translate systematically new discoveries into technological processes susceptible to industrialization or into production of sophisticated weapons to meet rising domestic and foreign demand. They were trained as administrators and production managers, not as scientists, weapons innovators, and salesmen. Technical proficiency and elegance in weapons design was valued over commercial advantage.

Except for such unique governmental organizations as the Atomic Energy Commission, most basic scientific research was carried out in university laboratories. The arms industry found few friends in this environment. The deep suspicion, shared widely by members of the scientific community, of the military establishment hampered Ministry of Defense access to sound scientific advice and assistance. University laboratories were also insulated from French industry. With a reward structure based on publications and teaching and with a work agenda focused more on theoretical than applied concerns, researchers had little incentive to be sensitive to the economic and marketing problems associated with production innovation, much less in arms development. Meanwhile in the 1950s and early 1960s, the Ministry of Defense and private industry were too weak to mount their own R&D programs to fill this void.[119]

To achieve its military strategic objectives, the de Gaulle regime needed to revamp the entire structure by which weapons were developed. A new scientific-technological-industrial complex had to be erected. The state and, specifically, the Ministry of Defense, as its agent, were assigned critical roles as the major organizing and coordinating bodies of this rebuilding effort. The American model of using defense contracts to command services and to set economic and military priorities was adapted to French ways of doing business. Through the use of generous defense-related research and development contracts, principally to corporations, direct subsidies to industry, and broad and varied support for exports, a new arms infrastructure was created. The arms industry was rapidly expanded beyond the narrow confines of the arsenal system. Brought within the arms complex were the universities, including their scientists and laboratories, private and semipublic corporations, particularly in aerospace and electronics, and governmental research units under the General Delegation for Armament and the Atomic Energy Commission. With an expanded industrial base linked to basic research and development centers, it was expected that commercially profitable products would be incidental spinoffs from progress in military technology. Annual Ministry of Defense reports dutifully catalogued self-proclaimed successes in civilian product design and innovation, resulting from asserted breakthroughs in military know-how.[120] The new spirit of cooperation between the defense establishment and the research community carried through the Mitterrand years. Aside from continued governmental support for university and corporate R&D, sketched below, special colloquia and convocations were organized to bring scientists, technicians, and military elites together; and consultative bodies were organized, including a national scientific defense advisory group, to institutionalize contacts.[121]

The actual pattern of defense spending on research and development followed a more unpredictable and meandering course than the unified and coherent vision of a new France projected by President de Gaulle and his technocratic advisers. Inherently scarce economic resources and techno-scientific talent, demanding international competition, unanticipated domestic welfare demands, and the narrow national base from which France began its effort to become a global economic power ruled out swift or conclusive realization of the Gaullist design. Forced on the French were unpalatable choices that ran counter to widely shared notions of an independent France: desirable civilian and military programs were abandoned or their progress retarded; international cooperation and its inevitable constraints and inconveniences had to be accepted; and even American economic, technological, and military dependency had to be grudgingly acknowledged.

Table 3-8 traces French spending for civilian and military research and development from all public and private sources.[122] Several patterns emerge. First, notable increases in governmental R&D expenditures, particularly for military purposes between 1963 and 1968, highlight Gaullist strategic and technological priorities in favor of the force de dissuasion. Military R&D expenditures during this period comprise approximately 40 percent of all spending for R&D estimated in current dollars. Total spending for R&D from all sources tripled between 1958 and 1963.[123] By 1965 over one-fifth of the defense budget and 50 percent of the procurement portion were devoted to arms R&D. This level of spend-

Table 3-8. Total Expenditures for Civilian and Military Research and Development from All Sources: 1963-1980
(In billions of current and constant 1970 dollars)

		1963	'64	'65	'66	'67	'68	'69	'70	'71	'72	'73	'74	'75	'76	'77	'78	'79	'80
Civilian R&D	Current	.7	1.0	1.1	1.4	1.6	1.9	2.0	2.1	2.4	2.8	3.4	3.8	4.9	5.0	5.6	6.7	8.0	8.7
	Constant	.9	1.2	1.3	1.6	1.9	2.3	2.2	2.1	2.4	2.6	2.8	2.4	3.3	3.1	3.3	3.8	4.0	4.0
Military R&D	Current	.6	.7	.9	.9	.8	.8	.7	.6	.6	.7	.9	1.0	1.2	1.2	1.2	1.7	2.2	2.7
	Constant	.7	.9	1.0	1.1	.9	1.0	.7	.6	.6	.7	.8	.6	.8	.7	.7	.9	1.1	1.2
Total R&D	Current	1.3	1.7	2.0	2.3	2.6	2.7	2.7	2.7	3.0	3.5	4.3	4.8	6.1	6.2	6.8	8.4	10.2	11.4
	Constant	1.6	2.1	2.4	2.7	3.0	3.2	2.9	2.7	2.9	3.3	3.5	3.0	4.1	3.9	4.0	4.7	5.1	5.2
% Military R&D in current dollars		46.2	41.2	45.0	39.1	30.8	29.6	25.9	22.0	20.0	20.0	20.9	20.8	19.7	19.4	17.6	20.2	21.6	23.7
Total R&D as % of GNP	Current	1.8	2.1	2.3	2.4	2.5	2.5	2.2	2.1	2.1	2.0	1.9	2.1	2.0	2.0	2.1	2.0	2.1	2.1
	Constant	2.2	2.6	2.7	2.8	2.9	2.9	2.4	2.1	2.1	1.9	1.6	1.3	1.4	1.3	1.2	1.1	1.0	.9
Military R&D as % of GNP	Current	.8	.9	1.0	.9	.8	.7	.6	.5	.4	.4	.4	.4	.4	.4	.4	.4	.4	.5
	Constant	.9	1.1	1.1	1.2	.9	.9	.6	.5	.4	.4	.4	.3	.3	.2	.2	.2	.2	.2
Military R&D as % of Defense Spending	Current	15.8	17.5	21.4	20.0	16.7	15.7	13.7	12.2	11.5	11.3	11.5	12.5	11.8	11.4	10.1	11.3	12.2	12.9
	Constant	18.4	22.5	23.8	24.4	18.8	19.6	13.7	12.2	11.5	11.3	10.3	7.5	7.8	6.7	5.9	6.0	6.1	5.7
GNP	Current	73.7	82.0	87.7	94.9	103.7	110.0	121.0	125.6	140.8	171.4	223.1	233.8	300.6	307.7	330.3	416.4	489.7	551.8

Sources: For 1963-1970, see Jean-Bernard Pinatel et al., *L'Economie des forces* (Paris: Les Cahiers de la Fondation pour les Etudes de Défense Nationale, 1976), p. 160; for 1971-1980, see France. Assemblée Nationale. Commission des Finances (1980), *Rapport sur le projet de loi de finances pour 1981, Défense: Considérations Générales, Dépenses en Capital*, No. 1976, pp. 161-162. Exchange rates and industrial index deflators are drawn from Table 3-3, note j.

ing, while gradually declining in the late 1960s, still averaged approximately one-third of the government's outlays for R&D during this period, even in the lean years of the middle 1970s.[124]

Much of the fillip in R&D spending in the early years of the Fifth Republic was attributable to France's nuclear industry. Throughout this period, more funds were transferred from the defense budget to the Atomic Energy Commission than was spent on all other military R&D programs.[125] The Ministry of Defense underwrote more than $5 billion in new construction for the nuclear industry, including over $1 billion for the enrichment plant at Pierrelatte, a half-billion dollars for the reprocessing facility at la Hague, and an additional half-billion dollars or more for two Celestin reactors and the Gymnote, the prototype nuclear power plant for France's strategic submarine fleet.[126] The economic fruits of these expenditures were realized a decade later when France emerged as a leading civilian nuclear exporter capable of furnishing services, material, and know-how covering the entire fuel cycle.

Second, after 1968 and for the decade thereafter, French spending on military R&D declined, whether measured as a proportion of overall governmental spending, GNP, or defense expenditures. Two factors explain the downturn. The most important again was the May uprising in 1968 which compelled overall lower defense spending and, within the defense budget, a higher rate of expenditures on military personnel and welfare than before. The second and less visible factor was the preference of the Pompidou and the early Giscard-Barre governments for increased spending on civilian R&D directly rather than for awaiting the trickle-down effects of defense spending, relied upon by the de Gaulle administration. Military R&D as a percentage of GNP or of the defense budget remained essentially static throughout the period of the third program-law from 1970 to 1975.

One unanticipated effect of the temporary shift away from governmental financing of military R&D was to catalyze arms industry leaders to expand arms exports and to multiply cooperative accords with other producers to gain access to needed outside funding for increasingly costly R&D programs.[127] Following the logic, if not the spirit, of Gaullist thinking, R&D funds were actually siphoned from the arms side of the industries supporting weapons production to the civilian side of these units. These shifts were most pronounced in the aerospace and electronics industries. Contrary to Gaullist assumptions, the arms industry was supposed to lead civilian sectors, not to be leaned upon, with possible adverse repercussions on its long-term competitiveness in international markets.

Figures 3-10 and 3-11 suggest these trends. Figure 3-10 plots current and constant dollar spending on military R&D. The hump in the 1960s is

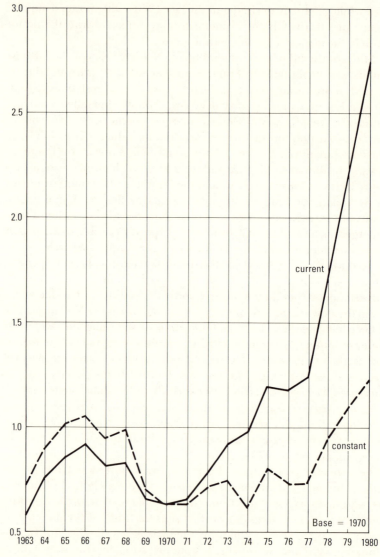

FIGURE 3-10

Current and Constant Military Research and Development Expenditures: 1963-1980 (In billions of dollars)

SOURCE: See Table 3-8 and Table 3-3, note j.

FIGURE 3-11

Total Civilian and Military Research and Development Expenditures: 1963-1980 (In billions of constant dollars, base 1970)

SOURCE: See Table 3-8.

attributable to the force de frappe. The 1969-1970 trough reflects decreased spending on defense forced by domestic upheaval. The dip in R&D spending in 1973-1974, measured in constant 1970 dollars, is attributable to the oil crisis and a steep rise in the rate of inflation. An upturn in military R&D does not occur until 1977, the first year of the fourth program-law. Figure 3-11 compares civilian and military spending for R&D in constant dollars. While military spending continues on an even course, spending on civilian R&D mounts through the 1970s. This includes government outlays and increased reliance on self-financing by firms. Between 1966 and 1975, the share of R&D funds contributed by industry as a percentage of the national total rose from 53.8 percent to 64.4 percent. Half of this increase occurred in 1969 and was due to increased governmental expenditures on welfare.[128]

In response to sustained internal criticisms within the government, rising principally from the Gaullist wing of the governmental coalition, the rate of military R&D spending was increased in the late 1970s, a trend continued under the Socialist government at a higher level than a decade earlier. By one accounting, the proportion of central governmental expenditures for military R&D climbed through the late 1970s from 32.5 percent in 1976 to 39 percent in 1979.[129] In the last year of the Giscard d'Estaing administration, spending for military R&D reached, as Table 3-8 notes, almost 24 percent of all spending from public and private sources. The Mitterrand government appears to have, proportionately, slipped somewhat below this high. Through the early 1980s, military R&D accounted for about one-third of all governmental expenditures for R&D and about 70 percent of what flowed to this area from all avenues.[130] Viewed from still another perspective, the proportion of the defense budget devoted to R&D broke through the 12 percent barrier in 1982, rising to 13.6 percent but subsequently dropping again to 12.5 percent in 1983 and 1984. Economic setbacks in 1982 made it difficult to sustain the higher rate.[131]

The modest upturn in R&D spending in the late 1970s and 1980s did not prevent serious program cuts. The Future Combat Aircraft had to be scrapped and the Air Force had to settle for the single-engine Mirage 2000 whose technology approached that of the F-16, which was on line for almost a decade before the appearance of the French fighter. In 1977 the Army dropped plans for a new generation of helicopters. A year later slowdowns were ordered on several important programs, including the cruise missile, observation satellites, and low altitude radar. The Navy was also prevented from initiating needed studies on several projects. A Ministry of Defense study warily concluded that "such a situation was all the more harmful since, alone, a sustained policy of research had permitted the Directorate for Naval Construction to achieve the development of weapon systems competitive on an international level and capable of assuring arsenals of export outlets."[132] The huge sale of naval and air defense equipment to Saudi Arabia may soften the edge of this criticism, but the problem facing the arms industry of remaining viable in all areas of military technology remains formidable.

The Mirage 2000 program and the cancellations and cutbacks experienced in other areas, particularly in conventional arms, have underscored a serious problem for France's arms industry. There is the grave risk that weapons programs will be completed at so late a date through continued delays and slowdowns that the weapons which are produced will be obsolete before they become operational. French forces may not be equipped to match their battlefield opponents. French arms exports may also be threatened as clients turn to other suppliers, particularly to the superpowers, to meet their enlarging needs. The Saudi insistence on the American F-15 aircraft, a twin-engine fighter superior to the Mirage 2000, suggested how important technological progress is for the maintenance of France's arms industry. The French were dealt another blow when Riyadh turned to the Tornado over the Mirage 2000. France's comparative advantage may well erode if the prestige and military effectiveness enjoyed by clients in purchasing state-of-the-art weapons as well as friends in western capitals offset the political advantages that France can offer.

The expectations of the de Gaulle government about the civilian benefits of a modernized arms industry have been only partially realized. The success of the civilian nuclear energy program, whatever its drawbacks, cannot be gainsaid. The same cannot be said for France's efforts to enter the civilian aircraft market. Billions of dollars were lost on the Concorde, Mercure, and A-300 projects with no appreciable impact being made on the American share of the global market for medium- and long-haul civilian aircraft. Several of the sixteen Concordes that were produced have yet to be sold and production has terminated. As a short-distance carrier, Dassault's Mercure was a commercial failure. It was forced on government-controlled airlines in France, but flopped with foreign carriers. The initial Airbus program with Great Britain also suffered major losses until it was reorganized under Franco-German direction. Important parts of the A-300 B follow-on aircraft were purchased off the shelf from American producers rather than redeveloped at great cost by European firms.[133]

French security interests and technological aspirations were also hampered by foiled efforts to penetrate the world computer field. Prompted partly by the refusal of the United States to sell France scientific computers needed for the operation of the force de frappe, French planners developed the ill-fated Plan Calcul to make France a leader in computer technology. American firms controlled 75 percent of France's computer market and threatened to expand their predominant position through takeovers of French firms, like Machine Bull, by General Electric (GE). Plan Calcul led to the formation in 1967 of CII (Compagnie Internationale de l'Informatique), a creature of three French electronics firms (CSF, CGE, and Schneider). Aided by government subsidies, tariff protection, and a guaranteed domestic market, CII was designated the national champion to do battle with American firms for France's home market. Once having gained a strong base of operations on the domestic front, it was expected to sally forth into the international arena. Chronic financial losses and slow technological progress in swiftly moving competitive markets forced the Giscard d'Estaing government to cut CII loose and sell control of the firm to Honeywell-Bull, which had since purchased GE's share of Machine Bull. American dominance of France's computer market and the throttling of its national champion have seriously limited French aspirations to be fully autonomous and competitive in world markets in this key defense-related industry.[134]

These setbacks in computer or other high technology areas, like color television, can be exaggerated.[135] Despite reversals and the dashed hopes of the Mitterrand government to engineer a rapid economic recovery, France is still a major industrial and trading power, thanks partly to the success of arms and military technology sales. On the other hand, key technologically advanced industries and the principal firms within them are still heavily dependent on military production for their revenue and, increasingly, on foreign markets to maintain production and R&D programs at accustomed levels. Thomson-Brandt, France's major electronics firm, owes much of its turnaround in profits in the middle 1980s to the sale of an air defense system to Riyadh which builds on the Shahine ground-to-air missile designed for Saudi armed forces.[136] There is something to be said for the proposition that the Fifth Republic was more successful in building a profitable arms industry than in using the arms industry to develop economically competitive high technology industries in the civilian sector. Reconversion from military to civilian production has been more difficult than anticipated by French political and industrial leaders.[137] For many in the arms industry such a reorientation away from arms production is a dubious alternative since it would weaken France's comparative advantage in weapons production. From this perspective, the growth of France's arms exports and the dependency of the arms industry on them is viewed more as an opportunity than as a threat. Table 3-9 traces business turnover in the arms industry from 1960 to 1980. It comes as no surprise that exports comprise an increased share of the value of all arms produced. Approximately 40 percent of the productive capacity of the French arms industry was devoted to exports in 1980. Less than 10 percent was sent abroad in 1960, and as late as 1971, arms exports were below 20 percent of business turnover.

It should be noted that the value of arms production relative to GNP was slightly less in 1980 (2.76 percent) than in the period 1965-1967 at

Table 3-9. Business Turnover Measured as the Sum of Domestic Arms Procurement (Title V and VI) and Arms Deliveries: 1960-1980 (In billions of current dollars)

	Domestic Procurement (A)	Delivery of Arms to Other States (B)	Total (A) + (B)	Percentage of Arms Deliveries to Arms Produced	Percentage of Arms Deliveries to Domestic Procurement
1960	1.21	.10	1.31	7.6	8.3
1961	1.15	.20	1.35	14.8	17.4
1962	1.17	.20	1.37	14.6	17.1
1963	1.57	.30	1.87	16.0	19.1
1964	1.84	.40	2.24	17.9	21.7
1965	2.11	.40	2.51	15.9	19.0
1966	2.28	.40	2.68	14.9	17.5
1967	2.49	.50	2.99	16.7	20.1
1968	2.53	.50	3.03	16.5	19.8
1969	2.49	.40	2.89	13.8	16.1
1970	2.31	.50	2.81	17.8	21.6
1971	2.37	.50	2.87	17.4	21.1
1972	2.83	.80	3.63	22.0	28.3
1973	3.58	1.20	4.78	24.1	31.8
1974	3.55	1.40	4.95	27.2	37.5
1975	4.45	1.90	6.35	30.4	43.7
1976	4.38	2.40	6.78	37.7	55.6
1977	4.87	3.00	7.87	38.1	61.4
1978	6.31	3.80	10.11	37.6	60.2
1979	7.83	4.80	12.63	38.0	61.3
1980	9.44	5.80	15.24	38.1	61.4

SOURCES: See Table 3-3. Export data are taken from International Monetary Fund, *International Financial Statistics, 1977*, XXI, No. 5 (May 1977).

the height of spending on the force de frappe when arms exports were below 20 percent of total military production. In these three middle years, the ratio of arms production to GNP ranged between 2.82 and 2.88 percent. The arms industry has therefore expanded in tandem with the growth of France's economy while contributing more than most domestic industries to its progressive foreign orientation. The gross formation of fixed capital in the 1970s reflects this pattern. National accounts indicate that fixed capital in the arms industry grew at a rate comparable to the growth in the national economy, which doubled in current value between 1973 and 1979.[138]

The aerospace and electronics industries remain heavily dependent on arms production for business turnover and on foreign sales to show a profit and to finance their research and development programs. Figures 3-12 and 3-13 sketch the evolution of business turnover, respectively, for professional electronic equipment and aerospace materiel. Receipts from foreign and domestic military orders have always been more than 50 percent of business turnover in this sector of the electronics industry. Exports have also steadily grown to replace the declining demand of the domestic defense establishment. The dependency on military production is even more pronounced in the aerospace industry. In 1977 and 1978, military deliveries made up 74 percent of the industry's production. Three-fifths of this amount was sent abroad.

These patterns of dependency of high technology industries on arms production and foreign sales are reinforced if one examines what is happening at the individual firm level. Table 3-10 selectively identifies major French arms producers for 1978 and 1983. It profiles the percentage of business activity devoted to civilian and military production as well as the relative ratios of French military purchases to foreign arms sales of France's leading arsenals, firms, and nationalized corporations in the arms industry for 1978.[139] Most of its units are either run by the government (arsenals and personnel of DGA) or controlled through public corporations (SNIAS, SNECMA, SNPE), or directed through government ownership of a majority share of stock (Dassault, Matra, Thomson-Brandt).

In the aerospace industry, all of the major firms depend on military contracts for most of their work. France's four leading aerospace firms are especially tied to foreign arms sales. Aérospatiale (SNIAS), France's largest aerospace group, depends on military sales for approximately 60 percent of its receipts; 40 to 50 percent of its activity is attributable to foreign military sales, principally tactical missiles and helicopters. A separate division within Aérospatiale is responsible for developing strategic missiles for France's ground- and sea-based deterrents. In 1978,

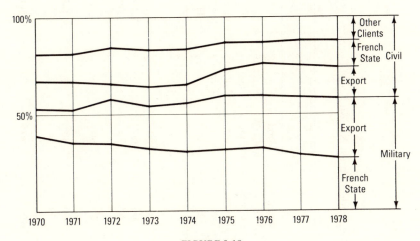

FIGURE 3-12

Business Turnover of the Professional Electronic Equipment Industry: 1970-1978
SOURCE: France, Ministère de la Défense, *Données économiques sur les dépenses militaires* (Paris, 1978), Chapter 10.

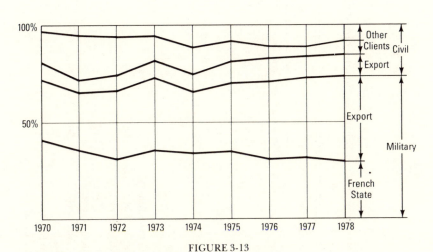

FIGURE 3-13

Business Turnover of the Aerospace Industry: 1970-1978
SOURCE: France, Ministère de la Défense, *Données économiques sur les dépenses militaires* (Paris, 1978), Chapter 10.

Table 3-10. Proportion of Business Turnover of Major Arms Producers Dependent upon National and Foreign Arms Purchases: 1978 and 1983

	Ranking[a] Among French Firms in Turnover A	1978 Civilian: French and Foreign Purchases B	1978 Percentage of French arms Purchases C	1978 Percentage of Military Exports D	1978 Total Military Business Turnover E	1983 Total Military Business Turnover[c] F	1983 Percentage of Military Exports G	1983 Workforce H
Aeronautics								
DGA	—	—	100	—	100	100	—	53,000
SEP (Missile Propulsion)	—	40	59	1	60	60	—	3,300
SNECMA (Aircraft Motors)	73	17	36	47	83	75	60	13,000
Turbomeca (Aircraft Motors)	210	47	35	18	53	60	60	4,500
SNIAS (Helicopters, Missiles, Aircraft)	30	40	29	41	60	60	50	34,000
Matra (Missiles)	63	41	27	32	59	40	75	6,000
Dassault-Bréguet[a] (Fighter Aircraft)	38	9	22	69	91	90	70	15,800

Ground armaments								
DGA (Arsenals)	—	0.5	57	42.5	99.5	100	40	7,500
Manurhin	205	21	19	60	79	80	60	4,500
Luchaire	181	66	13	21	34	35	60	5,000
Thomson-Brandt[b]	—	88	1	11	12	—	—	—
Panhard	—	—	1	99	100	100	95	800
Naval armaments								
DGA (Arsenals)	—	4	91	5	96	95	5	12,500
CMN	—	3	1	96	97	—	—	—
Electronics								
EMD[a]	—	23	26	51	77	70	70	2,000
Thomson-CSF[b]	—	47	18	35	53	70	60	107,000
Explosives								
SNPE	189	36	42	22	64	70	50	6,900

SOURCES: For 1978, France, Ministère de la Défense, *Données économiques sur les dépenses militaires* (Paris, 1978), Chapter 8. Figures for 1983 are adapted from Pierre Dussauge, *L'Industrie française de l'armement* (Paris: Economica, 1985), pp. 19-23.

[a] Includes Dassault-Bréguet and Electricité Marcel (later Serge) Dassault.

[b] Thomson-Brandt, one of France's leading corporations and multinationals, has an armaments division, Brandt Armement, which exports 80 percent of its production of ground equipment, munitions, and aerospatial material. Thomson-CSF is an affiliate of Thomson-Brandt and is France's principal firm devoted to military electronics.

[c] Columns E and F compare, respectively, turnover due to military sales for 1978 and 1983. Column E is the sum of percentages of columns C and D.

Dassault, France's second largest aerospace firm, relied on foreign sales for almost 70 percent of its business turnover. Throughout the 1970s and into the 1980s, more than 60 percent of its annual production, on the average, was for foreign governments.[140] Over 90 percent of Dassault's production was military. The next largest aeronautics firms, SNECMA and Matra, owed 47 and 32 percent respectively of their business receipts in 1978 to foreign military buyers. While both are attempting to diversify their production to civilian purposes, their military sales still rely heavily on exports, actually increasing for Matra in 1983.

Other important sectors of the French arms industry are similarly dependent on foreign contracts. National arsenals producing ground equipment export over 40 percent of their work to other countries. Manurhin, a high technology firm in ground equipment, earns three times as much from military exports as from domestic arms purchases by French armed forces. Panhard, a producer of motorized small armor, primarily exploits the international arms market. The electronics firm of Dassault exports approximately three-quarters of its military production. Thomson-CSF, France's principal military electronics firm, owed more than a half of its business turnover in 1983 to military exports, increasing its dependency over the 1970s, largely as a consequence of the multibillion-dollar sale of air defense equipment to Saudi Arabia.

As Table 3-10 suggests, exports of naval vessels have lagged behind those of other arms sectors. The government-run yards principally respond to French needs, primarily surface ships and nuclear submarines. Smaller private firms, like Construction Mécanique de Normandie (CMN), build fast patrol boats, mine sweepers and coastal craft, primarily for foreign purchasers. Finally, the Société Nationale des Poudres et Explosifs (SNPE) owed one-fifth of its production to foreign arms contracts in 1978, increasing to one-half in 1983.

Whether France's arms industry will continue to be responsive to the needs of its military forces and to flourish as an important sector of France's economy will depend on its ability to keep pace with rapid technological change and the rising cost of creating and manufacturing new arms. Its past achievements as a producer of modern arms, as a technological innovator, and as a national commercial asset cannot obscure the problems that lie ahead. France's limited resources and the sharp domestic constraints that have been placed on defense spending and on research and development programs trace the parameters of the ability of France's arms industry to provide French forces the weapons they need. Arms sales have extended but not effaced these limits.

Trouble signs are everywhere. As Chapter 6 details, France faces increased competition from arms suppliers in western Europe and the developing world. Since the 1960s France has also been a net importer of technology. In 1973 technological deficits stood at approximately $71 million and jumped to $250 million just a year later. The deficits in 1975 and 1976 were also high, reaching almost $200 and $250 million, respectively. The French have also been unable to cover their technological purchases abroad. Even in 1975, one of France's best years, the rate of coverage of technological imports over exports was only 51.2 percent. The trend in technological exports over imports does not appear encouraging. If one uses an index of imports and exports of technological transfers based on 1963 prices, spending on foreign technology progressed from 100 in 1963 prices to 324 in 1974, while receipts received by French firms progressed from 100 to 289. France's relative position with respect to the value of technological imports during this period did not improve and may be said to have even slipped somewhat.[141] At the same time, France's competitors forged onward. The Pentagon's budget for R&D is at least six times as large as France's for military R&D; the United States spends 1.7 times as much as the entire European Community on civilian and military R&D.[142] France stands behind Japan, Canada, and West Germany in the percent of funds expended by businesses for R&D. It also is far below other developed states in the number of scientists and engineers engaged in R&D per 10,000 labor force members. With 30 per 10,000, France was in 1978 surpassed by West Germany (45), Japan (50), the United States (58), and the Soviet Union (82).[143]

Domestic restraints, a faltering international economic position, and an unbridled superpower arms race confront France with a difficult choice—to continue along a national course in arms production and development and risk being outdistanced, or to break sharply with the past and seek greater cooperation with its Western allies whether in a European or Atlantic framework, but at the expense of its political and economic independence. French leaders are not oblivious to the choice. Witness the initiatives and pronouncements of President Mitterrand and Defense Minister Charles Hernu, discussed earlier. Cooperation in selected arms development programs with other European states has been rationalized as an economic and technological necessity. So also has tolerance of foreign influence and control over key segments of French industry which are closely associated with arms development. These deviations from the norm of French conduct do not suggest necessarily a wholesale abandonment of principle. That may be forced on French leaders if the domestic and foreign limits within which the defense industry must operate cannot be extended or if they grow narrower and more financially and technologically problematic in the future.

Conclusions

The arms industry merges the security and welfare functions of the French state. This fusion overcomes previous attitudinal, conceptual, and institutional obstacles that had previously tended to separate the state's defense and economic activities. Military preparations, even among the patriotically motivated, had been viewed traditionaly in negative terms as a burden on the national treasury and a lien on private gain and corporate profits. The creation of the force de dissuasion, linked to the larger postwar effort to renovate and modernize the French economy, transformed the image of the military establishment as a barrier to France's reemergence as a world industrial power, to one of a center for scientific discovery and technological innovation, and an asset in the production of national wealth.

Attitude and image gave way to a new conception of the role of defense in responding not only to security but also to the state's welfare imperatives. The elites in control of the state's machinery and the arms industry became convinced and perpetuated the view that the arms industry generated both security and welfare benefits. Arms production could stimulate economic growth. As an integral part of the development of the French economy, the arms industry would make resources available for more and better arms. The choice, then, was not between guns and butter. There would be more butter if France produced more guns—especially to meet rising foreign demand.

The decision to produce more arms for domestic and foreign consumption was never put to an electoral or legislative test as it had been in England in the 1960s or, given the vicissitudes of American politics, as it has been periodically posed in the self-contradictory approach of the United States to arms and military technology sales since World War II. The choice to produce and sell increasingly more arms was taken at the highest levels of the French government during the Gaullist years and subsequently reaffirmed, with different degrees of enthusiasm and acquiescence, by succeeding administrations on the Right and Left.

Elites across the political spectrum and the French public now accept the arms industry as a national asset. It has assumed something of the sacred-cow status of the force de dissuasion. Support for the arms complex, as for nuclear weapons, has been built from the top down. Consent has been minted in the coinage of the comparative advantages marking the arms industry: successful penetration of foreign markets; a global sales network; universally marketable, if lethal, products; a high ratio of domestic added value to the market worth of arms exports; a major source of job creation and maintenance, especially in advanced technological sectors; significant contribution to France's balance of payments solvency arising from sustained surpluses of arms exports over imports; and the availability of a wide array of equipment and weapons with which to barter for raw materials in short supply.

The Ministry of Defense is at the center of the decisional process of arms acquisition and sales. In command of the largest budget within the government and with access to approximately 4 percent of disposable GNP, the Minister of Defense has a pervasive impact on the priorities of the French economy and on its structure. The defense ministry plays a critical role in determining how much will be spent on arms for military preparations; the division between arms production for domestic consumption and foreign sales; the level and direction of research and development expenditures; the degree to which the state will direct these spending and production activities or consign them to market forces; the proportion of national resources that will be invested in the arms industry to meet future security and economic needs; and the use of arms sales (or their prohibition and regulation) to promote the foreign and security objectives of the nation.

The contradictory demands of national security and solvency are by no means resolved by housing them within the defense establishment or in delegating them to the techno-scientific-military-industrial complex for decision. The next two chapters outline the industrial concentration of the French arms industry and the decisional process within the French security community concerned with the acquisition and transfer of arms and military technology and assess the effectiveness of this decisional process in balancing security and welfare imperatives and in meeting minimal norms of democratic conduct.

Part III.
Arms and the State

CHAPTER 4

National Champions and
the French Fifth Republic

BY THE 1970s, as the preceding chapters argue, public consensus had been reached on two controversial issues: France's nuclear strike force and the level of permissible defense expenditures. The election of the Socialist government in 1981 confirmed the commitment of the Left to the force de dissuasion. Spending limits on defense were also affirmed. This broadly based consensus established the outer boundaries of the political authority of the arms complex viewed as an autonomous political system within the governmental structure and decisional processes of the Fifth Republic.

Within the political sphere marked by the evolving consensus on military strategy and expenditures, the arms complex has become a government within a government with its own rules, interests, aims, and priorities. While its power and prosperity ultimately depend on how well it responds to governmental and societal needs for security and welfare, it also has formidable resources and influence to elicit the political and economic support for what it wants as the price for its cooperation. Through skillful self-promotion it can also create demands for its goods and services. The widely shared belief of elites within the arms industry, that the production and sale of arms stimulates civilian economic development and strengthens France's competitive position in world markets, has not been seriously challenged by opponents at home or abroad. While there is no want of public lament about France's dependence on arms sales, there has been no serious attempt to curb the arms industry. Indeed, the spending limits on domestic arms purchases and the decreasing rate of governmental expenditures devoted to defense have spurred the leadership of the arms complex to expand sales abroad, to strike cooperative arrangements with other foreign producers, and even to seek foreign investment—witness the accords with South Africa and Saudi Arabia—to ensure its stability and influence. The arms complex enjoys considerable prestige, and its claims on resources within the defense community, particularly for its most technologically advanced sectors in avionics and missiles, electronics, and nuclear energy, remain steady and strong.

How then is the arms acquisition and production system organized and who are the principal players? How are actors directed and governed, and how are weapons and arms priorities decided? And to what extent are the arms complex and its governing mechanisms susceptible to democratic accountability, defined by electoral and parliamentary controls?

The French have answered the first question through the concentration of the arms industry within its principal sectors, including avionics and missiles, electronics, ground and naval equipment, nuclear energy, conventional munitions and propulsion systems. This chapter traces the gradual centralization of the arms industry and the nationalization of its principal components. Chapter 5 describes the governmental process within the arms complex, how weapons systems are chosen, priorities established, and arms sales regulated. It also evaluates arms politics and governance from the perspective of democratic control and accountability.

WHAT IS THE ARMS INDUSTRY?

It is well to keep in mind that defining the arms industry is a more difficult task than may at first appear. From a military or strategic perspective, it is seen primarily as an extension of the armed forces. Viewed in this light it is part of the equipment, logistics, and repair system of the armed forces. From this vantage point, what counts is weapons performance in battle, their timely availability in adequate quantities and quality to impose coercive controls on an enemy, and their ability to deter attacks on vital state interests. This is the common understanding of the arms industry defined by the lethal character of its products. The arms industry becomes simply all those units which make arms.[1]

The French also look at the arms industry as a producer of saleable items in international markets. Buyer preferences turn only partially on weapons performance. Terms of sales, repair services and spare parts, instruction of cadres in weapons use, and opportunities for licensed production become critical features of the arms industry, understood as a commercial enterprise. The commercialization of arms requires a global sales structure and promotional campaigns, after-sale (après vente) training and service, export subsidies, and the availability of credit and financing for potential buyers. These activities imply a larger number of institutional arrangements than are traditionally included within an arms industry rubric. Included within the arms industry must be banking and commercial credit institutions, insurance, export agencies, and the assumption of enlarged commercial responsibilities by the armed forces. Brought into play, as suggested earlier, is an entirely new tier of support and services from the private and public sectors. These units are, if you will, valets, serving the many needs of a complex arms master.

The arms industry may also be seen not as a product but as a process. The engineers and technocrats in control of the arms complex are particularly attracted to this characterization. Under this guise, the lethality of the product or its commercial possibilities are of lesser consequence than the scientific, technological, and industrial processes—or the collection of these processes—that animate the work of those engaged in designing and producing arms and military know-how. Protecting and perfecting these processes assume new historic dimensions under conditions of nuclear weapons. Nuclear arsenals are created and subsequently modernized to prevent wars, not fight them. If military preparedness is more important than mobilization, it follows that maintaining an up-to-date nuclear weapons plant that meets the changing techno-scientific requirements of deterrence is of equal importance with the weapons themselves. Modern arms are like the tires of an automobile which must be changed while the car is in motion. What is ultimately important in an era of rapid scientific discovery and technological innovation is the arms industry's capacity for change and adaptability; otherwise it will be unable to respond to the needs of the military services.

The same reasoning may be applied to conventional arms whose performance characteristics—destructive power, range, accuracy, reliability, and vulnerability—are subject to scientific findings and their technological and industrial exploitation lie well beyond the use or threat of arms governed by military tactics and strategy. Nor is it enough to look at arms as a commercial product, like any other, to capture the notion of an independent system of activity that is the source of the lethality and saleability of weapons products. An implication of this line of reasoning, as one leading member of the French arms complex suggests,[2] is that the so-called civilian fallout of military arms production should not be defined by products but by industrial processes. Fallout is measured by the advancement of technological units and economic agents capable of survival and growth in an international market. From this perspective it is more important that the arms complex survives and grows as a competitive system than that it simply sells goods and services, classified as military or civilian end-items.

Both arms products and processes may also be seen as status symbols of a nation's power and position. The arms industry becomes as much an end in itself as a tool of foreign policy. This is a persistent theme of official French pronouncements and a perennial of the French political landscape, long recognized by close observers of French industrial development.[3] It also explains such commercially doubtful ventures as the Concorde. Pride in what the French have wrought on their own in new areas of technology—nuclear energy, avionics, electronics—characterizes the promotional materials issuing from the arms industry.[4] French arms makers have even had the cheek to chide their allies when French arms have been successfully employed to destroy or damage allied military forces. Aérospatiale purchased a full-page ad in the *Economist* to vaunt the lethal efficiency of Exocet missiles in sinking British warships and cargo vessels in the Falklands War.[5] These feats are viewed as France's answer to the challenge posed by competitors, principally identified as American multinationals, which are portrayed as determined to undermine French competitiveness and independence.[6] Recapturing French industry and domestic markets to prevent foreign domination by multinational corporations has been a widely shared value among elites within the arms complex and a persistent theme of French industrial policy. The concentration of resources on a national champion within key industrial sectors of the arms industry has been the preferred strategy in doing battle with foreign competitors.

Concentration of the Armaments Industry

A glimpse of the concentration process also reveals the rocky and tortuous path along which industrial consolidation has progressed. The forces urging concentration were by no means mutually reinforcing nor were those groups pressing for concentration within and outside the bureaucracy always in lock step either with respect to the priorities and interests that were to be served or to the timing and opportunities for each move leading to greater centralization of weapons design and production.

While mapping the entire play of aims and actor interests over the concentration issue falls beyond the scope of this study, some understanding of this struggle and its outcome is important to explain French resistance to international controls on the sale of military technology and arms. It cautions against the easy but suspect expectation that French cooperation in controlling arms transfers can be readily achieved once the dangers of arms sales are exposed. The leadership of the military-industrial complex ultimately captured the concentration process and shaped it to suit its own needs and interests. Nationalized and private firms and arsenals have enlarged their clout in dealing with other segments of the French administrative state which might seek to curb their activities or to compel them to accept restraints. When the needs of French arms makers in adapting to the competitive demands of the international market conflict with proposed arms control accords, the arms complex disposes powerful means to have its way and say within the bureaucracy and French state.

A distinction should be drawn first between the principles of concentration and nationalization. The Right and Left have generally favored concentration in the arms industry. Majority sentiment in each camp has shared many of the same aims associated with concentration: large economic units to compete effectively against multinational corporations, particularly American and, increasingly, Japanese firms; reconquest of France's domestic markets from foreign competitors; the utility of foreign competition as a spur to domestic efficiency as compensation for the gradual suppression of internal competition; the necessity to concentrate resources in specialized firms—national champions—to meet the rising costs of research and development, especially in high technology areas in the civil and military sectors; a French-based arms plant to meet national defense needs; the maximization of corporate profits, whether under private or public management; and the preservation of technical prowess and entrepreneurial dynamism at the unit or firm level to assure all of the above.[7]

Aside from matters of principle, pitting advocates of free market against those favoring a socialized economy, opposition to nationalization was grounded in several reinforcing concerns: that it would be costly and regressive and that it would retard progress toward the concentration and rationalization of French industry to serve the shared economic goals of the Right and Left. The long involvement of the state in economic affairs also tempered the intensity and scope of opposition to nationalization. As one critic of the Mitterrand government's scheme to nationalize key segments of the arms industry remarked: "I remain confounded to see the . . . Secretary of State, M. Le Garrec, write: 'We will not play with tinker toys.' Incredible! It is not clear why one nationalizes. . . . If it is in order to rigidify firms without striving for reorganizations and reinforcements of the structure, it is absurd! What does nationalization serve if not to rationalize [the industrial structure]?"[8] Concentration was not the issue. Achieving it in a way responsive to global competitive imperatives was at the center of concern of opponents and proponents of nationalization.

Concentration raised several questions to which nationalization offered partial answers. Who would lead and manage the arms industry and the sprawling array of its separate units? Should the leadership be concentrated in the hands of public officials or corporate firms? Who would control the balance of power in arbitrating differences over objectives, strategies, and resource allocations? Who also would bear the burdens and enjoy the benefits of industrial concentration—corporate owners and managers, political leaders and functionaries, technicians or workers, consumers, or the general public? The battles over industrial concentration have been fought over these questions rather than over the principle of concentration per se. The nationalization program of the Mitterrand government, the third such surge in this century, may be viewed as an assertion of previously disenfranchised groups to participate in the concentration process, to exercise influence in areas of the public domain from which they had been previously excluded, and to extract material benefits and even ideological and psychic satisfaction from the nationalization of those few remaining large firms outside the reach of state ownership and control. As the following chapter suggests, it is by no means clear that public ownership of the means of production will narrow the discretionary power and authority of public managers and elites, including highly skilled technicians and administrative personnel, to assert their interests over those of passing political authorities in quest of support from a volatile and distracted electorate. Nor can it be said that nationalization will ensure larger and more effective expression of worker, consumer, and citizen interests in the allocation of corporate authority and public resources, as proponents of nationalization claim.[9]

A brief sketch of the process of concentration within the armaments sector suggests how entrenched are elite, business, and bureaucratic interests. More importantly, such a review highlights the tight resource constraints within which the French decision-makers must work as they attempt, through industrial reorganization efforts like those of the armaments industry, to meet the competing imperatives of national independence and economic welfare within what is still a liberal trading system at home and abroad. The French face these dilemmas: on one hand, a credible national defense may be erected on an indigenous industrial base, but at an intolerable public cost and at the risk of destroying the international competitiveness of the French economy; on the other hand, the international competitiveness of French industry may be promoted but along lines of comparative advantage and specialization within an evolving global division of labor that, if accepted by the French, risks sacrificing national independence, resulting in a loss of control over national defense, arms design and production, and one's home markets. Not surprisingly, French planners have resisted these choices. Industrial concentration—a policy of designated national champions—has been one of the principal means used by French planners to relax the dilemmas confronting the French economy.

Aerospace Industry

Fighter Aircraft, Transport, and Missiles. Figure 4-1 sketches the concentration of the French airframe and engine industry from the first nationalization wave of the 1930s to those of the 1980s. The concentration is hardly unique to France. The high costs of research and development, the long lead times in producing civilian and military aircraft, and the risks of failure have led to mergers throughout the industry. These economic and technological factors are distinguishable from the political aims driving the nationalization of French firms in the 1930s, the immediate postwar period, and the takeovers of the 1980s. Partisans of nationalization have sought a larger public share of the profits of companies receiving governmental assistance; a greater degree of public participation in the direction and management of these industries; and, some, but a distinct minority, the eventual conversion of the arms industry to civilian production.

Currently, France's aerospace industry is a distant second to that of the United States whose business turnover is approximately six times greater and whose exports are three times as large. With half the number of personnel, the French aerospace industry has been able to surge slightly ahead of Great Britain and remains about twice as large in business turnover as West Germany, which is fourth worldwide. France's four principal aerospace firms are in the top twenty globally: Aérospatiale (9), Dassault-Bréguet (12), SNECMA (16), and Matra (18). In 1980, airframes and space accounted for 63 percent of turnover, while motors and equipment divided the remainder.[10]

The dominant position enjoyed by Avions Marcel Dassault-Bréguet Aviation (AMD-BA) was by no means clear and assured after World War II. Dassault's design teams were in competition with those of nationalized corporations and private firms, like Bréguet, for dominance of fighter aircraft production. Dassault's pursuit aircraft, the MD 450, powered by a Nene motor produced under license by Hispano, proved superior to the English Vampire, which SNCASE was planning to manufacture under license. A French Air Force order for 25 preseries and 300 copies of the Ouragan (not to mention Indian and Israeli purchases) aided Dassault in bringing its Mystère series to profitable production. American offshore purchases of 225 Mystères and French Air Force orders of an additional 100 copies built governmental confidence in the Dassault Corporation. Dassault's Mirage series proved so militarily effective and commercially promising that nationalized firms were gradually eased out of military airframe competition by the government. The war in Algeria and developing plans for a nuclear strike force also induced the Fourth Republic to concentrate on the Mirage.

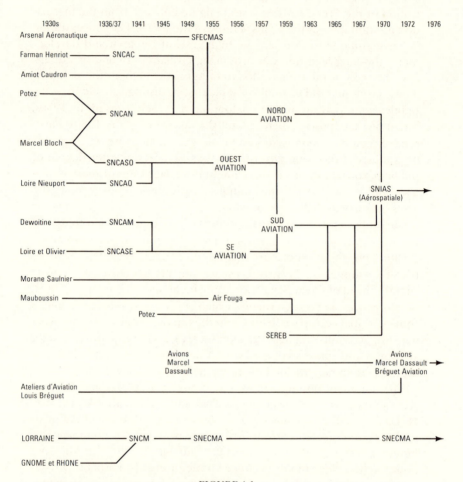

FIGURE 4-1

France: Airframe and Engine Company Mergers, 1930-1976

SOURCE: Yves Morau, "L'Aéronautique," *L'Industrie en France*, eds. Bertrand Bellon and Jean-Marie Chevalier (Paris: Flammarion, 1983), p. 255; Monique Bouleau, *Les Industries et l'exportation d'armes françaises en 1970*, Mémoire pour Diplôme d'Etudes Supérieures (Paris I, October 1972), p. 25.

Orders for Bréguet's Deux Pont aircraft and 50 Nord 2506 cargo planes from Nord-Avion were canceled. Support was withdrawn for studies by Sud-Aviation on the Super Vautour as was aid for the Trident III developed by Sud-Ouest.[11]

Dassault counted on research and development funds from the French government to mount its private ventures. Once it became the sole supplier for French fighter aircraft, this flow of assistance became progressively more steady and institutionalized, though relations between Dassault and the general staffs of the Air Force have not always been smooth. It has never been fully clear who tells whom what planes Air Force combat wings will fly.

The Dassault Corporation enjoyed still other forms of government assistance which strengthened the firm's monopolistic position. These included continuing aid for prototype development, export subsidies (e.g., 28 percent of the Mystère IV contract to India), and coverage of industrial tooling costs. The company expects a minimum of about 25 percent of its business turnover from the state to maintain its military programs.[12]

Assistance was also extended to Dassault for the purchase of F1 M53 aircraft to assist the firm's bargaining position in the sale of jet aircraft to NATO countries, although the Air Force was initially cool about the order which was made over its objections.[13] As noted earlier, the Air Force also had to absorb 50 Mirage fighters embargoed from delivery to Israel in 1967.[14]

The Dassault corporation has also had to adjust to the industrial policy of consolidation pressed by the de Gaulle, Pompidou, and Giscard d'Estaing administrations and, more recently, by the Socialist government. In 1967, as part of the policy of the second program-law to consolidate the aircraft industry, the Dassault Corporation was prodded to absorb financially ailing Bréguet Aviation. There was concern about Bréguet's ability to keep up its end of the Jaguar project with Great Britain. Dassault assumed oversight of the program, although management had serious reservations about the mediocre performance of the aircraft and the problems it posed for selling Mirages.[15]

Pressures for consolidation and greater governmental oversight of Dassault operations came from a different source in the 1970s. Marcel Dassault's reputation for behind-the-scenes influence over governmental policy had already become legendary. Dassault's personal manner—at once jealously private and publicly ostentatious—cultivated the image of a man apart; even one above the laws or limits binding lesser mortals. Few outsiders penetrated the inner councils of the Dassault

Corporation. Fears and suspicions about the reach of the corporation and its wily and ingenious head inevitably multiplied. Dassault's public success and demeanor fueled opposition. He used his parliamentary seat and senior status within the National Assembly to promote his corporation's interests. Large contributions were made to Gaullist party coffers. Constituents received parliamentary and personal favors to sustain electoral support for Dassault's retention of his legislative seat. A slick magazine and expensive ads in newspapers, promoting Dassault corporate and personal interests, rounded out the image of Dassault, as persona and corporate baron, in shameless pursuit of private gain over public good.

In the wake of embarrassing revelations about dubious in-house financial mismanagement practices in the early 1970s, the Dassault Corporation became a prime candidate for nationalization. The Common Program of the Socialist and Communist parties put Dassault at the top of its wish list for state ownership. It also became the target of an extraordinary parliamentary inquiry inspired by a coalition of Socialist and Communist deputies, in 1977, when details of financial embezzlement and hanky-panky by an officer of the firm were revealed in the press. To quiet domestic criticism, the Giscard d'Estaing administration, which had pursued an industrial policy favoring the private sector, felt constrained to acquire 20 percent of Dassault's equity in exchange for releasing the firm from reimbursements owed the state through production and export advances made by the government. Although the government failed to purchase the required one-third share to gain a legal veto over corporate policies, the voting that it retained in a personal arrangement with Dassault essentially provided the government with veto power over corporate decisions.[16]

Like Pauline in her perils, Dassault stayed the execution of nationalization once more after the Socialist victory of 1981. Marcel Dassault, as owner of the bulk of nonstate holdings in the firm, voluntarily relinquished 26 percent of his stock to the state, partly in compensation for a state waiver of inheritance taxes. The state was expected to purchase an additional 5 percent of Dassault holdings in the open market in order to gain majority control when combined with shares already owned. As a condition of Dassault's grant to the state, the Dassault firm was to be insulated from reorganization for five years, well within the period of the next legislative elections. Dassault's delaying tactics were vindicated in 1986 with the victory of a coalition of the Right opposed to nationalization.[17]

Figuring prominently in the negotiations with the government was the worry that any major change in Dassault management or leadership would have a damaging effect on the firm's competitiveness. Even its critics grudgingly concede Dassault's success, although they prefer to attribute Dassault profits to public support, assured by Marcel Dassault's *bras long*—his long political arm—as a major Gaullist financial supporter and parliamentarian rather than to his and his corporation's enterprise and skill.

The critical role played by the Dassault Corporation within the aeronautics industry is suggested by a comparison of Dassault's business turnover and exports with those of the industry as a whole. In the middle 1970s, Dassault accounted for approximately one-third of the business receipts of the air industry and almost one-half of its exports. Military exports[18] bulked large in Dassault's exports; less than 10 percent of its foreign and domestic deliveries were for civilian aircraft.[19] The business generated by AMD-BA for other French firms was also significant. Over one-half of the receipts received in purchase of the Mirage III and 5 were garnered by Aérospatiale and French subcontractors. A little more than 40 percent of the receipts on the F1 was earned by these latter firms. The firm of AMD-BA received approximately one-third of the receipts for the Mirage III and 5 and a little less than 45 percent of the receipts for the F1.[20] Between 1976 and 1980 the price of Dassault stock rose from 245 francs to 1,105, or slightly more than four times.[21] Its principal products today include F1 fighters, Jaguar assault and ground support aircraft, Super Etendards and Alpha-Jets. The Mirage 2000 is its major hope for export sales in the 1980s and 1990s. The French Air Force expects to have approximately 130 of these planes in its inventory by 1988. The twin-engine Mirage 4000 has, however, not received assistance from the government, nor has foreign investment been found for a plane whose estimated cost will be in considerable excess of the already expensive Mirage 2000.[22]

Dassault's potentially major competitor in airframe construction, Société Nationale Industrielle Aérospatiale (SNIAS), has been directed to concentrate on civilian aircraft, military transport, missiles, and helicopters. Its genesis may be traced to the nationalization of the 1930s. The five nationalized firms surviving after World War II were eventually regrouped by 1957 into two firms—Sud-Aviation and Nord-Aviation. Beginning in the middle 1960s, the last phase of consolidation was mounted by the government over the objections of the industrial groups. Potez, a private firm, was attached to Sud-Aviation. After five years of painful negotiation, Aérospatiale was formed in 1970. It absorbed Nord- and Sud-Aviation and the Société d'Etude et de Réalisation d'Engins Balistiques (SEREB).[23]

Aérospatiale is composed of four divisions: aircraft, helicopters, tactical missiles and strategic missiles, and space. Throughout the 1970s, its aircraft division suffered continuing financial setbacks. The failure of the Concorde and the absence of any other civilian large-carrier program after the end of the successful Caravelle series accounted for much of the firm's problems. It also had no military aircraft programs of consequence on line. By the early 1970s, the life spans of the Transall and Nord 262 were nearing an end. It required the rest of the decade to launch the medium-carrier Airbus program as a successful commercial enterprise before the airframe division could begin to climb out of the red. Building trainers (Fouga 90 and Epsilon) and filling a contract for 25 more Transalls could hardly keep the division afloat. The division's difficulty is suggested by the high level of governmental support required during the decade to cover its losses.[24] The Aérospatiale helicopter division, meanwhile, enjoyed brilliant commercial success with its fleet of helicopters—Alouette, Gazelle, Dauphin, Puma, Super Frelon, Lynx, Lama, and Ecureuil.

Aircraft Motors. Since 1946, with the nationalization of Gnome and Rhône and the creation of SNECMA (Société Nationale d'Etudes et de Construction de Moteurs d'Aviation), French production of major military and civilian aircraft motors was concentrated in one firm. Dassault and Aérospatiale were generally obliged to use SNECMA for the design of their aircraft. Penalization of Gnome and Rhône for collaboration with the Nazi regime and Vichy was as much a factor in its takeover as economic considerations in the postwar period. The monopoly position enjoyed by SNECMA, however, has posed serious problems for French competitiveness. Relations between France's two airframe companies and SNECMA, particularly between Dassault and SNECMA, have not always been easy. Also, SNECMA has been unable to match the technical perfection of Pratt-Whitney and General Electric engines. The Atar 9C and the Atar 9K50, powering the Mirage and F1, respectively, lack the power, range, and acceleration available from comparable American motors. This drawback obviously did not appreciably hinder Mirage exports, but it placed French aircraft at a disadvantage in competition with General Dynamic's F-16, McDonnell Douglas' F-15, and Northrop's F-18. The M53 motor of the Mirage 2000, while an improvement over previous propulsion systems, has not closed the technology gap between the United States and France and raises doubts that French military aircraft will be able to compete in the 1990s and beyond. As French technology approaches the performance characteristics of the F-16 with the Mirage 2000, American developers are already busily occupied with follow-on aircraft and new and more powerful motors for the next century.

Cooperation between SNECMA and General Electric in civilian motor development has produced positive commercial results. The CF6-50 motor powers the Airbus A-300 B. Development of this large motor has led to the creation of smaller motors, including the 12- to 18-ton CFM-56, an option for the Boeing 707, and the 13- to 17-ton CF6-32.[25]

Turboméca continues as a private firm within a largely nationalized or state-controlled industry. Its major roles are to supply engines for Aérospatiale's helicopter division and turbine engines for small aircraft. By 1970, it had received orders for over 1,200 motors with slightly less than half earmarked for export.[26]

Propulsion Systems and Strategic and Tactical Missiles. Aérospatiale's ballistic and space systems division, partially an outgrowth of SEREB, is principally responsible for the development of French sea- and ground-based strategic missiles. Approximately one-third of Aérospatiale's military turnover is attributable to ballistic missile development. None of its missiles is for export. The ballistic missile division also develops civilian propulsion systems for launching satellites into space. While the leading firm in this area, it cooperates with SNPE (Société Nationale des Poudres et Explosifs), SEP (Société Européenne de Propulsion), SNECMA, and Matra.[27] Ariane, a French-developed missile, serves as Europe's principal propulsion system for its space program.[28]

Aérospatiale's tactical missile division is the largest manufacturer of missiles in France. With Matra, it dominates the production of tactical missiles; the national arsenals are a distant third. A wide range of air-, sea-, and ground-launched missiles has been developed, leading to the production of over a half-million units since World War II.[29] Aérospatiale has produced variously designated antitank, surface-to-surface, surface-to-air, and air-to-surface missiles. Its air and sea Exocet missiles are widely exported and have been used by antagonists in several regional conflicts, as in the Falklands War. Aérospatiale is also responsible for the development of Pluton and Hadès tactical nuclear missiles. Its cooperative program with MBB in developing Hot, Milan, and Roland has already been covered in Chapter 3.

Matra possesses a minority share of the tactical missile market. Like Dassault, it was also earmarked for nationalization. Its civilian and military functions, however, were so intertwined that the Socialist government decided to seek majority control of the company rather than nationalize only the armaments branch of the firm.[30] Separating the firm into two branches threatened its life as a viable unit. Matra has had considerable success in developing tactical missiles, particularly its air-to-air systems, including Magic 550 and Super 530. In cooperation with Great Britain, it developed the Martel and, with Italy, the sea-to-sea missile

Otomat. Its Durandel, a bomb designed to destroy airfields, has also been exported and is found in the inventory of the American armed forces.

Aerospace Research and Space Programs. The French military aerospace program, given its weight within the aeronautics industry, quite naturally extends to a network of national research and test centers and to French participation in the European-based space program. Besides the laboratories and development programs supported by the industrial sector, there is also ONERA (Office National d'Etudes et de Recherches Aérospatiales) and ISL (Institut de St. Louis). Created in 1946 for the study of aerodynamics, ONERA has assumed over the years additional responsibilities of interest to industrial developers and the armed forces, such as air resistance in helicopter, aircraft and missile flight experiments, and static tests of airframes. More than 1,500 professional, technical, and support personnel are employed by ONERA. The St. Louis installation was organized around German missile scientists and engineers captured after World II. It has been under binational French-German direction since the repatriation of German personnel. It is concerned with ballistics, lasers, and flight measurement problems.[31] Added to these laboratories are the test centers and research and development facilities organized within the DGA to support ONERA and ISL and to provide services for French aerospace firms. Most notable among these test centers are those of the DCAé (Direction des Constructions Aéronautiques) and the DEN (Direction des Engins).[32]

The French space program has been developed within a European framework. As in other areas of the aerospace field, firms have been assigned primary responsibility, with some overlap, for specific space programs. Matra shares with Aérospatiale work on satellite platforms as well as satellite components regarding flight altitude, thermal controls, and solar generators. Thomson-CSF is the principal contractor for internal workings of the satellites,[33] including electronic circuits and their components. It also cooperates with SEP and Telespace in developing ground telecommunications and observation posts. By the end of 1984 the Europeans had conducted nine launchings of various kinds of meteorological, communications, navigational, and observation satellites. These firms work closely with CNES (Centre National d'Etudes Spatiales), a research center established in 1961 for space exploration and placed under the direction of the Ministry of Research and Industry.

Electronics

The problem of identifying the arms industry as a set of activities or enterprises apart from the structure of French industry as a whole and its umbilical ties to centers of scientific discovery and technological innovation is most acute when one tries to describe the military electronics component of the electronics industry. One may as well attempt to stipulate which leg of a three-legged stool is the most important for its support. First, the rapidity of technological developments and the speed with which these advances are exploited for commercial advantage submit the electronics industry to incessant pressures for changes in organizational structure to keep pace with international competitive demands. These run the entire gamut from laboratory and development centers to industrial facilities for series production. Heavy R&D costs and the high risk of failure necessitate large and stable financial support to meet current competition while preparing for the next cycle of competition. These entrance fees have necessitated increasingly deeper French governmental involvement in the organization of the electronics industry to induce the consolidation of inherently scarce technological, economic, and financial resources within the private sector.

Governmental aid—through direct subsidies, forced purchases of French-made materials by governmental agencies, and export assistance—has also been indispensable in keeping the electronics industry afloat. This investment and support structure has been itself put under strain by competing demands from other industrial and defense sectors for governmental assistance. Within this field of conflicting pressures, the financial structure of the electronics industry has been in perpetual crisis. Neither industrial concerns nor the government, separately or in union, has so far been able—as the failure of Plan Calcul and the problems surrounding nationalization attest—to stabilize the industry's precarious organizational structure.

It is also somewhat arbitrary, in attempting to define the industry, to separate military and civilian components. More than any other industry, its development depends on French scientific and technological advances along a wide front. French economic competitiveness *and* the independence of its national defense depend on the broad socioeconomic reforms within France and upon the success of French science and industry. The arms production and export elements of the industry are merely the end products of this larger, more pervasive, civilian front-end, composed of parts drawn from large segments of French business, governmental science and engineering units, and educational institutions.

Third, the armaments portion of the electronics industry cannot be easily contained within one armed service. Each of the military branches maintains its own electronics sections with their own separate ties to the electronics industry, part of which is located within the arsenal system itself. It is very difficult to isolate electronics from, say, aircraft, submarine, or tank design and development since electronic systems are so integrated with the other components of a weapons system. One study of the 1969 French defense budget, for example, attributed 40 percent of naval construction and 25 percent of aeronautics expenditures to electronics.[34] The decreasing share of French military spending in the industry's business turnover for professional electronic equipment (between 1970 and 1975 the military's share fell from 39 to 25 percent),[35] and the increasing portion of military electronics exported abroad further complicates the task of defining precisely what to include or exclude within the arms sectors of the industry. Military and civilian electronics exports, e.g., in radar, navigation, telecommunications, and computers, are so intermingled that caution should be exercised in drawing a line between one and the other.

These qualifications aside, the French electronics industry may be divided into three parts: consumer products (*biens de consommation*), basic components (*biens intermédiares*), and capital goods (*biens d'équipement*).[36] The first does not directly concern the military. Components refer to the production of integrated circuits, semiconductors, and microchip processors. Capital goods encompass computers, especially large processing units, professional materials (telecommunications networks, radar, electromagnetic detection, navigational devices), and industrial measurement equipment.

French industry has had mixed success in controlling domestic markets and in selling abroad in all three areas. The situation facing France is similar to the problem facing the entire European electronics industry. As one analyst concluded: "Despite . . . technical success, notably in France, it is difficult to speak of the success of computers. The champions of old Europe are neither technologically independent nor dependably profitable, nor assured of their future. More troubling is the situation in electronic components. Two-thirds of the microprocessors used in the EEC are imported; the rest, produced usually under license, are neither profitable, despite substantial subsidies, nor represent the latest advanced techniques. The situation is worse for consumer goods."[37] France could take some comfort in having recorded surpluses in its professional electronic equipment accounts although these were offset in the 1970s by continuing deficits in other electronics markets, including consumer goods, component parts, and computers.[38] Not surprisingly, military electronic equipment comprised the largest segment of French professional exports. Thomson-Brandt's affiliate, Thomson-CSF, was largely responsible for these surpluses. In 1980, it was France's largest arms exporter, exceeding Dassault and Aérospatiale.[39] As early as 1970, Michel Debré had already publicly announced that "the government had strongly encouraged the activities of Thomson-Brandt and CSF."[40]

Thomson-Brandt's strong export position may be traced to decisions taken a decade earlier. The Pompidou government's decision to finance a plan to expand Thomson-CSF's professional electronic equipment sector over other competitors assisted the firm's export success. Progress in military electronics was, however, at the expense of positioning France favorably in the components market. Lacking funds, the government was in no position to underwrite a major components plan. The disarray in the electronics industry and the government's inability to halt damaging domestic industrial competition precluded an efficient allocation of resources to orient investment choices.[41] Thomson-CSF developed a recognized specialization in automated air defense systems, radar, and naval, air, and ground guidance to add to the other military export outlets of the firm.

The failure of Plan Calcul illustrates the resource constraints facing the French government in assisting the French electronics industry. It also reveals the fundamental dilemma confronting governmental intervention. The dilemma derives from the limited resources available to the French nation and the problems of governmental choice that arise when, simultaneously, the state attempts to pursue a policy of economic, technological, *and* military independence. French governments can permit a wider range of initiative to be left to private firms in adjusting to international competition. Such a policy promises a more competitive French industry but one increasingly specialized as it accepts its place within an evolving global division of labor. It is by no means clear that a national champion, implying a large firm and a complex structure, is best suited for the quick pace and intense competition of the international electronics industry. Backing several minichampions goes against the grain of French industrial thinking and ingrained bureaucratic practice. It also obviously enjoys little support from giants like Thomson-Brandt. As French firms gain in competitiveness, measured by increasing profits, capital for new investment, high employment, and balance of payments stability, there is a risk that the responsiveness of the industry to defense needs or to governmental control will be diminished. The choice is posed between remaining autonomous at the risk of lowered productivity and a slower rate of technological advancement or maintaining an internationally competitive electronics industry. Increased governmental controls and oversight, spurred by nationalization, facilitate the creation of an industry responsive to governmental directives and to the pursuit of across-the-board independence, but such a strategy cannot guarantee either a commercially successful or a technologically advanced industry. Worse, it may be unable to produce military equipment and systems to match those of the superpowers.[42]

Partly in response to the refusal in 1963 of the United States to sell Control Data computers, needed for France's force de frappe, and to American trade dominance in computer technology, efforts were launched within the French government to assure French defense needs, technological independence, and a share of the computer market. France's Machine Bull was the state's prime candidate for support. A request by General Electric to purchase 20 percent of Bull's stock was initially turned down in 1964, but the company's precarious position led Finance Minister Valéry Giscard d'Estaing to relent, accepting further American penetration of the French market already dominated by American firms, with IBM at the head of the list.

Under the impulse of Finance Minister Michel Debré, who succeeded Giscard, a Plan Calcul was formulated to achieve French computer independence by governmental officials and representatives of CGE (Compagnie Générale d'Electrique) and the Schneider group. A special post of Delegate for Computers was also created within the Ministry of Industry to coordinate governmental and industrial efforts. Compagnie Internationale de l'Informatique (CII) was formed in 1967 and designated the state's primary agent for the development of France's computer industry. The state signed a compact promising financial aid for a new line of computers which would be "original with no relation to American technology."[43] Majority control of the firm was divided between CGE and Thomson-CSF, which had been absorbed in 1967 by Thomson-Brandt. Majority control subsequently passed to Thomson-CSF as part of a "Yalta" accord in 1969, dividing the industry between France's two giants. Meanwhile, GE sold its share in Machine Bull to Honeywell. A proposal to reject the sale and join CII and Machine Bull got nowhere as neither CGE nor Thomson-Brandt was prepared to assume a new financial burden while confronted with a major reorganization of their activities.[44]

Despite 1.8 billion francs in government subsidies between 1966 and 1974,[45] CII was unable to develop a solvent position. It was placed between two unpalatable solutions: it would have to join either a European or an American firm to maintain at least a portion of its corporate existence. The first entailed creation of Unidata, a joint enterprise of CII, Dutch Phillips, and German Siemens. The second was the proposal to merge CII and Machine Bull and wed them to Honeywell International. The latter option was finally chosen and CII-Honeywell-Bull was created. While 53 percent of the stock was owned by French firms, control of the firm rested in Honeywell's hands, notwithstanding substantial French governmental subsidies and credited to sustain CII-Honeywell's operations and to give priority to CII-Bull products in governmental purchasing.[46]

The nationalization program of the Mitterrand government marked a new phase in French attempts to create an independent electronics industry. CGE and Thomson-Brandt have also been nationalized, although Thomson-CSF has been left untouched. Majority state control over CII-Honeywell-Bull, under the published terms of the nationalization, provided that Honeywell would voluntarily diminish its equity in CII-Honeywell-Bull from 47 to 19 percent. This change in ownership would not change the company's competitive position nor necessarily assure it privileged access either to investment funds or governmental subsidies. Thomson-Brandt and CII were running deficits at the time of their takeovers, both well in excess of 5 billion francs.[47] CGE's profit position, estimated at 500 million francs in 1982,[48] was based substantially on assured contracts with the state amounting to 80 percent of its turnover.[49] A second Yalta accord between CGE and Thomson-Brandt was reached in September 1983. CGE became France's leading firm in telecommunications while Thomson-Brandt assumed primary responsibility for consumer products, components, and military electronics.[50] A new, dynamic leadership and the success of the military division, witnessed by the multi-billion dollar sale of air defense equipment to Saudi Arabia, breathed new life into Thomson-Brandt and CSF, making them solvent by the time of the Socialist defeat in the legislative elections of 1986.

Munitions: Nuclear and Conventional

The Atomic Energy Commission or CEA (Commissariat à l'Energie Atomique) has had a monopoly over the development of military uses of nuclear energy since its formation in 1945. It was not until the 1950s that a special Directorate for Military Applications (DAM, Direction des Applications Militaires) was created. The CEA remains the monopoly supplier of nuclear arms, although it depends primarily on funds from the Ministry of Defense to supply required military needs and to conduct research and testing. The CEA has jealously guarded its autonomy since its inception. While it is formally placed within the Ministry of Research and Industry, it retains considerable latitude for independent action.

Arms are furnished to the armed forces through a series of governmental decrees that have created the juridical structure for close cooperation between the CEA and DAM within the General Delegation for Armament. The Minister of Defense is responsible for choosing the nuclear systems. The Minister of Research and Development, essentially through the CEA, conducts the research and testing to provide nuclear weapons ordered by the armed forces. A nuclear armaments committee prepares decisions concerning the orientations of nuclear research. It is composed of the armed forces chief of staff, the General Delegate for Armament, the Secretary General for Administration, and the General Administrator and High Commissioner of the CEA. These representatives of the Minister of Defense are also members of the CEA's administrative committee. This is a six-member committee composed of three representatives each from the CEA and the armed forces. Presided over by a representative of the Minister of Defense, it is charged with overseeing the execution of approved programs. The DGA coordinates and finances the realization of military programs. These functions are executed by a special branch or mission within DGA which is responsible for nuclear affairs.

Coordination between the CEA, monopoly supplier for nuclear weapons, and the Ministry of Defense, monopoly purchaser of these arms, has apparently worked well enough to quell periodic calls for a reorganization of the CEA's military activities and their incorporation within DGA. As long as the arrangement works, there are no strong pressures to concentrate activities following the pattern in other arms areas. Even if they were present, it is not clear how much weight they would have since the CEA has traditionally, and quite successfully, resisted efforts to share its monopoly position for developing nuclear weapons with other agencies. The CEA has also expanded its civilian functions without retarding its response to military requests for new programs in tactical and strategic nuclear arms. As a former head of the DGA (then called DMA) observed: "It is wise to recall that the best (theoretically) is the enemy of the good (practically). I do not recommend and, as long as things will be as they are, I will not recommend the annexation of the CEA to the DMA."[51]

Conventional munitions are the monopoly of SNPE (Société Nationale des Poudres et Explosifs), a nationalized company along the lines of Aérospatiale and SNECMA. The state holds over 99 percent of the firm's equity. The SNPE's responsibilities for munitions were previously within the domain of the Directorate for Munitions (Poudres) within the DMA. These activities had been part of the French state's arsenal system for several centuries. Reorganization along more commercial lines was necessitated by obligations incurred by France under the Rome Treaty, which forbade member states from exercising a production or commercial monopoly. The shift to a semipublic firm also conformed to the orientation of successive French administrations to allot an increasing segment of military production to the private sector or to nonarsenal outlets.

There are five divisions in SNPE: propulsion, munitions and explosives, chemistry (largely of volatile materials), engineering, and research. It also assumed control of six munitions plants previously under the Directorate for Munitions. The latter was downgraded to a technical service within DGA. The reorganization has had the desired effect of increasing the business turnover and commercialization of SNPE. Exports now bulk larger in its operations.[52]

Ground Equipment

The state arsenal under the Directorate for Ground Armaments (DAT, Direction des Armements Terrestres) is primarily responsible for equipping France's ground forces with tanks, heavy armor, and artillery as well as mortars and small arms. In line with the efforts to make the arsenals more sensitive to market forces and commercial opportunities, the government created in 1971 an industrial grouping within DAT. The Groupement Industriel des Armements Terrestres (GIAT) is divided into four divisions: weapons systems research, commerce, production, and administration. It controls ten factories whose production capabilities span the gamut of major ground arms, including the entire family of AMX-10 and -30 armored vehicles: tanks and combat infantry carriers, self-propelled artillery, missile carriages for Pluton, Roland, and Milan, portable bridges, command and observation vehicles, 120 mm. tracked vehicles, and ambulances.[53]

Communications systems (e.g., RITA), battle reconnaissance equipment, and command information processing materials are also produced by GIAT. Its independence from DAT is suggested by the development of the AMX-32 tank for export, although the Army general staff had not defined a requirement for it.[54] Some of its centers have even branched into the production of civilian electro-nuclear materials. In the mechanics industry, GIAT is among France's largest firms. Its business turnover doubled between 1971 and 1976 in large part due to export sales that comprised more than a third of its output, a proportion of sales that continued into the 1980s.[55] During this period, combat vehicle production increased 50 percent (987 to 1,420) and armored infantry equipment more than doubled (790 to 1,900 units). Its 17,000 employees exceed Dassault's, and its business turnover is comparable to those of SNECMA and Saviem.[56]

Clustered around GIAT are several private firms specializing in ground armaments. Panhard, with almost a century of experience in military vehicle production, produces the AML-60 and -90 series of armored cars and, more recently, the VTT series. It is estimated that as of 1980 over 4,000 of the AML series had been produced for the French and for foreign armies.[57] Panhard concentrates almost totally on exports. Saviem of the nationalized Renault group makes tank engines and, with Berliet, produces heavy ground transport vehicles, many designed for special needs. Creusot-Loire also manufactured the now outmoded AMX-13 light tank.

Naval Warships and Equipment

Most of the Navy's ship construction is done in state-controlled arsenals under the Directorate for Naval Construction (Direction des Constructions Navales, DCN). Of 166 new naval vessels under construction or completed, 118 were done in state shipyards.[58] Of these, most major ships have been constructed under arsenal direction. Private firms have been tendered government contracts for special projects. Penhoët at St. Nazaire helped construct the cruiser *Jean Bart* and hulls for the aircraft carriers *Foch* and *Clemenceau* under exacting DCN supervision.[59] Like GIAT, the naval system is a major industrial grouping. Its 32,000-member work force and business turnover of approximately 6 billion francs in 1980 makes it comparable in size to Gaz de France and CII-Honeywell-Bull.[60] Besides new construction, the naval arsenals have the major responsibility for service and repair of the fleet, special functions that create an especially close bond between the French naval command, interested in controlling all facets of its logistics system, and the arsenal complex.

The main seaboard installations are at Cherbourg, Brest, Lorient, and Toulon. Cherbourg, where France's strategic submarine force was built, has specialized in conventional and nuclear powered submarines. A sixth submarine was completed in 1985. The first nuclear-powered attack submarine was also to be built at Cherbourg. Conventional submarine production included the Narval (modernized in the late 1960s), Daphne, Agosta series and the experimental submarine *Gymnote*. Lorient has concentrated on service and repair of conventional submarines and of light- and middle-size vessels (under 8,000 tons). Brest, the second largest seaboard installation with a work force of 7,000, is capable of large-ship construction. It has built five destroyers, an antiaircraft cruiser, the helicopter carrier *Jeanne d'Arc*, and the aircraft carriers *Clemenceau* and *Foch*. It also services the submarines of the strategic nuclear force and ships of the fleet assigned to Brest. Toulon, the largest establishment, services and repairs the Mediterranean fleet, all of the Navy's aircraft and helicopters, and some civilian ships. It also produces specialized aeronautic equipment and runs an acoustics laboratory.[61]

Three other important arsenals which are not at major ports are St. Tropez, Indret, and Ruelle, the latter dating back to the middle of the eighteenth century. St. Tropez manufactures torpedoes; Indret concentrates on conventional propulsion systems and produces elements for nuclear-powered vessels; Ruelle works on naval fired missiles, including Masurca, Exocet, and sea- and ground-launched strategic systems. Ruelle is also involved in manufacturing naval artillery, submarine equipment, and aeronautic materials. There are also installations at Dakar and Papeete; the Tahitian base services French ships in the Pacific and supports France's nuclear test program.[62]

Several private firms and dockyards are involved in military construction, service, or repair. Among the most important are Alsthom-Atlantique at St. Nazaire, Chantiers Navals de la Ciotat, Chantiers de France Cherbourg and CNIM (Constructions Navales et Industrielles de la Mediterranée) at Toulon. All have a capacity to construct major vessels. CNIM produces frigates, landing craft, torpedoes, and rocket launchers. Dubigeon Normandie at Nantes constructs Daphne class submarines; CMN (Constructions Mécaniques de Normandie) specializes in mine sweepers and fast patrol boats, like those produced for West Germany, Iran, and Israel. Like most private yards, its production is primarily for exports.[63]

Until very recently, DCN concerned itself almost totally with construction, repair, and service for the French fleet. Like GIAT, it is becoming more sensitive to its potential commercial role. In 1983 DCN began citing exports for the first time in its promotional material as among its principal activities.[64] Much of France's naval military exports in the 1960s and 1970s was left to private yards, like CMN, Dubigeon, Brest, Le Trait, and Carthagène.[65] The multibillion-dollar contract signed in 1980 with Saudi Arabia (Sawari program) and others with Iraq and Pakistan have plunged the DCN and its production centers into the export market. Under the Saudi program, France will build and train crews for 4 frigates, 2 oil tenders, and 24 Dauphin helicopters. For more than half of the 1980s, the Saudi contract will represent 50 percent of France's naval military program (38,000 tons), during which time approximately 1,400 sailors and technicians will have been trained in DCN schools. The Lorient shipyards will be principally responsible for the initial phase of heavy naval construction.[66] Three additional frigates and two tenders are scheduled to be built by Ciotat.[67]

CHARACTERISTICS OF THE FRENCH ARMS INDUSTRY

The French arms industry is increasingly concentrated around a set of monopoly suppliers. In aerospace, Dassault, Aérospatiale, SNECMA, and Matra are the principal agents; in electronics, Thomson-CSF commands the heights, a position reinforced by the nationalization of Thomson-Brandt and the second Yalta accord between CGE and Thomson; in munitions, the CEA and SNPE supply French armed force needs. The DCN and GIAT under DAT furnish, respectively, the bulk of France's naval and ground equipment. All are heavily dependent on exports of military technology, arms, training, and service and repair of materials.

Concentration has been a clear trend throughout the Fifth Republic, although it has not always been direct or smooth. Each successive consolidation has been prompted by conjunctural opportunities, seized upon by the government, to advance its long-term goal of consolidation. Opposition, sometimes strong, has dogged reformist attempts. Nationalized aircraft firms bitterly resisted Dassault's appointment as France's sole fighter aircraft firm. For much of the 1960s, they also blocked their incorporation into Aérospatiale. Within Aérospatiale these formerly independent firms still operate to some degree as separate units. As a result, Aérospatiale often appears more as a collection of autonomous entities than as a fully integrated corporation.[68] Dassault assumed reluctant control over Bréguet. Thomson-CSF has embraced its military role, including computers and components, but only after being lavishly plied with carrots in the form of governmental subsidies, assured orders, and export support. If SNPE marks a clean institutional break with the past, success in moving the ground and naval arsenals into a commercial mode has been slow, impeded by traditional military concerns for an arsenal system exclusively keyed to armed force needs, outdated and costly financial management controls, and a resistant work force jealous of its privileged status within the state personnel system which guarantees employee retention whether the arsenal mills turn or not.

Second, concentration has also been equated with suppression of competition in domestic and foreign markets. Created has been an almost totally insulated domestic market dominated by national champions who hold essentially monopoly positions as suppliers. There is general consensus on this policy "of means." The Left and Right agree that competition should cease among home units to husband resources for what is perceived as the economic war being waged by American, German, and Japanese multinationals. Discord turns on who should direct the national champions—private interests or state-appointed managers. All want competitive industries but also units sensitive to the varied social and political aims of France's political parties.

Over the course of the Fifth Republic, successive governments have moved from a policy of favoring the private sector of the armaments industry to its nationalization under the Socialist government of François Mitterrand. What is interesting to note was the hesitancy of the Socialists in nationalizing major segments of the arms industry in 1981. Wholesale expropriation was rejected in favor of a complex formula defined by the competitive needs of each firm and industry and the bargaining power and leverage of their corporate managers. Dassault, Matra, and Thomson-CSF were not fully nationalized. Their stocks remain quoted on the Bourse, the Paris stock exchange. Efforts have been made to keep the design teams of these corporations intact and to insulate these firms from the inevitable political buffeting of the nationalization process.

Third, the presence of state officials throughout the consolidation process has been pervasive. Each step toward concentration has been under the prodding or oversight of a host of interested political leaders and civilian and military functionaries. It is a process of consolidation marked, once authorizing legislation had been passed, by the absence of any significant intrusion by parliamentary influence or public opinion. Like the protagonists of *Animal Farm*, many of the heads of arms-producing units continue to act under nationalization as they did before. Nationalization may yet carry the social struggle for popular control into the government or *pouvoir*, but the early years of the nationalization movement have not registered any decisive changes either in corporate behavior or in the range of initiatives available to industrialists who now are essentially public agents.[69] Arms managers and makers remain jealous of their autonomy while energetic in their pursuit of governmental subsidies and support.

Within a protected domestic market of monopoly suppliers, will the French arms industry remain competitive, measured by the effectiveness of their arms or by the price tags they carry? Governmental officials have attempted to answer that question by relying on four principal devices to promote competitiveness: (1) foreign arms purchases; (2) maintenance of alternative industrial facilities that can be brought into service in the case of nonperformance by a monopoly supplier; (3) tight cost controls; and (4) international competition.[70] The first two approaches, while often threatened, have rarely been employed. After a generation of trumpeting independence in weapons production, it seems hardly plausible that foreign purchases would be readily available to any French government or the armed services. The latter have at times shown an interest in buying abroad (e.g., Hawk and AWACS). Complaints from the armed forces tend to focus more on the lack of finances to buy additional arms from French industry than on the quality of the weapons themselves. These reservations were once again expressed before a special commission empaneled by Prime Minister Mauroy to evaluate the policies of his predecessor.[71] Maintaining parallel production facilities also appeared as a foregone option as the pace of concentration has intensified.

International competition is also no sure check on the arms industry.

It may provide a measuring rod to check domestic efficiency, but there is no clear way of knowing whether it will be applied or how it might be used to conserve resources and to maintain competitiveness. Arms sales, as more than one study has shown,[72] depend as much on political and strategic factors as on price. French manufacturers bargain over the technical performance of their equipment rather than over its price, which is generally higher than often can be found by buying from American or other foreign suppliers. The political concessions and reliability of French arms suppliers further enhance the French position. In any event, it would be years after the development of a weapons system before it could be determined whether the government had made a wise economic investment or not. The performance of French arms may, indeed, keep pace with technological changes in superpower arsenals, but it is not clear that the international arms market is sufficiently sensitive to price fluctuation to be of much use in holding the French arms industry to account. What is left is governmental control and oversight to ensure cost efficiency, arms effectiveness, and competitiveness in international arms markets. Chapter 5 sketches the governance of the arms complex and the mechanisms used by its principal actors to resist pressures for greater public exposure and accountability.

CHAPTER 5

The Politics of Arms Transfers:
The Arms Oligarchy and Democratic Norms

GOVERNANCE OF ARMS PRODUCTION AND TRANSFERS

Rule by State Oligarchs

RESOURCE CONSTRAINTS require the creation of governmental institutions and processes to define objectives, to orient the arms industry toward national needs, to establish priorities, and to adopt strategies for the achievement of these aims. Democratic imperatives imply, moreover, a government accountable to the public and its chosen representatives. Who, then, in France decides what weapons will be produced, in what quantities, and for whom? How are decision-makers held accountable for these choices, and how are these choices legitimated to meet democratic tests of governance?

This mediating process of decision and accountability itself is not politically neutral since it is necessarily driven by the security and welfare imperatives confronting the government as well as by the personal and bureaucratic interests of the units participating in the governing process. Behind the façade of a hierarchically ordered, centralized, and unified state, the process by which arms decisions are reached is dominated by elites whose influence is largely defined by the organizational positions that they enjoy within the design, production, control, and user segments of the arms complex. Where they sit affords them special standing and access to the decisional centers setting the aims and priorities for the arms complex.

As Chapter 4 argues, industrial concentration and the certification of national champions have made the corporate heads of favored state enterprises key actors within the governing system of the arms complex. They are rivaled in influence only by the military engineers and technocrats who run the General Delegation for Armament (Délégation Générale pour l'Armement, DGA). Within the Ministry of Defense, with the Minister of Defense acting, alternately, as arbiter but more often as conciliator and coordinator, the corps of arms engineers competes as an equal with the chief of the general staff of the armed forces and the top leadership of the military services. These actors form the inner core of the governing system. On a second tier stand a disparate array of units and individuals who oversee important economic, industrial, financial and technological resources needed by the arms industry. Most important among them are the Minister of Economics, Finance, and the Budget (portfolios that have been integrated or divided according to momentary needs), the Minister of Research and Industry, and the Minister of Foreign Affairs. Other ministries, like those devoted to foreign commerce and transportation, also play significant roles in specific areas, such as in civilian and military aircraft development and sales.

This second-tier group, which has service responsibilities beyond those of the arms industry, may be viewed as the inhabitants of the immediate environment that must be controlled by the arms complex if its needs and interests are to be served. As the discussion below relates, the agents of the arms complex are strategically placed throughout this second tier. Through an elaborate process of external administrative conditioning, financial manipulations, clever bureacratic alliances, cooptation, cajolery, and raw use of power, the arms complex—aided and abetted by successive French presidential administrations—has largely had its way in bureaucratic infighting where much of governmental decision-making about arms production and sales is made.

The Socialist nationalization program which extended state ownership over key portions of the private sector of the arms industry has not significantly changed the governing structure of the arms industry. If anything, it has added new layers of insulation between the arms industry and French society and public opinion. After nationalization, the arms complex was less vulnerable to the charge that governmental policy had been "privatized" and made a creature of corporate giants like Dassault and Thomson-Brandt. Arms and arms export decisions are more than ever shielded from public debate and from societal pressures, which are still too weak and scattered to force a fundamental reform of the armaments system. Nationalization created more the illusion than the reality of public accountability and elected governmental control. When the state is everywhere, there is the risk that its influence is nowhere, the public authority invested in the state having devolved by choice, neglect, bureaucratic entrepreneurship, and happenstance to its agents whose organizational and personal needs vie with public interest claims on national resources.

General Delegation for Armament

The DGA is the hub around which the French arms industry turns. Created in 1961, the DGA (known first as the DMA, Délégation Ministérielle pour l'Armement) has broad authority to control, guide, and oversee all phases of arms research, development, production, and sales. It occupies a unique place in the hierarchy of the powerful Ministry of Defense. Its prestige is enhanced by the privileged position of the Minister of Defense within the Council of Ministers. At its inception the DGA was placed directly under the Ministry of Defense but, within the ministerial hierarchy, *above* the chief of staff of the armed forces and those of the three military services. The DGA reported directly to the Minister of Defense. Its director owed his loyalty to the minister and, in turn, to the prime minister and president. Potential conflict between the Minister of Defense and the DGA head never materialized since defense ministers, like Pierre Messmer and Michel Debré, barons within the Gaullist party, had the confidence of President de Gaulle. Those appointed as DGA directors were either proven civil servants with a passion for anonymity (e.g., Jean Blancard), industrial leaders with circumscribed political ambitions (e.g., Jean-Laurens Delpech) or, as has been the pattern since the late 1970s, armaments engineers (e.g., Jean Martre who later headed Aérospatiale).

Although the DGA's hierarchical standing was lowered in 1977 when the DMA became the DGA, ostensibly to bring it into line with special delegations in other ministries, its political influence has not perceptibly diminished.[1] The efforts of the chiefs of staff of the military services and, particularly, the armed forces chief to be placed on an equal administrative footing with the DGA director have been more symbolically than substantively successful.[2] The delegated authority, critical hierarchical positions, and broad public powers enjoyed by the DGA and its units are so wide and pervasive that the DGA and its leadership remain a powerful force within the Ministry of Defense and throughout the French governmental system and economy.

The seeming downgrading of the DGA and the appointment of an armaments engineer to head the organization had what appears to have been the intended effect of actually strengthening the DGA's governmental position and its hold over the armaments industry. Bureaucratization provided additional layers of insulation for the DGA and its director—chosen for his technical expertise and not his partisan connections—from party contests between the Left and Right for control of the parliament. Partisan conflict threatened to draw the military-industrial complex into the domestic factional struggle.[3] The proposals of the Socialist and Communist parties to nationalize key segments of the arms industry, advanced during the presidential and the legislative elections of 1974 and 1978, respectively, risked politicizing the DGA. Changing the name of the agency and harmonizing its status on standard organizational charts with similar though much less powerful units in other ministries provided protective covering for the DGA, shielding

it from the political limelight and the heat resulting from partisan conflicts and too visible and potentially damaging public exposure. Both
the DGA and its director preferred to be cast in the role of technical and
administrative agents of governmental policy rather than as politically
tainted appendages of a particular political regime or party.[4]

Despite claims that the DGA is on an equal plane with similar agencies
in other ministries, the DGA remains a hybrid within the governmental
hierarchy. Given its extensive powers and responsibilities, it is something more than a mere directorate within the Ministry of Defense since
it has directorates under its supervision; yet, formally, it is something
less than a politically designated ministerial delegation. If precedent
had been followed, as in 1916 and 1938, when similar posts were temporarily created, the DGA head would have been made a special minister
of state. Such a post would have corresponded more closely in form to
the broad powers exercised by the DGA in practice. Since the 1970s,
Fifth Republic governments have preferred officially to treat the DGA
director "only as a technician . . . charged to procure the best arms at
the lowest price in the shortest possible time."[5] Publications of the DGA
equally portray it narrowly as an administrative and technical service.[6]
So modest a position is belied by the fact that the DGA director is still the
highest ranking officer below the Minister of Defense. In peacetime, he
takes precedence in official functions over the chief of staff of the
armed forces except before military personnel or during hostilities. In
all other cases he stands higher than the general secretaries for administration and the chiefs of staff of the military services.[7]

The missions formally attributed to the DGA, while on the surface circumscribed, obscure rather than reveal the critical institutional roles
played by the DGA and the powers it wields in advancing governmental
military and economic objectives and in shaping these objectives, particularly those associated with the expansion of France's arms exports, to
suit administration policies and its own interests. The governmental decree of April 5, 1961, which created the DGA, asserted that "a national
policy for the fabrication of arms—and notably the fabrication of the
most modern arms—required a concentration of authority and of
means which favor a better use of men, a higher return from the industrial infrastructure, and a more effective use of credits."[8]

The DGA was charged (1) to prepare—in collaboration with the chief
of staff of the armed forces and the service chiefs—arms research, development, and production programs for approval by the Minister of
Defense; (2) to guide the activities of public and nationalized arms firms
and to oversee private arms development and production; and (3) to repair military equipment whether on the request of the Army or Air

Force or in cooperation with the Navy's chief of staff.[9] Publications of the DGA also note that "while it is not explicated in the original texts creating the DGA, it is necessary to cite a fourth mission because it has acquired, in the course of the last several years, a particular importance: the animation and oversight of cooperation between France and foreign governments in armaments as well as in imports and exports in this area, within the framework of the policy fixed by the government."[10] The afterthought hardly does justice to the critical economic functions discharged by the DGA, nor to its role in fixing governmental policy.

Centralization of arms development authority within the DGA in 1961 was the logical result of the decision to create a strategic nuclear force under the direct authority of the French president. Separate weapons directorates among the armed services were overtaken by two new conditions: advances in science and technology that cut across traditional service missions, and the political decision of the Gaullist government to abandon France's empire and the traditional army structure and weapons on which it rested. The primary task of the DGA's armaments engineers was initially to construct a force de dissuasion. A necessary first step was to weaken the tie between the armed services and their arms engineers and orient the latter to the newly defined military needs of the Gaullist government. The traditional directorates for the fabrication of ground, naval, and air arms were regrouped under the DGA. Liaison with the Atomic Energy Commission was assured through the creation of a special mission for atomic weapons. The Directorate for Munitions and a new directorate for research and testing were added to these agencies.[11] The upgrading of civil authority through the DGA and the integration of the corps of arms engineers under a central direction were in keeping with the efforts of the de Gaulle government to gain control over a rebellious military officer corps that had toppled the Fourth Republic and threatened the foundations of the Fifth Republic.

A unified engineering corps promised to be more responsive to the need for integration and modernization of French armed forces than separate technical branches under the eye and control of each of the armed forces staffs. Endowed with a separate institutional personality, the arms engineers, already inclined by educational background, professional interests, and temperament to promote technological innovation in arms development, became a natural lobby within the defense community for the modernization of the military services. The officer corps of the traditional services, especially those in the ground army, were indelibly marked by their experience in France's colonial wars. Rather than work only through the resistant medium of the armed services to discipline them to conform to a Gaullist strategic design, the de Gaulle government also constructed a parallel institutional mechanism dedicated primarily to the technological advancement of the military services and to the needs of the government in its pursuit of a new international order, enhancement of French independence and power, and national grandeur. With respect to atomic weapons, arms engineers were more than a match for their counterparts in the armed services. Special expertise resided in technical training and skills. Experience in battle or field operations carried less weight within the promotional system and status of a technically trained officer corps. Emphasis would shift from a large conscript force to a professional army utilizing sophisticated weapons systems, not massed armies. Managers of violence, not warriors, were in the ascendancy.

In 1965, administrative notice was taken of the DGA's increasing responsibility for the development of France's arms industry and exports. Three functional directorates for personnel, industrial affairs, and international programs (cooperation and exports) were created along with a fourth technical entity, the Technical Directorate for Missiles (Direction Technique des Engins, DTEn), later renamed the Directorate for Missiles (DEN). The commercialization of the French arms industry was advanced further in 1971 with the creation of GIAT and the transformation of the Directorate for Munitions into SNPE. These reorganizations clarified the manufacturing and state oversight functions of the DGA. GIAT became the industrial arm of DAT; a service was created within DEN to survey the munitions industry. In 1977 the Directorate of Research and Testing (Direction des Recherches et Moyens d'Essais, DRME) was renamed the Directorate for Research, Development, and Techniques (Direction des Recherches, Etudes et Techniques, DRET). It absorbed a research unit of the DAT while transferring two test centers to the DEN.[12] Under Defense Minister Charles Hernu, the DGA was again streamlined. The technical directorates all dropped the term "technical" from their former designations and came more closely under the direction of DGA which was specifically authorized "to manage the means of research, study and production relevant to its direct authority (the industrial installations of the DGA)"[13]

Organizational Structure of the General Delegation for Armament. To gain some notion of the principal players in the governance and politics of the DGA itself and, from this vantage point, the centrality of the DGA within the security community and its hold over other segments of the French governmental structure, one must have some idea of the DGA's organizational structure and the legal authority and delegated responsibilities of its component units. A succeeding section will attempt to suggest the impact of the DGA and its units on the French economy by describing how arms requirements and weapons programs appear to be defined and how arms and military technology sales are concluded and executed. A sketch of these two interlinked processes of decision, viewed against the backdrop of the DGA's organization, powers, and responsibilities, suggests the fluid and supple character of DGA rule of the arms complex and highlights the influence of other significant actors within the French arms complex. The latter include, as suggested earlier, the leadership of industrial enterprises (including DGA arsenals), the military services, and the political officials within the Ministry of Defense as well as the prime minister and president. Outside France, recipients of French arms and military technology and those cooperating with the French arms industry on joint programs also exercise an appreciable influence on arms production and arms flows. The DGA is thus the critical hinge between French armed forces and the French industry and between the arms industry and French civil industry and economy. It acts as a buffer between the arms industry and those segments of the bureaucracy charged with oversight and direction of the nonmilitary segments of the economy. The DGA is also the principal institutional vehicle through which France's foreign relations in arms transfers are conducted. In principle, the Ministry of Foreign Affairs is still ascendant in foreign affairs; in practice, the DGA and the sprawling network of information flows and controls over which it presides is the key instrument of the government's arms transfer policy as well as its primary maker and mover.

Figure 5-1 sketches the organization of the DGA. The DGA is composed of a set of central administrative and mission-oriented units, two high level delegations for industrial policy and international relations, two functional directorates, and five technical or operational directorates closely tied to the armed services. The organizational structure, formal authority, and duties of the DGA and its units are detailed in an enlarging web of laws, decrees, and administrative regulations that have accumulated through the years.[14] From the perspective of internal administrative control, the arms industry is closely regulated within France. This legal and administrative structure, important segments of which predate the creation of the DGA, is taken very seriously by the DGA and its subordinate units. Legal authority for control and initiative and their position in the DGA hierarchy legitimize the actions taken by these units and "arms" them in their disputes with each other within the DGA and between them and other parts of the state establishment. The investment of "public power" (*puissance publique*) in these units makes them formidable players within the French bureaucracy and strong competitors in intergovernmental politics.

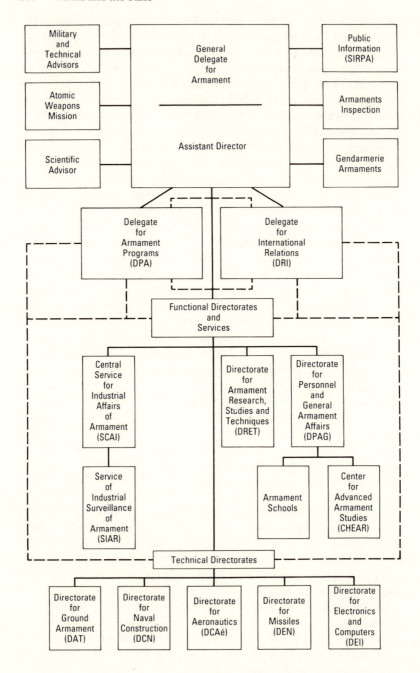

FIGURE 5-1

Organization of the General Delegation for Armament

Source: France, Ministère de la Défense, *Délégation Générale pour l'Armement* (Paris, 1983, 1985, 1986).

Within the central administration, there is a unit to handle public relations (SIRPA), liaison officers between DGA and the general staffs of the armed forces (*conseillers techniques et militaires*), a scientific mission, usually headed by a distinguished scientist (*mission "recherche"*), the cabinet of the General Delegate, an arms and financial inspection team, and a unit concerned with armaments for the gendarmerie. An atomic weapons group (*mission atome*) assures close ties with the Atomic Energy Commission for the development of France's nuclear forces.

Technical Directorates. There are five technical or operational directorates maintaining close day-to-day contacts with the arms industry. These include the DAT and DCN, already noted, the Directorate for Aeronautics (Direction des Constructions Aéronautiques, DCAé), the Directorate for Missiles, and the Directorate for Electronics and Computers created by the Mitterrand government. All are expected to ensure that French forces are equipped with the most modern ground, naval, and air arms within the technological and financial possibilities of the French nation. They cooperate closely with the military services in setting military requirements and in defining research, development, and production programs and priorities. They also oversee segments of the defense industry with which they are, in part, in competition for contracts. All are also expected to facilitate arms exports. These general functions cover what are generally referred to as "state" responsibilities as distinguished from industrial activities.

The technical directorates differ in how they organize and execute these varied state functions and the industrial responsibilities associated with them. The DAT and DCN direct large, complex arsenals that meet most of the ground and naval needs of their respective military services. The DCAé and DEN, which do not have industrial facilities under their direction, rely on private and nationalized firms to produce the equipment demanded by the armed services. This varied pattern may be explained partly as a product of history. The arsenal system for naval and ground arms is centuries old. Despite the creation of the DGA, the military services and engineering corps are still attached to the arsenal concept. The army and navy general staffs view the arsenals as more responsive to their military requirements than private industry.

The DAT and DCN have responded differently to the DGA's explicitly designated military *and* implicitly assigned economic responsibilities. Figures 5-2 and 5-3 suggest these differences. Figure 5-2 distinguishes between DAT's state functions and GIAT's industrial activities. The DAT prepares, directs, and manages approved arms programs. A central technical service within DAT is assigned overall responsibility for a program. Since most weapon systems, like the AMX-30 heavy tank, require a range of expertise and technical advice, engineers and specialists are

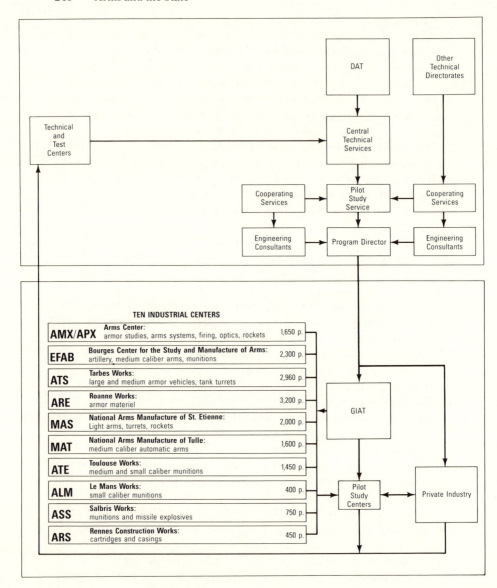

FIGURE 5-2

Organization of the Directorate for Ground Armament (DAT) and the Industrial Group
for Ground Armament (GIAT)

SOURCE: France, Ministère de la Défense, *Direction Technique des Armements Terrestres* (Paris,
1976), pp. 17, 27, and France, Ministère de la Défense, *Délégation Générale pour l'Armement*
(Paris, 1985).

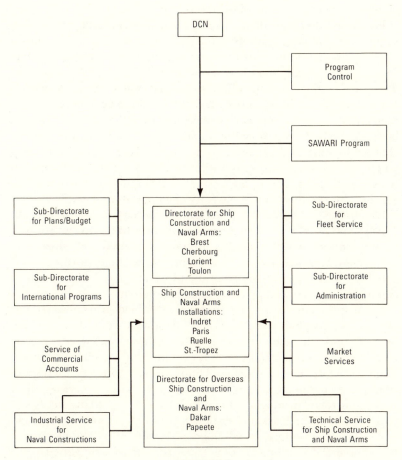

FIGURE 5-3

Organization of the Directorate for Naval Construction (DCN)

Source: France, Ministère de la Défense, *Délégation Général pour l'Armement* (Paris, 1983, 1985), and Ingénieur Général Ballet, "Technique des constructions et armes navales," *L'Armement*, No. 50 (April 1978), 175.

assigned to the program from other services within DAT. A director is designated as the responsible head of a program. Similarly, other technical directorates and services of DGA are enlisted into service, and cooperating services and technical personnel are assigned to the program. This team directs GIAT and its various units and private industry, where appropriate, to develop and produce the weapon. Once these industrial tasks are completed, DAT and officials of the ground army test the equipment before its admission into service.[15]

Figure 5-3 describes the DCN's less formally defined separation between state and industrial responsibilities. The DCN has direct control over eight domestic and two overseas installations variously responsible for research, development, and construction of ships and armaments. The Navy's industrial units within its arsenal system serve as the principal means for refitting, repair, and service of the fleet and its equipment. The Army has less of a requirement than the Navy in this area because much of these operations and maintenance activities are discharged by units at the operational level. The Navy's concern to keep and to control these functions within its arsenal system is registered in the stipulation of the DGA's responsibilities that repair and maintenance are the joint responsibility of the Navy chief of staff and DCN.[16]

Like the DAT, the DCN enjoys access to a special commercial account which separates the DAT's commercial and industrial activities from its state responsibilities. Separate accounting is supposed to sensitize arsenal personnel to the costs of production and to the opportunities offered by marketing abroad ground and naval arms.[17] The record of commercial success and personnel adaptation to market opportunities is less clear than those pressing for greater flexibility in arsenal accounting practices, inventory control, and investment would have one believe. To underline their service obligations, the arsenals were expressly forbidden, until recently, to work for commercial advantage or profit. Many within the arsenal system still find it difficult to accept the responsibility not only of producing weapons for the armed services but of promoting their "products" for export. The Ministry of Finance also resists placing arsenal accounting practices on a level with nationalized firms. That the budgetary, administrative, and attitudinal barriers to the commercial development of DCN may be eroding is suggested by the creation of a special unit within the DCN responsible for the Sawari program with Saudi Arabia.[18] The DCN appears to be adapting gradually to the dual orientation—toward French military and commercial needs— following the path already taken by DAT and GIAT.

The arsenals remain somewhat in limbo—no longer simply arms production units to meet national military needs yet not fully adjusted to the demands for increased commercialization and accountability made

upon them.[19] The DCN and DAT's GIAT cannot produce goods in anticipation of foreign sales, use "profits" to develop new products, cover
risks of operations, or speed orders to subcontractors. Under these circumstances, GIAT is hampered in meeting foreign competition and in
keeping production lines open. One DGA director complained that he
could not produce in anticipation of orders—a normal commercial
practice of private firms. This restriction hampered the arsenals in
meeting foreign competition and in keeping production lines open:

> Do I feel myself to be the director general of DGA? Frankly, no . . . in
> the usual sense of the term. . . . First, because I have no power in so-
> cial matters. The public sector is inserted in such a network of general
> rules that I can decide nothing alone in this area. . . . This absence of
> power stems directly from the state of quasi-financial irresponsibility
> in which I find myself. The rules of public accountability leave me no
> latitude neither in buying nor, what is worse, in selling. At the time
> that our exports are considerable, I do not have the right to draw on
> profits to use for . . . investments. I cannot even, as any boss, support
> my operations from the treasury.
>
> I characterize myself often as a Gulliver in Lilliput, rendered finan-
> cially and socially inert by an immense network of tight ties which
> prohibit the least movement.[20]

For historic reasons, the DCAé and the DEN approach the DGA's state
and industrial functions differently. Their practices are at once simpler
and more complex. They are simpler than those of the DAT and the DCN
because they do not have arsenals under them. They are not in the awk-
ward position of directing themselves and of evaluating their own efficiency. There is also no need to keep track of commercial production.
Military service needs are met through private or nationalized firms.
Relations with industry are more complex because there are greater
opportunities for conflicts of interest over programs, prices, controls,
and client needs. These arise at several levels: between industrialists,
between them and the technical directorates and the armed services,
and between all of them and other administrative agencies and ministries within the French bureaucracy. The directives, under which the
DGA, DCAé, and DEN work, confuse as much as clarify the interests of
these parties.

The problems facing the DCAé illustrate some of these difficulties.
French directives assign the DCAé some of the responsibility for guidance (*tutelle*) of the entire aeronautics industry, including its civilian and
military development. Opinions differ widely, however, on how to
translate tutelle into practice. At one extreme, some would restrict the
state to financial and administrative backing for the industry, leaving it

free to manage its own affairs.[21] Not surprisingly, this view is widely held among industrial leaders of nationalized and civilian firms. Even after the nationalizations of 1981-1982, industrial interests have viewed themselves as possessing "public power," independent of the governing agencies charged to oversee them.[22] Since both the nationalized industries and governmental units, like DCAé, are state agents, disputes between them are between governmental organs, not between the state and private firms. Nationalization blurred, not sharpened, the line where the authority of one begins and the other ends. Industrialists and administrators of nationalized firms can reasonably claim to be as invested with public authority as any DGA official and to represent the public interest. One Socialist minister was chided for leaving too little discretion and initiative to the nationalized industries.[23] Socialist Minister of Research and Industry Jean-Pierre Chevènement was reportedly dismissed from his post for having meddled too much in the affairs of nationalized firms.[24] His successor, Laurent Fabius, later to become François Mitterrand's second prime minister, attempted to steer a middle course between industrial freedom to facilitate competition in international markets and the government's interests in an industry responsive to its military and varied welfare needs.[25]

The DCAé feels these pressures daily. The high and mounting costs of aircraft development and the monopolistic character of the French aerospace industry impose special control responsibilities on the DCAé to promote technologically advanced civil and military aircraft near or at prevailing market rates in the absence of internal competition. The DCAé must replace the controls on price and quality normally associated with domestic competition, yet cooperate with the industry to maintain high profits, full employment, and continued investment to meet foreign competition and to keep pace with military advances made by other states. It is also cross-pressured between foreign clients and the industry. The DCAé provides product control services to foreign buyers of military aircraft. Increasingly, military aircraft sent abroad depart from French armed service specifications. "This tendency," as one DCAé official has conceded, "is not without its delicate problems for the DCAé whose services and test centers find themselves confronted, often at the last moment, with equipment which they must certify but about whose development and configuration they are poorly acquainted."[26] It is no easy task serving as agent of the military services and foreign clients while being held responsible for the economic health and technological progress of the aeronautics industry.

Added to these conflicting tasks are the special concerns of the civilian sectors of the aerospace industry which must be attentive to ecological demands, carrier security, and the "lively and fierce domination of the American industry."[27] These varied roles and divided responsibilities mean that the DCAé must elicit adherence to its recommendations more through persuasion and financial incentives rather than through administrative directives. It must coordinate its oversight and leadership functions with those of other governmental agencies which have overlapping authority and duties as well as special clients to service. Relations are far from smooth; frictions and discord are frequent enough to prompt at least one DGA head to complain: "The [DGA's] tutelle [of the aeronautics industry] in my eyes, is not satisfactory and, structurally, it cannot be. What is worse is that one has difficulty imagining how it could be less ineffective. Note, first of all, that four ministers are concerned and that, unfortunately, they are [all] quite legitimate."[28]

The size of the DCAé suggests how seriously it takes its oversight functions. It employs slightly less than 9,000 employees who are divided among three central services, three test centers, two repair facilities, and several schools for specialized training. The service units provide technical information on aircraft developments and telecommunications as well as prepare long-range production programs. The test centers, which employ almost half of DCAé's personnel, furnish the industry with a full gamut of developmental and industrial facilities for the testing of aircraft and motors. These units work closely with ONERA and the laboratory at St. Louis. Workshops at Bordeaux and Clermont-Ferrand repair and maintain military aircraft. Technical schools prepare personnel for the industry and the armed forces.[29]

The DEN has a more narrow focus and is less crosspressured by conflicting roles than the DCAé. Approximately half the size of the DCAé, its personnel are grouped into three technical services (ballistic and tactical missiles and munitions), four laboratories, and a small central administrative unit.[30] It must rely on France's industrial establishment for the development and production of ground- and sea-launched missiles. It also has control over the tactical nuclear program and new missile programs to arm the Mirage 2000, as well as ground and naval forces.[31] Established tactical missile programs (e.g., Martel, Masurca) and antitank missiles fall, depending on their military function, within the purview of the DAT and the DCN. In space, it plays a dual civilian and military function. It is charged with developing military satellites and with assisting in the design and perfection of civilian launchers and space systems. In the latter capacity, DEN representatives participate in working groups of the surveillance committee for Ariane. These broad civilian roles ensure that the interests of the Ministry of Defense will receive a serious hearing in the development of France's civilian space program.

Since 17 percent of the military capital budget passes through DEN, the defense establishment can use its financial leverage to insinuate its interests into planning for civilian space programs.

In 1985, the service unit concerned with electronics and computer technology was upgraded to directorate level. The Directorate for Electronics and Computers (Direction de l'Electronique et de l'Informatique, DEI) combines the activities of the technical or operational directorates as well as the functional or crossunit tasks of the functional directorates, discussed below. In the former capacity, it develops transmission, communications, and command systems linked to electronic media. It is specifically charged with the responsibility for command and control of nuclear forces. Its Center for Electronic Armaments (Centre d'Electronique de l'Armement, CELAR) near Rennes, with a staff of over 700, including approximately 200 military and civilian engineers, conducts tests and evaluation of electronic equipment destined for the armed services. In its functional role, it has a wide range of responsibilities, including the development of an industrial electronics and computer policy, coordination of armed forces electronics programs, and support for the development of the electronics industry and foreign exports.[32]

Functional Directorates. There are currently two functional agencies in the DGA. The Directorate for Personnel and General Armament Affairs (Direction des Personnels et Affaires Générales de l'Armement, DPAG) is charged with the overall management, recruitment, and training of DGA personnel. The training and professional development programs for personnel are well structured and articulated. Skilled workers and technicians are divided into six recruiting categories. At the lowest levels, students, some younger than sixteen years old, are recruited through competitive examinations and given training for two to four years in specialized tasks, like electronics, leading to a Bachelor's degree. These students may enter either advanced technical schools (Ecole Technique Nationale, ETA) at Arcueil and Brest, or they may pursue specialized training at the Ecole Technique Normale de l'Armement (ETNA) at St. Etienne and Latresne near Bordeaux.

The training of engineers as well as technical and administrative staff is more extensive and elaborate. Three categories of personnel are sought. At the pinnacle stand the armament engineers who enter into DGA service largely through the celebrated Ecole Polytechnique or, less so, through competitive examination. Those entering through this route are earmarked from the start to ascend the promotion ladder to higher offices. Recruits go either to the Ecole Nationale Supérieure des Techniques Avancées (ENSTA) in Paris or the Ecole Nationale Supérieure de l'Aéronautique et de l'Espace (ENSAE) at Toulouse for two years where they develop along specific career lines in applied military engineering, covering naval construction, engine and aircraft design, communications, or ground armaments.

A second level of recruits is designated engineers of arms studies and technique (Ingénieurs des Etudes et Techniques d'Armement, IETA) and are drawn from civilian engineering and technical schools through competitive examinations. Recruits are normally sent to the Ecole Nationale Supérieure des Ingénieurs des Etudes et Techniques d'Armement (ENSIETA) for two to three years or to the Ecole Nationale d'Ingénieurs de Construction Aéronautique (ENICA). Finally, technical and administrative cadres are formed through training at the Ecole d'Administration de l'Armement (EAA) for two years to study the legal and economic dimensions of arms production.

The recruitment and training process for DGA personnel accents the point that French arms production in France is a long-term, highly developed *state* enterprise and not a partisan concern subject to the vicissitudes of a passing government. Created are cadres of engineers and specialists who are expected to work for the state in developing new and better arms—and to sell them abroad. The incentives of national service and the pursuit of personal gain and high social status are thus joined and sanctioned by the state. A large and differentiated bureaucratic structure within the Ministry of Defense, as well as ample opportunities for advancement in the arms industry, encourage high morale and cohesion.[33] Formed is a dedicated corps of some of France's most talented and accomplished individuals who are committed to the development, production, and sale of arms. The marriage of national service and personal interest is a major force for expanded arms sales and their promotion. France has not only been in the arms business a long time, but its manpower policies, keyed to the pursuit of national independence, sustain its continued success. New and talented personnel, spurred by ambition, by the prospect of high status and financial rewards, and by a desire for public service, continually replenish the ranks of the DGA and the military-industrial complex.

The Directorate for Research, Studies, and Techniques (Direction des Recherches, Etudes et Techniques, DRET) links the private and public sectors of the scientific community in France, including university laboratories, to the weapons industry.[34] It conducts and coordinates research with military applications; provides scientific data and results to the military services; evaluates the evolution of scientific exploration and technological developments; and manages or initiates study of new technologies applicable to military purposes. Created in May 1977,

DRET is a relatively new unit within DGA. It absorbed most of the responsibilities previously executed by the Directorate of Research and Testing (Direction des Recherches et Moyens d'Essais, DRME). Operating seven test and data centers that cover a wide range of activities from communications to data processing, DRET is expected to track new scientific discoveries and relate them to military uses. It exercises a guidance role over ONERA and the Franco-German Institute of Research at St. Louis. It is also at the center of a complex of ties to university laboratories, corporate research units, and governmental agencies, especially the General Delegation for Scientific and Technical Research (Délégation Générale à la Recherche Scientifique et Technique, DGRST).

It is difficult to summarize DRET's activities because it is charged with oversight of the entire range of scientific discovery and technological development. It must accomplish these tasks with a modest budget and a relatively small staff of approximately 2,000, resources smaller than the funds and personnel under the control of the military services and technical directorates.[35] The DRET organizes and often presides over working teams of engineers and service specialists concerned with a specialized technology like lasers or optics. These teams are charged with the responsibility of drawing up research programs to be funded from service budgets. Distinguished scientists regularly sit on its board of review and consult with DRET, the services, and the technical directorates. Every second year, the Academy of Sciences recognizes a distinguished scientist for his contribution to DRET's program.[36]

There exists no overall plan for civilian and military R&D programs. The latter have developed over time and have gradually become institutionalized within the French budget, industry, and university laboratory activities. The DGA is able to shape significantly the orientation and pace of these programs since the Ministry of Defense commands approximately one-third of the government's R&D expenditures. In setting priorities DRET plays a secondary role. One administrator characterized its role as a "notary" who recorded the contracts, let primarily by the technical directorates working in close cooperation with the military services.[37]

The Minister of Research and Industry, while technically in control of approximately three-quarters of the civilian R&D budget, has actually less say about the direction of R&D in France than the Minister of Defense. Most of the funds assigned to the Ministry of Research and Industry are earmarked for established programs like the Atomic Energy Commission and National Center for Scientific Research (Centre National de la Recherche Scientifique, CNRS). In the early 1980s a billion francs was left to the ministry for the entire French industry, including claimants linked to arms development.[38] Similarly, large sums assigned to the Ministry of Transport for civil aviation also come under DGA and DCAé oversight.

Almost all of the R&D funds available to the Ministry of Defense are divided among the CEA, the directorates within DGA, and industry. In 1981, CEA and the DGA were allocated 26 percent of the government's R&D expenditures, while industry received the lion's share of 73 percent. Universities received a paltry 1 percent. Table 5-1 lists the benefiting industries under Column A, with the exception of atomic energy, and the areas of study and development under Column B. Electronics, engines and missiles, nuclear industries, and aeronautics have the highest priority. Within these industries, preference is given to chemical energy, propulsion, and explosives (24 percent), computers (17 percent), and mechanics (15.5 percent). The flow of information and priority setting tends to be one way at the national level. Representatives of the DGA regularly sit on interministerial committees, including the Plan, but often for security or administrative reasons information is not shared with civilian agencies.[39]

Delegates for Industrial Policy and International Relations. Shortly after the election of the Chirac government in 1986, the newly appointed

Table 5-1. Percentage of Military R&D Listed by Industry and Branch of Study

Industry		Branch of Study	
A	%	B	%
Electronics	26.8	Computers	17.0
Aeronautics	14.5	Telecommunications	10.3
Engines and Missiles	22.1	Physics	5.0
Naval Construction	2.6	Optics	13.5
Ground Vehicles	2.3	Solid State Physics and Electronic Components	2.0
Conventional Arms	10.8	Mechanics and Physics of Fluids	15.5
Nuclear	20.9	Chemical Energy, Propulsion, Explosives	24.0
	100.0	Structural Materials	10.0
		Scientific and Human Biology	4.5
			100.0

SOURCE: "L'Effort public de recherche et de développement technologique," *Le Progrès Scientifique* (November-December 1981), 24-25.

General Delegate for Armament created two units for industrial policy and international relations, headed by special assistants, each with the title of delegate, directly responsible to him. These were, respectively, the Delegate for Armament Programs (Délégué aux Programmes d'Armement, DPA) and the Delegate for International Relations (Délégué aux Relations Internationales, DRI). The two directorates that had been previously responsible for these areas were abolished. These were the Directorate of Armaments Programs and Industrial Affairs (Direction des Programmes et Affaires Industrielles de l'Armament, DPAI) and the Directorate of International Affairs (Direction des Affaires Internationales, DAI).

The reorganization strengthened the DGA's industrial and commercial roles. It culminated a long evolutionary process of organizational transformation, underway for over twenty years, during which the DPAI and the DAI gradually grew from support agencies within DGA to superdirectorates acting as the DGA's principal instruments for the adaptation of the arms industry to France's overall industrial needs and for the expansion of arms exports and joint development and production programs with other states. The DPAI's broad reach across the DGA and the defense establishment, other governmental bureaucracies, and French industry was not reflected in its status as a DGA directorate. The DPA's absorption of the DPAI's general oversight functions and its elevation in rank and power within DGA bring into closer alignment the sweeping organizational grasp of the unit with its reach.

The DPA directs and supervises the preparation and execution of research, design, and industrial programs; repair work on arms equipment; and the preparation of plans for industrial development, including financial and technical support for their execution over annual and five-year budget and program cycles. These administratively prescribed responsibilities are subordinated to an unstated but implied political imperative: the preservation and promotion of an ever-modernizing arms industry within an internationally competitive French industrial system. In the final analysis, as one DGA official once observed, "there is no arms industry," since France's capacity to meet its arms requirements depends on the growth of France's economy and on its continued scientific and technological development.[40] The DPA's enhanced position within DGA facilitates its tasks in orienting the work of the arms industry and of harmonizing its activities with those of other French industries within the broad economic planning goals of the French government. Pressures are intense within the DGA for favor from those interested in aerospace or electronics or the improved commercialization of ground (GIAT) and naval arsenals. The DPA can manage these rival claims more easily on behalf of the DGA's General Delegate as Delegate for Armament than from the trenches as a directorate in combat with organizational equals.

Like the DPAI, the DPA exercises overall control of the formulation and direction of DGA industrial policy and how it is executed through DGA's directorates and services. While the DPA is in constant contact with all of the DGA's functional and technical directorates and services, day-to-day oversight of the arms industry and detailed forward planning is discharged by a newly created service that disposes those powers and responsibilities not otherwise assigned to DPA. The Central Service for Industrial Affairs of Armament (Service Central des Affaires Industrielles de l'Armement, SCAI) prepares data and evaluations to improve the competitiveness and profitability of the French arms industry; sets out guidelines for defense contracts and industrial practices; specifies the financial and organizational arrangements needed to preserve the independence of the arms industry; and suggests ways to enhance the contribution of the arms industry to the nation's industrial development and commercial competitiveness.

The 1986 reorganization also introduced additional organizational clarity in the execution of the DGA's *tutelle* role over the aerospace industry. While the responsibility for furnishing technical advice and assistance about civilian aircraft and helicopters still resides in the DCAé, the overall responsibility for defining the economic and commercial development of the civilian and military components of the aerospace industry is more clearly lodged in SCAI, whose work is guided by DPA leadership. Conversely, the SCAI, as a DGA service, is expected to be responsive to the needs of the technical and functional directorates rather than to operate on its own as a competitor.

In contrast to the technical directorates, the DPA has a long-term vision of France's industrial needs, emphasizing industrial development and trade expansion rather than immediate arms production. The DPAI often interceded on behalf of industrialists caught short by a lack of work or in need of rescheduling authorization in meeting French armed service deadlines because they had to fill foreign arms orders. The DPAI had been known, too, to have found financial support for production lines or design and research teams whose contracts had been terminated.[41] The DPA can be expected to follow these precedents largely by relying on other DGA units to supply needed aid.

Merely illustrating DPA's concern for the health of the arms industry scarcely describes its importance. Through the DPA, in cooperation with SCAI and other DGA units, French industry is profoundly shaped and oriented toward the arms needs of the Ministry of Defense. DPA guides the French industrial plant to meet France's arms requirements and, with DRI, to compete in foreign arms markets. It strives, and is expected, to present a unified DGA front toward other governmental agencies, the Plan, and the industrial community. Given the resources at the disposal of the Ministry of Defense for research, development, and arms and supply purchases, the DGA, now assisted by a more flexibly organized DPA, may be said to have the largest weight among an array of less organized and endowed governmental bodies responsible for France's industrial growth. The weakness of internal economic planning within France and the gradual enfeeblement of the Plan as an institutional mechanism afford the Ministry of Defense multiple opportunities in allocating its contracts and deploying its administrative organs to mark French industrial planning indelibly with an arms imprint. What is particularly striking is the success of the DGA and the DPA in making their influence felt, quietly and unobtrusively, behind the veil of interministerial groups hidden from public view and within the corporate board rooms of France's leading firms. The DPA is clear about its industrial bias over immediate service needs (though the latter are hardly neglected) and its interest in strengthening the arms segment of French industry. As one DGA official argued: "The role of the Army is not confined to national defense; it ought equally to reinforce the national structure, notably industry. Any time that we can facilitate a reorganization, we intervene without hesitation. We have been at the origin of the reorganization of Bréguet-Dassault or the constitution of CII."[42]

The DPA leads more by persuasion than by command. It must coordinate the work of the other directorates which have their own historical and legal standing, access to public and governmental support, special bureaucratic interests, and client groups. Within the DGA, the DPA argues for long-term industrial and economic needs over immediate service demands. It must convince rather than order the technical directorates to invest in research with no immediate arms payoff and to be sensitive to the economic and financial constraints within which industry lives. Outside the DGA, it orients French industry toward the military and economic objectives of arms production and foreign sales. It presides over, more than rules, a sprawling collection of industrial units, each with its own particular concerns but all linked to arms development and production. Whether the arms industry tilts toward economic or military imperatives, the thrust since the 1970s depends on the delicate balances the DPA is able to negotiate within the DGA, the French bureaucracy, and the industrial community on developmental and production priorities. This balancing act is largely conducted within the DPA. The five-year defense plans, annual updates, and administrative and industrial adjustments to projected plans or, alternatively, changes in planning goals to respond to constraints or opportunities before the armed forces or industry are orchestrated through DPA with the help of SCAI. The DPA cues those sections of the arms ensemble that will be given emphasis while guiding other parts to play a subordinate or supporting role. While it has little or no power to eliminate any of the players, it has a significant impact on what contribution they will make, in what sequence, and in combination with what set of players.

What makes the DPA's work particularly difficult is that its broad responsibilities for promoting France's industrial and economic growth and for meeting France's arms needs must be harmonized with its equally important state obligations to oversee the production quality and financial and administrative accountability of the French arms industry. These state activities raise role problems and conflict of interest issues for DPA. Among its several roles, played simultaneously, the DPA is the state-as-client, when it intervenes on behalf of the military services, the state-as-economic promoter, the state-as-exporter and agent on behalf of foreign buyers, and the state-as-auditor and substitute for the market in allocating resources and in assuring the efficient production of quality arms.

France's arms industry qualifies as the most highly regulated among the liberal democracies. The complex rules and requirements under which the industry must operate are incorporated in a corpus of laws, governmental decrees, administrative regulations, and informal arrangements governing the relations between bureaucratic units and between the government and the industrial community. The modern legislative foundation on which the regulatory foundation of the arms industry rests was laid in the 1930s, well before the creation of the DGA or the DPA.

The National Assembly accorded the government broad powers over the arms industry. Essentially all arms production, importation, and exportation are prohibited without explicit governmental authorization. Laws passed in 1935 and 1939, along with the first nationalization wave in 1936, defined the range of the government's power to intervene in industrial affairs concerned with arms. The initial thrust of this legislation was to preclude arms manufacturers from making excessive profits from the arms trade. To this reformist urge were added over time other governmental objectives that have become increasingly important. These include means to verify the quality of arms before they are admitted into use, careful study of development and production costs to ensure competitiveness, and careful auditing practices to guard against waste and fraud. An arms manufacturer is obliged by 1935 legislation to furnish "at production sites . . . all accounting and statistical documents asked of it . . . as well as justifying materials."[43] Under laws passed in 1939, governmental control extends over all technical and accounting operations, notably . . . production, improvements realized in manufacture, profits, and spending for publicity and representation. . . ."[44] Arms producers must also permit representatives of the government to "penetrate into every part of their enterprise" to assess the entire range of a firm's activities extending even to social legislation and salary policies.[45]

Two agencies of particular interest are the Service of Industrial Surveillance of Armament (Service de la Surveillance Industrielle de l'Armement, SIAR) and the Government Commissioners (Commissaires du Gouvernement), attached to the controller general of the armed forces, outside the direct purview of the DGA. Examination of the work of these units provides a useful shorthand of the complex legislative rules and administrative regulations within which the arms industry operates.[46]

Created in 1964, SIAR is under SCAI's direction.[47] It groups within one unit the quality control personnel previously attached to each of the armed services. It verifies the technical quality of arms produced by French industrialists and certifies equipment purchased by the armed services and foreign governments. To carry out its missions, SIAR's 2,400 personnel operate six regional units and a central office in Paris. These establish a tight network of relations at the factory level between SCAI and industrial firms. Specialists in the weapons systems of the armed services are stationed permanently at these production sites or periodically visit these sites to inspect manufacturing processes and products. Only SIAR can authorize the substitution of industrial quality controls for its own procedures. Personnel from SIAR also assist in assessing developmental and production costs and keep track of orders, production schedules, and inventory. Its authority is clearer with respect to private or nationalized firms than to arsenals. Toward the latter, a SIAR publication observes, "It does not have in its domain of responsibilities the fabrication or repair of materials produced by the establishments and arsenals of the Minister of the Armed Forces."[48] Its oversight of arsenal activities must be mediated through the technical directorates. In the corporate sectors of the arms industry, SIAR's presence is pervasive. It binds the SCAI, the DPA, and the DGA to the day-to-day operations of the defense industry and keeps them closely abreast of industrial developments at the shop level.

The corps of Government Commissioners precedes the formation of the DGA and SIAR. Created in the 1930s, the Commissioners guaranteed that the arms industry hewed closely to governmental directives and to proscriptions against excess profits. The corps has gradually broadened its functions and administrative purview, partly in response to the growing complexity of the arms industry. A record of solid achievement and growing confidence in the professionalism and objectivity of the Commissioners prompted new responsibilities to be assigned to the corps. The primary task of the Commissioners is "to assure, for the benefit of the Minister of Defense and the General Delegate for Armament, rapid, accurate, and continued information about the situation and activity of arms enterprises under [all] administrative, financial, accounting, and economic aspects."[49] One of the principal duties of the Commissioners is to produce a series of annual reports on the major arms enterprises. These 60 or so units are regularly covered by the small but elite group of approximately 13 military officers who, although attached to no service branch, hold the rank of general. The reports of the nationalized firms (Aérospatiale, SNECMA, SNPE) are filed with the Cour de Comptes—a unit similar to the U.S. General Accounting Office—which is responsible for post audit of firm accounts.[50] Commissioners also sit on the governing board of the major aircraft firms and exercise a veto power of their activities. In their capacity as a *fonctionnaire coordonnateur*, they also serve as a conduit of information for all agencies of government with respect to specific arms firms. As special agents of the Minister of Defense, and not of the DGA, they can review the activities of arsenals. Through practice, they have exercised particularly close review of the pricing policies of the electronics industry and engineering firms while leaving many of these responsibilities in the aeronautics and mechanical industries to SIAR. The Commissioners have also been employed by the government for delicate political tasks such as preparing Dassault and Matra for nationalization or by the National Assembly to determine, in its investigation of the industry, how aeronautics firms have utilized public funds.[51]

If the DPA is critical for the internal operation of the DGA and its oversight and direction of the arms industry, the DRI is indispensable as the principal administrative vehicle by which both are linked to international arms markets and to potential foreign clients. The DRI also facilitates cooperation between France and other arms producers on joint developmental and manufacturing programs. Until 1986, the DRI was a functional directorate—the Directorate of International Affairs—and was placed on a line with DPAI, DRET, and DPAG. Like DPAI, the DAI's purview and responsibilities were too broad and its penetration too deep of the DGA and the armed services, the governmental bureaucratic apparatus, and French industry to be permanently equated in power and significance with the DGA's other functional and technical directorates and services. Its elevation to delegate level confirmed the power it had informally wielded since it was first upgraded and its responsibilities enlarged in the early 1970s. The change in title from international "affairs" to "relations" also underscored the increasing importance of joint projects with other arms producers in the work of the DGA. Now the DPA and the DRI work hand in glove as arms of the DGA in promoting France's industrial development, exports, and multilateral cooperation with other states.

The DRI's importance is somewhat in inverse proportion to its size. In keeping with the varied tasks that must be done to make the arms sales machine operate smoothly, its personnel force (approximately 150 in 1986) is a rich mixture of varied professional orientations and experience. Included in its ranks are arms engineers (knowledgeable about the major weapon systems), diplomats, commercial and financial experts, and public relations specialists. Among their responsibilities are liaison with the ministries of foreign affairs and finance to promote sales and facilitate their execution, advertising through arms fairs, and support for DRI's role as the agency principally responsible for the preparation of dossiers reviewed by the interministerial committee charged with approving industrialist requests to promote or sell arms.

Most of DRI's overseas work is carried out through its four operational subdivisions. Three are geographically oriented. One focuses on North Africa and the Middle East where most of France's arms went in the 1970s and early 1980s. Another concentrates on cooperation with other producers in weapons development and production. Most of the work of this latter group deals with Western Europe, toward which the DRI is increasingly oriented in the 1980s as sales to developing states slacken. A third subdivision is concerned with the general problem of expanding French arms exports and industrial cooperation in those regions not covered by the other DRI units. A fourth group concerns itself with the execution of contracts and their implications for service, professional training, and technical assistance.[52]

The DRI's structure, one set focused inside the French government with the other facing outward toward foreign clients and cooperating states, reflects DRI's dual orientation: to make the French bureaucracy, within and outside the Ministry of Defense, responsive to arms and technology sales and to find new outlets and markets for the French arms industry. Neither French civil servants nor the military officer corps nor industrialists were fully equal to the first task throughout much of the 1960s despite the export success of selected manufacturers like Dassault. The diplomats of the Quai d'Orsay were ill-equipped to assume an expanded commercial role. The military services viewed the arms industry as an extension of their logistics system. They were not interested in assisting other states in repairing and servicing French arms, in training foreign personnel, or in promoting French equipment through fairs and demonstrations. They were also concerned about the transfer of high technology items whose use by other states might prove damaging to French strategic interests. Arms engineers within the arsenal system, by habit and formation, saw themselves primarily as weapons makers to meet national defense requirements, not as arms salesmen. French law was a tangle of restrictions on selling arms and military technology and a drag on initiative and risk-taking. Private and nationalized arms manufacturers were hesitant to embark on a search for arms markets abroad without government support and subsidies. They were not keen on selling arms to states with a dubious reputation for meeting their financial obligations. Financing and insurance for arms sales were not readily available. The arsenals were particularly resistant to change. A revolutionary decree of 1791 (*décret d'Allarde*), proscribing sale of ground and naval arms and munitions, was often cited by arsenal managers to blunt pressures coming from within the government to sell abroad.

French law hobbled foreign sales. The decree-law of April 18, 1939, forbade the export of arms or associated war materials without express governmental authorization. In 1955, a governmental order assigned an interministerial committee the responsibility of authorizing variances from this blanket prohibition on arms exports. The Interministerial Committee for the Study and the Export of War Materials (Commission Interministérielle pour l'Etude et l'Exportation des Matériels de Guerre, CIEEMG) includes representatives from the ministries of defense, foreign affairs, economy and finance, and foreign commerce.[53] On behalf of the prime minister, it passes on "requests for authorization relative to the production and export of war materials" and is responsible for recommending changes in arms sales policy.[54]

While the committee is formally chaired by the secretary-general of national defense, a staff agency under the prime minister, effective leadership of the group has devolved to the DRI (formerly the DAI) director. He prepares all dossiers for committee approval, covering requests to make contact with foreign purchasers, negotiations over proposed sales, and permission to deliver material. Until the installation of the Socialist government, decisions were taken on a case-by-case basis. There existed no formally defined criteria to guide decisions. These were implicit, not explicit, and were defined by the CIEEMG board on a pragmatic basis, depending on the government's economic and strategic aims or conjunctural needs.[55]

The CIEEMG members reflect the special interests of their ministeries.

Since the Directorate for Foreign Economic Relations (Direction des Relations Economiques Extérieures, DREE), within the Ministry of Foreign Commerce, promotes and finances exports, the representative of the Ministry of Economy is concerned with the advisability of loaning public funds to a foreign client to purchase arms and with the rate and terms of such credit extensions. Government backing and intercession on behalf of a client in national financial markets is an additional area of interest. The Quai d'Orsay must worry about the adverse repercussions on foreign policy of a sale abroad—or the refusal to make a transfer. Only the DRI director has an overall view of France's arms transfer policy and of the network of obligations and institutional ties that it engenders.[56] He is in a unique position to orient French arms and military technology transfers. Enjoying privileged bureaucratic status within the powerful Ministry of Defense, the DRI director approaches in importance the DGA director and the service chiefs in the day-to-day influence that he exercises throughout the French governmental apparatus on marketing arms. His special status derives from his position as France's principal arms promoter, presiding over a global sales network. When economic arms transfer considerations clash with foreign and security concerns, he has a powerful say in determining which claims—those of the ministries of defense and foreign affairs—will prevail. As an arms salesman, the DRI director views the Quai d'Orsay and the armed forces as service agencies which are expected to facilitate, not retard, his entrepreneurial activities. In a sense, he is in business for himself, and the Quai and the armed forces are expected to consider seriously his representations.

The ascendancy of Michel Debré, a proven and unswerving Gaullist loyalist, to the post of Minister of Defense in 1969 marked the transformation of the Directorate of International Affairs from a service unit to an external promoter of French arms. The organizational implications of this fundamental shift in orientation came to fruition in the creation of DRI in 1986. Under Debré's leadership the DAI changed from just another functional directorate within the DGA to a superagency with tentacles reaching to most key sectors of the French bureaucracy and to foreign and military establishments around the globe. Debré was driven by the Gaullist vision of a powerful and independent France once again possessed of its lost grandeur. To these ends he dedicated his extraordinary talents as well as his ability for the skilled and, if necessary, ruthless use of power in executing Gaullist designs. Vauban and Colbert appeared to be his inspiration. Like the former, Debré was devoted to a strong defense; like the latter, he strove to erect that defense on the solid foundation of an outward-looking economy capable of competing for markets and raw materials abroad.

Debré concluded that the institutional structure of the French bureaucracy had to be fundamentally reformed to foster, not frustrate, arms sales. Following Gaullist thinking, Debré moved first to appoint a new leadership team experienced in bureaucratic maneuvering and dedicated to reshaping the system to serve a new arms order. The occasion for the shift was inadvertently presented to Debré by the embarrassing *vedette* incident. In violation of French law and the arms embargo imposed by the de Gaulle government against Israel in the late 1960s, Israeli agents, in collusion with French officials, spirited several patrol boats out of Cherbourg harbor. General Louis Bonte, the DAI director, was dismissed over the affair, and Hughes de l'Estoile was appointed in his stead as Debré's chosen instrument to accomplish two major tasks: (1) to focus the personnel, finances, and regulatory power of the French bureaucracy, within *and* outside the defense ministry, to facilitate arms sales and (2) to eliminate obstacles, psychological and institutional, blocking arms sales.

Estoile's two tasks were to be discharged simultaneously. Industrialists, from arsenal heads to the directors of nationalized and private arms producing firms, were urged to take advantage of the state's enlarged supportive role and of expanding opportunities for sales abroad, partly generated by the DAI director and his able and enterprising staff. Administrative ground-clearing and institutional reforms were launched on several fronts to create a more flexible and responsive framework to exploit possibilities for increased sales. An administrative order of April 1973 conferred greater power on the DAI to speed authorization and execution of foreign sales. The list of arms requiring authorization was updated to account for technological advances not covered in the original list which was assembled in the 1930s.[57] Creation of the SNPE better positioned the arsenals to sell munitions. The finance law of December 21, 1970, established a special account for exports, permitting arsenals to invest "profits" made on sales to expand their market outlets.

The military services were also induced to provide training, after-sale service and repair, and arms demonstrations for current and prospective clients. Under Paul Assens and Gérard Hibon, Estoile's successors, the armed forces gradually expanded their contribution, not without reservation, to the national sales effort. Chief of Staff General Guy Méry complained more than once that the "technical assistance load [of the armed forces] for after-sales service (detachments of specialists to foreign governments and foreign students in [military] schools) had reached a saturation point."[58] More, not less, was expected of the armed forces to support the DAI's sales effort. Multibillion-dollar sales to Saudi Arabia alone increased *après vente* services several fold.

The pro-sale posture of the DAI (now the DRI) cued industrialists that a new, permissive practice and an active promotional arms sales policy were in vogue.[59] Successful arms merchants, like Panhard and Dassault, needed little encouragement. Others, in the electronics and mechanics industry and in the arsenal system, had to be nudged and nurtured to be more aggressive in searching for new markets rather than being satisfied with their share of a restricted national outlet. The arms approval process was streamlined and speeded up. The DAI assumed the role of advocate rather than arbiter of industrial requests to sell arms. As the agency primarily responsible for preparing requests to seek arms buyers, negotiate sales, and deliver arms—each a separate approval process—the DAI worked to overcome internal governmental obstacles to sales while lobbying actively to promote more sales.[60]

The elaborate system of approving requests for the prospection, sale, or delivery of arms, while formally retained, was increasingly short-circuited. The DAI often entered the process early by searching out orders or by placing would-be buyers in contact with French arms makers. Meanwhile, the DAI director prepared the CIEEMG agenda to approve arms contracts which it had a direct hand in negotiating. While French law still prohibited arms sales unless an exemption was specifically authorized by the prime minister, the DAI director enjoyed new and expanded opportunities to wire the CIEEMG process to produce the desired result of increasing arms sales. French officials might well insist that the controls governing arms sales were tighter than those of other liberal democracies, but this claim lost much of its force in light of the latitude granted to the DAI director to sell arms. Sales became more the rule than the exception to the blanket prohibition on sales embodied in French law.

The encouraging winks and nods emanating from higher political authority urged the DAI on as advocate, gadfly, promoter, lobbyist, and arbiter of arms sales. The special concerns of the military within the Ministry of Defense could, of course, not be ignored, nor could the particular demands of other ministries represented on the CIEEMG be brushed aside. This said, the DAI held the strongest cards in CIEEMG deliberations. According to one participant in the process, the DAI controlled 65 percent of that body's decisions, DREE and the Treasury about 25 percent, and foreign affairs 10 percent. The DRI's organizational position is even stronger than that of the DAI, its predecessor. The DRI occupies a top rung in the DGA hierarchy, equal in status to that of the DPA and just under the General Delegate for Armament.[61]

The DRI's work, to promote arms sales, is eased somewhat by the broad range of assistance available to French industrialists. The arms industry is accorded special treatment because of the high costs of research and development, the artisanal character of many of its products, and the corporate risks run in designing arms that might not be purchased by national or foreign armed forces. There are also extensive tax- and nontax-related incentives to spur arms exports. Working with the DPA and industrialists, the DRI can exploit these programs to underwrite machine tools, purchases of primary materials and special component parts, basic research, and ongoing developmental expenses. In some areas, like electronics, the government is expected to pay for half or more of the costs of doing business.[62] It also assists in inducing foreign buyers, like Saudi Arabia, to assume R&D costs and to share risks in developing weapons for their own use.

Aid to exports is impressive. Public funds are available to develop new materials for export. In principle these extensions of credit are reimbursable, but as one close observer of DGA activities notes, "the 'line' above which begin the first reimbursements is fixed at a number of copies which are rarely attained."[63] In more than one instance, even this obligation has been waived as in the case of Dassault. Both Dassault and SNECMA were criticized by the Cour des Comptes for failure to repay advances, respectively, on the Mirage F1 and M53 motor,[64] both ventures with which the DAI was closely involved.[65] The government may also induce French armed forces to purchase arms to "guarantee" the quality of equipment destined for foreign clients as in the case of the proposed sale of F1 M53 aircraft to NATO states, or, it may provide facilities (e.g., testing sites at ONERA), use of patents without charge, and special guarantees or compensatory reimbursements to exporting industrialists.[66]

The DRI runs a worldwide marketing network. It has offices in Bonn, London, and Washington to furnish technical and sales advice to prospective clients. They are linked to France's military attachés around the world who double as arms salesmen. French ambassadors are also expected to support this sales effort as a significant part of their responsibilities.[67] Arms exhibits, presentations, and fairs are routine elements of DRI's sales promotion campaigns. Foreign personnel are sometimes employed to show their French wares to best advantage. Before the break with Tel Aviv, Israeli pilots on several occasions demonstrated the capabilities of Mirage aircraft for foreign buyers.[68]

Every two years, fairs are held for air, ground, and naval equipment. The Paris air show, which dates from the prewar era, is a world-class event. Hundreds of manufacturers from states around the globe present their civilian and military equipment. According to GIFAS, the industrial association representing French aerospace firms, these numbers have grown in the 1980s. French military aircraft and armaments are normally given prominent display.[69] Ground arms are demonstrated at a closed session for selected invitees at Satory, an army base near Versailles. At a show in the middle 1970s, 115 firms exhibited 900 military models of ground-related equipment to 93 foreign delegations. The Navy exposes its wares at salons at Bourget, Lorient, and Toulon. At a 1976 show, for example, representatives reportedly from 78 foreign navies inspected French equipment for possible purchase. These fairs have grown each year since the 1960s, reaching an ever larger number of states with an expanding panoply of weapons and support equipment.[70]

The DRI and France's arms makers also have created a commercial network of sales agencies to stimulate foreign purchases. These trading houses are owned or controlled in whole or part by the state. Among the most important are the following:

> L'Office Général de l'Air (OGA), created in 1921, concentrates on aircraft and avionics sales to Arab states.
> L'Office Français d'Exportation de Matériel Aéronautique (OFEMA), organized in 1936, facilitated delivery of aircraft to Israel and, since the embargo, focuses on states other than those in the Middle East interested in aerospace materials.
> La Société Française de Matériels d'Armement (SOFMA), established in 1939, sells on behalf of France's ground arms industry, including GIAT.
> La Société Française de Vente et Financement de Matériels Terrestres et Maritimes (SOFRANTEM) assists in marketing naval and ground arms and equipment.
> La Société Française d'Exportation d'Equipements et Matériels Spéciaux (SOFREMAS) concentrates on markets in the Far East and Africa and complements SOFMA in selling ground arms.
> La Société Française d'Exportation d'Armement Naval (SOFREXAN) organizes naval expositions and promotes sales.

Buttressing this commercial system are specialized technical services to assist foreign clients in the use and maintenance of French military equipment. These include the Société d'Etudes Techniques et de Gestion (SODETAG) with approximately 3,500 employees, roughly half of whom are engineers. The Compagnie Française d'Assistance Specialisée (COFRAS) works with industrialized firms and with developing states in a wide variety of areas from the installation of turn-key plants to coastal defense.[71]

Financial support for arms exports is also as varied as it is extensive. There is, first of all, the Banque Française du Commerce Extérieur

(BFCE) to assist overall French exports.[72] Banks interested in arms sales have also created SOFRANTEM. Banks, like Crédit National, have full-time personnel devoted to solving the financial problems associated with arms sales.[73] These varied forms of financial assistance are succintly summarized by two analysts of French export policy:

> In light of the traditionally close relations between French business and government, it is no surprise that France has, and uses, one of the largest government batteries of explicit export promotion tools. The French government affects the performance of its export sector in several ways, ranging from state ownership positions in several of France's leading industrial export firms, to the use of official export credits and assistance, cash grants, loans by the Ministry of Industry, financing by the Caisse Centrale through loans, grants and mixed credits, and insurance guarantees by the COFACE, to more indirect measures such as tax-related incentives directly and indirectly tied to exports, and the political push to increase export orders provided by the disbursements of French aid in the form of official export credits, tied aid, technical assistance, and training programs.[74]

Tax-related incentives include special business deductions to spread trading risks and promotional charges. Tax havens have also been created. Income from arms exports or service and from coproduction activities abroad is exempt from taxation or is taxed at lower rates, while losses may be deducted from tax obligations. Direct credits for all exports amounted to an estimated $22.5 billion in 1977, four times more than in 1970.[75] Exports to developing states, while lower in amount than to industrialized states, were given favored treatment.[76] Loans have generally been soft to arms merchants.[77] Through the Compagnie Française d'Assurance pour le Commerce Extérieur (COFACE), the French government insures arms exports, including guarantees against war, catastrophe, defaults, hedges against inflation, exchange fluctuations, and start-up costs in launching foreign investments and sales.[78]

Who Decides French Military Requirements and Arms Transfers

This one question, often raised in discussions of French arms sales policy, is really two. Making arms for one's forces and selling them, while related activities, have been progressively differentiated in the evolution of French strategic and economic policy. Different aims and diverse interests drive arms production and sales. One can well argue that France's record in pursuing independence through the provision of indigenously produced weapons to its armed forces has been impressive.

Even if this assumption is made, however, it does not follow necessarily that the rise in arms exports in the 1970s or the level maintained in the 1980s can be explained solely by reference to military needs—or as a net contribution to public welfare. Neither the French government nor spokesmen of the arms complex make much of an effort to distinguish the two activities. Supporters of French arms sales policy contend that arms have been defined strictly in terms of national military requirements. Arms transfers are seen as derivatives of French military requirements and justified as an indispensable economic and technological support for them—not to mention alleged foreign and security policy influence exercised by France in selling arms.[79] From this perspective, arms exports are portrayed as the excess of France's productive capacity after French needs have been met. British practice, which is pictured as melding commercial possibilities with national military needs, is invidiously contrasted by arms spokesmen with the alleged purity of French practice.[80] Critics of French arms transfer behavior, on the other hand, like to characterize French sales abroad as risking French security by depriving French forces of the quantity and quality of the weapons that they need to meet the nation's security needs.[81]

As the discussion below suggests, neither view is entirely correct. The force de dissuasion, for example, is not for sale. Its weapon system requirements are invariably assigned top priority. In contrast, nonnuclear weapons and technology are sold to almost all takers outside the Soviet bloc to keep the arms industry solvent. Deciding what balance should prevail between national arms requirements and sales opportunities is at the heart of the weapons choice process. If we distinguish between the making and selling of arms, we will be in a better position to assess the effectiveness of the French arms complex as an instrument of French security and welfare policy and to evaluate the democratic controls and policy considerations guiding arms production and sales.

Deciding Arms Requirements Actors and Interests. Four principal actors, besides political leaders associated with arms and defense policy, shape the definition of French military requirements as well as the quantity and the quality of arms that will be produced for national and foreign forces. These include French armed forces, especially their military staffs, the arms engineers dominating the DGA, with outposts throughout the arms industry, industrial elites at the head of design and production units, and foreign decision-makers responsible for cooperating with France in developing or purchasing arms. Evidence suggests that the initial definition of French military requirements begins with the military services, but rarely does it end with them.

Figure 5-4 presents the classic, idealized portrayal of how weapon systems are supposedly defined. It sketches a flattering self-portrait of

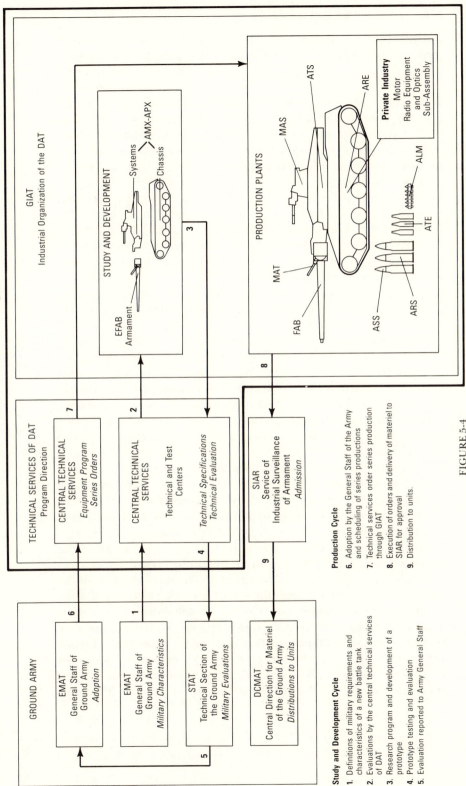

FIGURE 5-4

Design and Production of the AMX-30 Tank: Industrial Group for Ground Armament (GIAT) and Directorate for Ground Armament (DAT)
SOURCE: France, Ministère de la Défense, *Direction Technique des Armements Terrestres* (Paris, 1976), pp. 32-33, and France, Ministère de la Défense, *Délégation Générale pour l'Armement* (Paris, 1985).

Study and Development Cycle

1. Definitions of military requirements and characteristics of a new battle tank
2. Evaluations by the central technical services of DAT
3. Research program and development of a prototype
4. Prototype testing and evaluation
5. Evaluation reported to Army General Staff

Production Cycle

6. Adoption by the General Staff of the Army and scheduling of series productions
7. Technical services order series production through GIAT
8. Execution of orders and delivery of materiel to SIAR for approval
9. Distribution to units.

DAT's decision-making process for heavy tanks. Step 1 of the process begins with a definition of military requirements and characteristics of a new battle tank. These are presented to the central technical services of the DAT for evaluation (Step 2). A research and development program is launched and a prototype built (Step 3). Then DAT's plants are engaged to produce the component parts. The prototype is tested and evaluated by representatives of the technical services and the military staff (Step 4). The team evaluation and recommendation is returned to the army general staff for approval (Step 5). Once authorized (Step 6), the new tank falls again within the responsibility of the DAT and the SCAI which schedule series production (Step 7). In cooperation with GIAT units, GIAT—DAT's industrial arm—produces and equips the tank, following specifications defined by the army general staff and DAT's technical advisers (Step 8). The SIAR checks each tank before its acceptance and its admission by the Army's materiel command which distributes the equipment to designated units (Step 9).

Experience often departs, sometimes sharply, from this ideal picture. Budgetary shortfalls, technological constraints, and the claims of other competing weapons programs preclude realization of armed services' expectations regarding the number and quality of arms that will be available to them. French nuclear strategy has lowered the priority previously assigned to ground forces. When cutbacks are required, it is not surprising to discover that the Army has been among the first to lose its place in the production line. It is also hampered in acquiring enough funds to close the technology gap with Germany, the United Kingdom, and the United States in tank design, armor plating, armaments, and propulsion systems.

Export demands have also placed strains on the Army from time to time. Foreign contracts for armored vehicles have sometimes been given higher priority than national orders. As noted earlier, the Army has been ordered on occasion to deplete its own stocks to meet temporary emergencies occasioned by delivery deadlines for foreign clients. The export account established for arsenals facilitated the development of the AMX-32, paid for by "profits" from previous foreign deliveries, with little attention given to the opposing views of the army staff. The tank was built for export over the objections of army planners who set no requirements for the weapon system. Several other armored vehicles have been produced by GIAT for the international market. The AMX-13B with a 105 mm. gun is for export only; French forces are equipped with 90 mm. guns. A variety of armored personnel carriers are also built for export only, or as modified versions for export. The VBC-90 and the ERC-90 are strictly export items. The AML

M3 VTT, the VCR, versions A through E, and the VLRA/ALM are all export items based on the AML series.[82]

In contrast to official claims, the arsenals, like their corporate counterparts in the arms industry, march at times to their own drum in responding to the cues for greater commercialization directed at them by higher political authority and mediated through DRI, DPA, SCAI, and the export-minded sectors of the DAT.[83] There are, however, limits to how much enthusiasm to sell arms will be tolerated. The director of the GIAT arsenal at Tarbes, for example, was dismissed in the early 1970s because his efforts to boost civilian and military sales conflicted with private industrial interests and deflected attention from the military programs assigned to his unit.[84]

There are limits, moreover, to the degree to which expert consideration can transgress the implicit alliance between the military services, industrial interests, and the arms engineering corps, the latter itself divided within its ranks between those oriented more toward the military or toward the economic missions of the DGA. Ambivalence is a way of life within the arms complex. As suggested in Chapter 2, conflict cannot always be contained and managed within the governing process of the arms complex over which the DGA presides if the vital interests of a key group are threatened. Dassault's proposal of the 1970s, supported by the DAI, to sell F1 M53 aircraft to Belgium, the Netherlands, Denmark, and Norway, as France's champion in the competition for the so-called sale of the century, ignored these limits at the peril of unity within the arms complex.[85] The general staff of the Air Force opposed the sale on these terms because it decreased the number of F1 fighters at its disposal. Of even greater concern was the delay, even possible cancellation, of the program for a new multipurpose fighter. The Air Force signed a contract with Dassault in February 1973 for the development of a two-engined aircraft to replace the Mirage III force as France's front-line fighter. Work on this project was deflected when Dassault, in league with the DAI, pressed its smaller NATO allies to purchase the Mirage F1 with an M53 engine that was still to be developed, but with radar and avionics tied more to the technology of the 1970s than of the future. Without consulting the Air Force, which was kept in the dark by the Ministry of Defense and the DAI, the French government agreed to purchase the F1 M53 on behalf of the French Air Force to assure its NATO allies of the fighter's military viability.

The proposed sale split the arms complex. Air Force officers bridled at the DAI-Dassault *démarche*. They pressed instead for the future combat fighter program (Avion de Combat Futur, ACF). The sale also divided the DGA. The DGA director, the DCAé, and the Air Force pitted themselves against elements in the DAI and DPAI. Marcel Dassault used his access to Gaullist Prime Minister Jacques Chirac to contain internal governmental opposition to the sale and to neutralize any attempt by President Giscard d'Estaing to place obstacles in the path of the Dassault juggernaut. The choice of the F-16 over the F1 M53 by the four NATO states was greeted with relief by Air Force partisans bent on developing an advanced fighter with new avionics and increased engine performance. "We cheered when the French lost the sale," said a high DGA official, "because it saved the Air Force."[86] Once this crisis in confidence had passed, the arms oligarchy again closed ranks. The Air Force settled for the Mirage 2000 in lieu of the ACF whose projected costs proved prohibitive. Dassault received government funds to develop the Mirage 2000. On its own, it also launched the Mirage 4000, a two-engine fighter for export, and sought foreign investments, principally from Saudi Arabia, for the venture since the French Air Force was cool to the proposal.

"We learned our lesson from the episode of the 'sale of the century,'" observed one longtime DGA official. "We cannot go beyond certain limits in forcing any of the armed forces to purchase weapons that it does not want."[87] Similarly, Ministry of Defense officials insisted that despite the quarrel between the Army and its arsenals over the AMX-32, "We are not going to make the Army buy any equipment that it has rejected."[88] That the services can get their way when they are firm and unwavering is suggested by Aérospatiale's criticism of the Epsilon trainer requested by the French Air Force. Aérospatiale had hoped to mount an engine and employ a design more suitable for the export market than the Air Force's conception of its needs. The DCAé and the military services held their ground, and industrialist pressures to change the aircraft's design and propulsion proved unavailing.[89]

Cooperative development and production programs also raise problems for coherent arms design. France's experience with cooperation has been mixed. It has fared well in helicopter production with Great Britain and, similarly, with West Germany for antitank and air defense missiles. It has not had the same success in aircraft development. The high cost of the Jaguar program did not yield an aircraft with performance characteristics to warrant the level of expenditure devoted to it. The Transall and Alpha Jet, while closer to French than German specifications, never fully satisfied either the French or German general staffs. The animus for these developmental programs was primarily political, not military.[90]

Deciding Arms Exports: Actors and Interests. The actors, described above, stand in a different relation to each other when the question of exports is strictly posed. Within the DGA, the DPA and especially the DRI are in the ascendancy. The technical directorates participate to meet export orders through their arsenals and shipyards, but not to decide which states will receive arms. The DGA, which normally is expected to represent French armed service interests in negotiations with industrialists, finds itself on the same side of the bargaining table when exports are being discussed. The military services have no explicit role in the search for arms outlets, although military attachés play important parts in DRI's promotional program. They can also voice objections to arms transfers on security grounds within the Ministry of Defense. As already noted, their responsibilities begin *after* a sale has been consummated since military personnel are detailed to service and repair equipment sold abroad and to train foreign personnel in its use.

The key roles played by the corps of armaments engineers in making France's arms complex run can hardly be exaggerated. Drawn largely from the Ecole Polytechnique, the most prestigious of France's "Grandes Ecoles," the army engineers form a unique and cohesive corps throughout their careers that lead almost inevitably to the highest posts within the Ministry of Defense, the DGA and, increasingly, to leadership positions throughout the nationalized and private sectors of the arms industry and to important civilian posts as well. Sharing a common schooling and formation, they have an engineer's and technocrat's way of looking at issues. Political objectives and priorities are ostensibly defined elsewhere, not by the corps or the DGA. The distinction between ends and means is a useful tact to disarm critics but not very persuasive in practice since what the DGA does *is* governmental policy. Members of the corps rationalize their roles as instruments of announced public policy. Their task is to find solutions to problems whose resolution promotes the interests of the state (and, incidentally, those of the corps as its chosen tool). Bureaucratic demarcations mean less to the corps than the discreetly shared loyalty that binds corps members to each other and to their view of how the state—and their personal interests and ambitions—should be served.[91]

Gradually, the notion has taken hold that members of the corps can serve in various roles that previously were conceived to be incompatible with its intended creation. The engineering corps traditionally took pride in its ability to conceive and develop arms of high proficiency. Technical skill, even aesthetic elegance in designing a weapon, was valued over commercial activities. The latter activity was denigrated as of a lower order of state responsibility or as an object of demeaning commercial concern.

The security and welfare demands upon the government in the postwar period elicited the need for a new kind of arms engineer—one who combined Vauban's devotion to military perfection with Colbert's keen sense of enterprise and mercantilist opportunity. Some corps members preferred the traditional ideal; others, like Hughes de l'Estoile, responded to the call for the new entrepreneur-engineer, given *imprimatur* by Gaullist barons like Michel Debré and Pierre Messmer. Those with the first orientation have tended to gravitate to the technical directorates or to the design and engineering workshops of the arms industry. Those who are comfortable with Colbertism drift toward the SCAI, DPA, and DRI or assume leadership posts in the arms industry. Those who are unable to adjust to the new environment are either isolated or led to resign of their own accord.[92]

The network of corps ties goes deeper and is more extensive than the organization charts of the arms industry or of the DGA can capture. The arms engineers who are liberally distributed throughout the weapons complex are the glue that holds the system together. Increasing numbers of the corps have no difficulty rationalizing their service to the state from the perspective of an industrialist or functionary since both activities are viewed as different aspects of a single national policy to make and sell arms. In contrast to American practice where conflict of interest law between private and public responsibilities is well developed and articulated (if not always observed), French practice is less sensitive to these distinctions. This difference in attitude among arms industrial elites in the two countries should not be surprising, nor is American practice necessarily of a higher moral order. The pervasive influence of the French state makes it difficult for even purists to know when to draw a line between private interests and public responsibilities when the activities of the corps are taken in name of the state and its policies.

Role confusion and conflict of interest inevitably arise, as in the sale of the century, but these eruptions are viewed by participants in the French system more as an exception than as the rule. There appears to be an unwritten rule that it ill serves corps interests to air these differences in the open. The easy slide of corps members from government to industry and back again might well be impeded or blocked by too much of a public fuss. There has evolved instead a subtle process of resolving differences over perspective or interest as they arise and of confining these conflicts within the institutional framework of the arms complex and, specifically, within the DGA. The upshot is a corps of engineers, within and outside the government, bent on making and marketing arms and convinced, with few nay sayers, that their interests, personally and collectively, lie in promoting and protecting the arms complex.[93] The informal leadership of the corps, defined by the high positions formally held in the governmental and corporate units of the arms complex, controls the recruitment, training, and incentives—salary, rank and status, and professional opportunities—of those working in the arms system. They are powerful levers in quieting dissent and in eliciting loyalty or acquiescence.

ARMS EXPORTS AND DEMOCRATIC CONTROLS

To what degree is the arms transfer policy process subject to public scrutiny and democratic control? This is not an easy question to answer. There is little agreement on which criteria should be applied to meet a democratic test. Discord turns not only on whether substantive or procedural measures should be used, but also on the priorities that should be assigned to order governmental objectives. Meeting these tests, however defined, may not necessarily result in sound public policy. A majority of French citizens supported prewar security policies with disastrous results for France. Similarly, democratically elected governments waged costly and ultimately hopeless colonial wars in Indochina and North Africa. It required a coup d'état to force the Algerian issue to a head and a subsequent countercoup by the de Gaulle government against rebellious officers to extricate France from colonial strife and, ironically, to preserve France's democratic tradition.

At the risk of simplifying the complexity of the problem of democratic consensus and effective policy-making, one can stipulate that a democratic decision-making process for arms transfers should have at least three characteristics: (1) a free flow of information about the purposes and implications of arms transfers for France's security, foreign policy, and economic interests; (2) continuing evaluation of policy choices and the posing of alternatives to maximize announced objectives; and (3) the clear assignment of responsibility for decisions about policy and their execution, viz., public accountability. The governing process of the arms complex falls short on all these counts.

Information Flow

As for the first test, the arms transfer policy process, as suggested earlier, scores low. Information about arms production and transfers—about their cost, size, composition, scheduled manufacture, financing and destinations—is hard to come by. While the annual parliamentary reports on the defense budget are the principal source for gross estimates of the value and regional distribution of arms deliveries, it is impossible to know from these economic data, who gets what arms, when, and at what price. One has to rely often, as the notes in Chapter 7 illustrate, on newspaper accounts of sometimes doubtful reliability or on a disparate array of fragmentary foreign sources to keep track of arms transfer decisions. These data problems are major impediments to a satisfactory evaluation of French arms sales behavior. One valuable source, the monthly journal *Armement*, is essentially restricted in circulation to subscribers within the DGA and to arms firms and contractors. It is designed as a house organ to inform operatives, not the general public, about the doings of the military-industrial complex. *Défense*, another in-house organ devoted to security issues, with occasional articles on the arms industry and exports, is also limited to à select list of subscribers within the French security community.

French governmental practice discourages a sustained flow of public information. Restrictions, justified for raisons d'état—military and economic, shroud the interest of political leaders and functionaries within the arms bureaucracy and industry in maintaining a protective glacis to protect their discretionary authority from public scrutiny or higher governmental control. Since the government and its agents control information flows, they have a significant say about how their own behavior should be understood and evaluated. Penetrating this realm is difficult even for governmental officials and bureaucrats outside the security community. One learns early, as a recent inductee into the DGA observed, to be discreet in divulging information about industrial practices, program financing, or commercial arrangements.[94]

The arms complex also has powerful muscles to flex when threatened by criticism from within the French bureaucracy. Internal evaluations of the arms industry have been squashed when embarrassing revelations touched important officials within the arms complex. The Mayer report, commissioned by the Minister of Defense and the Minister of the Economy and Finance, has never been made public nor has any government responded to parliamentary requests to air its findings. These reportedly criticized the government's failure to spend enough for military research and development to maintain the competitiveness of the arms industry and for varied lapses, including its mismanagement of the Roland contract with the United States. Specific officials were identified for their incompetence. Pierre Mayer himself, although a respected inspector of finance, was not spared attack. He was induced to seek refuge in the Ministry of Justice as a special assistant to the minister to escape the counteroffensive mounted against him for having had the temerity to trespass, even when ostensibly authorized, on the preserve of the military-industrial complex.[95]

In contrast to American practice where investigatory reporters, Congressional committees, and private associations are locked in a never-ending struggle to expose governmental shortcomings, a clear distinction is drawn in France between *le pouvoir*, the installed government exercising the state's power as the latter's agent, and French society. There are few effective institutional checks outside the state apparatus to oversee the daily activities of its agents on a continuing basis; absent are a well-established tradition of investigative reporting—*Le Canard Enchâiné* notwithstanding—and a well-developed network of independent security and arms control research centers which might be alternative sources for information and evaluation of policies.[96]

The National Assembly also stands outside le pouvoir. While the Prime Minister and his cabinet can be dismissed by parliament, the President of the Republic, who nominates the Prime Minister, is directly elected and draws his authority from the Constitution and the French electorate. Parliamentary inquiries, like the probe of the aircraft industry and of alleged financial irregularities perpetuated by the Dassault corporation, are extraordinary events, not routine exercises of legislative oversight. Parliamentary reports (written often by administrative personnel detailed temporarily to the National Assembly), are sparse about internal governmental operations and decision-making. The government commission established by the Socialists to assess the record and policies of President Mitterand's predecessors, while a departure from usual practice, was diluted in impact by the closed-door procedure adopted in soliciting testimony from military and bureaucratic officials.[97]

Once in power, former critics of the government tend to rely upon many of the same techniques used by their predecessors to control information flow. When out of office, Minister of Defense Charles Hernu joined with his Socialist colleague, Jean Pierre Cot (briefly Minister of Cooperation), in proposing legislation to oblige the government to consult and inform the National Assembly about the transfer of arms, licenses, and technology. The Hernu-Cot bill also stipulated that parliamentary approval would be required for contracts over a billion francs and discretionary above 100 million francs.[98] The National Assembly has never acted on this formula. The Socialist government's pledge to inform the National Assembly about arms transfers resulted, ironically, in less, not more, information about arms transfers. Annually reported data about orders *and* deliveries no longer regularly appear as they did earlier in the Senate and National Assembly reports on capital defense expenditures. Under the Socialist government, information about arms orders (presented in gross percentage amounts by region but not by country) was sent to the National Assembly every six months, but these slim data confuse more than clarify current commitments and long-term trends with respect to export dependency regarding what arms will be produced for what countries over what period of time.

After 1980, data about deliveries no longer appeared; only semiannual reports were communicated to the parliament. As a rule of thumb, it would appear that as more is said about providing information about arms transfers, less is rendered public.

The growth of the state's ownership and control of the sprawling arms complex has not increased public access to information about how it works and how resource allocation and authoritative decisions are reached on policies and programs. Hidden still are the limits of discretion at the disposal of elites directing the arms system. Cloaked from view are the varied roles and relative power of governmental elites—elected or appointed political officials, technocrats and administrative leaders within the arms bureaucracy—who share responsibility for making the arms complex work. Obscured, too, are the opportunities for initiative of powerful figures, particularly industrial leaders of favored arms firms, to direct governmental resources and financial credit their way.

The closed decisional process in France confronts the analyst with a dilemma. Any considered treatment of French arms production and transfer policy implies an analysis of its governing mechanisms and processes. Those in a position to verify findings are at once reserved about sharing confidences and privy information yet quick to find error with those whose evaluation of the system cite the arms complex for falling short in meeting tests of economic efficiency, military effectiveness, or public and democratic accountability. The instigators of the Mayer report soon discovered, when their critical findings were communicated to the government, that they were subject not only to verbal abuse, but their very personal positions and reputations within the French bureaucracy were assaulted.

These hazards aside, there is a public record available, if supplemented by personal interviews, that provides a provisional, albeit partial, image of the politics and governance of the arms complex in France. Part of the reason for piecing together a mosaic is to provide a target for critics to reveal more than we now know about the French arms complex and to furnish a point of departure for further scholarly research and evaluations to correct and to focus more sharply the refracted image of the arms decisional process that is projected below.

Evaluating Performance

A free flow of information is necessary for the evaluation of policy results and the posing of alternatives to maximize security and welfare objectives as well as to conserve public resources. On these scores, the arms transfer policy process may be faulted on several grounds. Neither critical evaluation of arms transfer results nor long-term alternatives to heavy reliance on selling arms and military technology can be expected from the arms complex itself. Those in the system are ill-suited by training, orientation, or interest to become their own critics. It is expecting too much to believe that participants in the arms complex who have been courted by privileged governmental treatment, will suddenly contemplate dismantling their imperial holdings. Published evaluations or public statements issuing from governmental sources about arms sales are invariably positive. Yet it has long been an open secret within the arms transfer bureaucracy that no clear foreign policy guidelines direct arms transfer decisions.[99] The Socialist government's attempt to define such guidelines has, thus far, had no appreciable impact on arms transfer decisions except to pariah regimes, like South Africa and Chile, which were already on the proscribed list.

One looks in vain for a public analysis of opportunity costs to the civilian economy from sustained investment in indigenously produced arms. Those that appear arise normally outside the arms producing complex or, as in the case of the Mayer report, are suppressed before they can stir public debate. Since only the DGA has the data to make these evaluations, critics are hampered in mounting an authoritative challenge to governmental findings and policies. The DGA jealously guards access to this information, alternately claiming national security or industrial competitive requirements as the basis for the withholding.[100] These data are withheld as much from other agencies—much to their chagrin—as they are from the public. A suggestion from one high civilian servant involved in the CIEEMG process that data about sales and deliveries be consolidated in a computer file accessible to governmental officials with an interest in exports, but outside the DGA, was dismissed without study.[101]

The DGA may well be right that the arms industry is run efficiently because its inspectors in SIAR and the technical directorates apply more exacting standards and exercise closer supervision over production and cost control than their counterparts in other arms producing states, but this claim remains untested. Arms sales may make good business and alternative investments may yield less return, but again there is no way of knowing without asking the interested agencies to make a self-critical assessment of their claim to public funds.

The statistical data furnished by the Ministry of Defense to the National Institute of Statistics and Economic Studies (Institut National de la Statistique et des Etudes Economiques, INSEE) are of questionable value. The data from INSEE are sharply at odds with the reports of arms industry firms and parliamentary reports. They show considerably less economic activity in the arms industry than these latter data sources or even those issued by the Ministry of Defense. There exists, moreover, no agency within or outside the government, including emerging university centers like INSEDD, which systematically evaluates the economic effectiveness of decision-making or the decisional process itself from a security, welfare, or economic developmental perspective.[102]

Information flow on research and development also tends to move along a one-way street—from the other ministries, including the Plan, to the Ministry of Defense but not vice-versa. It is by no means certain that the R&D funds channeled by the technical and functional directorates of DGA to new technological areas, like lasers and electronics which appear to have high military potential, will actually produce either the weapons that are needed or the broad-based scientific foundation that a modern state must have to maintain a competitive edge in meeting foreign challenges. The small percentage of the Ministry of Defense's R&D expenditures that are earmarked for basic science and university laboratory work—only 1 percent of R&D contracts—suggests the "applied" orientation and short-run payoff priorities that shape R&D spending, a criticism reportedly raised in the Mayer report. A comprehensive plan for R&D investment can hardly be made if over one-third is preallocated to military purposes. A five-volume study on research and development and industrial growth, sponsored by the Ministry of Research and Industry in the early Mitterrand years, was fundamentally flawed from the start since participants were precluded from examining military expenditures for research. The seminar that produced the study bordered on a "dumb show" since conference delegates were supposed to be "blind" to over a third of the government's R&D budget.

Looking beyond France's borders, there is no bureaucratic concern for the impact of French and rival arms suppliers' behavior on regional and global security or on economic development in the Third World. The French military-industrial complex can hardly look with equanimity on the prospect of decreased spending on arms by developing countries. Little or no attention is given to the impact on local stability of advanced weapon systems introduced into a region, such as supersonic aircraft in Latin America. Nor is much concern expressed for the arms races that might be provoked by the unregulated transfer of arms to a region such as South Asia or the Middle East where France has furnished arms to most of the principal rivals in the region at one time or another.

Public Accountability

The blocked or impeded flow of information and the absence of sustained and publicly debated evaluations of the economic and security implications of arms transfers—shortcomings inherent in the organization of the French arms complex—point to a third flaw in the system of decision-making. While responsibility for arms transfers may well be fixed in the DGA, working in close collaboration with industrial leaders, accountability about results is less clearly defined. Accountability demands data, evaluation of policy outcomes, and the development of alternatives to existing practices. Lacking these elements, higher political authority is poorly positioned to define policy or direct administrative execution. Elected or appointed political officials become the prisoners of the options favored by the arms complex.

However much the institutionalization of the arms production and sales system within French political and economic life can be traced to the intervention of major political leaders, the system that they have wrought lives beyond them and generates its own interests and priorities. If political leaders, like Pierre Messmer and Michel Debré, had once had to prod the DGA to expand its purview and to urge industrialists to prospect for foreign markets, such initiative from higher governmental authority no longer appears to be needed. The co-option process has now been reversed. Witness the ease with which the Socialist leadership abandoned its efforts to "moralize" arms transfers, as Prime Minister Pierre Mauroy frequently proclaimed, or to refocus French economic resources elsewhere than arms production and sales. President Mitterrand like President Giscard became more the captive than the keeper of the industry. Dependent on Gaullist support in the National Assembly and tied to a Gaullist prime minister, President Giscard d'Estaing was reduced to the role of an interested observer as his temporizing over the Stehlin affair suggested. Neither General Stehlin's frontal criticisms of the F1 M53, albeit self-interested, nor the Air Force revolt could stir the president to confront Dassault and its supporters in the DGA.[103]

The Arms Oligarchy and The Fifth Republic

The DGA and the French Bureaucracy

What factors explain the success of the arms complex within its defined but steadily expanding governmental and industrial domains? What explains the blockage of information flow, the absence of clearly defined and long-term alternatives to dependence on the transfers of arms and military technology as a spur to civil industry, and the broad discretionary power and initiative exercised by the armament engineers within the government and their homologues in industry? First, nothing succeeds like success—or at least the appearance of success. The mixed record of the civilian economy and the weakness of French exports and competitive position abroad in nonmilitary areas provide a powerful argument to continue the arms business as usual. Opportunity costs are difficult to assess. Investments in new civilian enterprises must inevitably appear risky and imprudent when compared to the tangible profits accrued and those still to be made from arms sales. The leaders of the arms complex lose few opportunities to advertise their successes and, not surprisingly, expect to be supported for doing what they genuinely believe that they have been told to do. The arms complex has powerful symbols at its disposal which are useful in eliciting governmental and popular support: the security of the hexagon, the welfare of the French citizen, technological progress, international competitiveness, and, on the part of the corps of arms engineers, the image of selfless service to the state.[104]

Second, the question of arms transfers has also become progressively depoliticized in French politics. At an ideological level, arms sales approach the sanctity of the force de dissuasion, which was put outside partisan politics, as the foundation of France's security strategy, with the victory of the Left in 1981. Selling arms has also become something of a national trust. The arms complex and its leadership are progressively insulated from partisan attacks and upheaval. The nationalization of the remaining important segments of the arms industry or state assumption of majority control of corporate enterprises, like Dassault and Matra, effectively neutralized attacks on these firms as arms merchants seeking private profits. They are now invested with a public interest, ostensibly under governmental control and subject to popular will. The Jacobin urge toward centralization in French politics is served without a corresponding expansion in democratic control of the arms industry either at higher political levels by the mass-based parties, or by society at large. One has public ownership, but not necessarily public control defined by minimal standards of access to data about performance, informed debate over policy alternatives, or increased parliamentary, media, and party oversight.

Since the heyday of the Estoile period, the DGA, the DAI, and now the DRI have assumed a lower political profile. In anticipation of the possible election of the Left in the legislative election of 1978, Jean-Laurens Delpech, a political appointee as head of the DGA, was replaced by Henri Martre, an arms engineer, to underline the nonpolitical character of arms making and selling. Martre assumed the post of director of the General Delegation for Armament when the ministerial title was dropped to signify the nonpartisan character of the post.[105] A career diplomat, Gérard Hibon, replaced Estoile. Martre later replaced

Jacques Mitterrand, President Mitterrand's brother, as head of Aéro-spatiale. Hibon accompanied Martre to Aérospatiale, leaving the DAI directorship to Marc Cauchie, an arms engineer and a longtime DGA functionary. The DRME, headed successively by two eminent Sorbonne scientists, was transferred into the DRET and also placed under the direction of an arms engineer.[106]

The colonization of the private and nationalized sectors of the arms industry by the corps of arms engineers lends additional neutral political coloring to the arms complex. The notion of national service shared by arms engineers extends increasingly beyond the traditional bureaucratic outlets for their talents. It extends to the engineering and technical branches of arms firms and to corporate board rooms. When Hughes de l'Estoile moved to a high post within the Dassault Corporation, few eyebrows were raised—conflict of interest questions notwithstanding. Nor is French law a bar to such easy personnel transfers despite a formal legal requirement, honored as much in the breach as in the observance, for a period of grace in changing from the regulatory sector of the arms complex to the regulated side. *Pantouflage*—the French term for such movement from the public to the private sector—is now commonplace as is the reverse process. In a perverse sense, nationalization has institutionalized two-way *pantouflage* within the structure and practices of the state bureaucracy.

The noticeable absence of interest in conflict of interest problems also reinforces the position of the arms complex within the French bureaucracy and economy. The DGA plays a number of governmental roles. It is at once (1) an agent of the state in purchasing arms (client), (2) a manufacturer and supplier of arms to national forces and to the international market, (3) a promoter of French industrial development, (4) the overseer of French industry, including its own manufacturing plants, to enforce quality and cost control, and (5) a major exporter and export service. These roles furnish powerful legislative and administrative authority to DGA officials in their bargaining with other government agencies. The funds which DGA officials and engineers have at their disposal also provide the arms complex with crucial leverage in interagency negotiations. Control of information and data flow and privileged access to higher political authority reinforce the decisional weight of the arms complex in interministerial deliberations. The DGA's colonization of other bureaucracies and the seconding of its personnel as liaison officers in other agencies provide useful listening posts and lobbyists on station for the arms complex. For example, DGA personnel can be found in the Ministry of Research and Industry as well as in important posts concerned with arms exports in the General Secretariat for National

Defense (Secrétariat Général de la Défense Nationale, SGDN), the principal staff agency for the Prime Minister.[107]

Countervailing power to the arms complex and its spread does, of course, exist within the state bureaucracy. The Ministry of Economy and Finance and the Quai d'Orsay are not without influence. The military services, as parts of the arms complex and as natural enemies of its commercial bent, have limited the degree to which security considerations can be ignored. It would also be a gross exaggeration to contend that the arms complex, revolving around the DGA and industrial interests, is cohesive and always moves in lock step. Battle lines within the complex have to be chosen with care. Today's allies may be tomorrow's adversaries. Besides, all of the players can claim to be exercising governmental authority and to be responding to state needs—all the more so in the wake of the nationalization program. Open conflict within the government merely invites political intervention from otherwise preoccupied ministers, or risks arousing a distracted parliament and a poorly informed electorate.[108]

Conflicts of interest and perspective within the DGA have been resolved either through gradual consensus among key actors and units about the proper roles of the arms complex, or these differences have been institutionalized and managed *within* the agency. The DGA's overlapping and sometimes conflicting roles are portrayed often as a virtue, allegedly giving new power and purpose to the organization.[109] Where differences cannot be papered over or rationalized, units within the DGA, while pressing their particular point of view, stay within the implicit rules of the game that have evolved within the DGA for settling or learning to live with divergent points of view. As noted earlier, DPA, DRI, and DRET take a long-term view of industrial growth; the technical directorates generally work within a shorter time horizon and are normally tilted toward service over industrial interests. Arms engineers, with different temperaments and attitudes toward arms production and sales, gravitate to one or the other of these units or to the industrial sector and specialized branches of the arms complex.

Having gained some impression of the organization, varied roles, functions, and formal powers of the DGA, it may now be useful to attempt to portray them graphically as a way of capturing through a picture how the DGA cues and co-opts the governmental and industrial apparatus and insulates itself from party and public controls. Figure 5-5 identifies the principal actors of the arms complex, the formal authority structure (solid lines), and the influence patterns (dotted lines) of the DGA throughout the French bureaucracy and industry. The President

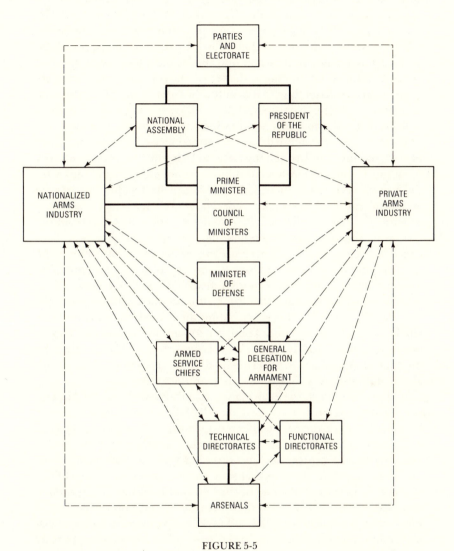

FIGURE 5-5

Formal Governing System and Field of Political Influence of France's Military-Industrial Complex

of the Republic, the prime minister, and the Council of Ministers sit atop the French political system and astride the arms complex. Their authority derives from periodic elections organized and conducted by France's multiple political parties. The president nominates the prime minister. All laws and finance bills must be passed by the National Assembly. The prime minister and his cabinet, including the Minister of Defense, retain office as long as they enjoy the confidence of a majority of the National Assembly.[110] It is in this broader arena of presidential appointment, legislative responsibility, and party and electoral support that the political framework within which the DGA acts is defined.

The Minister of Defense directs the armed services through the chief of staff and the DGA through the General Delegate for Armament. As a matter of formal organizational status, the DGA enjoys equal rank with the armed services and their military chiefs of staff within the defense establishment. Formal equality is deceptive. Whereas the armed services are essentially confined to their military duties, the tentacles of the DGA spread throughout the French state and industry. The DGA is engaged in a ceaseless effort to organize the resources and priorities of the French government and economy to address its needs and aims. The influence of the arms makers is identified by the multiple broken lines extending to the President, the Prime Minister, the National Assembly, and the Ministry of Defense, including the armed services and their chiefs, the DGA and its units. These are too numerous and complex to be incorporated into one figure. What is important to recognize are the multiple lines of access to governmental decision-making that are available to nationalized and private arms manufacturers.

Within the limits of the evolving political framework sketched in Figure 5-5 (defined partially by the demands of the arms complex), the DGA has broad powers, formally conferred and informally acquired through entrepreneurial self-promotion, to execute its multiple roles in discharging key governmental functions. As suggested earlier, its power and influence stem from several sources: its leadership and technical cadres are composed of some of the best and brightest of the French elite, specifically recruited for their security and economic roles; it enjoys easy and continuing access to France's top political and industrial leadership; and it has been accorded strong and sustained support by successive Fifth Republic regimes on the Right and Left.

Figure 5-6 extends Figure 5-5 and focuses specifically on the DGA's roles and state responsibilities. The DGA is the hub of the arms complex. While only the principal lineaments of the DGA's formal authority and influence can be captured by Figure 5-6, they are sufficiently clear to

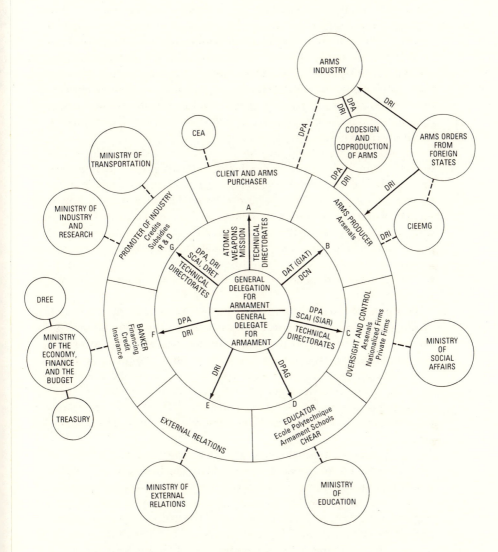

FIGURE 5-6
Roles and Functions of the General Delegation for Armament

highlight not only the insularity of the decision-making process within the arms complex but also the satellite roles—note the outer rings revolving around the DGA—of the other segments of the French bureaucracy in those spheres which are of interest to the DGA. Other ministries are expected to service the DGA and its needs. The DGA has at its disposal the talent, resources, political clout, and a historically sanctioned accretion of powers and privileges, parlayed from a generation of impressive economic and technical achievements, to work the French bureaucracy and industry to its advantage.

The DGA is invested with impressive governmental authority to discharge the multiple and often conflicting roles assigned to it. These are depicted by the large outer ring in Figure 5-6. The inner ring identifies the key DGA units associated with each role. The DGA and the armed services work together in their joint capacities as clients of the arms complex (A). They place their orders directly with the arsenals that are under the technical directorates, nationalized industries, and private firms comprising France's arms industry. The Atomic Energy Commission (CEA), while independent, works in tandem with the DGA's Atomic Weapons Mission.

Through its arsenal system, the DGA is also an arms producer (B). While it has direct control over arsenal activities through authority by the DAT and DCN, it also has close working ties with the governing boards and managerial and technical direction of nationalized industries (or those parts devoted to arms production) to ensure that armed service weapons requirements are filled. The top management of these key producing centers, like Aérospatiale and Dassault-Bréguet, and DGA personnel move freely between these varied organizational structures.

Closely associated with the DGA's producer role is its responsibility for the oversight and control of the arms industry, including the arsenals as well as nationalized and private firms (C). The SCAI and SIAR are the major players, charged with guaranteeing firm compliance with state directives, with ensuring responsiveness of the arms complex to orders arising from French and foreign clients, and with certifying tested products of acceptable quality. The DPA must be attentive to the entire range of state regulations and socio-economic policies concerned with labor relations, wage rates, worker rights, and health and safety codes. Making and selling arms must be harmonized with social welfare legislation. Perpetual vigilance must also be exercised to protect the special privileges accorded management and labor within the arms complex.

The DGA, as educator (D), directs the Ecole Polytechnique, an extensive network of armaments schools and training centers, and the Center for Advanced Armament Studies (Centre des Hautes Etudes de l'Armement, CHEAR). These functions, exercised through the DPAG, inevitably bring the DGA within the field of operations but not within the gravitational pull or directing authority of the Ministry of Education.

The DGA's DRI has a particularly critical extramural role within the French bureaucracy and economy. It motors and directs the decisions of the CIEEMG, which approves foreign arms sales. It is also expected to coordinate the efforts of the ministries of external affairs, finance, and defense to facilitate the sale and service of French arms. The Minister of External Relations is supposed to promote arms, less so to regulate their flow (E). Whether arms diplomacy or the diplomacy of arms sales prevails depends, as Chapter 7 details, on pragmatic adjustment to conjunctural opportunities and restraints.

The Ministry of Economy, Finance, and the Budget, through its various units, acts as banker, credit regulator, and export promoter of the arms complex (F). The DRI has a special interest in arranging attractive credit and finance terms for foreign arms buyers, in guaranteeing loans, in providing insurance for industrialists and banks against the special risks and hazards associated with the arms trade, and in assisting the promotion and subsidy of exports.

As a promoter of French industry (G), the DGA works through the DPA and SCAI. This role, as discussed earlier, overlaps and even conflicts with those of the DGA as producer, controller, and client of the arms complex. The DGA views the Ministry of Research and Industry as a satellite whose function is to improve the overall efficiency of the arms industry and its competitiveness abroad. The SCAI and the DCAé are specifically charged to promote the civil aeronautics industry, a responsibility that brings them within the ambit of the Ministry of Transportation. By overlapping the functions and responsibilities of the DGA with those of other ministries concerned with French industry, a favorable hearing is assured for the arms complex in governmental decision-making affecting subsidies, credits, and regulations to guide industrial affairs. Co-operative arms design and production accords with foreign arms makers furnish the arms complex and the DGA additional leverage in their bargaining with political leaders and ministries whose activities must be controlled and whose resources—material and political—must be enlisted into the service of the arms group. These various forms of leverage and diverse opportunities for intervention in the French bureaucracy and economy to promote industrial development are also joined to the allocation of research funds that are channeled through the DGA's functional and technical units whose resources exceed those of the Ministry of Research and Industry.

The DGA and the French Public: Weak Legislative and Societal Checks

Since there exists broad party, bureaucratic, and industrial support for the arms complex, one could hardly expect the National Assembly to offer much criticism or provide much effective opposition to making and selling arms—a policy that successive assembly majorities have urged and supported. Legislative criticism has been aimed more at the shortcomings of France's sales effort, such as the initially weak after-sale service system,[111] than at curtailing foreign sales. Periodic expressions of anxiety over dependency on arms sales have not been translated into legislative opposition to such sales. If the opinion poll commissioned by the DGA is an accurate indicator of public sentiment, a majority of French citizens favor arms sales as an economic necessity and as a requirement of an independent foreign policy.[112] Of those polled, however, only 16 percent of the national sample of 1,066 respondents had ever heard of the DGA and 50 percent would not respond or venture a guess about the extent of France's cooperative arms programs with other countries.[113] Even if one concedes that public support for arms transfers does not rest on much information or knowledge, there was little encouragement in these figures for skeptical legislators to attack the arms establishment. Another poll of students, taken in early 1985, revealed that two-thirds favored arms sales.[114]

Legislators accept a subordinate role in making defense and arms sale policy. They resist the temptation to delve deeply into government policy. "From everything that I have just said," observed a former chairman of the National Assembly's Committee on National Defense before an audience of military personnel, "it follows that my committee does not participate in the determination of defense policy: it is an attribute of the President of the Republic and the chief of staff of the armed forces, who make it in the Defense Council."[115] As noted earlier, the bill proposed by Charles Hernu and Jean-Pierre Cot, as Socialist deputies, to increase parliamentary control over arms sales was quietly shelved when both became ministers in the Socialist government.[116]

Societal checks on the arms industry and its patrons in government and bureaucracy are no less weak and fragmentary than those faintly discernible within the parliament or parties. Criticism has come from three main sources: churches, peace groups, and unions. None has had a perceptible impact on governmental policy. As early as April 1970, the Catholic episcopate voiced misgivings about the rising tide of French arms sales to developing states. The Bishop of Arras questioned the sale of Mirage aircraft to Libya.[117] Protestant and Catholic leaders mobilized their forces in the next two years and published a joint tract, condemning the sale of arms on moral grounds.[118] The bishops called for more public debate and information about the allegedly damaging economic, political, and moral consequences of arms transfers. Recognized, too, were the international dimensions of the problem and the need to find solutions to convert the arms industry to civilian production without increasing unemployment. Envisioned were increased cooperation among suppliers to control or regulate the arms traffic and a more effective international security organization as a prerequisite for dampening incentives to make and sell arms.

These declarations initially prompted debate within confessional circles and elicited self-justifying governmental retorts. Hughes de l'Estoile rebutted the bishops' note of reflection on arms sales: "It took me seven minutes to read; that is to say it contains little."[119] From the podium of the National Assembly, Michel Debré criticized the prelates for weakening civic virtue and for having no understanding of defense.[120] General André Beaufre, a well-known French strategist, dismissed the bishops' attack as "ridiculous," advanced "in the name of a vague and irresponsible idealism."[121] Public indifference, more than hostility, blunted the impact of the attack by the churches. Efforts to raise questions about the advisability of mounting arms exports continued through the 1970s, but with equally meagre results.

Pacifist and peace groups have been no less vocal nor more successful than the Catholic and Protestant clergy in reducing arms transfers. These groups form a loose collection of associations variously opposed to the arms race, nuclear weapons, or the arms traffic. J. M. Müller, a longtime opponent of arms sales, advocates a policy of nonviolence in constructing France's foreign and security relations with other states.[122] This orientation stops short of advocating civil disobedience except in those instances where moral and religious questions are clearly at stake. Those associated with the movement tend to assume one of two postures: to refuse association with any national military force or arms transfers or to engage in efforts aimed at changing on a global level the international structure within which arms are produced and exchanged.

Other groups, like the Centre Local d'Information et de Coordination pour l'Action Non-Violente (CLICAN), see no possibility for a final solution to the arms sales problem unless the anarchy of the international system, based on national loyalties, is overcome. Socialist and capitalist states are viewed in a similar light, each seeking to press its respective interests. The long-run answer proposed by these groups is an

informed world public opinion united in opposition to further armament.[123] The fight for French national opinion has not been won. These
groups, like the active branches of the Christian churches, currently
stand outside the mainstream of national sentiment.

The absence of a coherent, broadly based countervailing movement
within French society, balanced in political weight to that of the military-industrial complex, is best exemplified by the self-contradictory
stances assumed by France's two principal unions, the Confédération
Générale du Travail (CGT) and the Confédération Française Démocra-
tique du Travail (CFDT). The leaders of these two Left-leaning unions
have repeatedly condemned arms sales. Their bill of charges against
arms exports is well known: a stimulant to regional and global arms
races; a waste of national resources; an impediment to economic development; a contribution to international tensions; a support for "racist
and fascist" regimes; and a profit-making venture of private corporations.[124] The CFDT has been particularly active in mobilizing member
sentiment against continued high defense spending and arms sales. Its
Nantes meeting, assembling 1,700 delegates from its local branches,
passed a resolution criticizing the government's arms export policies. In
particularly harsh terms, the CFDT

> Observe[d] that the present conflicts in the world, open and latent,
> are reinforced by the spectacular development of French [arms] ex-
> ports;
> Accuse[d] the collusion of the French Patronat and government
> for amplifying by this commerce the power of oppression and ex-
> ploitation over Third World peoples through fear and imperialistic
> violence; [and]
> Reject[ed] the false arguments advanced to justify this commerce
> (maintenance of employment, increased effectiveness and independ-
> ence of national defense) which camouflage[d] a will to integrate
> workers to this policy of grand capitalism.[125]

The CGT, while supporting these charges, tends to stress the need for a
strong national defense and an indigenous arms production base.[126]

Union recommendations to control the arms trade and profiteering
fall into several well-grooved formulae. French support of disarmament is generally stressed to relax the need for armaments. The manufacture of national arms, however, is to be concentrated in the arsenal
system and nationalized firms to preclude arms production for profit.
Plans for the reconversion of the arms industry and for broadening the
civil industrial base of the industry are continuing parts of the union position. The capstone is nationalization of key private arms industries to

ensure state control and worker access to policy-making to preserve their jobs and to shape the terms of employment.[127]

There has been widespread worker-leadership accord on these principles. Nationalization has enjoyed considerable rank-and-file support because it potentially affords a greater say by workers over the issues that most concern them: jobs, wages, and work rules. Unionization has been weakest within private industry. An estimated 10 to 15 percent of all workers are unionized in private arms firms. These percentages rise to approximately 50 percent for nationalized firms and about 70 percent for arsenals. While figures vary, the CGT enjoys the support of an estimated 40 to 45 percent of the unionized personnel followed by the CFDT with 22 percent and the Force Ouvrière (FO), under a more conservative leadership, with 18 percent.[128]

Workers have been more interested in protecting their jobs and job status than in pressuring the government to cut back on arms production or sales. "Why," asks a CGT brochure, "were there no orders for AMX-30 tanks in 1976? Why hasn't the Minister of Defense programmed more for 1977?"[129] Similar petitions and demonstrations to keep arms facilities open or to continue or increase national purchases of arms sales, to assure a larger share of government arms spending for unionized labor are recorded annually.[130] Efforts of the Barre government in 1979 to weaken the civil service status of workers were met by strikes and the burning down of the review stand constructed for the launching of the first nuclear attack submarine. The government was forced to capitulate.[131] Leadership reservations notwithstanding, the unionized workers in the arms industry have become natural allies of the Ministry of Defense and tacit supporters of arms sales abroad.

CONCLUSIONS

The French military-industrial complex is largely a state creation. It is among the most closely regulated industries of its kind in the world. State power permeates the system. State leadership in pressing arms sales is no less extensive. Nationalization represents more a logical working out of a process begun before World War II than a departure from past practices. While it raises new problems for governance and role definition among governmental units, it does not appear to have changed the orientation of the arms complex bent on increasing sales abroad or the weight of the arms system in policy circles.

Partisans of the arms production and export systems work from a position of strength within the Ministry of Defense. The alliance of the corps of arms engineers, the general staffs of the armed services, weapons-making industrialists and, tacitly, the arms work force hinder attempts to evaluate independently the economic and military performance of the arms industry or to propose feasible and practical alternatives to the heavy reliance on foreign arms exports in maintaining economic productivity and in supporting French technological development and competitiveness. The arms oligarchy controls information flows about arms making and selling, and perpetuates a favorable image of its activity and interests while insulating itself from public scrutiny and oversight. The impressive size, pervasive organizational structure, and formidable political influence of the arms industry within the government and within the French economy and society create a subgovernmental system that sustains and reinforces the commitment of the Fifth Republic to an "open-door" arms sales policy.

The military-industrial complex has its own governing institutions, processes of decision, symbols of legitimacy, and payoff schedules—negative and positive—to regulate and resolve internal conflict. Participants and players in the system owe it an allegiance that often transcends loyalties to party, church, or union. Personal ambitions and loyalties are harnessed to the system which successfully competes for allegiance with France's most powerful political and social institutions. The military-industrial complex is alive and well in France. While it must respect the limits set on defense spending and respond to the welfare demands of parties and the public, its influence and powers are the envy of other governmental agencies. A state-created oligarchy thrives within the broadly defined democratic contours of the Fifth Republic—a persistent challenge to presidential, ministerial, and parliamentary control.

Security and welfare imperatives are critical determinants of French arms production and sales behavior. The arms complex gives these imperatives shape and form. In pressing its own bureaucratic needs and interests, it buttresses the commitment of the Fifth Republic to making and marketing arms. It links governmental aims to governmental execution and fuses both to party and public support. These bonds, forged from the union of parochial interest and high purpose, undergird the stability and underwrite the legitimacy of the Fifth Republic. At this juncture of history, the fate of the arms complex and the French republic appear inextricably entangled.

Part IV.
Arms and Foreign Policy

CHAPTER 6

The Nation-State System and Modernization: Drive Wheels of Militarization

INTRODUCTION

To WHAT DEGREE have traditional foreign policy considerations directed French arms transfer behavior? These are usually distinguished from domestic concerns—low politics—associated with internal governance, the struggle of elites and parties for power, and economic and welfare problems. Foreign policy has been characteristically reserved for the projection of a state's power to shape the regional and global environment within which it acts and to influence the behavior of other states in ways congenial to its security, economic interests, and political values. The transfer of arms and military technology is one form of power among others to produce beneficial outcomes in these domains.

The utility of arms transfers as an instrument of foreign policy—i.e., as high politics—may be viewed from two perspectives. The first refers to the use of arms sales to shape the overall international structure of power within which the French state acts. As Chapter 2 suggests, French foreign and security policy—certainly as it was practiced in the Gaullist years—has been marked by its attention to the East-West and North-South conflict and by its persistent efforts to change the distribution of power along these axes to France's advantage. The pursuit of national independence, a shared objective of the French Right and Left, implies that France should have a capacity to enhance its power along these lines of competition or, alternatively, to insulate itself from their damaging effects. The Mitterrand government, like its predecessors, reiterated these systemic objectives as central to its foreign policy concerns. It accepted the strictures of the Gaullist opponents who insisted on a key role for France in international politics. The country's significant position as a major arms supplier gave voice to this aspiration.

A second level of analysis focuses on the use or denial of arms transfers to other states to achieve particular, desirable results in France's relations with other states or regions within the international system. Using arms transfers to achieve specific local outcomes may, but need not, have significant implications either for the structure of the global arms transfer system or for the overall distribution of power among states. Nor is the contrary proposition necessarily true. As the third largest arms supplier, France inevitably enjoys high status in the hierarchy of arms exporting states, yet as the analysis below reveals, the diplomatic success of French arms sales in high politics circles—in enhancing France's influence with specific states or in increasing its political weight in various regions—is not all that clear. On more than one occasion— arms sales to Iraq, Libya, and Argentina illustrate the point—France has had to pay in the coinage of high politics for the low politics gains that it has sought.

Aside from the problems raised by existing data sources regarding global arms transfers,[1] there are at least three formidable impediments hindering a fully satisfying evaluation of the foreign policy dimensions of French arms transfer behavior. First, as suggested above, the widely used distinction between foreign and domestic politics—or high and low politics[2]—is often artificial and strained where arms transfers are concerned. Granting or denying the request of a third state for arms may answer critics at home, confound domestic opponents, or assuage governmental critics. Sales to South Africa or to the military regime in Chile were a constant source of embarrassment to successive governments on the Right in France, while selling modest amounts of arms to the Sandinista government in Nicaragua by the Socialist government quieted ideologues bent on supporting Leftist revolutions.

No major public figure in France argues that foreign policy should not promote domestic welfare and wealth or that there is an incompatibility between the two. All accept an independent arms production system as a security imperative and, with comparable consent and commitment, the need to sell arms to sustain that effort and to meet the demands for national social and economic betterment. Creating a favorable environment for selling arms is as much a part of foreign policy as using them to shape the behavior of particular states for specific diplomatic purposes. French diplomacy has been as much in the service of selling arms and technology as using these transfers to promote other political aims. Boosting sales *is* a major foreign policy goal, motored by the welfare aims and bureaucratic interests outlined in the previous chapters. What one close observer of British behavior suggested as the animating motivation underlying a major dimension of British foreign policy—viz., to sell arms abroad—may be applied to French Fifth Republic policy as well.[3]

Despite this caveat there still appears to be a domain of French arms transfer behavior that resists reduction to the welfare and bureaucratic factors outlined earlier, however compelling these still are or have been. Enhancing France's global power and reputation—grandeur, if you will—deciding questions of peace and war (Arab-Israeli conflict), influencing the outcomes of interstate conflict (the Iran-Iraq war), developing cooperative relations with other states, supporting regimes favorable to the French Fifth Republic (Morocco and Zaire), or simply limiting damage to French interests (e.g., submission to the U.N. arms boycott of South Africa) are also considerations that cannot be overlooked in explaining French arms sales—or sales denials. It is at this point in the analysis that the other two problems, referred to earlier, are encountered.

First, French declaratory policy has been primarily confined, as Chapter 2 indicates, to the general and imprecise objective of breaking the superpower monopoly by encouraging the development of a multipolar system. French arms are supposed to provide other states an alternative source of arms. Pressures to align with Washington and Moscow are presumably lowered if states are not dependent for their security, including their arms, on either superpower. Evaluating the effectiveness of France's efforts to decentralize the international system is not as easy. Establishing France's role as a significant arms supplier does not ipso facto establish France's claim to have broken or decreased superpower dominance of the system. All that can be safely argued is that France has contributed to multipolarity, giving it legitimacy and voice in a Gaullic idiom.

The superpowers, ironically, have contributed more to the decentralization of military capabilities around the globe than France or other lesser suppliers. Their competition for allies, clients, and surrogates has led them to become the principal arms suppliers of the international system. Their generous arms supply policies, particularly outside their blocs, have not assured the compliance of recipients to their wishes or bidding.[4] To the extent that the superpowers have failed to hold the allegiance or command the loyalty of an arms recipient, French interest in a multipolar system may well have been advanced, but not necessarily as a consequence of anything the French may have done. Signs of independence from superpower pressure cannot be simply attributed to the availability of French arms. They arise from various structural elements of the system: the irresistible force of decolonization and national self-determination; the offsetting power of Moscow and Washington; the limits of force in resolving international conflict; the importance of factors other than military force—like economic productivity (Japan), control of primary resources (OPEC and oil), or religious and ideological fervor (Islamic fundamentalism)—in affecting foreign policy outcomes; the decisions by states to assert their

interests and independence despite superpower pressures (Egypt and
Indonesia vis-à-vis the U.S.S.R., or Iran and Cuba vis-à-vis the U.S.);
and the growth of new economic and technological production centers
that are based on indigenous national resources.[5] The fissiparous tendency of the international system derives from forces deep within the
system of independent states. French behavior as much reflects these
forces as it gives specific impulse and form to them.

One confronts the paradoxical situation where France's systemic impact may well be argued to have been greater than the influence that it
has specifically derived from arms sales. Its systemic design—to break
the superpower hold—was critically aided and abetted by the breakup
of colonialism and the globalization of the nation-state system. The expansion of French sales of arms and military technology may be viewed
as more a response to this systemic change sweeping the world community than as the principal instrument of its construction. The genius
of the Gaullist Fifth Republic was to embrace history by adapting to the
modernization process reconstructing the international system.

Second, French arms transfer policy is not cast in terms of concrete
foreign policy objectives. Policy guidelines that might have directed
specific arms sales were never written down until the flawed attempt of
the Mitterrand administration to spell them out, particularly with respect to the sale of arms to so-called fascist or racist regimes. Even these
guidelines have never been published or publicly confirmed.[6] Since the
foreign policy considerations underlying approval or disapproval of
sales are normally not available except in rare circumstances when they
are touched by scandal or crisis, the analyst must piece together patterns from the fragmentary evidence and incomplete accounts found in
public sources of varying degrees of reliability and authenticity and
supplemented by interview data bearing on specific sales and deliveries
with appropriate (but not easily accessible) French officials. Little institutional memory or codified written documentation to record experience apparently exist within the French policy-making community to
orient arms decisions.[7] Absent are any clear, publicly visible bench-
marks by which one can assess whether the announced intentions of the
government in making or denying a sale have been realized.

The notion of political guidelines should be distinguished from the
detailed and meticulous budgetary, financial, and bureaucratic regulations that control agents within the French arms production and transfer process. French apologists for French arms transfer policy often cite
the latter as evidence of political control and direction.[8] This attention
to form, if consistent with centuries-old French insistence on strict and
detailed bureaucratic regulations and accountability, masks the per-

sonal aims and bureaucratic interests often driving arms sales forward. Ostensibly informed opinion is also a dubious guide in determining the number of times that the French government has refused to sell arms to other states and the importance of these rejections. Estimates range from the view that few clients capable of paying for arms are denied them to statements that "two-thirds of the exports envisioned by French industrialists are not realized for reasons linked to control."[9] Since these denials are rarely publicly revealed or confirmed to avoid backlash or embarrassment on the part of the denied party, it is difficult to know whether they ever occurred at all. Proving a nonhappening is not easy when the analyst is confronted with the pervasive secrecy surrounding the decision-making process and the confusions and contradictions among observers, close and distant, of what supposedly went on behind closed doors.

These many obstacles notwithstanding, there still exists a great deal of data, in the public domain or accessible through interviews, to assess, albeit provisionally, the foreign policy implications of French arms sales. This chapter defines France's overall position as an arms supplier relative to its competitors. It attempts to sketch the gross dimensions of France's arms transfer effort in proportion to the level of activity of other suppliers since the inception of the Fifth Republic. Against this global background, it traces the pattern of French arms transfers at a regional level. France's importance as a supplier, relative to other suppliers, is viewed from three general perspectives: its role as sole, principal, or multiple supplier; the economic value of its deliveries to the major regions of the globe; and the amount and quality of the arms transferred to other states.

The various measures that are presented in the tables below provide a composite picture of France's standing as an arms seller. Once a "bird's-eye" view of worldwide arms transfer patterns has been completed, Chapter 7 shifts to a "worm's-eye" look at what appear to be the specific foreign policy considerations influencing French decisions to transfer or to refuse to transfer arms to a country or region. Identified will be the geopolitical constraints and perceived opportunities that appear to have channeled and directed French behavior in a region. These factors should be distinguished from the structural factors—security, welfare, economic, and bureaucratic and elite interests—identified earlier. These are, let us concede from the outset, almost always at play in any decision to sell arms. What we want to know now is how broader foreign policy considerations have added to the equation explaining French arms sales policy. The discussion will attempt, through an inductive process of reasoning, to define the rules of behavior and objectives that appear to animate French arms policy toward the major regions of the globe.

GLOBAL ARMS SUPPLY PATTERNS AND TRENDS

Multilateralization of Arms Supplies

Since the 1960s, there has been a pronounced trend toward the multilaterization of arms supplies. French arms sales have contributed to this development as former sole or principal clients of the superpowers have turned to other states, including France, to meet their arms and military technology needs and as new states, seeking to broaden their supply base, have entered the arms market. Similarly, France has seen its position as a sole or principal supplier decline in many areas of the world. In partial compensation for losses in a particular region, like Western Europe, it has expanded its regional outlets for arms and strengthened its position as one of several suppliers for an increasing number of states, especially in the developing world.

Table 6-1 summarizes the trend toward increasing multilaterization. Sole suppliers are defined as those which provided 96 percent or more of all weapons imported by a state; principal or dominant suppliers furnished 56 to 95 percent; and a multiple-supplier relationship was established if no single supplier furnished more than 55 percent of all major imported weapons. The United States, France, and Great Britain, as major arms suppliers, lost ground as sole or principal suppliers between 1963 and 1980. The total number of states in a multiple-supplier relationship rose, meanwhile, from 29 of 132 states in 1964-1973 to 62 of 142 states in 1976-1980.

The United States was the sole supplier for 13 countries and the principal supplier of 29 others between 1964 and 1973. These figures shrank, respectively, to 4 and 16 a decade later. In Asia, withdrawal from Vietnam accounted for the American loss of its role as sole supplier of Laos, Cambodia, and South Vietnam. The U.S. also slipped from sole to principal supplier of the Republic of China, South Korea, the Philippines, and Thailand. Japan, a special case, continues to buy the bulk of its arms from the United States. In Africa, Liberia traded places with Cameroon as the only African state solely dependent on the U.S. for arms. In Latin America, Panama was the only state to rely totally on the United States at the end of 1970s.[10] In the Middle East, the United States replaced France as Israel's principal, then sole, supplier after the Six Day War in 1967. Washington has also lost its place as the principal supplier of Iran and Saudi Arabia: the Khomeini-led Islamic revolution sharply reduced dependence on American arms; Saudi Ara-

Table 6-1. Number of States by Supplier Relationship with Major
Suppliers: 1964-1980

	U.S.	U.S.S.R.	France	G.B.	Total Out of All States in Region[a]
SOLE SUPPLIER					
1964-1973					
Africa	1	1	3	1	6/42
East Asia	7	—	—	—	7/16
Europe	1	5	—	—	6/29
Latin America	4	1	—	1	6/23
Middle East	—	—	—	—	—
South Asia	—	1	—	—	1/6
TOTAL	13	8	3	2	26/116[b]
1973-1977					
Africa	1	—	3	1	5/47
East Asia	3	1	—	—	4/16
Europe	32	—	—	—	2/29
Latin America	3	1	—	1	5/24
Middle East	2	—	—	—	2/16
South Asia	—	—	1	—	1/6
TOTAL	11	2	4	2	19/138[b]
1976-1980					
Africa	1	3	—	1	.5/47
East Asia	1	2	—	—	3/15
Europe	—	2	—	—	2/29
Latin America	1	1	—	1	3/25
Middle East	1	1	—	—	2/16
South Asia	—	1	—	—	1/6
TOTAL	4	10	—	2	16/138[b]
PRINCIPAL OR DOMINANT SUPPLIER					
1964-1973					
Africa	3	6	8	1	18/42
East Asia	2	2	—	—	4/16
Europe	7	3	1	—	11/29
Latin America	9	—	—	—	9/23
Middle East	4	6	1	2	13/16
North America	1	—	—	—	1/2
Oceania	2	—	—	—	2/2
South Asia	1	2	—	—	3/6
TOTAL	29	19	10	3	61/136[b]

Table 6-1 (*cont.*)

	U.S.	U.S.S.R.	France	G.B.	Total Out of All States in Region[a]
1973-1977					
Africa	1	8	3	1	13/47
East Asia	4	1	—	—	5/16
Europe	5	7	—	—	12/29
Latin America	—	1	—	1	2/24
Middle East	2	4	2	—	8/16
North America	1	—	—	—	1/2
Oceania	1	—	—	—	1/4
South Asia	—	3	—	—	3/6
TOTAL	14	24	5	2	45/144[b]
1976-1980					
Africa	—	14	3	—	17/47
East Asia	5	1	—	—	6/15
Europe	6	5	—	1	12/29
Latin America	—	1	2	1	4/25
Middle East	2	3	1	1	7/16
North America	1	—	—	—	1/2
Oceania	2	—	—	—	2/4
South Asia	—	1	—	—	1/6
TOTAL	16	24	6	3	49/144[b]
MULTIPLE SUPPLIERS					
1964-1973					
Africa	7	7	5	6	10/42
East Asia	3	1	2	3	3/16
Europe	3	—	4	3	5/29
Latin America	6	—	6	6	8/23
Middle East	—	—	1	1	1/16
South Asia	2	2	1	2	2/6
TOTAL	21	10	19	21	29/132[b]
1973-1977					
Africa	5	8	13	7	20/47
East Asia	3	1	1	2	4/16
Europe	9	1	5	4	10/29
Latin America	13	—	6	5	13/24

Table 6-1 (*cont.*)

	U.S.	U.S.S.R.	France	G.B.	Total Out of All States in Region[a]
Middle East	5	2	4	4	5/16
Oceania	1	—	—	1	2/4
South Asia	2	2	1	1	2/6
TOTAL	38	14	30	24	56/142[b]
1976-1980					
Africa	8	4	13	8	21/47
East Asia	3	2	3	2	5/15
Europe	6	1	3	4	8/29
Latin America	12	—	8	5	16/25
Middle East	6	2	6	5	7/16
Oceania	—	—	—	—	2/4
South Asia	1	3	2	3	3/6
TOTAL	36	12	35	27	62/142[b]

SOURCES: U.S., Arms Control and Disarmament Agency (ACDA), *World Military Expenditures and Arms Transfers, 1963-1973* (Washington, D.C.: U.S. Government Printing Office, 1975), pp. 67-70; *idem, 1968-1977*, pp. 155-158; and *idem, 1971-1980*, pp. 117-120.

[a] The total number of states listed here in a sole-, principal-, or multiple-supplier relationship by regions may not equal the total number of states in that region if some states received only marginal supplies of arms.

[b] Refers only to the total number of states in all regions which contain states with the respective supplier relationships.

bia, while still a major recipient of U.S. arms, received about 60 percent of its arms imports, measured by their economic value, from other states by the end of the 1970s. Only Jordan continued through this period to be a principal Middle East recipient of U.S. arms, while the U.S. remained Israel's sole supplier.

Europe and North America, as Chapter 3 indicates, are special cases. In the period 1976-1980, the U.S. was the principal supplier to seven western countries, mostly NATO allies. Excluding other major NATO arms producers, American clients included Belgium, Denmark, Greece, Netherlands, Norway, Switzerland, and Canada.

Like the other major suppliers in Table 6-1, the United States bolstered its role as a multiple supplier. Its clients rose from 21 to 36 states in this category between 1964 and 1980. Arms supply relationships were particularly fluid in Africa. The United States was the principal supplier to Ethiopia, Tunisia, and Zaire in the 1960s and early 1970s and a major arms provider of Morocco (slightly over 50 percent). It was a multiple supplier for Tunisia, Morocco, Nigeria, Liberia, Zaire, and South Africa. Kenya and Sudan were added in the late 1970s. In the Middle East, the U.S. moved from one multiple-supplier relationship in 1964-1973 (United Arab Emirates) to seven a decade later, including Saudi Arabia, Bahrain, Cyprus, Egypt, Kuwait, Lebanon, and Qatar. Twelve countries in Latin America assumed a multiple status with Washington in contrast to seven a decade earlier. A similar pattern is evidenced in West Europe where the U.S. position, as only one of a multiple set of suppliers, rose from three to seven states between the 1960s and 1970s. In Asia the U.S. held its multiple-supplier status with Indonesia, Malaysia, and Pakistan through most of this period.

The Soviet Union departed slightly from the trend toward multilateralization. It actually expanded its position as a sole supplier to ten states after a previous high of eight in 1964-1973 and a lapsed period in 1973-1977 when it had only two single source clients. Most notably, it replaced the U.S. as sole supplier for Laos and Vietnam and held its positions as the sole supplier of Cuba and Afghanistan between 1964 and 1978. The drop as sole supplier in East Europe from five to two is a somewhat misleading statistic because the Soviet Union still supplied approximately 80-90 percent of Warsaw Pact arms needs; the remainder was largely furnished by other bloc states, principally Czechoslovakia and Poland. Only Finland, where the Soviet Union fell from sole- to multiple-supplier status by the end of the 1970s, can be listed as a loss.

The Soviet Union also improved its position as a principal supplier, adding to its list of states since 1973. Major gains were scored in Black Africa. Fourteen states received the preponderant proportion of their arms from Moscow. If it lost Somalia and slipped badly in Sudan, it made new inroads in Ethiopia, Angola, Mozambique, Madagascar, Libya, Tanzania, Uganda (since lost), Benin, and Zambia. In East and South Asia, Moscow was the principal supplier, respectively, of Mongolia and India, the latter a particularly significant market. In the Middle East, the Soviet Union preserved its dominant states in Iraq, Syria, and Yemen (Sanaa and Aden), but lost important ground in Egypt. Only Peru, after Cuba in Latin America, imported the bulk of its arms from the Soviet Union.

Not surprisingly, the Soviet Union strengthened its position only slightly as a multiple supplier while it was advancing as a sole or principal supplier. Again Africa headed the list of client states. In Europe neither superpower was able to cross the line between the two blocs. In East and South Asia, Moscow was a multiple supplier in the 1976-1980 period to Kampuchea (Cambodia), North Korea, Bangladesh, Sri Lanka, and Pakistan. The arms relationship with Islamabad was largely severed by the Afghanistan invasion and by the Pakistani tilt toward the U.S. as an arms supplier.

France's experience as an arms supplier fits the evolving multilaterization pattern characterizing the arms transfer process. It no longer is sole supplier of any state and can count only six states in the principal-supplier category in the 1976-1980 period—Ivory Coast, Niger, Gabon, United Arab Emirates, Ecuador, and El Salvador. The latter position has since been relinquished to the United States. On the other hand, it provided arms to 35 states in the 1976-1980 period as a multiple supplier against only 19 in 1964-1973. Based on ACDA figures, its largest gains, like those of the Soviet Union, have been in Africa where French recipients rose from 5 to 13. The rise may be inflated since, as the discussion below of African arms transfers suggests, France has maintained a semicolonial relationship with many of its former West African colonies. France was their principal arms supplier, having transferred old and outdated equipment, including American material, to these countries on independence. Nine African states, including Morocco, received 33 to 50 percent of the value of their arms from France in 1976-1980. However, within this grouping it is clear that these African states are pursuing a multiple source strategy. On the whole, France has lost some of its firm footing in Africa as it has moved from a principal- to a multiple-supplier relationship with 9 states between 1963 and the end of the 1970s (Cameroon, Chad, Ivory Coast, Madagascar, Mauritania, Senegal, Togo, Upper Volta [later Burkina Faso], and South Africa).

In the Middle East, France is a multiple-source supplier. What is interesting is the gradual widening of France's stance in the region. It essentially serviced only one state—Israel—in the 1960s. As its ties with Israel slackened, France successfully penetrated 7 Arab Middle East markets. France also slowly broke the American monopoly in Latin America. Its coverage grew from 6 to 10 states between the 1960s and 1970s. Asia has proved, however, less receptive to French arms than Africa, the Middle East, and Latin America. In 1976-1980, 5 out of 21 states in East and South Asia received French arms—all as multiple-source purchasers.

Table 6-2 compares the value of arms transferred to the developing world for 1966-1975 and 1976-1980. Not only is France shown as having increased its share of the global market from 4.5 to 9.6 percent

Table 6-2. Percentage Shares of Arms Transfers to the Developing
World for the U.S.A., U.S.S.R., France and Others: 1966-1975 and
1976-1980

	1966-1975	1976-1980
U.S.A.	51.8	25.0
U.S.S.R.	28.6	38.7
France	4.5	9.6
Others	15.0	26.6
TOTAL	99.9	99.9

SOURCES: U.S., Arms Control and Disarmament Agency, *World Military Expenditures and Arms Transfers, 1966-1975* (Washington, D.C.: U.S. Government Printing Office, 1976), pp. 77-80, and *idem, 1971-1980*, pp.117-120.

(based on ACDA figures), but other arms producers also reinforced their positions, accounting for 26.6 percent of the value of transfers in 1976-1980 against 15 percent a decade earlier. Among the leaders were France's West European allies: the United Kingdom, West Germany, and Italy, which accounted for almost half of the 26.6 percent total. In three of the eight years between 1978 and 1985, the four major European arms suppliers (France, Great Britain, Italy, and West Germany) exceeded the value of arms delivered by the U.S. During this period, these European suppliers also surpassed the value of arms agreements signed by each superpower in 1978, 1980, and 1985. European arms sales accords accounted for 31.3 percent of all arms orders. Great Britain was the major gainer, surpassing France in 1985 for the first time in the value of arms agreements in one year with developing states, due largely to the sale of Tornado aircraft to Saudi Arabia. Developing states currently control only a small percentage of the world arms market, estimated by one recent study at 1.5 percent. As developing states industrialize and expand their technological base, they can be expected to follow the French example and export arms as much for economic as for security purposes. Israel and Brazil, which accounted for about 75 percent of Third World arms sales in the middle 1980s, fit this pattern.[11]

Table 6-3 lists the principal developing states engaged in producing and selling arms and military technology between 1970 and 1980.[12] During the decade of the 1970s, 21 developing countries exported approximately $6.2 billion in arms. One-third produced 10 or more weapons. Of these, China, Brazil, and India were able to design or develop

Table 6-3. Rank Listing of Arms Exporting by Less Developed States
by Total Sales: 1970-1980 (In millions of current dollars)

Country and Rank	Total Sales [a]	Number of Weapons Systems Produced [b]
1. China	2,190	All Types
2. Israel	835	19
3. Korea (South)	730	6
4. Brazil	510	22
5. Korea (North)	480	5
6. South Africa	230	12
7. Egypt	170	4
India	170	21
Iran	170	—
8. Cuba	160	—
9. Libya	135	1
Saudi Arabia	135	—
10. Singapore	70	2
11. Pakistan	60	3
12. Jordan	51	—
13. Argentina	40	18
14. Taiwan	25	11
15. Morocco	15	1
Syria	15	—
16. United Arab Emirates	10	—
17. Vietnam	5	—

SOURCES: U.S., Arms Control and Disarmament Agency, *World Military Expenditures and Arms Transfers, 1963-1973,* and *idem, 1972-1982* (Washington, D.C.: U.S. Government Printing Office, 1983); and Andrew L. Ross, *Arms Production in Developing Countries: The Continuing Proliferation of Conventional Weapons,* No. N-1615-AF, RAND Corporation Note (Santa Monica, Calif., 1981), pp. 16-19. The Ross study was updated with data from the Stockholm International Peace Research Institute, *World Armaments and Disarmament, SIPRI Yearbook 1974,* pp. 250-258, and *idem, Yearbook 1980,* pp. 168-173 (New York: Crane, Russak and Company, Inc., 1980). Publishers vary for SIPRI *Yearbooks.* Note that SIPRI in the period 1977-1980 lists Brazil and Israel as the major arms suppliers in the developing world, accounting for 62 percent of all sales—Brazil at 33.1 percent and Israel at 28.9 percent; only South Korea is cited in the top thirteen, at 3 percent. *Le Monde Diplomatique,* April 1982.

[a] Entries were recorded only if they were equal to, or exceeded, $5 million between 1970 and 1980.

[b] Refers to the number of different systems of aircraft, ground equipment, missiles, or naval vessels which are produced indigenously, either under license agreements or as nationally developed systems.

or independently produce under license 20 or more systems, with Israel (19) and Argentina (18) not far behind. The entry of these states into the world arms market demonstrates the strong trend toward multilaterization of arms suppliers and, as noted below, the increased competitive pressures felt by the superpowers and West and East European arms suppliers to find outlets for their excess arms production capacity. One should not exaggerate, however, the significance of Third World states (excluding China) in global arms trafficking. In 1980-1984, the period of greatest export success for these states, the Third World share of the world market has been calculated at about 3 percent, including reexports.[13] What is noteworthy is the import substitution and indigenous production policy pursued by an increasing number of states over an expanding list of major weapon systems and the continuing trend toward greater Third World participation in the global arms transfer system.[14] The same pressures that pushed France and other West European states to become major arms producers and suppliers are now pushing new states in a similar direction.

Among developing states, Israel and Brazil have enjoyed notable success as arms suppliers, measured by the value and number of systems that have been transferred.[15] Israel has reached world stature as a supplier of quality lethal products.[16] Some are indigenously produced, like the Gabriel surface-to-surface missile, or adapted from arms and technology purchased abroad, like the Kfir fighter, patterned after the French Mirage airframe and powered by U.S.-built GE engines. Israel sells military arms and equipment to a wide range of customers, including West Germany, Indonesia, South Africa, Singapore, Taiwan, Chile, Ecuador, Mexico, Honduras, Guatemala, and, until recently, Nicaragua. It has reportedly sold war material to Iran, although diplomatic relations between the two states have been severed. Its Dagger aircraft, capable of being armed with air-to-ground missiles, are currently being used by Argentine air forces. It also produces civil aircraft, all forms of tactical missiles, patrol boats, armored vehicles, artillery and small arms, radar systems, communication and navigation systems, industrial and shipborne monitoring and control systems, medical electronics, microelectronics, computers and computerized communications systems, fire control systems, security systems, air and ground crew equipment, ground-support equipment, and microwave components.[17] ACDA lists exports of $260 million for 1981 and $360 million for 1982, figures that are likely to be conservative.[18]

Brazil has also captured markets in the Middle East and Africa and must be considered an important arms supplier.[19] In the Middle East, it has sold equipment, especially light armored vehicles, to Libya, Qatar, and Iraq. The Cascavel, a light armored vehicle that mounts a 90 mm. cannon and carries laser range-finders, has seen service with Iraqi armed forces in the war with Iran. Brazil's state-owned Empresa Brasileria de Aeronautica (EMBRAER) is the world's sixth largest aviation firm. It sells the twin-engine Bandeirante aircraft worldwide and also manufactures the Xavante jet under Italian license. Brazilian arms are also attractive to developed states. The United States Marines seriously evaluated a Brazilian light tank for possible purchase, and France has purchased the Xingu, a Brazilian light transport aircraft, for its armed forces. Brazil is likely to continue to invest in its arms industry in the future. As one student of Brazilian politics and foreign and security policy observes: "Brazilian arms are especially attractive to third-world countries since they are comparatively simple, high quality, and free of ideological ties. Because of the growing demand for Brazilian arms, and given that Brazil must increase exports to compensate for rising petroleum prices, the state continues to assign a high priority to investment in what already is the largest and most sophisticated conventional-weapons industry in South America. As a major arms supplier, Brazil will be able to exert greater pressure on its neighbors and to increase its influence in the emerging commercial markets of black Africa, the Middle East, and Asia."[20]

Modernization and Militarization: France as Role Model

Many factors explain the trend toward the multilateralization of arms production, supplies, and purchases. Only key elements and their apparent mutually reinforcing character can be traced here. On the demand-pull side, the growth in the number of nation-states after World War II gave impulse to the development of indigenous production centers and to foreign arms acquisitions.[21] In a self-help international system, states perceive a need for arms alternatively as an external security imperative, an internal regime requirement, and a symbol of national independence. Regional conflicts and arms races—the latter stimulated in some instances by the entrepreneurial initiative of governmentally sponsored arms marketeers—trigger pressures for more and better arms. Since technological innovation makes military equipment rapidly obsolescent, military planners characteristically demand the most up-to-date arms.[22] The development of an indigenous arms production capacity is closely associated, as in France's case as Part I argues, with the requirement of state control over the arms supply process. Many Third World elites concerned with state development and national security share the view of Brazilian Air Force Minister Joelmir Campas de Araripe Macedo: "The time has come to free ourselves from the United

States and the countries of Europe. It is a condition of security that each nation manufacture its own armaments."[23] Successive French regimes over centuries have essentially pursued arms policies based on the same assumptions of national independence.

As welfare demands and the socio-economic modernization process progress, governmental leaders like their French counterparts before them, seek strategies that can reconcile competing security and foreign imperatives, on one hand, and the realities of scarce resources and the demands of national elites and populations for economic growth and a move equitable distribution of wealth. Again, the creation of an independent arms production capacity appears as a viable option to relax, if not resolve, these conflicting imperatives. As a state's military-industrial complex develops to decrease dependency on foreign suppliers and to conserve limited international reserves, the interests of civilian elites— scientists, engineers, civil servants, industrial managers—fuse with those of a nation's larger security community. External national security and regime needs for internal control conspire with demands for welfare, technological innovation, social reform, and economic development—varied and not necessarily compatible facets of the global modernization process—to drive governments to adopt an independent arms production policy similar to the strategy pursued by the French government. The choice facing governmental elites is no longer posed in the classical terms of guns versus butter. Making arms appears—and is publicly presented—more as an appealing opportunity than as an unwanted burden: "More 'guns' mean more 'butter.' "[24]

Once a nation has embarked on this path, blazed by developed states like France, incentives to sell arms or transfer technology also inevitably arise for much the same reasons outlined in the previous chapters. It is no accident that Israel, Brazil, and an increasing number of developing states have entered, or are at the threshold of entering, the arms market as suppliers. What may have begun as a demand-pull response ends as a supply-push policy to sell arms. These national strategies combine and propel the arms and military technology transfer system forward. Global transfers progressively become self-sustaining and decreasingly dependent on any one state for the maintenance of the overall network of supplier-client relations.[25]

Table 6-4 lists the growing number of states in the developing world which have joined the ranks of arms producers while remaining major arms importers. It provides prima facie evidence for the link between indigenous arms production, nation-state building, and modernization. Noted in the survey between 1960 and 1980 are the number of states, totaling 29, which have achieved some level of independence in arms

Table 6-4. Arms Production in Developing States: 1960, 1970, 1980

	1960		1970		1980	
	No. of States	No. of Systems	No. of States	No. of Systems	No. of States	No. of Systems
Aircraft						
Fighters	1	2	3	4	6	10
Trainers (Jet)	3	3	4	4	3	5
Trainers (Basic)	6	7	5	6	11	13
Maritime (Re-connaissance)	—	—	—	—	2	2
Transports	1	1	4	6	8	11
Aircraft (Engines)	1	1	2	2	6	8
Helicopters	1	1	2	2	11	15
Avionics	—	—	—	—	3	3
TOTAL [a]	7	15	8	24	18	67
Naval Vessels						
Frigates	1	1	1	1	4	5
Corvettes	2	2	2	2	1	1
Patrol Craft	8	8	13	13	20	25
Submarines	—	—	—	—	3	3
Amphibious Craft	1	1	2	2	4	4
Support Craft	6	6	4	4	7	7
TOTAL [a]	13	18	15	22	25	45
Ground Equipment						
Tanks	—	—	3	3	5	6
Armored Personnel Carriers	—	—	1	2	5	6
Armored Cars	—	—	2	2	2	2
Reconnaissance Vehicles	—	—	—	—	2	2
Armored Bridgelayers	—	—	—	—	1	1
TOTAL [a]	—	—	5	7	6	17
Missiles						
Surface-to-Air	—	—	—	—	5	6
Air-to-Ground	—	—	1	1	3	3
Air-to-Air	1	1	2	2	5	5

Table 6-4 (*cont.*)

	1960		1970		1980	
	No. of States	No. of Systems	No. of States	No. of Systems	No. of States	No. of Systems
Surface-to-						
Surface	1	1	1	1	3	4
Antitank	—	—	1	1	7	8
TOTAL [a]	1	2	5	5	9	26

SOURCE: Andrew L. Ross, *Arms Production in Developing Countries: The Continuing Prolif-eration of Conventional Weapons*, No. N-1615-AF, RAND Corporation Note (Santa Monica, Calif., 1981), pp. 16-19. The Ross study was updated with data from the Stockholm International Peace Research Institute, *World Armaments and Disarmament, SIPRI Yearbook 1974*, pp. 250-258, and *idem, Yearbook 1980*, pp. 168-173 (New York: Crane, Russak and Company, Inc., 1980). A more comprehensive set of arms producing states (51), but grouped together in more general categories of production (i.e., ammunition, small arms, aircraft, armored vehicles, missiles, and ships), is found in Michael Broszka and Thomas Ohlson, eds., *Arms Production in the Third World* (London: Taylor and Francis, 1986), p. 16.

[a] Numbers of systems do not overlap; numbers of states frequently do.

design or production within four major weapons categories—aircraft, armored vehicles, tactical missiles, and naval vessels. Cited also are the number of systems that states within each weapons category are producing. The levels of independence range from licensed assembly at the lowest point of capability to licensed component production, licensed system production, system modification and reverse engineering, dependent R&D and production, and independent R&D and production at succeedingly higher levels on the scale.[26]

In each of the weapons categories that are listed in Table 6-4, the number of states producing a particular item has grown; in several cases they have more than doubled in the decade between 1970 and 1980. During this time frame, the number of states producing fighters grew from 3 to 6; basic trainers from 5 to 11; and helicopters from 2 to 11. Overall, the number of states in the developing world producing aircraft more than doubled from 8 to 18.[27] Similarly, the number of developing states constructing naval vessels climbed from 15 to 25;[28] most notable is the increase in the number of states producing patrol and support craft, rising from 13 to 20 states in a decade.

Production of armored vehicles and tactical missiles has grown more slowly. Over the decade since 1970, the number of states producing tanks increased from 3 to 5 and armored personnel carriers from 1 to

5. The total number of producing states rose from 5 to 6.[29] The producers of tactical missiles increased in the same period from 5 to 9.[30] Producers of SAM missiles leaped from 0 to 5;[31] those producing anti-tank weapons, from 1 to 7.[32] Six states (Argentina, Brazil, India, Israel, China, and South Africa) produced arms at some level of independent capability in all four major categories.

These figures also imply a high stage of technological development since aircraft, missiles, electronics, and aircraft engines require a broad scientific, engineering, and industrial base. While many countries like China or India may still be considered underdeveloped, measured by GNP and per capita income figures, they have accumulated the technological know-how and industrial plant to produce advanced military equipment. One can metaphorically speak of a "Belgium" emerging from India or a "Netherlands" arising from an otherwise underdeveloped China. The same process of modernization, with military technology employed by nations as the spearhead, may be seen to be operating in other states, like Brazil, Pakistan, and Argentina.[33] Modernization is seen by elites in many states throughout the southern tier of developing nations as a critical, if not totally dependent, function of a technologically advanced warfighting system, linked to a capacity to make and sell arms and military technology.

Modernization, a global process, is mediated through the nation-state system. It touches every important layer of contemporary societal development. Military technology is viewed as a key, if not the only, motor force of this complex process. Modernization may be viewed from several related perspectives. Among these, some of the most important refer (1) to the development of national consciousness and unity over tribal, religious, ethnic, or linguistic barriers to internal cohesion; (2) to the reform of domestic political institutions and the gradual elimination of feudal arrangements as well as class, caste, and racial distinctions; (3) to the preoccupation of revolutionary groups and governments with the socio-economic welfare of national populations; and (4) to the growth of the size and technical proficiency of the military establishment and arms production complexes, viewed both as an instrument and as an object of reform.

The modernization process has been synchronous, if not synonymous, with the experience of violent conflict and with the steady growth of military centers of power around the globe.[34] While these characteristics of modernization have occurred in many parts of the globe without resort to force or its threat, militarization and modernization, as France's history suggests, are not strangers to each other; their histories are entwined; and they enjoy intimate company in the theories of political change advanced by social scientists and political reformers.[35] The triumph of the nation-state, as the provisional but fundamentally flawed solution to the security problem confronting all peoples and the world community, is joined by the revolutionary force of modernization (the reactionary response of the Khomeini's Iran notwithstanding). Together these powerful systemic forces provide much of the explanation for the militarization of the world in the postwar period, including the developing states. France's development as an arms producer and supplier is now being acted out on a global stage. France is both a role model for other states to follow and part of the supporting cast contributing to the institutionalization of the nation-state system, the spread of modernization, and the growth of militarization, defined as the growth of independent centers for the organized and legitimate use of violence.

The rapid diffusion of military technology from developed to developing states has sped the modernization process along. Diffusion is both a demand-pull and supply-push phenomenon. The incentives to receive or transfer technology are much the same as those for arms. Developing states are increasingly reluctant to limit their imports to arms themselves. There has been a trend to tie arms contracts to licensing accords for production and to continued access to original technology. France has been in the forefront of arms suppliers disposed to transfer technology as well as arms to retain a competitive edge. Table 6-5 summarizes the licensing arrangements created by France with its arms clients, affording them the know-how and techniques needed to develop their own arms industries. Agreements for the transfer of military technology have been signed with 23 countries over the entire range of conventional arms produced by France. Most, while signed in the 1970s, continue in force into the 1980s. The preference of arms recipients for licensing over direct sales is not confined to the French experience. It appears as a general trend and a progressively more significant component of arms supply arrangements with recipient states.[36] The value of indigenously produced over licensed arms production by Third World states between 1950 and 1984 (excepting China) has been estimated, respectively, at $6.4 billion and $12.7 billion, with the rate of increase for licensed production continuing at twice that of indigenous production since the middle 1970s until 1984.[37]

Superpower Dominance: A Regional Perspective

A trend toward the multilateralization of supplies should not be confused with the equalization of military production and power among states. Some are more equal than others and will remain so for the fore-

Table 6-5. Licensing Agreements for French Weapons Systems: 1950-1983

	Licensor	Licensee	Year of License	Year Production Started	Total Plan
Aircraft-High Performance					
Mirage III	France	Switzerland	—	—	98[a]
	France	South Africa	—	—	36[b]
	France	Australia	—	1964	106
Mirage 5	France	Belgium	—	1969	106
Mirage F1	France	South Africa	1971	1979	100[c]
Alpha-Jet	France (F.R.G.)[d]	Belgium	1975	1978	17
	France (F.R.G.)[d]	Egypt	1978[e]	—	160
Aircraft-Other					
CM 170 Fouga-Magister	France	F.R.G.	—	—	188[f]
	France	Finland	—	—	62[f]
	France	Israel	1957	—	100[g]
MS 760 Paris	France	Argentina	1957	—	32
Helicopters[h]					
SA-316	France	India[i]	1962[j]	1965	221+
Alouette III	France	Pakistan	1968	1972	10[k]
	France	Switzerland	1969	1971	60
	France	Romania[i]	1971	1971[l]	200+[l]
SA-315 Lama	France	India[i]	1970[m]	1972[m]	140
	France	Brazil[i]	1978	1979	30
SA-342 Gazelle	France (U.K.)[d]	Yugoslavia[i]	1971	1978[n]	132
		Yugoslavia[i]	1982	—[n]	—
AS-350 Ecureuil	France	Brazil[i]	1978[o]	1979	200
SA-330 Puma	France	South Africa	1973	1973	20
	France	Indonesia	1977	1977	25
	France	Indonesia[i]	1980	1982	8[p]
	France	Romania[i]	1977	1978	124[q]
	France	Brazil	1980	—	34[r]

Table 6-5 (*cont.*)

	Licensor	Licensee	Year of License	Year Production Started	Total Plan
Lynx	U.K. (France)[d]	Egypt	1978[s]	—	280
SA-365 Dauphin	France	People's Republic of China	1980	—	50
AS-332 Super Puma	France	Egypt[i]	1983	—	—
		Indonesia[i]	1980	1982	26[p]
Engines					
Helicopter And Fouga-Magister Engines	France	Israel	1969	—	—
Atar Spare Parts for Mirage III	France	Israel	1966	—	—
30mm.[t] Aircraft Cannon	France	Israel	—	—	—
Ground Equipment					
AML-60/90	France	South Africa	1965	1966	1,000
AMX-13	France	Argentina	1968[r]	1969[u]	60 + [r]
AMX-30	France	Spain	1972	1974	180
	France	Spain	1975	1978	200
	France	Spain	1980	1980	100
VAB	France	Argentina[d]	1981	1981	—[v]
Missiles					
AS-20	France	F.R.G.	1969[w]	—	1,056[w]
SS-11	France	India	1970	1971	3,000 + [x]
	France	U.S.	—	—	50,000[y]
Roland I	France (F.R.G.)[d,z]	Brazil	1972	1977	80
Roland II (FRG)[d]	France	U.S.[i]	1974	—	595
Crotale/Cactus	France	South Africa[i]	1974	1978	—[aa]

Table 6-5 (*cont.*)

	Licensor	Licensee	Year of License	Year Production Started	Total Plan
Milan	France	U.K.[i]	1976	1978	50,000
	(F.R.G.)[d]	Italy[i]	1980	—	23,000
		India[i]	1981	—	10,000[bb]
R-550 Magic	France	India	1977[cc]	—	—
Entac	France	India[dd]	—	—	—
Harpon	France	India[dd]	1971	—	—
Ships					
Submarines					
Daphne Class	France	Spain	1968	1968	4
Agosta Class	France	Spain	1974	1975	4[ee]
S-70 Class	France	Spain[i]	1975	1982	8[ff]
Surface Warships					
A69 Aviso Frigate	France	India	1974	1975	25-30[gg]
Joao-Coutinho Frigate	France (F.R.G.)[d]	South Africa[hh]	1975	—	6
Combattante III Guided Missile Patrol Boat	France	Greece	1975[ii]	1978	6
Combattante II Guided Missile Patrol Boat	France	Greece	1976[ii]	—	—
Batral Type Landing Ship	France	Chile[i]	1979	1982	2
Durance Class Support Ship	France	Australia[i]	1977	1980	1

SOURCES: See the Note on Sources in the Appendix and notes below.

Table 6-5 notes (*cont.*)

The primary sources for this data were the SIPRI *Yearbooks*. Confirmation on SIPRI data was sought from the other sources where SIPRI data were ambiguous. Greater reliance was placed on later sources for corrections of previously published information. Conflicts, lapses, and unclarities in the listings are footnoted.

ᵃ The 1962-1963 *Jane's All the World's Aircraft* first mentions this agreement. It cites that 2 Mirage IIIs would be purchased and 98 more built under license. No specific dates are available.

ᵇ The SIPRI *Arms Trade Registers* only mentions that 36 Mirage IIIs were to be produced under license in South Africa. No dates are available.

ᶜ The 1977 and 1978 SIPRI *Yearbooks* list 48 orders of which 16 were to be directly imported and 32 were to be assembled in South Africa. SIPRI lists a total planned production of 100 aircraft. Later *Yearbooks* do not mention further details of the licensing agreements.

ᵈ Coproducer of weapon system, not included in formal licensing agreement.

ᵉ The 1979 SIPRI *Yearbook* cites 1978 as the licensing year; the 1980 edition estimates that the license was confirmed in 1979. No further details are available.

ᶠ The 1969-1970 *Jane's All the World's Aircraft* cites that the F.R.G. received 250 Magisters of which 188 were built under license. Similarly, Finland received a total of 82, of which 62 were built in Finland. No dates are available.

ᵍ The 1969-1970 *Jane's All the World's Aircraft* cites 52 Fouga-Magister orders or deliveries to Israel. Of these 36 were built in Israel. The SIPRI *Arms Trade Registers* lists a total of 125 delivered. Of these, 25 were former German stock, while another 100 were said to have been built under license between 1960 and 1964.

ʰ *Le Monde*, May 23, 1972, notes that besides countries noted in the table, Italy, the United States, and West Germany also secured licenses to produce French helicopters. The United Kingdom has a special codevelopment and coproduction arrangement with France.

ⁱ Current license as of 1984.

ʲ The 1980 SIPRI *Yearbook* indicates that the 1962 license may have been renegotiated in 1979. Editions from 1981 through 1984 no longer mention this. The 1984 *Yearbook* only comments that as of 1983, 221 SA-316 helicopters have been built.

ᵏ The SIPRI *Yearbooks* indicate that manufacture of the Alouette III would proceed in two stages, from assembly to an increasingly substantial portion of locally made parts. No numbers are given. The SIPRI *Arms Trade Registers* cites four deliveries in 1968 and ten more licensed-produced helicopters in 1972.

ˡ The SIPRI *Yearbooks* from 1975 through 1979 indicate that production of Alouette III helicopters in Romania began in 1971. The 1980 through 1982 editions cite 1977 as the first year. Up through 1981 the *Yearbooks* list a total of 130 planned Alouette IIIs, the 1982 and 1984 editions state that more than 200 had been produced by 1981.

ᵐ Prior to the 1979 *Yearbook*, SIPRI lists 1970 as the licensing year and 1972 as the year production started. In the 1979 through 1984 editions, 1971 is listed as the licensing year and 1973 as the year production started.

ⁿ The 1980, 1981, 1982, and 1984 SIPRI *Yearbooks* list 1978 as the first production year. Prior editions cite 1973. The 1984 edition also cites a December 1984 contract for the L-version of the Gazelle. No further information about production is available.

ᵒ The 1979 SIPRI *Yearbook* lists 1977 as the year of the licensing agreement for the Ecureuil. Thereafter the helicopter is listed as the AS-350M Esquilo, with a licensing agreement dated in 1978. This helicopter is to be produced over a ten-year period in a new company of which France owns 45 percent. See also *Le Monde*, February 4, 1978.

ᵖ The 1982 SIPRI *Yearbook* cites a 1980 license and a start of production in 1981 with a total plan for fifteen Pumas. The 1983 and 1984 *Yearbooks* estimate a planned production of only eight and the first production year is cited as 1982. The 1984 SIPRI *Yearbook* also mentions a license for the AS-332 Super Puma. Only the production start in 1982 is confirmed. The number of Super Pumas to be produced, as well as the licensing year, are estimates. No other *Yearbook* lists this license.

[q] The 1984 SIPRI *Yearbook* indicates the production of 20 to 30 Puma helicopters per year. It is estimated that between 1978 and 1983 a total of 124 Pumas were built.

[r] The 1982 SIPRI *Yearbook* estimates that 34 Pumas will be "obtained."

[s] The 1980 SIPRI *Yearbook* only cites that a license production contract for 280 helicopters was signed in 1978. No other information is available.

[t] *Le Monde*, June 2, 1973.

[u] The 1973 SIPRI *Yearbook* reports a 1968 license; the 1979 edition reports 1969 as the licensing year. No production figures are cited in the 1973 edition, but the 1979 *Yearbook* cites a current annual production of 12 for 1978. The SIPRI *Arms Trade Registers* mentions the licensed production of 60 AMX-13 between the 1969 and 1971 only. *Le Monde*, February 28, 1968, notes a licensing accord with Argentina.

[v] The SIPRI *Yearbooks* from 1982 through 1984 comment that two prototypes have been received for evaluation. It is unclear whether these are the two VABs listed as "produced" in Argentina. These same editions also estimate that the license was granted in 1981. No further information is available.

[w] The 1975 SIPRI *Yearbook* cites this agreement but gives no dates. The 1974-1975 *Jane's All the World's Aircraft* mentions that in 1968 it was decided to produce a slightly modified version of the AS-20 in Germany. It is not mentioned whether a licensing agreement was concluded that year. *Le Monde* (July 31, 1969) refers to an impending license to produce the AS-20 in 1969.

[x] The SIPRI *Arms Trade Registers* reports a licensing agreement for the SS-11 for the period from 1971 to 1973. The 1975 SIPRI *Yearbook* then notes that in 1974 complete production rights have been handed over to India, and the 1981 *Yearbook* estimates that 8,600 missiles had been produced by 1980.

[y] The 1963-1964 *Jane's All the World's Aircraft* first cites a license for the U.S. to produce the SS-11. *Brassey's Infantry Weapons of the NATO Armies* notes that 50,000 were made under license in the U.S.

[z] In the 1977 and 1978 SIPRI *Yearbooks*, both France and Germany are listed as licensors. The 1980 edition lists only France.

[aa] The 1980 through 1984 SIPRI *Yearbooks* only cite an annual production of 100 missiles.

[bb] The 1984 SIPRI *Yearbook* estimates the planned production of 10,000 Milan missiles.

[cc] Only the 1979 SIPRI *Yearbook* cites the 1977 agreement. No further data were available in later SIPRI editions.

[dd] *Le Monde* (January 9, 1971) reports an Indian license for the Harpon missile. On November 8, 1971, the Entac license is reported by the same source. No other confirmations of these licenses could be found. The Entac is an antitank version of the SS-10 surface-to-surface missile, while the Harpon is an antitank version of the SS-11.

[ee] The SIPRI *Yearbooks* give conflicting numbers on the total number of Agosta class submarines to be produced in Spain. The 1975 through 1978 editions list two, the 1979 edition six, and the 1980 through 1982 editions cite four. *Le Monde* (March 3, 1975) cites the license date as of July 16, 1966.

[ff] Only the 1984 SIPRI *Yearbook* cites this license. This edition also comments that four of the eight submarines are for Egypt.

[gg] Only the 1975 and 1976 SIPRI *Yearbooks* list this agreement. Later editions no longer mention it.

[hh] The 1977 and 1978 SIPRI *Yearbooks* cite this agreement, noting that construction was announced as indigenous, but that the frigates were "perhaps originally to have been built in Portugal."

[ii] The 1979 SIPRI *Yearbook* lists 1974 as the year of the licensing agreement, the 1980, 1981, and 1982 editions list 1975.

[jj] Only the 1979 and 1980 SIPRI *Yearbooks* list this agreement. No further data were available.

seeable future. The East-West conflict continues to shape the principal patterns of the worldwide network of arms and technology transfers. As Table 6-2 records, Moscow and Washington still dominate the global arms market for major weapons systems, although they must share a decreasing slice of the world market with an increasing number of suppliers. Neither tolerates arms transfers across bloc lines in Europe. Except for Romania's import of French civil aircraft and its licensing accords to produce French helicopters and British BAC-111s,[38] the Eastern bloc is hermetically sealed to nonbloc access. Similarly, western states buy from each other; and, within NATO, the United States has a commanding lead as an arms supplier. Even the transfers of economically sensitive materials that do not unambiguously fall within the purview of NATO's list of proscribed materials—e.g., oil drilling equipment, machine tools, and piping—are subject to close American scrutiny.[39]

Table 6-6 compares the percentage of arms deliveries within NATO and Warsaw Pact countries by suppliers over three time periods. While both superpowers, as noted earlier, control a smaller share of their respective bloc markets in 1976-1980 than they did a decade earlier, transfers within the bloc are still largely confined to suppliers within the bloc. In the overlapping periods covered by Table 6-6, France, Italy, and West Germany have managed at different times to dent the virtual

Table 6-6. Percentage Shares by Suppliers of Arms Deliveries to NATO and Warsaw Pact States: 1964-1973, 1973-1977, 1976-1980

	U.S.	U.S.S.R.	France	U.K.	Italy	Canada	F.R.G.	Others
Europe (NATO)								
1964-1973	83	—	5	1	—	1	7	3
1973-1977	62	—	12	3	5	1	7	11
1976-1980	69	—	3	5	2	—	11	9

	U.S.	U.S.S.R.	France	U.K.	Czechoslovakia	Poland	Others
Europe (Warsaw Pact)							
1964-1973	—	70	—	—	11	18	1
1973-1977	—	71	—	—	14	11	4
1976-1980	—	59	1	—	24	13	3

SOURCES: U.S., Arms Control and Disarmament Agency (ACDA), *World Military Expenditures and Arms Transfers, 1963-1973* (Washington, D.C.: U.S. Government Printing Office, 1975), pp. 67-71; *idem, 1968-1977*, pp. 155-158; and *idem, 1971-1980*, pp. 117-120. Overlapping time periods are the result of ACDA presentation of data in its annual volumes.

American monopoly, but have not succeeded in breaking the American grip on NATO. The shift to a bloc-partner supply pattern is more pronounced within the Warsaw Pact. Czechoslovakia, a traditional center for arms supply throughout most of this century, supplied almost a quarter of Warsaw Pact needs outside the Soviet Union in 1976-1980. Poland follows, accounting on the average for 14 percent of all Soviet bloc arms supplies.

With some obvious exceptions (U.S./Israel and U.S.S.R./Cuba), the superpower hold on the developing states appears to be slipping. Both are compelled to compete with each other or other suppliers. While the superpowers accounted for 50 percent of all transfers to developing states in the 1970s, with the exception of Latin America, they have been able to increase their share only in South Asia. In all other regions, both faced increasingly stiffer competition from third suppliers, including the developing states themselves. Table 6-7 traces the shares controlled by major suppliers to developing states on a regional basis in three overlapping periods between 1973 and 1980. Developing states have increasingly enlarged their portions of the world market. In the Middle East and East Asia, developing states doubled their slices of the regional transfers pie while expanding their portions by about half as much in Africa (Arab and Black Africa) and Latin America. France's losses in Africa to the superpowers and other suppliers in Africa were more than compensated, in terms of real value increases, by its stronger showing in the Middle East and slightly improved position in Latin America. It has also maintained a modest but reliable market in South Asia.

Superpower dominance, within a context of increasing third-state supplier importance, is also illustrated by an examination of the actual weapons systems transferred by suppliers. These data provide a more useful measure of the security and arms control implications of weapons transfers since they furnish information about the lethality and sophistication of these arms, and not merely their economic value. For the period 1972-1981, Appendix C plots deliveries of major weapons systems to developing countries. Included are deliveries of supersonic combat aircraft, subsonic combat and support aircraft, helicopters, surface-to-air missiles, major and minor surface warships and guided missile patrol boats, submarines, light armor, and tanks and self-propelled guns.

During the ten-year period covered in Appendix C, West European states and France accounted for approximately one-quarter of helicopters, ships, and naval craft supplied to developing countries, one-fifth of the light armor and subsonic aircraft, and one-tenth of tanks, supersonic aircraft, and surface-to-air missiles. These impressive figures ob-

Table 6-7. Percentage Shares by Major Suppliers of Arms Deliveries to Developing States: 1964-1973, 1973-1977, 1976-1980

	U.S.	U.S.S.R.	France	U.K.	Others[a]
Africa					
1964-1973	17	27	26	11	19
1973-1977	6	47	15	2	30
1976-1980	4	52	11	2	31
East Asia					
1964-1973	74	16	—	1	9
1973-1977	75	12	—	4	9
1976-1980	50	26	2	5	17
Latin America					
1964-1973	43	13	16	8	20
1973-1977	18	29	13	16	24
1976-1980	11	29	18	11	31
Middle East					
1964-1973	34	50	3	5	8
1973-1977	45	32	6	5	12
1976-1980	37	32	9	7	15
South Asia					
1963-1973	9	55	9	4	23
1973-1977	5	61	10	3	21
1976-1980	6	63	10	4	17

SOURCES: U.S., Arms Control and Disarmament Agency (ACDA), *World Military Expenditures and Arms Transfers, 1963-1973* (Washington D.C.: U.S. Government Printing Office, 1975), pp. 67-71; *idem, 1968-1977*, pp. 155-158; and *idem, 1971-1980*, pp. 117-120. Although ACDA sources overlap data for the three time periods reviewed in Table 6-7, the trend toward the multilateralization of arms suppliers is not essentially distorted.

[a] The following developing states are included: Algeria, Argentina, Brazil, China (PRC), China (Taiwan), Cuba, Egypt, India, Iran, Iraq, Israel, Jordan, Korea (North), Korea (South), Libya, Morocco, Pakistan, Saudi Arabia, Singapore, South Africa, Syria, United Arab Emirates, and Vietnam (North).

scure the differential impact of West European and French transfers as well as those of other nonsuperpower suppliers. The role of these suppliers is more critical than a narrow focus on total arms shipments may reveal, both with respect to particular countries and to the composition of the arms exports.

Appendix D displays the regional distribution of the arms shipments listed in Appendix C for the Near East and South Asia, sub-Saharan Africa, Latin America, and East Asia and the Pacific over two time periods, 1972-1976 and 1977-1981. In the Near East and South Asia, the superpowers, France, and other suppliers were locked in a fierce competition for markets across a wide range of weapons systems. Within each weapons category, the position of any one supplier tended to vary with the aggressiveness, enterprise, and opportunities of its competitors. Market shares varied throughout the period. France was, comparatively, a slight gainer in the Near East and South Asia, having improved its market share in seven of nine areas, most notably in tanks, light armor, minor surface vessels, and helicopters. In 1977-1981, the superpowers supplied 50 percent or more of the tanks, light armor, major warships, supersonic aircraft, helicopters, and surface-to-air missiles (SAMs). With the exception of helicopters, this same pattern of superpower dominance holds for sub-Saharan Africa.

Of the two superpowers, the Soviet Union clearly emerged as the leading arms supplier to the Near East and South Asia in the 1970s. If submarines are not counted (only one was transferred in a decade), the Soviet Union is first in five weapons systems categories (tanks, light armor, supersonic aircraft, minor naval craft, and SAMs) and second in the remaining three (major ships, subsonic aircraft, and helicopters). It was essentially the only supplier providing clients with surface-to-air missiles. The United States was behind the Soviet Union in most categories. It also trailed France in submarines, patrol boats and, most notably, helicopters. The penetration of arms sellers other than France or the superpowers was a characteristic feature of the supplier-recipient relations of the area. The United Kingdom, West Germany, Italy, Yugoslavia, and China all made headway as major arms suppliers.

The African pattern tended to be replicated in Latin America, once a U.S. preserve. Suppliers other than the superpowers and France were the major gainers, with the United Kingdom, West Germany, and Italy in the forefront. The value of French deliveries was higher, largely because France was a leading supplier of costly supersonic aircraft and helicopters. Other suppliers, however, led in six of the eight categories of weapons listed in Appendix C. These again included the major West European suppliers. The Soviet Union was first in shipping supersonic aircraft and SAMs, although these were confined principally to Cuba and Peru.

East Asia and Oceana presented a more confusing picture, largely as a consequence of the American withdrawal from Vietnam. While the United States declined as a regional supplier, the stock of the Soviet Union rose. In proportional terms, the United States lost ground in each weapons category and the Soviets increased their deliveries between the first and second halves of the 1970s. France's position improved in tanks, light armor, and, characteristically, helicopters. Other suppliers also advanced in sales of helicopters, subsonic aircraft, and ships and small naval craft.

CONCLUSION

However confusing the pattern of supplier-recipient relations may be at a regional level, the trend toward the multiplication of production centers and the multilateralization of arms and military technology supply appears deeply chiseled in the behavior of states around the world. The traditional state struggle and the new, globalized force of modernization in its various modes drive the militarization of the international system. The superpowers, as the principal arms movers of the system, have accelerated arms proliferation and the creation of independent centers of arms design and development. France has doubled in brass, giving example and impetus to the diffusion of arms around the globe. The developed states, especially those in western Europe are on an infernal and perpetual treadmill largely of their own creation. New developing states have achieved various levels of independence in armaments. Arms suppliers, like France, are impelled increasingly to sell quantities of arms of enhanced sophistication and to ease access to military technology in order to compete with other states, including former dependencies and colonies, in world markets. The developing states swell the ranks of arms producers and suppliers, forcing France to run even harder in order to stand still in offsetting import substitution policies of the developing states or the export competition posed by these states as they enter the world market.

The incentives and constraints within which nation-states act, emanating principally from the self-help nature of the international system and the pervasive modernization process within which they are entangled, press them to acquire arms through indigenous production, cooperative arrangements with other states, or outright purchases or licensing grants. A vicious circle arises: the nation-state struggle and modernization create a global arms production and transfer system which in turn animates these primal international forces.

What is not at all clear is whether the accumulation of more arms by more states from new production sources decreases the probability of armed conflict or enhances their security. The multiplication of arms production centers and the growing lethality at the command of an increasing number of states set arms races in motion—witness the Middle East and South Asia—and increase tension between states. Once hostilities erupt, as the Arab-Israel, Iran-Iraq, and India-Pakistan conflicts suggest, they tend to be of great intensity and destructiveness if for no other reason than that states are now better armed. The tangle of supply-recipient relations draws extraregional states, as France discovered in the Gulf war, into conflicts against their will or interest—precisely the dilemma that the de Gaulle Fifth Republic sought to avoid in resisting both superpower collision and collusion by pressing for a multipolar international system. Now that we have some picture of the systemic role and status of France as an arms supplier, it may be useful to examine how the Fifth Republic has used arms transfers as an instrument of diplomacy in promoting its security interests and its specific regional objectives around the globe.

CHAPTER 7

Arms Transfers as Aim
and Instrument

REGIONAL PATTERNS OF FRENCH ARMS DELIVERIES

To WHAT EXTENT have traditional foreign policy considerations, beyond those associated with French opposition to a superpower-dominated system, shaped French behavior? How has France used arms
sales to define regional military balances to favor some contestants over
others, to support or undermine political regimes, and to win friends
and influence other governments and events by granting or withholding arms? A case-by-case examination of French transfers provides a
provisional answer to these questions. What emerges is a crazy-quilt
pattern of behavior that admits to no easy—or sure—generalization.
While certainly more is at play than simply economic or welfare considerations or raw security imperatives, something less than purely foreign
policy concerns drive French arms policy. In some regions, particularly
West Europe and Black Africa, security and foreign policy aims appear
as important as economic and welfare considerations in explaining
French transfers of arms and military technology. In the Middle East,
where the superpowers have been the major actors and where the regional states have important leverage, French transfers appear more directly related to domestic economic needs. These same concerns also
are very much at the surface of French sales in Latin America and the
Far East. In all these regions, however, calculations of political and diplomatic influence—whether in breaking the U.S. arms monopoly in
Latin America or in assuring the Soviet Union on European détente by
restricting Communist Chinese access to French arms—are discernible
in French decision-making.

Table 7-1 provides a regional road map of French arms transfers for
the period from the early 1950s to 1983. It confirms the trade data
found in Chapter 3 which indicate that the Middle East and, especially
before 1970, West Europe were the largest recipients of French arms.
What is also important to note is not only the relative importance of
these two regions to each other and other parts of the globe, but the se-
quential ordering of French arms deliveries. For reasons to be discussed shortly, the Middle East, principally the oil producing states, re-

Table 7-1. Total French Arms Deliveries by Region and Weapon Category
as of 1983

Region	Attack Aircraft[a]	Support Aircraft[b]	Helicopters[c]	Missiles[d]	Armor[e]	Ships[f]
North Africa	262	88	134	672	903	42
South Africa	120	13	173	2,022	1,600	5
Southern Africa (Francophone)	51	166	68	184	260	45
Southern Africa (non-Francophone)	53	80	197	290	790	19
Central America	34	7	30	—	72	2
South America	215	114	233	3,171	734	18
East Asia	55	91	153	588	1,664	41
South Asia	336	48	408	2,823	150	7
Middle East	582	208	482	15,351	3,646	46
Western/Eastern Europe	574	487	1,095	15,429	2,506	54

SOURCES: See Appendix A and the Note on Sources in the Appendix. French retransfers of foreign-made equipment are also included.

KEY: Only countries that have received French weapons are included. The countries grouped in each region are:

North Africa: Algeria, Libya, Morocco, Tunisia.

South Africa: South Africa.

Southern Africa (former French colonies): Benin, Cameroon, Central African Republic, Chad, Djibouti, Gabon, Guinea, Ivory Coast, Madagascar, Mali, Mauritania, Niger, People's Republic of the Congo, Senegal, Togo, Upper Volta (Burkina Faso).

Southern Africa (former non-French colonies): Angola, Burundi, Ethiopia, Ghana, Guinea-Bissau, Kenya, Malawi, Mozambique, Nigeria, Rwanda, Somalia, Sudan, Uganda, Zaire, Zambia, Zimbabwe/Rhodesia.

Central America: Dominican Republic, El Salvador, Honduras, Mexico, Nicaragua.

South America: Argentina, Bolivia, Brazil, Chile, Colombia, Ecuador, Peru, Venezuela.

East Asia: Brunei, Burma, Cambodia (Kampuchea), Indonesia, South Korea, Laos, Malaysia, People's Republic of China, Singapore, South Vietnam, Taiwan, Thailand.

South Asia: Bangladesh, India, Nepal, Pakistan, Sri Lanka.

Middle East: Abu Dhabi, Bahrain, Dubai, Egypt, Iran, Iraq, Israel, Jordan, Kuwait, Lebanon, North Yemen, Oman, Qatar, Saudi Arabia, Syria.

Western/Eastern Europe: Austria, Belgium, Denmark, Federal Republic of Germany, Finland, Greece,

placed Western Europe as the major outlet for French arms in the 1970s and early 1980s. If North Africa is added to the Middle East, the region stretching from the Atlantic shoulder of North Africa to Turkey and Iran—largely Arab states—has received the bulk of French arms. Sub-Saharan Africa follows in importance if all of the states of the area, including South Africa, are counted. South and Central America are next in importance with East Asian sales lagging behind all other regions.

Western Europe

Western Europe is an interesting test case of the proposition that French arms sales are driven simply by commercial gain. The contrary appears closer to the truth, if France's failure to maintain its hold on the European market is a test of intent. French insistence on political and military independence, antagonism to bloc politics, and withdrawal from NATO's integrated military structure have seriously hobbled its ef-

---

Table 7-1 notes (*cont.*)

Ireland, Italy, Netherlands, Norway, Portugal, Romania, Spain, Sweden, Switzerland, Turkey, United Kingdom, Yugoslavia.

Also included are weapons produced under license as well as foreign arms in France's inventory that were retransferred to third states.

[a] Includes 16 models, the most important of which are the Mirage III/5, F1, Jaguar, Alpha-Jet, Mystère, and Ouragan.

[b] Includes 28 models, the most important of which are the Broussard, Cessna 337, Magister, Noratlas, Paris MS-760, and Transall.

[c] Includes 12 models of which the most important are the Alouette II and III, Gazelle, Lama, Puma, and Super Frelon.

[d] Includes several models within different sets of missiles: air-to-air (R-530/550), air-to-surface (AS-11, -12, -30), surface-to-air (Crotale, Roland), surface-to-surface (MM-38, Otomat, SS-10, -11, -12), and antitank (Entac, Harpon, Hot, Milan).

[e] Includes 24 models. Of special note are AML-60/90, Panhard's AML VTT, ERB 75, Eland 2 (S. Africa), M-3, self-propelled artillery (AMX-105 and -155), and light and heavy tanks and associated equipment (AMX-10, -13, and -30). In some cases, it could not be determined whether the French supplied U. S. or French APCs (M-3). Tank chassis carry different mountings. The AMX-10, for example, comes in at least eight versions carrying 105 mm. cannon, Hot missiles, or support equipment. All AMX transfers are counted as tanks because rarely are these differences recorded in ACDA, SIPRI, or IISS data.

[f] Includes 46 different types. The bulk are naval craft below 500 tons, including gunboats, missile-firing boats, armed patrol and coastal vessels, torpedo boats, support and landing craft, and submarines (Agosta, Albacora, and Daphne classes). Naval craft that could not be identified by specific type, but were French-supplied, are counted and listed on worksheets drawn from Appendix A. See the Note on Sources in the Appendix for counting rules and procedures.

forts to sell arms to its western allies. France's foreign policy stance on the East-West split has also hindered efforts to elicit cooperation from West European arms suppliers or joint projects to confront the U.S. monopoly with a European common front. It has also weakened allied confidence in France as a reliable partner and, by extension, as an arms supplier, a view strengthened by arms boycotts imposed at different times on such varied states as Israel, Chile, Libya, and Nigeria. As much as the ambiguity of the Fifth Republic's commitments to allied objectives and its periodic flirtations with neutrality in the Cold War struggle have helped France penetrate Third World arms markets, these same characteristics of French policy have limited its access to lucrative arms contracts in the West.

Illustrative of the French dilemma is the decision, discussed earlier, of four NATO states to replace their aging American F-104 Starfighters with General Dynamics' F-16 fighter over Dassault's Mirage F1 M53. The political cards were stacked against France from the outset of the competition. The two Scandinavian states—Denmark and Norway—were traditionally oriented to Anglo-Saxon producers. Dutch political and military leaders, always wary of French political motives—stemming from their repeated unrewarding encounters with de Gaulle directed at revising the framework of European security cooperation through the Fouchet Plan—insisted on conditions that were tantamount to a reversal of France's decision to withdraw from NATO as a prerequisite for their consideration of the Mirage fighter. The Dutch sought not only to coordinate small state purchases of new fighter aircraft but also plans on how these fighters, including those purchased by the French Air Force, would be integrated into NATO strategy.

Belgium was France's only strong suit. Belgium was a major purchaser of French arms. Dassault planes were known and valued. The Belgian aeronautics firm of SABCA, 51 percent of whose stock was owned by Dassault, profited from producing Mirage 5s; it anticipated a similar profitable relationship from the contract let by the Belgian government in September 1973 for the Dassault-Dornier Alpha-Jet. These pluses were offset by a number of negative factors working against the French: internal opposition, especially from Flemish sources, the pressures of Belgium's small-state allies to buy American, bungling by French negotiators, and the hard sell mounted by Washington. The Belgians finally caved in. In an unkind cut, Brussels announced its decision to reject the French offer during the Paris Air Show in June 1975.[1]

To offset Atlanticist critics in the four states, French leaders played a "European" card. Early in the campaign to win the fighter contract,

Prime Minister Jacques Chirac raised the possibility that France might relax its reservations about sharing political authority within a revived Europe of Nine. Specifically singled out for closer political and economic integration was Europe's aeronautics industry. In a formal address during a state visit to Denmark in August 1974, Chirac declared that France wished to promote among the European Nine "the greatest [possible] cooperation, going so far in some sectors to the transfer of sovereignty."[2]

French President Giscard d'Estaing echoed the same sentiments in promoting France's case. On May 31, a week before the Belgian announcement of its rejection of the Mirage F1, President Giscard d'Estaing squarely placed responsibility for the future of Europe's aircraft industry on Belgium: "The Mirage F1 still has a good chance. The Belgian government is studying with much care this important decision on which . . . depends in large part the future of European avionics. . . . It is less a question of business interests than a test of the capacity of certain Europeans in authority to make Europe."[3] When the Belgians opted for an Atlantic solution, Chirac accused his European partners of abandoning the ideal of European unity:

> France, faithful to [the] option concerning the imperative realization of European union . . . , believes in the necessity of progressing in all areas where progress can be accomplished. In this spirit, France believes in the utility of a European aeronautic policy resting on the development of a European aeronautics industry. . . . The decision taken [by the four NATO states to buy the F-16] constitutes, for the Parliaments and the governments in question, a responsibility which does not bear essentially, and I will not say principally, on the facts and on the economic and financial consequences of a sale, but on [this] point, . . . whether there exists among European leaders of Europe the genuine will to permit our continent, formerly a pioneer in aviation, to find again the place that its industry and its technical capacity makes it possible to hold.[4]

Remonstrances and passionate appeals to European independence failed to overcome the deep suspicions of France's NATO partners. France's plea for unity appeared to be a thin cover for French aggrandizement and economic gain. Rhetorical commitment to a United Europe squared badly with the ambiguity of France's strategic doctrine in defending Europe, its long resistance to British entry into the Brussels grouping, and its insistence on national sovereignty over community authority. As Jacques Isnard, *Le Monde*'s highly respected defense analyst, concluded in the aftermath of the sale of the century: "It would be with some ill-grace for the French government to deny any abandonment of the European idea and to accuse its neighbors of contributing, by their choice, of consolidating United States supremacy when it is far from having clarified the whole of its European policy and, in particular, its European defense doctrine."[5] Ingemar Dörfer, the biographer of the sale of the century, also shares the view that Gaullist-shaped French strategic and foreign policy objectives prevailed over commercial considerations: "The French policy of independence on the one hand and foreign sales on the other worked beautifully in the Third World. But here in Northwest Europe the French withdrawal from NATO military cooperation now hurt for the first time: for once the French specific road to glory cost money."[6]

One should be cautious in assigning too great a weight to foreign policy either in explaining French behavior or the reasons for its failure to sell Mirages to its European partners. First, the F1 and F-16 appear to have been mismatched. Most observers agreed that the General Dynamics fighter was a superior fighter in avionics, electronics, and engine capability.[7] It was also priced lower than the French aircraft. Cost offsets proposed by General Dynamics through subcontracting were as financially attractive to prospective clients as the sole-source arrangements dangled by Dassault.[8] There was the added attraction of access to more advanced aeronautics technology in associating with American industry instead of France. The French government had itself opted for association with the United States in nuclear energy (Westinghouse), computers (IBM and Honeywell), and even in aircraft engines (General Electric).[9] The decision of the U.S. Air Force to buy the F-16 also opened the possibility of not only lower unit costs and greater NATO standardization but also increased third state sales in which the European states would participate.

Second, the French weakened their case in ways quite apart from the disingenuousness of their newly found Europeanism. Earlier chapters have already recounted resistance of the French Air Force to the F1 M53. The French first offered to purchase 30 copies of the fighter, then increased the total to a sum equal to the largest number bought by any of the European states. If the French armed forces balked at purchasing the Mirage F1 M53, it was hard to see how much enthusiasm could be generated among the four small states about the aircraft. The French also haggled over price, discoloring the image of high purpose and staunch Europeanism that French governmental leaders had attempted to project.[10] The French were no less wary about sharing decisions on third state sales with their European partners. The Dutch and Scandinavians shared reservations about selling to many states with which France already carried on a profitable arms trade.

Finally, hard American selling of the F-16 put the French at a disadvantage. Aside from the quality of the F-16, Washington went full tilt in pressing its case. Unlike France, the armed forces and the American bureaucracy were unified. The American firms were also not about to relinquish the NATO market to a European state; much less were they prepared to be beaten by the French with whom they competed for arms markets around the world. Even before its announced withdrawal from NATO in 1966, France had already suffered major setbacks in its efforts to supply NATO forces. The F-104 Starfighter had been chosen over the Mirage III, and the French lost to Italy in a NATO-sponsored competition for an all-alliance light attack aircraft. Congressional concern about European burden-sharing and standardization also increased American pressures on Europe to purchase the American fighter.

The French sales position in Europe remains weak. As Chapter 3 suggests, its strategy of joint contracting with European states has, after some initial success, not kept pace with changes in military requirements and new technologies. The British, Germans, and Italians went their own way with the Tornado, leaving France to fend for itself in the highly competitive market of advanced fighter aircraft. Belgium, a traditional French preserve, also chose to modernize its armed forces with American tanks rather than continue with French systems.[11] Efforts to rely on a revived Western European Union (WEU) as a vehicle for greater European military industrial cooperation have not borne much fruit. That may change as the possibility of a superpower arms control accord, potentially at the expense of Europe, prompts France to forge a common stance with its European allies on defense. France's à la carte approach to penetrating the European arms market has serious shortcomings. High politics may still be the road to greater industrial cooperation and arms sales in Europe. Britain has already signaled greater interest in the WEU.[12] A reluctant Bonn may yet follow.

Until recently, there was not much left for France after the United States carved out its near-monopolistic share of the European arms market and indigenous production by the major West European states met national military requirements. What markets remain are with neutral states—Austria, Switzerland, Sweden, and Finland—and with West European states on the periphery of the NATO alliance—Spain, Portugal, and Greece. Among the neutral states, Switzerland was France's most important buyer in the 1960s, having ordered 100 Mirages and other equipment. Since then, a series of scandals surrounding the purchase of Dassault aircraft, a taint associated with sales to other states, Swiss interest in developing their own arms production capacity, and a successful American sales campaign to increase sales to Switzerland have cooled interest in French arms.

Among southern-tier western states, France has fared slightly better. Throughout the 1970s they were steady clients of France. France offered the Franco regime a counterweight to the United States in Spain's bargaining over bases in return for civilian and military assistance. A series of protocols was signed in the 1970s with the Spanish government to buy French Mirages, helicopters, ships, and ground armor, and to jointly produce tanks and submarines.[13] Portugal used French equipment, particularly helicopters, to retain, as long as it could, its hold on its tattered empire in southern Africa. The Greek colonels, the Karamanlis regime, and then the Socialist government, which came to power in Greece in 1981, found France a ready arms supplier and an alternative to the United States. Washington, according to Greek critics, was tilted in favor of Ankara over Athens on the Cyprus question. Paris was willing to sell arms to the Greek military over the objections of its European allies and in spite of the condemnation of such sales by the Council of Europe.[14] The French also winked at the use of their arms to suppress local resistance either to Spanish rule in the western Sahara or to Portuguese control over its colonies in southern Africa.[15]

Competitors from the United States and France's West European allies pose serious obstacles to sales in Europe. Portugal progressively prefers to rely on Washington for its arms purchases. Neutral states which had previously purchased French arms, especially aircraft, missiles, and armor, are either meeting their own needs or turning to other West European suppliers.[16] Spain's entry into the Atlantic Alliance also threatens France's long-term role as one of Spain's principal European arms suppliers. Madrid's decision to buy 84 McDonnell Douglas F-18s rather than the Mirage 2000 was symptomatic of the problem.[17]

To meet the American challenge, France entered into a comprehensive military agreement with the Spanish government in November 1983 which surpasses previous levels of cooperation, including the 1970 protocol. The accord covers joint arms production, training, and the sharing of facilities for ships, aircraft, and transport. "The new agreement," noted the Spanish Defense Minister, "places Spain and France on an absolutely equal footing—something which was not the case with the 1970 agreement; that is, it allows that the exchange of licenses in arms manufacture and cooperation in weapon systems is extended to missiles and satellites, which was not envisaged in the previous agreement."[18] France would not only freely grant Spain licenses for the production of weapons, but joint manufacture was also contemplated.

Parallel to the Spanish accord, Mitterrand's France extended its cooperation with Greece, particularly in military avionics. "Greece," explained French Defense Minister Hernu, "has an important industrial base in different sectors and it hopes to develop them further in order to increase its technology and military independence."[19] The French ostensibly had an added advantage over the United States, since France had more consistently supported the Athens government over disputes with Turkey than the United States. The Socialist Papandreou government was also ideologically closer to the Mitterrand regime than to Washington. These assets contributed to the decisions of the Greek government to purchase 40 Mirage 2000 fighters, although they were not sufficient to forestall Greek purchase of 40 F-16s as part of the offset accords defining American access to Greek bases and naval facilities.[20]

MIDDLE EAST

The French-Israeli Alliance

The need for oil and markets notwithstanding, foreign policy considerations have been consistently at the surface of French arms transfer behavior in the Middle East. The dramatic swings in French-Israeli arms relations illustrate the point. The alliance between Tel Aviv and Paris, from roughly the inception of the Israeli state to the end of the Algerian War in 1962, was founded on different but complementary security interests threatened by the Arab states bordering the Mediterranean basin—Israel's very life as a state and nation and France's empire, identified by the Fourth Republic as a prerequisite of national survival and grandeur. Whatever stymied or stifled the Arab states in overthrowing French colonial rule or the Israeli state was viewed from Tel Aviv and Paris as mutually beneficial. Franco-Israeli collusion in launching the Suez War reflected these converging perspectives.[21] The pan-Arab movement, led by Egypt's President Gamal Abdel Nasser, simultaneously menaced the Israeli state and French colonial rule. Arming Israel was tantamount to arming the French nation, as France's enemy was also Israel's. Table 7-2 summarizes French arms transfers to Israel between 1950 and 1962.

The Israeli Air Force was essentially made in France. Its ground forces were largely equipped with French armor or with American-made surplus items transferred (not always with permission from Washington) to Israel. Certainly these sales assisted the expansion of

Table 7-2. Deliveries of Major French Weapons Systems to Israel: 1950-1962

Year	Fighter Aircraft	Support Aircraft	Ground Armor	Missiles	Heli-copters	Naval Vessels
1950	60 Mosquito (Great Britain)					2 Torpedo Boats
1953		5 Broussard				7 Torpedo Boats
1954			150 AMX-13			
1955	24 Mystère 15 Ouragan MD 450		300 M-2 M-3 (U.S.) 30 AMX-105 100 Sherman Tanks (U.S.)	200 SS-10		
1956	36 Mystère 45 Ouragan MD 450	8 Noratlas				
1957	24 Vautour					
1959	24 Super Mystère					
1960	100 Fouga-Magister CM 170	6 Noratlas			5 Alouette III	
1962	72 Mirage III			150 Entac 150 SS-11 300 AS-30		

Sources: See Appendix A and Note on Sources in the Appendix for counting rules.

France's arms industry, particularly Dassault's emergence as a major world producer of fighter aircraft, but the dominant concern was arming for mutual survival against a common Arab foe. During this period, French arms streamed into Israel. French military technology and assistance accompanied the arms flow. Ezer Weizman, former Israeli Minister of Defense, characterized how close these French-Israeli ties had become when he recounted his participation in the decision in 1958 to buy 72 Mirage IIIs to counter the MIG-21s promised Egypt by the Soviet Union:

The most crucial decision I ever took was the purchase of the Mirage. I'll be bold as to say that the way Israel and France worked together on the Mirage was something unique. When we bought our previous planes from France, a lot of French know-how had already been built into them. But the Mirage went into squadron service with the French and Israeli air forces simultaneously. Nothing like this had ever happened anywhere else before. . . .

We did not choose the Mirage simply because we had no other alternative and could not get Lightnings or F-104s. We bought the Mirage because it's a damn good plane. . . . The plane had its problems. After all, there's no perfect woman in the world. But the Mirage was just right for us.[22]

As noted earlier, French-Israeli nuclear cooperation continued. This led to the construction of the Dimona reactor and joint development of the Gabriel surface-to-surface missile, potentially capable of carrying a nuclear warhead.

The Evian accords of 1962, dissolving the last major remnant of France's colonial empire, implicitly ended the marriage of convenience between Tel Aviv and Paris. With Algeria independent and with Morocco and Tunisia no longer French protectorates, a critical obstacle to a French-Arab détente—and eventual entente—was removed. The same could not be said for Israel. The Evian peace accords boded ill for Israel. France henceforth had an interest in distancing itself from Israel as a condition for improved relations with the Arab states.

Even after Evian, arms continued to flow to Israel. Between 1962 and 1967, these included 15 Alouette IIIs, 6 Super Frelons, 100 R-530 Matra air-to-air missiles, 18 Noratlas transports, and quantities of spare parts. Orders for almost a billion dollars in equipment were also placed in the six months preceding the Six Day War.[23] These arms flows, however, were guided by a worldview and strategy entirely different from that of the Fourth Republic. What changed with the Evian settlement was the geopolitical context within which the Gaullist government directed French foreign policy conduct. After 1962, Israel was viewed more as a client than as an ally. France's willingness to arm Israel was subordinated to a postcolonial geostrategic policy based more on France's techno-scientific competitiveness and diplomatic finesse than on the direct use of its military power (outside the Francophone area) to enlarge France's regional and global role. In the Mediterranean, the Gaullist stance dictated a more even hand toward all parties—Arabs and Jews—to prevent armed conflict which would open the area to superpower penetration, reducing the political influence that France could exert in region.[24]

The de Gaulle government's ambitions did not match France's capabilities. The Six Day War defined the limits of its power to moderate and arbitrate the Arab-Israeli rivalry. Although French-made Mirage fighters dominated the desert skies, destroying Soviet combat aircraft on the ground and in the air, France had little say about the political outcome of the war. The total defeat of Arab forces so polarized the region that France was forced to choose between Israel and the Arab states, a choice that it had resisted for half a decade since the Evian agreement. The war also precipitated deeper superpower entry into the region, creating the worst of all worlds for French policy objectives. The two conflicts, regional and global, fed each other. The prospects of a superpower clash increased while the European détente, initiated by France and confirmed by its withdrawal from NATO, was jeopardized. The superpowers flooded the region with arms, dwarfing the French effort and influence. Meanwhile, domestic unrest, economic recession, and the oil crises of the 1970s cast France in the unattractive role as *demandeur* in Middle East politics.

France's ill-fated arms embargo against Israel on June 2, 1967, revealed the impotence of French arms supply policy to manage or moderate the Arab-Israeli dispute. It failed to restrain Israel from resorting to force or from using French arms in its preemptive attack against the Arab states in 1967 or in its assault on the Beirut airport in December 1968. The superpowers shouldered France aside. The United States swiftly met Israeli demands for arms while the Soviet Union launched a massive resupply of the defeated Arab states. With arms came superpower presence and influence. Israel speeded development of its arms industry. By the 1970s it was competing with France for markets in Europe, Latin and Central America, and Africa.[25] Damaged, too, was France's reputation as an arms supplier as well as its claim that, unlike the superpowers, it placed no restrictions on the use of French arms by a state in defense of its security interests.

The de Gaulle government entangled itself in a self-made mesh of contradictions and hypocritical posturings as it attempted to steer a middle course in the Arab-Israeli dispute and manage a serious domestic challenge to its embargo policy from Israeli sympathizers who were also key supporters of the regime.[26] The June embargo covered only so-called offensive arms. These extended exclusively to 50 Mirage 5s purchased and paid for by Israel but impounded and later absorbed by the French Air Force after restitution of Israel's payment, with interest, had been made. Despite the announced embargo, arms shipments continued to Tel Aviv. These included 25 Fouga-Magister aircraft, 7 Super Frelon helicopters, and 7 of 12 missile-firing patrol boats as well as substantial amounts of ammunition and spare parts. Turboméca also initiated and constructed an engine plant at Bet Shemish during this period of selective embargo.[27]

The Israelis defied French proscriptions on "offensive" use of French equipment by attacking the Beirut airport in December 1968, reportedly using at least one recently acquired Super Frelon. Paris interpreted the attack as a challenge to the French state and a blow to French standing among the Arab states. President de Gaulle characterized the Israeli action as an excessive act of violence "committed by the regular forces of a state on a civilian airport of a peaceful country and on a long-time friend of France."[28] The destruction of French-owned Caravelles only added to the distress of Paris.

Under heavy Arab pressure, a full arms embargo against Israel was announced on January 3, 1969. The finality of this prohibition was, however, subject to no less doubt than the previous embargo. In reply to a parliamentary inquiry, Gaullist deputy Alexandre Sanguinetti said, "As Chairman of the National Defense Committee for five years, I can assure you that the spares that we sent Israel permitted it to reconstruct totally its Mirages."[29] The day after the announcement of the full embargo, the seventh of twelve missile-firing patrol boats left France for Israel. Eleven months later on Christmas Eve, Israeli sailors, with the complicity of French military and civilian officials, spirited the remaining five patrol boats from Cherbourg under the guise of a purchase by a Norwegian company whose name was illicitly used to repurchase the vessels.[30] The head of the Directorate of International Affairs of DMA was sacked over the affair, although no formal charges of complicity were ever brought against him.[31] Projected was a picture of collusion between highly placed French and Israeli officials and of slipshod internal security procedures. French arms policy was not only ineffective in disciplining Israel, but the vaunted integrity of the French administration appeared to have been penetrated by foreign agents and compromised without the knowledge of leading governmental officials.

Tilt toward the Arab States

Extension of the Israeli embargo to "belligerents on the field of battle in the Middle East"—i.e., Israel, Jordan, Egypt, and Syria—preserved the image of neutrality while tilting France toward the Arab states. Since the Arab states, particularly Egypt and Syria, were being supplied by the Soviet Union, the French embargo was effectively aimed at Israel. France also entered into serious arms negotiations with Iraq, Saudi Arabia, Algeria, and Libya—states which in one way or another had supported the Arab cause. Between the 1967 and 1973 Middle East wars, including the war of attrition, Iraq received 15 Alouette IIIs and

70 armored vehicles (AML-60/90); Saudi Arabia, 5 Alouette IIIs and 220 armored vehicles; Algeria, 28 Fouga-Magisters; Lebanon, 14 Mirage IIIs; and Libya, some 65 Mirages out of a total order of 110 Mirage IIIs and 5s.[32] The French government ignored Israeli charges that Iraq had fought in the Six Day War and that Saudi finances were fueling the Arab war effort.[33] Algeria and Libya were also vociferous opponents of Israel. In contravention to French restrictions on arms retransfers, Libya sent Egypt some 24 Mirages to aid in the Yom Kippur War against Israel.[34]

The French advanced several explanations for their duplicitous behavior. They clung to the distinction between belligerents and nonbelligerents, insisting that Iraq and Saudi Arabia were not directly implicated in the Six Day War or the subsequent war of attrition. Paris also ignored the objections of Kurdish leaders who feared that French helicopters and armor would be used by Iraq to suppress their efforts to gain national independence, although French arms sales were supposed to ensure, not preclude, national self-expression.

The sale of Mirages to Libya produced the most elaborate, if no less contradictory, exhibition of French hypocrisy. By 1970, oil and markets were looming larger than ever in the French arms sales equation. A $400-million contract, tied to oil, was too tempting to reject on grounds of political bias in the Arab-Israeli split. If France turned Libya down, the Soviet Union was seen to be the alternate supplier; better that France furnish arms than Russia. French officials also privately denigrated Libya's ability to fly or maintain the aircraft, minimizing the threat to Israel. The *coup de Libye* was heralded as part of France's Mediterranean policy to keep the basin safe from the risk of superpower conflict. Argued Foreign Minister Maurice Schumann in defending the Libyan sale: "There is a Mediterranean policy for France which . . . has only one aim: to prevent . . . the western Mediterranean . . . and if possible . . . the whole of the Mediterranean basin, from becoming again, or from remaining a theater of the cold war and a supplementary state in the rivalry of the great powers."[35]

To those still not persuaded by the reasoning underlying the tilt toward the Arab states, Gaullist France rationalized an Arab need to offset Israeli military superiority and expansionism at the expense of Palestinian independence and Arab territory. Schumann alluded to Israel's "inclination to annex" and to its "inability to define its position on its fundamental problem, the fact of the occupied territories and that of one million Arabs."[36] In the aftermath of the June war, de Gaulle referred to the Jews as "an elite people, sure of itself and dominating. . . ."[37] A new calculus of principle and interest pointed in the direction of long-term alignment on Arab, not Israeli, concerns. Prime Minister Michel Debré was candid about French motivation: "If the French do not think first about their country, who will do it for them? No one. This policy is naturally guided by our interests, because every people has the duty to defend its interests."[38]

The intricate tissue of scholastic rationalization clothing French arms sales in the Middle East was rent finally when Egyptian President Anwar Sadat confirmed in 1974 what had been widely believed, viz., that some of the French Mirages sold to Libya had been used in the Yom Kippur War.[39] This belated revelation prompted the Giscard d'Estaing government on August 28, 1974, to abandon its "no arms for states on the field of battle" policy. This veiled embargo, aimed more against Israel than the Arab states, was not working anyway. Its perverse consequences went contrary to French expectations and aims. The superpowers and other arms-producing states filled the vacuum left by selective French self-restraint. The no-retransfer clauses of French arms contracts obviously had little effect on recipients since there were no serious penalties for noncompliance. Worse, the embargo hindered access to lucrative Arab arms and commercial markets, which had become irresistible in the wake of the oil boycott and a quadrupling of oil prices.[40]

Arab capitals were generally pleased by the shift in French policy. Three months before in April 1974, five Arab states—Kuwait, Saudi Arabia, Abu Dhabi, Iraq, and Libya—placed orders for over a billion dollars of military equipment.[41] The August lifting of the boycott gave ex post facto sanction to the spring sale. According to a *Le Monde* report, Saudi Arabia also ordered 38 Mirage IIIs in late 1973 in the aftermath of the Yom Kippur War. These aircraft were eventually destined for Egypt. Had the embargo not been raised, the anticipated transfer would have contravened not only the aim of the embargo but ostensibly unauthorized third state transfer restrictions routinely written into French arms contracts.[42] Kuwait's prime minister, expressing widely shared Arab sentiment, hailed the open-door arms policy announced by Paris: "We consider the raising of the embargo as a positive decision on the part of the French government. We hope that this decision is going to offer the Arab countries the possibility to buy French arms of all kinds. . . ."[43] The Israeli government was understandably more reserved. Since lifting the embargo did not assure resumption of French arms sales to Israel, Tel Aviv preferred a dual stance—criticizing the French for having imposed the boycott yet violating its spirit in selling arms to Arab states while pressing Paris to maintain its embargo, however porous it had become, to hamper Arab purchases of French arms.[44]

Israeli fears were soon confirmed. Table 7-3 summarizes French deliveries of arms to Arab states in the decade following the end of the arms embargo. French arms of all kinds flowed in a steady stream to the Arab states. Principal recipients were Saudi Arabia and Iraq, France's major oil partners. The sales to these states opened the way to major arms purchases by Egypt, Syria, and the Persian Gulf states and to increased French military cooperation and assistance to the region.

The Saudi connection was strongest and, though its political dimensions remain largely hidden from view, the most entangling. France has become Saudi Arabia's principal supplier of ground armor, major naval vessels, and air and coastal defense systems. The first of three major waves of contracts developed not long after France had lost in its bid to sell F1 M53s to NATO. Riyadh made a key decision in the middle 1970s to rely on French ground armor for its army. Heavy AMX-30 and lighter AMX-10 tanks became the backbone of Saudi ground forces. Hundreds were delivered to Saudi forces while the French Army, lacking resources, was unable to order new tanks to meet planning goals. Saudi purchases of French armor were supplemented by a panoply of specially designed vehicles utilizing the basic AMX chassis.[45] Of particular significance was the Saudi contract for a readaptation of the Thomson-Brandt's Crotale antiaircraft surface-to-air missile to meet desert conditions.[46] Development of the Shahine formed the kernel of a research and development effort that fused the interests of France's arms industry and those of the Saudi regime and its security needs in the Middle East.

In early 1984, the Saudi government signed a contract valued in excess of $4 billion for a comprehensive air defense system, including advanced radar technology and ground-to-air missiles. This contract evolved over several years during which the Saudi government subsidized research and development of a new version of the Shahine missile to fit its air defense needs. Once in place, the French system is designed to meet Saudi air defense needs against low and high flying aircraft. Added to these purchases, Riyadh placed orders in 1985 for the modernization of its fleet of 400 self-propelled armored cars and the purchase of 600 armored reconnaissance vehicles.[47] The multibillion-dollar air defense contract and the purchase of armored vehicles surpassed even the ambitious contract let in 1980 for four frigates, two refueling ships, and a fleet of helicopters. All of these sales entailed the commitment of several thousand military and civilian technicians to assist in training and operating French equipment. The air defense contract marked the largest foreign weapons contract in French sales history. The Saudis viewed the arrangement as a counter to dependence on the

Table 7-3. Deliveries of Major Weapons Systems to Arab States: 1974-1983

	Fighter Aircraft	Support Aircraft	Armor	Missiles	Helicopters	Naval Vessels
Bahrain[a]						
Egypt	73 Mirage III 28 Mirage 5 10 Alpha-Jet [5 Mirage 2000][b] [14 Mirage 5][b]	1 Falcon	110 Panhard/M-3	24 MM-38 Exocet 100 R-550 Matra 624 Hot 24 AS-12 20 Crotale 30 Otomat [96 Crotale][b] [60 Otomat][b]	66 Gazelle	
Iran		5 Falcon		36 AS-12 (?) MM-38 Exocet		12 Patrol Boats
Iraq[c]	36 Mirage F1 5 Super Etendard	2 Falcon	100 ERC 50 AMX-10 100 AMX-30 100 VCR-6 [50 AMX-10][b]	144 R-550 Matra 180 Hot 120 AM-39 Exocet [100 Crotale][b] [50 Roland 2][b] [250 AM-39 Exocet][b]	36 Alouette III 60 Gazelle 40 Puma 12 Super Frelon	
Jordan	23 Mirage F1				11 Alouette III	
Kuwait	20 Mirage F1		20 AMX-155 34 AMX-13	1,200 SS-11 120 R-550 Matra, 120 R-530	24 Gazelle 10 Puma	

	Aircraft		Armored Vehicles	Missiles	Helicopters	Ships / Other
Lebanon[d]	4 Fouga-Magister		5 VAB 13 AMX-13 [9 AMX-13][b] [9 VAB][b]	200 Milan 96 SS-11 96 SS-12	6 Alouette III 6 Puma 4 Gazelle	3 Patrol Boats, 1 EDIC Class Tank Landing Ship
Oman	12 Jaguar	1 Falcon		72 R-550 Matra 60 MM-38 Exocet 6 MM-40 Exocet	4 Puma	
Qatar[e]	3 Mirage F1 8 Alpha-Jet [14 Mirage F1][b]		136 VAB 30 AMX-10 24 AMX-30 [8 VAB][b]	16 MM-40 Exocet	4 Gazelle 3 Puma	2 La Combattante
Saudi Arabia[f]		2 Falcon	500 AML-60/90 749 AMX-10 [480 AMX-30][b] [53 AMX-30 30 mm.][b] [4 AMX-30 Shahine][b]	2,000 SS-11 2,000 Harpon [100 R-440 Crotale][b] 96 Shahine	22 Alouette III	[Sawari Program: 4 Frigates, 2 Re-fueling Vessels, Fleet of Helicopters][b]
Syria[g]		2 Falcon	246 Hot [108 Hot][b]		66 Gazelle 15 Super Frelon	
U.A.E. (Abu Dhabi et al.)	18 Mirage III 32 Mirage 5	1 Falcon	16 AMX-155 150 AML-60/90	3,650 Harpon 2,000 AS-11/12 100 R-440 Crotale 24 MM-40 Exocet	5 Alouette III 5 Puma	

SOURCES: See Appendix A and the Note on Sources in the Appendix.

[a] Egypt. *Mirage 2000*: The order for 5 Mirage 2000s, plus an option for 20 more, was placed in 1982. The 1982 SIPRI *Yearbook* estimates that the first 5 aircraft were delivered in 1983.

Mirage 5: SIPRI sources indicate that Egypt received as many as 62 Mirage 5s. *The Military Balance* only cites 14. These 14 additional (to the 28 confirmed by SIPRI) deliveries are estimated to have occurred between 1980 and 1981.

Crotale: Only SIPRI sources cite a 1982 order for 96 Crotale SAMs. Delivery of 48 is estimated to have occurred in 1982 and 1983 respectively.

Otomat-2: Egypt may have received both versions of the Otomat. The presence of the Otomat-1 is confirmed. It is a ship-to-ship missile supplied by Italy. The Otomat-2 is the coastal defense version supplied by France. Only SIPRI sources estimate the delivery of the Otomat-2 between 1980 and 1981.

[b] Estimates; see respective country footnotes.

[c] Iraq. *AMX-10*: Only SIPRI sources cite the additional 50 AMX-10s. They list the order and a 1981 delivery, but the quantity of 50 is an estimate.

Crotale: SIPRI sources indicate delivery of Crotales in 1981 and 1982; about 50 were estimated to have been shipped each year.

Roland II: The presence of Roland SAMs is confirmed by both SIPRI and *The Military Balance*. SIPRI lists a 1981 order for 150 and estimates that 50 were delivered in 1982. *The Military Balance* cites Rolands in the Iraqi force structure in its 1981-1982 edition, but it gives no numbers.

Mirage F1: A total of 89 F1s were ordered by Iraq. *Le Monde*, February 7, 1983.

Exocet: Ibid., March 17 and 18, 1985.

Lebanon. *AMX-13*: *The Military Balance* through 1983-1984 lists only 13 AMX-13s in service in Lebanon. The 1983 SIPRI *Yearbook* estimates that an additional 9 were delivered in 1982.

VAB: The 1983 SIPRI *Yearbook* estimates that another 9 VABs were delivered to Lebanon in 1982. The presence of 5 VABs is confirmed by both SIPRI and *The Military Balance*.

[e] *Qatar: Mirage F1*: SIPRI sources cite a 1980 order for 14 Mirage F1s. The 1983 *Yearbook* then states that these were delivered in 1981 and estimates 7 each for 1982 and 1983. The difference between the order for 14 and the 17 estimated deliveries is not explained. *The Military Balance*, through its 1983-1984 edition, still only cites an order for 14 Mirage F1s.

VAB: SIPRI sources cite an order for 136 VABs, but proceed to estimate deliveries of 144 between 1980 and 1983. *The Military Balance* indicates deployment of 136 in its 1982-1983 and 1983-1984 editions.

[f] Saudi Arabia. *AMX-30*: Orders and deliveries for the AMX-30 differ widely in the sources. The SIPRI *Yearbooks* indicate orders ranging from 359 to 600 and annual deliveries of 55 or 60 from 1976 through 1983. *The Military Balance* cites orders between 300 and 650, but deployed numbers vary widely from 280 in the 1980-1981 edition, to 480 in the 1981-1982 edition, to 300 in the 1983-1984 edition.

AMX-30 30 mm. and *Shahine*: Only SIPRI sources list a 1975 order for 4 AMX-30 Shahine and 53 AMX-30 30 mm. The delivery of these systems is estimated to have occurred between 1979 and 1982.

R-440 Crotale: The 1982 SIPRI *Yearbook* cites a 1980 order for Crotale SAMs, stating that this order was placed in addition to the Shahine (a version of the Crotale). Deliveries of 50 for both 1980 and 1981 are estimated.

Sawari Program: Orders.

[g] Syria. *Hot*: The total number of Hot missiles supplied to Syria is uncertain. Between 1977 and 1978, 246 missiles were delivered, while an order for 108 Hot is cited in the 1982 SIPRI *Yearbook*. Delivery is estimated to have occurred between 1980 and 1981.

United States, which had previously supplied Saudi Arabia with F-15 fighters and a $8.5 billion AWACS system (Airborne Warning and Control System).[48] What was noteworthy about the Saudi contract were the constraints reportedly placed on French use of its own equipment. Saudi leaders asserted that the large sums granted to France to develop the air defense system gave Saudi Arabia a veto over its use either by France or any third state.[49] Paris has never publicly denied Saudi claims, according them a potential lien on French arms that France has steadfastly resisted in its relations with other states.

Iraq was the second largest recipient of French arms. Withdrawal from dependence on the Soviet Union has been gradual and by no means complete. Access to French arms has been conceived by Iraqi leaders as a hedge against reliance on Soviet supplies, not as a substitute. Delivery of arms, particularly ground armor and tactical missiles, began not long after the Six Day War. The pace of deliveries intensified during the late 1970s and reached its peak in the early stages of the Iraq-Iran war. Between 1980 and 1982, approximately $7 billion in arms were ordered.[50] Iraq received F1 fighters (a total of 89 were ordered),[51] assorted French armor and tactical missiles, and some 150 helicopters. As fighting mounted, large quantities of this equipment passed through Saudi ports.[52] Ignoring Gaullist strictures, the Giscard d'Estaing and Mitterrand governments allowed France to be drawn into the Iraqi orbit, pushed sequentially, with reinforcing compulsion, by several factors: the search for arms markets and secure oil supplies, Saudi and Arab Gulf state urgings, and fear that the pan-Islamic revolution unleashed by the Iranian regime of Ayatollah Khomeini might spread. As the war dragged on and Iraqi resources were strained to the limit, the French weighted official neutrality in favor of the Hussein government.

The decision in the fall of 1983 to "lend" Iraq five Super Etendard attack aircraft and air-to-surface Exocet missiles—so deadly against British vessels in the Falklands War and the U.S. frigate *Stark*—revealed the depth of French support for Iraq and the Hussein regime. Aside from the considerations already noted, pressing France to tilt toward Iraq rather than Iran, the Baghdad government also owed France several billion dollars for past arms purchases. These debts could not be repaid until Iraqi oil could again begin flowing through the Persian Gulf and across the Syrian pipeline closed by Damascus in support of Iran. The Super Etendards were supposed to force the Iranian hand by threatening Iranian oil shipments—which rapidly proved to be an illusory expectation. Paris vacillated for several months in 1983 between concern for protecting its risky political and economic investments in

Iraq and its standing among the Gulf states and the fear of enlarging the war and of incurring lasting Iranian hostility that could be costly if Teheran prevailed.[53] The French government, although confronted by billions of dollars in trade deficits, felt compelled to relax Iraq's schedule of payments.[54] It was repaid for its loyalty by Iraqi use of Exocet missiles launched from Super Etendards and Super Frelons against Iranian ships and by an expanded campaign of Iraqi attacks on Gulf shipping.[55] By 1985, some 250 Exocets were delivered to Iraq.[56] As in the Libyan and Saudi cases involving Mirage aircraft, once arms were transferred, Paris had little control over their use.

The obverse of increased French commitments to Iraq and the Hussein regime was decreased access to Iran, the Khomeini regime, and to Iran's Arab supporters, principally Syria. As in the case of the Six Day War where the choice was Israel or the Arab states, French regimes now had to choose between warring Arab factions and between rivals for dominion of the Persian Gulf. The Iranian market had been closed to French arms dealers since the U.S. implanted itself in Teheran after the fall of the Mossadeq regime and the Shah's restoration in 1953. What credit had been accumulated in offering political asylum to Ayatollah Khomeini was quickly lost in France's grant of asylum to opponents and former collaborators of the Khomeini regime and its support of Washington's position on the hostage issue. The Mitterrand regime completed delivery of twelve patrol vessels. The remaining three vessels of this order had been blockaded in Cherbourg, stranding a complement of Iranian sailors pending final payment on the ships. Subsequent Iranian overtures to buy French equipment, however, were rebuffed, although the possibility of secret negotiations and arms shipments by France to Iran cannot be ruled out in light of the discovery in 1986 that the Reagan administration had pursued a duplicitous policy toward Teheran, condemning the regime while sending arms to enhance its position with Iran. Future disclosures may reveal that France played a similar two-handed game. Nevertheless, French Defense Minister Charles Hernu declared in February 1983 that "if Iran asked for arms, Paris would refuse."[57]

In tilting toward Iraq and the Hussein regime, French governments simultaneously pitted themselves against Syria, Iran's ally, and against the Hassad government committed to Hussein's overthrow. Sales to Syria, while not negligible,[58] never approached the impressive sales to Iraq and Saudi Arabia, which were several times larger. Deliveries were concentrated in tactical missiles and helicopters. Antitank missiles, coproduced with West Germany, were sent to Syria over Bonn's objections.[59] Damascus shifted progressively toward dependence on the Soviet Union for arms.

Avoiding a clash with Syria became doubly difficult as the Giscard d'Estaing and Mitterrand governments became embroiled in the Lebanese civil war and the growing Syrian-Israeli confrontation. Lebanon had maintained close ties with France since its independence in 1944, after more than twenty years as a mandate of France under the League of Nations. The Lebanese intelligentsia and business communities were oriented toward France. French was the preferred European language. Cordial relations were maintained with Paris throughout the decolonization period. Lebanon was the first Arab state to receive substantial arms after the end of the Algerian War. Arms to Lebanese armed forces tended to solidify these historic ties. Sentiment seemed to sway French sympathy for Lebanon's plight in contrast to calculated, if sometimes hastily estimated, self-interest in Saudi and Iraqi security affairs.

Once France's power and arms were engaged in the Lebanese civil war, its prestige as a reliable ally and arms supplier came inevitably under close scrutiny by its principal arms clients in the region. France's behavior appeared motivated by several negative concerns: to stem Israeli occupation of southern Lebanon, Soviet-backed Syrian expansion, the spread of Islamic fundamentalism, and, subsequently, hostage-taking of French citizens. There was also a demand, voiced loudest in Saudi Arabian quarters, that the Palestine Liberation Organization (PLO) under Yasir Arafat be protected against its Arab foes and internal enemies and that the issues of Palestine and Jerusalem be addressed by Israel.

As early as March 19, 1978, the Giscard d'Estaing government agreed to send French troops to southern Lebanon as part of the United Nations Interim Force in Lebanon (UNIFIL) to restore peace in the area and monitor Israeli occupation and withdrawal. As the U.N. operation bogged down, France, with U.S. backing, advanced a plan for an international peace-keeping force with an enlarged mandate to separate the warring elements. The Soviet Union vetoed the plan in April 1981. A year later in July 1982, a multinational force was again proposed by the United States to oversee withdrawal of the Palestine Liberation Organization from Beirut in the wake of the Israeli invasion of Lebanon. The Mitterrand government agreed to send French parachutists to join U.S., Italian, and British troops to supervise the PLO departure. The French left with the other troops in September 12, 1982, only to return a fortnight later to restore order in the aftermath of massacres perpetrated by Christian militia in Palestinian refugee camps.

The return of the multinational force thrust the Mitterrand government deeply into the Lebanese civil war and into the growing Syrian-Israeli conflict. France found itself beset on all sides. In April 1983, Paris announced a proposed $100-million program to arm the

Lebanese Army. Meanwhile, its support for the Gemayel government met with stiff criticism from Arab sources. French forces, like those of the United States, came under repeated terrorist attacks from factions opposed to the Lebanese-Israeli treaty. The French government was also pressured by its Arab clients to undermine the Gemayel government's decisions to compromise on Israeli demands. Washington countered these pressures by insisting on preserving the Lebanese-Israeli pact as the basis for the end of foreign occupation of Lebanon. The Mitterrand government also pledged itself to improve French-Israeli relations. President Mitterrand's official visit to Israel in 1982 signaled a desire, never fully realized in light of countervailing Arab pressures, to deal with Arab-Israeli issues in a more evenhanded way than before.

French forces were too weak (never numbering much more than 2,000) and the multinational force too small and divided to halt the civil war, to arbitrate Syrian-Israeli differences, or even to defend themselves. In October 1983, 58 French troops and over 250 American Marines were killed in terrorist attacks launched simultaneously against them. President Mitterrand put a brave face on the crisis. Affirming support for the Gemayel government, he said, "A country is great as a result of its strength of spirit, its resolve, as well as its friendships and the respect which it inspires. That is why France remains and will remain faithful to its history and its commitments to Lebanon."[60] Less than a half year later on March 24, 1984, the French government announced the withdrawal of its remaining contingent. Too many crosscutting pressures undid the efforts of the Mitterrand government to maintain French forces in Lebanon. The Reagan administration's military attacks against Syrian and Arab positions threatened to widen the conflict and put France and the multinational force directly at odds with Damascus. Paris was embarrassed, too, in having to denounce American belligerency as excessive while conducting independent French military strikes against the bases of terrorist groups in Lebanon enjoying tacit Syrian assistance. Pleasing Baghdad, Riyadh, Damascus, and Tel Aviv all at once was impossible.

French protection of Yasir Arafat's Palestinian forces, first against Israel and later against Syrian-supported PLO rebels, proved useful but of marginal import. The French escorted Palestinian forces from Beirut and subsequently provided naval cover for Arafat Palestinians from Tripoli after their defeat by Syrian-backed PLO rebels. They could neither prevent the Israeli invasion of Lebanon—anymore than de Gaulle's arms boycott could stop the Six Day War—nor shield the Arafat wing of the PLO from extremist attacks within the organization. There is little consolation to be drawn from the fact that the superpowers could not boast much more success in regulating Middle East conflicts or the Lebanese civil war. To cut their losses, the French withdrew their remaining forces.

There was at least one bright side to the Saudi-Iraqi arms connection. It led, not surprisingly, to expanded sales to the Persian Gulf emirates and some inroads in penetrating the Anglo-American monopoly in Jordan. As early as January 1969, Defense Minister Pierre Messmer toured the area in search of arms outlets.[61] The diplomatic status of the Gulf states was upgraded, with the naming of a full ambassador to the United Arab Emirates, as more attention was paid to these small oil-rich Arab states. Even before the raising of the Middle East boycott, Abu Dhabi, Kuwait, and Oman ordered a wide range of sophisticated materials, including Mirage III, F1, and Jaguar aircraft, Puma and Gazelle helicopters, and an assortment of tactical missiles.[62] Abu Dhabi alone placed orders for 38 Mirage 2000s, only one of four countries by January 1985 to have placed orders for the advanced fighter.[63] Saudi Arabia, blocked from additional purchases of F15s, opted for the Tornado. Particularly noteworthy about these purchases was the engagement of Pakistani flyers and technicians to train local forces and to maintain French equipment.[64] Qatar followed the example of its Arab neighbors in placing similar orders for advanced arms.[65] Alpha-Jets, Mirage F1s, Gazelles, and AMX-30 and AMX-10 tanks were delivered in the early 1980s. The heavy Saudi investment in French coastal and air defense systems set the stage for similar purchases by the other Gulf states. Bahrain, Oman, and Qatar received naval surface-to-surface Exocets, and the latter commissioned a 400-ton missile-firing gunboat, the largest ever built by a French naval yard.[66]

The French arms connection with Egypt was especially complex. The wounds of Suez did not heal quickly. They were produced by forces—anticolonialism, pan-Arabism, modernization—that cut as deep as worries about oil. Except for a small delivery of armored vehicles before the Six Day War, there were no significant French arms shipments to Egypt in the 1960s. The Soviet Union and the Eastern bloc were Cairo's principal suppliers. After the Six Day War, France's embargo prevented any change in Egypt's supply pattern. Saudi and Gulf state purchases and the subsequent Saudi transfer of 38 Mirage fighters to Egypt eased suspicions between the Sadat regime and opened the way to expanded cooperation.

French access to the Egyptian market survived the Egyptian-Israeli rapprochement and the Camp David accord of 1977. These alignment shifts ruptured previous Saudi-Egypt comity. Riyadh officially withdrew its financial support for Egyptian arms purchases and for Cairo's plans to expand its arms production base.[67] Despite these setbacks, Cairo was dogged in its determination to widen its western contacts and broaden its arms supply network. Previous German objections to increased cooperation with Egypt in producing tactical missiles and Alpha-Jets, jointly produced by France and West Germany, dissipated after 1975.[68] Mirage III, 5, and F1 aircraft were delivered to Egypt. In January 1982, Egypt signed a contract for 20 Mirage 2000s, with an option to purchase an additional 20, counterbalancing 40 F-16s sent by the United States in a $3-billion aid package growing out of the Camp David agreement. Ironically, Egypt's ability to buy French equipment was being inadvertently subsidized by American military assistance which released pressures on Egyptian foreign reserves. The level of French-Egyptian military cooperation topped $1.5 billion in 1983. Facilitating these sales were French licenses to the Egyptian arms industry to assemble some French weapons, including the Mirage 2000, and to sell selected systems to developing states.[69]

Tracing French arms transfers in the Middle East provides a sketch of the broad political choices French decision-makers have faced in the region. Arms sales have been alternately used by France to favor one or the other of the contestants in the region. Arms clients, in turn, have used their buying power to curry French favor. The Fifth Republic initially maintained the tacit alliance with Israel, inherited from its predecessor. After Evian, however, the tilt was decidedly in an Arab direction. Realignment has created new problems as Paris has had to steer between competing Arab states and the factions within them. Oil put France squarely on the side of Saudi Arabia and the Arab Gulf states. French troops provided discreet support for the Riyadh regime during the crisis over the sacred mosque, temporarily seized by Moslem extremists. French coastal and air defense systems, overseen and staffed partially by French technicians and military personnel, provide a thin security cover for the fragile principalities lining the Persian Gulf. Radical regimes, like Khaddafy's Libya and Khomeini's Iran, have had difficulty securing French arms. The Mitterrand government signed no new arms contracts with the revolutionary government in Iran. Libya has been placed under varying restrictions since the Mirage sale of 1970, depending on the bargaining needs of Paris and Libya's interventions in Chad and the western Sahara. The Lebanese civil war also forced unwanted choices between rival factions, between Israeli and Syrian demands, and between the conflicting representations made by Washington and the Gulf states. Meanwhile, French citizens were held hostage by extremist factions in Lebanon, forcing Paris to negotiate secretly with Damascus and Teheran for their release at the risk of contravening the support accorded Iraq and Arab moderates.

It is difficult to distinguish arms transfers as an aim or as an instrument of French policy or to assess how successful either has been in the Middle East. The Israeli embargo proved counterproductive as an instrument as Israel turned to the United States and expanded its own arms industry and weapon sales abroad; arms sales to Saudi Arabia and Iraq ensnared France in the Middle East tangle; access to Iran, nurtured in extending asylum to Khomeini, was abruptly arrested once the Iranian revolution turned radical and fed on its progeny. Iraq used French arms to inflame the Gulf war and attack oil shipments to the West. Paris was also forced into uneasy alignment with Washington in the region and induced to carry, as in Lebanon, the unwanted baggage of Washington's ties to Tel Aviv. Historical and sentimental ties with Lebanon promoted both arms transfers and the assumption of commitments and responsibilities without compensating political benefits. Relations with another former mandate, Syria, were also inevitably strained as France joined the American-initiated international force while siding with Arafat's wing of the PLO. In retrospect, French arms policy, entwined inextricably with France's temporizing stances in the Middle East, was both a success—valued in billions of dollars of trade—and a failure if measured by political investments, high risks, and negative foreign policy returns.

North Africa

North Africa, as the geographical hinge between the Middle East and Black Africa, shares many of the problems of these regions and contributes its own to the agenda of global conflicts. From the perspective of the Fifth Republic, the Algerian War held center stage until 1962. French arms to the region were dictated by the imperatives of the war. The Evian accords radically transformed the problems facing French diplomacy. France now had to deal with the states of the region as independent nation-states with their own interests and aims. For them France was just another arms supplier whose need to sell arms complemented their need to buy weapons, but the motivations driving these needs were by no means the same. In transferring arms to these states, France could not be indifferent to the impact of arms on regional divisions, on conflicts in the Middle East and Black Africa, or on France's ability to withstand superpower competition for privileged access and strategic and economic advantage in the area.

The Libyan Connection

France's arms sales to Libya serve as a touchstone for the set of conflicting foreign policy choices confronting French decison-makers in the post-Evian period. The overthrow of King Idris in 1969 brought to power colonel Muammar Khaddafy, an obscure army officer obsessed with spreading his own brand of radical Arabism and Islamism throughout the Middle East and North Africa. The Khaddafy regime has posed serious problems for France. It has consistently supported the intransigent wings of the Arab states that refuse to compromise with Israel. Libya has sent troops, financial aid, and arms, including French Mirages, to fight Israel. It reportedly supports terrorist activities in the Middle East and North Africa and assists terrorist and revolutionary movements in such distant points as Northern Ireland and the Philippines.[70] It has supported efforts to overthrow regimes in Egypt, Sudan, Tunisia, and Morocco. It has supported, with economic aid and arms, the Polisario rebellion in the western Sahara against Morocco. The Khaddafy regime has also occupied the Aouzou strip in northern Chad since 1974 and has repeatedly intervened in the Chadian civil war since the late 1960s. French leaders have had to weigh the benefits of selling arms to Libya against the costs of reinforcing Tripoli's ability to intervene in regional conflicts and even to confront French armed forces with their own weapons.

Several factors encouraged French leaders to sell large quantities of sophisticated arms to Libya. First, there was simply the persistent need to sell arms. Libya's oil and its possession of large international monetary reserves, produced by oil, have been magnets too powerful to resist. In the early 1970s, Libya was one of France's principal oil suppliers. It also paid in hard currency for French weapons. Second, French planners banked on the possibility of drawing Libya into the Maghreb as part of a French sphere of influence encompassing Algeria, Tunisia, and Morocco.[71] These states were to be made key parts of a larger Mediterranean grouping of states which the French hoped could be progressively insulated from superpower influence and made responsive to French suggestion. These expectations rationalized the *coup de Libye*—the decision to sell 112 Mirage fighters to Tripoli.

Third, in selling arms to Tripoli, Paris moved into the vacuum created by the toppling of the Idris regime. It stole the march on Britain and the United States, which had previously enjoyed preponderant political influence in the former Italian colony. With the closing of Wheelus Air Force base, France saw an opportunity to prevent Soviet and East European influence from replacing Anglo-Saxon dominance. Communist bloc arms were already flowing into the area as Algeria turned to the Soviet Union as its principal supplier.

Finally, the French have relied, alternately, on arms sales, on stipulated controls on arms sent to Libya, and on temporary and selective embargoes on arms deliveries or on new contracts to conciliate, discipline, or block the Khaddafy government from taking actions damaging to French interests in the Mediterranean basin. A brief review of French arms transfers to the region illustrates the unreliability of using or withholding arms as a diplomatic instrument to shape the behavior of strong-willed regional states like Libya. There is little evidence that the Khaddafy government has been disciplined or deterred by threats to cut off arms sales or swayed by blandishments of more and better arms. It is difficult to identify any link between French willingness to sell or send arms and fleeting displays of accommodation by Libya to French remonstrances and representations. Libya remains outside the Francophile camp and appears, as evidenced by the Chad episode, impervious to French pressures. The Communist bloc and other states have been at the ready to fill the void left by the French. Even when Libya enjoyed open access to French arms, the Khaddafy regime was not deflected from turning to the Soviet Union and the Communist bloc for arms and military advisers.

The opening to Libya began auspiciously enough. The 112 Mirage IIIs and 5s orderd by Tripoli provided an estimated $400 million to meet France's oil bills and balance its commercial deficit, deepened by the events of 1968. SS-12 missiles armed British patrol boats acquired by the Idris government. Alouette and Super Frelon helicopters and Crotale air defense missiles were also dispatched. Paris ignored Anglo-American criticism and opposition from Israeli supporters at home. The lure of oil and markets steeled President Pompidou during an official visit to the United States to demonstrators protesting France's pro-Arab policy and the Mirage sale. In February 1974, Libyan Prime Minister Abdessalem Jalloud asserted that Libya was "banking on France. . . . Arabs count only two friends in Europe, Yugoslavia and France."[72] Tripoli's reliance on French permissiveness was confirmed shortly thereafter with the revelation that Libyan Mirages had participated in the Yom Kippur War. Paris imposed no penalties on Libya for having transferred the planes in violation of contractual obligations forbidding such retransfers.

Even before the Mirage sale, there were reports of Libyan intervention in the Chadian civil war and support for rebel forces opposed to Moroccan rule of the western Sahara. France's military intervention in Chad, its garrisoning of troops in Africa, and its biased neutrality favoring the Hassan II regime became sources of deepening irritation between Tripoli and Paris. Renewed overtures for French arms by the Sadat regime in Egypt, sobered and conciliatory after the 1973 war, increased tensions between the two capitals. For its pains to please Khaddafy, Tripoli accused France of being a "cannon merchant" and of following "archaic" colonial policies in Africa.[73]

These signs of discord did not prevent the signing of a contract for ten fast patrol boats to be armed with Otomat missiles. The sale of these ships, important for the lagging French naval industry, prompted an internal debate within the French administration. The Libyan threat to acquire comparable naval craft from the Soviet Union, to be equipped with Scud missiles, sealed the contract with France despite the lack of any assurance that these ships would not be employed against French friends and clients, not to mention French forces themselves.[74] Contracts were also signed for antitank Gazelle helicopters, air-to-air R-550 Matra missiles, and ship-to-ship Exocet missiles.

These conciliatory gestures, combined with a French decision to withdraw militarily from Chad, whetted, not satiated, Libyan interventionist inclinations. The Giscard d'Estaing government in March 1979 decided to end French involvement in the Chadian civil war. France had intervened off and on in Chad since 1968. During much of the 1960s, 30 percent of France's military assistance program was earmarked for Chad. Withdrawal was attractive for several reasons. The Organization for African Unity (OAU) appeared on the threshold of reaching accord on recognizing the Transitional Government of National Unity (GUNT) as the legitimate ruling body in Chad. Paris also counted on the OAU to check Libyan pretensions. There was also the hope that Colonel Khaddafy, as next in line to become the chairman of the OAU, would have an incentive to be restrained in interfering in Chadian politics.[75]

Khaddafy showed little interest in the role for which he was cast by Paris. Libya appeared to become more aggressive as the prospect of French withdrawal grew imminent. Tripoli temporarily suspended payments on military contracts to protest French intervention in the Central African Republic as well as the detention of 37 Libyan military advisers in Bangui and the confiscation of several tons of Libyan military equipment, later redistributed to France's African allies.[76] France also refused to sell Libya light aircraft capable of carrying rockets because they appeared destined to be used against Morocco in the western Saharan war.[77] In January 1980, Libyan irregulars attacked the Tunisian border city of Gafsa. American and French military assistance was swiftly sent to bolster the Bourguiba regime.[78] Tunisia had already received or purchased modest amounts of French armored vehicles, AMX-13 tanks, patrol boats, helicopters, and missiles. French support of the Tunisian government prompted the burning of the French embassy in Tripoli and the sacking of the consulate in Benghazi.

Despite these incidents, the French withdrawal from Chad continued on schedule. A month after the departure of French forces in May 1980, Libya signed a cooperation accord with Oueddi Goukouni, head of GUNT. Fighting again broke out between Goukouni supporters and those of Hissène Habré. Libyan troops intervened in Chad during November 1980 in support of Goukouni and GUNT. The protest of the Giscard d'Estaing government to Libyan intervention, as contrary to the August 1979 Lagos agreement, fell on deaf ears. The understanding envisioned a political settlement of the Chadian civil war under OAU auspices. Facing elections in the spring, President Giscard d'Estaing resisted pressures from France's West African clients to reintroduce French troops into Chad. He argued that no treaty with Chad legitimated such a move, although such accords had not blocked French intervention in Africa before GUNT was portrayed in Paris as having legitimately requested Libyan aid.

While temporizing on Libyan intervention, Paris also sent confusing signals to Tripoli regarding Libyan expansionism. Thirty-seven tons of French military equipment arrived in Libya, and maintenance contracts on Matra missiles and French military equipment were executed with the Tripoli government even as its military intervention was publicly condemned. In December 1980, fourteen days after the fall of N'Djamena to Libyan troops, a pilot of UTA airlines was disciplined for refusing to fly helicopter parts to Libyan forces.[79] French statements, affirming that an arms embargo had been placed on arms to Libya, lost much of their credibility.[80] Meanwhile, Elf-Erap, France's state-owned oil company, signed agreements with Libya to expand its oil explorations. A governmental commission, established by President François Mitterrand after his election in the spring of 1981, concluded that the "inconsistencies" of his predecessor's management of the Libyan invasion "gave plausibility to the idea that French diplomacy was too dependent on mercantile considerations, whether arms sales or petroleum prices."[81]

The Mitterrand government hardly presented a more resolute posture than its predecessor when it proposed lifting the embargo on arms to Libya in July 1981 on the condition that the Libyans withdraw from Chad and that the French consular building be rebuilt. The conciliatory stance of the Mitterrand government was keyed to the creation of an OAU peace-keeping force to replace Libyan forces and to pry GUNT and Goukouni loose from Libyan control. A month after President Mitterrand met Goukouni in Paris in September 1981, small quantities of French arms reached GUNT forces. The Mitterrand tactic appeared at first to be working. The Goukouni-led GUNT requested Libya's withdrawal opening the way for the entry of the OAU peace-keeping force composed of troops from Nigeria, Zaire, and Senegal.

Unexpectedly, Hissène Habré's forces, sheltered in Sudan, again took to the offensive after the Libyans departed. By June 1982, Habré occupied N'Djamena. As Habré's successes mounted, Paris again agonized about which Chadian faction it would support. As early as January 1982, French arms to GUNT ceased. Paris rationalized that it could not support any group as long as the civil war could not be halted, even though its embargo against GUNT could only aid Habré. By the fall, Habré's forces controlled most of Chad except the Aouzou strip and Libyan-controlled enclaves in the north where Goukouni forces took refuge.

In a quick about-face, President Mitterrand threw his government's support behind Habré while calling for an OAU-sponsored settlement. The belief that the civil war had finally been resolved by force of arms proved premature. Less than a year later, Libyan troops again backed a rebellion by Goukouni supporters. In the summer of 1983, they established control of northern Chad, effectively dividing the country in half. To prevent the collapse of the Habré regime, France again intervened unilaterally in August 1983. Only two months earlier, governmental sources were reportedly ruling out French intervention. American pressures to stop Libyan expansion, viewed from Washington as Moscow-incited, and demands for French reentry from France's West African clients backed a reluctant Mitterrand government into the Chadian quagmire. Strategic interests and reputation as a reliable ally overrode Socialist party sentiment, voiced by President Mitterrand himself and several of his ministers, against military intervention.[82]

As in the Middle East, France found itself uncomfortably aligned in Chad with the United States. President Mitterrand's criticism of American support of Habré's forces and Washington's dispatch of military advisers to Sudan barely hid the parallel interests bonding Washington and Paris. By September, France had 3,000 troops stationed in Chad.[83] They established an east-west defense line below Faya Largeau to stem further Libyan expansion. Fourteen Jaguars and Mirage F1s sent to Chad provided cover for Habré's troops. Crotale units protected N'Djamena against air attack. Small arms and antitank and antiaircraft missiles were supplied to Habré's army along with armored vehicles, mortars, rocket launchers, and radar and telecommunications equipment, manned by French technicians. The on-again-off-again arms embargo against Libya was reinstated, but not before the first of the ten missile-firing fast patrol boats previously ordered by Libya was delivered.[84]

Until 1987, French prospects in Chad looked unpromising. Libya violated an agreement reached with the Mitterrand government in 1984 to withdraw its troops and appeared to have tightened its hold on northern Chad. French policy was portrayed at home as self-defeating. "It is very difficult," editorialized *Le Monde*, "to pursue a policy when you distrust your ally as much as your adversary."[85] It was as if the French had ordered their opponents in Chad to be shot by a firing squad arrayed in a circle.

French fortunes changed dramatically in 1987 when Hissène Habré's forces decisively won pitched battles at Fada in January and at Ouadi Doum and Faya-Largeau in March. By April, Khaddafy's army was retreating in disarray, leaving large stocks of arms and much of northern Chad under Habré's control. Several factors contributed to the rout. Patient training of Chad forces by French advisers and improved equipment from French and American stores created an effective fighting force, something that had been absent from the Chadian civil war since its inception. Habre also demonstrated an unexpected daring in exploiting French logistical and air support, small covert French forces, and American satellite intelligence in defeating Libya's more heavily armed but demoralized forces. French arms (with timely assistance from the United States) rather than arms sales and diplomacy had succeeded, at least temporarily, in checking Khaddafy's ambitions in Chad.[86]

Maghreb and Western Sahara

The influence and alignment patterns in the Maghreb were no less complex or more coherent than those reflected in the Chadian civil war. The impact of French arms transfers on political conflicts in the area was, not surprisingly, similarly refracted and ambiguous. At the center of conflict in the mid-1980s was the rebellion in west Africa against Moroccan rule. Algeria and Libya, having longstanding differences with Morocco over borders, ideology, and Middle East and Black African policy, provided safe haven for the Polisario and ease of transit for Soviet arms destined for rebel forces. With arms and sanctuary at the disposal of the Polisario, the Moroccan Army was stymied in its efforts to defeat the rebels.

The Hassan II regime found itself torn in different directions by the fighting. While it faced a costly and seemingly unwinnable war since the keys to a resolution of the conflict were in Algers and Tripoli, not Rabat, national sentiment and army intransigence precluded a compromise with the Polisario. Meanwhile, domestic pressures mounted from the Left for a greater share of political power and for faster economic development. Faced with these unyielding demands, Rabat turned to the West for economic and military assistance. The United States and France became the principal supporters of the monarchy, discreetly aided by the Saudi Arabian treasury.[87] This alignment in the western Sahara was solidified by Moroccan support for a compromise solution to the Arab-Israeli conflict, notwithstanding Moroccan military participation in Arab offensives against Israel. Western aid was also tributary to Morocco's military assistance to the beleaguered Zaire government. In 1977, American and French transports carried Moroccan troops to Shaba province to quell rebellions against the Kinshasa government. Zaire returned the favor by temporarily stationing over 2,000 troops in Chad to sustain the forces of Hissène Habré and to extend a fig leaf of international legitimacy to the French intervention.[88]

The politics of the region is murkier than the array of forces over the western Sahara might suggest. France has made a determined effort to preserve close economic and political ties with Algeria. The bitter disputes with Algeria in the late 1960s over a series of issues—French oil concessions, Algerian workers in France, compensation for French citizens for property seized by Algeria—did not deter Algiers and Paris from keeping lines of communication open.[89] Paris has also tried to maintain a neutral stance in Algerian-Moroccan disputes despite major arms sales to Morocco.[90] It has also attempted, with considerably less success, to adopt the same position in the west Saharan conflict. Although Algeria depends primarily on the Communist bloc for arms and military assistance, the French maintain a training mission in Algeria. In 1982, they won a contract to supply 44 Panhard armored personnel carriers to the Algerian gendarmerie.[91]

As France's long-range effort to wean Algeria from Soviet and Communist bloc dependency proceeded, it was also confronted with two economic barriers to the expansion of French influence in the Maghreb. The United States replaced France in the 1970s as Algeria's major trading partner, purchasing much of its gas and oil. The Soviet Union also entered into a barter arrangement with Morocco, valued at approximately $2 billion, to develop its phosphate industry.[92] The infrastructure created by Soviet technicians, including roads and rail beds, bolstered the Moroccan government's ability to resist the Soviet-supported rebellion in the western Sahara while providing the Soviets access to valuable mineral resources capable of being transformed into uranium.

Against this threatening background of superpower penetration, French arms transfers have had to serve several masters. As in the Middle East and with Libya, economic gain remained, as always, a French concern. Sales, while modest, have not been negligible. Between 1976 and 1983, deliveries to Morocco were conservatively estimated at $1.1 billion, more than twice U.S. arms exports. Those to Tunisia were estimated at $120 million.[93] Underlining the importance of prompt and proper payment, France has on at least one occasion held up shipment of arms and spares to Morocco for failure to meet its contractual obligations, despite Rabat's urgent need for more arms.[94] The economic significance of sales to Morocco gained prominence in the late 1970s as Morocco attempted to impose a military solution on the west Saharan rebellion. In the late 1970s and early 1980s, contracts were signed for 6 light (90-ton) and 2 heavy (400-ton) naval patrol boats, 3 landing ships, 50 F1 fighters, 24 Alpha Jets, a Crotale air-defense system, 100 AMX-10 tanks, varied armored vehicles, and tactical missiles and ammunition.[95] This equipment was added to Fouga-Magisters, Alouette and Puma helicopters, R-550 Matra missiles, AML-60/90 armored vehicles, and AMX-13 tanks already in the Moroccan inventory.

France was drawn into a suppliers' arms competition with the United States. The Carter administration touched off the race when it raised the embargo on arms to Morocco in 1978. Approval was granted to sell 20 F-5 fighters and V-Bronco helicopters to Rabat. The Reagan administration traded military equipment and credit for arms and base concessions. In May 1982, Hassan II signed an accord providing the United States access to air facilities in Morocco; in exchange Morocco received 108 M-60 tanks, armor, electronic equipment, missiles, and ammunition.[96] Increased American arms to Rabat were premised on a set of mutually supportive, but differing, needs. The survival of the Hassan II regime was tied to the successful termination of the Saharan conflict. Assistant Secretary of State Morris Draper summarized American expectations in testimony before Congress: "Morocco is firmly opposed to the Soviet invasion of Afghanistan. . . . Twice it has sent troops to Zaire to confront subversion fomented from abroad. . . . While it has supported the hostile Arab consensus to the Israeli-Egyptian treaty and to the Camp David accords, it is a voice of reason and pragmatism in world councils. . . ."[97] Morocco also assumed a new strategic importance with the organization of a rapid deployment force begun under the Carter administration. Moroccan bases were made a part of the logistical network linked to other base agreements with Egypt, Oman, and Somalia. These facilities were stepping stones to still others in Liberia as well as in Senegal and Zaire, deep within France's sphere of influence. During a meeting of a mixed Moroccan-American military committee at Fez in 1982, an American official characterized the Maghreb as a "vital zone" which had acquired an importance that it did not have 20 or 30 years ago. The United States "now considers the entire Mediterranean as a part of its strategic zone of access to the Middle East."[98]

In arming Morocco, France was drawn against its will in two directions. First, it was increasingly difficult to maintain a pretense of neutrality as French and American equipment poured into Morocco. France had earlier sent Jaguars to Mauritania to protect French technicians and their families as well as investment projects against terrorists linked to the Polisario.[99] The Polisario repeatedly complained about the shipment of French arms to Morocco.[100] To counter these criticisms, France pressed for a compromise acceptable to all of the warring parties. The preferred forum was the OAU; the U.N. was a secondary possibility but less desirable since consensus, already tenuous within the OAU, was even less likely within the world body and certainly less favorable to French interests. Foreign Minister Claude Cheysson hailed Morocco's decision in 1983 to submit the Saharan controversy to a referendum, despite the unlikelihood of its implementation.[101] Rabat's arming for parley preceding a referendum offered no incentive for OAU or Polisario cooperation.

Second, France risked being reduced, as in Chad and in the Middle East, to an appendage of American strategic policy aimed more at confronting a globally expanding Soviet Union than at resolving or managing local conflicts on their own merits. For France, distancing itself from Washington was becoming increasingly difficult in areas outside of Europe. The American weight was too great to ignore or manipulate, yet it was needed to contain Soviet expansionism and Libyan mischief. There was the added need for American cooperation in Europe. France's and Europe's security depended, as much as before, on U. S. arms and military presence. No less did Europe's and France's economic health hinge on American trade and on its monetary and fiscal policies. Opposition to United States policies and resistance to its demands had to be evaluated in terms of these grating requirements.

France found itself in a similar competition with the United States for Tunisian favor. After the Gafsa raid by Libyan-supported terrorists, both countries rushed military assistance and arms to Tunisia. Tunisia's defense budget was increased and requests for arms and aid were made simultaneously to Paris and Washington. American credit for military equipment reached $140 million for 1983, almost 50 percent higher than the preceding year. These advances permitted Tunis to buy 12 F-5s and 54 M-60 tanks, equipment that had been discussed in talks with French arms officials.[102] France did sell Crotale and Milan missiles, radar equipment, Ecureuil helicopters, self-propelled machine guns, and three patrol ships armed with Exocet missiles. France also has an edge over the United States in providing military training and technical services to Tunisia.[103]

SUB-SAHARAN AFRICA: BLACK FRANCOPHONE, ANGLOPHONE, AND LUSOPHONE AFRICA, AND SOUTH AFRICA

The patterns of arms and military technology transfers to sub-Saharan Africa contrast sharply with those in other regions. As Table 7-4 reveals, White South Africa, until 1978, received the overwhelming share of French arms sent to the region. The quality of these arms was comparable to the best conventional weapons furnished French armed forces. Between 1950 and 1978, a year after the French boycott of all arms to Pretoria, South Africa received over two-thirds of the armored vehicles and tanks (1,600 out of 2,601), over 70 percent of the supersonic fighters, including Mirage III and F1 aircraft, approximately 40 percent of all helicopters, and all of the submarines (3 Daphne class). France also delivered or signed joint production contracts for a wide range of tactical missiles.[104]

The backbone of South Africa's Air Force is composed of Mirage III and F1 fighters. In the late seventies, South Africa's 4 Air Force helicopter squadrons were entirely French equipped, including Alouette IIIs, Pumas, and Super Frelons. Twelve additional Alouettes were assigned to the Navy. Nine Transalls, purchased in 1969, provided long-range logistical capability to supply South African troops in Namibia and to support forays outside South African territory against rebel forces.[105]

The Black African states were a distant second to South Africa in all major weapons categories except light logistical aircraft and small naval vessels. French transfers to Black Africa have been largely concentrated in support aircraft, armored and ground vehicles, and helicopters. Support aircraft have been composed, in significant part, of obsolete transport, liaison, and small carrier airplanes, including American World War II equipment transferred from French stocks to the armed forces of its former dependencies. France assigned an appreciable number of Max Holste, Broussard, Noratlas, and American C-47 aircraft to each of its colonies at independence. These were outright grants and might properly be categorized as French military assistance rather than as arms sales. Many older Alouette helicopters were also given to local forces during this early period. As for ground and armored vehicles, South Africa again received more equipment than all of the Black African states combined. What is also interesting to note is that the former

Table 7-4. French Arms Transfers to Sub-Saharan Africa: 1950-1983

	Tanks and Self-Propelled Guns	Armored Vehicles and Personnel Carriers	Patrol Boats and Ships	Submarines	Supersonic Aircraft	Other Aircraft	Helicopters
South Africa	—	1,600	—	3	120	13	173
Former French Colonies and Mandates	10	250	45	—	17	200	68
Belgian Colonies	—	331	12	—	17	35	65
Non-Francophone Africa	39	420	7	—	24	57	132
TOTAL	49	2,601	64	3	178	305	438

SOURCES: See the Note on Sources in the Appendix for basic sources and for guidelines used in calculations. The specific problems associated with this table are described in detail in the author's "Security Interests and French Arms-Transfer Policy in Sub-Saharan Africa," in Arms for Africa, ed. Bruce Arlinghaus (Lexington, Ma.: Lexington Books, 1983), pp. 141-143.

Belgian colonies, particularly Zaire, and non-Francophone African states received more ground equipment than did the Francophone states.

Few supersonic aircraft have been sold to sub-Saharan states other than South Africa. Deliveries have been restricted to small numbers of aircraft to Gabon (7 Mirage 5s),[106] Zaire (17 Mirage 5s),[107] and Sudan (24 Mirage 50s). Even when deliveries in 1980 of Alpha-Jets to Nigeria (12) and Ivory Coast (6)[108] are taken into account, the number sold to sub-Saharan Black regimes is only slightly more than half the 120 Mirage aircraft, including the more advanced Mirage F1 and III, delivered or licensed for local production to South Africa.

Until the Giscard d'Estaing government reluctantly imposed an arms embargo on South Africa in 1977, France, as South Africa's principal arms supplier,[109] tried to maintain the fiction that its sale of sophisticated military aircraft, helicopters, missiles, armored ground equipment, submarines, and naval craft contributed exclusively to South Africa's external security needs and were not "susceptible to be used for police or repressive action."[110] As early as October 1963, French representatives to the United Nations informed the Security Council that the French government "would take every measure . . . to prevent the sale to the South African government of arms usable for repression."[111]

It was difficult, for example, to reconcile French assurances with the delivery of helicopters and the licensing to Pretoria of Panhard armored vehicles. These weapons were highly effective against Black separatist guerrillas being harbored in states bordering on South Africa and against the security forces of these states. Since the South African government identified national security interests with the maintenance of apartheid, it failed to distinguish between weapons allegedly designed for one or the other aim. Nor did South African rebels see much difference between arms for national defense and arms used to suppress dissent or revolt. Arms for the White state of South Africa were ipso facto support for the Pretoria government and its racial policies. The Black African states were not persuaded that the sale of French Mirages to South Africa was consistent with the U.N.'s embargoes since these aircraft could be used against rebel camps in countries neighboring South Africa. They were skeptical of official assurances, voiced by France's ambassador to the United Nations that Mirages were "only useful for exterior defense and . . . not for internal suppression."[112]

Pressures mounted throughout the 1970s to stop arms sales and military assistance to South Africa. Staunch French clients in Francophone Africa, like Senegal, joined the protesting chorus. Only with difficulty was France able to stifle dissension among its closest allies (Gabon, Ivory Coast, Madagascar, and Dahomey).[113] The OAU was given little comfort by President Georges Pompidou's promise, made to President Kenneth Kuanda during a visit to Paris on behalf of the OAU, that France would desist from selling helicopters and light armor to South Africa. French licensing accords to Pretoria made South Africa self-sufficient in the production of light arms and armor.[114] The OAU stepped up its attacks. French arms to Portugal, ostensibly in support of western alliance needs, but used by Lisbon to combat subversion in its African colonies, deepened African resentment.[115] Reports that South Africans used French Super Frelons against Black nationalist guerrillas widened the split between Paris and the Black African states.[116] The nonaligned states, meeting in Colombo, joined the OAU in condemning French arms sales to Pretoria.[117]

The French government was compelled to fall back either on legal fictions to justify its arms sales to South Africa or on stricter definitions of what kinds of weapons would be sold to Pretoria in order to soften international criticism. Paris objected that the U.N. was interfering in the domestic affairs of South Africa—precisely what was intended by the embargo and economic sanctions.[118] On August 9, 1975, during a visit to Zaire, President Giscard d'Estaing narrowed the French commitment to Pretoria. While existing contracts would be honored, France would no longer sell "long-range or aerial" arms to South Africa.[119] This tightening of the French arms net still did not preclude naval arms and armaments from slipping through as contracts for two submarines and two escort ships went forward.

French efforts to gain Black African approval of a policy of selective restrictions proved unavailing. Threatened by economic reprisals and diplomatic isolation, President Giscard d'Estaing declared in Mali on February 14, 1977, that every effort was being taken by France "not only to prohibit any new provision of ground or air material destined for South Africa but equally to assure that no delivery might take place."[120] French credibility had sunk to such a low that even this concession was greeted with widespread skepticism. Foreign Minister Louis de Guiringaud cut short an official visit to Tanzania in August 1977, when he was greeted on deplaning by demonstrations protesting French arms policies to South Africa.[121] Paris finally relented in its efforts to save the naval contracts. They were canceled and the South African government's down payment was returned.[122] The French government discreetly excluded from its total embargo weapons under licensed production by South Africa. These permitted Pretoria to manufacture French Mirage IIIs and F1s, ground armor and machine guns, and tactical missiles, like Cactus and 550-Magic air-to-air missiles.[123] Charges from Black African leaders of French supply of spare parts for aircraft and helicopters and technical assistance in producing licensed equipment continued into the 1980s.[124] Deflections of arms through third states, like Argentina, also afforded another avenue through which French arms and spare parts could slip past French internal controls to reach the Pretoria regime.[125]

Far more complicated factors than the commercial considerations underlying France's arms trade with South Africa explain its minimalist approach to Black Africa. First, African nations are generally too poor and underdeveloped to service France's mercantilist needs. Of 31 countries cited by the United Nations as the most poor and deprived, 21 are in Africa. Black Africa also has had the lowest rate of economic growth of any region in the world. According to one estimate, the rate of annual growth has not exceeded 5 percent while military expenditures have moved upward on the average at 8 percent.[126] The increase in defense spending has not been uniform—more for resource-endowed countries, like Nigeria, much less for poorer states. This selective growth has had little impact on overall spending by Black African states whose military expenditures are among the lowest in the world. Excluding South Africa, France's arms deliveries to Black Africa have never been a significant part of the volume of its global sales, averaging only about 3 percent of total sales and reaching a high of 5.3 percent in the 1980s.[127]

Second, most Black African military forces are simply incapable of absorbing large amounts of sophisticated military weaponry. The low level of education of the population, linguistic barriers, and tribal divisions hamper the development of a modern army. Indigenous military forces, left after the withdrawal of the colonial powers, were poorly trained and lacked experienced officer cadres. They were hardly prepared to assume the responsibilities of an up-to-date fighting force. Even today, most Black African states have weak or nonexistent air and naval forces which elsewhere are in the forefront of technologically advanced military establishments. The fighter squadrons of Gabon, Ivory Coast, Nigeria, and Zaire, for example—which are in the lead in sub-Saharan Africa—are minuscule by the standards of other regions, not to mention NATO and Warsaw Pact nations.

Third, and closely related to the economic underdevelopment and technological backwardness of the newly independent states of Africa, the regional security and economic system created by the French Fifth Republic with its former African dependencies relaxed the need for large arms transfers. Treaties signed by France with newly independent Black African states implicitly assumed that large expenditures on arms would neither be in the economic developmental interest nor consistent with France's expectation that it would maintain its dominant hold on Francophone Africa and, from this base, project its influence throughout the continent. With the loss of its colonial empire, its claim to big-power status hinged almost totally on its regional economic and security roles in Africa.[128] Its pretensions were served more effectively, as sketched below, by restricting arms to its former colonies rather than lavishing military equipment upon them—a strategy pursued along parallel lines by the United States in Latin America until it was challenged in the 1970s by France and other arms suppliers.

French concern for Africa's economic development has been genuine enough. It has been a consistent theme in French foreign policy since the independence of its colonies until the present. France has resisted increased military spending by the African states as detrimental to their economic development (while hewing, incidentally, to an opposite line in rationalizing its own spending on technologically advanced military systems). France invariably exceeds richer states, like the United States, West Germany, and Japan, in the proportion of GNP devoted to foreign assistance. In the early 1980s, over 10,000 French *coopérants* served in Black Africa alone as teachers, technicians, and language specialists. Approximately one billion dollars in French economic aid was earmarked for sub-Saharan Africa and special programs were organized to combat famine in the Sahel.[129] Thousands of African students pursued degrees and technical training in France. France was also firm in insisting that the European Community's development funds assist its former colonies, accounting for more than one-quarter or $150 million of the fund's assets.[130] It has strongly supported special trade concessions to the Black African states under the Yaounde and Lome conventions. The example of France's purchase of Algerian oil above market rates was advanced as a model for other states to follow to provide economic assistance to developing states through negotiated commodity accords.

The economic barriers raised by France to increased expenditures by the sub-Saharan states on arms, while real, masked more determinant geo-political considerations resistant to a rapid military buildup and modernization of African armed forces. Increased arms flows to sub-Saharan Africa undermined France's hold on its former colonies. The poorly equipped armed forces of African clients could not match French forces based in their countries nor those stationed in France for rapid deployment overseas. Continued dependence on France for military equipment fostered French hegemony. While an open arms trade policy elsewhere in much of the developing world served French economic and strategic interests, a reverse policy of restricting arms was designed to preserve French influence and to protect its monopoly over local markets and resources. In controlling arms flows to the Francophone states, Paris could also maintain military balances in the region to its liking and essentially preclude an attack by one client on another.[131]

In the wake of Black African independence in the early 1960s, Gaullist France created a complex network of bilateral treaties with its former colonies covering every aspect of their foreign activities—diplomatic, security, economic, monetary, postal, and cultural relations.[132] Central to these arrangements were sets of bilateral and multilateral security accords with most of the Francophone states.[133] Of the fifteen states formed from the French Union, twelve signed defense accords regulating their security relations.[134] Except Congo (Brazzaville), all also agreed in 1965 to accord French forces various logistical privileges covering the stationing of troops, as well as overflight, landing, and transit rights.[135] Those not signing these collateral agreements were Guinea, Mali, and Upper Volta. Guinea refused to join the French Community or be subject to French control; Mali denounced its defense accords with Paris on assuming independence; Upper Volta (later Burkina Faso), while resisting a defense treaty with Paris, accepted French military assistance in exchange for limited French access to its territory.

Under these treaties, France was given great liberty to intervene in the domestic and foreign affairs of its former dependencies. Protocols attached to most of these accords defined France's responsibilities for maintaining local order. Under these arrangements, aid could be indirect (logistical support, supplies) or direct (military intervention by French forces). Requests for assistance were normally to be made by a head of government, although French officials retained considerable discretion over the timing and conditions of French intervention. Elaborate bilateral and multilateral military consultative and planning bodies were also envisioned by the treaties, but these were never really empaneled on a regular basis.[136] Only Togo and Dahomey (later Benin) resisted the formal extension to France of a right to intervene.[137] A special assistant to the President of the Republic for African affairs was created to underline the special importance of French-Francophone security ties and to ensure direct presidential control over French covert and overt intervention in Africa. Under the de Gaulle government, Jacques Foccart acted as the French President's viceroy over West Africa; Guy Penne, while more constrained in his role, performed a similar oversight role for President Mitterrand.[138]

Complementing France's postcolonial defense treaties with its former dependencies were technical agreements regulating military assistance. These accords, signed by all of the Francophone states except Guinea, assured France a privileged role in the organization, instruction, and equipment of African national forces. These agreements transferred modest amounts of military equipment, primarily transport and logistics capabilities, to the newly independent African states. Also included in some of these agreements were codicils to standardize weapons by purchasing arms exclusively from France, a commitment gradually relaxed in the 1970s in the face of stiff competition from other arms suppliers and demands for greater autonomy voiced by France's African clients.[139] Six states signed additional understandings covering the provision of strategic raw materials to France.[140]

Black African security interests rested on a three-tiered defense structure: French-trained and equipped local forces; French contingents based in the African continent; and an intervention force, composed of ground, air, and naval units, stationed in France for rapid deployment to crisis spots in Africa. From independence until the late 1970s these components have been rather indifferently maintained. During this period, French policy might be characterized as one of benign neglect with intermittent surges of interest when a crisis erupted in one of the Francophone states. Yearly real military aid over the eighteen-year period from 1960 to 1978 remained essentially static. Increased Soviet penetration of Africa, witnessed by successes in the Horn and Angola, prompted a reevaluation of French policy under President Giscard d'Estaing, leading to an increased priority assigned to the African continent, measured in economic and military assistance and in the gradual bolstering of France's intervention forces.[141] Between 1977 and 1978, French military assistance jumped from 414 million francs to 644 million; it then climbed steadily each year, reaching an estimated high of over 800 million francs in 1985.[142]

The implied, if not announced, aim of France's military assistance program was to make African armed forces dependent on France. Africans were trained to adopt French ways and habits in their soldiering skills. French military officers often exercised greater control over indigenous forces than their titular national commanders. By far the most significant element of French military assistance was for the support of French military personnel on training missions with African armies. Equipment represented less than 30 percent of total French military aid through the 1960s, and hovered around 30 percent until the end of the 1970s. Local armed forces received very little in the way of weapons and training materials.[143] Between 1960 and 1973, over 12,000 Black African officers and noncommissioned personnel spent varying amounts of time in France on training missions.[144] The major beneficiaries of French aid were Senegal, Ivory Coast, Cameroon, Gabon, and Chad. In 1974, Chad received three times as much military assistance as any other state.[145] Less favored were Niger, Upper Volta (Burkina Faso), Togo, and Benin (Dahomey). Other Francophone states (Madagascar, Mauritania, Mali, Congo, and the Central African Republic) enjoyed varying levels of assistance, depending on French needs and local demands. Zaire received most of the assistance given to Belgium's former colonies.

If French military assistance until 1978 did not do much to organize and equip indigenous military forces, the deployment of French forces in Africa did little to compensate for these shortcomings in France's discharge of its security role in sub-Saharan Africa.[146] French military strength in Africa receded, falling from a high of 58,500 in 1960 to 5,279 in 1973.[147] In 1984, there were approximately 10,000 troops in sub-Saharan Africa, if the expeditionary force of about 3,000 troops in Chad is included.[148] On the African continent, principal bases are at Bangui and Bouar in the Central African Republic, Ouakam in Senegal, Libreville in Gabon, Port-Bouet in the Ivory Coast, and Djibouti.[149] Naval bases at Dakar in Senegal and Djibouti in the Horn are key *points d'appui* for French forces and western allies, as British use of Dakar during the Falklands War suggests.[150]

Troops from Communist bloc countries are more than three times more numerous than French forces in Africa. The largest concentrations of Soviet and East European military personnel are found in Angola, Ethiopia, Benin, Libya, Mozambique, and Guinea-Bissau. Cuban troops on military missions are stationed in twelve African states with large concentrations in Angola (18,000-21,000) and Ethiopia (11,000-12,000). In 1985, Cuba was estimated to have had 35,000-37,000 troops in Africa. The former Portuguese colonies offered a particularly favorable climate for Soviet and Cuban penetration. Socialist bloc troops in Angola and Mozambique anchor Soviet presence in southern Africa. With the help of its East European (especially German) and Cuban surrogates, the Soviet Union also established a major hold on the Horn of Africa and put pressure on the French contingent of approximately 3,000 troops in Djibouti.[151]

France's third line of African defense, its intervention forces, falls short of expectations as an effective deterrent or defensive force. The Mitterrand government, following the lead of its predecessor in paying greater attention to conventional forces, attempted to meet France's overseas commitments by strengthening France's intervention forces. In 1983, a Rapid Action Force (Force d'Action Rapide) was organized, largely from prevailing units, bolstered by a concentration of helicopter-transport and gun ships to increase mobility and firepower. These forces are primarily designed to reinforce NATO and French troops stationed in Germany and, as a complementary mission, to intervene outside Europe in defense of French interests and treaty commitments in Africa. The core of the overseas intervention forces is composed of units attached to the 11th Parachute Division (15,000) based in southwest France, the 9th Marine Infantry Division (7,600) stationed in Brittany, and the 31st Brigade (3,500) in Provence.[152] Of 47,000 troops assigned to FAR, only about 10,000 can be immediately counted upon to be dispatched quickly to quell an uprising or to meet an attack on an African ally. These include paratroop regiments stationed at Carcassone and Castres, amphibious units at Vannes, and Foreign Legion paratroops in Corsica.[153] Whether these forces can perform a dual role in different operational theaters with dramatically contrasting climatic and environmental demands is somewhat problematic. Given a tight defense budget, France's Rapid Action Force will necessarily be assigned a lower priority than its European conventional or strategic nuclear forces, despite the generally accepted view that the French position in Africa is likely to be under heavy strain.[154]

French forces will be incapable of long, sustained, or costly operations in Africa. They lack adequate logistics capability, equipment, and material to conduct extensive field operations. Air transport depends primarily on 73 first- and second-generation Transall aircraft with limited delivery payloads (8 metric tons over 5,000 kilometers or twice that over only 1,800 kilometers).[155] Sealift is slow and not very useful in central Africa. Dependence on U.S. logistical support is politically risky and strategically tenuous. European assistance is all but unavailable except perhaps for strictly humanitarian operations. A large-scale intervention would seriously detract from France's European military missions. It would also cripple domestic welfare spending and even slow France's nuclear modernization program. Unless interventions are quick, punctual, and of short duration, as in Shaba I and II, the French military forces risk overextension. Almost alone, France patrols a long and exposed western salient.

French Military Intervention in Africa

Table 7-5 lists French intervention in the Black African states since 1956. In almost every case (later Chad an exception), intervention was directed at internal unrest, not overt, external aggression. Even in the Shaba I and II incidents Kinshasha was menaced by Katangese dissidents based in Angola. French intervention does not imply the existence of a defense accord with a beleaguered regime. French forces op-

Table 7-5. French Military Interventions in Sub-Saharan Africa:
1956-1986

Year	Countries	Nature of Intervention
1956-1963	Mauritania	Maintenance of internal order
1960	Cameroon	Repression of the members of the L'Union des Populations du Cameroun
	Congo	Maintenance of public order
	Gabon, Congo	Settlement of a local dispute
1960-1962	Chad	Maintenance of internal order
1961	Cameroon	Repression of the U.P.C.
	Mauritania	Maintenance of internal order
1962	Congo	Maintenance of internal order
1963	Chad	Maintenance of internal order
	Niger	Military support to President Hamani Diori
1964	Gabon	Reestablishment of President M'ba in power
1968	Chad	Maintenance of internal order
April 1969	Chad	Suppression of members of the FROLINAT and maintaining order
January 1971[a]		
September 1975[b]		
1977	Zaire	Logistical aid to Zairean National Army
1978	Mauritania	Protection of French technical assistants
	Zaire	Protection of French nationals and European technical assistants against Katangese elements
	Chad	Maintenance of internal order
1979	CAR	Overthrow of Bokassa regime
1983-1986	Chad	Check on Libyan influence and support of Hissène Habré forces
1986	Togo	Maintenance of internal order

SOURCES: Déclaration de M. A. Peyrefitte, A.F.P. *Bulletin quotidien de l'Afrique Noire*, No. 316, March 4, 1964; W. A. Nielsen, *The Great Powers and Africa* (London, 1969); R. Buijtenhuijs, *Le Frolinat et les révoltes populaires au Tchad, 1965-1978* (Paris: Mouton, 1978); and Pascal Chaigneau, *La Politique militaire de la France en Afrique* (Paris: CHEAR, 1984), pp. 93-100.

[a] The official date of French intervention in Chad.

[b] Repatriation of French military expeditionary corps.

erated in Cameroon before the formal implementation of a defense treaty. France also had no security agreement with the Kinshasa regime when it intervened in Zaire. Having an agreement with Paris does not ensure intervention in a crisis. France did not send troops to the Congo in 1963, when Bishop Philibert Youlou was confronted with an internal revolt, although a defense accord was in place. As Alain Peyrefitte, French Minister of Information, explained, "Our troops began to intervene but President Youlou having himself resigned, our troops stopped their intervention."[156] The de Gaulle government relied on the absence of a defense treaty with Togo to justify its refusal to intervene following the assassination of President Olympio. In October 1963, Paris stood by as President Maga of Dahomey was forced to resign under pressure. These examples suggest that having or not having a defense treaty within Francophone Africa neither bars nor guarantees French intervention.

France's pragmatic approach characterizes its interventions in the other cases cited in Table 7-5. Its support for African leaders appears motivated by shifting policy considerations and conjunctural needs. Leon M'ba was apparently restored to power in Gabon to protect French access to Gabonese mineral resources, including uranium and oil. Similar economic and strategic objectives appeared at play in Zaire and Mauritania. France's military operation in Mauritania, as suggested earlier, may be seen as an effort to protect French workers and technicians operating mining enterprises in the country and, at the same time, to bolster the Moroccan campaign against the Polisario. The Shaba interventions were conditioned by humanitarian aims as well as by concern for Zaire's strategic position and its mineral wealth. On the other hand, the overthrow of the Bokassa regime in the Central African Republic (CAR), with the complicity of Gabon, Ivory Coast, and Zaire, seemed impelled by several factors: Emperor Bokassa's murder of schoolchildren demonstrating against his regime, scandalous levels of corruption, and the threat of Libyan intervention at Bokassa's request.[157] The subsequent removal by army officers of Bokassa's successor, President David Dacko, with tacit French complicity, suggests that factors other than humanitarian purposes animated France's nonintervention in CAR politics. That the French garrison stationed in Bangui did not move to save President Dacko indicates how tenuous French political support can be. Contrasting cases are offered by Gabon in 1964 and the CAR in 1980 where French forces intervened without benefit of a local request for assistance.

Except for Chad and Biafra, France's selective interventionism has worked reasonably well for Paris. It prudently avoided interference in the Somali-Ethiopian conflict and in the Eritrean rebellion in the Horn of Africa. It also maintained good relations with Portugal's former colonies after independence. France broke with Washington and recognized the Neto regime in Angola. On the other hand, the Chadian tangle, already reviewed, resisted the "quick fixes" applicable to most of France's other interventions. France's tentative and indecisive approach to the Nigerian civil war was a case where local and superpower forces overwhelmed France and where French support—itself too little and too late—was mischievous in its impact and counterproductive for French interests and influence.

In contrast to the superpowers and Britain, France tilted early toward the Biafran cause, despite the formal announcement in June 1968 of an embargo on arms to all parties in the civil war. There seems little doubt that geopolitical and strategic objectives motivated France's intervention into the Nigerian civil war since it was willing to risk significant economic interests in siding with the Biafran rebels. Most French investments and the oil drilling concessions extended to SAFRAP, France's government-controlled oil company, were in areas controlled by the federal government. These concessions were suspended and diplomatic relations ruptured when the central government won the civil war.[158]

On July 31, the ministerial council of the French government, no doubt acting on presidential directive, issued a call for negotiations on Biafran claims for self-determination. President de Gaulle's press conference on September 9 inched further toward recognition of the insurrection: "France," said de Gaulle, has "helped Biafra within her possibilities. She has not accomplished the act which for her would be decisive: the recognition of the Briafran Republic. For she thinks that the gestation [sic] of Africa is first of all an African business. Already, there are East and West African states which have recognized Biafra. Others seem to be heading toward recognition. It means that for France, the decision which has not yet been taken, cannot be considered as excluded in the future."[159] Permission to open a Biafran information center was as far as the de Gaulle government was willing to go toward recognition.

The arms embargo apart, French arms shipments to Biafra commenced in appreciable amounts at the end of September 1968 in conflict with the government's own ban on military equipment and munitions to Nigerian belligerents. Press articles cited deliveries of 75 mm. cannons, mortars, and heavy machine guns.[160] These were delivered by planes based in Gabon and Ivory Coast,[161] two of Biafra's staunchest supporters in West Africa. The French government also permitted

Libreville and Abidjan to draw on their stocks of French weapons to supply Biafran forces. The arms reaching Biafra, including an estimated $5 million in French equipment,[162] were enough, as one commentary concluded, to "permit [Biafra] to survive,"[163] but not enough to win the war. Biafran troops succeeded temporarily in relieving pressures on Umuahia, in breaking the federal government's defensive line south of the capital, and in launching several counterattacks against government forces. These successes extended the war and the suffering, but did little to turn the war in Biafra's favor.

Several conflicting considerations explain France's intervention and its ineffectual pursuit of this decision. There was, first of all, the Gaullist principle of national self-determination and resistance to hegemonies. Nigeria's emergence as the dominant state in West Africa was a threat to France's influence in the region. Hegemonies, local or global, were to be hobbled wherever they might limit French cultural and political influence.

These potential benefits cut, however, against the grain of French interests and strategy in Francophone Africa. There was the possibility "that Biafra's success might well inspire dissident Housas in southern Niger, thousands of Ibo residents in western Cameroon, and Yorubas in eastern Dahomey (Benin) to seek greater autonomy."[164] National self-determination applied to dissident elements in West Africa, and the western Sahara was a potential threat to France's clients in Francophone Africa. The Biafran issue also split the Francophone states. If Gabon, Ivory Coast, and Senegal lobbied hard for the Biafran cause, Mali, Upper Volta (Burkina Faso), and Niger, no less front-line states, cleaved to the Nigerian federal government. Finally, massive French arms and aid to Biafra risked greater Soviet and British involvement in the war and even American intrusion, raising the local war to global proportions, well beyond France's capacity to influence or control. After the May riots in 1968, moreover, the loss of French investments and oil concessions in Nigeria could no longer be dismissed as marginal.

These cross-pressures advised hedging. Arms shipments to Biafra, under cover of Gabon and the Ivory Coast, permitted France to deny a charge of intervention. The negotiated settlement, pushed by Paris, offered the prospect of some measure of autonomy for Biafra, of weakening Nigeria's federal government, and of advancing long-term French influence in Nigerian domestic politics. It also promised to limit superpower influence since the civil war, once settled, would discourage foreign intervention. Throughout, French diplomacy could claim unswerving commitment to national self-determination and a humanitarian concern to end the fighting and mass starvation occasioned by the war and the federal government's strategy of attrition.

None of the expectations of the Gaullist government was realized. The Biafrans suffered hundreds of thousands of casualties, many of whom were noncombatants—children, women, the old and infirm. French arms, though modest, helped to lengthen the war without bringing it to a successful end for the Biafran cause. The strife divided Francophone Africa. The Soviet Union's African stock rose for its ready supply of arms and assistance to the federal government. Nigeria's opposition to French military presence in Africa was intensified. Diplomatic and economic ties between Lagos and Paris were disrupted. The residue of French involvement in the civil war still embittered relations a decade later when France sought to rely on Nigeria and the OAU to limit Libyan intrusion in Chad. Increased sales of arms to Nigeria in the 1980s of 24 Alpha-Jets, 18 Jaguars, and air defense equipment suggested closer cooperation, but only in the aftermath of a decade of relations marked by sharp disagreements, deep suspicion, and mutual recrimination.[165]

France's Prospects in Sub-Saharan Africa

The balance sheet of France's long-term prospects in Africa is mixed. First, France's military presence will be necessarily circumscribed. As Chapter 6 indicates, it has lost ground as an arms supplier to the West African states. Its forces stationed in Africa and the Metropole are slim and overextended. Their staying power is questionable and public support for extended ventures cannot be assured. Indigenous forces are not fully reliable in bolstering its policing role. In Chad, France was able to call on Zaire, not a traditional Francophone client, for troop support, but the Kinshasa regime, as Shaba I and II suggested, proved unable to sustain its effort in the field. As a new generation of leaders comes to power in Ivory Coast, Senegal, Cameroon, and Gabon, France's access to local forces or to bases promises to be weakened.

Second, the superpowers and their clients have been more active and effective in the 1980s than France in extending their presence and influence throughout the region. France's maneuverability along East-West and North-South axes of conflict has been narrowed. Cuban troops in Africa, particularly in Ethiopia and Angola, outnumber French local forces and pose a serious challenge to them in any confrontation, far more than that of any opposing African state. Libya's defeat in 1987 may resolve the Chadian civil war, but Libya's withdrawal from Chadian soil will not guarantee its elimination as a regional force. Approximately 1,000 French military advisers are spread thinly over twenty sub-Saharan states. Their importance in shaping African armed forces, while not negligible, especially in those Francophone states where French influence has been traditionally greatest, appears to be in long-term decline relative to the roles being played now by other powers.[166]

Third, the African states themselves have sought a greater degree of independence from France. The defense and military assistance accords of the early 1960s have since been revised.[167] Several Black African states objected to the broad prerogatives accorded France to intervene in their affairs. Others, like Mali, Congo (Brazzaville), Benin, and Madagascar drifted toward the Soviet Union. These states increasingly relied on the Soviet Union, the Eastern bloc, and Cuba for arms, assistance, and military advisers. In 1977, sixteen countries, including the former Belgium colonies of Burundi, Rwanda, and Zaire, had technical assistance accords with France. Of the twelve states which initially signed defense accords, only five remained faithful in 1977 (Central African Republic, Gabon, Ivory Coast, Senegal, and Togo). After 1977, military agreements were added with newly independent Djibouti to permit the stationing of France's largest force in Africa. A technical assistance agreement was signed with Comoros to train its thousand-man army. While these accords are formally still in force, their practical import depends primarily on how much cooperation is desired by France and an African state.

Fourth, the expansion of the European Community and increased interest of France's European allies in expanding their ties with sub-Saharan Africa has decreased France's capacity to magnify its regional influence by drawing on the political weight and economic resources of the Community. Paris competes with London, Bonn, Rome, and Brussels for African favor and access, while, since the 1970s, drawing on Community help to sustain its position. It can hardly expect its European partners to extend credit without some fair return for aiding French interests. France has had to accept the principle of equalization of treatment of all Community states in trade with its former West African dependencies. These states, too, have seen advantages in widening their economic relations with the other members of the European Community and the United States to increase trade and aid.

Fifth, increased reliance on the United States, even if tacit, by Paris, had serious shortcomings for French interests. France risked being drawn into the superpower struggle as a client of the United States. Its claim to evenhandedness in opposing superpower hegemony would then have been seriously impaired. Its access and influence in the developing world resided critically on its ability to maintain its independence both as a model for other states to follow and as an autonomous source of diplomatic and strategic support and military and economic assistance. Criticism of American saber rattling toward Chad in 1983, resistance in 1985 of President Mitterrand to meeting with President Reagan before the U.S.-Soviet summit meeting in Geneva, coolness in joining American punitive measures over terrorism against Libya in 1986, and recognition of the Luanda regime and the sale of combat helicopters to Angola were consistent with French efforts to preserve a position—even a pose—of independence. In a Socialist government the need was doubly important: not only for exterior credibility but also the internal cohesion within a Left ostensibly dedicated to antihegemonic and strictly qualified intervention policies.[168]

Finally, French policy-makers have had second thoughts about building France's future in Africa or in the developing world simply by confining itself to its Francophone sphere. The foreign ministry in the middle 1970s was reorganized and arranged along regional, not linguistic, lines.[169] Aid to non-Francophone states was increased and emphasis shifted progressively from bilateral to multilateral assistance.[170] Trade and investment were directed to other developing areas to widen France's access to other markets, to increase its global competitiveness, and to encourage greater initiative and risk-taking among French firms used to their comfortable ways but restricted in opportunities in the Francophone zone.

Despite sharp differences of opinion among French analysts and decision-makers about the economic importance of Francophone Africa—as a market or as a source of raw materials—it would appear that the clear trend of French economic regional policy toward Africa is to escape from a nationally created ghetto. The view of one close observer of French policy toward Africa appears essentially consistent with French behavior: "In recent years, trade with Francophone Africa has declined sharply as a proportion of total French trade, even if it remains an important market. This is not to say that France would be indifferent to problems in African countries which affected the economic interest of the government or of private companies, but only that such a threat would not be the sole or the primary cause of French *military* action."[171]

LATIN AMERICA

Arms sales to Latin America raise three separate but related political and strategic problems. First is France's challenge to U.S. domination of the region and the potentially adverse implications for hemispheric arms control as a consequence of the opening of Latin America to the global arms supply network. Second, there is the problem of human rights and civil liberties. Since many Latin American states have long been ruled by military juntas, French arms have inevitably supported authoritarian rule, an embarrassment for successive French governments which have had trouble squaring their mercantilist needs with the liberal stance assumed by Fifth Republic regimes. Third, in keeping its book orders for arms amply filled, France has had to make hard choices between support for its western allies—e.g., the British in the Falklands War—and its claim as champion of Third World self-determination and social reform. The Falklands War notwithstanding, Latin America appeared to pose fewer problems for France in engaging in an arms free-for-all than the war-prone Middle East or Africa.

Challenging the United States was an integral part of the Gaullist attack on the superpowers. Much like France in Francophone Africa, the United States had pursued in Latin America a minimalist arms policy. The policy bolstered American domination of the region and, not without irony, limited the amount and sophistication of the arms flowing to the American states.[172] French penetration of these arms markets made good business sense and, as an added boon, eroded American influence. In his triumphal tour of Latin America in 1967, President de Gaulle spared no opportunity to attack American hegemony in the western hemisphere. France's resolution of the Algerian War and its determination to use Algeria as a showcase for exemplary North-South relations contrasted with the American-Cuban impasse. Under the Gaullist banner of self-determination and aided by the record of success of French arms in the Six Day War, enterprising French arms sellers invaded the Latin American market, bending if not breaking the American hold on the region.

The sale of high performance Mirage fighter aircraft, first to Peru in 1968, provoked the most controversy. By the end of the 1970s, seven Latin American countries had acquired Mirage III, 5, or F1 fighters, accounting for approximately 10 percent of the Mirages sold abroad.[173] Other sales followed: Jaguars (Ecuador), helicopters, tactical missiles, tanks and armored vehicles, and ships. French engines power and French 20 mm. cannons arm the Pucara, an Argentinian-designed ground support and counterinsurgency aircraft.[174] Paris also sweetened its sales by granting licensing accords to produce French weapons, aiding Latin American industries to become arms producers *and* suppliers.

France also purchased 41 Brazilian-made Xingu trainers to instruct French pilots flying transport and liaison aircraft. This purchase, which prompted Pentagon objections over France's alleged failure to buy

American, was part of a larger military assistance and industrial cooperation strategy to link the French arms and industrial plant with a
modernizing Brazil. In May 1981, the Mitterrand government approved a loan of approximately a half-billion dollars to Brazil for industrial development.[175] A year later a technical assistance accord was
signed with the Brazilian Navy.[176]

The Pentagon's criticism of France's purchase of Xingu aircraft gave
a reverse twist to repeated complaints made by Washington about
French arms sales to Latin America. To meet the French sales offensive,
the Johnson administration, egged on by Congress, launched a campaign to sell American Skyhawks to Latin America. Special appeals
were made to the ABC countries—Argentina, Brazil, and Chile.[177] Secretary of Defense Melvin Laird charged that French arms sales disrupted local relations and undermined the American position in the region. France was pictured as having unfairly intruded upon the
monopoly enjoyed by American suppliers who were obligated to meet
the Pentagon's needs in Vietnam.[178] By June 1972, a year particularly
bountiful in Mirage deliveries to Latin America,[179] the Nixon administration convinced Congress, otherwise reluctant to expand presidential
power, to double American arms sales to Latin America.[180] Throughout
the decade, American and French arms sellers saw themselves locked in
a no-holds-barred competition for the arms and pocketbooks of Latin
America's ruling military establishments.[181]

What was not fully foreseen was the rapidity with which other arms
suppliers would follow the French lead and the degree to which the
Latin American states would become world-class arms producers. As
in other regions, the trend has been toward the multilateralization
of arms supplies. If the Soviet Union's special arms relation with Cuba
is discounted, France remains the major supplier of arms to Latin
America in the period 1978-1982, but it is pressed closely by Italy, the
United Kingdom, and West Germany, whose collective sales exceed in
value those of France—$2.1 billion versus $1.9 billion, with a trailing
United States at $650 million.[182] Of particular interest is that all other
suppliers—e.g., Israel, Brazil, Belgium et al.—exceed the major western suppliers (again excluding the Soviet Union) with sales to Latin
America totaling $2.3 billion over this five-year period.[183] Annual Is-
raeli sales in the late 1970s were estimated to be between $200-300 mil-
lion.[184] Dagger fighters, a modification of the Mirage, were sold to Argentina. Only American refusal to permit the sale of GE engines,
powering the Israeli Kfir, a modification of the Mirage III, precluded
sales to Ecuador.[185] Israel also gradually replaced France as a major
supplier of small arms to Central American juntas and assumed main-

tenance contracts on French equipment previously held by French firms.[186] By the early 1980s, Latin America was the subject of bidding wars between major and minor arms suppliers, including Latin American states. Small-scale arms races erupted between Argentina and Brazil, Argentina and Chile, and Peru and Ecuador; Columbia and Venezuela joined the race to keep pace with their neighbors.

The overthrow of the Allende government in Chile in 1973 dramatized the second problem—support for military and authoritarian regimes in Latin America. Arms sales to Chile became a rallying point for Socialist and Communist opposition while out of power to France's permissive arms transfer policy. The contract to sell AMX-155 mm. artillery to Chile, signed with the Allende government, was honored despite the coup d'état engineered by General Augusto Pinochet. Reported governmental opposition to sales to Chile in 1974 by Creusot-Loire and Thomson-Brandt of AMX-13s and electronic equipment was overcome by the end of the 1970s.[187] Contracts were subsequently signed for 16 Mirage fighters, 50 AMX-30 tanks, 40 Puma helicopters, and an assortment of AS-11, AS-12, 550-Magic, and Exocet missiles.[188]

On entering office, the Socialist government imposed a ban on arms deliveries to Chile and on new arms contracts. Twenty-nine of the 50 AMX-30 tanks still undelivered to Santiago were impounded. Spares for the 21 tanks already sent were blocked. These moves did little to stop Spanish supply of this equipment, thanks to license arrangements signed between Spain and France during the 1970s. The Mitterrand government, relying on the tried but not always true distinction between counterinsurgency weapons and arms for legitimate national self-defense, announced that it would not send arms to a state which "could contribute to the maintenance of order or to domestic repression."[189] This self-imposed limitation did not preclude arms sales to military governments in Brazil and Peru of coastal patrol boats, tactical missiles, or the extension of technical assistance; 24 Mirage 2000 aircraft have also been ordered by the Peruvian government.[190] Reports that French-built helicopters were used to put down peasant unrest in Brazil have not impeded sales.[191] Overriden, too, has been the objection that French coastal patrol boats can be used to track and control domestic opponents.[192]

As the case of Argentina over the Falklands War suggests, the ability of a repressive government to meet national security imperatives impinges directly on its domestic authority, legitimacy, and control of its own population. French supply of high capability aircraft, sophisticated weapons systems (Roland to Brazil), and munitions to authoritarian regimes demonstrated their ability to gain access to world arms markets—even to democratically ruled suppliers—and their capacity to provide for national security needs. The Mitterrand government persisted in relying on the threadbare distinction between arms for suppression or for external defense to justify arms sales to military regimes. This ill-fitting tissue of rationalizations covered French vital interests in selling arms to developing states hardly more effectively than when it was used by Mitterrand's opponents to conceal the commercial thrust of French arms transfers so roundly condemned by the Socialists when they were out of office.

Selling arms to Argentina also posed the issue of choosing between arms sales and allies. France was the largest single supplier of military equipment to Argentina in the five years preceding the Falklands War. According to ACDA, it delivered $575 million in military equipment to Argentina during this period out of a total of $1.8 billion received by the military junta.[193] At the start of the Falklands War, Argentina reportedly had 19 Mirage IIIs and 9 Super Etendards as well as 68 American Skyhawks (sold earlier to meet French competition), and 26 Israeli Daggers. These aircraft were supplemented by approximately 58 Pucaras, Italian Macchi MB-339 trainers, 32 older MS-760A Paris IIs from previous purchases from France, and several aging British Canberra bombers. French Mirage aircraft were armed with Magic 530 and AS-11 and AS-12 air-to-surface rockets. Also available to Argentina were 5 newly developed Exocet air-to-surface missiles capable of being fired by the land-based Super Etendards.[194]

Despite the varied foreign equipment used by Argentina in the Falklands War, including American and British arms,[195] the French came under particularly sharp attack because of the number of French arms in the Argentinian inventory and the wide media attention given to the sinking of two British naval ships, the destroyer *Sheffield* and the *Atlantic Conveyor*,[196] by French Exocet air-to-surface missiles. A modified Exocet rocket, launched from land, damaged but did not disable the light cruiser *Glamorgan*. Rocket-firing Puma helicopters also took part in attacking British ships, and at least one battery of Roland missiles, acquired shortly before the outbreak of hostilities, engaged five British Harrier fighters.[197] The countries supplying the weapons systems and munitions which destroyed three other naval ships—the destroyer *Coventry* and the frigates *Ardent* and *Antelope*—and damaged twelve other ships received less attention in western media coverage.[198] American Skyhawks and Israeli Daggers were presumably involved in some of these attacks since so-called "iron bombs" were used by Argentinian attack aircraft and some of these aircraft were shot down by English gunners.

The Mitterrand government closed ranks quickly with Britain at the onset of hostilities. France supported a European Community ban on

Argentinian imports and exports and imposed a total ban on arms and spares to Buenos Aires.[199] Contract talks with Argentina over the sale of AML-90 armored vehicles and over French assistance for the production of a new light tank were suspended. Shipments of Exocet missiles to Peru were halted for "technical reasons," according to French officials,[200] to preclude their transshipment to Argentina. These moves were matched by public support of Britain's military action and British access to French facilities at Dakar.[201] These supportive moves only partially overcame British annoyance. The Exocet affair and France's swift lifting of the arms embargo on August 10, a little more than a month after the British retook the Falklands, rankled the Thatcher government as did French support for U.N. efforts to seek a negotiated and compromise solution.[202]

Socialist France faced a similar Hobson's choice between its ideological commitments and American urgings that it support pressures on the Nicaraguan Sandinista government to limit its Marxist revolution and to end its arms supply of El Salvadoran rebels. The Mitterrand government irritated the Reagan administration early on by joining with Mexico in a search for a negotiated settlement in Central America and, worse, by signing on December 21, 1981, a contract with Nicaragua to supply approximately $16 million in arms, useful for counterinsurgency, including 45 heavy trucks, 2 patrol boats, 2 used Alouette III helicopters, and several thousand air-to-ground rockets.[203] Paris, seeking to separate itself from the Sandinista regime, later announced that no more arms sales were contemplated with Managua.[204] One can speculate about the reasons for this gradual narrowing of U.S. and French differences. The weakness of the French economy and dependency on the United States for recovery may have played a role. Worry about Soviet expansionism, through clients as in Chad or saber rattling in Europe, may also have induced the Mitterrand government to line up with Washington.[205] Whatever the reasons for the Mitterrand government's belated reserve toward Nicaragua, the limits imposed on sales to Managua have hindered sales to other Central American states, like Guatemala, Honduras, and El Salvador, previous recipients of arms from France. These states have turned to other suppliers, the United States and Israel in particular, to meet their needs. Socialist ideological qualms would appear to have advised a go-slow policy in selling arms to junta-ruled states of Central America.

OCEANA AND SOUTH AND EAST ASIA

Considering the vast territory covered by the states of these regions and their large populations, it is somewhat surprising that France has not been able to make much headway in penetrating these arms markets. Its most dramatic achievement was the sale of 116 Mirage aircraft to Australia in the early 1960s, much to the voiced chagrin of the Kennedy administration. As a member of the ANZUS security treaty, Australia was expected to arm itself with American fighters. The financial arrangements and opportunities for coproduction offered by Dassault proved too attractive to turn down. Quarrels between Australia and France over French nuclear testing in the south Pacific and heightened American sales pressures blocked duplication of the feat in the early 1980s when the Mirages were scheduled for replacement. Canberra opted for the F-18 of McDonnell Douglas over the Mirage 2000.[206] The French had to settle for a consolation prize of 18 Ecureuil helicopters as Australia slipped back within the American arms fold.[207] The potential loss was substantial. In the eight-year period between 1974 and 1982, Australia ordered over $5 billion in American military hardware.[208]

South Asia, dominated by the Indian-Pakistani conflict, offered a more lucrative market for the French arms industry. French commercial interests drove much of the French sales effort to these two warring clients. Sales to India were especially important in the early stages of France's efforts to create an independent arms industry after World War II. India and Israel helped launch Dassault as a world-class producer of fighter aircraft. During the 1950s, India purchased 164 Ouragan MD 450s and 110 Mystères to match Pakistan's acquisitions of American advanced fighters, including F-86 Sabres and F-104 Starfighters. It also ordered Bréguet Alize transports and 150 AMX-13 tanks.

A profit-motivated French arms industry was no match, however, for the Soviet Union which became India's principal arms supplier in the 1960s. France could not compete with a Soviet offer of $600,000 a copy for its MiGs against a price of $900,000 set for the Mirage III.[209] Throughout most of the 1960s and 1970s, France had to content itself with licensing arrangements for Alouette helicopters and antitank missiles.[210] India produced these in substantial numbers—more than 100 Alouettes and approximately 2,150 SS-11s, weapons that saw multiple service in India's clashes with Pakistan.

A potential breakthrough of tight Soviet control came in the late 1970s with the announcement of an Indian decision to order 200 Jaguars. Forty were to be built by Britain and France and the remainder by India. To solidify the decision, the British government dispatched 18 Jaguars of the Royal Air Force to India.[211] Debate in India over the high cost and mediocre performance of the aircraft raised second thoughts among Indian planners. Pakistan's purchase of American F-16s, M-48A tanks, and TOW antitank missiles prompted, as in the 1950s, a major switch in Indian procurement priorities. In 1982, India signed a contract for 150 Mirage 2000s at a cost of $3.3 billion, a sum surpassing any previous contract for a single weapons system with a foreign state.[212] Despite these inroads, the Soviets remain India's major arms supplier, providing the bulk of its supersonic aircraft except for the hedge represented by the Jaguars and the Mirage 2000s.

Pakistan also looked elsewhere than France for most of its arms—primarily to China and the United States. It was a major purchaser of Mirage aircraft and tactical missiles.[213] It also bought five French-built submarines—three of the Daphne and two of the Agosta class, the latter being repurchased from South Africa after the imposition of the 1977 embargo.[214] On at least one occasion, France also imposed an embargo on arms to Pakistan. In 1971, arms were blocked to Islamabad in response to Pakistan's military intervention in West Bengal. The embargo was temporarily extended to the entire region with the outbreak of the third India-Pakistan war in 1971.[215]

As suggested earlier, Pakistan was important to France's arms industry in ways that went beyond the purchase of equipment. France drew upon Pakistani military personnel to support its services to clients in the Persian Gulf and the Middle East. As Moslems, Pakistani pilots, soldiers, advisers, and technicians were welcome in Saudi Arabia, Kuwait, Libya, and Abu Dhabi as instructors and as maintenance personnel of their French equipment. For the French, Pakistan offered access to relatively inexpensive sources of trained personnel useful in selling arms to fetching markets in the Middle East. There was also good will and a reputation for arms to draw upon. Pakistan's President Zia had, for example, directed Jordanian troops against Palestinian rebels in 1970. Pakistani forces were also available to bolster the Riyadh regime.

East Asia completes this *tour d'horizon* of French arms transfers and the political and geostrategic considerations shaping France's behavior. With France's withdrawal from Southeast Asia in 1954, its influence in the region declined rapidly and, correspondingly, so did its prospects as an arms supplier. Unlike other regions of the world, no Mirages criss-crossed the skies of these states. Orders were confined to scattered purchases of Alouette, Gazelle, and Puma helicopters and small orders for tactical missiles and armor. A contract with Indonesia for 1,000 armored vehicles in 1979 is among the few notable sales made by France to East Asian states.

The Chinese market, while potentially large, was essentially limited in its prospects. The Chinese had limited means and meager international reserves at their disposal with which to pay for French equipment. Active Soviet opposition to sales of French arms beyond the Super Frelons and a license to produce a small number of Alouettes, reportedly weighed heavily in French calculations about selling arms, to China. Détente in Europe was held partly hostage to arms for China. American concern, not to mention French worries, about transferring high technology equipment to a possibly resurgent China, only recently entering the global arena, also dampened enthusiasm to press arms sales to China. Beijing also preferred to be its own arms supplier. However much it craved access to western technology, it was reluctant to become dependent on another power.

CONCLUSIONS

Arms sales have served several masters. Explaining French arms transfers in simple commercial terms seriously distorts the shifting aims underlying French behavior and the evolving internal and external pressures and constraints shaping the movement of French arms across state borders. If welfare and economic considerations remain overriding in the 1980s, military strategic and traditional foreign policy objectives—particularly support for friendly regimes—figure prominently in French decision-making. To explain the amount, composition, and timing of arms transferred to a particular state—or the French refusal to respond to outside requests—prompts reference to a host of particular political considerations and conjunctural constraints and opportunities that are otherwise hidden from sight if French transfers are viewed solely through a commercial prism.

In Europe, France's independent nuclear strategy, linked to its withdrawal from NATO's integrated military structure, has cost the French arms industry valuable arms contracts. In the 1960s, sales to Europe constituted the primary outlet for French arms. After 1966, France faced increasing difficulty in meeting American and allied competition. This would have undoubtedly been the case even if France had stayed within the western integrated system, but as the F-16 case suggests, Gaullist independence worked against French arms sales. Neither the Pompidou nor the Giscard d'Estaing regime was prepared to abandon Gaullist-defined national autonomy to assuage allied suspicions about French reliability. When the Netherlands joined Denmark and Norway in favor of the F-16 over the Mirage, their combined weight tipped Belgium in the same direction.

In the Middle East and North Africa, a prima facie case can be made for the dominance of economic and welfare concerns in selling arms. Until Algerian independence, French arms sales policy was keyed more to strategic and security concerns than economic profit. Arms to Israel served French imperial interests. With the end of empire, political and economic ties with the Arab states multiplied, and arms naturally followed this realignment at Israel's expense. French security and economic interests were tied to Arab interests based more on a mutual exchange between states than on the direct exercise of French power in support of an imperial system. The significant economic value of arms sales to Arab states carried their own political costs which were not clearly foreseen at the outset of the massive push to become a major Middle East weapons supplier. Pressed by the Gulf states, especially Saudi Arabia, French security and welfare interests were joined in France's costly interventions in Lebanon. Italy and Britain, under the same pressures, assumed lower profiles than France. France was caught in a web of its own creation: arms transfers, essential for the autonomous development of its arms industry, raised political expectations of support and forged obligations with recipient states, while France's heightened determination to play a major role in the Middle East, whether under the Fourth or Fifth Republic, encouraged an active and extensive arm sales effort.

France's interventions in Chad and the western Sahara also illustrate how arms sales and implied commitments, many of which are costly and unwanted, to recipient states feed on each other. French aspirations in the Maghreb have been in no small part defined by French arms sales to the area. Libya has been both a benefactor of France's arms industry and a burden for its armed forces and diplomacy. Morocco and Tunisia are also bound to an arms umbilical cord. Paris has not abandoned the hope of drawing Algeria closer through arms sales, although Algiers has been careful to keep its distance, notwithstanding a more favorable disposition to receive more French arms and military assistance in the 1980s than before.

Sub-Saharan Africa presents its own unique political demands. A strategy of arms denial was implicitly pursued in the postcolonialist period to preserve French hegemony, while arms sales to Portugal and South Africa helped to extend the life of white rule. France has been forced to yield to international pressures, most especially those from Black African states, to relinquish its profitable trade with Pretoria. Portugal has left the imperial scene of its own accord. Meanwhile, competition from other arms suppliers, especially the superpowers, weakens France's hold on its former colonies. As its grip slips, it has turned its attention to non-Francophone Africa, particularly Nigeria, to recoup its strength. The record, if intervention in the Nigerian civil war is any indication, has not been brilliant. Recent arms sales to Nigeria suggest

French relations with the Black African states are on the mend, but the going does not promise to be easy, given a recent history of mutual suspicion and antagonism.

While it cannot be gainsaid that arms sales both lead and follow French foreign policy preferences, it is equally, if paradoxically, true that French sales have preserved a remarkable quality of neutrality toward regional rivals and groups locked in civil war. France sold arms and military technology to Pretoria long after the United States and Britain were compelled by foreign pressures and domestic criticism to join the embargo against South Africa. Even under the Socialists—bitter critics of arms sales to racist and authoritarian regimes—arms have continued to flow with little interruption or slackening of promotional vigor. Only Chile appears proscribed from receiving arms on regime grounds. Since 1958, governments of almost every stripe have received French arms. In Europe, Franco's Spain, Salazar's Portugal, and the Greek junta of the early 1970s were important French clients, as were the democratic rivals who have replaced them. In the Middle East and North Africa, radical and moderate Arab states as well as democratic Israel have been accorded French weapons. The juntas of Latin America have all had relative ease in buying French arms. So also have the military governments of Pakistan and the democratic regimes of India. Human rights protests have not noticeably reduced the overall level of French arms contracts. Whereas human rights considerations have assumed at different times the status of an overriding national interest in American arms transfer policy, they have normally been subordinated in French practice to the welfare, strategic, and foreign policy concerns discussed earlier.

The French have also armed regional rivals around the world. French arms have had an important, sometimes a decisive, impact on the strategic balance of a region and on the outcome of a test of arms. Israel's military successes in Suez and the Six Day War critically depended on French arms. Israel's enemies have also received large quantities of French equipment and munitions. Iran and especially Iraq have French arms in their arsenals. Libya and Morocco, at odds over the western Sahara, have modernized their forces with French equipment. Here the French risked too much success in pushing arms. The Chadian intervention to stop Libya's advance raised the possibility that French forces might be defending themselves against their own weapons. Indian Ouragans and Pakistani Mirages, not to mention the French armor and tactical missiles possessed by both states, have confronted each other in all of the wars of the Indian subcontinent since the 1950s. In the Falklands War, Argentina inflicted heavy losses on British naval forces using French Mirages and Exocet missiles, while Britain's order of battle included French equipment.

The impact of French arms on intra- and interstate conflict should not be exaggerated. One must remember that there are other suppliers at the ready to fill orders should the French falter in supplying arms. The superpowers still dominate the arms transfer system. France's European allies are also serious competitors. New developing states, many possessing French arms know-how, contest France for contracts. Arms supplies are becoming increasingly multilateralized with the effect, recognized by the Mitterrand government, that France must redouble its efforts to sell abroad to maintain its share of the world market. New incentives—e.g., more inclusive joint design and production contracts or better after-sale follow up—are being offered to clients. France's arms industry must run harder just to stand still in the global arms sales race.

If emulation is the highest form of flattery, the French example of selling arms has become a policy instrument relied upon increasingly by developing states as they attempt to assert their independence and meet the rising expectations of their elites for political power, status, and legitimacy, and those of their populations for material welfare and personal and national identity. Not surprisingly, they are modeling their behavior on the French experience and on the other developed industrial states which in greater or lesser measure have used arms production and sales, especially in the post-World War II period, to cope with the conflicting security demands of the nation-state system and with the modernization process engulfing political regimes around the globe.

Part V.
Arms and Global Security and Welfare

Making and Marketing Arms: A Rational Strategy and an Irrational International System

EXPLAINING why France makes and markets arms and military technology is both easy and difficult: easy, because the specific aims guiding French policy—national independence and security, economic and technological development, diplomatic influence, and prestige—are clear enough despite their variable significance; difficult, because the systemic imperatives prompting these aims are not always evident, yet they critically orient and shape French arms policy.

French arms behavior responds to two structural imperatives inherent in the contemporary international system: external pressures generated by the incipient anarchy of the international community and domestic demands for increased well-being. These imperatives impelled the reform and modernization of France's internal economic and political institutions to ensure greater security as well as public and private welfare, civilian and military. These systemic factors warrant particular attention, since they also impact, as Chapter 6 suggests, in varying measure on other developed and developing states and drive the militarization of the international system.

French arms behavior provides significant evidence to support the proposition that the gradual but inexorable emergence of new weapons production centers around the globe and the expansion of the arms trade, including hardware and know-how, can be explained by reference to these systemic determinants. They generate powerful incentives for the making and marketing of arms. They prompt national governments to create military-industrial-techno-scientific complexes to address their security and welfare needs. Ideology—whether characterized as capitalist or socialist or cast as authoritarian or democratic—offers an unsatisfactory explanation for the militarization of the international system and for the mushrooming of centers dedicated to the design, production, and sale of weapons and hostile technologies. Fifth Republic governments on the Right and on the Left have pursued security and welfare policies based on the assumptions of an indigenous arms industry and on the sale of arms and military technology to a global market. These should be considered expected outcomes of the pressures intrinsic to the current nation-state system and to the modernization process sweeping the globe.

From a national perspective, the making and marketing of arms is a rational response to the incentives arising from the international system within which states are ensnared. These incentives may be viewed essentially as constraints shaping national strategies and orienting the scarce allocation of resources in pursuit of national aims and interests. The implications of these responses for the stability of the international system do not appear to be as clear as the result that is intended by states in embarking on a policy of indigenous arms production and sale. The result is an international system bent and biased in favor of producing arms in increasing numbers, sophistication, and lethality and of transferring weapons and hostile technologies across state borders. French behavior is symptomatic of the system as a whole. Systemic imperatives, eliciting rational national strategies keyed to weapons, produce an unexpected and irrational outcome—the militarization of the globe—which, in the long run, risks yielding less security for the nations of the system and less well-being for their populations.

ARMS AND THE SECURITY DILEMMA

The French Fifth Republic addressed the age-old security dilemma in the same way as its predecessors: by arming. Postwar pursuit of an independent strategic policy required the reconstruction of France's arms industry. However much they may have differed in methods and strategies, the Fourth and, more assertively, the Fifth Republic reaffirmed France's traditional policy of providing for its own defense through its own means. On this score all French regimes have been in essential agreement.

What is of interest about the reconstitution of France's arm industry is the rationale advanced by the de Gaulle government to justify a modern weapons industry. The Gaullist Fifth Republic broke sharply with France's imperial past. In liquidating France's foreign holdings, de Gaulle essentially contended that the empire had divided the French nation at home and sapped its strength abroad. Algeria, the last remnant of France's colonial past, could not be held against the historic tide of nationalism, first unleased by the French Revolution and later exported to Europe and to other regions and peoples around the world. Nor could France stand alone against the relentless expansion of the United States and the Soviet Union whose struggle replaced the Eurocentric system as the principal organizer and drive wheel of the nation-state system and of world politics after World War II. France needed allies in the developing world to halt or at least hobble the spread of superpower influence and to diffuse the impact of their conflict on European and global politics. France's unreserved embrace of the principle of self-determination and its application to the developing world was the precondition for the formation of a grand, if inevitably loose, coalition to balance the superpowers. The Third World and the Old World were needed as counterweights to the superpowers, each with its own vision of global order based on incompatible principles of political legitimacy and interest.

De Gaulle's bold abandonment of empire released French domestic politics and foreign policy from a self-imposed bondage. The Fifth Republic forged a coalition of the Right and Left, however else partisans of each were divided, opposed to superpower rule. De Gaulle cast France in the role of champion of the developing states. The hegemonial drives of the superpowers were condemned as unstable and illegitimate. Instability was defined by de Gaulle as the inclination of the superpower competition toward war, either as the consequence of miscalculation or mismanagement of their conflict, or as a result of client manipulation or commitments that might propel them into an unwanted but inevitable global conflagration. Conversely, the ability of the superpowers to regulate their differences and to constrain the freedom of other states infringed critically on the principle of national independence. Both superpower collision and collusion had to be resisted in creating, over time, a new global order.

For de Gaulle, France's capacity to make its own arms was a precondition of a successful challenge to superpower domination. To consign this function to another state or to a consortium of states—say the Atlantic or European Community—would be tantamount to renouncing the key function that, according to Gaullist assumptions and logic, justified a state's claim to sovereignty and independence. The de Gaulle regime posed this issue in the sharpest and clearest light. Its response— the force de dissuasion—appeared to afford France a measure of control over the overriding issue of peace and war. It also provided psychological and political bargaining power with which to resist allied demands for alliance conformity and U.S. economic and military expansionism in the 1960s and to counter rising Soviet military power during the 1970s and 1980s.

The force de dissuasion also served as a foundation for France's initiation of détente well before its western allies embraced this negotiating stance to relax and resolve the Cold War. With nuclear arms, Paris could presumably bargain from a position of strength with the superpowers. As an added benefit, France assumed a preeminent military position among western continental powers. Its only potential challenger was a divided Germany precluded from acquiring its own nuclear arms by treaty with its European allies and by implicit postwar Big Four accord. National unity gradually crystallized around a national nuclear force whose legitimacy was confirmed in the election of the Left in 1981.

The Fifth Republic has also marketed arms and military technology around the world and at levels of economic value and lethality unprecedented in French history. Gaullist France and its successors rationalized France's provision of arms and military know-how to other states as an indispensable means to contest superpower rule of the international system. An open-door sales policy strengthened the prospects of a multipolar system which was viewed as more compatible with France's aspirations and more congenial to its interests and aims than the bipolar system of the immediate postwar period. Selling arms and military technology is as much an essential element of French security policy as the force de frappe. Any diminution of French effort in this domain would be tantamount to a slackening commitment to an independent nuclear deterrent since arms sales and production, as well as the arms complex so painstakingly organized after World War II, are intimately woven together with France's nuclear policy.

ARMS, WELFARE, AND MODERNIZATION

An arms sales policy *tous azimuts* also responded to rising civilian and military welfare demands. It was a strategy calculated to reconcile security and welfare imperatives by stimulating France's socio-economic and political modernization after World War II. France's scientific base was broadened and deepened to serve the nation's military needs and to promote its economic development. National champions were designated to battle for a global leadership role in nuclear energy, avionics, electronics and computers—areas critical for the development of a modern, post-industrial society and of a leading military power. To stimulate internal competition, the French market was opened to foreign competitors. French industries were urged and ordered to expand and adapt to a world market. Thanks to specialization and the emerging global division of labor, France achieved a comparative advantage in the 1970s in making, marketing, and servicing arms. French leaders strove to avoid the traditional choice between guns and butter by wedding the imperatives of security and economic development. From this marriage of necessity was born the transformation of France's industrial and techno-scientific base and the modernization of its socio-economic structure. These changes—particularly the rise of large, internationally organized state-dominated corporations and the emergence of a state-led techno-scientific-military-industrial complex—unleashed forces that have profoundly shaped French contemporary politics and institutions. These forces are now widely abroad, shaping the global system in ways foreshadowed in the French case.

The transformation of France's strategic posture, economic system, and techno-scientific structure was accomplished within the political framework established by the Fifth Republic—itself partially the product of the irresistible modernizing process unleashed by the superpower struggle, decolonization, the globalization of the national-state system, and rising expectations of peoples everywhere for material well-being. When viewed against the record of previous French republics and their successive collapse, the reforms midwifed by the Fifth Republic were truly impressive. During the interwar period, the Third Republic had internal consensus on the policy of appeasement and on a military strategy based on a defensive posture at home and empire abroad, but it failed to stem the Nazi invasion and its own collapse. The Fourth Republic imploded after a chain of colonial defeats from Southeast Asia to North Africa, unable to reconcile external security and foreign policy imperatives with the requirements of domestic cohesion and democratic rule.

The Fifth Republic and the arms complex on which it depends fashioned a new strategy simultaneously responsive to security and welfare demands and disciplined to France's material capabilities and possibilities. The arms complex guarantees an independent nuclear force and ensures its continual modernization. It also provides saleable—albeit lethal—products and techniques in world markets to strengthen French competitiveness and to promote domestic welfare. It comes then as no surprise that the arms complex enjoys wide popular support. With the victory of the Left in 1981, an independent nuclear deterrent and a liberal arms sales policy have been raised to a level of sacred practices beyond partisan politics to affect or ideology to dispute. Nationalization by the Left reaffirmed and symbolically legitimated the policy of concentrating key defense industries pursued by the Right. Both factions were in essential accord on the indispensability of an indigenous arms industry and on France's role as a world supplier of advanced weapons and military technology.

Making and Marketing Arms: An Assessment

There is, of course, a negative side to the arms production and transfer policies pursued by the Fifth Republic. This side of the balance sheet, as Chapter 5 suggests, has never been fully or openly debated and evaluated by the French people and parties. Democratic consent has been elicited but within a political process that controls information flow and that precludes a probing evaluation of the weapons and welfare performance of the military-industrial complex. The politics of arms production and sales is largely insulated from the heat of partisan debate and the glare of public disclosure.

The security costs and risks of French arms production and selling practices merit examination. Concerns arise that the arms industry will be increasingly dependent on exterior sales and coproduction agreements to remain solvent. The postwar dependency of the Fourth Republic on the United States for arms supplies and economic support is being transformed into a dependency on foreign arms purchasers under the Fifth Republic. There is the real worry that the military requirements of recipient states more than French national needs will shape weapons design, development, and production priorities; that military personnel may be deflected from primary missions to service French equipment and to train foreign armed forces in its use; that the missions of the French military establishment will be distorted in promoting arms sales abroad; and that France will, through the backdoor of arms sales, acquire unwanted and potentially costly and dangerous security obligations.

The credibility of the force de dissuasion remains problematic. Two of the three elements of France's nuclear forces—its Mirage IV aircraft and IRBMs on the Albion Plateau—are more targets than deterrents, easy marks for Soviet theater and strategic nuclear forces. The French force of six nuclear submarines, while formidable as a first-strike system and increasingly more powerful through MIRVing and greater missile accuracy, must confront Soviet nuclear attack submarines and the possibility of breakthroughs in antisubmarine warfare and ABM defenses. Only three submarines are on station at any time. The short range of French missiles relative to their American and Soviet counterparts compels French submarines to operate in the confining waters of northern Europe. Communication is not easy and would very likely be disrupted in a postattack environment.

Slighted, too, in French estimates are serious asymmetries in political risks run by France and the Soviet Union in threatening nuclear war. In a nuclear exchange, Soviet cities are traded for the entire French nation. That is not much of a bargain. Meanwhile, uninhibited by arms control limitations, the superpowers are building in the late 1980s and into the 1990s vastly more powerful offensive nuclear weapons than they have now and are developing new defensive systems potentially damaging to third states possessing small nuclear forces. The superpowers not only threaten each other but are—and will be—increasingly capable of neutralizing or disarming third-state nuclear forces as well.

Despite the ominous trends running against the French nuclear force, Fifth Republic governments remain suspicious of arms control negotiations as a complement to their nuclear strategic policies and posture, and reticent about placing restraints on superpower nuclear forces lest they be applied to France. Until the 1970s, Fifth Republic regimes pursued an empty-chair policy in arms control and disarmament negotiations. French planners preferred to draw benefit from superpower self-imposed limitations for the enhancement of French strategic forces rather than advance arms control measures or pressure the superpowers and other nuclear states to accept limitations as a way to stabilize the nuclear environment, to prepare for reductions in nuclear arsenals, and to slow and regulate military technological development. France certainly bears far less responsibility for the lethality and instability of the global nuclear arms race than the superpowers. Relative to its resources, however, it has contributed its proportional share to global instability. It is by no means certain that the force de dissuasion is a long-term solution to France's security dilemma. The French consensus on defense policy, supported by the Right and the Left, precludes the exploration of options and approaches other than the traditional one of *si vis pacem, para bellum.*

While part of the explanation for France's reservations about arms control negotiations is rooted in a concern for maximum freedom in developing nuclear weapons, other internally directed welfare and bureaucratic considerations also hamper France's pursuit of a more ambitious arms control strategy than it has adopted until now. Strong incentives arising from domestic need and the benefits of comparative advantage significantly limit French interest in restricting arms and military technology sales or in restraining nuclear and conventional arms proliferation. The leadership of France's arms complex, within the government, bureaucracy, and industry, have consistently resisted American, allied, neutral state, and Soviet pressures to impose checks on the export of nuclear materials, know-how and equipment. Nothing less than India's dramatic explosion of a nuclear device in 1974 was needed to shock the complacency of France's political leadership and to force the proliferation issue onto the French policy agenda—and then only over the objections of powerful elements within the arms complex. It required the direct intervention of President Giscard d'Estaing to establish tighter national controls on proliferation and to orient France toward a policy of increased cooperation with other suppliers in order to slow proliferation. This shift did lead to restrictions on previous French permissiveness which had catered to the nuclear appetites of South Korea, Pakistan, Iraq, and South Africa. Tighter restrictions on access to French nuclear materials, facilities, and equipment were finally adopted, but not before these states, as Israel before them, had received substantial French assistance in advancing their military nuclear programs.

French resistance to conventional arms limitations remains strong. Paris continues to impose conditions on initiating regional or global conventional arms talks. French weapons and support equipment have armed—and continue to arm—regional belligerents on opposing sides in the Middle East, North Africa, Black Africa, South and East Asia, and Latin America. Argentina and Britain faced deadly French weapons in their war over the Falklands. France and its trading partners in the European Community run risks in shipping goods to the Gulf states and in transporting needed oil to run their industries because French-equipped Iraqi forces, armed with F1 fighters and Exocet missiles, destroy neutral shipping. Regional arms races must be stimulated to keep the French arms industry solvent and profitable.

France has also taken the lead in transferring know-how and technology to developing world states. To win contracts, France has had to tempt foreign buyers not only with advanced weapons but with progressively greater access to technological know-how for producing sophisticated weapon systems. French arms contracts with Argentina, Brazil, Israel, India, and South Africa have accelerated the diffusion of arms and military technology. Indigenous arms production systems have multiplied in number and in the capacity of these centers to develop and produce an increasingly wider range of advanced weapons. Retention of France's comparative advantage in weapons production and sales hinges more and more on its responsiveness and sensitivity to market demands for state-of-the-art techniques in designing and developing weapons and less and less on the weapons themselves.

The welfare imperatives pressing France to sell more arms and military know-how—to run faster to keep abreast with the increased number of national suppliers that French arms and technology transfers have helped to create—crowd out consideration of alternate strategies to ensure economic development which might dampen global and regional demand for arms. French planning for economic growth and technological advancement is harnessed to the French war-production machine. The evaluation of the economic performance of the military-industrial complex is hindered by the tight control over information and the definition of performance criteria maintained by its leadership. While the Fifth Republic meets the broad tests of an open society in deciding its military strategy and arms sales policies, bureaucratic constraints and the oligarchical governance of the arms complex, in insulating weapons making and marketing from public scrutiny and evaluation, impair the democratic process.

Serious questions also remain unanswered with respect to the problem of reconciling popular consent, however achieved, with policies that are effective in meeting France's security, welfare, and broader modernization needs over the long run. Sir Henry Maine, no friend of popular government, wrote over a century ago that "there can be no grosser mistake than to have an impression that Democracy differs from Monarchy in essence. . . . The tests of success in the performance of the necessary and natural duties of government are precisely the same in both cases."[1] The "natural duties of government" today are broader and more complex than those understood by Maine and his contemporaries a century ago and before. France's answer to the competing demands of the security state and the welfare state—*production et ventes d'armes tous azimuts*—is by no means a riskless or cost-free strategy. Certainly the case is far from closed that it is a winning one.

IMPLICATIONS OF THE FRENCH EXPERIENCE

The French experience in producing and transferring arms and military technology helps to explain the behavior of other developed and developing states around the globe. As Chapter 6 suggests, the systemic imperatives eliciting French behavior also animate, in greater or lesser measure depending on the specific security needs and developmental state of each state, the arms production and transfer policies of other states. The insecurity generated by the anarchy of the international system drives the militarization of the world political community. Witness the growth of independent centers of military power, increases in the quantitative and qualitative destructive power of national arsenals, and the emergence of indigenously based arms production complexes.

The global modernization process, which is mediated through the nation-state, also fuels militarization. Arming and arms making are viewed by a growing number of key regional powers as preconditions of national welfare. They are seen as transmission belts for technological advancement and diffusion, economic development, and social reform. Thus the nation-state system and demands for increased human welfare and modernization—what the populations of the world and their governing elites care about most—militarize the international system.

The French record suggests how daunting—if not utopian—will be the quest for cooperation among states to slow the militarization of international relations. National leaders cannot easily ignore the apparent success enjoyed by the Fifth Republic in producing and selling weapons and know-how: national security and independence have been strengthened; economic and technological growth stimulated; bureaucratic and industrial interests protected and promoted; and governmental power and legitimacy enhanced. Viewed from the perspective of the international system as a whole or from the narrower perspective of domestic politics, arms transfers appear to have admirably served the needs—real and perceived—of the French Fifth Republic, its ruling elites, and a majority of the electorate. A strong, if rebuttable, brief can be made for the proposition that French arms policy has been, by and large, a rational response to the constraints and opportunities of international and national politics.

But what are the prospects for international stability, peaceful change, and economic development if every state, whether wittingly or not, emulates the French example, as much current research and experience suggest is the case? What may have begun at a national level as a rational response to systemic and domestic imperatives may well end, if current trends continue, by creating an international environment shaped by the uncontrollable militarization of state-to-state relations and the deflection of scarce resources from long-term economic development and social progress. These ironic and unsought outcomes of rational national conduct—sources of support for a perverse international system—require serious attention if the world community is to be spared destructive and potentially catastrophic war and if large segments of the world's populations are to escape chronic poverty and penury.

The French experience contributes to our knowledge and understanding of the global incentive structure that deepens the security and welfare dilemmas facing the international community today. The design of this study is applicable to an examination of other states and their arms production and transfer behavior. What we already know of the behavior of regional powers suggests that the French experiment is being repeated in different measure around the globe. Examples are plentiful: in Latin America, Argentina and Brazil; in the Middle East, Israel and Egypt; in South Asia, Pakistan and India; in East Asia, China and the two Koreas; and in Africa, South Africa. Understanding the sources of our present discontents which are linked to arming and selling arms is a prerequisite for fashioning realistic national and international arms control measures to manage and ameliorate them. Cooperative national arms control policies must address powerful systemic forces whose needs are now met, however provisionally, by fabricating and selling ever-larger quantities of arms and advanced military technology.

The French case is a window to the world. By tracing French behavior and by exposing French aims and motives in making and marketing arms, one is introduced to the global arms production and transfer system that gives form and impulse to the behavior of states within the international community. Revealed is an arms subsystem responsive to powerful and seemingly uncontrollable security, welfare, and modernization imperatives that propel the international system forward. It marches to its own drum, progressively insensitive to the seemingly rational, calibrated, and prudent national arms strategies pursued by the states and governments of the system. Rational national behavior produces outcomes that frustrate the intentions of statesmen, undone by the countermoves of opponents—and even allies—in their efforts to enhance their security and improve their well-being.

The seeming success of the French experience prompts concern for the long-term prospects of international stability and development. Pressures to produce arms and to diffuse them and the technology to make them through the global community show no signs of relaxation or reversal. Secular trends appear to be biased upward despite brief, periodic downturns due to conjunctural factors of passing moment. Arms and arms transfers appear to be highly flexible and fungible instruments of state power and purpose. Supple and subservient, they serve many state needs—and do so simultaneously. A conflict-ridden international setting—rent by ideological, national, racial, and ethnic strife—generates few countervailing pressures to offset the will to arm. When militarization is joined to benign and benevolent purpose—modernization and public welfare—the compulsion to make and market arms appears overwhelming. One would need the optimism and naïveté of Candide to be cheered by the French example and what the French experience portends for the future of the international system.

Appendixes

As a general rule, French governmental documents and parliamentary reports are the principal sources for figures covering the economic value, number, and types of arms produced and delivered by France to its own armed forces and to other states. When comparisons are made to other arms producers and suppliers, these primary materials are supplemented by several other widely used sources, noted below. Among these, the *Yearbooks* of the Stockholm International Peace Research Institute and the annual *Military Balance* of the International Institute for Strategic Studies of London are extensively consulted for the transfer of major weapon systems, including fighter and support aircraft, missiles, armor, and ships.

The annual reports of the United States Arms Control and Disarmament Agency, *World Military Expenditures and Arms Transfers*, are used primarily for comparison of the economic value of arms supplied by France and by other countries to the world market. Some of the problems associated with reconciling primary French sources with ACDA data are discussed in the author's "Measuring French Arms Transfers: A Problem of Sources and Some Sources of Problems with ACDA Data," *Journal of Conflict Resolution*, XXIII, No. 2 (June 1979), 195-227, and will not be repeated here. It should be noted that the major finding of the article—that French estimates of the economic value of its arms deliveries were higher by a factor of two to three when compared to ACDA data—has gradually been narrowed in the 1980s as ACDA has raised its estimates of the value of French deliveries, bringing them into closer alignment with official French sources, although they are still lower than those cited by the French government.

To the degree feasible (defined by the length and the complexity of footnote citations and by considerations of redundancy), source notes are placed as close to the material being supported as possible to assist the reader. These are usually cited in full under each table or figure. For example, Table 2-5 cites the major sources for French arms production to 1980 since exclusively French sources were consulted.

The problems associated with identifying the value, number, types, and dates of delivery of arms and military technology by France and other suppliers are so formidable that space limits dictated a different strategy of citation and source consultation. The number of these sources, their varying reliability and accuracy, the many gaps and discrepancies within each source and between them required the definition of counting rules and procedures to develop as coherent and as systematic a set of delivery data as possible that would integrate original French and secondary data.

Data for foreign deliveries are derived from the following sources which are the bases for the deliveries cited throughout the text and for the detailed regional transfer tables of the following Appendixes.

The International Institute for Strategic Studies (iiss), *The Military Balance, 1960-1985* (London: iiss, 1960-1985).

Jaffee Center for Strategic Studies, *Arms Transactions with Middle Eastern and North African Countries, 1982-1984*, Digests No. 1, 2, and 3 (Tel Aviv: Tel Aviv University Documentation Service, 1982-1985).

Jane's All the World's Aircraft (through 1984-1985) (London: Jane's Publishing Company Limited).

Jane's Armour and Artillery (through 1983-1984) (London: Jane's Publishing Company Limited).

Jane's Fighting Ships (through 1984-1985) (London: Jane's Publishing Company Limited).

Stockholm International Peace Research Institute (sipri), *The Arms Trade Registers* (Cambridge: The MIT Press, 1975).

sipri, *Worksheets* (unpublished data on weapons transfers to Western Europe).

sipri, *World Armaments and Disarmament, SIPRI Yearbooks 1973-1984* (New York: Taylor and Francis, 1984). (Publishers vary over this decade; only the latest is cited.)

U.S., Arms Control and Disarmament Agency, *World Military Expenditures and Arms Transfers* (Washington, D.C.: U.S. Government Printing Office, 1975-1985).

F. M. von Senger und Etterlein, *Tanks of the World* (Annapolis, Md.: The Nautical and Aviation Publishing Company of America, 1983).

Other relevant sources were used on occasion to verify figures. These included, *inter alia*, major U.S., British, and French newspapers, *Aviation Week and Space Technology*, and the Foreign Broadcast Information Service. Only principal sources are cited here. Reference to these supplementary materials is made when a particular source is pertinent in supporting a specific point in the text or in a table or figure.

The weapons deliveries indicated throughout the text and the Appendixes only represent confirmed deliveries as established by the following set of counting procedures:

1. If a discrepancy in figures appeared between sipri sources and *The Military Balance*, the larger figure was counted and the discrepancies were noted in worksheets for regional tables that appear in Chapter 7.

Since these contradictions in the data are too numerous to publish here, the author will be pleased to share his worksheets with interested researchers. For example, 149 discrepancies were noted between SIPRI and IISS and within each set for the Middle East. Another 151 discrepancies were identified for western Europe.

2. Where delivery data fluctuated over years within one of the sources, or between them, the number that was most consistent over time or that was most consistently cited by both sources was quoted. The objective was to arrive at a figure for deliveries that was as reliable as possible over time while taking into account the many lapses, lacunae, and discrepancies within the data.

3. Where delivery data were available only over a span of years, the total was entered in the first year and the span noted in the regional tables.

4. Delivery figures that were estimates were specifically noted in the footnotes to the regional tables. They were counted only if they were confirmed by a second source.

5. Data supplied by only one source were counted, but specifically footnoted in the author's worksheets.

6. All contracts for assemblage or licensed production were counted as transfers of French weapons. Where France cooperated in developing and producing arms, the products were counted as French transfers, even if the coproducer supplied them.

7. Third-party transfers of French arms were not counted.

There are notable discrepancies between reported deliveries, cited by SIPRI and IISS, and those found in French sources. It has only been possible to record these differences, not reconcile them.

Also vexing are the discrepancies to be found between sources for domestic and foreign deliveries and those for orders. The figures for orders cited in Table 2-6 for French aerospace products would appear to be authoritative since they derive from industry sources. Thus, for arms no longer in production, like the Alouette II, the higher figures cited in Table 2-6 would appear to be more reliable than the deliveries (not orders) found in Appendix A. However, deliveries and orders for Alouette IIs and IIIs should be the same since they are no longer manufactured in series. The higher figures, based on French sources, would appear to be correct, but there is no independent method of definitively verifying deliveries and orders.

Table 7-3, summarizing French arms deliveries to the Middle East, illustrates three common problems in reconciling sources.

The first relates to the contradictions within the same source over time, or between different sources, concerning dates and quantities of deliveries. The 1975 SIPRI *Yearbook*, for example, reports a Saudi Arabian order for an unknown number of "Thomson-CSF/Matra Crotale Shahine" missiles. Deliveries were expected to occur between 1975 and 1979. In the 1977 through 1979 editions, SIPRI revised that citation to an order for Shahine, with the expected delivery to begin in 1980. The 1982 edition cites no deliveries, but mentions a 1980 order for R-440 Crotale SAMs, of which 50 were estimated to have been delivered in 1980 and 1981, respectively. The 1983 edition lists a 1975 order for 4 AMX-30 Shahine, estimating that 2 each were delivered in 1980 and 1981. On the other hand, the 1981-1982 *Military Balance* lists 6 Crotale missiles. The 1980-1981 edition mentions these SAMs but gives no numbers. The 1982-1983 and 1983-1984 editions no longer cite Crotales, but list Shahines without indicating numbers. The Shahine is a version of the SAM Crotale, modified to Saudi specifications.

These problems were the most frequently encountered, but they are also representative of the second pattern: i.e., the frequent lack of specific information on weapons. The 1976 SIPRI *Yearbook*, for example, lists the delivery of 2,000 AS-11/12 missiles to Abu Dhabi in 1975. It also estimates that 3,650 SS-11/Harpon antitank missiles were delivered during that same year. Although all four of these missiles are similar, they are distinct versions. Similarly, the 1982 SIPRI *Yearbook* estimates that 15 M-3s were delivered to Bahrain in 1981. The 1981-1982 *Military Balance* lists 110 Panhard AML-90s and M-3s. The two vehicles are quite distinct in appearance and design capabilities.

Finally, the third pattern of problems relates to the question of who ordered, who paid for, and who supplied what? The first two questions arise, for example, with regard to Saudi Arabia. The 1975 and 1976 SIPRI *Yearbooks* report a 1974 order for 38 Mirage IIIEs, that "included tanks and missiles" for a total of $860 million. Only the 1977 edition reports that the aircraft were ordered for Egypt. No *Military Balance* ever mentions this order. Similarly, the 1983 SIPRI *Yearbook* indicates the delivery of 17 Mirage F1Cs to Jordan, stating that they were financed by Saudi Arabia. The 1982-1983 *Military Balance* lists 16 Mirage F1Cs; the 1983-1984 edition cites 23; but neither makes a reference to Saudi financing of the aircraft.

The question of who supplied what usually arises when coproduced weapons are transferred. The 1981 and 1982 SIPRI *Yearbooks* estimate, for example, that Egypt received 30 Otomat-2 coastal defense missiles in 1980 and 1981 from France. During those same years, Egypt also received the naval version (Otomat-1), which is Italian and was installed on British-made Ramadan fast patrol boats. The 1981-1982 through 1983-1984 *Military Balances* only cite Otomats in service on patrol boats and others on order. They do not indicate suppliers or versions of the missile.

Researchers familiar with arms transfer data are well acquainted with these problems. Additional commentary on these and related problems is found in the notes to Tables 6-5 and 7-4 as well as in briefer remarks throughout the manuscript.

There is an urgent need to develop a more reliable and accurate set of arms production and delivery data, including transfers of technology, as a key monitoring device of the international security system. The data from SIPRI, IISS, and ACDA are indispensable tools of analysis, but all have shortcomings. What is needed is a well-funded, fully computerized data bank covering number and types of weapons as well as consistent economic measures to estimate the value of transfers over time. It is also important that such an effort be as free as possible of governmental control to have an independent source to check governmental figures. Reliance on indigenous sources of information is also important. As the French case suggests, there is far more material available in the open record, particularly in open societies, than has been systematically reviewed and exploited by current research efforts. Gathering these data is a prerequisite for theory building, either in explaining global arms production and transfer or their implications for international stability, and for moderating hostilities and terminating them when they erupt. This case study has been framed in a way that is potentially applicable to the examination of other arms producers and suppliers. Systematic application of this research design and counting rules promises to develop a data base and theoretical framework of analysis that can yield insights about the present and future behavior of the global security system. No individual researcher can hope to cover so broad a field on a systematic, up-to-date effort. Only a team effort can do so.

French Arms Exports by Regions, Countries and Major Weapon Categories: 1960-1983

SOURCE: See the Note on Sources in the Appendix.

Table A-1. North Africa

Country	Attack Aircraft	Support Aircraft	Helicopters	Missiles	Armor	Naval Vessels
Algeria		28 Magister	8 Hughes 269A 7 SA-330 Puma		50 AML-60/90	
Libya	52 Mirage III 60 Mirage 5 32 Mirage F1 32 Mirage 50	5 Falcon	3 Alouette II 14 Alouette III 30 SA-341 Gazelle 9 Super Frelon	60 R-440 Crotale 20 MM-38 Exocet 60 Otomat 48 SS-12		9 La Combattante 1 CNIM Tank Landing Ship
Morocco	50 Mirage F1 24 Alpha-Jets	2 Beech Twin Bonanza 2 MS 760 Paris 6 MS 733 Alycon 6 MS 500 Criquet 8 Magister 12 Broussard 1 DH 114 Heron	5 Alouette II 4 Bell 47 40 SA-330 Puma 1 SA-365 Dauphin	300 R-550 Matra 96 R-440 Crotale 32 MM-38 Exocet	100 AML-60/90 40 M-8 Greyhound 36 Panhard EBR-75 15 AMX-105 135 AMX-13 36 AMX-155 400 VAB 30 AMX-10	1 Chamois Class Corvette 1 Frigate 1 Fougeux Class Patrol Boat 1 Patrol Vessel 1 PR-72P Fast Patrol Boat 1 Submarine Chaser 6 CMN Type 92 Fast Patrol Boats 1 Landing Craft (under 500 t.) 3 Transport Ships (over 500 t.)
Tunisia	12 F-86 Sabre	12 NA-T6 Texan 3 Flamant 3 Noratlas 2501	8 Alouette II 4 Alouette III 1 SA-330 Puma	48 SS-12 8 MM-40 Exocet	13 AML-60/90 15 Panhard EBR-75 33 AMX-13	1 Aviso A 69 Destroyer Escort 1 Corvette 1 Accia Coastal Mine Sweeper 3 P 48 Patrol Boats 9 Patrol Vessels 1 La Combattante
TOTAL	262	88	134	672	903	42

Table A-2. South Africa

Country	Attack Aircraft	Support Aircraft	Helicopters	Missiles	Armor	Naval Vessels
South Africa	72 Mirage III 48 Mirage F1	4 Airbus A-300 Tanker 9 Transall C-160	7 Alouette II 70 Alouette III 80 SA-330 Puma 16 Super Frelon	96 R-530 Matra 1,848 AS-12 60 AS-20/30 18 R-440 Crotale	1,500 AML-60/90 100 Panhard Eland 2	2 Aviso A-69 Class Destroyer Escort 1 Daphne Class Submarine (830 t.) 2 Daphne Class Submarine (350 t.)
TOTAL	120	13	173	2,022	1,600	5

Table A-3. Southern Africa (Francophone)

Country	Attack Aircraft	Support Aircraft	Helicopters	Missiles	Armor	Naval Vessels
Benin (Dahomey)		1 Cessna 337 1 Aero Commander 500 2 Broussard 5 Douglas C-47	1 Alouette II		15 M-8	
Cameroon	8 Alpha-Jet	6 Magister 7 Broussard 5 Douglas C-47 3 Flamant	2 Alouette II 3 Alouette III 2 SA-330 Puma 4 SA-342M Gazelle	48 Milan 8 MM-40 Exocet 8 SS-12	8 M-8	2 P-48 Type Patrol Boats 5 Patrol Vessels 3 Plascoa-Cannes Coastal Patrol Boats 1 La Combattante
Central African Republic	10 Douglas A-1D Skyraider	1 Falcon 8 Broussard 3 Douglas C-47 1 DC-4 2 Rallye 235 GT	1 Alouette II		5 VAB	
Chad	6 Douglas A-1D Skyraider	5 Cessna 337 3 Broussard 2 Douglas C-47 1 DC-4 1 C-212-200	1 Alouette II 4 SA-330 Puma		4 ERC-90 20 Panhard M-3	
Djibouti			2 AS-350 Ecureuil			1 Tecimar Type Gun Boat

Table A-3 (*cont.*)

Country	Attack Aircraft	Support Aircraft	Helicopters	Missiles	Armor	Naval Vessels
Gabon	4 Jaguar 7 Mirage 5	2 Cessna 337 2 Falcon 4 Broussard 3 Douglas C-47 3 Nord 262 A-1 Fregate	2 Alouette II 6 Alouette III 4 SA-330 Puma	12 SS-12	30 AML-60/90 15 M-3	2 Patrol Vessels 1 Esterel Type 42M Coastal Patrol Boat
Guinea			2 Alouette III 1 SA-341 Gazelle 1 SA-330 Puma			
Ivory Coast	6 Alpha-Jet	3 Cessna 337 2 Falcon 4 Cessna 150 4 Broussard 3 Douglas C-47 1 Flamant	2 Alouette II 3 Alouette III 4 SA-365 Dauphin 4 SA-330 Puma	24 SS-12	17 AML-60/90 15 M-8 10 AMX-13	2 CN-Darachon Fast Patrol Boats 1 P-48 Type Patrol Boat 2 Patrol Vessels 1 Submarine Chaser
Madagascar		4 Cessna FR-172 7 Broussard 3 Douglas C-47 2 Flamant	2 Alouette II 1 Alouette III 1 Bell 47		15 M-8	1 Patrol Vessel (over 500 t.) 2 Patrol Vessels (under 500 t.) 2 YMS Type Patrol Boats 1 DTCN Batran Class Landing Craft

Niger		2 Cessna 337 4 Broussard 4 Douglas C-47 1 Flamant 4 Noratlas			8 M-8 8 M-20 30 AML-60/90	1 Patrol Vessel
People's Republic of the Congo		3 Broussard 1 Douglas C-47 2 Nord 262 A-1 Fregate	1 Alouette II 5 Alouette II/III			
Senegal		1 Cessna 337 2 Magister 4 Broussard 3 Douglas C-47 6 F-27 Friendship 1 DHC-6 Srs 300 4 Rallye 180T/235CA	2 Alouette II 2 Bell 47 1 SA-341 Gazelle	62 Roland 22 SS-12	15 AML-60/90 15 M-8	3 P-48 Type Patrol Boats 2 Patrol Vessels 3 VC-Type Patrol Boats 1 EDIC Class Landing Craft 2 PR-72 Fast Patrol Boats
Togo	5 Mirage 5 5 Alpha-Jet	2 Cessna 337 5 Magister 2 Broussard 1 Douglas C-47 1 Transall C-160	1 SA-315 Lama 1 SA-330 Puma		15 APC	2 P-32 Type Coastal Patrol Boats 3 Patrol Vessels 1 River Boat
Burkino Faso (Upper Volta)		1 Cessna 337 1 Aero Commander 500 3 Broussard 2 Douglas C-47 2 Nord 262 A-1 Fregate	2 SA-365 Dauphin		15 APC	
TOTAL	51	166	68	184	260	45

Table A-4. Southern Africa (Non-Francophone)

Country	Attack Aircraft	Support Aircraft	Helicopters	Missiles	Armor	Naval Vessels
Angola		6 Noratlas	30 Alouette III 17 SA-365 Dauphin			
Burundi			5 Alouette II/III		12 ACs 18 AML-60/90 9 M-3	
Ethiopia			4 Alouette II 10 Alouette III 1 SA-330 Puma		56 AML-60/90	
Ghana			5 Alouette III			
Guinea-Bissau		1 Cessna 337				
Kenya			3 Alouette III 10 SA-330 Puma		30 AML-60/90 10 Panhard M-3	
Malawi			1 Alouette III 1 SA-330 Puma			
Mauritania		8 Cessna 337 4 Broussard 3 Douglas C-47 1 Douglas C-54			20 AML-60/90 15 M-8	3 Patrol Vessels 1 Patra Class FAC
Mozambique						
Nigeria	12 Alpha-Jet	2 B-26	4 Alouette II/III 4 Alouette II/III 6 Alouette III 13 SA-330 Puma	36 MM-38 Exocet 18 Otomat	144 AML-60/90 28 AMX-30 Roland	3 La Combattante Guided Missile Patrol Boats

Rwanda		3 Magister 2 Douglas C-47 1 Rallye 235 GT	1 Alouette II 2 Alouette III 6 SA-342 Gazelle 15 SA-330 Puma		12 AML-245	
Sudan	24 Mirage 50				50 AMX-10 11 AMX-155 15 M-3	
Uganda				200 SS-11	80 SAVIEM AC	
Zaire	17 Mirage 5	20 Cessna 337 9 Magister	5 Alouette II 15 Alouette III 30 SA-330 Puma 1 Super Frelon	37 AS-30	250 AML-60/90 30 Machine Gun Carriers	12 Patrol Vessels
Zimbabwe		20 Cessna 337	8 Alouette III			
TOTAL	53	80	197	291	790	19

Table A-5. Central America

Country	Attack Aircraft	Support Aircraft	Helicopters	Missiles	Armor	Naval Vessels
Dominican Republic			2 Alouette II 1 Alouette III 1 SA-365 Dauphin		20 AMX-13	
El Salvador	4 Super Mystère 18 Ouragan MD 450	7 Magister	1 Alouette III 3 SA-315 Lama		12 AMX-13	
Honduras	12 Super Mystère		1 Alouette II			
Mexico			7 Alouette II 8 Alouette III 3 SA-330 Puma		40 ERC-90 Lynx	
Nicaragua			3 Alouette III			2 Patrol Craft
TOTAL	34	7	30		72	2

Table A-6. South America

Country	Attack Aircraft	Support Aircraft	Helicopters	Missiles	Armor	Naval Vessels
Argentina	45 T-28 Fennec 30 Mirage III 13 Mirage 5 14 Super Etendard	48 MS 760 Paris 10 Broussard	2 Alouette II 10 Alouette III 3 SO 1221 Djinn 2 Lynx 15 SA-330 Puma	90 R-530 Matra 36 AS-11/12 30 AS-12 24 MM-38 Exocet 20 SS-11 20 AM-39 Exocet 72 Roland 48 MM-40 Exocet	24 AMX-155 120 AMX-13 24 AML VTT	3 Aviso A-69 Class Destroyer Escort 2 La Combattante Guided Missile Patrol Boats
Bolivia					4 Tanks	
Brazil	12 T-28 Fennec 9 Mirage III	30 MS 760 Paris 7 Magister 7 Atlantique 1150	10 SA-315 Lama 12 Lynx 6 SA-330 Puma 20 AS-350M Esquilo	72 R-530 Matra 1,152 AS-11 576 AS-12 80 Roland 36 MM-38 Exocet		
Chile		3 PBY-SA Catalina	12 Alouette III 6 SA-315 Lama 40 SA-330 Puma 1 AS-332 Super Puma	150 AS-11 300 AS-11/12 150 AS-12	47 AMX-13 71 AMX-30	1 Oiler
Colombia	18 Mirage 5 12 Jaguar 18 Mirage F1		27 SA-315 Lama			
Ecuador		3 Magister	8 Alouette III 4 SA-315 Lama 2 SA-330 Puma 4 AS-332 Super Puma	4 MM-38 Exocet 8 MM-40 Exocet 84 R-550 Matra 30 MM-40 Exocet	27 AML-60/90 6 AMX-155 81 AMX-13	
Peru	28 Mirage 5	5 MS 760 Paris 1 Mystère 20	6 Alouette II 18 Alouette III 5 SA-315 Lama	33 AS-30 84 MM-38 Exocet	118 AMX-13	6 PR-72P Patrol Boats
Venezuela	10 Mirage III 6 Mirage 5		20 Alouette II/III	36 Otomat 36 Otomat	30 AMX-155 40 AMX-13 142 AMX-30	6 Esterel-Cannes Type 32 M Patrol Boats
TOTAL	215	114	233	3,171	734	18

Table A-7. East Asia

Country	Attack Aircraft	Support Aircraft	Helicopters	Missiles	Armor	Naval Vessels
Brunei				36 MM-38 Exocet 48 SS-12		
Burma						
Cambodia	30 Douglas A-1D Skyraider	27 MS 733 Alcyon 4 Magister 6 Flamant 12 Garda 6Y-80 Horizon	13 Alouette III 10 Alouette II 2 Alouette III		15 AML-60/90 15 M-3 20 AMX-13 50 Military Vehicles	1 Gunboat 5 Patrol Vessels 1 EDIC Class Landing Craft 6 Landing Craft (under 500 t.)
Indonesia		3 Noratlas	17 Alouette III 19 SA-330 Puma 13 Super Frelon 11 SA-365 Dauphin	200 Entac 36 MM-38 Exocet	1,000 AMX VCI 280 AMX-13	
People's Republic of China						
Laos		1 Cessna 185 Skywagon 10 MS 500 Criquet	2 Alouette II 4 Alouette III		15 M-3 15 M-8 Greyhound	
Malaysia			33 Alouette III 13 SA-341 Gazelle	88 MM-38 Exocet 96 SS-12	44 Panhard AML VTT	4 La Combattante Guided Missile Patrol Boats
Singapore		12 T33-A	8 Alouette III		150 AMX-13	
South Korea			8 Alouette III			
South Vietnam	25 Grumman F-8F Bearcat	16 Douglas C-47			50 AMX-13 10 M-24 Chaffee	1 Patrol Vessel 3 YMS Type Mine Sweepers 16 Landing Craft (under 500 t.) 2 Landing Ships (over 500 t.) 1 Oiler 1 Training Ship
Taiwan						
Thailand				24 Otomat 60 MM-38 Exocet		
TOTAL	55	91	153	588	1,664	41

Table A-8. South Asia

Country	Attack Aircraft	Support Aircraft	Helicopters	Missiles	Armor	Naval Vessels
Bangladesh						
India	110 Mystère IV 104 Ouragan MD 450 16 Jaguar	12 Magister 30 Alice 1050	4 Alouette III 247 Alouette III 100 SA-315 Lama	50 Entac 50 AS-30 2,150 SS-11	150 AMX-13	
Nepal			1 Alouette III 2 SA-330 Puma			
Pakistan	36 Mirage III 70 Mirage 5	1 Falcon 5 Atlantique 1150	14 Alouette III 35 SA-330 Puma 4 Super Frelon	312 R-550 Matra 192 R-530 Matra 60 AM-39 Exocet 9 R-440 Crotale		2 Agosta Class Submarines 5 Daphne Class Submarines
Sri Lanka			1 SA-365 Dauphin			
TOTAL	336	48	408	2,823	150	7

Table A-9. Middle East

Country	Attack Aircraft	Support Aircraft	Helicopters	Missiles	Armor	Naval Vessels
Abu Dhabi (*U.A.E.*)	18 Mirage III 32 Mirage 5		5 Alouette III 5 SA-330 Puma	3,650 Harpon 2,000 AS-11/12 100 R-440 Crotale 24 MM-40 Exocet	16 AMX-155 150 AML-60/90	
Bahrain						
Dubai (*U.A.E.*)		1 Falcon		24 MM-38 Exocet	110 Panhard M-3	
Egypt	73 Mirage III 28 Mirage 5 10 Alpha-Jet [5 Mirage 2000]	1 Falcon	66 SA-341 Gazelle	100 R-550 Matra 624 Hot 24 AS-12 20 R-440 Crotale 30 SS-10 30 Otomat	20 AMX-105 20 AMX-13	
Iran		5 Falcon 1 MS 760 Paris	16 Super Frelon	36 AS-12 500 SS-11 500 SS-12		12 Kaman Class Fast Patrol Boats
Iraq	36 Mirage F1 5 Super Etendard	2 Falcon	36 Alouette III 60 SA-341 Gazelle 40 SA-330 Puma 12 Super Frelon	144 R-550 Matra 180 Hot 120 AM-39 Exocet	70 AML-60/90 100 ERC-90 50 AMX-10 100 AMX-30 100 VCR-6	

	Combat Aircraft	Trainers / Transport	Helicopters	Missiles	Armor	Naval
Israel	72 Mirage III 60 Mosquito 60 Mystère IV 24 Super Mystère 60 Ouragan MD 450 24 SO 4050 Vautour	125 Magister 5 Broussard 32 Noratlas	20 Alouette III 13 Super Frelon	100 R-530 Matra 150 Entac 300 AS-30 2 MD-660 200 SS-10 150 SS-11	80 AML-60/90 300 M-2/3 100 M-5 30 AMX-105 150 AMX-13 100 M-4 Sherman	12 Saar Class Gunboats 9 Torpedo Boats
Jordan	23 Mirage F1	1 Falcon	18 Alouette III	120 R-550 Matra 120 R-530 Matra 1,200 SS-11	20 AMX-155 34 AMX-13	
Kuwait	20 Mirage F1		24 SA-341 Gazelle 10 SA-330 Puma			
Lebanon	14 Mirage III	12 Magister	4 Alouette II 19 Alouette III 4 SA-341 Gazelle 6 SA-330 Puma	15 R-530 Matra 200 Milan 96 SS-11 96 SS-12	30 Panhard AML VTT 77 AMX-13 5 VAB	3 Byblos Class Patrol Boats 4 Patrol Vessels 1 EDIC Class Landing Ship
North Yemen			2 Alouette III			
Oman	12 Jaguar	1 Falcon	4 SA-330 Puma	72 R-550 Matra 60 MM-38 Exocet 6 MM-40 Exocet		
Qatar	8 Alpha-Jet 3 Mirage F1		4 SA-341 Gazelle 3 SA-330 Puma	16 MM-40 Exocet	136 VAB APC 30 AMX-10 24 AMX-30	2 La Combattante
Saudi Arabia		12 Cessna FR-172 2 Falcon	30 Alouette III	2,000 Harpon 2,000 SS-11 96 Shahine	720 AML-90 749 AMX-10 480 AMX-30	
Syria		2 Falcon 6 Douglas C-47	66 SA-341 Gazelle 15 Super Frelon	246 Hot		3 CH Class Patrol Boats
TOTAL	582	208	482	15,351	3,801	46

Table A-10. Western/Eastern Europe

Country	Attack Aircraft	Support Aircraft	Helicopters	Missiles	Armor	Naval Vessels
Austria		18 Magister	16 Alouette II 25 Alouette III		70 AMX-13	
Belgium	135 Mirage 5 33 Alpha-Jet	4 Falcon 50 Magister 2 MS 730	83 Alouette II 3 Alouette III 5 SA-330 Puma 11 Sikorsky S-58	95 Entac 96 MM-38 Exocet 50 SS-10 800 Milan 100 SS-11	700 AMX-13	
Denmark			11 Alouette II 7 Lynx	20 Otomat		
Federal Republic of Germany	90 Alpha-Jet	15 Atlantique 1150 108 Noratlas 89 Transall		1,793 Milan[a] 100 Roland[a] 28 MM-38 Exocet 350 SS-11	100 Armored Vehicles	20 Type 140 Guided Missile Boats
Finland		80 Magister				
Greece	40 Mirage F1		8 Alouette II 5 Alouette III	540 Milan 66 MM-38 Exocet	100 Armored Vehicles 240 AMX-10 285 AMX-30	4 Gunboats 14 La Combattante Guided Missile Patrol Boats 2 Missile Boats
Ireland		13 Cessna FR-172 6 Magister	8 Alouette III 2 SA-341 Gazelle 1 SA-330 Puma		52 AML-60/90 30 Panhard AML VTT	

Italy		18 Atlantique 1150		2,000 Milan		
Netherlands		9 Atlantique 1150	26 Lynx 60 Alouette III	20 Milan	131 AMX-13	
Norway		1 Falcon	6 Lynx	40 Roland II Launchers		
Portugal		32 Cessna 337 4 Broussard 12 Noratlas	7 Alouette II 80 Alouette III 12 SA-330 Puma 45 Alouette III		100 Panhard EBR-75	4 Daphne Class Submarines
Romania			35 SA-330 Puma			
Spain	30 Mirage III 47 Mirage F1	4 Falcon	13 Alouette III 21 SA-330 Puma	60 Hot	188 AML-60/90 275 AMX-30	4 Daphne Class Submarines
Sweden			28 Alouette II			
Switzerland	68 Mirage III		62 Alouette II 88 Alouette III 4 SO-1221 Djinn	45 AS-30	200 AMX-13	
Turkey	5 Republic RF-84F	20 Transall		2,480 Milan 100 SS-11		1 Boom Defense Vessel
United Kingdom	126 Jaguar[a]		17 Alouette II 214 SA-341 Gazelle[a] 75 Lynx[a] 40 SA-330 Puma[a]	5,000 Milan 1,000 AS-30 396 MM-38 Exocet 250 SS-10		
Yugoslavia		2 Falcon	40 Alouette III 38 SA-341 Gazelle[a]		35 AMX-13	1 Corvette 1 Destroyer 3 Mine Sweepers
TOTAL	574	487	1,096	15,429	2,506	54

[a] Coproduced with France; see Table 3-2.

Selected Major Weapons Systems by Recipient Country: 1950-1983

Aircraft, High Performance

Alpha-Jet: Belgium, Cameroon, Egypt, F. R. Germany, Ivory Coast, Morocco, Nigeria, Qatar, Togo

Jaguar: Ecuador, Gabon, India, Oman, United Kingdom

Mirage F1: Ecuador, Greece, Iraq, Kuwait, Jordan, Libya, Morocco, Qatar, South Africa, Spain

Mirage III: Abu Dhabi, Argentina, Australia, Brazil, Egypt, Israel, Lebanon, Libya, Malaysia, Pakistan, Saudi Arabia, South Africa, Spain, Switzerland, Venezuela

Mirage 5: Abu Dhabi, Argentina, Belgium, Colombia, Egypt, Gabon, Libya, Pakistan, Peru, Togo, Venezuela, Zaire

Mirage 50: Libya, Sudan

Mystère IV: India, Israel

Ouragan: India, Israel, El Salvador

Super Mystère: El Salvador, Honduras, Israel

Transport, Trainer, and Other Aircraft

Alize: India

Atlantique 1150: Brazil, F. R. Germany, Italy, Netherlands, Pakistan

Broussard: Argentina, Benin, Cameroon, Central African Republic, Chad, Gabon, Israel, Ivory Coast, Madagascar, Mauritania, Morocco, Niger, People's Republic of the Congo, Portugal, Senegal, Togo, Upper Volta

Magister: Algeria, Austria, Bangladesh, Belgium, Brazil, Cambodia, Cameroon, Ecuador, El Salvador, Finland, Ireland, Israel, Lebanon, Morocco, Rwanda, Senegal, Togo, Uganda, Zaire

Noratlas: Angola, F. R. Germany, Indonesia, Israel, Niger, Portugal, Tunisia

Transall: F. R. Germany, South Africa, Togo, Turkey

Helicopters

Alouette II: Argentina, Austria, Belgium, Benin, Cambodia, Cameroon, Central African Republic, Chad, Denmark, Dominican Republic, Ethiopia, Gabon, Greece, Honduras, Ivory Coast, Laos, Lebanon, Libya, Madagascar, Mexico, Morocco, People's Republic of the Congo, Peru, Portugal, Rwanda, Senegal, South Africa, Sweden, Switzerland, Tunisia, United Kingdom, Zaire

Alouette II or III (not specified): Burundi, F. R. Germany, Mozambique, Nigeria, People's Republic of the Congo, Venezuela

Alouette III: Abu Dhabi, Angola, Argentina, Austria, Bangladesh, Belgium, Burma, Cambodia, Cameroon, Chile, Dominican Republic, Ecuador, El Salvador, Ethiopia, Gabon, Ghana, Greece, Guinea, India, Indonesia, Iraq, Ireland, Israel, Ivory Coast, Jordan, Kenya, Laos, Lebanon, Libya, Madagascar, Malawi, Malaysia, Mexico, Nepal, Netherlands, Nigeria, North Yemen, Pakistan, People's Republic of China, Peru, Portugal, Rhodesia, Romania, Rwanda, Saudi Arabia, Singapore, South Africa, South Korea, Spain, Switzerland, Tunisia, Yugoslavia, Zaire

Gazelle: Egypt, Guinea, Iraq, Ireland, Kuwait, Lebanon, Libya, Malaysia, Qatar, Rwanda, Senegal, Syria, United Kingdom, Yugoslavia

Lama: Bolivia, Chile, Colombia, Ecuador, El Salvador, India, Peru, Togo

Lynx: Argentina, Brazil, Denmark, Netherlands, Norway, United Kingdom

Puma: Abu Dhabi, Algeria, Argentina, Belgium, Brazil, Cameroon, Chad, Chile, Ecuador, Ethiopia, Gabon, Guinea, Indonesia, Iraq, Ireland, Ivory Coast, Kenya, Kuwait, Lebanon, Malawi, Mexico, Morocco, Nepal, Nigeria, Oman, Pakistan, Portugal, Qatar, Romania, South Africa, Spain, Sudan, Togo, Tunisia, United Kingdom, Zaire

Super Frelon: Iran, Iraq, Israel, Libya, Pakistan, People's Republic of China, South Africa, Syria, Zaire

Missiles

R-530 Matra: Argentina, Brazil, Israel, Kuwait, Lebanon, Pakistan, South Africa

R-550 Matra: Ecuador, Egypt, Iraq, Kuwait, Libya, Morocco, Oman, Pakistan

Entac[a]: Australia, Belgium, Canada, India, Indonesia, Iran, Israel, Morocco, Norway, South Africa, Switzerland, United States

Harpon[a]: Abu Dhabi, F. R Germany, Iraq, Kuwait, Saudi Arabia

Hot: Egypt, Iraq, Spain, Syria

Milan[b]: Belgium, F. R. Germany, Greece, Italy, Lebanon, Libya, Netherlands, Syria, Turkey, United Kingdom

AS-11: Brazil, Chile

AS-12: Argentina, Brazil, Chile, Egypt, Iran, South Africa, United Kingdom

R-440 Crotale: Abu Dhabi, Egypt, Iraq, Libya, Morocco, Pakistan, Saudi Arabia, South Africa[c]

Roland: Brazil, F. R. Germany, Norway, Senegal

AM-39 Exocet: Iraq, Pakistan

MM-38 Exocet[d]: Argentina, Australia, Bahrain, Belgium, Brazil, Brunei, F. R. Germany, Greece, Indonesia, Libya, Malaysia, Morocco, Nigeria, Oman, Peru, South Africa, Syria, Thailand, United Kingdom

MM-40 Exocet: Argentina, Cameroon, Colombia, Ecuador, Oman, Qatar, Tunisia, United Arab Emirates

SS-10: Belgium, Egypt, Israel, Nigeria, United Kingdom

SS-11: Argentina, Belgium, F. R. Germany, India, Iran, Israel, Kuwait, Lebanon, Saudi Arabia, Turkey, Uganda, United States

SS-12: Argentina, Brunei, Cameroon, Gabon, Iran, Ivory Coast, Lebanon, Libya, Malaysia, Senegal, Tunisia

Armor

AML-60/90: Abu Dhabi, Algeria, Burundi, Cambodia, Ecuador, Ethiopia, Gabon, Iraq, Ireland, Israel, Ivory Coast, Kenya, Mauritania, Morocco, Niger, Nigeria, Pakistan, Rwanda, Saudi Arabia, Senegal, South Africa, Spain, Tunisia, Zaire

AMX-10: Greece, Indonesia, Iraq, Qatar, Saudi Arabia, Sudan

AMX-13: Argentina, Austria, Belgium, Cambodia, Chile, Dominican Republic, Ecuador, Egypt, El Salvador, Guatemala, India, Indonesia, Israel, Ivory Coast, Kuwait, Lebanon, Morocco, Netherlands, Peru, Republic of Yemen, Singapore, South Vietnam, Switzerland, Tunisia, Venezuela, Yugoslavia

AMX-30: Chile, Greece, Iraq, Nigeria, Qatar, Saudi Arabia, Spain, Venezuela

Patrol Boats[e]

CMN Type 92: Morocco

Esterel-Cannes Type 32M: Venezuela

Kaman: Iran

La Combattante: Argentina, Cameroon, Greece, Libya, Malaysia, Nigeria, Qatar, Tunisia

P-48: Cameroon, Ivory Coast, Senegal, Tunisia

PR-72P: Morocco, Peru

Saar: Israel

Type 140: Germany

Submarines

Agosta Class: Pakistan
Daphne Class: Pakistan, Portugal, South Africa, Spain

Destroyers, Corvettes

Aviso A69: Argentina, Portugal, South Africa, Tunisia
Chamois Class: Morocco

SOURCES: See the Note on Sources in the Appendix.

[a] The Entac and Harpon are versions of the SS-10 and SS-11 respectively.

[b] According to *Le Monde* (February 7, 1978), the Milan is deployed by 16 countries. Not all may have been supplied by France, as the manufacturer (Euromissile) is a French-German venture.

[c] The R-440 Crotale is labeled the Cactus in South Africa and Shahine in Saudi Arabia.

[d] *Le Monde* (October 25, 1978) indicates that Exocet missiles can be found in 23 navies around the world.

[e] Includes naval craft of less than 500 tons. The specific types listed here are only a select sample of the identifiable exports. Data on these craft tend to be fragmentary and scattered, as designation of types may vary by recipient countries. In addition, small naval craft are often fitted and refitted at different dockyards within France or in other countries. For a more complete list of French small naval craft deliveries, see Appendix A.

APPENDIX C

Major Conventional Weapons Systems Delivered to the Third World by Major Suppliers: 1972-1981

Supplier	1972	1973	1974	1975	1976	1977	1978	1979	1980	1981	Total	%
Supersonic Combat Aircraft[a]												
U.S.S.R.	235	395	280	250	310	440	355	525	490	425	3,705	54.3
Other European Communist[b]	—	35	—	—	—	—	—	—	—	—	35	0.5
United States	70	150	175	220	235	190	160	125	50	165	1,540	22.6
Major West European[c]	(65)[d]	74	(45)[d]	(45)[d]	30	(65)[d]	(60)[d]	(55)[d]	32	(35)[d]	136	2.0
France[e]	115	36	85	56	30	116	69	56	53	71	687	10.0
Minor West European[f]	15	—	5	—	—	—	—	—	—	—	20	.3
Others[g]	90	70	20	125	20	30	90	100	120	40	705	10.3
TOTAL	525	760	565	651	625	776	674	806	745	701	6,828	100.0
Subsonic Combat and Other Military Aircraft												
U.S.S.R.	70	115	110	45	105	145	100	190	100	100	1,080	13.7
Other European Communist	40	40	30	55	105	70	55	40	50	85	570	7.2
United States	720	580	355	315	375	405	235	35	65	150	3,235	41.1
Major West European	113	186	135	132	104	(65)[d]	115	102	106	73	1,066	13.6
France	2	14	20	33	36	82	35	8	24	12	266	3.4
Minor West European	45	30	30	80	75	15	90	70	105	130	670	8.5
Other	45	50	120	150	65	100	80	90	150	125	975	12.4
TOTAL	1,035	1,015	800	810	865	817	710	535	600	675	7,862	99.9

Helicopters

U.S.S.R.	95	105	60	85	90	70	185	270	190	195	1,345	24.5
Other European Communist	—	—	—	—	—	5	10	20	30	35	100	1.8
United States	550	740	145	120	155	55	30	30	95	15	1,935	35.3
Major West European	112	110	106	93	115	(205)[d]	22	53	63	75	749	13.6
France	58	40	59	152	160	217	228	117	92	70	1,193	21.7
Minor West European	—	5	—	20	—	5	5	5	5	5	50	0.9
Other	—	5	25	30	5	5	25	10	5	5	115	2.1
TOTAL	815	1,005	395	500	525	357	505	505	480	400	5,487	99.9

Surface-to-Air Missiles

U.S.S.R.	1,340	1,900	2,180	2,500	3,650	6,015	920	3,845	600	300	23,250	63.0
Other European Communist	—	—	50	50	50	50	50	50	—	—	300	0.8
United States	400	—	115	870	645	2,340	965	2,780	1,295	480	9,890	26.8
Major West European	170	157	230	116	485	837	1	(10)[d]	510	27	2,533	6.9
France	40	78	—	9	—	78	24	167	—	13	409	1.1
Minor West European	—	—	—	—	—	—	—	45	85	—	130	0.4
Other	—	—	180	—	—	—	—	—	—	200	380	1.0
TOTAL	1,950	2,135	2,755	3,545	4,830	9,320	1,960	6,887	2,490	1,020	36,892	100.0

Major Surface Warships

U.S.S.R.	2	4	3	3	2	4	6	9	6	7	46	17.8
Other European Communist	—	—	—	3	1	3	2	3	—	1	13	5.0
United States	5	14	25	20	7	9	2	7	4	10	103	39.9

Appendix C (cont.)

Supplier	1972	1973	1974	1975	1976	1977	1978	1979	1980	1981	Total	%
Major West European	3	6	5	4	3	5	8	7	8	15	64	24.8
France	—	—	1	—	—	1	2	2	—	1	7	2.7
Minor West European	—	1	—	—	1	—	1	1	5	3	12	4.6
Other	—	—	—	—	—	2	2	3	2	4	13	5.0
TOTAL	10	25	34	30	14	24	23	32	25	41	258	99.8
Minor Surface Warships and Guided Missile Patrol Boats												
U.S.S.R.	28	16	19	30	14	27	32	51	48	21	286	24.6
Other European Communist	1	4	—	4	—	—	—	—	5	—	14	1.2
United States	28	17	62	55	21	6	3	6	19	5	222	19.1
Major West European	30	12	15	55	50	40	4	33	22	24	285	24.5
France	—	5	14	7	7	9	15	7	4	5	73	6.3
Minor West European	—	—	—	33	—	2	1	10	10	24	80	6.9
Other	34	18	10	31	15	11	19	29	25	9	201	17.3
TOTAL	121	72	120	215	107	95	74	136	133	87	1,161	99.9

Submarines												
U.S.S.R.	2	—	7	1	1	—	2	2	1	1	17	23.6
Other European Communist	—	—	—	—	—	—	—	—	—	—	—	—
United States	5	5	8	3	—	2	1	—	—	—	24	33.3
Major West European	3	1	1	3	3	5	1	—	1	4	22	30.6
France	—	—	—	—	1	1	—	1	1	—	4	5.6
Minor West European	—	—	—	—	—	1	—	—	—	—	1	1.4
Other	2	—	2	—	—	—	—	—	—	—	4	5.6
TOTAL	12	6	18	7	5	9	4	3	3	5	72	100.1
Light Armor												
U.S.S.R.	955	1,225	955	1,090	1,340	1,855	2,250	1,915	1,635	1,005	14,225	36.5
Other European Communist	300	30	125	250	95	110	20	—	35	—	965	2.5
United States	910	1,060	1,565	905	1,820	2,560	1,275	1,025	2,890	470	14,480	37.2
Major West European	(450)[d]	75	(195)[d]	250	600	(425)[d]	455	(930)[d]	350	626	2,356	6.0
France	856	110	402	—	—	737	320	1,205	290	259	4,179	10.7
Minor West European	—	30	50	—	—	—	15	50	55	30	230	0.6
Other	110	130	190	185	320	460	145	800	90	85	2,515	6.4
TOTAL	3,131	2,660	3,287	2,680	4,175	5,722	4,480	4,995	5,345	2,475	38,950	99.9

Appendix C (cont.)

Supplier	1972	1973	1974	1975	1976	1977	1978	1979	1980	1981	Total	%
Tanks and Self-Propelled Guns												
U.S.S.R.	770	2,220	1,500	590	1,075	1,430	1,150	2,435	990	1,060	13,220	40.5
Other European Communist	280	525	215	645	695	435	560	530	340	325	4,550	13.9
United States	430	760	1,110	1,030	890	850	930	450	734	255	7,440	22.8
Major West European	(205)[d]	235	408	(210)[d]	42	(325)[d]	(275)[d]	(70)[d]	(55)[d]	(110)[d]	685	2.1
France	231	30	12	226	218	481	409	260	317	112	2,296	7.0
Minor West European	—	—	—	—	45	55	165	150	95	140	650	2.0
Other	700	575	480	255	420	305	130	280	185	455	3,785	11.6
TOTAL	2,411	4,345	3,725	2,746	3,385	3,556	3,344	4,105	2,662	2,347	32,626	99.9

SOURCES: French delivery data were obtained from: Stockholm International Peace Research Institute (SIPRI), *World Armaments and Disarmament, SIPRI Yearbooks 1972-1982* (Cambridge: Oelgeschlager, Gunn, and Hain, 1982). Publishers vary over this decade. The International Institute for Strategic Studies (IISS), *The Military Balance, 1972-1982* (London: The International Institute for Strategic Studies, 1982). All other delivery data were taken from U.S., Department of State, *Conventional Arms Transfers in the Third World, 1972-1981*, Special Report No. 102, August 1982 (Washington, D.C.: Bureau of Public Affairs, U.S. Department of State), pp. 14-17. These data from a U.S. State Department document are based on data supplied by the American intelligence community. They are supplied to the Arms Control and Disarmament Agency for its annual *World Military Expenditures and Arms Transfers* (interviews, Washington, D.C., 1978, 1981, and 1982).
[a] The classification of weapons systems was taken from the U.S. Department of State, *Conventional Arms Transfers in the Third World, 1972-1981*, Special Report No. 102, August 1982. These classifications are:
Supersonic combat aircraft: all supersonic combat aircraft.

Subsonic combat and other military aircraft: These are two State Department categories combined into one. Included are subsonic bombers, fighters, attack aircraft, armed trainers and light strike planes, transports, communication or utility aircraft, antisubmarine warfare aircraft, and unarmed trainers.

Helicopters: all helicopters.

Surface-to-air missiles: all surface-to-air missiles.

Major surface warships: destroyers, destroyer escorts and larger size, tank landing ships, and larger amphibious warfare units.

Minor surface warships and guided missile patrol boats: patrol escorts and smaller naval vessels, mine sweepers, landing craft, and guided missile patrol boats. As a general rule the 500-ton mark was used to divide major and minor surface ships.

Submarines: all submarines.

Light armor: armored personnel carriers, infantry combat and armored reconnaissance vehicles, and scout cars.

Tanks and self-propelled guns: includes light, medium, and heavy tanks, as well as self-propelled guns.

[b] "Other European Communist": Albania, Bulgaria, Czechoslovakia, East Germany, Hungary, Poland, Romania, and Yugoslavia.

[c] "Major West European": West Germany, Italy, the United Kingdom, and France.

[d] Because of the serious discrepancies between SIPRI, IISS, and State Department sources with respect to deliveries by France, Britain, West Germany, and Italy, a complicated set of counting rules was adopted: In those instances where Major West European deliveries, as cited by the State Department, exceeded figures based on SIPRI and IISS data, I subtracted these latter figures from the totals given by the State Department; in those instances where the French deliveries, based on SIPRI and IISS, exceeded Major West European totals (including France as cited by the State Department), I noted the discrepancy by placing the number cited by the State Department in parentheses. Those numbers cited in parentheses are not included in the total for Major West European suppliers.

[e] French data were largely obtained from *The Military Balance* and SIPRI *Yearbooks*. For specific counting guidelines see the Note on Sources in the Appendix.

[f] "Minor West European": Austria, Belgium, Finland, Greece, Ireland, the Netherlands, Norway, Portugal, Spain, Sweden, Switzerland, and Turkey.

[g] "Other": Brazil, Israel, China, and other states or private arms dealers.

APPENDIX D

Regional Distribution of Major Weapons Systems by Suppliers: 1972-1976, 1977-1981

NEAR EAST AND SOUTH ASIA

Tanks and Self-Propelled Guns

Supplier	1972–1976 No.	%	1977–1981 No.	%
U.S.S.R.	4,640	40.5	5,205	46.4
U.S.	2,525	22.0	2,430	21.7
France	378	3.3	1,096	9.8
Other	3,907	34.1	2,480	22.1
TOTAL	11,450	99.9	11,211	100.0

Subsonic Combat and Other Military Aircraft

Supplier	1972–1976 No.	%	1977–1981 No.	%
U.S.S.R.	230	19.2	250	19.6
U.S.	500	41.8	320	25.1
France	29	2.4	46	3.6
Other	436	36.5	659	51.7
TOTAL	1,195	99.9	1,275	100.0

Light Armor

Supplier	1972–1976 No.	%	1977–1981 No.	%
U.S.S.R.	4,285	43.0	6,500	38.1
U.S.	3,280	32.9	7,210	42.3
France	30	0.3	1,100	6.5
Other	2,360	23.7	2,210	13.0
TOTAL	9,955	99.9	17,020	99.9

Minor Surface Warships/Guided Missile Patrol Boats

Supplier	1972–1976 No.	%	1977–1981 No.	%
U.S.S.R.	56	27.0	43	23.1
U.S.	23	11.1	10	5.4
France	8	3.9	16	8.6
Other	120	58.0	117	62.9
TOTAL	207	100.0	186	100.0

Helicopters

Supplier	1972–1976 No.	%	1977–1981 No.	%
U.S.S.R.	280	20.8	620	49.4
U.S.	285	21.1	15	1.1
France	302	22.4	431	34.3
Other	478	35.5	189	15.1
TOTAL	1,345	99.8	1,255	99.9

Submarines

Supplier	1972–1976 No.	%	1977–1981 No.	%
U.S.S.R.	7	87.5	3	33.3
U.S.	—		1	11.1
France	1	12.5	3	33.3
Other	—		2	22.2
TOTAL	8	100.0	9	99.9

Major Surface Warships

Supplier	1972–1976 No.	%	1977–1981 No.	%
U.S.S.R.	13	40.6	19	42.2
U.S.	2	6.2	7	15.5
France	1	3.1	1	2.2
Other	16	50.0	18	40.0
TOTAL	32	99.9	45	99.9

Supersonic Combat Aircraft

Supplier	1972–1976 No.	%	1977–1981 No.	%
U.S.S.R.	1,250	59.7	1,635	64.9
U.S.	470	22.5	430	17.0
France	203	9.7	233	9.2
Other	170	8.1	222	8.8
TOTAL	2,093	100.0	2,520	99.9

Surface-to-Air Missiles

Supplier	1972–1976 No.	%	1977–1981 No.	%
U.S.S.R.	10,595	80.1	9,495	56.0
U.S.	1,695	12.8	5,595	32.9
France	69	.5	228	1.3
Other	861	6.5	1,642	9.7
TOTAL	13,220	99.9	16,960	99.9

SUB-SAHARAN AFRICA

Tanks and Self-Propelled Guns

Supplier	1972–1976 No.	%	1977–1981 No.	%
U.S.S.R.	475	62.9	1,140	59.8
U.S.	10	1.3	25	1.3
France	—	—	61	3.2
Other	270	35.8	680	35.7
TOTAL	755	100.0	1,906	100.0

Subsonic Combat and Other Military Aircraft

Supplier	1972–1976 No.	%	1977–1981 No.	%
U.S.S.R.	80	16.0	150	35.3
U.S.	10	2.0	40	9.4
France	44	8.8	76	17.9
Other	366	73.2	159	37.4
TOTAL	500	100.0	425	100.0

Light Armor

Supplier	1972–1976 No.	%	1977–1981 No.	%
U.S.S.R.	910	37.0	1,590	48.9
U.S.	30	1.2	50	1.5
France	1,338	54.4	711	21.9
Other	180	7.3	894	27.6
TOTAL	2,458	99.9	3,245	99.9

Minor Surface Warship/Guided Missile Patrol Boats

Supplier	1972–1976 No.	%	1977–1981 No.	%
U.S.S.R.	26	19.1	49	47.1
U.S.	—	—	—	—
France	17	12.5	14	13.5
Other	93	68.4	41	39.4
TOTAL	136	100.0	104	100.0

Helicopters

Supplier	1972–1976 No.	%	1977–1981 No.	%
U.S.S.R.	40	21.0	125	38.8
U.S.	5	2.6	—	—
France	68	35.8	152	47.2
Other	77	40.5	45	14.0
TOTAL	190	99.9	322	100.0

Major Surface Warships

Supplier	1972–1976 No.	%	1977–1981 No.	%
U.S.S.R.	1	25.0	5	18.5
U.S.	—	—	—	—
France	—	—	2	7.4
Other	3	75.0	20	74.1
TOTAL	4	100	27	100

Submarines

Supplier	1972–1976 No.	%	1977–1981 No.	%
U.S.S.R.	—	—	—	—
U.S.	—	—	—	—
France	—	—	—	—
Other	1	100	—	—
TOTAL	1	100	—	—

Supersonic Combat Aircraft

Supplier	1972–1976 No.	%	1977–1981 No.	%
U.S.S.R.	120	57.7	220	60.3
U.S.	—	—	20	5.5
France	58	27.9	70	19.2
Other	30	14.4	55	15.1
TOTAL	208	100	365	100.1

Surface-to-Air Missiles

Supplier	1972–1976 No.	%	1977–1981 No.	%
U.S.S.R.	600	51.5	1,575	99.3
U.S.	—	—	—	—
France	18	1.5	—	—
Other	547	47.0	10	.6
TOTAL	1,165	100.0	1,585	99.9

Appendix D (cont.)

LATIN AMERICA

Tanks and Self-Propelled Guns

Supplier	1972—1976 No.	%	1977—1981 No.	%
U.S.S.R.	330	34.8	80	14.6
U.S.	295	31.1	15	2.7
France	314	33.1	97	17.7
Other	10	1.1	355	64.9
TOTAL	949	100.1	547	99.9

Minor Surface Warships/Guided Missile Patrol Boats

Supplier	1972—1976 No.	%	1977—1981 No.	%
U.S.S.R.	17	16.3	35	31.8
U.S.	31	29.8	3	2.7
France	4	3.8	10	9.1
Other	52	50.0	62	56.4
TOTAL	104	99.9	110	100.0

Subsonic Combat and Other Military Aircraft

Supplier	1972—1976 No.	%	1977—1981 No.	%
U.S.S.R.	5	0.7	70	10.4
U.S.	240	35.3	200	29.8
France	27	4.0	20	3.0
Other	408	60.0	380	56.7
TOTAL	680	100.0	670	99.9

Light Armor

Supplier	1972—1976 No.	%	1977—1981 No.	%
U.S.S.R.	55	4.1	175	31.2
U.S.	910	67.1	30	5.3
France	—	—	—	—
Other	390	28.8	355	63.4
TOTAL	1,355	100.0	560	99.9

Submarines

Supplier	1972—1976 No.	%	1977—1981 No.	%
U.S.S.R.	—	—	3	23.0
U.S.	19	65.5	2	15.3
France	—	—	—	—
Other	10	34.5	8	61.5
TOTAL	29	100.0	13	99.8

Helicopters

Supplier	1972—1976 No.	%	1977—1981 No.	%
U.S.S.R.	40	16.3	35	17.5
U.S.	120	48.9	35	17.5
France	69	28.2	104	52.0
Other	16	6.5	26	13.0
TOTAL	245	99.9	200	100.0

Major Surface Warships

Supplier	1972—1976 No.	%	1977—1981 No.	%
U.S.S.R.	—	—	1	2.7
U.S.	33	82.5	5	13.8
France	—	—	3	8.3
Other	7	17.5	27	75.0
TOTAL	40	100.0	36	99.8

Supersonic Combat Aircraft

Supplier	1972—1976 No.	%	1977—1981 No.	%
U.S.S.R.	40	25.8	130	51.2
U.S.	—	—	15	5.9
France	61	39.4	64	25.2
Other	54	34.8	45	17.7
TOTAL	155	100.0	254	100.0

Surface-to-Air Missiles

Supplier	1972—1976 No.	%	1977—1981 No.	%
U.S.S.R.	380	85.3	435	81.3
U.S.	—	—	—	—
France	40	9.0	54	10.1
Other	25	5.6	46	8.6
TOTAL	445	99.9	535	100.0

EAST ASIA AND THE PACIFIC

Tanks and Self-Propelled Guns

Supplier	1972—1976 No.	1972—1976 %	1977—1981 No.	1977—1981 %
U.S.S.R.	710	19.8	640	27.2
U.S.	1,395	38.9	750	31.9
France	25	0.7	325	13.8
Other	1,455	40.6	635	27.0
TOTAL	3,585	100.0	2350	99.9

Light Armor

Supplier	1972—1976 No.	1972—1976 %	1977—1981 No.	1977—1981 %
U.S.S.R.	315	12.0	395	16.6
U.S.	2,045	77.9	930	39.2
France	—	—	1,000	42.1
Other	265	10.1	50	2.1
TOTAL	2,625	100.0	2,375	100.0

Major Surface Warships

Supplier	1972—1976 No.	1972—1976 %	1977—1981 No.	1977—1981 %
U.S.S.R.	—	—	7	18.9
U.S.	36	97.2	20	54.0
France	—	—	—	—
Other	1	2.7	10	27.0
TOTAL	37	99.9	37	99.9

Minor Surface Warships/Guided Missile Patrol Boats

Supplier	1972—1976 No.	1972—1976 %	1977—1981 No.	1977—1981 %
U.S.S.R.	8	4.2	52	41.3
U.S.	129	68.6	26	20.6
France	4	2.1	—	—
Other	47	25.0	48	38.1
TOTAL	188	99.9	126	100.0

Submarines

Supplier	1972—1976 No.	1972—1976 %	1977—1981 No.	1977—1981 %
U.S.S.R.	4	40.0	—	—
U.S.	2	20.0	—	—
France	—	—	—	—
Other	4	40.0	2	100.0
TOTAL	10	100.0	2	100.0

Supersonic Combat Aircraft

Supplier	1972—1976 No.	1972—1976 %	1977—1981 No.	1977—1981 %
U.S.S.R.	55	9.6	250	46.3
U.S.	380	66.6	225	41.6
France	—	—	—	—
Other	135	23.7	65	12.0
TOTAL	570	99.9	540	99.9

Subsonic Combat and Other Military Aircraft

Supplier	1972—1976 No.	1972—1976 %	1977—1981 No.	1977—1981 %
U.S.S.R.	130	6.0	165	17.4
U.S.	1590	73.8	325	34.0
France	5	.2	19	2.0
Other	430	20.0	441	46.4
TOTAL	2155	100.0	950	99.8

Helicopters

Supplier	1972—1976 No.	1972—1976 %	1977—1981 No.	1977—1981 %
U.S.S.R.	80	5.5	130	27.1
U.S.	1,285	88.3	175	36.4
France	30	2.1	37	7.7
Other	60	4.1	138	28.8
TOTAL	1,455	100.0	480	100.0

Surface-to-Air Missiles

Supplier	1972—1976 No.	1972—1976 %	1977—1981 No.	1977—1981 %
U.S.S.R.	—	—	175	12.2
U.S.	335	85.9	1,260	87.8
France	—	—	—	—
Other	55	14.1	—	—
TOTAL	390	100.0	1,435	100.0

Source: See Appendix C.

CHAPTER 1

1. Robert Villers, *Cours d'histoire des institutions politiques et administratives du moyen âge et des temps modernes* (Paris: Sorbonne, 1967-1968), pp. 35-36.

2. A. Bigant, *La Loi de nationalisation des usines de guerre* (Paris: Editions Domat-Montchrestien, 1939), provides a brief survey of the development of the French armaments industry and the exercise of state control over its operations. Longer but of lesser use is H. L. Marquand, *La Question des arsenaux: guerre et marine* (Paris: Plon, 1923).

An edited volume which contains a great deal of useful bibliographical sources on European war preparations and arms production is *War and Economic Development*, ed. J. M. Winter (Cambridge: Cambridge University Press, 1975), especially pp. 257-292.

The literature on arms production is sparse compared to the many volumes on the evolution of French and European arms and armaments. Extremely helpful is William H. McNeill's *The Pursuit of Power* (Chicago: University of Chicago Press, 1982). Some of the following are useful, although they provide little information about the organizational structure for *making* arms: Phillipe Contamine, *Guerre, état et société à la fin du moyen âge* (Paris: Mouton, 1972); Ferdinand Lot, *L'Art militaire et les armées au moyen âge* (Paris: Payot, 1946); and André Corvisier, *L'Armée française* (Paris: Presses Universitaires de France, 1964); Charles John Ffoulkes, *The Armourer and His Craft from the XIth to the XVIth Century* (London: Methuen, 1912); Claude Blair, *European Armour: 1066-1700* (New York: Macmillan, 1959); John Hewitt, *Ancient Armour and Weapons in Europe* (Vienna: Akademische Druck-und Verlagsanstalt, 1967), 2 vols.; M. P. Lacombe, *Arms and Armour in Antiquity and the Middle Ages*, trans. Charles Boutell (New York: Appleton, 1870); and Auguste Demmin, *Guide des amateurs d'armes* (Paris: Renouard, 1869).

3. Bigant, *La Loi de nationalisation*, pp. 14-17.

4. Villers, *Cours d'histoire*, p. 44.

5. *Ibid.*, pp. 50-51.

6. *Ibid.*, pp. 60-61; Lacombe, *Arms and Armour* pp. 228ff.

7. Ernest Picard, *L'Artillerie française au XVII* (Paris: Berger-Levrault, 1906). The most comprehensive treatment of Gribeauval's contribution to the development of French arms is Pierre Nardin, *Gribeauval: Lieutenant général des armers du roi (1715-1789)*, Cahiers No. 24 (Paris: Les Cahiers de la Fondation pour les Etudes de Défense Nationale, 1982).

8. Villers, *Cours d'histoire*, pp. 80-81; Lacombe, *Arms and Armour*, pp. 234-235.

9. A useful source was Maurice Loir, *La marine française* (Paris: Hachette, 1893). It traces the evolution of the French navy and ship construction from ear-

liest times to the end of the nineteenth century. Richelieu's efforts in building a royal navy are reviewed in J. Caillet, *L'Administration en France sous le ministère de Cardinal de Richelieu* (Paris: Didot Frères, 1857), especially pp. 287-315. Two books by Louis E. Chevalier are informative, although they tell us little, in contrast to the Loir volume, about how ship construction and armaments were organized: *Histoire de la marine française de 1815-1870* (Paris: Hachette, 1900), and *Histoire de la marine française pendant la guerre de l'indépendance française* (Paris: Hachette, 1877). There is also the six-volume work of Charles de la Roncière, *Histoire de la marine française* (Paris: Plon, Nourrit, 1899-1932).

10. Villers, *Cours d'histoire*, pp. 91ff.

11. *Ibid.*, pp. 94-95.

12. D. J. Buisseret, "The French Mediterranean Fleet under Henri IV," *The Mariner's Mirror*, L (1964), 297-306.

13. Villers, *Cours d'histoire*, pp. 104-111.

14. Norman Hampson, *La Marine de l'an II: Mobilisation de la flotte de l'océan, 1793-1794* (Paris: Librairie Marcel Rivière, 1959), pp. 187-189.

15. Norman Hampson, "Les Ouvriers des arsenaux de la marine au cours de la révolution française, 1789-1794," I, *Revue d'Histoire Economique et Sociale*, XXXIX, No. 3 (1961), 287-329; II, XXXIX, No. 4 (1961), 442-473.

16. Hampson, *La Marine de l'an II*, pp. 219-240.

17. *Ibid.*

18. Indispensable for an understanding of arms production between 1815 and 1914 are two articles by François Crouzet in the *Revue Historique*. See also his extensive citations of other sources. The discussion of this period is principally drawn from Crouzet, and my great debt to him is freely acknowledged: "Recherches sur la production d'armements en France," *Revue Historique*, No. 509 (January-March 1974), 45-84, and "Remarques sur l'industrie des armements en France du milieu du XIXe siecle à 1914," *ibid.*, No. 510 (April-June 1974), 409-422.

19. *Ibid.*, Nos. 509-510.

20. *Ibid.*, No. 510, 409-422.

21. See also Maurice Tardy, "La Nationalisation et le contrôle des industries de guerre," *Revue de France* (1 September 1938), 84-108, and Bigant, *La Loi de nationalisation*, pp. 18-19. On the arms merchant literature, see Robert Harkavy, *The Arms Trade and International Systems* (Cambridge, Mass.: Ballinger, 1975), p. 251, n. 20.

22. For an overview, see Richard D. Challener, *The French Theory of the Nation in Arms, 1866-1939* (New York: Russell and Russell, 1965). William L. Shirer also briefly discusses the obtuseness of the French High Command in adjusting to new weapons and the novel strategies and tactics that they implied. William L. Shirer, *The Collapse of the Third Republic* (New York: Simon and Schuster, 1969), pp. 83ff.

23. See Barbara Tuchman, *The Guns of August* (New York: Dell, 1964), *passim*, on French strategic thinking. For the Schlieffen Plan, consult Hajo Holborn, "Moltke and Schlieffen: The Prussian-German School," in *Makers of Modern Strategy*, ed. Edward Mead Earle (New York: Atheneum, 1967), pp. 172-205.

24. J.F.C. Fuller, *The Conduct of War: 1789-1961* (New York: Minerva Press, 1961), pp. 175-176.

25. Shirer, *Third Republic*, p. 133. See also Judith M. Hughes, *To the Maginot Line: The Politics of French Military Preparation in the 1920's* (Cambridge, Mass.: Harvard University Press, 1971), p. 12.

26. There are several excellent works that might be consulted for a critical evaluation of French interwar strategy. These include the works by Challener and Hughes already cited, and Robert J. Young, *In Command of France* (Cambridge, Mass.: Harvard University Press, 1978); *idem*, "La Guerre de longue durée: Some Reflections on French Strategy and Diplomacy in the 1930s," in *General Staffs and Diplomacy before the Second World War*, ed. Adrian Preston (London: Croom Helm, 1978), pp. 41-64.

For a general discussion of French foreign policy, two works of interest, among many others, are Arnold Wolfers, *Britain and France between Two Wars: Conflicting Strategies of Peace since Versailles* (New York: Harcourt, Brace, 1940), and Jacques Néré, *The Foreign Policy of France from 1914 to 1945* (London: Routledge and Kegan Paul, 1974).

27. Quoted in Shirer, *Third Republic*, p. 177.

28. Quoted in *ibid.*, p. 179.

29. General Narcisse Chauvineau, *Une Invasion est-elle encore possible?* (Paris: Berger Levrault, 1939). Pétain's views are echoed in General Maxime Weygand, "How France Is Defended," *International Affairs*, xviii, No. 4 (July-August 1939), 72ff.

30. Quoted in Shirer, *Third Republic*, p. 178.

31. The best single source on military arms production in the interwar period is Robert Jacomet, *L'Armement de la France: 1936-1939* (Paris: Lajeunesse, 1945). Jacomet was a former comptroller general of the Army, who was imprisoned during World War II by the Vichy government for having allegedly contributed, through malfeasance and incompetence, to the French military debacle in 1940. Jacomet makes a spirited defense of his management and leadership of the arms industry. His views about French preparedness, defined by the availability of adequate stores of weapons and munitions, is lent support by Ingénieur Général Molinié, "L'Effort industriel d'armement en France de 1918 a 1940," *Armement*, No. 61 (June 1980), 26-37: "In June 1940, the amount of modern French armored combat equipment was effectively equal to that of German equipment with characteristics of superior armor protection and on the whole more advantageous armament. . . . Our artillery had been motorized as the German artillery. Our antitank cannons . . . remained effective against German tanks. The German 37AC was ineffective against our armor. Only the 88 cannon was worthwhile" (p. 26). See also n. 39 below.

32. Jacomet, *L'Armement*, pp. 95-96.

33. E. H. Carr, *International Relations between the Two World Wars, 1918-1939* (New York: Harpers, 1947), pp. 42-43.

34. See Harkavy, *Arms Trade*, especially pp. 60ff.

35. Jacomet, *L'Armement*, p. 114.

36. *Ibid.*

37. Shirer, *Third Republic*, p. 534.

38. See Carr, *International Relations, passim*.

39. Jacomet, *L'Armement*, pp. 43ff. and p. 117, describes the dilapidated state of the French arms industry before rearmament.

40. *Ibid.*, p. 152.

41. For a discussion of nationalization, see nn. 2 and 21 above and Paul Reuter, "La Nationalisation des usines de guerre," *Revue d'Economie Politique*, LIII (1939), 740-756.

42. Tardy, "La Nationalisation," pp. 89-108.

43. See André Charriou, "Quinze ans d'industrie aéronautique française." *Revue de Défense Nationale* (December 1948), 649-666; and Tardy, "La Nationalisation," pp. 89-108. These articles review government consolidation efforts and cite installations that were absorbed in the state system.

44. The major purpose of Jacomet's book is to dispel the notion of French unpreparedness. According to Jacomet, Germany "outgeneraled" France, not outproduced it in arms. Relevant also are Matthew Cooper, *The German Army: 1933-1945* (New York: Stein and Day, 1978), pp. 159-166, and pp. 209-216; A. Goutard, *The Battle of France, 1940*, trans. A.R.P. Burgess (London: Frederick Muller, 1958); R.H.S. Stolfi, "Equipment for Victory in France in 1940," *History*, LII, No. 183 (February 1970), 1-20; and Ingénieur Général Molinié, "L'Effort industriel d'armement en France," pp. 26-37.

45. See sources for Table 1-10. Young argues France's inferiority in men, industrial resources, and arms. See also his critique of French air forces and their insufficiency. Robert J. Young, "The Strategic Dream: French Air Doctrine in the Inter-War Period, 1919-39," *Journal of Contemporary History*, IX, No. 4 (October 1974), 57-76. For a more favorable assessment of prewar combat aircraft production, see Jan Truelle, "La Production áeronautique militaire française jusqu'en juin 1940," *Revue Historique de la Deuxième Guerre Mondiale*, XIX (1969), 75-110.

46. *Ibid.*, pp. 89, 103.

47. *Ibid.*, pp. 107-108.

48. *Ibid.*, pp. 107-109. See also selected bibliography, pp. 109-110.

49. John McVickar Haight, Jr., "Les Négotiations relatives aux achats d'avions américains par la France, *Revue Historique de la Deuxième Guerre Mondiale*, XV (1965), 1-34.

50. Shirer, *Third Republic*, p. 521.

51. Quoted in Jacomet, *L'Armement*, p. 293.

52. *Ibid.*

53. Charles de Gaulle, *Mémoires de guerre: L'Appel, 1940-1942* (Paris: Plon, 1954), p. 40.

54. Lieutenant-Colonel Rose, "Les Aviations allemandes, françaises, et anglaises," *Revue de Défense Nationale* (February 1951), 175-176. Additional information on aircraft production before World War II is found in Charriou, "Quinze ans d'industrie aéro-nautique," pp. 649-666, and Molinié, "L'Effort industriel d'armement en France," pp. 26-37.

55. Charles de Gaulle, *Discours et messages* (Paris: Plon, 1970), I, 3.

56. Much of the history of the provisional government's foreign policy is ably covered in Anton W. DePorte, *De Gaulle's Foreign Policy: 1944-1946* (Cambridge: Harvard University Press, 1968). For a brief overview, consult Edgar S. Furniss, Jr., *France: Troubled Ally* (New York: Praeger, 1960), pp. 3-23. Indispensable are de Gaulle's own memoirs (see n. 55 above).

57. DePorte, *De Gaulle's Foreign Policy*, p. 81.

58. There are several excellent studies of the French Army under the provisional government and the Fourth Republic. Among those that might be consulted are Paul-Marie de la Gorce, *The French Army*, trans. Kenneth Douglas (New York: George Braziller, 1963); John Ambler, *The French Army in Politics, 1945-1962* (Columbus: Ohio State University Press, 1966); Edgar S. Furniss, Jr., *De Gaulle and the French Army* (New York: Twentieth Century Fund, 1964); George Kelly, *Lost Soldiers: The French Army and Empire in Crisis, 1947-1962* (Cambridge, Mass.: MIT Press, 1965). The most thorough sociological study is in Michel Martin, *Warriors to Managers* (Chapel Hill, N.C.: University of North Carolina Press, 1981).

59. DePorte, *De Gaulle's Foreign Policy*, pp. 271-276. The other important reason for his resignation, and most likely the more critical, was the refusal of the French parties to strengthen executive authority under the Fourth Republic. The experience with the debate over the military budget and opposition to strong executive leadership as an antidote to fluid and often ineffective party government convinced de Gaulle that neither he nor his ideas would have much chance under such a constitutional arrangement.

60. Brief but useful summaries of the Fourth Republic's strategic and foreign policy are found in Martin, *Warriors to Managers*, pp. 14-19; Michael M. Harrison, *The Reluctant Ally* (Baltimore: The Johns Hopkins University Press, 1981), pp. 6-48; and Wilfrid L. Kohl, *French Nuclear Diplomacy* (Princeton: Princeton University Press, 1971), pp. 15-47.

61. France, Assemblée Nationale, Commission des Finances (1946), *Rapport: Section Commune, Guerre, Budget annexe de fabrications d'armements*, No. 4718, p. 36.

62. France, Assemblée Nationale, Commission des Finances (1947), *Projet de loi, portant fixation du budget extraordinaire* (Dépenses militaires pour l'exercice 1947), No. 2092, p. 10.

63. Assemblée Nationale, *Rapport*, No. 4718, pp. 46-47.

64. Furniss, Jr., *France: Troubled Ally*, pp. 165-235, 440-455.

65. Alfred Grosser, *Les Occidentaux* (Paris: Fayard, 1978).

66. Quoted in Tony Smith, "The French Colonial Consensus and People's War, 1946-58," *Journal of Contemporary History*, IX, No. 4 (October 1974), 226. The Smith article relates the reluctance of successive French republics to relinquish France's colonies to widely shared public and elite values. See also Raoul Girardet, *L'Histoire de l'idée coloniale en France de 1871 à 1962* (Paris: Fayard, 1972). For alternate views that blame more the political institutions and party structure than the French nation and its ruling elites, see Guy de Carmoy, *Les*

Politiques etrangères de la France, 1944-1966 (Paris: La Table Ronde, 1967), and Alfred Grosser, *La Quatrième république et sa politique extérieure* (Paris: Colin, 1961).

67. Quoted in Smith, "French Colonial Consensus," p. 221. For Soustelle's view, see Jacques Soustelle, *Le Drame algérien et la décadence française: réponse à Raymond Aron* (Paris: Plon, 1957).

68. Harrison, *The Reluctant Ally*, pp. 15-33, carefully traces these efforts to enhance Fourth Republic status within the alliance.

69. Illustrative are the following: Jacques Soustelle, "France and Europe: A Gaullist View," *Foreign Affairs*, xxx, No. 4 (July 1952), 545-553; General de Monsabert, "North Africa in Atlantic Strategy," *ibid.*, xxxi, No. 3 (April 1953), 418-426; E. J. Debau, "La France vue de Washington à travers l'O.T.A.N.," *Revue de Défense Nationale* (March 1956), 332-336; Georges R. Manue, "La Leçon de Suez," *ibid.* (October 1956), 1155-1164; Colonel Parisot, "Valeur stratégique de l'Afrique pour l'O.T.A.N.," *ibid.* (March 1958), 430-435; and Général J. Allard, "Verités sur l'affaire algérienne," *ibid.* (January 1958), 5-41; and Général Paul Ely, "Notre politique militaire," *ibid.* (July 1957), 1033-1051.

70. For a general treatment of French revolutionary warfare, consult Peter Paret, *French Revolutionary Warfare from Indochina to Algeria: The Analysis of a Political Doctrine* (New York: Praeger, 1964); Kelly, *Lost Soldiers*, pp. 107-142. Additional citations may be found in Martin, *Warriors to Managers*, p. 29, n. 10.

71. See Smith "French Colonial Consensus," and Girardet *L'Histoire de l'idée coloniale*, n. 48.

72. Jean Godard, "L'Aide américaine à la France," *Revue de Science Financière*, xlvii, No. 3 (July-September 1956), 446. The exchange rate was set at approximately 214 francs to the dollar before devaluation.

73. *Ibid.*, pp. 448-449, 454-457.

74. *Ibid.*, p. 457.

75. Jean Godard, "La Contribution alliée aux charges militaires de la France," *Revue de Défense Nationale* (April 1956), 436-445.

76. *Ibid.* and U.S., Department of Defense, *Foreign Military Sales and Military Assistance Facts* (December 1978), p. 17. For a general discussion of U.S. support of France during the Vietnamese War, see R.E.M. Irving, *The First Indochina War: French and American Policy, 1945-54* (London: Croom Helm, 1975).

77. Colonel Robert E. Peters, "U.S. Policy of Offshore Procurement," Army War College, Carlisle Barracks, Pennsylvania, 1954, p. 42.

78. William A. Brown and Redvers Opie, *American Foreign Assistance* (Washington, D.C.: Brookings Institution, 1953), p. 491.

79. Capitaine Valentin, "Les Fabrications d'armement depuis la libération," *Revue de Défense Nationale* (July 1946), 108-112.

80. France, Assemblée Nationale, Commission des Finances (1947), *Projet de loi: dépenses militaires pour l'exercice 1947*, No. 2092, p. 13.

81. France, Assemblée Nationale, Commission des Finances (1948), *Budget militaire: dépenses militaires pour 1948*, No. 4720, p. 2.

82. Valentin, "Les Fabrications d'armement," p. 110.

83. Assemblée Nationale, *Projet de loi*, No. 2092.

84. France, Assemblée Nationale, Commission de la Défense Nationale (1947), *Rapport sur le sociétés nationales des constructions aéronautiques*. The report is also known as the Pellenc Report after its principal author, Inspector General Pellenc.

85. France, Assemblée Nationale, Commission des Finances (1949), *Rapport sur le projet de loi portant sur du budget extraordinaire: dépenses militaires*, No. 2228, p. 18.

86. Derived from Godard, "L'Aide americaine à la France," pp. 451-453.

87. Martin, *Warriors to Managers*, pp. 61-79.

88. France, Assemblée Nationale, Commission de la Défense Nationale (1950), *Rapport sur le projet de loi portant fixation d'un programme aérien*, pp. 2-3.

89. *Revue de Défense Nationale*, "Chroniques Militaires" (June 1951), 242-243. This monthly review of armed force programs catalogues the development of the offshore program.

90. *Ibid.*, p. 242.

91. *Ibid.*, p. 243.

92. *Ibid.* The need for a return to France's policy of independent arms production was, of course, expressed throughout the 1940s (see ns. 70 and 78 above). See also France, Assemblée Nationale, Commission des Finances (1950), *Avis presenté sur le projet de loi portant fixation d'un programme aérien*, No. 10753; and André Charriou, "L'Industrie aéronautique dans le monde," *Revue de Défense Nationale* (January 1948), 222-242.

93. Peters, "Offshore Procurement," p. 22.

94. Quoted in *Business Week*, No. 1122, March 3, 1951, pp. 136-138.

95. Peters, "Offshore Procurement," p. 78.

96. *Ibid.*, p. 79.

97. *Ibid.*, p. 18.

98. *Revue de Défense Nationale*, "Chroniques Militaires" (March 1951), 357.

99. *Ibid.*, *passim*.

100. Pellenc Report, pp. 235-237.

101. *Jane's All the World's Aircraft* (London: Jane's Publishing Company Limited, 1947-1955), *passim*.

102. *Ibid.* (1954-1955), p. 136.

103. *Ibid.* (1957-1958), *passim*.

104. *Ibid.* (1961-1962), *passim*.

105. *Revue de Défense Nationale*, "Chroniques Militaires" (November 1960), 1891.

106. Sipri, *The Arms Trade Register* (Cambridge: The MIT Press, 1975), p. 89.

107. *Ibid.*, *passim*.

108. The evolution of France's nuclear military program under the Fourth Republic has been sketched elsewhere and need not be repeated in detail. See especially Bertrand Goldschmidt, *L'Aventure atomique* (Paris: Fayard, 1962). Also of use in understanding the evolution of the French atomic energy program is his *Rivalités atomiques 1939-1966* (Paris: Fayard, 1967). The Fourth Republic's nuclear program is also covered in these helpful sources: Lawrence Scheinman, *Atomic Energy in France under the Fourth Republic* (Princeton: Princeton University

Press, 1965); Kohl, *French Nuclear Diplomacy*, pp. 3-47; Wolf Mendl, *Deterrence and Persuasion* (New York: Praeger, 1970), pp. 122-154; and Robert Gilpin, *France in the Age of the Scientific State* (Princeton: Princeton University Press, 1968), pp. 151-187.

109. These are cited in full by Scheinman, *Atomic Energy in France*, pp. 227ff. See, for example, Colonel Charles Ailleret, "L'Arme atomique, arme à bon marché," *Revue de Défense Nationale* (October 1954), 315-325 and succeeding articles by Ailleret in the following three monthly numbers of the Revue.

110. In a discussion of de Gaulle's directorate scheme, see the author's *French International Policy under de Gaulle and Pompidou: The Politics of Grandeur* (Ithaca: Cornell University Press, 1974), pp. 69-122; Kohl, *French Nuclear Diplomacy*, pp. 48-81, 207-266; Harrison, *The Reluctant Ally*, pp. 86-98, and Lothar Ruehl, *La Politique militaire de la V⁰ république* (Paris: Fondation Nationale des Sciences Politiques, 1976), pp. 41-55.

111. See Gilpin, *France*, and Kohl *French Nuclear Diplomacy*, pp. 29-44.

112. See Goldschmidt *L'Aventure atomique, passim*, for a discussion of alliance cooperation and atomic development. See also his latest work in this same vein: *Le Complexe atomique: histoire politique et techniques* (Paris: Fayard, 1980).

113. Kolodziej, *French International Policy*, pp. 447-448.

114. De la Gorce, *The French Army*, pp. 373-374; Martin, *Warriors to Managers*, pp. 64-66. The dismantling prompted the resignation of General Guillaume, chief of staff of national defense, and General Zeller, Army chief of staff. On the point of army modernization the French military command was closer to American thinking than the political leadership of the Fourth Republic, beset by the conflicting demands of colonial war and European security and between force structures appropriate to revolutionary and atomic warfare.

CHAPTER 2

1. Since the focus of this section is the impact of French international policy on arms production and transfers, it goes beyond the scope of this discussion to review the evolution of French exterior behavior under the Fifth Republic. The literature is rich and only a few works can be cited as a guide to other useful studies. These include Stanley Hoffmann, "De Gaulle's Memoires: The Hero as History," *World Politics*, xiii (October 1960), 140-154; *idem*, "Obstinate or Obsolete? The Fate of the Nation-State and the Case of Western Europe," *Daedalus*, xcv (Summer 1966), 862-915; Inge and Stanley Hoffmann, "The Will to Grandeur: De Gaulle as Political Artist," *ibid.*, xcvii (Summer 1968), 829-887; Alfred Grosser, *French Foreign Policy under de Gaulle*, trans. Lois Ames Pattison (Boston: Little, Brown, 1965); W. W. Kulski, *De Gaulle and the World* (Syracuse: Syracuse University Press, 1966); Edmond Jouve, *Le Général de Gaulle et la construction de l'Europe, 1940-1966*, 2 vols. (Paris: Librairie de Droit et de Jurisprudence, 1967); and Philip G. Cerny, *The Politics of Grandeur* (London: Cambridge University Press, 1982). Also see Carmoy, *Politiques étrangères de la France*; Harrison, *The Re-*

luctant Ally, and Kohl, *French Nuclear Diplomacy*. See also the author's *French International Policy under De Gaulle and Pompidou*, where the systemic thrust of French strategic and foreign policy is emphasized.

Indispensable also are the memoirs, speeches, and pronouncements of General de Gaulle. See France, Ambassade de France, Service de Presse et d'Information, *Major Addresses, Statements, and Press Conferences of General Charles de Gaulle, 1958-1964* (New York, 1964), hereinafter cited *Major Addresses*; Charles de Gaulle, *Discours et messages* (Paris: Plon, 1970), 5 vols.; idem, *Memoires de guerre* (Paris: Plon, 1954-1958), 3 vols.; idem, *Memoires d'espoir: Le renouveau, 1958-62* (Paris: Plon, 1954-1958); and Volume Two, *L'Effort* (Paris: Plon, 1971). Useful is the compendium organized according to subject matter of André Passeron, *De Gaulle parle, 1962-1966* (Paris: Fayard, 1966).

The yearly handbook, *L'Année politique*, is also helpful as well as the semiannual publications of *La Documentation française* which reproduce the foreign policy statements of French presidents, key ministers, and governmental spokesmen. Also of value are two dossiers of the Minister of Defense, issued by the press division, Service d'Information et de Relations Publiques des Armées (SIRPA), *La Politique de défense de la France*, Dossier d'Information No. 75 (Paris, 1984) and the Socialist Government's Military Program for 1984-1988: SIRPA, *La Programmation militaire, 1984-1988*, Dossier d'Information No. 72 (Paris, 1983).

For a recent, up-to-date analysis of French strategic policy, both comprehensive and insightful, see David S. Yost's two-part study: *France's Deterrent Posture and Security in Europe*, Part I: *Capability and Doctrine*, Adelphi Paper No. 194, and Part II: *Strategic and Arms Control Implications*, Adelphi Paper No. 195 (London: International Institute for Strategic Studies, 1985). Also of relevance are two articles by Robbin F. Laird, "The French Strategic Dilemma," *Orbis*, XXVIII, No. 2 (Summer 1984), 307-328, and "French Nuclear Forces in the 1980s and 1990s," *Comparative Strategy*, IV, No. 4, 387-412. The findings of these articles are incorporated in Laird's monograph, *France, the Soviet Union, and the Nuclear Weapons Issue* (Boulder, Colo.: Westview Press, 1985). Jolyon Howorth also presents a useful and informed review of Mitterrand's defense policy in his "Defense and the Mitterrand Government," in *Defense and Dissent in Contemporary France*, ed. Jolyon Howorth and Patricia Chilton (London: Croom Helm, 1984), pp. 94-134. See also Howarth's spirited critique of Mitterrand security policies in "Of Budgets and Strategic Choices: Defense Policy under François Mitterrand," in *Continuity and Change in Mitterrand's France*, ed. Stanley Hoffmann and George Ross (forthcoming).

A bibliography of commentary and documentation covering the Mitterrand years to 1984 is found in *Politique Etrangère* (February 1985), 454-457. See also articles covered in the symposium on French foreign policy, 1981-1985, which is covered in this volume, pp. 309-447.

2. For references in de Gaulle's statements about the pernicious effect of Yalta, see Passeron, *De Gaulle parle*, pp. 107, 110, 212, 216, 291.

3. De Gaulle, *Discours et messages*, IV, 358.

4. See Kohl, *French Nuclear Diplomacy*, Harrison, *The Reluctant Ally*, and Lothar Ruehl, *La Politique militaire de la Ve république* (Paris: Presses de la Fondation des Sciences Politiques, 1976), for parallel analyses of the French nuclear force.

5. This is the central thesis of Harrison's informed study. See, for example, the news conference of President François Mitterrand of January 1983 confirming France's commitment to a nuclear deterrent, *New York Times*, January 3, 1983.

6. *Livre blanc*, i, 54.

7. *Le Monde*, September 1, 1974.

8. See below pp. 107ff. for a discussion of France's arms control and disarmament policy.

9. Even before President Mitterrand's government was installed in office, administration officials worked around the clock reviewing French arms contracts, largely approving what its predecessor had done. Thus, arms sales ranked in priority among the most important areas of concern of the new regime. Interviews, Paris, October 1981.

10. *New York Times*, July 13, 1982.

11. France, Ministère de la Défense, *La Politique de défense de la France*, Dossier d'Information No. 69, May 1982 (Paris: sirpa, 1982), p. 18.

12. News conference of September 5, 1960, de Gaulle, *Major Addresses*, p. 95. Extensive treatment of the de Gaulle memorandum is found in Kohl, *French Nuclear Diplomacy*, pp. 67-81, and *passim*, and the author's *French International Policy*, pp. 71-86.

13. *Major Addresses*, p. 95.

14. *Ibid.*

15. *L'Année politique, 1959*, pp. 479-480.

16. De Gaulle, *Discours et messages*, v, 19.

17. Two useful overviews of Gaullist European policy are Robert Bloes, *Le "Plan Fouchet" et le problème de l'Europe politique* (Bruges: Collège d'Europe, 1970), and Susan J. Bodenheimer, *Political Union, A Microcosm of European Politics, 1960-1966* (Leiden: A. W. Sijthoff, 1967). Other citations and a sketch of the Fouchet talks can also be found in the author's *French International Policy*, pp. 292-340.

18. For a review of the mlf affair, seen from an alliance perspective, see Richard Neustadt, *Alliance Politics* (New York: Columbia University Press, 1970).

19. John Newhouse, *Collison in Brussels: The Common Market Crisis of 30 June 1965* (New York: W. W. Norton, 1967); also Miriam Camps, *European Unification in the Sixties* (New York: McGraw-Hill, 1966).

20. De Gaulle, *Discours et messages*, v, 74-78.

21. France, Ambassade de France, Service de Presse et d'Information, *French Foreign Policy* (January-June 1967), p. 103.

22. For an analysis on French franc diplomacy, see Jacques Wolff in *Revue de Science Financière*, No. 4 (October-December 1968), 782-829; *ibid.*, No. 1 (January-March 1969), 5-76; and *ibid.*, No. 2 (April-June 1969), 205-234.

23. Gilpin, *France in the Age of the Scientific State.*

24. See three works by Robert Lieber: *Oil and the Middle East War: Europe in the*

Energy Crisis (Cambridge: Harvard Center for International Affairs, 1976); "Energy, Economics and Security in Alliance Perspective," *International Security* (Spring 1980), 139-163; and *The Oil Decade: Conflict and Cooperation in the West* (New York: Praeger, 1983).

25. French parliamentarians who reviewed the government's proposal to create a force de dissuasion placed particular emphasis on their perception of a declining American nuclear deterrent as a consequence of the growing U.S.–Soviet nuclear balance as a major justification for a nationally developed and controlled nuclear force. See France, Assemblée Nationale, Commission des Finances (1960), *Rapport sur le projet de loi de programme relative à certains équipements militaires*, No. 870, October 16, 1960, pp. 41-43 and *idem*, Commission de la Défense Nationale et des Forces Armées (1960), *Avis sur le projet de loi relative à certains équipements militaires*, No. 882, October 13, 1960, pp. 29-30. These committees of the National Assembly will be hereinafter cited, respectively, as CF and CDNFA.

26. *Ibid.*

27. Prominent French strategic thinkers—Pierre Gallois, a former Air Force general and consultant to Dassault; André Beaufre, a former Army general; General Charles Ailleret, former armed forces chief-of-staff; and Lucien Poirier—owe much to early French deterrence thinkers. See, e.g., Pierre Gallois, *Balance of Terror*, trans. Richard Howard (Boston: Houghton Mifflin, 1961) and *idem, Paradoxes de la paix* (Paris: Presses du Temps Présent, 1967); André Beaufre, *Deterrence and Strategy*, trans. R. H. Barry (New York: Praeger, 1966); Lucien Poirier, *Des Stratégies nucléaires* (Paris: Hachette, 1977); and notes 4 and 5 above and 28 below.

28. General Gerardot, "Plaidoyer pour l'attaque," *Revue de Défense Nationale* (March 1956), 285-305. See Reuhl, *Politique militaire*, pp. 163ff. for a more complete discussion.

29. See, for example, General Charles Ailleret, *L'Aventure atomique française* (Paris: Grasset, 1968); General Pierre Gallois, "Limitations des armes à grand pouvoir de destruction," *Revue de Défense Nationale* (December 1956), 1485-1496.

30. General Charles Ailleret, "Evolution nécessaire de nos structures militaires," *Revue de Défense Nationale* (June 1965), 949. See also his "Défense 'dirigée' défense à tous azimuts," *ibid.* (December 1967), 1923-1932.

31. *Livre blanc*, I, 9.

32. *Ibid.*

33. General Jean Noiret, "Les Formes de la guerre et de l'armée future," *Revue de Défense Nationale* (January 1963), 5-22, and *ibid.* (February 1963), 204-213. See Ruehl, *Politique militaire*, pp. 173-189 for an analysis of Noiret's ideas within the context of the French debate over nuclear strategy.

34. General Le Puloch, "Avenir de l'armée de terre," *Revue de Défense Nationale* (June 1964), 947-960.

35. General André Martin, "L'Armée de l'air dans le contexte nucléaire," *Revue de Défense Nationale* (October 1964), 1499-1517.

36. The views of Pierre Messmer are sketched in "Notre politique militaire,"

Revue de Défense Nationale (May 1963), 745-761 and "L'Armée de demain," *Revue de Deux Mondes* (February 1962), 481-493; and five years later "L'Atome, cause et moyen d'une politique militaire autonome," *Revue de Défense Nationale* (March 1968), 395-402.

37. Chirac's remarks appear in "Au sujet des armes nucléaires tactiques françaises," *Revue de Défense Nationale* (May 1975), 11-16.

38. *Livre blanc*, I, 21.

39. General d'Armée Aérienne M. Fourquet, "Emploi des différents systèmes de forces dans le cadre de la stratégie de dissuasion," *Revue de Défense Nationale* (May 1969), 757-767.

40. General Guy Méry, "Une Armée pour quoi faire et comment?" *Revue de Défense Nationale* (June 1976), 11-34.

41. *Ibid.*, p. 15.

42. Valéry Giscard d'Estaing, "Allocution," *Défense Nationale* (July 1976), 17, quoted in Yost, *France's Deterrent Posture*, I, 9. See Yost, Part I, and Harrison, *The Reluctant Ally*, for an excellent review of the meanderings over French defense policy.

43. U.S., Foreign Broadcast Information Service, *Western Europe*, January 3, 1983, p. K1. Hereinafter cited FBIS.

44. *Ibid.*, December 3, 1982, p. K4.

45. *Programme commun de gouvernement du parti communiste et du parti socialiste* (Paris: Editions sociales, 1972), pp. 171-176.

46. FBIS, December 3, 1982, p. K5.

47. Yost, *France's Deterrent Posture*, I, 9-13, covers these points extensively. Consult also the extensive literature from French sources on Mitterrand security policy which are listed in the *Politique Etrangère* symposium, n. 1 above.

48. *La Politique de défense de la France*, p. 22.

49. *Ibid.*, p. 23.

50. Yost, *France's Deterrent Posture*, I, 11.

51. *Ibid.*, p. 13.

52. Quoted by Yost, *ibid.*, p. 52, from General Jeannon Lacaze, "La Politique Militaire," *Défense Nationale* (November 1981), 10. Italics in the original. For a review and analysis of these changes, see Yost, *France's Deterrent Posture*, I, 48-54, and II, 26-31.

53. For an excellent brief summary of French strategic and nuclear force capabilities, consult Laird, "French Nuclear Forces," pp. 387-412.

54. For example, Robert S. Rudney, "Mitterrand's New Atlanticism: Evolving French Attitudes Toward NATO," *Orbis*, XXVIII, No. 1 (Spring 1984), 83-101. Soviet analysts draw this same conclusion: Laird, *France, The Soviet Union, and the Nuclear Weapons Issue*, pp. 89ff.

55. For a more extended analyses of this argument, see Jolyon Howorth, "Consensus of Silence: The French Socialist Party and Defense Policy under François Mitterrand," *International Affairs* (London), IX (Autumn 1984), 579-600.

56. See Laird, *France, The Soviet Union, and the Nuclear Weapons Issue, passim.*

57. FBIS, December 9, 1982, p. K2.

58. *Ibid.*, October 12, 1982, p. K3.

59. For a more favorable extensive analysis of French conventional forces and of FAR than can be attempted here, see David S. Yost, *France and Conventional Defense in Central Europe*, European-American Institute for Security Research Paper No. 7 (Marina Del Rey, Calif., 1984). *Le Monde* also published a useful dossier on the Army reorganization scheme and its implications in its issue of December 19, 1984.

60. That French planners understood and even enthusiastically embraced these implications of their foreign and strategic policies may be discerned from the annual reports of the Ministry of Defense which detailed the execution of successive program-laws. These reports were published for fifteen consecutive years. They were abruptly terminated in 1975 by the Giscard d'Estaing regime in a move to weaken National Assembly critics of its management of defense policy and its modest reorientation in favor of conventional arms. These reports were not widely circulated and are difficult to acquire. See the series from 1960-1975: from 1960-1964, these are published as the *Rapport sur le programme d'équipement militaire*; from 1965-1975, they appear as *Compte rendu sur le programme d'équipement militaire*. President Charles de Gaulle, a generation earlier, had already evidenced a keen awareness of the critical importance of an independent arms production system. Charles de Gaulle, "Mobilisation économique à l'étranger," *Revue Militaire Française*, LIV (January 1934), 62-88.

61. These changes in priority were deliberately taken by government officials. Interviews, Paris, 1977-1978.

62. France, Assemblée Nationale, CDNFA (1982), *Avis sur le projet de loi pour 1983, Défense: Politique de défense de la France*, No. 1188, October 21, 1982, pp. 10 and 20.

63. France, Ministère de la Défense, SIRPA, *Le Budget de la défense*, Dossier d'Information No. 76 (Paris, 1985), pp. 4-8.

64. Yost, *France's Deterrent Posture*, I, 19.

65. Laird, "French Nuclear Forces," pp. 403-404.

66. *Times* (London), November 6, 1986; *Le Monde*, July 29-30, 1986; and France, CDNFA, *Avis*, No. 1188, 1982, pp. 20-22. See also the NATO Report, October, 6, 1986.

67. Debate still rages over how effective and invulnerable the French nuclear force really is. The Mirage IV and ground-based S-3 systems are highly vulnerable to attack by Soviet SS-20 missiles deployed in western Russia. The submarine fleet, with three submarines normally on station, poses a serious threat to the Soviet Union. For a useful evaluation, see n. 1 above, especially Yost, *France's Deterrent Posture*, and Laird, *France, The Soviet Union, and the Nuclear Weapons Issue*, and Paul Stares, "The Future of the French Strategic Nuclear Force," *International Security Review*, V, No. 2 (Summer 1980), 231-232, and the author's "French Security Policy: Decisions and Dilemmas," *Armed Forces and Society*, VIII, No. 2 (Winter 1982), 185-222 and "Modernization of British and French Nuclear Forces: Arms Control and Security Dimensions," in *The Uncertain Course: New Weapons Strategies and Mind Sets*, ed. Carl Jacobsen (London: Oxford University Press, 1987), pp. 239-253.

68. See, for example, Ministère de la Défense, *Compte rendu sur le programme d'équipement militaire*, pp. 31-33.

69. France, cf, *Rapport*, No. 870, 1960, pp. 45-48; France, cdnfa, *Avis*, No. 882, 1960, pp. 34-40; *idem* (1964), *Avis sur le projet de loi de programme relative à certains équipements militaires*, No. 1192, November 26, 1964, pp. 25-32; *idem* (1970), *Rapport sur le projet de loi de programme relative aux équipements militaires de la période 1971-1975*, No. 1372, October 2, 1970, pp. 45-50.

70. This trend is exhaustively detailed in Martin, *Warriors to Managers*, and continues under a Socialist government. See the remarks of Defense Minister Charles Hernu, fbis, October 12, 1982, p. K3.

71. iiss, *The Military Balance, 1984-1985* (London: iiss, 1982), pp. 36-38.

72. France, cdnfa, *Avis*, No. 882, 1960, p. 34.

73. France, cf, *Rapport*, No. 870, 1960, p. 46.

74. France, cdnfa, *Avis*, No. 882, 1960, p. 38.

75. France, cf, *Rapport*, No. 870, 1960, p. 46.

76. France, cdnfa, *Avis*, No. 882, 1960, p. 38.

77. Martin, *Warriors to Managers*, pp. 63-64.

78. France, cdnfa (1976), *Rapport sur le projet de loi portant approbation de la programmation militaire pour les années 1977-1982*, No. 2292, May 13, 1976, pp. 31-33.

79. Amiral Yves Leenhardt, "Réflexions pour une stratégie navale d'avenir," *Défense Nationale* (August 1985), 11-33. Also the *Economist*, October 25, 1986.

80. *Ibid.*, p. 29.

81. France, Assemblée Nationale, cf (1964), *Rapport sur le projet de loi de programme relative à certain équipements militaires*, No. 1195, November 26, 1964, p. 28.

82. France, cdnfa, *Avis*, No. 1192, 1964, p. 28.

83. Martin, *Warriors to Managers*, p. 76.

84. iiss, *The Military Balance, 1977-1978* (London: iiss, 1977), pp. 24, 37.

85. *Ibid.*, p. 25.

86. *Ibid.*, pp. 13-15.

87. France, Assemblée Nationale, cf (1980), *Rapport sur le projet de loi de finances pour 1981, Défense: Considérations Générales, Dépenses en Capital*, No. 1976, October 9, 1980, p. 118.

88. *Ibid.*, p. 121.

89. International Monetary Fund, *International Financial Statistics, 1977, Supplement, Annual Data: 1952-1976*, xxi, No. 5 (May 1977), pp. 166-167.

90. France, cdnfa, *Rapport*, No. 2292, 1976, p. 11.

91. France, Ministère de la Défense, sirpa, *Le Budget de la défense*, p. 12.

92. Cited by Jolyon Howorth "Of Budgets and Strategic Choices" (forthcoming).

93. France, Ministère de la Défense, sirpa, *La Programmation militaire, 1984-1988*, Dossier d'Information No. 72 (Paris, 1983).

94. General Bernard Capillon, "L'Armée de l'air d'hier à aujourd'hui: le fait aérien, une nouvelle dimension de la défense," *Défense Nationale* (June 1985), 23-29.

95. For a brief critique, consult Howorth, "Of Budgets and Strategic Choices." A brief evaluation of French Army capabilities is found in the *Economist*, June 23, 1984, pp. 37-40.

96. The report was written by Pierre Mayer, an experienced and highly placed inspector of finance, whose career was reportedly damaged by the sharp personal attacks that the report delivered against individuals within the arms complex, particularly those associated with the Roland affair. Interviews, Paris, 1977-1978.

97. The author's efforts to gain access or additional information about the report through interviews with key actors associated with the report proved unavailing. Interviews, Paris, 1977-1978. Jean-Bernard Pinatel et al., *L'Economie des forces* (Paris: Les Cahiers de la Fondation pour les Etudes de Défense Nationale, 1976), develops some useful lines of critique.

98. See, for example, the brief in favor of the arms industry, written by high French functionaries in the arms industry in response to a critique of the French military-industrial complex in *Le Monde*, March 16, 1978. In a reply see Roger Godement, "Le Triomphe des Thanatocrates," *ibid.*, April 12, 1978. Read also Michel Theoval, "Is France a Paper Tiger—or an Illusive Wildcat?" *Armed Forces Journal International*, CXVI, No. 3 (November 1978), 22-26, a rejoinder to a critique written by Beau Morris, "Why France's Arms Exports Make It a Paper Tiger," *ibid.*, CXVI, No. 2 (October 1978), 19-23.

99. *Le Monde*, May 23 and 24, 1971.

100. France, CDNFA, *Avis*, No. 2292, 1976, p. 107.

101. Interviews, Paris, 1978-1979. A brief review of the ACF program is found in France, Assemblée Nationale, CDNFA (1975), *Avis sur le projet de loi de finances pour 1976, Défense: Dépenses en Capital, No. 1919*, pp. 74-77.

102. Morris, "France's Arms Exports," p. 19 and *L'Express*, November 21-27, 1977, p. 100.

103. Jean-François Dubos, *Ventes d'armes: une politique* (Paris: Gallimard, 1974), p. 440. Chapter 7 below details arms sales to Iraq.

104. Pinatel et al., *L'Economie des forces*, p. 25.

105. Morris, "France's Arms Exports," p. 23, and *L'Express*, November 21-27, 1977, p. 100.

106. Theoval, "Paper Tiger," p. 26.

107. Interviews, Paris, 1977-1978, 1981-1982.

108. FBIS, November 19, 1982, p. K1.

109. *Le Monde*, November 18 and 19, 1976.

110. Quoted by Morris, "France's Arms Exports," p. 19.

111. R. Crespin and J. Besançon, "Ventes d'armements et relations entre pays industrialisés et pays en voie de développement," *Défense*, No. 9 (May 1977), 45.

112. This is one of the principal implications of Strobe Talbot's *Deadly Gambits* (New York: Vintage Books, 1985).

113. For a more detailed discussion of French disarmament and arms control policy since de Gaulle than can be covered in this discussion, which is concerned primarily with the transfer of military technology and arms, see Yost, *France's Deterrent Posture*, II, 35-60. Also relevant is the author's "French Arms Control

and Disarmament Policy: International and Domestic Dimensions and Determinants," *Jerusalem Journal of International Relations*, IV, No. 3 (1980), 14-42. See,
for example, the turnabout of Bertrand Goldschmidt, in his "Le Contrôle de
l'énergie atomique et la non-prolifération," *Politique Etrangère*, XLII, Nos. 3-4
(1977), 413-430, and France, Documentation Française, *Une Politique de défense
pour la France, Actualité: Documents* (Paris, 1981). Goldschmidt played a key role
for over forty years in defining French nuclear policy and diplomacy. He has
gradually become more sensitive to the proliferation issue. Contrast his *Politique
Etrangère* article with his *L'Aventure atomique* and *Les Rivalités atomiques: 1939-
1966* (Paris: Fayard, 1967). He remains, however, a strong advocate of civilian
nuclear development. See his latest, *Le Complexe atomique* (Paris: Fayard, 1980),
published also in revised form by the American Nuclear Society: *The Atomic Complex* (La Grange, Ill., 1982).

114. The French attitude toward disarmament is authoritatively sketched in
Jean Klein, "Continuité et ouverture dans la politique française en matière de
désarmement," *Politique Etrangère*, XLIV, No. 2 (1979), 213-247.

115. See the author's *French International Policy*, pp. 447-554.

116. France, Ambassade de France, Service de Presse et d'Information (New
York), *Speeches and Press Conferences*, No. 208, July 23, 1964, pp. 7-9. Hereinafter
cited S&P.

117. This is one of the themes developed in the author's *French International
Policy, passim*. See also Yost, *France's Deterrent Posture*, II, 35-39.

118. Quoted in Jean Klein, "Désarmement au 'arms control': La position française sous le Ve république," *Etudes Internationales*, III (September 1972), 56.

119. De Gaulle, *Discours et messages*, III, 134-135.

120. S&P, April 27, 1967, p. 58.

121. For a summary of the defense policies of the Giscard d'Estaing administration, see Pierre Lellouche, "La France, les SALT, et la securité de l'Europe,"
Politique Etrangère, XLIV, No. 2 (1979), 249-272.

122. France, Ministère de la Défense, Service d'Information et de Relations
Publiques des Armées (SIRPA), *Information Bulletin*, No. 69 (Paris, May 1982), pp.
5-9. Also statements of President Mitterrand, *New York Times*, January 3, 1983.

123. SIRPA, *France's Defense Policy*, pp. 14-15.

124. De Gaulle, *Major Addresses*, pp. 181-182.

125. Stockholm International Peace Research Institute (hereafter cited as
SIPRI), *World Armaments and Disarmament, SIPRI Yearbook 1982* (London: Taylor
and Francis, 1982), p. 440.

126. FBIS, June 2, 1981, p. K1.

127. SIPRI, *Yearbook 1982*, pp. 429-430.

128. See *New York Times* coverage of the Greenpeace affair, especially September 23-27, 1985.

129. *Ibid.*, p. 493.

130. SIPRI, *World Armaments and Disarmament, SIPRI Yearbook 1981* (London:
Taylor and Francis, 1981), p. 433.

131. For a thorough review and an interpretation of French policy that sug-

gests more French disinterest and objectivity than portrayed here, see Klein, "Continuité et ouverture dans la politique française."

132. Michel Debré, "France's Global Strategy," *Foreign Affairs*, LXIX, No. (April 1971), 395-406.

133. *Ibid.*, p. 397.

134. *Le Monde*, September 26, 1971, p. 1.

135. Klein, *Etudes Internationales*, p. 378, discusses this outcome in his informed review of French arms control and disarmament policy. For the early period, see also his "Les SALT et la sécurité en Europe" *Revue Française de Science Politique*, XXIII (August 1973), 849-853.

136. *Le Monde*, September 26, 1981.

137. *Le Monde*, January 12, 1979. See also Lellouche, "La France, les SALT, et la securité de l'Europe."

138. SIRPA, *France's Defense Policy*, p. 8.

139. *Ibid.*

140. *Ibid.*, pp. 13-14. For budgetary reasons, the government of Jacques Chirac announced the suspension of work on a neutron bomb.

141. IISS, *The Military Balance, 1984-1985*, p. 134, lists 378 deployed in two modes carrying one and three warheads respectively: Model 1 has a single 1.5 mt. warhead, while model 2 came with three 150 kt. warheads.

142. FBIS, July 8, 1981, p. K1.

143. *Ibid.*, November 30, 1982, pp. K1-K2. Also see remarks of Prime Minister Mauroy, *France's Defense Policy*, pp. 15-16.

144. For an overall review of the Giscard d'Estaing initiatives in disarmament *and* arms control, see Klein, "Continuite et ouverture dans la politique française." The implications of the superpower arms spiral for French interest in participating in superpower nuclear arms talks are extensively explored in the author's "French Arms Control."

145. This is the thrust of Pierre Lellouche's position in "La France, les SALT, et la sécurité de l'Europe." This view is also reflected in the views of Jacques Huntzinger, director of research of the Socialist party, in his "La France et SALT III," *Défense Nationale* (April 1980), 15-32. Huntzinger agrees with other French strategists that France should stay clear of SALT (and presumably START) talks but is a partisan of arms control negotiations.

146. The current status of the French civilian program is outlined in a speech by Michel Pecquer, Commissariat à l'Energie Atomique, *Notes d'Information*, Nos. 1-2 (January-February 1982), 3-13.

147. Quoted in France, Documentation Française, "La Non-Prolifération Nucléaire," *Problèmes politiques et sociaux*, No. 434 (February 1982), 30.

148. SIPRI, *Yearbook 1981*, pp. 415-416.

149. See "Les Nouvelles orientations de la politique énérgetique," *Revue Générale Nucléaire*, No. 5 (September-October 1981), 474-495, and *ibid.*, No. 2 (March-April 1982), 188.

150. France, Documentation Française, "Le Désarmement: Limitation, réglementation, côntrole," *Problèmes politiques et sociaux*, No. 336 (May 12, 1978), 30.

151. *Ibid.*

152. By March 1977 the London Group had expanded to include fourteen countries: the U.S., the U.K., France, the U.S.S.R., West Germany, Japan, Canada, Belgium, Czechoslovakia, East Germany, Netherlands, Poland, Italy, and Sweden. Switzerland attended as an observer and Austria and Finland agreed to adhere to group guidelines. French participation in the Suppliers Group is discussed in Benjamin N. Schiff, *International Nuclear Technology Transfer* (London: Croom Helm, 1984), pp. 141ff.

153. Goldschmidt, "La Contrôle de l'énergie atomique," p. 424.

154. Jean Klein, "Peut-on limiter la prolifération des armes nucléaires?" *Défense Nationale* (October 1976), 72.

155. *Problèmes politiques et sociaux* (May 12, 1978), 30.

156. *Ibid.*

157. *Le Monde*, August 25, 1978. Also Lewis A. Dunn, *Controlling the Bomb* (New Haven: Yale University Press, 1982), p. 33.

158. *The New York Times*, Special Features, "The Birth of the Islamic Bomb," June 15, 1980; and Steve Weissman and Herbert Krasney, *The Islamic Bomb* (New York: Times Books, 1981). For a useful overview of U.S.-European differences, see Pierre Lellouche, "Breaking the Rules without Quite Stopping the Bomb: European Views," in *Nuclear Proliferation*, ed. George H. Quester (Madison: University of Wisconsin Press, 1981), pp. 39-58.

159. The most comprehensive review of developing world nuclear proliferation is Leonard S. Spector's *Nuclear Proliferation Today* (New York: Vintage, 1985). The Pakistani case is covered in pages 70-110.

160. For an account of the Israeli program, see Robert E. Harkavy, *Spectre of a Middle Eastern Holocaust: The Strategic and Diplomatic Implications of the Israeli Nuclear Weapons Program* (Denver: University of Denver Monograph Series in World Affairs, 1977), especially pp. 5-19 and notes which briefly describe France's nuclear relations with Israel. See also Fuad Jobber, *Israel and Nuclear Weapons* (London: IISS, Chatto and Windus, 1971), and Times (London), October 5, 1986.

161. Goldschmidt, *The Atomic Complex*, pp. 185-187. Spector, *Nuclear Proliferation*, estimates Dimona at 24 mw, p. 119.

162. *Ibid.*, pp. 118-121.

163. See the author's *French International Policy*, pp. 489-551.

164. The IAEA lists Osiraq at 40 mw.; Spector, *Nuclear Proliferation*, p. 168 and n. 13.

165. Useful is the article by Shai Feldman, "The Bombing of Osiraq—Revisited," *International Security*, VII, No. 2 (Fall 1982), 114-142; and Spector, *Nuclear Proliferation*, pp. 277-310.

166. *Ibid.*, pp. 68-69.

167. *Ibid.*, pp. 183-184.

168. See, e.g., Dunn, *Controlling the Bomb*, pp. 53-56.

169. FBIS, November 16, 1982, p. K3.

170. Spector, *Nuclear Proliferation*, p. 296.

171. J. Baumier, J. Charles, and M. Labrousse, "Les Tendances économiques

à long terme des surrégénérateurs et leur place dans les contextes énergétiques mondiaux et français," *Revue Générale Nucléaire*, No. 6 (November-December 1979), 570-581; and Ingénieur Général Bonnet, "Les Surrégénérateurs: Comment? Pourquoi? Pour qui?" *Armement* (December 1977), 22-38.

172. *Le Monde*, May 27, 1978; *ibid.*, February 11, 1978.

173. Relevant is the useful review of French MBFR policy provided by Jean Klein, "European and French Points of View on Mutual and Balanced Force Reductions in Europe: Historic and Current Perspectives," *Stanford Journal of International Studies*, XIV (Spring 1979), 53-70. Also Yost, *France's Deterrent Posture*, II, 42-46.

174. *Ibid.*, p. 43.

175. *Ibid.*, pp. 46-50.

176. SIPRI, *Yearbook 1982*, p. 54.

177. *Le Monde*, January 26, 1978. Unlike the arms transfer control proposals of the Carter administration which were aimed at supplier accord, French arms transfer controls envisioned supplier and recipient accords.

178. *Ibid.*, February 11, 1978.

179. FBIS, June 23, 1981, p. K3.

180. *Ibid.*

181. Interviews, France, October 1983.

182. *Ibid.*, June 1, 1981.

183. *Ibid.*

184. The logic of the security dilemma is developed by Robert Jervis in his *Perception and Misperception in International Politics* (Princeton: Princeton University Press, 1976), especially pp. 58-116.

185. This is the thesis of SIPRI's *The Arms Trade with the Third World* (London: Paul Elek, 1971), pp. 249-270.

CHAPTER 3

1. Jean-Bernard Pinatel et al., *L'Economie des forces*. The most recent and comprehensive analysis of the impact of defense expenditures and activity on the French economy is the excellent monograph by Jacques Fontanel and Ron Smith, *L'Effort économique de défense* (University of Grenoble: Arès, 1985).

2. The marriage of France's economic modernization, as a widely shared political objective, to the development of a military and civilian aeronautics industry as a key instrument of this design is described in revealing detail in Claude Carlier, *L'Aéronautique française, 1945-1975* (Paris: Lavauzelle, 1983), Part I, 21-210. Postwar French economic policies are sketched in several sources. Among the most useful are the following: François Caron, *The Economic History of Modern France*, trans. Barbara Bray (New York: Columbia University Press, 1979); Warren C. Baum, *The French Economy and the State* (Princeton: Princeton University Press, 1958); Jean-Jacques Carré et al., *La Croissance française* (Paris: Seuil, 1972); John Sheahan, *Promotion and Control of Industry in Postwar France*

(Cambridge: Harvard University Press, 1963); John H. McArthur and Bruce R. Scott, *Industrial Planning in France* (Boston: Graduate School of Business Administration, Harvard University, 1969); Charles P. Kindleberger, "The Postwar Resurgence of the French Economy" in *In Search of France*, Stanley Hoffmann et al. (Cambridge: Harvard University Press, 1963), pp. 118-158; Robert Gilpin, *France in the Age of the Scientific State*; and Stephen S. Cohen, *Modern Capitalist Planning: The French Model* (Berkeley: University of California Press, 1977).

3. Martin, *Warriors to Managers*.

4. See note 2 above. Especially useful are the articles on Fifth Republic economic policies found in *The Fifth Republic at Twenty*, ed. William G. Andrews and Stanley Hoffmann (Albany: SUNY Press, 1981), p. 204-329; and *France in the Troubled World Economy*, ed. Stephen S. Cohen and Peter A. Gourevitch (London: Butterworth, 1982), especially Chapters 2-3 by Cohen, pp. 21-75.

Calls for greater French competition and industralization came from a variety of private and public sources in 1970s. See W. Allen Spivey, *Economic Policies in France, 1976-1981*, Michigan International Business Studies No. 18 (Ann Arbor: University of Michigan Press, 1982) for a useful review and the citation of relevant sources. For a brief sketch of the principal objectives of French industrial policy under President Valéry Giscard d'Estaing, see Ministère de l'Industrie, *Politique industrielle: Le Modèle français, 1974-1981* (Paris: Actualités Documents, 1981). Annual OECD reports on France are also helpful as is the recounting of yearly French economic policy found in *L'Année économique et social* and *Le Monde*'s annual review of the French economy, *L'Année économique et social, 1978-1982*.

5. For an initial effort to model the economics of arms production, transfers, and acquisition, see Arthur Alexander, William P. Butz, and Michael Mihalka, *Modeling the Production of International Trade of Arms: An Economic Framework for Analyzing Policy Alternatives* (Santa Monica, Calif.: RAND Corporation, March 1981), p. 1.

6. Cohen, in Cohen and Gourevitch, *France*, p. 30.

7. Quoted in Pinatel, *L'Economie*, p. 81. For an analysis of the unit cost of weapons development, see Pierre Massonneuve, "Prix des matériels d'armement," *Défense Nationale* (July 1980), 65-80. Massonneuve argues that the cost of weapons has largely paced the rise in growth of GNP. If so, the cost would be less a burden than is assumed in my analysis and the evidence cited in notes 8 and 9 below. For details on unit costs of selected French weapons, see France, Assemblée Nationale, Commission des Finances (1978), *Rapport sur le projet de loi de finances pour 1979, Considérations générales et dépenses en capital*, No. 570, p. 143.

8. U.S., Department of Defense, Statement of William Perry, Assistant Secretary of Defense for Research and Engineering, Fiscal Year 1980, January 1979, pp. 1-8. See also Jon S. Eckert, *Trends in U.S. Air Force Tactical Fighter Life Cycles* (Ithaca: Cornell University Peace Studies Program, No. 1, 1979).

9. Jacques Gansler, *The Defense Industry* (Cambridge: The MIT Press, 1980), p. 16.

10. France, Ministère de la Défense, *Livre blanc sur la défense nationale* (Paris, 1972), I, 54-55.

11. sirpa, *La Programmation militaire, 1984-1988*, p. 6.

12. Interviews, Paris, 1978.

13. *Livre blanc*, i, 45.

14. *Le Monde*, January 30, 1971.

15. French announced objectives in international cooperative arms accords are developed in a series of speeches and articles that stretch over a decade. The following provide a *tour d'horizon*: Colonel Muller, "Aspects de la coopération internationale dans le domaine des armements," *Armement* (December 1968), 47-57; Jean-Laurens Delpech, "La Standardisation des Armements," *L'Artilleur* (October 1976), 20-29; Ingénieur Général Marc Cauchie, "French Armament Policy and Interoperability," before the Assembly of the Western European Union (weu), at A European Armaments Policy Symposium, March 3-4, 1977, Paris, pp. 21-24; *idem, Meeting Report, Third International Symposium on NATO Standardization and Interoperability*, before the American Defense Preparedness Association, March 20-21, 1979, Washington, D.C., pp. 21-26; *idem*, "Prospects of Bi- and Multi-lateral European Cooperation," before the Assembly of the weu, Paris, 1979, pp. 30-33; *idem*, "Conférence prononcée le 8 Mai 1980," Symposium 1980 de l'American Institute of Aeronautics and Astronautics, Washington, D.C. (mimeo.); and *idem*, "Coopération internationale dans le domaine des armements," *Défense Nationale* (June 1980), 25-42.

Also of interest are the following articles of Marc Defournaux, Ingénieur en Chef de l'Armement, "La Coopération internationale en matière d'armement," *PCM*, No. 3 (March 1978), 23-28; "France and a European Armament Policy," *NATO Review*, No. 5 (1979), 19-25; "Indépendance nationale et coopération internationale en matière d'armement," *Défense Nationale* (February 1979), 35-48; and "Coopération et l'indépendance technologique," *ibid.* (March 1983), 105-118.

16. Mark A. Lorell, *Multinational Development of Large Aircraft* (Santa Monica, Calif.: RAND Corporation, 1980), pp. 31-47. Lorell provides an accurate description of French priorities in entering cooperative arms accords. So also do Herschel Kanter and John Fry, in *Cooperation in Development and Production of NATO Weapons: An Evaluation of Tactical Missile Programs* (Arlington: Institute for Defense Analyses, 1980), especially Chapter 3, pp. 33-76. Kanter and Fry cover nato and weu policy.

17. Lorell, *Multinational Development*, pp. 4-5, and Pinatel, *L'Economie*, pp. 96-109, are skeptical about the claims of decreased national costs through cooperation.

18. Delpech, "La Standardisation des Armements," p. 28.

19. Lorell, *Multinational Development*, p. 76.

20. See *ibid.*, pp. 71-81, which summarizes Lorell's sensible conclusions about European cooperation on large military and civilian aircraft.

21. Quoted by Cauchie, "Conference," 1980 (mimeo.), pp. 4-5.

22. *Ibid.*, p. 8.

23. Defournaux, "La Coopération internationale," pp. 26-28, sketches these various organizational arrangements.

24. See Defournaux and Cauchie, n. 15. Also consult Chapters 4 and 5 below for an extensive analysis of the dga.

25. Defournaux, "Coopération et l'indépendance," p. 114.

26. Lorell, *Multinational Development*, pp. 8-9. Jacques Vernant suggests that French interest in arms cooperation with Germany was motivated more by the urge to exercise control of the German arms industry than to promote standardization: Jacques Vernant, "Initiatives françaises sur le contrôle et la production des armements," *Revue de Défense Nationale* (January 1955), 91-95. Carlier's evaluation of France's early experience (in *L'Aéronautique française*, pp. 504ff.) with bilateral projects with West Germany and Great Britain closely parallels the discussion above.

27. Lorell, *Multinational Development*, pp. 31-47, 73-76, provides an excellent evaluation of the Transall program.

28. Quoted in *ibid.*, p. 47.

29. Kanter and Fry, *Cooperation*, p. 85.

30. Franco-German cooperation has also been successful in the development of the Airbus A-300 B. Discussion of civilian programs goes beyond the scope of this analysis. See Lorell, *Multinational Development*, pp. 48-70.

31. Interviews, Paris, 1977-1978.

32. Interview, NATO Brussels, June 1980. Problems surrounding Anglo-French collaboration on the Jaguar project are discussed in Martin Edmonds, "International Collaboration in Weapons Procurement: The Implications of the Anglo-French Case," *International Affairs* (April 1967), 252-264.

33. Quoted in Lorell, *Multinational Development*, p. 73. For sharp criticism of the Jaguar program, see France, Assemblée Nationale, CDNFA (1971), *Avis sur le projet de loi de finances pour 1972, Défense nationale: Dépenses en Capital*, No. 2013 1971, p. 24.

34. Interviews, Paris, 1977-1978. Cost overruns on the Jaguar project were also disconcerting to the French. John Simpson and Frank Gregory, "West European Collaboration in Weapons Procurement," *Orbis*, XVI, No. 2 (Summer 1972), 452.

35. Lorell, *Multinational Development*, p. 76, outlines R&D overruns.

36. For a review of early NATO arms cooperation, see Francis A. Beer, *Integration and Disintegration in NATO* (Columbus: Ohio State University Press, 1969), pp. 131-175; Robert Rhodes James, *Standardization and Common Production of Weapons in NATO* (London: Institute for Strategic Studies, 1967); and Brigadier General Elliott E. Vandervanter, Jr., *Coordinated Weapons Production in NATO: A Study of Alliance Processes* (Santa Monica, Calif.: RAND Corporation, 1964).

37. Quoted in Beer, *Integration and Disintegration in NATO*, p. 159.

38. The definitive study of this sale is Ingemar Dörfer's *Arms Deal: The Selling of the F-16* (New York: Praeger, 1983). All relevant citations to secondary literature are found in Dörfer.

39. *Ibid.*, p. 208.

40. The literature on RSI speaks volumes and constitutes the basis for a separate study. Through the late 1970s the pages of the military journals and NATO publications are filled with articles on the problem. See *NATO Review, International Defense Review, Strategy,* and *Fifteen Nations*. A comprehensive study of RSI is found in Robert A. Gessert et al., *The Impact on the Rationalization of European*

Defense Industry of Alternative U.S. Approaches to Transatlantic Defense Cooperation (McLean, Va.: General Research Corporation, 1979), 4 vols. The GRC report is especially useful for comparative purposes: *Arms Exports and Weapons Cooperation in NATO: Summary and Analysis of a Data Base* (McLean, Va.: General Research Corporation, 1980). Gessert summarizes his views in his informed article, "Industrial Considerations in Transatlantic Weapons Cooperation—Part 1: European Industry and Political Perspectives," *International Defense Review* (June 1979), 921-930. See also the annual Department of Defense reports, *Rationalization/Standardization within NATO.* An overview of European views may be found in U.S., General Accounting Office, *Standardization in NATO: Improving the Effectiveness and Economy of Mutual Defense Efforts* (Washington, D.C., 1978); U.S., Cong., House, Committee on Armed Services, *Hearing before the Special Subcommittee on NATO Standardization*, 95th Cong., 2d Sess., 1979; and Egon Klepsch, *Future Arms Procurement* (London: Brassey's, 1979). For a useful overview, see William Bajusz, "The Collective Management of Defense: Collaborative Weapons Acquisition in NATO" (Unpublished Ph.D. dissertation, University of Wisconsin, 1981). Bajusz also reviews the Jaguar program on pp. 168 and 245-252. He presents a more favorable evaluation than that presented above; see n. 33 above. Also see n. 52 below.

41. The standardization and redundancy issue was given initial impetus by a report written by Thomas A. Callaghan, Jr. An expansion of his critique of NATO armaments policy is found in *U.S./European Economic Cooperation in Military and Civilian Technology* (Washington, D.C.: Center for Strategic and International Studies, Georgetown University, 1975).

42. Delpech, "La Standardisation des Armements," pp. 20-21.

43. Kanter and Fry, *Cooperation*, pp. 97-123.

44. William J. Perry, *The Department of Defense Written Statement on NATO-Improved Armaments Cooperation*, before the Research and Development Subcommittee of the Senate Armed Services Committee, 96th Cong., 1st Sess., 1979.

45. Kanter and Fry, *Cooperation*, pp. 33-54, provide a useful brief overview of official European views. Gessert is also well informed in this score; see n. 40 above.

46. Cauchie and Defournaux, n. 15 above.

47. Based on the assumption of shared strategic objectives within the alliance (an admittedly dubious assumption), the American case for arms cohesion was compelling. Elliott R. Goodman, "France and Arms for the Atlantic Alliance: The Standardization-Interoperability Problem," *Orbis*, XXIV, No. 3 (Fall 1980), 541-571, makes a strong plea for the American position. For a French reply, see Pierre Gallois, "Réponse à Elliott R. Goodman: Arsenal moderne et veilles recettes ou standardisation, coopération, illusions," *Politique Internationale* (Summer 1980), 261-266.

48. U.S., Arms Control and Disarmament Agency (ACDA), *World Military Expenditures and Arms Transfers, 1967-1976* (Washington, D.C.: U.S. Government Printing Office, 1978), *passim.*

49. Defournaux and Cauchie make this point repeatedly. See Cauchie, "Conference," 1980 (mimeo.). Also instructive of the French position is Colonel Jean-Marie de Gonneville, *Armées d'Aujourd'hui* (April 1978), pp. 28-29.

50. ACDA, *World Military Expenditures, 1967-1976, passim.* Also Kanter and Fry, *Cooperation*, pp. 17-19.

51. Quote in Bernard Udis, "Lessons from Aerospace: The Prospects for Rationalization in NATO," *Orbis*, xxv, No. 1 (Spring 1981), 178.

52. Cauchie, WEU, March 3-4, 1977, p. 22, and interviews, Paris, 1977-1978 and NATO Brussels, June 1980. An optimistic appraisal of the Roland contract containing useful detail about the program is the study of Donald K. Malone, *Roland: A Case for or against NATO Standardization?* (Washington, D.C.: National Defense University, 1980). A less supportive evaluation that parallels French sentiment is found in Phillip Taylor, "Weapons Standardization in NATO: Collaborative Security or Economic Competition?" *International Organization*, xxxvi, No. 1 (Winter 1982), 95-112, especially 108-112.

53. A well-researched Congressional view of the Roland case that is also more exhaustive than the Malone or Taylor discussions is Richard Charles Fast's "The Politics of Weapons Standardization in NATO" (Unpublished Ph.D. dissertation, University of California, Santa Barbara, 1981), pp. 372-447, and Interviews, NATO Brussels, Headquarters, 1980.

54. *Le Monde*, May 30, 1984, and NATO *Report*, October 6, 1986.

55. FBIS, September 11, 1984, p. K20.

56. *Ibid.*, p. 21.

57. See the following for sensible discussions of weapons cooperation in Europe: Kanter and Fry, *Cooperation*; Bernard Udis, "Lessons from Aerospace"; and Roger Facer, *The Alliance and Europe: Part III Weapons Procurement in Europe—Capabilities and Choices* (London: International Institute for Strategic Studies, 1975), pp. 36-48, provides an overview of NATO cooperation.

The most comprehensive discussion of the economics of cooperation in NATO, with special regard to the aeronautics industry, is the excellent study by Keith Hartley, *NATO Arms Co-operation* (London: George Allen and Unwin, 1983).

58. See, France, Ministère de la Défense, *Compte rendu sur le programme d'équipement militaire, Années 1960-75, passim.*

59. See, for example, n. 68 below for illustrations.

60. Interviews, Paris, 1977-1978, 1980, and 1982.

61. National Assembly reports and ministerial documents stress the civilian benefits of arms production and foreign sales. E.g., see France, Ministère de la Défense, *Compte rendu.* For a vigorous defense of the arms industry, see the brief written by anonymous "high functionaries" in the government, *Le Monde*, March 16, 1978. Commentary on the shared views of governmental and industrial leaders in the arms industry about the necessity of exports is found in Jannic Hervé, "Complexe militaro-industriel à la française," *L'Expansion* (January 1971). For a recent statement of essentially the argument in favor of a strong arms industry as a net contributor to economic prosperity, see Henri Azam, "Industrie d'armement et politique industrielle de défense," *Défense Nationale* (April 1982), 5-30.

62. *Le Monde*, December 2, 1974.

63. Ministère de la Défense, *Livre blanc*, i, 45.

64. FBIS, September 14, 1982, p. K1.

65. The value of the franc to dollar fell from 4.22 in 1980 to 8.74 in 1984, more than half. International Monetary Fund, *International Financial Statistics* (Washington, D. C., 1985), p. 200.

66. Converted to dollars, the value of deliveries slipped each year between 1981 and 1984: 1981, $5.2 billion; 1982, $4.4 billion; 1983, $4.3 billion; 1984, approximately $4.1 billion. *Ibid.*

67. Estimates are based on French arms delivery data drawn from French sources. Arms exports for other suppliers are provided by ACDA, *World Military Expenditures and Arms Transfers, 1971-1980* (Washington, D.C.; U.S. Government Printing Office, 1983), *passim*. See notes to Table 3-3 for a discussion of data sources. Higher estimates for French arms exports are used than those cited by ACDA and otherwise widely used even by French officials like General Cauchie, who preferred to downplay the magnitude of French arms sales. Interviews, Paris, 1977-1978.

68. Cited by Pierre Dussauge, *L'Industrie française de l'armement* (Paris: Economica, 1985), pp. 66-67.

69. Sources, drawing on official figures, differ slightly in the estimates of the value of French arms exports. Compare Dussauge, *ibid.*, pp. 64-66; François Heisbourg, "Défense et sécurité extérieure: le changement dans la continuité," *Politique Etrangère*, No. 2 (Summer 1985), 398; and Ministère de la Défense, SIRPA, *Armament in France*, Dossier d'Information No. 77 (May 1985), p. 28. A study of the Ministry of Defense calculates arms exports at 6.14 and 6.87 percent in 1981 and 1982, respectively, dropping to 4.59 percent of exports in 1983. Ministère de la Défense, *Analyse économique des dépenses militaires* (November 1984), 13.

70. *Le Monde*, April 17, 1985. Arms orders are discussed in France, Assemblée Nationale, CDNFA (1981), *Avis sur le projet de loi de finances pour 1982, Défense: Politique de défense de la France*, No. 473, p. 120, and *idem* (1982), *Défense: Politique de défense de la France*, No. 1168, p. 61. See also Dussauge, *L'Industrie*, pp. 64-66.

71. Figures are calculated from data drawn from Table 3-3 and France, Ministère de l'Industrie du Commerce et de l'Artisanat, *Les Usines Clef en Main: Réalité et Perspective pour la France, 1978*, cited in Lawrence G. Franko and Sherry Stephenson, *French Export Behavior in Third World Markets*, Significant Issues Series, II, No. 6 (Washington, D.C.: Center for Strategic and International Studies, 1980), p. 57; and France, Centre Français du Commerce Extérieur, *Commerce Extérieur de la France, 1977* (Paris, 1978), p. 10, and *idem, Commerce Extérieur de la France, 1978* (Paris, 1979), p. 12.

72. This statistic is drawn from the annual report of the Ministry of Defense on the execution of successive military five-year plans: *Compte rendu, 1962-1975, passim*.

73. *Ibid.*

74. Data on orders are drawn from annual parliamentary reports devoted to spending on military equipment. They are issued by the Committee on National Defense and the Armed Forces. The full title is given below only for 1975. The others follow a similar format with the number and year of the report changing on an annual basis: France, Assemblée Nationale, CDNFA (1975), *Avis sur le projet*

de loi de finances pour 1976, Dépenses en Capital, No. 1919, p. 43; No. 2532 (1976), p. 57; No. 3150 (1977), pp. 102-103; No. 573 (1978), p. 149; No. 1295 (1979), pp. 44-45; No. 1979 (1980), p. 42; No. 473 (1981), p. 119; and No. 1168 (1982), p. 61. As late as 1973 a report of the Committee on National Defense and the Armed Forces, in answer to domestic critics of French arms transfer, insisted that the bulk of these exports went to developed states: No. 684 (1973), p. 42. Technically, the response was correct since deliveries until that time were to industrialized states; however, the flow of orders for arms had already been reoriented to the developing countries.

75. Data cover 1974-1981, inclusive, and the first six months of 1982.

76. Citations are those found in n. 68.

77. Hard data for exports to specific regions and states are difficult to acquire. These regional percentages are cited in an unpublished paper by two French analysts acquainted with the French arms industry: Pierre Dussauge and Christian Schmidt, "L'Industrie française de l'armement" (Paris: 1982), pp. 16-17 (mimeo.). Published results appear in n. 101.

78. Commission de la Défense Nationale (1982), No. 1168, p. 61.

79. ACDA, *World Military Expenditures and Arms Transfers, 1970-1979* (Washington, D.C.: U.S. Government Printing Office, 1982), pp. 58-59, 63, 80, 100-101, 105, 122. Italy does not follow this pattern; arms exports in the 1970s grew at a slower rate than defense expenditures.

80. U.S., Department of Defense, news release, December 1985.

81. Interviews, Paris, 1977-1978.

82. Percentages are derived by dividing exports to developing states, including oil producers, by arms transfer data found in Table 3-3. Export data are drawn from International Monetary Fund, *Direction of Trade, Yearbook 1982* (Washington, D.C., 1983), pp. 160-162.

83. *Ibid.*

84. There are numerous treatments of European and, specifically, French energy policy. For a general review of European policy, see Robert J. Lieber, *The Oil Decade* (New York: Praeger, 1983). Useful, too, is the earlier work by Guy de Carmoy, *Energy for Europe: Political and Economic Implications* (Washington, D.C.: American Enterprise Institute, 1972).

For French policy, specifically, see Horst Mendershausen, *Coping with the Oil Crisis: French and German Experiences* (Baltimore: The Johns Hopkins University Press, 1976); Robert J. Lieber, "Energy Policies of the Fifth Republic," in *The Fifth Republic at Twenty*, pp. 311-321; France, Conseil Economique et Social, *Les Moyens d'assurer la sécurité de l'approvisionment énergetique de la France, Journal Officiel*, March 11, 1973; Jean Choffel, *Le Problème pétrolier français. Notes et Etudes Documentaires*, No. 4279 (Paris: Documentation Française, 1976); Guy de Carmoy, "The New French Policy," *Energy Policy* (September 1982), 181-188, and N.J.D. Lucas, "The Role of Institutional Relationships in French Energy Policy," *International Relations*, v, No. 6 (November 1977), 87-121.

85. French oil politics and the Libyan sale are extensively discussed in the author's *French International Policy*, pp. 168-170 and 489-551.

86. Michel Béhar et al., "Un dépot d'armes: Le Moyen-Orient," *Géostratégie et économie mondiale, Cahier Français*, No. 201 (May-June 1981), 17-19.

87. Dussauge and Schmidt, "L'Industrie française de l'armement," p. 17.

88. *Ibid*.

89. Janice McCormick, "Thorns among the Roses: A Year of the Socialist Experiment in France," *West European Politics* (January 1983), 43-62.

90. Defournaux, "Coopération et l'indépendence," reflects the prevailing view within the General Directorate for Armament that France has a competitive advantage in arms sales that should not be relinquished.

91. Interviews, Paris, 1977-1978.

92. ACDA, *World Military Expenditures, 1963-1973*, p. 119.

93. *Ibid., 1966-1975*, p. 77.

94. *Ibid*.

95. *Ibid*. For a more detailed analysis, see Edward A. Kolodziej and Robert E. Harkavy, "Developing States and the International Security System," *Journal of International Affairs* (Spring-Summer 1980), 59-84.

96. Interviews, Paris, 1977-1978.

97. Quoted in Dussauge, *L'Industrie*, p. 96.

98. See *ibid*., pp. 127ff.

99. See the widely quoted report of Robert Perry, who evaluated the factors underlying Dassault's commercial success. Also of value is Hartley, *NATO Arms Co-operation, passim*. For background material, consult Claude Carlier, *Le Développement de l'aéronautique militaire française de 1958 à 1970* (Paris: Service Historique de l'Armée de l'Air, 1979), pp. 155-170.

100. *Ibid*., p. 161.

101. Christian Schmidt and Pierre Dussauge, "L'Armement" in *L'Industrie en France*, ed. Bertrand Bellon and Jean-Marie Chevalier (Paris: Flammarion, 1983), pp. 290-297.

102. See John Zysman for a thoughtful and informed critique of French industrial and trade policy from the perspective of a liberal economic viewpoint within which the role of the state would be minimal and basically noninterventionist: *Political Strategies for Industrial Order* (Berkeley: University of California Press, 1977).

103. International Monetary Fund, *Direction of Trade, Yearbooks 1970-1979, passim*.

104. Bela Belassa, "The French Economy 1958-1973," in *The Fifth Republic at Twenty*, p. 209.

105. *Ibid*., pp. 209-210.

106. *Ibid*., p. 210.

107. *Ibid*., p. 225. Spivey confirms Belassa's succinct analysis.

108. France, Ministère de la Défense, *Compte rendu, 1967*, p. 30. Government figures on employment are not consistent. They vary with respect to the total number and, specifically, with regard to the proportion devoted to arms exports. In the 1970s, sources place employment between 270,000 to 280,000 of which 45,000 to 75,000 were engaged in exports. The figures cited in Figure 3-8 appear closer to the mark than previous estimates although still somewhat low both in the total personnel in the arms industry and in the number assigned to exports. See, for example, *Livre blanc*, I, 45, and the citations noted in the author's "Determinants of French Arms Sales: Security Implications," in *Threats,*

Weapons, and Foreign Policy, ed. Pat McGown and Charles W. Kegley, Jr. (Beverly Hills: Sage, 1980), pp. 150-152; "France," in *The Structure of the Defense Industry*, ed. Nicole Ball and Milton Leitenberg (London: Croom Helm, 1983), p. 107; and "French Arms Trade: The Economic Determinants," in SIPRI, *World Armaments and Disarmament, SIPRI Yearbook 1983* (London and New York: Taylor and Francis, 1983), pp. 371-390. I have had to change the estimates for personnel working in the arms industry as new and more current data became available. Despite discrepancies, the parameters of arms industry personnel are fairly stable; what is more problematic is the proportion devoted to domestic and to foreign production.

109. France, Ministère de la Défense, *Données économiques sur les dépenses militaires* (Paris, 1978), Chapter 11 and *idem*, SIRPA, *Armament in France*, Dossier d'Information, No. 77 (May 1985), p. 8.

110. See n. 98 above.

111. Figures are drawn from Gessert and Brooks, *Arms Exports and Weapons Cooperation in NATO*, p. 25.

112. Stephen S. Cohen, "Twenty Years of the Gaullist Economy," in *The Fifth Republic at Twenty*, pp. 240-251.

113. Robert H. Ballance et al., *The International Economy and Industrial Development* (London: Wheatsheaf Books, 1982), p. 75.

114. *Ibid.*, pp. 74-76.

115. Compare Figure 3-8 with figures found in France, Assemblée Nationale, CF (1964), *Rapport sur le projet de loi relative à certain équipements militaires*, No. 1155, p. 40; and *Livre blanc*, I, 45.

116. France, Ministère de la Défense, SIRPA, *Budget 1983* (Paris, 1983), p. 26.

117. France, Assemblée Nationale, CDNFA (1980), *Avis sur le projet de lois de finances pour 1981, Dépenses en Capital*, No. 1979, p. 38, and ns. 98 and 105 above.

118. Carlier, *L'Aéronautique française*, makes the point that this reform effort began with the Fourth Republic but it lacked the means, will, and public support to transform the military establishment and to reform the economy.

119. The use of military R&D to reorganize France's scientific-technological-industrial base and to use defense spending to modernize the French economy is described in Gilpin, *France in the Age of the Scientific State*. For a brief sketch of the argument, see Robert Gilpin, "Science, Technology, and French Independence," in *Science Policies of Industrial Nations*, ed. T. Dixon Long and Christopher Wright (New York: Praeger, 1975), pp. 110-132.

120. See Ministère de la Défense, *Compte rendu, 1962-1975, passim*.

121. *Le Monde*, April 27, 1983, recounts a colloquium at the Ecole Polytechnique on defense research.

122. Accurate spending data for R&D are difficult to acquire. Accounting procedures differ from one source to another, and data bases are often not the same. These problems are signaled in George Menahem, *La Science et le militaire* (Paris: Seuil, 1976), pp. 116-119. Confusing and inconsistent sets of R&D data issue from various governmental sources. Since the list is so extensive, I have cited only those sources that I have actually used and that appear to be consistent. While these sources differ on specific amounts and percentages, they

are closer in terms of the trends that they describe as depicted in Table 3-6.

123. *Ibid.*, p. 107 and Table 3-8.

124. "L'Effort public de recherche et de développement technologique," *Le Progrès Scientifique* (November-December 1981), 24-25.

125. Pinatel, *L'Economie*, p. 160.

126. *Ibid.*, p. 53.

127. Jean Barberry, "L'Impact industriel du IIIe Plan Militaire," *Revue de Défense Nationale* (May 1970), 1755-1772.

128. France, Délégation Générale de la Recherche Scientifique et Technique, *Recherche et développement dans l'industrie* (Paris, 1975), pp. 14-15.

129. Ministère de la Défense, *Données économiques*, Chapter 12. Also Dussauge, *L'Industrie*, citing Ministry of Defense figures, notes a lower percentage (34) for 1979, p. 66.

130. *Ibid.*

131. *Ibid.*, and Commission de la Défense Nationale (1982), No. 1168, pp. 10-14.

132. Quoted in *Recherche et développement à fins militaires* (Paris: Les Cahiers de la Fondation pour les Etudes de Défense Nationale, 1978), p. 113. This is the most comprehensive evaluative study available in French of the military R&D program. This analysis draws extensively on this analysis.

133. Lorell, *Multinational Development*, pp. 48-81, discusses the Airbus program.

134. The French electronic industry is probingly discussed in Zysman, *Political Strategies for Industrial Order*. For a competent and informed coverage of the Plan Calcul fiasco, see Jean M. Quatrepoint and Jacques Jublin, *French ordinateur* (Paris: Alain Moreau, 1976).

135. McCormick, "Thorns among the Roses."

136. See the article of J. M. Quatrepoint in *Le Monde*, January 28, 1984.

137. For a discussion of the problems faced by Matra in attempting to reconvert to greater civilian production, see the articles by Quatrepoint in *Le Monde*, February 17, 1984, and by J. Gloaguen in *Le Nouvel Economiste*, February 1, 1985; and Dussauge, *L'Industrie*, pp. 176-199.

138. France, Institut National de la Statistique et des Etudes Economiques (INSEE), *Rapport sur les comptes de la nation de l'année 1980: Les Comptes et agrégats*, Séries C, 94-95, pp. 148-151.

139. The dependency of key French firms on arms exports is confirmed in Dussauge's independently calculated results, *L'Industrie*, pp. 40-44.

140. For confirmation of these figures, see Dassault-Bréguet Corporation, *Bilan*, 1980. Civilian orders in 1980 were above the average of preceding deliveries and amounted to 15.5 percent of Dassault's order book. See also *Le Monde*, June 8, 1979.

141. *Recherche et développement*, p. 110.

142. European Community, Committee on Scientific and Technical Research, *Government Financing of Research and Development: 1975-1981* (Brussels, 1982).

143. *Economist*, July 18, 1981, p. 19.

CHAPTER 4

1. This, for example, is the organizing principle of the useful description of the French arms industry found in Christian Schmidt and Pierre Dussauge, "L'Armement," in *L'Industrie en France*, pp. 219-250.

2. This broad conception of the arms industry is sketched in the confidential remarks of Hughes de l'Estoile, a key figure in the development of the French arms industry, before a closed group of arms designers, developers, and manufacturers: "Armement et vie économique," Conférence prononcée par Hughes de l'Estoile, Directeur du Centre de Prospective et d'Evaluation, October 27, 1969.

3. See Cohen, *Modern Capitalist Planning, passim*; Cohen and Gourevitch, *France, passim*; and Martin, *Warriors to Managers, passim*. See also Chapter 3, ns. 3 and 4.

4. See France, Ministère de la Défense, SIRPA, *Le Budget de la défense pour 1983* (Paris, 1983) and *idem, Direction Générale pour l'Armement* (Paris, 1983).

5. *Economist*, September 8, 1984, p. 37.

6. Interviews, Paris, 1977-1978, 1982, 1983.

7. The debates over nationalization are in many ways more interesting in what they say about shared French views about economic development than about their differences, especially with respect to a preference for large units. For the debate over nationalization, see André G. Delion and Michel Durepty, *Les Nationalisations, 1982* (Paris: Economica, 1982); Jacques Blanc and Chantal Brulé, *Les Nationalisations françaises en 1982, Notes et Etudes Documentaires*, Nos. 4721-4722, June 20, 1983 (Paris: Documentation Française, 1983); Janine Brémond, *Les Nationalisations* (Paris: Hatier, 1977); and the series of articles appearing in *Projet* (March 1982), 289-332.

8. Remarks of Lionel Stoleru, *Le Monde*, September 23, 1981.

9. These expectations are developed at length in a three-part presentation by Michel Bauer and Elie Cohen in *Le Monde*, September 24, 25, and 26, 1981.

10. Yves Morau, "L'Aéronautique," *L'Industrie en France*, pp. 251-280, and citations noted therein.

11. Claude Carlier, *Le Développement de l'aéronautique militaire française*, pp. 17-18. Carlier's 1983 study should be consulted for a detailed description of the evolution of French airpower from 1945 to 1975: *L'Aéronautique française*.

12. *Ibid.*, and interviews, Paris, 1983.

13. Dörfer, *Arms Deal*, pp. 154-177.

14. The French government was not so generous to the Manhurin Corporation for similar losses suffered during the Suez episode in the 1950s. Mohamed Adel El-Zaim, *Le Régime juridique du contrôle de fabrication de vente et d'exportation des matériels de guerre en droit française*, Mémoire pour le diplôme d'études supérieure de droit public (Paris: Université de Paris, 1969), pp. 88-89. This conclusion is also supported by the remarks of Bernard Waquet, a disaffected employee of the Dassault Corporation, before the parliamentary committee created to investigate governmental financial support of the aircraft industry, 1977 (mimeo.).

15. Interviews, Paris, 1977-1978, 1983.

16. See François-Xavier Donnadieu, *Le Contrôle des industries d'armements*, Thèse pour le doctorat d'état de droit public, Paris II, 1979, pp. 298-311 and 372-375.

17. Blanc and Brulé, *Les Nationalisations françaises*, pp. 28-29; *Le Monde*, September 15, 1981; and *Lutte Ouvrière*, September 19, 1981; interviews, Paris, 1977-1978, 1983.

18. France, Assemblée Nationale, CF (1977), *Projet de loi de finances pour 1978, Défense: Considérations Générales: Dépenses en Capital*, No. 3131, pp. 96-101.

19. *Ibid.*

20. *Ibid.*

21. Schmidt and Dussauge, "L'Armement," p. 288. Matra and Thomson-CSF also showed smart increases during this period: Matra rose from 533 to 2,562 francs; Thomson-CSF doubled from 243 to 579 francs.

22. France, Assemblée Nationale, CDNFA (1983), *Rapport sur le projet de loi portant approbation de la programmation militaire pour les années 1984-1988*, No. 1485, p. 67.

23. Carlier, *Le Développement de l'aéronautique française*," pp. 112-113.

24. Donnadieu, *Le Contrôle des industries d'armements, passim.*

25. Jean Ravaud, "L'Industrie aérospatiale française," *Défense Nationale* (June 1979), 32-36. Most of this number is devoted to the French aeronautics industry; see pp. 17-120. Only the most important corporate units of the industry can be described here. At least 130 different enterprises compose the principal elements of the industry.

26. Carlier, *Le Développement de l'aéronautique française*, p. 124.

27. France, Ministère de l'Industrie, *20 Ans de Conquête française de l'espace*, Etudes de Politique Industrielle, No. 31 (Paris: Documentation Française, 1981), pp. 51-53.

28. *Ibid.* describes the European space effort and French participation.

29. Guy Gauthier, *Délégation Générale pour l'Armement*, doctorat d'état, Paris, II, 1982, p. 46.

30. Blanc and Brulé, *Les Nationalisations françaises*, pp. 29-31, summarize the steps leading to governmental takeover.

31. Gauthier, *Délégation Générale*, pp. 130-132.

32. France, Ministère de la Défense, *Délégation Générale pour l'Armement* (Paris: 1983), pp. 41-47.

33. Ministère de l'Industrie, *20 Ans de Conquête française de l'espace.*

34. James W. Sterling, *The French Weapon Acquisition Process* (Charlottesville, Va.: Army Foreign Science and Technology Center, 1974), p. 45.

35. Raymond Manicacci, *L'Electronique française: électronique d'armement* (Paris I: Mémoire D.E.A., 1978), p. 19.

36. *Ibid.*, pp. 11-12.

37. André Danzin, "Nationaliser l'électronique et l'informatique: pour quelle stratégie?" *Projet* (March 1982), 309.

38. Manicacci, *L'Electronique française*, p. 16.

39. Schmidt and Dussauge, "L'Armement," pp. 219-250.

40. Quoted in Monique Bouleau, *Les Industries et exportation d'armes françaises en 1970*, Mémoire pour Diplôme d'Etudes Supérieures (Paris I, October 1972), p. 77.

41. Quatrepoint and Jublin, *French ordinateurs*, pp. 58-61.

42. The implications of these dilemmas are developed at length by John Zysman in *Political Strategies for Industrial Order*. See also his "French Electronics Policy: The Costs of Technological Independence," in *Industrial Policies in Western Europe*, ed. Steven J. Warnecke and Ezra N. Suleiman (New York: Praeger, 1975), pp. 227-245.

43. Quoted in Quatrepoint and Jublin, *French ordinateurs*, p. 34. Most of this account is taken from exhaustive investigative accounts of the Plan Calcul.

44. *Ibid.*, p. 67.

45. *Ibid.*

46. *Ibid.*, pp. 192-200ff.

47. London *Financial Times*, March 17, 1983.

48. *Ibid.* The export problems facing France's computer industry are reviewed by Robert Zarader in "L'Informatique," *L'Industrie en France*, pp. 219-250.

49. *L'Unité*, September 19, 1981.

50. See the series of articles by Quatrepoint, *Le Monde*, September 9, 20, and 21, and October 4, 1983.

51. Jean-Laurens Delpech, "Délégue Ministeriel pour l'Armement," *Armement* (October 1975), 10, and *idem*, "Entretien avec M. J.-L. Delpech," *Défense Nationale* (October 1974), 22.

52. SNPE, *Bilan, passim*, and Gauthier, *Délégation Générale pour l'Armement*, pp. 135-136.

53. See the special issue of *Armement* on GIAT, 1980, pp. 1-212; the brochure of the DAT (Paris, 1976); and the 1972 and 1983 editions of DMA, pp. 26-29 and DGA, pp. 31-34, respectively; Gauthier, *Délégation Générale pour l'Armement*, pp. 123-129; David Greenwood, *The Organisation of Defence Procurement and Production in France* (Aberdeen: Centre for Defence Studies, 1979), pp. 18-20; and Jacques Ramont, "Le G.I.A.T., ses moyens, ses produits," *Défense Nationale* (June 1981), pp. 25-36.

54. GIAT, *Armement*, p. 63.

55. DAT brochure and Gauthier, *Délégation Générale pour l'Armement*, p. 127.

56. DAT brochure.

57. Greenwood, *Organisation of Defence Procurement*, p. 33.

58. DMA brochure, 1972, p. 34.

59. *L'Expansion*, October 20, 1980, p. 77.

60. *Ibid.*, pp. 74-78; Gauthier, *Délégation Générale pour l'Armement*, p. 166; and Schmidt and Dussauge, "L'Armement," p. 297.

61. DGA brochure, 1983, pp. 35-37.

62. Gauthier, *Délégation Générale pour l'Armement*, pp. 116-122.

63. Greenwood, *Organisation of Defence Procurement*, p. 64.

64. Compare DMA, 1972, pp. 29-36 and DGA, 1983, p. 35.

65. Orders in the 1970s were grouped as follows:

Ship	Constructor	Destination
Aviso	Dubigeon	Portugal
Daphne submarines	Dubigeon(7)	Portugal(4)
	Brest(1)	South Africa(3)
	Le Trait(2)	Pakistan(3)
	Carthagène(4)	Spain(4)

Source: DMA, 1972, p. 35.

66. Jean Chaboud, "Le Programme Sawari," *Armées d'Aujourd'hui* (October 1982), 34-35.

67. *L'Expansion*, October 20, 1980, p. 78.

68. Interviews, Paris, 1977-1978.

69. Interviews, Paris, 1983. Opinion is mixed on this point of initiative, but most of those consulted in approximately twenty interviews saw little or no change in arms production and exports. All agree that under the Socialists the commercialization of arms production has intensified and the process of authorizing exports was streamlined with more active ministerial involvement than before.

70. Delpech, "Entretien avec J.-L. Delpech," *Défense Nationale* (June 1975), 15-38.

71. Interviews, Paris, 1983.

72. Schmidt and Dussauge, "L'Armement," *passim*. See also Dussauge, "L'Industrie française de l'armement."

CHAPTER 5

1. France, Ministère de la Défense, *Délégation Générale pour l'Armement* (Paris, 1983), p. 3; interviews, Paris, 1977-1978.

2. Interviews, Paris, 1977-1978.

3. Interviews, Paris, 1977-1978.

4. Interviews, Paris, 1977-1978.

5. Gauthier, *Délégation Général pour l'Armement*, p. 46.

6. See successive DMA and DGA brochures: 1972, pp. 4-6; 1978, pp. 5-7; 1983, pp. 3-4.

7. Gauthier, *Délégation Général pour l'Armement*, p. 28.

8. France, Ministère de la Défense, *Délégation Ministérielle pour l'Armement* (Paris, 1972), p. 3.

9. France, Ministère de la Défense, SIRPA, *Délégation Générale pour l'Armement*, Dossier d'Information No. 54 (December 1977); G. Lacoste, "Les Structures unifiées de la Délégation Ministérielle pour l'Armement," *Forces Armées Françaises* (June 1972), 13-15; and Jean Tison, "La Délégation Ministérielle pour l'Armement," *La Jaune et Rouge* (June 1970), 17-18.

10. DGA, 1977, p. 6.

11. Jean Girodet, "Des Techniques et des hommes: La Délégation Générale pour l'Armement à vingt ans," *Armées d'Aujourd'hui* (January-February 1981), 29.

12. *Ibid.*

13. France, Ministère de la Défense, *Délégation Générale pour l'Armement* (Paris, 1985).

14. The DGA's authority is codified in a lengthy administrative document: France, Ministère des Armées, Bulletin Officiel des Armées, *Organisation de la Délégation Générale pour l'Armement et des organismes rattachés*, May 17, 1977, 162 pp.

15. Additional descriptive material about the DAT and GIAT may be found in Jacques Ramont, *Défense Nationale* (June 1981), 25-36. Consult especially the issues of *Armement*, published under the auspices of the DGA. See the special 1980 number devoted to GIAT. *Armement* also periodically features articles on particular DAT units. For example, "Manufacture nationale d'armes de Saint Etienne, *Armement* (October 1971), 130-141; "L'Etablissement de la DTAT à Bourges," *ibid.* (December 1972), 84-107; "L'Atelier de construction de Tarbes," *ibid.* (April 1974), 108-125; "La Manufacture nationale d'armes de Tulle," *ibid.* (April 1975), 119-133; "L'Atelier de changement de Salbris," *ibid.* (December 1976), 122-137; and "Les Service aéroportés de la DTAT," *ibid.* (December 1977), 134-145.

16. Bulletin, *Organization de la Délégation Générale*, p. 9. Jean Mesmet outlines DCN functions in "La Direction techniques des constructions navales et ses activités," *Défense Nationale* (October 1982), 29-42. Additional material on DCN and its units may be found in *Armement*: "Etablissement des constructions et armes navales de Ruelle," *Armement* (February 1970), 100-108; "Etablissement des constructions et armes navales de Saint-Tropez," *ibid.* (February 1972), 153-172; "La Direction des constructions et armes navales de Brest," *ibid.* (October 1973), 162-181; "L'Etablissement des constructions et armes navales d'Indret," *ibid.* (June 1974), 156-169; and "La Direction des constructions et armes navales de Lorient," *ibid.* (February 1975), 121-137.

17. Ingénieur en Chef Crétinon, "Le Compte de Commerce de la DTCN," *Armement* (December 1979), 39-46.

18. France, Ministère de la Défense, *Délégation Générale pour l'Armement* (Paris, 1985).

19. This problem is briefly sketched by Ferdinand Varenne in "Exportations d'armements: diriger ou laissez faire," *Projet* (April 1983), 303-317. They are also touched upon in the remarks of Jean-Laurens Delpech, "Entretien avec M. J.-L. Delpech," pp. 21-26.

20. Jean-Laurens Delpech, "Délégue Ministériel pour l'Armement," *Armement* (October 1975), 13-14.

21. Ingénieur Principal de l'Armement Dubresson, "Réflexions sur la 'tutelle' de l'industrie aéronautique," *Armement* (April 1970), 73-77, argues against this stance.

22. Interviews, Paris, 1983.

23. Lionel Stoleru, *Le Monde*, September 23, 1981.

24. Interviews, Paris, 1983.

25. Interviews, Paris, 1983.

26. Ingénieur Général de Batz, "Le Rôle de la DTCA dans la conduite des programmes aéronautiques," *Armement* (February 1977), 22.

27. *Ibid.*, p. 32.

28. Delpech, "Delégue Ministériel," p. 11. The four ministries are Transportation, Research and Industry, Finance, and Defense.

29. The organizational structure and functions of the DCAÉ (known formerly as DTCA) are outlined in "Monographie de la DTCA," *Armement* (August 1977), 153-164. Additional discussion can be found in *Armement*: "L'Atelier industriel aéronautique de Clermont-Ferrand," *Armement* (April 1973), 119-135; and "L'Atelier industriel aéronautique de Bordeaux," *ibid.* (February 1974), 121-137.

30. Ingénieur en Chef Carnot, "La Direction Technique des Engines," *Armement* (April 1979), 8-13. Other facets of DEN are covered in *Armement*: "Le Centre d'essais des Landes," *Armement* (June 1969), 116-129; and "Le Centre d'achèvement et d'essais des propulseurs et engins," *ibid.* (April 1972), 144-159.

31. The DEN oversees France's tactical missiles, including Super 530, Magic, MM-38 and MM-40, AM- and SM-39, Crotale, Roland, and Hawk.

32. *Délégation Générale pour l'Armement*, 1985

33. DGA, 1983, pp. 9-13.

34. *Ibid.*, pp. 23-25.

35. Y. Le Henaff, "Les Armes de destruction massive et la politique de défense française," *PRI*, 1979-1980, p. 76.

36. *Ibid.* Some winners of the Prix Lamb are Y. Rocard for the atomic bomb (1960), P. Carrière for missiles (1970), A. Chesné and P. Faugeras for the H-bomb (1970), and R. Dautry for nuclear submarines (1974).

37. Interviews, Paris, 1983.

38. Interviews, Paris, 1983.

39. Interviews, Paris, 1983.

40. Interviews, Paris, 1983.

41. Interviews, Paris, 1983.

42. Georges Menahem, *Le Science et la militaire* (Paris: Seuil, 1976), p. 130.

43. Quoted by Contrôleur Général des Armées Audebaud, "Le Commissaire du Gouvernement auprès des sociétés industrielles d'armement," *Armement* (October 1982), 27.

44. *Ibid.*, p. 28.

45. *Ibid.*, pp. 28-30.

46. Space does not permit a full discussion of the legislative laws and administrative regulations governing the arms production and sales process or of all of the agencies charged with oversight functions. For an introduction to the vast legal and administrative literature covering the control mechanisms available to the government to control French industry and the economy, particularly those affecting the arms industry, consult Gauthier, *Delegation Général pour l'Armement* and the following: Ingénieur Général Maurice de Lorris, "Surveillance des fabrications d'armement dans l'industrie," *Armement* (June 1969), 68-84; Ingénieur en Chef Martre et le Contrôleur des Armées Blandin, "Animation et contrôle

de l'industrie d'armement," *ibid.* (June 1969), 32-51; Ingénieur Maurice de Lorris, "Le SIAR aura bientôt dix ans!" *ibid.* (October 1973), 58-81; Jean Faveris, "Contrôle des industries d'armement," *Défense Nationale* (February 1973), 49-70. The legal aspects of governmental controls are extensively treated by Donnadieu, *Le Contrôle des industries d'armements, passim,* and Andrée Jallon, "La Règlement de la fabrication et du commerce des armements," *Droit Administrative,* February 20, 1978, pp. 67-81.

47. France, DGA, *Service de la Surveillance Industrielle de l'Armement* (Paris, 1977).

48. *Ibid.,* p. 2.

49. Audebaud, *Commissaire du Gouvernement,* pp. 29-30.

50. For a discussion of the Cours de Compte, see Gauthier, *Délégation Général pour l'Armement,* pp. 218-222.

51. Audebaud, *Commissaire du Gouvernement,* pp. 29-34.

52. Gauthier, *Délégation Général pour l'Armement,* pp. 57-62, sketches DAI's organization. See also DGA, 1983, pp. 19-21.

53. The work of the CIEEMG is outlined in Claude Lachaux, "La Règlement des exportations des matériels de guerre," *Défense Nationale* (December 1977), 35-42.

54. Quoted in *ibid.,* p. 39.

55. Interviews, Paris, 1978-1979.

56. Interviews, Paris, 1977-1978, 1983. The specific units which participated in CIEEMG deliberations in the 1970s were the Bureau for Financial Policy and Technical Cooperation of DREE, the Bureau for Loans, Assistance, and Guarantees to Firms of the Ministry of Finance, and a section of the Ministry of Foreign Affairs concerned with control of arms exports and strategic materials. Interviews, 1977-1978, 1982, 1983. The importance of the DAI is also suggested in two articles written under a nom de plume by an arms engineer within DGA: Ferdinand Varenne, "Exportations d'armements: diriger ou laissez passer," *Projet* (March-April 1983), 303-315 and "Vente d'armements: le juridisme et l'incantation," *ibid.* (July-August 1983), 711-722.

57. Regulations covering arms exports are summarized in France, Journal Officiel, *Matériels de guerre, armes et munitions* (Paris, 1976).

58. Quoted in Varenne, "Exportations d'armements," p. 304.

59. *Ibid.*

60. Interviews, Paris, 1977-1978, 1982, 1983.

61. Interviews, Paris, 1983.

62. Interviews, Paris, 1977-1978, 1982, 1983.

63. Gauthier, *Délégation Général pour l'Armement,* p. 193.

64. *Ibid.,* pp. 220-221.

65. Dörfer, *Arms Deal,* pp. 154-177.

66. Gauthier, *Délégation Général pour l'Armement,* pp. 193-194.

67. Interviews, Paris, 1977-1978, 1982, 1983. See the case study of the sale of F-16s to NATO states in which the role of the foreign office as instrument of the French arms complex is described, Dörfer, *Arms Deal,* pp. 154-177.

68. Interviews, Paris, 1977-1978.

69. President Mitterrand ordered all French military aircraft at the Paris show

to be disarmed as a gesture of concern for arms sales. The act was more symbolic than substantive since, as Chapter 3 details, the Socialist government became as dependent on arms sales as its predecessors.

70. Centre Local d'Information et de Coordination pour Action Non-Violente (CLICAN), *Les Trafics d'armes de la France* (Paris: Maspero, 1978), pp. 38-39.

71. *Ibid.*, pp. 39-40 and Gauthier, *Délégation Général pour l'Armement*, pp. 362-364.

72. For a brief overview of French export-support institutions and programs, with bibliographic citations for further reading, see Christian Gavalda, "Institutions du commerce extérieur et en particulier de l'exportations," *Banque*, Fascicule 39 bis A. pp. 1-19 (1976) and "Financement et assurance crédit des exportations," *ibid.*, Fascicule 39 bis B, pp. 1-45 (1976). Formulae guiding laws and credits are outlined in Credit National, *Analyse des prêts consentés par le Crédit National dans le cadre de la procédure de financement des entreprises exportatrices*, May 1976.

73. Interviews, Paris, 1983.

74. Lawrence G. Franko and Sherry Stephenson, *French Export Behavior in Third World Markets* (Washington: Center for Strategic and International Studies, 1980), p. 16. Useful, too, for an overview of French financial instruments is John Zysman, "The Interventionist Temptation: Financial Structure and Political Purpose," in *The Fifth Republic at Twenty*, pp. 252-270.

75. Franko and Stephenson, *French Export Behavior*, p. 25.

76. *Ibid.*, p. 27.

77. Interviews, Paris, 1977-1978, 1982, 1983.

78. Franko and Stephenson, *French Export Behavior*, pp. 20-21. The most extensive discussion of COFACE is found in the doctoral thesis of Michèle Klein, *L'Assurance-crédit et les autres guaranties des riques dans le commerce international*, Thèse pour le doctorat d'etat en droit, Paris II, 1983.

79. Interviews, Paris, 1977-1978, 1982, 1983.

80. Interviews, Paris, 1983.

81. Interviews, Paris, 1977-1978.

82. Interviews, Paris, 1977-1978, 1982, 1983. For details of French export of armored vehicles, consult F. M. von Singer und Etterlin, *Tanks of the World, 1983* (Annapolis, Md.: Nautical and Aviation Publishing, 1983), p. 169.

83. Interviews, Paris, 1983.

84. Interviews, Paris, 1983.

85. Dörfer, *Arms Deal, passim* and especially pp. 154-177.

86. Interviews, Paris, 1977-1978.

87. Interview, Paris, 1983.

88. Interview, Paris, 1983.

89. Interview, Paris, 1983.

90. See Lorell, *Multinational Development*, pp. 31-47.

91. These conclusions are consistent with the remarkable studies of French elites by Ezra Suleiman, *Politics, Power, and Bureaucracy in France* (Princeton: Princeton University Press, 1974) and especially his *Elites in French Society*, (Princeton: Princeton University Press, 1978), which provides a penetrating

analysis of the critical role of the "polytechnicien" in the French economy and bureaucratic structure. Also consult Jacques Kosciusko-Morizet, *La "Mafia" polytechnicienne* (Paris: Seuill, 1973); Gerard Grunberg, "L'Ecole polytechnique et 'ses' grand corps," *Annuaire International de la Fonction Publique, 1973-1974*, pp. 383-407; for a more general discussion of elite behavior, see Jacques Birnbaum, *Les Sommets de l'état* (Paris: Point Politique, 1977). Birnbaum characterizes the Fifth Republic as a republic of technocrats. This is the point of Philippe Simonnot's analysis of French nuclear policy, *Les Nucléocrates* (Grenoble: Presses Universitaires de Grenoble, 1978).

92. Interviews, Paris, 1977-1978, 1982, 1983. Also of use is Roland Cayrol and Pascal Perrineau, "Governing Elites in a Changing Industrial Society: The Case of France," report presented at international colloquium on elites at Northern Illinois University, September 7-9, 1981.

93. These problems are covered in the author's "Measuring French Arms Transfers: A Problem of Sources and Some Sources of Problems," *Journal of Conflict Resolution*, XXIII, No. 2 (June), 195-227.

94. Interviews, Paris, 1983.

95. Interviews, Paris, 1977-1978, 1982, 1983.

96. Some notable exceptions are the Institut Français des Relations Internationales; the Institut National Supérieur d'Etudes de Défense et de Désarmement, under the direction of Professor Jacques Soppelsa, President of Paris I (Sorbonne); and the Centre Interdisciplinaire de Recherche sur la Paix et d'Etudes Stratégiques (CIRPES). See also David S. Yost, "Strategic and International Affairs Research in France," *Orbis*, xxv, No. 3 (Fall 1981), 801-805.

97. See the so-called Limouzy Report: France, Assemblée Nationale, Commission d'Enquête Parlementaire (1977), *Rapport sur l'utilisation des fonds alloués aux entreprises privées ou publiques de construction aéronautique*. The Mitterrand government's inquiry appears in a multivolume series issued by Documentation Française, *La France en mai 1981*, published under the auspices of the Commission du Bilan.

98. France, Assemblée Nationale, *Proposition de loi instituant un contrôle du Parlement sur les exportations de matériels de guerre*, No. 536, July 1, 1978.

99. Lachaux, "La Règlement des Exportations," p. 39, hints at this gap in his carefully worded review of CIEEMG processes.

100. Interviews, Paris, 1977-1978, 1982, 1983.

101. Interviews, Paris, 1983.

102. See Chapter 3 and n. 92 above for relevant comparative data.

103. Interviews, Paris, 1983. Dörfer's recounting of the Stehlin affair underscores the point that even at the presidential level one moves cautiously against the arms complex. See Dörfer, *Arms Deal*, pp. 166-170.

104. The presentations of Delpech, de l'Estoile, and defenders of the arms complex reflect a combination of self-satisfaction with France's arms sales record, self-interest of the arms complex, and an ideological commitment to Gaullist tenets of internal independence as a justification for the expansion of arms sales. These themes are all struck in a letter written by partisans of the arms in-

dustry in defense against attacks launched by the Left during the legislative elections of 1978. *Le Monde*, March 16, 1978. For a reply, see Roger Godement "Les Triomphe des Thanatocrates," *ibid.*, April 12, 1978.

105. Interviews, Paris, 1977-1978.

106. Gauthier, *Délégation Général pour l'Armement*, p. 26.

107. During the Socialist years, the principal officer within the SGDN, responsible for overseeing arms transfers, was an ex-arms engineer reportedly opposed to even the minimal constraints on transfers imposed by the Mitterrand government. Interviews, Paris, 1982, 1983.

108. This sentiment was expressed to me on more than one occasion. Interviews, Paris, 1977-1978, 1982, 1983.

109. See, for example, Henri Azam, "Industrie d'armement et politique industrielle de défense," *Défense Nationale* (April 1982), 5-30.

110. For a general discussion of constitutional relations between governmental institutions, consult, for example, Dmitri-Georges Lauroff, *Le Système politique française* (Paris: Dalloz, 1975).

111. See, for example, France, Assemblée Nationale, CF (1976), *Rapport sur le projet de loi de finances pour 1977*, No. 2525, pp. 66ff.

112. "Les Français et l'armement," *Armement* (June 1979), pp. 29-39.

113. *Ibid.*, pp. 31, 34.

114. *Le Monde*, April 6, 1985.

115. M. S. Voilquin, "Les Parlementaires et la défense," *Défense* (October 1976), 43. The limited role and influence of the National Assembly in defense is similarly described in the following discussions: Joël Le Theule, "L'Opinion publique, le parlement, et la défense," *Défense Nationale* (August-September 1977), pp. 39-46; and Hughes Tay and Michel Dobry, "Débats et travaux parlementaires," *Arès: Défense et Securité* (Paris: Economica, 1981), pp. 221-242; and Yost, "French Defense Budgeting: Executive Dominance and Resource Constraints," *Orbis*, XXIII, No. 3 (Fall 1979), 579-608.

116. See n. 97 above.

117. J. Demaldent, "La Cinquième république et le commerce des armes: études d'un mouvement de contestation" (Paris, 1978, mimeo.,), p. 107.

118. Conseil Permanent de l'Episcopat Français et Conseil de la Federation Protestante de France, *Note de réflexion sur le commerce des armes* (Paris: Centurion, 1973).

119. Demaldent, "La Cinquième république," p. 116.

120. *Ibid.*, p. 117.

121. *Ibid.*

122. J. M. Müller, *Stratégie de l'action non-violente* (Paris: Fayard, 1972). See also the numbers of the journal *Alternatives Non-Violentes* published by Christian Delorme and edited by Jacques Semelin.

123. CLICAN, *Les Trafics d'armes*.

124. Union views are reviewed in Demaldent, "La Cinquième république," pp. 139-198, and by Mohamed Makhlouka, *La CGT et la CFDT face à l'armement et au désarmement*, Paris I, DESS Science Politique, 1978-1979.

125. Quoted in Demaldent, "La Cinquième république, p. 153.

126. See Fédération Nationale des Travaileurs de l'Etat, *CGT and la politique d'armement* (Paris: n.d.)

127. See Makhlouka, *La CGT* and Demaldent, "La Cinquième république."

128. Fédération Nationale des Travaileurs de l'Etat, *CGT*, p. 14.

129. Makhlouka, *La CGT*, p. 23.

130. *Ibid.*, pp. 56-58, lists a number of such instances. For confirming evidence, see CFDT, *L'Action Syndicate* (January 1978), on worker rights in arsenals and other numbers of this house organ on CFDT personnel in the arsenal system; also examine CFDT, *Résolution générale*, 40th Congress, April 26-29, 1977. Work status is defended by A. Bilous, "Arsenaux: quelle défense du statut?" *CFDT Aujourd'hui* (January-February 1980), 32-44.

131. Gauthier, *Délégation Général pour l'Armement*, pp. 160-163.

CHAPTER 6

1. See the discussion in Chapter 5 and the Note on Sources in the Appendix.

2. Ingemar Dörfer, in his *Arms Deal*, for example, relies on this distinction to explain France's failure to sell its Mirage F1 M53 to NATO. Andrew Pierre makes the same distinction in his *Global Politics of Arms Sales* (Princeton: Princeton University Press, 1982), which highlights political over socio-economic, technological, and organizational explanations of arms transfers. Absent from these otherwise useful works is a systemic examination of the impact of modernization on arms production and technology transfers.

3. Lawrence Freedman, "British Foreign Policy to 1985: IV: Britain and The Arms Trade," *International Affairs* (July 1978), 377-392.

4. This is an increasingly well-established conclusion of much of the recent research on the security policies of developing states. See, for example, Adelphi Papers Nos. 133-134: *The Diffusion of Power*, Power I: *Proliferations of Force* and Part II: *Conflict and Its Control* (London: International Institute for Strategic Studies, 1977); Kolodziej and Harkavy, *Security Policies of Developing Countries, passim*; and Yehezkel Dror, "Nuclear Weapons in Third World Conflicts," in Adelphi Paper, No. 161, *The Future of Strategic Deterrence* (London: International Institute for Strategic Studies, 1980), Part II, pp. 45-52.

5. Recent works that shed considerable light on the arms production capacity of the developing states are Stephanie G. Neuman, ed., *Defense Planning in Less-Industrialized States* (Lexington, Mass.: Lexington Books, 1984); *idem*, "International Stratification and Third World Military Industries," *International Organization*, XXXVIII, No. 1 (Winter 1984), 167-197; James E. Katz, ed., *Arms Production in Developing Countries: An Analysis of Decision Making* (Lexington, Mass.: Lexington Books, 1984), especially the article by Neuman, pp. 15-38; Milton Leitenberg and Nicole Ball, eds., *The Structure of the Defence Industry* (London: Croom Helm, 1982); and Michael Broszka and Thomas Ohlson, eds., *Arms Production in the Third World* (London: Taylor and Francis, 1986). See also the ex-

tensive bibliography compiled by Nicole Ball in Stephanie G. Neuman and Robert E. Harkavy, eds., *Arms Transfers in the Modern World* (New York: Praeger, 1980), pp. 323-361.

6. Interviews, Paris, 1983.

7. Interviews, Paris, 1983.

8. Interviews, Paris, 1977-1978, 1980, 1981-1982.

9. Varenne, "Exportation d'armement," *Projet* (July-August 1983), p. 714, and Interviews, Paris, 1977-1978, 1980, 1981-1983.

10. Costa Rica, Dominican Republic, Guatemala, and Jamaica fell into a multiple-supplier category between 1970 and 1980.

11. Richard F. Grimmett, *Trends in Conventional Arms Transfers to the Third World by Major Supplier, 1978-1985* (Library of Congress: Congressional Research Service, May 9, 1986), pp. 30, 36.

The data of Table 6-2 are just one more example of the uncertain reliability of comparative data available to arms transfer researchers. In these periods, ACDA indicates a loss of more than half, from 51.8 percent to 25 percent of the U.S. share of the market to the developing world. SIPRI shows a net increase of arms supplied from 32.5 percent to 40 percent. For the U.S.S.R. the two sources indicate an inverse relationship, i.e., ACDA shows a 10 percent increase for the U.S.S.R. while SIPRI indicates a 6.5 percent loss over the two periods. ACDA indicates an almost doubling of France's share of the world market while SIPRI cites only a 1.8 percent increase. For all other suppliers, ACDA notes an increase from 15.0 percent to 26.6 percent while SIPRI shows a net loss of 1.8 percent.

Data from ACDA also estimate U.S.-U.S.S.R. shares to be quite different. In the 1966-1975 period, ACDA cites the U.S. in the lead by 13.2 percent. In the 1976-1980 period the reverse is true, with the U.S.S.R. having a 13.7 percent lead. Figures from SIPRI are closer for the superpowers. They indicate a U.S.S.R. lead of 7.3 percent in the first period and a U.S. lead of 6.7 percent in the second five years.

Only for France in the 1976-1980 period are both sources close in their estimates (ACDA = 9.6 percent; SIPRI = 10.6 percent). For all others they differ significantly in their market estimates.

Data from ACDA were used to estimate the value of superpower deliveries because they appear to be derived from a more comprehensive set of sources. Interviews, Washington, 1977-1978, 1980-1981, and Stockholm, 1977. See U. S., Arms Control and Disarmament Agency (ACDA), *World Military Expenditures and Arms Transfers, 1971-1980* (Washington, D.C.; U.S. Government Printing Office, 1983), *passim; idem, 1968-1977, passim; idem, 1963-1973, passim.*

For data about West European sales, consult Richard F. Grimmett, *Trends in Conventional Arms Transfers to the Third World by Major Supplier, 1978-1985* (Washington, D.C.: Congressional Research Service, 1985), pp. 1-2. For Third World sales, see Broszka and Ohlson, *Arms Production,* pp. 30-31, for the calculation of the 1.5 percent estimate. Additional support for the economic thesis, stressed in Chapters 3 and 6, is found, aside from Broszka and Ohlson, in Carol Evans, "Reapprising Third-World Arms Production," *Survival,* xxvii, No. 2 (March-April, 1986), 99-118.

12. Broszka and Ohlson, *Arms Production*, pp. 30-31, offer a slightly different listing, covering the period 1950-1984.

13. *Ibid.*, p. 30.

14. *Ibid.*, pp. 1-33, provides a balanced assessment of the implications of increasing arms production and exports by developing states. Sobering analysis is also found in Neuman, *Defense Planning*. Andrew Ross advances a more threatening interpretation of these trends in "World Order and Arms Production in the Third World," in *Sowing The Dragon's Teeth: The Implications of Third World Military Industrialization*, ed. James E. Katz (Lexington: Lexington Books, 1986).

15. Broszka and Ohlson, *Arms Production, passim*, devote separate chapters to major Third World arms producers.

16. See *ibid.*, pp. 163-192, as well as Aaron S. Klieman, *Israel's Global Reach: Arms Sales as Diplomacy* (Washington, D.C.: Pergamon-Brassey, 1985); Alex Mintz, "Military-Industrial Linkages in Israel," *Armed Forces and Society*, XII, No. 1 (Fall 1985), 9-28, and Robert Harkavy and Stephanie Neuman, "Israel," in Katz, *Arms Production*, pp. 193-224.

17. The list is drawn from Bernard Reich's analysis of Israeli security policy in Kolodziej and Harkavy, *Security Policies of Developing Countries*, pp. 216-217.

18. ACDA, *World Military Expenditures and Arms Transfers, 1972-1982*, p. 73.

19. Broszka and Ohlson, *Arms Production*, pp. 79-104.

20. David Myers quoted in Kolodziej and Harkavy, *Security Policies of Developing Countries*, p. 69.

21. These factors cannot be extensively treated here. Much of the vast library of literature on international conflict deals with these demand-pull factors. For general discussions, see SIPRI, *Arms Transfers and the Third World*, the annual SIPRI *Yearbooks*, and Pierre, *Global Politics of Arms Sales*.

22. One of the first and most innovative studies of the arms transfer problem, launched by the MIT group and Amelia Leiss, focused specifically on inventory obsolescence as a key indicator of demand. Private defense consulting firms, like Defense Marketing Services (DMS), collect data for corporate clients in terms of projected national inventory needs for major weapon systems. See, e.g., Amelia Leiss et al., *Arms Transfers to Less Developed Countries* (Cambridge: The MIT Center for International Studies, 1970); *idem*, "Changing Patterns of Arms Transfers," Report C/70-2 (Cambridge: MIT Center for International Studies, 1970).

23. Quoted in Michael Moodie, "Defense Industries in the Third World: Problems and Promises," in Neuman and Harkavy, *Arms Transfers in the Modern World*, p. 298. The Moodie article, pp. 294-312, also discusses the views of other Third World leaders. For an Indian perspective that mirrors these sentiments, see the views of K. Subrahmanyam, who was once head of Indian arms production: *Defence and Development* (Calcutta: Minerva Associates, 1973). Also relevant are Rajesh K. Agarwell, *Defense Production and Development* (New Delhi: Arnold-Heinemann, 1978) and K. Subrahmanyam, ed., *Nuclear Myth and Realities* (New Delhi: ABC Publishing House, 1981).

24. This point is elaborated in the author's "National Security and Modernization: Drive Wheels of Militarization," in *Arms Control* (London), VI, No. 1 (1985), 17-40.

25. The notion of a self-sustaining arms transfer subsystem of the international system is outlined in the author's "Arms Transfers and International Politics: The Interdependence of Independence," in *Arms Transfers in the Modern World*, pp. 3-26.

26. See Andrew L. Ross, *Arms Production in Developing Countries: The Continuing Proliferation of Conventional Weapons*, No. N-1615-AF, RAND Corporation Note (Santa Monica, Calif., 1981), pp. 16-19, for a definition of these levels. For a list of countries producing various systems between 1950 and 1980, see also Neuman, "International Stratification," pp. 172-173, 178-181.

27. States producing aircraft: Argentina, Brazil, Colombia, Egypt, India, Indonesia, Israel, Libya, Nigeria, North Korea, Pakistan, Peru, Philippines, South Africa, South Korea, South Vietnam, Taiwan, Thailand.

28. States producing naval vessels: Argentina, Bangladesh, Brazil, Colombia, Dominican Republic, Egypt, Fiji, Gabon, India, Indonesia, Israel, Ivory Coast, Malagasy Republic (Madagascar), Malaysia, Mexico, North Korea, Peru, Philippines, Singapore, South Africa, South Korea, Sri Lanka, Taiwan, Thailand, Venezuela.

29. States producing ground equipment: Argentina, Brazil, India, Israel, South Africa, South Korea.

30. Producers of tactical missiles: Argentina, Brazil, Egypt, India, Israel, Pakistan, South Africa, South Korea, Taiwan.

31. Producers of SAM missiles: Brazil, India, Israel, South Africa, and Taiwan.

32. Producers of antitank weapons: Argentina, Brazil, Egypt, India, Israel, Pakistan, Taiwan.

33. See articles on these three states, respectively, by David Myers, Stephen Cohen, and Edward Milenky, in Kolodziej and Harkavy, *Security Policies of Developing Countries*: "Brazil," pp. 53-72; "Pakistan," pp. 93-118; and "Argentina," pp. 27-52.

34. The relation between militarization and modernization is explored by Peter Wallenstein et al., *Global Militarization* (Boulder, Co.: Westview, 1985). See also the author's "Whither Modernization and Militarization?: Implications for International Security and Arms Control," in a symposium of the International Economics Association on defense and economics (London: Macmillan, forthcoming, 1987).

35. For an overview, see Kenneth Waltz, *Man, the State, and War* (New York: Columbia University Press, 1959). Also relevant are Robert Gilpin's *France in The Age of The Scientific State*, and his more general theoretical work, *War and Change in International Relations* (Cambridge: Cambridge University Press, 1981). Relevant, too, is McNeil, *The Pursuit of Power, passim*.

36. See SIPRI *Yearbooks, passim*, for confirmation. Demands for offsets arrangements are an increasingly significant part of U.S. arms contracts, as evidenced by the F-16 sale.

37. Broszka and Ohlson, *Arms Production*, pp. 8-9.

38. Frederic Pearson, "The Question of Control in British Defense Sales Policy," *International Affairs*, LIX, No. 21 (Spring 1983), 226.

39. Western differences over East-West trade are discussed in the following:

Angela Stent Yergin, *East-West Technology Transfer: European Prospectives* (Beverly Hills: Sage, 1980), and Stephen Woolcock, *Western Policies on East-West Trade* (London: Routledge and Kegan Paul, 1982).

CHAPTER 7

1. See Dörfer, *Arms Deal*, for a general review of this case.

2. *Le Monde*, August 2, 1974. Dörfer, *Arms Deal*, recounts these events at length: for Belgium, pp. 134-153, and for France, pp. 154-177.

3. *Le Monde*, June 2, 1975.

4. *Ibid.*, June 11, 1975.

5. *Ibid.*

6. Dörfer, *Arms Deal*, p. 209.

7. *Le Monde*, April 10, 1975, and June 8, 9, 10, 1975. The theme of American technical superiority is struck throughout Dörfer's analysis.

8. *Le Monde*, January 12, 1975.

9. For criticism of the French, see *Le Monde*, October 8, 9, November 17, 1974, and April 8, 1975.

10. Dörfer, *Arms Deal*, pp. 154-177.

11. *Le Monde*, June 14, July 26, 1979.

12. Speech of British Foreign Secretary Sir Geoffrey Howe, Brussels, March 16, 1987.

13. *Le Monde* traces these military ties over a decade: June 23, 24, December 12, 1970; March 17, 1973; April 20, 21, June 13, October 19, 25, 1974; December 28, 1976; November 9, 1977; June 27, 28, 1978; and July 16, 28, 1982.

14. *Ibid.*, April 5, 1973.

15. *Ibid.*, December 12, 1970.

16. *Ibid.*, July 16, December 25, 1982.

17. Jacques Isnard analyzes France's isolation as an arms supplier in Europe in *ibid.*, November 4, 5, 1979.

18. FBIS, November 2, 1983, p. K5.

19. *Ibid.*, February 11, 1983, p. K4.

20. *Le Monde*, January 12, 13, 1986.

21. There is a rich literature recounting the Suez crisis. See, e.g., Michel Bar-Zohar, *Suez: Ultra-Secret* (Paris: Fayard, 1964).

22. Jack Gee, *Mirage: Warplane for the World* (London: Macdonald, 1971), pp. 100-101.

23. *Le Monde*, October 16, 1970.

24. For the Mediterranean region, French policy is discussed at length in the author's *French International Policy under De Gaulle and Pompidou*, pp. 489-551.

25. The systemic thrust of Gaullist arms policy toward Israel and the Middle East is also the underlying theme of Yair Evron's "French Arms Policy in the Middle East," *The World Today*, XXVI, No. 2 (February 1970), 82-90.

26. *De Gaulle contre Israel: Documents sur l'embargo* (Paris: Jacques Lanzmann, 1970), and Raymond Aron, *De Gaulle, Israel, and the Jews*, trans. John Sturrock (New York: Praeger, 1969). For a favorable interpretation of the Gaullist em-

bargo, viewed from a pro-Arab perspective, see the two-part series of Paul Balta, "La France et le monde arabe: Les Réalités économiques," I, *Revue de Défense Nationale* (May 1970), 813-835, and "La France et le monde arabe: Les Réalités politiques," *ibid.* (June 1970), 924-934, and Nasser H. Aruri and Natalie Hevener, "France and the Middle East: 1967-1968," *Middle East Journal*, XXIII (Autumn 1969), 484-502.

27. *Le Monde*, January 7, 8, 1969.

28. Quoted by Eric Cerdan, *A . . . Comme armes* (Paris: Alain Moreau, 1975), p. 198. Also *Le Monde*, January 8, 23, December 28, 1969; and March 16, 1970.

29. Quoted in Jean Klein, "Commerce des armes et politique: le cas français," *Politique Etrangère*, XLI, No. 6 (1976), 576. *Le Monde* affirms the point in reports published on October 16 and 23, 1973.

30. The so-called vedette affair is traced in *Le Monde*: December 28, 1968, January 2, 4, 5, 8, 9, 11, and 17, 1969.

31. *Le Monde*, January 2, 1969. General Bonte is widely regarded as a scapegoat. Also, interviews, Paris, 1977-1978. He died shortly afterwards in an automobile accident.

32. Arab arms purchases in this period are traced in *Le Monde*: February 8, November 7, 1968; January 9, 11, 23, February 8, 16, April 10, 13, 1969; January 4, 5, 11, 1970; and October 21, 29, 1971.

33. *Ibid.*, January 8, 1970.

34. *Ibid.*, August 8, 9, 1973; and January 26, 1975.

35. France, Documentation Française, *Politique étrangère de la France* (January-June 1970), p. 144. Hereinafter cited PEF.

36. *Ibid.*, p. 31.

37. French Embassy, *French Foreign Policy* (July-December 1967), p. 137.

38. PEF (January-June 1968), pp. 47-48.

39. *Le Monde*, August 9, 1974, reviews the Sadat revelation and traces the reports of the appearance of Libyan Mirages in the Middle East conflict.

40. *Ibid.*, August 29, 30, 1974.

41. *Ibid.*, April 24, 1974.

42. *Ibid.*, January 9, 1974; and March 27, 1975.

43. *Ibid.*, August 30, 1974.

44. *Ibid.*, December 26, 1976.

45. Reports of AMX-30 purchases occur as early as July 1971. *Ibid.*, October 21, 29; and November 19, 1975.

46. *Ibid.*, December 6, 1974; and January 26, 1975.

47. *Ibid.*, June 14, 1985.

48. *Wall Street Journal*, January 17, 1984. The French air-defense system was made compatible with the U.S. AWACS system, *Le Monde*, February 4, 1984.

49. *Wall Street Journal*, January 17, 1984.

50. FBIS, April 16, 1983, pp. K6-K7.

51. *Le Monde*, February 7, 1983.

52. *Facts on File*, November 20, 1980.

53. Interviews, Paris, September-October, 1983. See also the following issues of FBIS in 1983: June 3, 24, August 26, September 1, 13, 19, 20, 22, November 3, 9, *passim.*

54. *Ibid.*, August 19, 1983, p. K3; and February 29, 1984, pp. K4-K6.

55. *The New York Times*, May 24, 1984.

56. *Le Monde*, March 18, 1985.

57. FBIS, February 18, 1983, p. K2.

58. ACDA estimates these at $600 million in deliveries between 1978 and 1982, *World Military Expenditures and Arms Transfers: 1972-1982*, p. 97.

59. *Le Monde*, February 7, 1978.

60. *Facts on File*, October 24, 1984, p. 814. This source is also useful in quickly tracing French policy toward Lebanon and the Middle East. See especially *Facts on File*, 1978-1984, *passim*. Dominique Moise reviews Mitterrand's Middle East policies in "La France de Mitterrand et le conflit du Proche-Orient: Comment concilier émotion et politique," *Politique Etrangère*, No. 2 (1982), 395-402.

61. *Le Monde*, January 23, 1969.

62. *Ibid.*, July 15, 1972; February 19, April 9, 18, 19, and May 9, 1974.

63. *Ibid.*, May 19, 1983, p. K6 and FBIS, January 16, 1985, pp. K3-K7.

64. *Le Monde*, July 15, 1972; January 9, March 16, and December 12, 1974.

65. *Ibid.*, March 17, December 21, 1977; September 28, December 6, 1980; May 25, August 27, 1981.

66. *Ibid.*, June 2, 1982.

67. *Ibid.*, October 4, 22, 23, 1978.

68. *Ibid.*, October 20, 1975.

69. *Ibid.*, July 7, 12, 1984.

70. Edward A. Kolodziej and Robert Harkavy, "Developing States and the International Security System," in *The Foreign Policy Priorities of Third World States*, ed. John J. Stremlau (Boulder, Co.: Westview, 1982), p. 44.

71. See the author's *French International Policy under the Fifth Republic*, pp. 489-551.

72. Quoted by Paul Balta in a review of French-Libyan relations, *Le Monde*, February 6, 1980.

73. *Ibid.*, February 11, 1976; and February 6, 1980.

74. *Ibid.*, July 12, 1984.

75. An excellent review of French policy in Chad is found in David Yost, "French Policy in Chad and the Libyan Challenge," *Orbis*, XXVI, No. 4 (Winter 1983), 965-997.

76. *Le Monde*, December 22, 1979.

77. *Ibid.*, February 6, 1980.

78. *Ibid.*, February 3, 1980.

79. Romain Yakemtchouk, "La Coopération militaire de l'Afrique noire avec les puissances," *Afrique Contemporaine*, No. 127 (1983), 15-17.

80. *Ibid.*

81. Quoted in Yost, "French Policy in Chad," p. 974.

82. FBIS, August-September 1983, traces the French intervention in Chad and the arms transferred to Habré's forces.

83. Yakemtchouk, "Coopération militaire," p. 16.

84. *Le Monde*, March 1, 1981.

85. *Ibid.*, December 13, 1984. Disagreements within the French government over Chad are recounted from the perspective of a biased observer, writing un-

der the pseudonym "Colonel Spartacus." The ministries of defense and foreign affairs came equally under attack over Operation Manta, the name assigned the Chadian intervention. *Les Documents secrets: Opération Manta, Tchad, 1983-1984* (Paris: Plon, 1984).

86. *Le Monde*, March 24-26, 28-29, 1987 and *Daily Telegraph* (London), April 4, 1987.

87. *Ibid.*, February 4, 1980, and *Le Monde Diplomatique*, July 1982.

88. FBIS, August-September 1983, *passim*, reports on Zaire's increasing military support.

89. See the author's *French International Policy under De Gaulle and Pompidou*, pp. 447-488, 529-543.

90. For a statement of its position, see the remarks of President Giscard d'Estaing when he attempted to justify arms sales to Morocco as consistent with French neutrality vis-à-vis Moroccan-Algerian differences, *Le Monde*, February 1, 2, 1976.

91. *Ibid.*, October 22, 1982.

92. U.S., National Foreign Assessment Center, *Communist Aid Activities in Non-Communist Less Developed Countries, 1954-79* (Washington, D.C.: U.S. Government Printing Office, 1980), p. 7.

93. ACDA, *World Military Expenditures and Arms Transfers, 1972-1982*, p. 95.

94. *Le Monde*, March 13, 1982.

95. *Ibid.*, February 4, May 11, June 6, 1978; March 29, 1980; and March 13, 1982.

96. *Le Monde Diplomatique*, July 1982.

97. *Ibid.*

98. *Le Monde*, April 29, 1982.

99. *Ibid.*, December 23, 1977.

100. *Ibid.*, September 29, 1979.

101. FBIS, May 6, 1983, p. K3.

102. *Le Monde*, August 28, 1981; and April 29, 1982.

103. *Ibid.*, August 28, 1981.

104. SIPRI, *Southern Africa: The Escalation of Conflict* (New York: Praeger, 1976), pp. 129-135.

105. *Ibid.*, p. 131.

106. The 1977 SIPRI *Yearbook* indicated five Mirage 5 interceptor/reconnaissance aircraft were delivered instead of Mirage IIIs as earlier SIPRI data had noted.

107. The number of Mirage aircraft sent to Zaire is not fully certain on the basis of SIPRI and IISS sources. The 1976 SIPRI *Yearbook* reports seventeen Mirage 5s delivered from 1975 to 1976. The 1977 SIPRI *Yearbook* reports fourteen Mirage 5s delivered in that time. For 1977-1978 and 1978-1979, the *Military Balance* lists seventeen Mirage 5s in the force structure. The 1979-1980 and 1980-1981 editions, however, report only thirteen and ten, respectively. Lower numbers are possibly due to attrition since delivery.

108. The 1981 SIPRI *Yearbook* lists four Alpha-Jet deliveries in 1980, leaving two to be delivered of the 1977 order of six. The 1980 SIPRI *Yearbook* asserts that six Alpha-Jets were ordered in 1977 and six again in 1978. The 1980-1981 *Mil-*

itary Balance only confirms an order of six Alpha-Jets. The two preceding editions cite the orders of twelve Alpha-Jets.

109. This relationship is extensively pursued in SIPRI *Yearbooks, passim.* See also *Le Monde Diplomatique,* April 16, 1976, and *Le Monde,* March 5, 1977, and August 20, 1977. Moshe Decter, "Arms Traffic with South Africa: Who Is Guilty?" (New York: American Jewish Congress, 1976, mimeo.), disputes claims of Israeli sales to Pretoria. Reent reports from U.S. sources indicate continuing Israeli, French, and European arms sales. *International Herald Tribune,* March 30, 1987.

110. Quoted by Jean Klein in his "Commerce des armes et politique: Le Cas Français," *Politique Etrangère,* No. 5 (1976), 578.

111. *Le Monde,* March 5, 1977.

112. *Ibid.,* September 8, 1971.

113. *Ibid.,* February 19, 1973.

114. *Ibid.,* October 21, 1970; January 20, 1973; and August 20, 1977.

115. *Ibid.,* April 24, 1973.

116. *Ibid.,* June 8, 9, 10, 1974.

117. *Ibid.,* August 21, 1976.

118. *Ibid.,* April 7, 1973.

119. *Ibid.,* August 8, 1975.

120. *Ibid.* See also Klein, "Commerce des armes," pp. 578-579.

121. *Le Monde,* August 20, 1977.

122. *Ibid.,* September 20, 1978.

123. SIPRI, *Southern Africa, passim.*

124. *Le Monde,* January 25, 1983.

125. *Ibid.,* January 12, 1985 and *International Herald Tribune,* March 30, 1987.

126. Yakemtchouk, "Coopération militaire," p. 5.

127. *Ibid.*

128. The fusion of France's big-power pretensions and retention of its grip on postcolonial Francophone Africa is explored in detail by Pascal Chaigneau, *La Politique militaire de la France en Afrique* (Paris: CHEAR, 1984). Early Gaullist thinking is outlined by Chaigneau, pp. 9-39. For a recent Left-of-Center affirmation of President Mitterrand's active African policy, see Jean-François Bayart, *La Politique Africaine de François Mitterrand* (Paris: Karthala, 1984), and remarks of the Defense Minister, *Défense Nationale* (December 1982), 7-22.

129. Louis de Guiringaud, "La Politique Africaine de la France," *Politique Etrangère,* No. 2 (1982), 441-455.

130. *Ibid.,* pp. 448-449, and ACDA, *World Military Expenditures and Arms Transfers, 1972-1982,* p. 9.

131. John Chipman advances the same thesis as Chaigneau in his *French Military Policy and African Security,* Adelphi Paper No. 201 (London: IISS, 1985).

132. For background material on the change from the colonial empire to the French community and, subsequently, to independence, consult Henry Grimal, *Decolonization: The British, French, Dutch, and Belgian Empires, 1919-1963,* trans. Stephan De Vos (Boulder, Co.: Westview, 1978), *passim.* Also pertinent is Miles Kahler, *Decolonization in Britain and France* (Princeton: Princeton University

Press, 1984). Pierre Lellouche and Dominique Moisi, "French Policy in Africa: A Lonely Battle against Destabilization," *International Security*, III, No. 4 (Spring 1979), 108-133, outline the varied accords signed by France with its former African dependencies.

133. These security and military assistance accords are discussed in detail by Jacques Guillemin in his "Coopération et intervention, la politique militaire de la France en Afrique Noire Francophone et à Madagascar," doctoral dissertation (Nice, 1979), pp. 1-32. They are also briefly reviewed in Pierre Dabezies, "La Politique Africaine du Général de Gaulle: 1958-1969" (Paris: Pedone, 1980), pp. 229-262.

134. The twelve included Cameroon, Central African Republic (CAR), Chad, Congo, Gabon, Ivory Coast, Madagascar, Mauritania, Niger, Senegal, and Togo.

135. Guillemin, "Coopération et intervention," p. 27, and Dabezies, "Politique Africaine du Général de Gaulle," pp. 235-244.

136. Chaigneau, *Politique militaire*, describes these now defunct arrangements, especially pp. 29-30, 41-43, and 69-71.

137. Guillemin, "Coopération et intervention," pp. 27-35.

138. Chaigneau, *Politique militaire*, p. 42.

139. Yakemtchouk, "Coopération militaire," p. 11.

140. Guillemin, "Coopération et intervention," pp. 32-33.

141. Chaigneau, *Politique militaire*, p. 80; Chipman, *French Military Policy*, pp. 12-15; and Daniel Bach, "La France en Afrique subsaharienne: contraintes historiques et nouveaux espaces économiques," in Samy Cohen and Marie-Claude Smouts, eds., *La Politique extérieure de Valéry Giscard d'Estaing* (Paris: Presses de la Fondation Nationale des Sciences Politiques, 1985), pp. 284-310.

142. Chaigneau, *Politique militaire*, p. 121 and Chipman, *French Military Policy*, p. 51.

143. This section of the discussion is based on the Edward A. Kolodziej and Bokanga Lokolutu, "Security Interests and French Arms-Transfer Policy in Sub-Saharan Africa," in *Arms for Africa*, ed. Bruce Arlinghaus (Lexington, Ma.: Lexington Books, 1983), pp. 125-152.

144. Dabezies, "Politique Africaine du Général de Gaulle," p. 250.

145. Guillemin, "Coopération et intervention," p. 63.

146. Kolodziej and Lokolutu, "Security Interests," pp. 134-136, compare foreign troop deployments in 1980. Libyan, French, and Zairean occupation in Chad is not covered because of the uncertainty about deployments.

147. Dabezies, "Politique Africaine du Général de Gaulle," p. 240.

148. This total does not include troops stationed in Mayotte and Réunion. Verifying troop levels is a difficult task since sources differ sharply in their estimates. See Kolodziej and Lokolutu, "Security Interests," pp. 134-136, for a discussion of some of the problems.

149. Thomas Jalloud, "La Coopération militaire, outil de contrôle," *Tricontinental*, I (1981), 110-111.

150. Chaigneau, *Politique militaire*, pp. 52-54. Chipman, *French Military Policy*, pp. 20-21, details French unit deployments.

151. Jalloud, "La Coopération militaire," pp. 111-112, and U.S., Department

of Defense, *Soviet Military Power* (Washington, D.C.: Government Printing Office, 1985), pp. 116-117.

152. Chaigneau, *Politique militaire*, p. 80.

153. *Ibid.*, p. 88.

154. *Ibid.*, pp. 85-89, discusses some of the operational weaknesses of the Rapid Action Force.

155. Chipman, *French Military Policy*, p. 17.

156. Quoted in Lellouche and Moisi, "French Policy," p. 118.

157. Bach, "France en Afrique subsaharienne," p. 296.

158. This appears to be the shared view of those who have looked closely at the war: John J. Stremlau, *The International Politics of the Nigeria Civil War: 1967-1970* (Princeton: Princeton University Press, 1977), especially pp. 224-233; Daniel Bach, "Le Général de Gaulle et la guerre civile en Nigéria," in *La Politique de Général de Gaulle: 1958-1969* (Paris: Pedone, 1980), pp. 330-344. Bach's article is based on his doctoral dissertation. Also of interest are Suzanne Cronje, *The World and Nigeria* (London: Sidgwich and Jackson, 1972), and John de St. Jorre, *The Nigerian Civil War* (London: Hodder and Stoughton, 1972).

159. Quoted in Stremlau, *International Politics*, pp. 228-229.

160. *Le Monde*, December 8, 1968.

161. Stremlau, *International Politics*, p. 231; Bach, "France en Afrique subsaharienne," p. 339.

162. Stremlau, *International Politics*, p. 230.

163. Bach, "Général de Gaulle," p. 339.

164. Stremlau, *International Politics*, p. 225.

165. *Le Monde*, August 4, 1983.

166. Chipman, *French Military Policy*, p. 24, lists French advisers abroad as of January 1985.

167. These are summarized in Kolodziej and Lokolutu, "Security Interests," pp. 132-133; and Yakemtchouk, "Coopération militaire," pp. 10-14.

168. See Bayart, *Politique Africaine de François Mitterand, passim.*

169. Guiringaud, "Politique Africaine," pp. 445-447.

170. *Ibid.*, pp. 448-450.

171. Chipman, *French Military Policy*, p. 31.

172. This is the interpretation given to American arms policy in Latin America by SIPRI, *The Arms Trade with the Third World*, pp. 249-270.

173. The countries are Argentina, Brazil, Chile, Colombia, Ecuador, Peru, and Venezuela.

174. *Le Monde*, July 6, 1978.

175. *Ibid.*, May 2, 1981.

176. *Ibid.*, May 18, 1982.

177. *Ibid.*, February 1, 1968.

178. *Ibid.*, May 17, 1970.

179. Argentina, Brazil, and Colombia received Mirage aircraft in 1972.

180. *Le Monde*, June 29, 1972.

181. See *ibid.*, March 28, 1980, for views of French DGA officials locked in battle with Breechcraft and Cessna over the purchase of Brazilian Xingus.

182. ACDA, *World Military Expenditures and Arms Transfers, 1972-1982*, p. 97.

183. *Ibid.*

184. *Ibid.*, p. 73.

185. *Ibid.; Le Monde*, November 9, 1978, and March 15, 1979.

186. *Le Monde*, August 8, 1980, and *Le Monde Diplomatique*, October 1982.

187. *Le Monde*, January 23, 1974; July 6, 1979; and April 3, 1981.

188. *Ibid.*, April 3, 1981.

189. *Ibid.*, February 26, 1982.

190. *Ibid.*, December 23, 1982.

191. *Ibid.*, October 12, 1980.

192. *Ibid.*, July 2, 1979.

193. ACDA, *World Military Expenditures and Arms Transfers, 1972-1982*, p. 97.

194. IISS, *Military Balance, 1981-82*, pp. 92-93; Norman Friedman, "The Falklands War: Lessons Learned and Mislearned," *Orbis*, XXVI, No. 4 (Winter 1983), 908-909; Appendix A-6; and *Le Monde*, November 7, 1982.

195. The retired British aircraft carrier *Colossus* was sold to Argentina in the 1960s.

196. The indexes of *The New York Times* and the *Times* of London covering the Falklands War make numerous references to French arms used by Argentina. E.g., see Drew Middleton's feature on Argentina's use of the Exocet against Great Britain, *The New York Times*, June 19, 1982. Also Jacques Isnard, *Le Monde*, July 10, 1982, and Friedman, "The Falklands War," pp. 907-940.

197. *Ibid.*, pp. 925, 929; *Le Monde*, July 10, 1982.

198. Friedman, "The Falklands War," p. 929.

199. *Le Monde*, April 8, 1982.

200. *Ibid.*, May 28, June 10, 1982; *The New York Times*, May 28, 1982.

201. *Ibid.*, May 24, June 5, 1982.

202. See, for example, *Le Monde*, August 12, November 7, 1982.

203. *Ibid.*, February 1, 1982.

204. *Ibid.*, July 14, 1982.

205. For an analysis of Mitterrand's foreign policy, see the author's "Socialist France Faces The World," in *France under Mitterrand*, symposium of *Contemporary French Civilization*, ed. Lawrence D. Kritzman, VIII, Nos. 1-2 (Fall/Winter 1983-1984), 158-180.

206. *Le Monde*, October 21, 1981.

207. *Ibid.*, August 25, 1982.

208. Richard Grimmett, "The Role of Security Assistance in Historical Perspective," in *U.S. Security Assistance*, ed. Ernest Graves and Steven A. Hildreth (Lexington, Ma.: Lexington Books, 1984), p. 16.

209. Gee, *Mirage*, pp. 66-67.

210. These are described in *Le Monde*, December 20, 1969; and November 7, 1971.

211. *Le Monde*, October 11, 22, 23, 1978.

212. Raju G. C. Thomas, "Defense Planning in India," in *Defense Planning in Less-Industrialized States*, ed. Stephanie G. Neuman, p. 257. See also *Le Monde*, May 22, 1981, and April 17 and October 19, 1982. How this contract and the

one for Jaguars, downgraded after the F-16 sale to Pakistan, will be executed is not fully clear at this writing.

213. SIPRI cites 74 deliveries by 1980; *Le Monde*, May 22, 1981, indicates that Pakistan acquired 96 Mirages.

214. *Le Monde*, November 7, 1979. A Daphne submarine was sunk in the 1971 war; *ibid.*, February 20, 1979.

215. *Ibid.*, July 8, December 12, 1971.

CHAPTER 8

1. Sir Henry S. Maine, *Popular Government* (New York: Henry Holt, 1886), pp. 60-61. The quotation is slightly paraphrased but with no distortion in meaning.

188-190; governance of, 239-240, 261; imperatives for, 3, 4, 397-398; before Napoleonic Wars, 5-9; from Napoleonic Wars to World War I, 9-18; and national security, 398-400; need for expansion, 83; output of, 29, 45, 129; private control over, 6, 15, 16, 25; producers of, 135-140; protectionist measures for, 191; quality control of, 262; rebuilding following World War II, 43-48; regulations covering, 6, 261-262; rising costs of, 140-143; royal control of, 5-7; shifting priorities of, 135-140; standardizations in, 7, 9; state control over, 5, 6, 202; targets of, 54; values of, 201-202; between the world wars, 18-32. *See also* arms industry, French

arms production, German, 12, 15-16, 29
arms production, Third World, 315-320
arms sales, French: after-sale (*après vente*) phase, 105-106; agencies for, 270; aggressive policy for, 268, 400; in American Revolution, 4; "banalization" of, 129; of conventional weapons, 126-130; decision making in, 271, 276-279; and French economic growth, 167-169; global network for, 3, 269; importance to French global policy, 59, 60, 130-132, 294, 301-306; Mitterrand as critic of, 60; multilateralization of, 306-315; purpose of, 54, 69, 71; regional pattern of, 332-334; restrictions on, 265; value of, 311; volume of, 169, 326; in World War I, 4; following World War II, 46. *See also names of individual customer countries;* arms exports, French

arms transfers. *See* arms sales
Army, French: American contracts to, 42; collaboration during World War II, 35; expenditures for, 11; forced to purchase AMX-30 tanks, 103; nationalized suppliers for, 28-29; nuclear forces in, 74, 80; reorganization of, 80; size of, after World War I, 19; under Third Republic, 12. *See also* armed forces, French
Arnold, Phillippe, 100
Arras, Bishop of, 294
arsenals: army, 6, 7, 17, 28; decision making by, 275; exports from, 206; in limbo, 250-251; navy, 8-9, 28, 234, 250; nu-

clear, 215; royal, 6, 7, 8-9; superpower, 108
artillery schools, 7-8
ASMP (medium-range air-to-ground missile), 79, 86
Assens, Paul, 267
Atar aircraft engine, 46, 103, 224
Atlantic Alliance (1949): and EC, 64; and French security, 36, 37, 39-40, 51, 61, 62, 63; as deterrent to Soviet Union, 68
Atlantic sea patrol planes, 92, 104, 157, 160
Atlantic Treaty. *See* Atlantic Alliance
ATLIS laser designator, 165
Atomic Energy Commission, French. *See* Commissariat à l'Energie Atomique
atomic (nuclear) weapons, American: refusal to accept on French soil, 63
atomic weapons. *See* nuclear weapons *entries*
"Atoms for Peace," 121
Australia: French arms sales to, 176, 389; protest over French nuclear testing, 113, 389
Austria: French arms sales to, 338; sales of armored cars by, 23
Aviation-Sud, *see* Sud-Aviation
avion de combat futur. See future combat fighter
Avions Marcel Dassault-Bréguet Aviation (AMD-BA), 141, 159, 219-223
AWACS (airborne warning and control system), 100, 237
Azores, missile development center in, 87

Backfire bombers, 115, 117
Bahrain: American arms sales to, 310; French arms sales to, 355
Banderante aircraft, 315
Bangladesh, Soviet arms sales to, 311
Banque Française du Commerce Extérieur (BFCE), 270-271
Barre, Raymond, 185, 297
Bayonne, royal port/arsenal at, 8
Beaufre, André, 295, 457n27
BEG. *See* Bureau d'Études Générales
Belgium: American arms sales to, 309; disturbed over Britain's exclusion from EC, 64; French arms sales to, 23, 46, 176, 335-336; French cooperation with, 160,

LIBRARY OF CONGRESS CATALOGING-IN-PUBLICATION DATA

Kolodziej, Edward A.
Making and marketing arms.

Includes index.
1. Munitions—France.   2. Military assistance,
French.   3. World politics—1945-   . I. Title.
HD9743.F82K64 1987   338.4'76234'0944   86-30567
ISBN 0-691-07734-7

EDWARD A. KOLODZIEJ is Research Professor of Political Science at the University of
Illinois and the Director of the European Arms Control Project. He is the author
of *French International Policy under De Gaulle and Pompidou: The Politics of Grandeur*
(Cornell) and *The Uncommon Defense and Congress, 1945-1963* (Ohio State).